The Fasti, Tristia, Pontic Epistles ... (the Metamorphoses. The Heroides ... The Amours ... And Minor Works) Of Ovid, Tr. Into Engl. Prose, With Notes, By H.t. Riley...

Publius Ovidius Naso

Nabu Public Domain Reprints:

You are holding a reproduction of an original work published before 1923 that is in the public domain in the United States of America, and possibly other countries. You may freely copy and distribute this work as no entity (individual or corporate) has a copyright on the body of the work. This book may contain prior copyright references, and library stamps (as most of these works were scanned from library copies). These have been scanned and retained as part of the historical artifact.

This book may have occasional imperfections such as missing or blurred pages, poor pictures, errant marks, etc. that were either part of the original artifact, or were introduced by the scanning process. We believe this work is culturally important, and despite the imperfections, have elected to bring it back into print as part of our continuing commitment to the preservation of printed works worldwide. We appreciate your understanding of the imperfections in the preservation process, and hope you enjoy this valuable book.

THE FASTI,

TRISTIA, PONTIC EPISTLES,

IBIS, AND HALIEUTICON

OF

OVID.

LITERALLY TRANSLATED INTO ENGLISH PROSE,
WITH COPIOUS NOTES,

BY HENRY T. RILEY, B.A.
OF CLARE HALL, CAMBRIDGE.

LONDON:
H. G. BOHN, YORK STREET, COVENT GARDEN.
MDCCCLI.

J. BILLING,
PRINTER AND STEREOTYPER,
WOKING, SURREY.

PREFACE.

If the following pages shall be found to express the meaning of the author, with fidelity and tolerable neatness of diction, the object proposed will have been accomplished.

Some few deviations have been made from the strict letter of the text, in cases where usage, or the idiom of our language, seemed to render such a course desirable. From the peculiar nature of Elegiac compositions, which mostly run in detached couplets, the use of the conjunction copulative occurs much more frequently than would be consistent with our ideas of euphony; and we often find the poet employing in the same sentence the present, perfect, and pluperfect tenses almost indiscriminately, a strict adherence to which, in the English language, would be extremely inelegant. In many instances of this nature, and in several, where the only alternative has been either a departure from the exact words of the author, or a violation of decorum, the former course has been adopted. The distinction between the use of the pronoun "you," and the more sententious "thou," which has been very generally neglected in prose translations of the classical writers, has been carefully observed throughout.

The several critical editions of the original text vary much in respect to punctuation; the translator has therefore adopted one or the other, according as it appeared to him the most clearly to elucidate the author's meaning. In the Fasti the text of Krebs has been followed, excepting in a few passages. In the Tristia and Pontic Epistles, he has used that given in Valpy's classics.

The Variorum editions, especially Burmann's *magnum opus*, and the editions of the 'Fasti' by Keightley, Thynne, and Stanford (productions which reflect considerable credit on their respective editors), have been carefully consulted, and many notes of especial value to the student selected therefrom. Dr. Smith's Dictionary of Greek and Roman Antiquities, and Mr. Keightley's Mythology of Ancient Greece and Italy, have also proved fertile sources of information.

A translation of the Fasti, by Dr. Butt, of Trinity College, Dublin, was published some years since; and the first three Books have been translated by Mr. Thynne, the editor of the Latin text. The former of these is unaccompanied by notes, and the annotations given in Mr. Thynne's translation are scarcely sufficient in the hands of the English reader, for the elucidation of a work so replete with allusions to the manners, customs, superstitions, and traditions of antiquity, and so abounding in passages of obscure and doubtful meaning.

A poetical translation of the Fasti, by John Gower, "Master of Arts, and sometime of Jesus Colledge," was published at Cambridge by Roger Daniel, the University printer, in 1640. It is an attempt to translate the poem into English verse, line for line. How the translator has performed his task will be seen from the accompanying specimens, which have been culled here and there from his work. The almost burlesque style generally employed by him, forcibly reminds us of Cotton's more famous Travesty of the first and fourth books of the Æneid, while the taste displayed is certainly not superior to that of Sternhold and Hopkins.

A poetical translation of the Fasti, assuming to be nearly literal, was published in 1757, by William Massey, "Master of a boarding-school at Wandsworth." So far as mere versification is concerned, it is somewhat better than Gower's translation, though it is by no means so faithful.

A poetical translation of the Tristia, by Wye Saltonstall, was published in the earlier part of the seventeenth century; and by its fidelity, and the terseness and fluency of its language, does considerable credit to its now forgotten author.

The Pontic Epistles do not appear to have been ever published in an English form, either verse or prose.

The Invective against the Ibis was "faithfully translated into English verse by John Jones, M.A., teacher of a private school in the city of Hereford," in 1658. The style is not much superior to that of Gower, and the book, with its notes and deductions, is a curious medley, to use the Translator's own words, of "Natural, Moral, Poetical, Political, Mathematical, and Theological Applications."

INTRODUCTION.

THE LIFE AND WRITINGS OF OVID.

The little that is known to us of the personal history of this poet has been principally gathered by the research of various scholars from detached passages in his works, which incidentally bear reference to himself or to his family. From contemporary writers we learn nothing of his history; and those of the succeeding age are almost equally silent respecting him.

Publius Ovidius Naso was born at Sulmo, a small town of Pelignum, situated in the Apennines, and about ninety miles from Rome, on the 20th of March, A.U.C. 711, or B.C. 43, being the year in which the consuls Hirtius and Pansa fell at the battle of Mutina. He was of Equestrian family, and had one brother, who was his senior by exactly a year, and who died at the early age of twenty.

The patrimonial property of his family appears to have been of limited extent; and he was trained by his parents to habits of strict frugality. In his writings he speaks of his hereditary estate at Sulmo, and of his house in the neighbourhood of the Capitol; and he also makes mention of his orchards in the vicinity of the Claudian Way.

By the desire of his father he proceeded to Rome, and, with his brother, commenced the study of law and rhetoric; but, finding that he was little fitted for these pursuits, and that his poetical tendencies ill-accorded with them, he neglected them as soon as he had adopted the "toga virilis," and thereby became his own master. Contrary to the advice of his father, who, as he tells us, often represented to him that poetry was a worthless pursuit, and that Homer himself died in poverty, he devoted himself entirely to poetical composition, and the Muses thenceforth became the chief objects of his veneration.

To complete his education, in conformity with the custom of the time, he proceeded to Athens, the great school of philosophy; and it was probably in his early years that he visited Sicily and Asia Minor.

With the view, perhaps, of obtaining political preferment, he assumed the senatorial badge of the "broad hem," or "Laticlave," a right which seems to have been conferred by Augustus on the sons of persons of Equestrian rank, as a prelude to their entering the Senate; and he soon after took office as one of the "Vigintiviri," or city magistrates. He afterwards acted as one of the "Centumviri," a body of one hundred and five officers elected from the thirty-five tribes of Rome, and whose duty was to assist the Prætor in questions where the right to property was litigated. He also occasionally acted as a private judge or arbitrator.

He was three times married; to his first wife, when, as he says, he was almost a boy; but neither that marriage nor his succeeding one was of long duration; and it is supposed that in both instances he had recourse to the then existing facilities of divorce. His last wife was of the Fabian family, and was a favourite of Marcia, the cousin of the Emperor Augustus. At the time of her marriage she was a widow, and had a daughter, who became the wife of Suilius, a friend of Germanicus. It was probably by her that the poet had a daughter, who, in his lifetime, was twice married, her second husband being Fidus Cornelius, a senator. It is not known whether he had any other children.

In the fifty-first year of his age he was banished from Rome by the edict of the Emperor Augustus. By the terms of his "relegatio," or banishment, he was ordered to reside at Tomi (sometimes called Tomis, or Tomos), the principal city of Pontus; but his rights as a citizen, he tells us, remained unimpaired. The place, whose site is now unknown, was situated in a bleak, inhospitable, climate, near the mouth of the Danube, a spot, in those days, on the very confines of civilization. The poet tells us that the people were immersed in barbarism, spoke the Getic language mingled with Greek, and wore "braccæ," or "trowsers," after the manner of the Parthians. Having soon learned their language, he wrote a poem in it, which secured to him the esteem and sympathy of the natives. The immoral nature of some of his earlier writings is said to have been the cause of his exile; and he informs us that they were excluded from the public libraries of Rome. There seems, however, to have been another and a more influential reason for his punishment, which he repeatedly hints at in his Pontic writings, but which he nowhere reveals. From his remarks it has been supposed by some that he had inadvertently been witness of an immoral act of a member of the family of Augustus. Perhaps, as Julia, the Emperor's grand-daughter, was about that period banished for her extreme profligacy, he had, prematurely and by accident, become acquainted with her guilt, and had failed to keep silence on the subject. Other writers suggest that he had an intrigue with Julia, which was discovered by Augustus; but there seem to be no good grounds for such a conjecture. The reason was, very probably, a political one.

His departure from Rome was very precipitate, being in the midst of winter. He embarked at Brundisium for Greece, whence he took ship to the coast of Thrace, and completed his journey by land.

He afterwards made repeated applications to Augustus and his successor, Tiberius, for a remission of his sentence; but his entreaties were in vain, for he died at Tomi, in the ninth year of his exile, and the sixtieth of his age. We learn from Eusebius that his remains were buried at that place.

His "Amores," or "Amours," were the work of his youth, and it is supposed that he destroyed the more objectionable portion of them. The "Epistolæ Heröidum," or "Epistles of the Heroines," were written by him in about his thirty-second year. He next produced his "Ars Amatoria," or "Art of Love," which was quickly succeeded by his "Remedium Amoris," or "Cure of Love." He then devoted himself to the "Metamorphoses," his principal work; which, when he received his sentence of exile, he committed, in an unfinished state, to the flames. Duplicate copies of that poem were, however, in the hands of his friends, and to this fact we are indebted for its preservation. It is uncertain whether the poet wrote six or twelve books of the "Fasti," or Roman Calendar. From a remark in his epistle to Augustus, in the sceond book of the "Tristia," it would appear, according to one mode of translating the passage, that he had written twelve books, one for each month, and that he was interrupted in the completion or revision of the work by his exile. Another meaning for the words there used by him, is, however, suggested in this Translation. Masson would interpret the passage as meaning that he had collected materials for the first six months only, and that he had worked them into a poem of six books. From the fact that allusions are made, in the Fasti, to political events which occurred very near to the close of his life, and the more striking circumstance, that among the very numerous quotations from that work by ancient writers, there is not one that is not to be found in the six books now possessed by us, we shall probably not err in the conclusion that either he wrote but six books, which he revised in his latter years, or that, if he wrote twelve, the last six were lost at his death. The four lines which are sometimes appended to the end of the sixth book of that work are placed in one of the Vatican MSS. as the commencement of a seventh book; but they are universally regarded as spurious. Gronovius, indeed, informed Heinsius that he had seen an old copy of Ovid, in which Celtes Protacius, an eminent German scholar, had written to the effect that the remaining six books of the Fasti were in the possession of a clergyman near Ulm, and that the commencement of the seventh book was—

"Tu quoque mutati causas et nomine mensis,
"A te, qui sequitur, maxime Cæsar, habes."

But Heinsius expresses it as his decided opinion that Protacius had been either misinformed or wilfully imposed upon.

During his journey to Tomi Ovid wrote the first book of his "Tristia," or "Lament:" the next two books were composed in the second and third years of his exile, and the others in the following years. After the latter period he addressed his friends in his "Pontic Epistles."

His poem, "In Ibin," "against the Ibis," and his "Halieuticon," or "Treatise on Fishes," were also composed during his exile. Two other trifling poems of his also exist, which are supposed to have been the productions of his youthful years. Among his lost works we have to include his Getic composition in praise of Augustus, his tragedy of Medea, his

Elegy on the Death of Messala Corvinus, his Epigrams, a version of the Phænomena of Aratus, a Poem on Bad Poets, one on the Battle of Actium, and another on the Illyrian Victories of Tiberius.

We are told that the poet was of delicate health, slight in figure, and of graceful manners. Like Horace, he was no lover of war; and he was moderate in his diet, while he tempered his wine with copious dilutions of water. Though too susceptible of the tender passion, we do not learn that he ever degraded himself by sensual indulgences, and his kind and gentle demeanour rendered him generally beloved by his friends.

The servility which he appears to manifest when addressing Augustus and Tiberius would certainly reflect much discredit on him, if it could be shown to be the spontaneous effusion of his breast; but, in justice to him, we ought to remember that adulation was the universal fashion of the day, and that, while he naturally longed for a return to his kindred, his friends, and his country, he was too sensible that he and his family were at the mercy of persons of no forgiving temper, and who would be satisfied with no homage short of servility. We shall, then, find some reason for palliating his conduct in this respect, and for, at least, considering him more excusable than many of his more ennobled and more favoured contemporaries, who did not disdain to swell the crowd of flatterers by which Augustus was surrounded.

ON THE RECKONING OF TIME AMONG THE ROMANS.

ACCORDING to Ovid, the year of Romulus consisted of ten months, commencing with the month of Martius, or March, and ending with December. Numa is said to have inserted two additional months, and we learn from the poet (in which statement, however, he is not confirmed by any other writer) that he prefixed January to March, and subjoined February to December, which order continued till the Decemviri placed February in its present position. The year of Romulus is supposed to have contained six months of thirty days, and four of thirty-one, making in all 304 days. The year of Numa originally consisted of 355 days, which falling short of the solar year, he supplied the defect by adding to every *second* year an intercalary month, which he called Mercedonius, consisting of twenty-two and twenty-three days alternately. This month was thrown in at the end of February in each year, and by this plan four years contained 1465 days, making an average annual excess of one day. This was corrected by reducing the number of days in the intercalarated month in every third "octennium," or period of eight years, by which means, in a cycle of twenty-four years, the Calendar was reduced to the same state as if every year had consisted of 365 days and a quarter.

The direction of the intercalations was left with the Pontifices, and it is supposed that they frequently lengthened or shortened the year at their own option, for the benefit or detriment of the Consuls and other public officers, and the farmers of the revenue, according as they were friendly or hostile to them.

These abuses, and the fact, that, as the fixed part of the year of Numa was not adapted to the sun's revolution, while the intercalary part did not observe the phases of the moon, the places of the seasons on the calendar were not exactly the same in any two consecutive years, influenced Julius Cæsar, when Pontifex Maximus, to reform the Calendar, as by virtue of his office he was empowered to do. This was the more necessary, when we consider that the first of January had at that time retrograded nearly to the Autumnal equinox. To bring that day to its proper place, he made the current year to consist of 445 days, by adding two intercalary months of sixty-seven days to the usual intercalary month Mercedonius. This year is generally called "the year of confusion." His chief alteration was, the abolition of the month Mercedonius, and the distribution of the ten days, which thereby became wanting, among some of the other months; and by this means the months became of their present length. As, however, this year was still too short by about a quarter of a day, he provided for the deficiency by the insertion, every fourth year, of an extra day immediately after the 23rd of February, which was to be esteemed as a duplicate of the 24th of February, or, as the Romans called it, the sixth of the Calends of March. It is this double day which gave the name of "Bissextile" to the Leap year. The months, which had previously been called Quintilis and Sextilis, then received the names of Julius and Augustus, in honour of the first two emperors. The Pontifices, soon after, mistook the proper method of intercalation, by making it every third year; but Augustus finally corrected the results of this error by omitting the intercalary day during twelve years.

The Romans did not, as we do, count the days of the month in a regular numerical succession, but reckoned them with reference to three principal points of time—the Calends, the Nones, and Ides. The first day of every month was entitled its Calends. In March, May, July, and October the Nones were the seventh, and the Ides the fifteenth of the month; in all the other months the Nones were the fifth and the Ides the thirteenth; and thus the Nones were always eight days before the Ides. After passing over one of these points, the Romans counted forward to the next, calling the day after the Calends so many days before the Nones, the day after the Nones so many days before the Ides, and the day after the Ides so many days before the Calends of the next month. The days were accordingly entitled with reference to the number backwards from each point to the preceding one; thus the thirty-first of January was "Pridie Calendas Februarias," or "the day before the Calends of February;" the day before that was reckoned as the third day before the Calends of February (as the Romans included both extremes in counting), and was called "Tertio Calendas Februarias," or "Calendarum Februariarum," which we translate "the third of the Calends of February," though it really means "the third day before the Calends of February." Pursuing this mode of enumeration, we find the fourteenth of January (the day after the Ides) to be the nineteenth "before," or, as we say, "of the Calends of February." So the day before the Ides of January was "Pridie Idus Januarias," and so on backwards to the Nones, the day before which was "Pridie Nonas," and the day before that was "Tertio Nonas Januarias." It should be remembered that the space between the Nones and Ides was the same in all the months; while those between the Calends and Nones and the Ides and Calends varied. The Calends were originally the day of the new moon, which received its name from the fact that on that day the Pontifex addressed the moon in presence of the people, in the words "Calo te,

Jana Novella," "I call upon thee, new moon," which was repeated as many times as intimated to his hearers the number of days before the arrival of the Nones. The Nones were so called from being always nine days before the Ides (including in the enumeration, according to the Roman custom, both the day of the Nones and the day of the Ides). The Ides derived their appellation from the Etrurian verb "iduare," "to divide," their place being in the middle of the month; and they originally represented the day about which the moon was full. In Cæsar's Calendar the year was divided into eight periods; the points which marked them were thus named:—

Bruma	The Winter Solstice . .	25th December.
Veris Initium . . .	The beginning of Spring .	9th February.
Æquinoctium Vernum .	The Vernal Equinox . .	25th March.
Æstatis Initium . . .	The beginning of Summer	13th May.
Solstitium	The Summer Solstice . .	26th June.
Autumni Initium . .	The beginning of Autumn	11th August.
Æquinoctium Autumni	The Autumnal Equinox .	24th September.
Hiemis Initium . . .	The beginning of Winter	11th November.

The civil day began at midnight. The artificial day was from sunrise to sunset, and was divided into twelve parts, called "horæ," which, though usually translated by our word "hours," really varied with the seasons. The night (from sunset to sunrise) was divided into four watches, of three "horæ" each.

The Romans had no week of seven days like ours; but from the recurrence of the "Nundinæ," or market-day, every eighth day, on which the citizens in the neighbouring country repaired to the city, they may be considered to have had a week of eight days. The "Nundinæ" were sacred to Jupiter, and originally no legal business could be dispatched on them; but the necessity, from the increase of numbers, of enlarging the "dies fasti," which alone were originally devoted to litigation, and a wish to promote the convenience of the residents in the country, induced the Consul, Hortensius, to make these days "fasti," or days of sitting in judgment for the Prætor.

The days were distinguished into "fasti," "nefasti," and "endotercisi" or "intercisi," which were marked in the Calendars with the letters F. N. and EN. The "dies fasti" were those on which the courts sat, and the Prætor, who was the chief judge, gave his decisions, which contained three words which were essential to his power of adjudication, "do," "I give," or "appoint," judges and the form of the writ; "dico," "I pronounce" sentence; "addico," "I adjudge" the property in dispute. On the "dies nefasti," these words were not allowed to be uttered; the prætor was consequently forbidden to adjudicate, and the courts of law were closed. These were the days set apart for religious ceremonials. The word "fasti" is derived from "for," or from the old Greek verb φάω, both signifying "to speak;" consequently the "dies fasti" were literally "the speaking days," and the "dies nefasti" the "non-speaking days," in allusion to the restrictions put upon the judgments of the Prætor.

The "dies intercisi," or "endotercisi," ("endo" being an old form for "in,") were certain days, partly "fasti" and partly "nefasti," on only a part of which the courts might sit and justice be administered. Thus, some days were "nefasti," while the victim was being killed; "fasti," from the minute of its death until the laying out of the entrails on the altar; and "nefasti," while the victim was being consumed.

The Romans had three kinds of public "Feriæ," or "holydays," which all belonged to the "dies nefasti," and were observed by the whole nation. These were the "Feriæ stativæ," "conceptivæ," and "imperativæ." The first were held regularly, and on stated days, marked in the Calendar. To these belonged the "Lupercalia," "Carmentalia," and "Agonalia." The "Feriæ conceptivæ," or "conceptæ," were moveable feasts, held at certain seasons every year, but not on fixed days; the time being annually appointed by the magistrates or priests. Among these we find the "Feriæ Latinæ," the "Sementivæ," the "Paganalia," and the "Compitalia." The "Feriæ imperativæ" were appointed on certain emergencies by the order of the Consuls, Prætors, or Dictator; and were mostly held, either to avert national calamities, or to celebrate great victories.

In reckoning longer periods than a year, the Romans used a measure of time called a "lustrum," which signified the period intervening between each Census or review of the people by the Censors. This interval averaged about five years, which was, consequently, the usual measure of a "lustrum." Sometimes, however, as in the Fasti (Book iii.

l. 165), a "lustrum" denotes only four years, and sometimes an indefinite number of years. Twenty-two "lustra" made a "seculum" of 110 years, the largest measure of time existing among the Romans.

ON THE RISING AND SETTING OF THE STARS.

BEFORE the age of Thales, the astronomer, only the settings and risings of the stars, as they were visible to the naked eye, were the subject of observation. Ever since that period, however, astronomers have divided these phænomena, with reference to the sun, into three classes. They are termed the cosmical, acronychal, and heliacal risings and settings. The cosmical rising or setting is the true one in the morning; the acronychal, the true one in the evening; and the heliacal the apparent rising in the morning or setting in the evening. A star or Constellation is said to rise cosmically when it rises at the same time with the sun; and to set cosmically, when it sets in the west, as the sun rises in the east. It rises or sets acronychally when it rises or sets at sunset. When it rises heliacally it emerges to the sight from the lustre of the sun's rays, where before it was hidden, and it arrives to such a distance from him as to be seen in the morning before the sun's rising; and when it sets heliacally, approaching the sun, it is lost sight of in his superior brightness. The heliacal rising of a star takes place from twelve to fifteen days after the cosmical rising, and the heliacal setting the same time before the acronychal setting. From the time of its heliacal setting to its heliacal rising, the star is over the horizon by daylight only, and is therefore invisible.

Thus we find that there are three risings and as many settings of a star, two of each of which are real and one apparent, namely:—

    The true morning rising . . . . the cosmical.
    The apparent morning rising . . . . . the heliacal.
    The true evening rising . . . . the acronychal.

    The true morning setting . . . . the cosmical.
    The apparent evening setting . . . . . the heliacal.
    The true evening setting . . . . the acronychal.

These few observations may be of some utility in the elucidation of the remarks which will be found in the Notes to the Fasti on the risings and settings of the various Constellations.

It is also worthy of notice that Julius Cæsar, in his arrangement of the year, intended to make the beginning of summer correspond with the heliacal rising of the Pleiades; that of winter, with the cosmical setting of the same Constellation; and that of autumn, with the cosmical setting of the Lyre. The blowing of Favonius or Zephyrus, the West wind, was, with the Romans, the sign of the arrival of spring.

THE ROMAN FASTI.

THE complex state of the Roman Calendar long remained one of the sources from which the priesthood and the Patrician order derived their power and influence over the Plebeians. For a long period of time, having no other method of ascertaining what days were "fasti," and what were "nefasti," the lower classes were obliged either to apply to the priests for information, or to await their proclamation of the various festivals which were about to take place. The priesthood also, in early times had the sole privilege of proclaiming what was to be the length of the ensuing month, and in their hands was the sole right of intercalating. The difficulties and uncertainty experienced by the commonalty very naturally tended to render them dependent upon the Patricians, who, by their superior opportunities for gaining knowledge on these subjects, were enabled to give them advice and assistance in all points, (especially legal matters), which in any way depended upon the effluxion of time.

At length, in the year A.U.C. 440, or B.C. 334, Flavius, the secretary of Appius Claudius Cæcus, made a code of forms for the regulation of litigation, and secretly transcribed the tables of the Calendar or plan of the year, and set them up in the Forum. Though this step gave considerable offence to the Senate, the people, in their gratitude to one who had rendered them so essential a service, elected him to the Ædileship, and subsequently to the Prætorship. These tables were called " Fasti," probably because this was the first word of their title; and, in time, this name was extended to all plans of the year, whether in reference to religious ceremonials or to matters of a purely civil or military nature. Of the latter kind, the most distinguished seem to have been the "Fasti Consulares," which, so far from containing directions and instructions intended for all future time, were simply records formed from year to year, containing the names of the yearly magistrates, and especially the Consuls. Events, as they occurred, being set down in them, formed, when grouped together, a series of annals; and though they had no character in common with the "Fasti sacri," or "Calendares," they became, as authentic records, of the greatest use to the statesmen and historians of Rome for chronological reference; to these, consequently, we are indebted for much of the knowledge that we possess, after the lapse of 2,000 years, relative to the history of that wonderful Republic.

THE ROMAN CALENDAR

FOR THE FIRST SIX MONTHS OF THE YEAR,

ACCORDING TO THE FASTI OF OVID.

(Those days are omitted on which there is nothing worthy of remark.)

JANUARY.—Book I.

1		The Calends.	The Consular procession, 75. The festival of Janus, 89. The dedication of the temples of Jupiter and Æsculapius, on the Sacred Island, 290.
3	III.	Nones.	The setting of the Crab, 311.
5		The Nones.	The rising of the Lyre, 315.
9	V.	Ides.	The Agonalia, 317. The rising of the Dolphin, 457.
10	IV.	Ides.	The middle of Winter, 459.
11	III.	Ides.	The Carmentalia, 461. The dedication of the temple of Juturna, on the Campus Martius, 463.
13		The Ides.	A wether is slain to Jupiter Stator, 587. The Provinces are restored to the government of the people, 589. Octavius receives the surname of Augustus, 590.
15	XVIII.	Calends of February.	The Carmentalia are repeated, 617. The sacred rites of the Deities Porrima and Postverta, 631.
16	XVII.	Calends.	The dedication of the temple of Concord in the Capitol, 637.
17	XVI.	Calends.	The Sun enters Aquarius, 651.
23	X.	Calends.	The Lyre sets, 653.
24	IX.	Calends.	The star on the breast of the Lion sets, 655. The Sementive moveable feast is proclaimed about this period, 657. The feast of the Paganalia, 669.
27	VI.	Calends.	The dedication of the temple to Castor and Pollux, near the Lake of Juturna, 705.
30	III.	Calends.	The dedication of an altar to Peace.

FEBRUARY.—Book II.

1		The Calends.	A temple is dedicated to Juno Sospita, 55. The people resort to the grove of the Asylum, 67. A sheep is sacrificed to Jupiter Tonans, 69.
2	IV.	Nones.	The setting of the Lyre, 73. The middle of the Lion sets, 77.
3	III.	Nones.	The Dolphin sets, 79.
5		The Nones.	Augustus is entitled the Father of his Country, 119. The middle of Aquarius rises, 145.
9	V.	Ides.	The beginning of Spring, 149.
11	III.	Ides.	Arctophylax rises, 153.
13		The Ides.	The rites of Faunus, 193. The anniversary of the slaughter of the Fabii, 195.
14	XVI.	Calends of March.	The rising of the Crow, the Snake, and the Cup, 243.
15	XV.	Calends.	The Lupercalia are celebrated in honour of Faunus, 267. The winds are changeable for six days, 453. The Sun leaves Aquarius, and enters the Fishes, 457.
17	XIII.	Calends.	The sacrifice to Quirinius, 475. The festival of Fools, 513. The Fornacalia, 527.
19	XI.	Calends.	The Feralia, or last day for propitiation of the Manes, 567. The rites of Muta, 571.
22	VIII.	Calends.	The Caristia, or feast of the relations, 617.
23	VII.	Calends.	The Terminalia, 639.
24	VI.	Calends.	The banishment of the Kings, 685. The arrival of the swallow, 853.
27	III.	Calends.	The Equiria, or horse-races in honour of Mars, 857.

MARCH.—Book III.

1		The Calends.	The laurels are replaced in the houses of the Flamens, the temple of Vesta, and other public buildings, and the fire of Vesta is rekindled, 137. The Matronalia, 170. The festival of the Salii, 259.
3	V.	Nones.	One of the Fishes sets, 399.
5	III.	Nones.	Arctophylax sets, 403.
6		Day before Nones.	Sacrifices to Vesta; the anniversary of the appointment of Augustus Cæsar to be Pontifex Maximus, 415.
7		The Nones.	The temple of Vejovis is consecrated, 429. The neck of Pegasus rises, 449.
8	VIII.	Ides.	The Crown of Ariadne rises, 459.
14		Day before Ides.	The Equiria are repeated in the Campus Martius, 517. Or on the Cælian Hill, 521.
15		The Ides of April.	The rites of Anna Perenna, 523. The death of Julius Cæsar, 697.
16	XVII.	Calends of April.	The Scorpion partly sets, 711. The Argei are visited on this and the following day, 791.
17	XVI.	Calends.	The Liberalia are celebrated in honour of Bacchus, 713. The assumption of the Toga Virilis, 771. The rising of the Kite, 793.
19	XIV.	Calends.	The Quinquatrus, in honour of Minerva, 809. The birth-day of Minerva, 811. The Minerval, or schoolmaster's fee, is paid, 829. The dedication of the temple to Minerva Capta, 835.
20	XIII.	Calends.	The second and three following days of the Quinquatrus celebrated with gladiatorial shows, 818.
22	XI.	Calends.	The Sun enters the Constellation of the Ram, 851.
23	X.	Calends.	The fifth and last day of the Quinquatrus; and the Tubilustria, 849.
25	VIII.	Calends.	The Vernal Equinox, 877.
29	IV.	Calends.	The festival of Janus, Concord, Health, and Peace, 879.
31		Day before Calends.	The rites of Diana on the Aventine Hill, 833.

APRIL.—Book IV.

1		The Calends.	The sacred rites of Venus, 133. The females bathe in honour of her, 139. Fortuna Virilis, 145, and Venus Verticordia are propitiated, 151. The Scorpion sets, 163.
2	IV.	Nones.	The Pleiades begin to set, 165.
4		Day before Nones.	The Megalesia, in honour of the Mother of the Gods, 179. Her games are celebrated for several days, 387.
5		The Nones.	A temple is dedicated to Fortuna Publica, on the Quirinal Hill, 373.
6	VIII.	Ides.	Juba is conquered by Cæsar, 377. Libra brings showers, 385.
9	V.	Ides.	Orion sets, 387.
10	IV.	Ides.	The games in the Circus, 389.
12		Day before Ides.	The games of Ceres, 393.
13		The Ides.	A temple is dedicated to Jupiter Victor, 621. A temple to Liberty is built, 623.
14	XVIII.	Calends of May.	Westerly winds prevail, with hail, 625. The victory of Augustus at Mutina, 627.
15	XVII.	Calends.	A pregnant cow is sacrificed to Tellus, 629.
16	XVI.	Calends.	Augustus is saluted Imperator, 675. The Hyades set, 677.
19	XIII.	Calends.	The horse-races in the Circus in honour of Ceres, 679. Foxes are set fire to on the last day of the Cerealia, 681.
20	XII.	Calends.	The Sun enters the Constellation of the Bull, 713.
21	XI.	Calends.	The Palilia, 721. The anniversary of the foundation of Rome, 806.
23	IX.	Calends.	The Vinalia, 863. The rites of Venus, 865; and of Jupiter, 878.
25	VII.	Calends.	The middle of Spring, 901. The setting of the Ram, 903. The rising of the Dog-star, 904. The Robigalia, 905.
28	IV.	Calends.	The commencement of the Floralia, 943. Vesta is received in the Palatium by Augustus, 949. This day is also partly dedicated to Apollo, 951; and partly to Augustus, 952.

INTRODUCTION. xxiii

MAY.—Book V.

1		The Calends.	The She-goat rises, 111. An altar is erected to the Guardian Lares, 130. The sacred rites of Bona Dea, 148.
2	VI.	Nones.	Argestes blows; the Hyades rise, 163.
3	V.	Nones.	The last day of the Floralia, 183. The Centaur rises, 379.
5	III.	Nones.	The Lyre rises, 415.
6		Day before Nones.	The middle of the Scorpion sets, 417.
9	VII.	Ides.	The Lemuria are celebrated, 419.
11	V.	Ides.	The Lemuria are continued, 419. Orion sets, 493.
12	IV.	Ides.	A temple is dedicated to Mars Ultor, 545. Games are held in the Circus in honour of Mars, 597.
13	III.	Ides.	The Lemuria are concluded, 591. The Pleiades rise, 599. The beginning of Summer, 601.
14		Day before Ides.	The Bull rises, 603. Images made of rushes are thrown into the Tiber, 621.
15		The Ides.	A temple is dedicated to Mercury, on his festival, 663.
20	XIII.	Calends of June.	The Sun enters Gemini, 693.
21	XII.	Calends.	The second Agonia, 721.
22	XI.	Calends.	The Dog-star rises [sets], 723.
23	X.	Calends.	The Tubilustria, in honour of Vulcan, 726.
24	IX.	Calends.	The day marked Q. R. C. F. 727.
25	VIII.	Calends.	A temple is built to Fortuna Publica, 729. The beak of the Eagle appears, 731.
26	VII.	Calends.	Boötes sets, 733.
27	VI.	Calends.	Hyas rises, 734.

JUNE.—Book VI.

1		The Calends.	The rites of the Goddess Carna, 101. Beans are eaten, 180. A temple is consecrated to Juno Moneta, 183. Sacrifice is offered to Mars near the Capenian gate, 191. A temple is dedicated to Tempest, 193. The Eagle disappears, 196.
2	IV.	Nones.	The rising of the Hyades and of the horns of the Bull, with rain, 197.
3	III.	Nones.	A temple is dedicated to Bellona, 199.
4		Day before Nones.	The temple in the Circus Flaminius is dedicated to Hercules Custos, 209.
5		The Nones.	A temple is dedicated to Sancus, Fidius, or Father Semo, 209.
7	VII.	Ides.	Arctophylax sets, 235. The fishermen's games in honour of the Tiber, 237.
8	VI.	Ides.	A temple dedicated to the Mind, 241.
9	V.	Ides.	The rites of Vesta, 249. An altar to Jupiter Pistor is dedicated, 349. Brutus conquers the Callaici, 461. Crassus is conquered by the Parthians, 465.
10	IV.	Ides.	The Dolphin rises, 469.
11	III.	Ides.	The Matralia, in honour of Mater Matuta, 473. The temple of Matuta built by Servius Tullius, 479. Rutilius and Didius are slain, 563. The temple of Fortune is built by Servius Tullius, 569. A temple is dedicated to Concord by Livia, 637.
13		The Ides.	A temple is dedicated to Jupiter Invictus, 450. The lesser Quinquatrus, in honour of Minerva, 651.
15	XVII.	Calends of July.	Thyene rises in the forehead of the Bull, 711. The temple of Vesta is cleansed, 713.
16	XVI.	Calends.	Zephyrus blows, 715. Orion rises, 717.
17	XV.	Calends.	The whole of the Dolphin is seen, 723. Posthumius Tubertus conquers the Æqui and the Volsci, 721.
19	XIII.	Calends.	The Sun leaves Gemini, and enters the sign of the Crab, 725. Pallas is first worshipped on the Aventine hill, 728.
20	XII.	Calends.	A temple is erected to Summanus, 729. Ophiuchus rises, 733.
23	IX.	Calends.	Flaminius is defeated at Lake Thrasymenus, 765.
24	VIII.	Calends.	Syphax is conquered, 769. Hasdrubal is slain, 770. The rites of Fors Fortuna, 771.
26	VI.	Calends.	The Belt of Orion is seen, 785. The Summer Solstice, 789.
27	V.	Calends.	A temple is dedicated to the Lares, 791. The temple of Jupiter Stator is built, 793.
28	IV.	Calends.	A temple is erected to Quirinus, 795.
30		Day before Calends.	A temple is consecrated to Hercules and the Muses, 797.

THE FASTI;

OR,

CALENDAR OF OVID.

BOOK THE FIRST.

CONTENTS.

The nature of the subject, and the Dedication, ver. 1—26. The division of the year by Romulus and Numa, 27—44. The different qualities of the days, 45—62. The calends of January, the invocation of Janus, and a prayer that the author may commence auspiciously, 63—74. The consuls enter upon their office in an assemblage of the people, 75—88. The mythology of Janus: who presents himself before the author with his badges of office, 89—99, and states, first, his origin, and the fact of his two-formed figure, 100—114; then, his duties and his various names derived therefrom, 115—132; then, the reasons for his peculiar form, 133—144. He next explains some matters relative to the calends of January; why the new year begins in the middle of winter, and not in the spring, 145—164; why on that day causes are pleaded, 165—170; why sacred rites are performed in his honour the first of all the Gods, 171—174; why words of good omen should be used, 175—182; why presents are made at the beginning of the new year, 183—226; why the ancient coin bore the figures of a ship and a double-head, 227—254; why he himself has his statue in one temple only, 255—277; why his temple is open in time of war, 278—288. The author then proceeds to examine the calendar. The dedication of the two temples of Æsculapius and of Jupiter, 259—294. Before treating of the rising and setting of the constellations, he commences with the praises of those who cultivate the science of astronomy, 295—310. The setting of the Crab and the Lyre, 311—316. The origin and meaning of the Agonalia, 317—334. An inquiry into the meaning of the terms 'Victima' and 'Hostia;' the ancient sacred rites and origin of the sacrifice of animals, in which he introduces the story of Aristæus, 335—456. The rising of the Dolphin, 457—8. The middle day of winter, 459—60. The Carmentalia, which introduces the arrival in Italy of Carmenta, Evander, and Hercules, together with the death of Cacus by Hercules, 461—586. The sacred rites of Jupiter, 587—8. Octavius is graced with the title of 'Augustus,' the meaning of which word he explains, 590—616. The return of the Carmentalia, on which Porrima and Postverta are propitiated, 617—636. The Temple of Concord rebuilt by Tiberius, to which Livia is a contributor, 637—650. The Sun enters Aquarius; the Lyre and the constellation of the Lion set, 651—656. The Sementive festivals; cessation from field labour, the rural rejoicings thereupon, the prayers of the husbandman for good crops, and the great blessing of Peace, 657—704. The temple of Castor and Pollux dedicated by Tiberius, 705—708. The altar of Peace is erected. The poet concludes with a prayer for eternal peace, and for the house of Cæsar, 709—726.

THE festivals,[1] arranged throughout the Latian year,[2] together with their origin and the constellations as they set beneath the earth and rise, I will celebrate. Receive, Cæsar Germanicus,[3] this work with benignant aspect, and direct the course of my timid bark;[4] and not disdaining a mark of attention thus slight, be propitious to this act of duty consecrated to thee. Thou wilt here review the sacred rites brought to light from the ancient annals,[5] and *see* by what memorable fact each day has been distinguished. Here, too,

[1] *The festivals.*]—Ver. 1. Literally, 'The times,' as set out for observance, and arranged for particular purposes.

[2] *The Latian year.*]—Ver. 1. The Latian year here spoken of was the Julian or solar year of 365 days and a quarter; so called because instituted by Julius Cæsar. (See Introduction.) The month of January received its name from the god Janus, and has retained it from the days of Numa to the present time, with an interval only in the reign of the Emperor Commodus, who called it 'Amazonius,' in honour of his mistress; but on his death the former name was restored by a decree of the senate. Latium was the name of that part of Italy in which Rome was situated.

[3] *Cæsar Germanicus.*]—Ver. 3. He was the son of Drusus Claudius Nero, and was adopted by his uncle Tiberius, at the express request of the Emperor Augustus. Drusus, the father of Germanicus having died shortly after his victory over the Germans, the senate conferred the title of Germanicus on his descendants. Germanicus died at an early age, and was the father of the Emperor Caligula.

[4] *Timid bark.*]—Ver. 4. Gower translates these lines in the following manner—

'Germanic Cæsar! O! accept our charge
With smooth aspect, and guide my feeble barge.'

Massey gives them in a single line—

'Support Germanicus, my feeble wing.'

While the one caricatures the metaphor, the other abandons it altogether.

[5] *Ancient annals.*]—'Annalibus—priscis.' Ver. 7. The Roman annals

thou wilt find the household festivals peculiar to thy own family.[6] Often must thy sire, often thy grandsire,[7] become the subjects of thy perusal. The rewards of honour distinguishing the painted calendar,[8] which they bear, thou, too, with thy brother Drusus,[9] shalt obtain.[10] Let others sing the arms of Cæsar; we will sing the altars[11] of Cæsar, and those days which he has added[12] to the festivals. Do thou favour me while endeavouring to recount the praises of thy kindred, and dispel from my breast its trembling fears. Show thyself propitious to me; then wilt thou have given me energy for my verses, for according to thy countenance does my genius stand or fall. My page,[13] about to be submitted to the judgment of a prince thus learned, is moved *with awe*, as though sent to the Clarian God[14] to be perused. For we

before the time of Ovid, were compiled by Hemina, Claudius, Afranius, Ennius, Attius, Quadrigarius, Piso, Fannius, Fenestella, Laberius, and Licinius. The principal annals were named 'Annales Maximi.' They were open to public inspection, and were kept by the Pontifex Maximus. At their discontinuance, in the time of Sylla, they amounted to eighty volumes.

[6] *Thy own family.*]—'Vobis.' Ver. 9. Either the Claudii, his family by birth, or the Julii, his family by adoption.

[7] *Thy grandsire.*]—Ver. 10. Augustus, who had adopted Tiberius.

[8] *The painted calendar.*]—Ver. 11. 'Pictos Fastos.' The Roman books were often decorated with colours, especially red; whence our word 'rubric.' These were most probably the 'Fasti Consulares,' kept in the temple of Janus, and not the 'Fasti Calendares,' which were originally only a calendar marking the days of religious observance.

[9] *Drusus.*]—Ver. 12. Drusus was the son of Tiberius, and the adoptive brother of Germanicus. The superior merits of the latter are supposed to have excited the jealousy of Tiberius, and to have caused his death by poison.

[10] *Shalt obtain.*]—Ver. 12. 'Feres.' Literally, 'shalt bear.' It was a high honour to be mentioned in the 'Fasti,' or annals; and the erasure of a name from them was a mark of extreme degradation.

[11] *Altars.*]—Ver. 13. Built and consecrated by Augustus; the passage most probably refers to the dedication by that Emperor of the altar of Concord.

[12] *He has added.*]—Ver. 14. Either by the revival of festivals; or by the institution of them in honour of the gods or of himself.

[13] *My page.*]—Ver. 19. 'Pagina.' This word is very appropriate, as paged books had been recently introduced into common use by Julius Cæsar, in substitution for those of the scroll form.

[14] *The Clarian God.*]—Ver. 20. The oracle of the Clarian Apollo was at Claros, near Colophon, in Asia Minor. According to Tacitus, it was consulted by Germanicus, to which circumstance the poet probably here alludes.

have felt how great is the fluency of thy polished eloquence, when it bore civic arms[15] in behalf of the trembling accused. We know, too, when inclination has impelled thee towards our arts,[16] how copious the streams of thy genius flow. If it is lawful and right,[17] do thou a poet guide the reins of a poet, so that under thy auspices the whole year may proceed favourably.

When the founder[18] of the city divided the periods, he appointed that there should be twice five months in his year. In good truth, Romulus, thou wast better acquainted with arms than with the stars, and thy greater care was to conquer thy neighbours. Yet, Cæsar, there is a reason which may have influenced him, and he has *a ground* on which he may defend his error. That period which is sufficient *to elapse* until the infant can come forth from the womb of its mother, he determined to be sufficient[19] for the year. During so many months after the funeral of her husband, does the wife keep up[20] the sad emblems of mourn-

[15] *Civic arms.*]—Ver. 22. According to Suetonius and Dio Cassius, Germanicus had pleaded in public with considerable success; indeed, every young man of the patrician class who pretended to any talent pleaded for his friends. Gower translates these lines thus—

'For we did taste those sweets your lips let fall,
When you did plead in causes criminall.'

[16] *Our arts.*]—Ver. 23. Germanicus made a Latin version of the astronomic poem of Aratus, which is still extant, and, according to Suetonius, he wrote several Greek comedies.

[17] *Right.*]—Ver. 25. 'Si licet et fas est.' This expression is strictly equivalent to, 'as far as consists with laws, human and divine,' or, 'with law and good conscience.'

[18] *The founder.*]—Ver. 26. Romulus. On the year of Romulus, see Introduction.

[19] *To be sufficient.*]—Ver. 34. That is to say, ten lunar months. Ovid is here in error; as ten lunar months would be at least fourteen days less than the ten complete months of the original Roman year.

[20] *Keep up.*]—Ver. 36. 'Sustinet in vidua tristia signa domo.' 'Sustinet' may mean either that she 'wears' the mourning garments, or that she 'keeps up' the emblems of mourning, such as the cypress branches hung up in the house, and exclusion from society. Numa regulated the time of mourning by the degree of kindred, and appointed to the widow the longest period, that of ten months, because that was the length of the original year, so that the poet has, in fact, here put the effect for the cause. Gower thus translates these lines—

'That time the widow, from the fatal burning
Of her dead mate, did wear the signs of mourning.'

ing in her widowed home. This then the care of Quirinus, arrayed in the regal robe,[21] regarded when he gave to the rude people[22] the ordinances pertaining to the year.[23] The first month was that of Mars;[24] the second that of Venus; she, the origin[25] of his family, he, the sire of *Romulus* himself. The third month was so called from the aged,[26] the fourth from the name of the young;[27] the rest that follow were denoted by their numerical place.[28] But Numa[29] passed by neither

[21] *Clad in the regal robe.*]—Ver. 37. 'Trabeati.' Literally, 'clad in the trabea.' The 'trabea' was a 'toga,' or robe, ornamented with purple horizontal stripes, and was worn by kings, consuls, and augurs. It very probably derived its name from the bars, or stripes, 'trabes.' Servius (Comm. Æn. VII., 612) mentions three kinds—one wholly of purple, sacred to the gods; another of purple and white; and another of purple and red, or saffron, worn by the augurs. The purple and white was the royal robe, and is assigned especially to Romulus, who is supposed to have derived the use of it from the Latin kings. It was worn by the consuls on festivals and public solemnities, such, for instance, as the opening of the temple of Janus. The 'equites,' or equestrian order, wore it on public festivals. The emperors, of whom Julius Cæsar was the first who assumed it, wore it entirely of purple.

[22] *Rude people.*]—Ver. 38. 'Populis,' perhaps, means 'tribes,' or 'clans,' not yet fused into one people.

[23] *Pertaining to the year.*]—Ver. 38. This may mean the rules and ordinances which were to be observed during the succeeding year till Romulus again met his people, or the general regulations regarding the year, for future observance. The latter is the preferable sense.

[24] *Of Mars.*]—Ver. 39. The Roman year originally began in March.

[25] *She, the origin.*]—Ver. 40. Venus, the mother of Æneas, was the ancestress of Romulus; Mars was his father. The poet here derives the name of March from 'Mars,' and the month of April (anciently written 'Aphrilis') from 'Aphrodite,' the Greek name of Venus, and formed from ἀφρὸς, 'sea-foam,' whence she is fabled to have sprung. He, perhaps, coined this very far-fetched derivation to please the Cæsars, who were said to have sprung from Venus through Æneas.

[26] *From the aged.*]—Ver. 41. May—'Maius,' or 'Majus,' as anciently spelt, he derives from 'the aged,' who were called 'majores natu.' 'More stricken,' or 'greater in age,' would be the nearest literal translation.

[27] *The name of the young.*]—Ver. 41. June, 'Junius,' he derives from the young, who were called 'juniores,' or 'juvenes.'

[28] *Numerical place.*]—Ver. 42. July, in the old year here spoken of, was 'Quintilis,' 'fifth month.' August was 'Sextilis,' 'sixth month,' and the names September, October, November, and December are respectively compounds of the numericals Septem, Octo, Novem, Decem, seven, eight, nine, and ten.

[29] *Numa.*]—Ver. 43. Numa Pompilius was a Sabine by birth, and the

Janus nor the shades[29] of his ancestors, and added two to the ancient months. That, however, you may not be ignorant of the privileges[30] of the various days, every light-bearing *day*[31] has not the same office; that will be inauspicious throughout which the three words[32] are not spoken, that auspicious throughout which it will be allowable for suits to be pleaded by law. But do not suppose that its own privileges last throughout the whole day; that which now will be auspicious, in the morning was inauspicious. For as soon as the entrails have been offered to the Deity, it is lawful to speak upon every subject,[33] and the Prætor, honoured *by his office*,[34] then has his decrees unobstructed. There is also the day on which it is the usage to shut the people within the *polling* inclosures[35] *for the purposes of election.* There is also *the market day*,[36] which always

second king of Rome. He added two months, January and February, to the year of Romulus.

[29] *The shades.*]—Ver. 43. 'Avitas umbras.' This alludes to the 'feralia' or rites to appease the 'Manes,' or shades of the dead, described in the second book, ver. 533, and following.

[30] *The privileges.*]—Ver. 45. The 'Jura' were the distinctive rights or privileges given to certain days by public order.

[31] *Light-bearing day.*]—Ver. 46. 'Lucifer' is properly 'the morning star.' As introducing the day, it is here put for the day itself.

[32] *The three words.*]—Ver. 47. On the subject of the 'auspicious and inauspicious days,' and the 'three words,' ('dies fasti' and 'nefasti,' and the 'tria verba,') see Introduction.

[33] *Speak upon every subject.*]—Ver. 51. On this subject see Introduction, in which reference is also made to the office of the Prætor, alluded to in the next line.

[34] *Honoured by his office.*]—Ver. 52. 'Honoratus,' 'Honored,' or, as we should say, 'Right worshipful, or right honourable.' This was the peculiar title of the 'Prætor Urbanus,' or city prætor.

[35] *The polling inclosures.*]—Ver. 53. Allusion is here made to the 'Dies Comitialis,' or day of Comitia, for making laws and electing magistrates. The 'Septum' was a boarded enclosure near the tribunal of the Consul, into which the 'centurii' went in their proper order when summoned by the herald. There was a plank called 'pons,' 'the bridge,' leading to the 'Septum,' over which each century passed in succession.

[36] *The market day.*]—Ver. 54. The 'Nundinæ,' so called from 'nonæ' 'ninth,' 'dies' 'day,' returned every eighth day, according to our reckoning; but, according to the Romans, who, in counting, included both extremes, every ninth day, whence the name. On this day the country-people came into the city to sell their wares, make their purchases, hear the new laws read, and learn the news. By the Hortensian law, the 'Nundinæ,' (which before were only 'feriæ,' or 'holidays,') were made

returns after the ninth revolution. The care of Juno claims for itself the Ausonian[37] calends;[38] on the ides, a white lamb,[39] of larger growth, falls in honour of Jupiter. The guardianship of the Nones is without the care of a Deity;[40] of all these (beware that you be not deceived) the morrow will be inauspicious.[41] The omen is *derived* from the event itself,[42] for on those days Rome sustained sad losses in adverse warfare. These circumstances, as being inherent to the whole of the festivals, will be here stated by me once for all, that I may not be forced to interrupt the order of the matters *treated of by me.*

Lo, Germanicus! Janus announces to thee a prosperous year,[43] and is present at the outset in my verse. O, Janus, thou of the two heads! origin of the year silently rolling on, thou who alone of the Gods above, dost behold thy own back, be thou propitious to our princes,[44] through whose toils both

---

'fasti,' or court days, that the country-people then in town might have their lawsuits determined.

[37] *Ausonian.*]—Ver. 35. Ausonia was properly the land of the Ausones, in the southern part of Italy; but the poets use it to signify the whole of Italy.

[38] *Calends.*]—Ver. 55. For an account of the Calends, Ides, and Nones, see Introduction. On all the Calends, the Pontifex minor and the Regina Sacrorum sacrificed to Juno.

[39] *A white lamb.*]—Ver. 56. A sacrifice of a lamb, called the 'ovis idulis,' was offered in the capitol to Jupiter, on the Ides of each month. On the Ides of January, the victim was always a wether.

[40] *Is without the care of a Deity.*]—Ver. 57. He means that on those days there are no sacrifices to any of the Gods.

[41] *Will be inauspicious.*]—Ver. 58. 'Ater,' literally 'black.' The epithet was perhaps derived from the custom of recording unlucky days by black marks set against them, as being 'carbone notandi,' 'to be marked in charcoal.'

[42] *From the event itself.*]—Ver. 59. The Romans had 'præliares' and 'non præliares,' 'fighting' and 'non-fighting' days. The days after the calends, nones, and ides, were 'non-præliares,' as they believed that there was of necessity something unlucky in the idea of 'post,' after. So a public calamity on any particular day of a month rendered that day 'ater,' or 'nefastus,' in every month. Many of their most memorable defeats happened on the Nones, which thence derived their inauspicious character.

[43] *Propitious year.*]—Ver. 63. As we should say in the present day, 'wishes you a happy new year.'

[44] *To our princes.*]—Ver. 68. The princes here alluded to are probably

the fertile earth and the sea enjoy undisturbed peace. Be thou, O Quirinus,[45] propitious to thy senators, and to thy people, and by thy nod *of approbation* unlock the white temples.[46] A favourable day is dawning, be ye propitious both in your language[47] and in your feelings; now on the auspicious day must auspicious language be used. Let our ears be relieved from strife, and forthwith let maddening discords be far away; and thou envious tongue, postpone thy occupation. Do you perceive how the sky is gleaming with the perfume-bearing fires,[48] and how the Cilician ear[49] is crackling[50] on the kindled hearths? The flame with its brightness irradiates the gold of the temples, and diffuses its tremulous beam throughout the highest part of the building. With unpolluted garments they go[51] to the Tarpeian

Tiberius and Germanicus. He may perhaps allude to the victory of Germanicus over the Catti, Cherusci and other German tribes, A. U. C. 770.

[45] *O Quirinus.*]—Ver. 69. The reading is 'Quirini;' but I have adopted Gierig's suggestion, 'Quirine.' The poet is addressing Janus, one of whose names was Quirinus, and would not ask him to 'be propitious to his own people.' Romulus also was called Quirinus, but it does not seem likely that allusion is here made to him.

[46] *White temples.*]—Ver. 70. Either white, as being built of marble, or whitened in appearance by the new white clothes of the worshippers. The temple of Janus only remained open during war; but the poet must not be understood as wishing it to be opened for that reason; but only that the gates of all the temples being open for sacrifice, the gate of that too might be opened for such a purpose. The Roman doors were fastened with a chain, at the end of which the 'sera,' or bolt, was fixed. When the door was shut the bolt was fastened in the door-post; when open it was drawn back.

[47] *In your language.*]—Ver. 71. 'Favete linguis,' 'be propitious in your language,' was an usual injunction at sacrifices, as a word of ill omen spoken during their celebration on the calends of January, was considered to have an influence on the whole year.

[48] *Perfume-bearing fires.*]—Ver. 75. Frankincense, cinnamon, saffron, and cassia, used to be thrown on the altars during the time of sacrifice.

[49] *The Cilician ear.*]—Ver. 76. 'Spica Cilissa' means the filaments of saffron from Mount Corycus, in Cilicia.

[50] *Is crackling.*]—Ver. 76. When the saffron was good, according to Pliny the Elder, it crackled while burning. Probably from this, as from the crackling of laurel (which was frequently burnt for the purpose), omens were derived

[51] *They go.*]—Ver 79. On the calends of January the new consuls, accompanied by the senate and the people, went in procession to the Capitolium, to solicit the protection of Jupiter for the state.

heights,[52] and the people itself harmonizes by the colour of its dress with the festival. And now the new fasces[53] precede, the new purple[54] glistens, and the much distinguished *chair of ivory*[55] is sensible of new weights. The steers unacquainted with toil, which the Faliscan herbage has fed on its own fields, offer[56] their necks to the blow. Jupiter, when he looks from his height over the whole earth, has nothing which he can behold but that which is *under* Roman *sway*. Hail! joyous day, and ever return more happy, worthy to be honoured by a people all-powerful throughout the world. But, O Janus, thou of the double form, what kind of deity shall I pronounce thee to be? for Greece has no divinity corresponding to thee.[57] Do thou, at the same time, declare the reason why thou alone of all the inhabitants of heaven lookest

[52] *The Tarpeian heights.*]—Ver. 79. The capitolian hill, on which the Capitol, or temple of Jupiter, was erected, was originally called 'Saturnius,' in honour of Saturn. It was afterwards called 'Tarpeius,' from the vestal virgin Tarpeia, whose fate is narrated below, line 261, and was the quarter allotted to the Sabines after they were incorporated with the people. The 'arx,' properly speaking, was the highest of the Roman hills, and the inferior part of the declivity was the 'Capitolium,' or 'mons Tarpeius.' The latter name was more especially applied to a steep rock on one side, whence criminals were thrown.

[53] *The new 'fasces.'*]—Ver. 81. The 'fasces' were a bundle of rods tied together, with an axe inserted in the middle. They were borne by the lictors, as the insignia of the consular dignity.

[54] *The new purple.*]—Ver. 81. The 'prætexta,' or consular robe.

[55] *Chair of ivory.*]—Ver. 82. The 'sella curulis,' was a seat inlaid with ivory, and at first used only by the kings, but afterwards by the consuls, prætors, censors, and the higher ædiles, when employed in their official capacity. These officers were from this circumstance named 'curule.' The name of the chair was perhaps derived from its being carried on the 'currus,' or 'chariot,' to be at hand when required by the officer in his official capacity, either in the senate-house, or at the tribunal of justice. It was borrowed from the Tuscans, and was in the form of the letter X, for the convenience of folding up.

[56] *Offer.*]—Ver. 83. As though of their own accord; for if the victim struggled, it was not considered to be an appropriate offering to the god. The Falisci were a people of Etruria: the fertility of the soil rendered their pastures greatly esteemed, and victims for sacrifice were sought from their fields. Their country was also famous for a stream which imparted extreme whiteness to the oxen that drank of it.

[57] *No divinity corresponding to thee.*]—Ver. 90. Janus was probably the same deity as 'Dianus,' who represented the sun. If so, we must only understand by this, that the Greeks had no god corresponding to him in form and attributes.

upon[58] that which is behind thee, and that which is before thee *at the same time*. While I was revolving these things in my mind, my tablets[59] being taken in hand, the house seemed to be brighter than it was before. Then the divine Janus, wondrous with his double form, suddenly presented his two-fold features to my eyes. I was struck with amazement, and felt my hair stiffen with terror, and my breast was frozen with a sudden chill. He, holding in his right hand a staff, and in his left a key,[60] uttered these accents to me from the mouth of his front face, "Having laid aside thy terror, thou poet, labouring at *the history of* the days, learn what thou dost ask, and in thy mind understand my words. The ancients (for I am a being of the olden time) called me Chaos;[61]—behold, of how remote a period I shall sing the transactions. This air, full of light, and the *other* three *elementary* bodies which remain, fire, the waters, and the earth, were one *confused* heap. When once this mass was broken up by the discord of its *component* parts, and, dissolving, passed away into new abodes, flame soared on high, the nearer place received the air, and the earth and sea settled in a middle position. Then I, who had been but a

[58] *Thou lookest upon, &c.*]—Ver. 92, 93. Gower translates these lines,

'Rehearse the reason why thou hast such odds,
Of looking both ways more than all the gods.'

[59] *My tablets.*]—Ver. 93. The 'tabulæ,' or 'tabellæ,' were thin pieces of wood, usually of an oblong shape, covered over with wax, upon which the ancients wrote with the 'stylus,' or 'pen' of steel.

[60] *In his left a key.*]—Ver. 99. The staff and key were the usual badges of office of the 'janitores,' or porters, among the Romans. Massey thus renders these lines—

'In his right hand a long battoon I see,
And in his left he grasps a pond'rous key.'

[61] *Called me Chaos.*]—Ver. 103. The name Chaos is derived either from χάω, 'to gape,' or χύω, 'to pour.' By it was signified that confused heap of matter which the ancients in general believed to have existed from all eternity. Ovid, Metam. book i. ver. 6, 7, says,

'Unus erat toto naturæ vultus in orbe
Quem dixere Chaos: rudis indigestaque moles.'

'There was but one aspect of nature throughout the whole world, which they called chaos: an unwrought and crude mass.' This, in their idea, the supreme power reduced to the state of order and harmony which prevails in the visible world.

mass and bulk without form, passed into a shape and limbs befitting a god. And even now, in me that part which is before, and that which is behind, appears to be the same, a slight mark of my former shapeless figure. Hear, too, what is another cause of the form *thus* inquired after *by thee*, that thou mayest at the same time learn this and my office. Whatever thou beholdest around *thee*, the sky, the sea, the air,[62] the earth, all these have been shut up and are opened by my hand. In my power alone is the guardianship of the vast universe, and the prerogative of turning the hinge is entirely my own. When it has been my pleasure to send forth Peace[63] from her tranquil habitation, then at liberty she treads her paths unobstructed *by the restraints of war*. The whole world would be thrown into confusion in deadly bloodshed, did not my rigid bolts confine imprisoned warfare. Together with the gentle seasons[64] I preside over the portals of Heaven; through my agency Jupiter himself doth pass[65] and repass. Thence am I called Janus,[66] to whom, when the priest lays on the altar the offering cake

[62] '*The air.*']—Ver. 117. 'Nubila' generally means 'clouds,' 'mist,' 'cloudy sky.' Here, however, it means the 'air,' or 'æther.'

[63] *To send forth Peace.*]—Ver. 121. He here personifies Peace and War, and represents them as committed to the custody of Janus. Some have supposed that the story of Janus is the corruption of a tradition that an Italian chief named Janus constructed doors and locks for the protection of the person and of property, and that from him doors received the name of 'januæ.'

[64] *The gentle seasons.*]—Ver. 125. The 'seasons,' or 'hours,' are mentioned by Hesiod, Theog. 903, as three goddesses, the daughters of Jupiter or Zeus, and Themis. He calls them Eunomia (good order), Diké (justice), and Eiréne (peace), and represents them as watching over the affairs of men. They appear to have been originally considered as the presidents of the three seasons, into which the ancient Greeks divided the year. The day being similarly divided, they were regarded as presiding over its parts also; and, when it was afterwards divided into hours, these also were placed under their charge, and named from them. They presided over law, peace, and justice, and were the guardians of order and harmony among mankind.

[65] *Jupiter himself doth pass.*]—Ver. 126. It has been suggested, and with some probability, that allusion is here made to the etymology of his name, as Cicero derives the name 'Janus, or 'Eanus,' from 'Eundo,' the act of going or passing.—De Nat. Deor. Book 2.

[66] *Thence am I called Janus.*]—Ver. 127. Either from the root mentioned in the last note, or from 'janua,' a 'door' or 'gate.'

of bread corn[67] and the spelt mixed with salt,—(thou wilt smile at my epithets,) for I, the same deity, am at one time called Patulcius,[68] and at another time Clusius,[69] by the lips of the sacrificer. In good truth, that rude antiquity wished by the changes of my name to express my different duties. My power has now been related. Next learn the reason of my shape, although thou already perceivest it, in some degree, at least, *from what I have already said.* Every gate has two fronts, one on either side, of which the one looks out upon the people, but the other *looks inward upon* the household shrine;[70] and as the gate-keeper among you mortals, sitting near the threshold of the front of the building, sees both the goings out and the comings in, so do I, the door-keeper of the vestibule of heaven, at the same time look forth upon the regions of the east and the west.[71] Thou seeest the faces of Hecate[72] turned in three directions, that

[67] *Cake of bread corn.*]—Ver. 127, 128. 'Libum Cereale.' Literally, 'the cake pertaining to Ceres.' Ceres was the goddess of corn and husbandry, the daughter of Saturn and Ops, and the sister of Jupiter. She was especially worshipped in Sicily, and at Eleusis, in Attica, where the Eleusianian mysteries were celebrated. The 'libum,' or cake, here mentioned, was of a peculiar kind, offered exclusively to Janus, and thence called 'Janual.' The spelt, mixed with salt, was coarsely ground, and then strewed over the victim.

[68] *Patulcius.*]—Ver. 129. From the verb 'pateo, patere,' 'to lie open.'

[69] *At another time Clusius.*]—Ver. 130. From the verb 'claudo, claudere, clausus,' 'to shut.'

[70] *The household shrine.*]—Ver. 136. Literally 'the lar,' or, (the plural being denoted by the singular), 'the lares.' It may either mean literally the spot in the house where the 'lar,' or 'household god,' stood; or, figuratively, 'the family,' as opposed to the 'populus,' the people, outside. These little idols were kept near the hearth, and in the 'lararium' (here probably referred to,) which was a recess formed for that purpose, and in which prayers were offered up by the Romans on rising in the morning.

[71] *East and the west.*]—Ver. 140. 'Eoas partes Hesperiasque.' Literally 'the parts pertaining to the eastern star and the western star.'

[72] *The faces of Hecate.*]—Ver. 141. This goddess, who was the patroness of magic, is sometimes confounded with Diana. She was invoked as potent to avert evil, and was regarded as a beneficent deity. Her triple statues were set up before houses and in places where three ways met; hence the name 'Trivia,' one of her titles. This office was conferred on her by reason of a tradition, that when an infant she was exposed by her mother at such a spot. According to Hesiod, in his Theogony, she was the daughter of Cœus and Phœbe.

she may watch the cross roads *where they are* cut into three pathways; to me, too, it is given, in order that I may not lose time in the bending of my neck, to look two ways without moving my body." He had said *thus far*, and by his countenance acknowledged that he would not be difficult to *be moved by* me, if I wished to make further inquiries. I took courage, and, undismayed, gave thanks to the deity, and looking upon the ground, spoke a few words. "Say, now, *I pray thee*, why the new year begins with the frost of winter, which might better have been begun in the spring? Then all things are blooming, then is the youthful season of the year, and the young bud is swelling from the teeming shoot. Then the tree is covered with the newly formed leaves, the corn blade shoots from the seed to the surface of the ground; the birds, with their melodies, soothe the genial air, and the flocks gambol and disport in the meadows. Then is the sunshine refreshing; and the stranger swallow[73] comes forth, and builds her fabric of clay beneath the lofty rafter. Then, too, is the field subjected to cultivation,[74] and renewed by the plough. This, in justice, should have been called the opening of the year." I had made my inquiry in many *words;* he causing no delay by many, thus compressed his words into two lines. "The winter solstice[75] is the first day of the new, and the last of the old sun; Phœbus[76] and the year take the same *period for* commencement." After these things I was wondering, and inquired why the first day was not exempt from the litigation *of the courts*.[77] "Understand

[73] *The stranger swallow.*]—Ver.157. The poet here refers to the martin or window swallow, which builds in the corner of windows, under roofs, or against rocky places, and returns year after year to the situation it has once adopted, only repairing its nest. It mixes earth and straw, and after moistening it with its mouth, sticks it against the wall as a foundation for its nest. At noon it ceases work, that the portion built may dry by next morning, and in about a fortnight its nest is completed.

[74] *Subjected to cultivation.*]—Ver. 159. 'Patitur,' literally 'suffers,' or 'endures.' This term is appropriately used; for the ground, before this period, has been so hard, that it would not, literally speaking, suffer or endure cultivation. Now, however, the crumbling soil is ready to admit the plough and spade.

[75] *The winter solstice.*]—Ver. 163. 'Bruma.' The winter solstice is the time when the sun has completed his progress northward on the ecliptic, and begins to return.

[76] *Phœbus.*]—Ver. 164. Phœbus, or 'the shining,' was one of the titles of Apollo, the god of the sun.

[77] *Litigation of the courts.*]—Ver. 165. See Introduction.

the reason," says Janus; "I have assigned the very earliest hours of the year for the transaction of business, lest the whole year might be spent in idleness from *a bad* precedent. For the same reason, each person takes a slight taste of his calling by doing something *on that day*, but does no more than merely give evidence of his ordinary employment.[78] After that I *asked*, "Why, although I am propitiating the power of other *gods*, do I, O Janus, present the frankincense and the wine to thee, the first of all?" "That by means of me,[79] who guard the threshold, thou mayst have," says he, "access towards whatever deities thou mayst wish." "But why are congratulatory expressions[80] uttered in thy calends, and why do we then give and receive *in return* good wishes?" Then the god, leaning on the staff which his right hand bore, answers, "Omens *of the future* are wont to be derived from beginnings. To the word first spoken, ye mortals, turn your timid ears: and the augur[81] observes the bird that is first seen by him. Then the temples and the ears of the gods

[78] *Evidence of his ordinary employment.*]—Ver. 170. It was usual with the Romans for all classes of people in the calends of January, as an omen of future prosperity and industry, and not for lucre, to practise a little at their respective callings. The mechanic did some trifling job, the farmer a little work in the fields, and the pleader exercised his lungs a little in the forum.

[79] *By means of me.*]—Ver. 173. Fabius Pictor, an ancient Roman historian, says that the reason was, because Janus first taught the Latins to use spelt, 'farra,' and wine in sacrifice. Macrobius says it was because he first erected temples to the gods in Italy.

[80] *Congratulatory expressions.*]—Ver. 175. It was the Roman custom on the calends of January to express good wishes and anxious prayers for the safety of friends. Our practice of wishing each other a happy new year, and the French custom of making presents on that day, are, no doubt, derived from this origin.

[81] *The augur.*]—Ver. 180. The augur, or diviner by birds, derived his name from 'avis,' a 'bird,' and 'gero,' to 'carry,' or from some unknown Etrurian origin. According to Plutarch, in his life of Romulus, they were anciently called 'auspices,' and are supposed to have been three in number, one for each tribe. They were confirmed in their office by Numa, and a fourth was afterwards added, probably by Servius Tullius, when he divided the city into four tribes. They derived the 'signa,' or 'tokens of futurity,' from five sources—celestial phenomena, (such as thunder and lightning),—the singing and flight of birds,—the quantity eaten by the sacred chickens,—quadrupeds,—and from extraordinary accidents and casualties, called 'diræ,' or 'dira.' Among the birds which gave omens by the voice, 'oscines,' were the raven, the crow, the cock, the owl, &c. Those giving omens by flight, 'præpetes,' were the eagle, vulture, &c.

are open, no tongue utters unheeded prayers, and all that is said has its due weight." Janus had concluded, and I made no long silence, but with my words followed close on his last accents. "What means," said I, "the palm-date, and the shrivelled *dried* fig, and the white honey given *as a present*,[82] in the snow-white jar?"[83] "A fair omen," said he, "is the reason, that the like grateful flavour may attend upon our transactions, and that the year may in sweetness go through the course which it has begun." "I see," *said I,* "why sweets are given as presents: add the meaning of the little coin[84] *also given*, that no part of thy festival may be imperfectly understood by me." He smiled and said, "Oh! how little are the habits of thy own times known to thee, who canst suppose that honey is sweeter than the acquisition of money. Scarcely did I see any one, even when Saturn reigned,[85] to whose spirit gain was not sweet. With

[82] *Given as a present.*]—Ver. 186. These new year's gifts were called 'strenæ.' They consisted of fruit, occasionally covered with gold-leaf, honey, and sometimes a trifling piece of coin. The fig derived its name 'carica,' from Caria, now Anatolia, in Asia Minor.

[83] *In the snow-white jar.*]—Ver. 186. The best honey was white, and was especially given on this day in a white jar, as bearing the best omen. Honey was more frequently yellow, and the 'cadus,' or jar, of red earthenware, according to Martial, i. 56. 10. Pliny tells us that a white 'cadus' was sometimes made from a kind of whitish stone. Gower renders these lines,

> 'What means dry figs and palm-fruit I wot not,
> And honey offered in a fine white pot.'

[84] *The little coin.*]—Ver. 189. The 'stips' was a trifling coin of the smallest value, given frequently to beggars, and sent as a new year's present, merely by way of good omen, and not for any intrinsic value. The nominative 'stips' does not occur in any of the Latin classics. According to Suetonius, book v. ch. 42, Augustus condescended to take new year's gifts, and to receive the 'stips,' and in such quantities that his new year's presents must have been not only of good omen, but of great value. 'He proclaimed that he too at the beginning of the year would receive new year's gifts (strenæ), and stood in the vestibule of the temples on the calends of January, to receive the coin (stipes), which a crowd of all classes showered before him from their hands and laps.' Queen Elizabeth and James the First, and others of our sovereigns, expected a new year's gift (generally a piece of plate) from each member of the nobility, and gave a present in return, though the balance of gain was generally on the side of the sovereign.

[85] *When Saturn reigned.*]—Ver. 193. Saturn, the god of Time, was the son of Uranus and Terra, or Vesta. When dethroned by his son

time, increased that love of acquiring, which is now at its height, and has scarcely a further point to which it can proceed. Wealth now is more valued than in the years of the olden time, while the people still were poor, while Rome was but newly built, while a little cottage received Quirinus,[86] the begotten of Mars, and the sedge of the stream afforded him a scanty couch. In those times scarcely could Jupiter stand at full length in his narrow temple,[87] and in his right hand was a thunderbolt of clay.[88] Then used they to adorn the capitol with boughs, which now *they adorn with gems*;[89] and the senator himself used to tend his own sheep. Nor was it *then reckoned* a disgrace to have enjoyed undisturbed slumber on the bed of straw, and to have heaped the hay as a pillow under one's head. The consul used to give laws to the people, the plough being but just laid aside, and the possession of a small ingot of silver was *deemed* a crime.[90] But after the Fortune of this place

Jupiter, he fled into Italy, and gave name to Latium, because he was concealed there, from 'lateo,' to lie hid. Janus, who was the king of Etruria at the time, received him hospitably, and Saturn afterwards reigned on the Latian side of the Tiber. Under Saturn was the golden age, which, as Janus here tells us, was not entirely proof against the charms of lucre.

[86] *Quirinus.*]—Ver. 199. This was a name of Romulus, as well as an epithet of Janus. According to Macrobius, in his Saturnalia, it was derived from the Sabine word 'curis,' 'a spear,' and signified one skilled in the use of that weapon.

[87] *In his narrow temple.*]—Ver. 201. Either the temple of Jupiter Feretrius, built by Romulus on the Capitol, which was not sixteen feet long, or that built by Numa. However, the sitting posture was frequently assigned to the god by the taste of the artist, and the reverential feelings of the worshippers, as an attitude of repose and majestic dignity, irrespectively of the limits of the temple.

[88] *A thunderbolt of clay.*]—Ver. 202. 'Fictile,' of baked clay. In the early times the images of the gods were of baked clay. Tarquinius Priscus employed Etrurian artists to make a Jupiter of pottery for the Capitolium; and the four-horse chariot, which was placed on the Capitoline Temple when first built, was of baked clay.

[89] *They adorn with gems.*]—Ver. 203. Augustus, at one time, presented sixteen thousand pounds weight of gold and jewels of an enormous value to the temple of Jupiter Capitolinus.

[90] *A crime.*] — Ver. 208. There was an ancient law which prohibited the possession by the same person of more than five pounds of silver. Fabricius, the censor, in the year A.U.C. 478, expelled from the senate Cornelius Rufinus, who had been dictator and twice consul, for having ten pounds' weight of silver plate in his possession.

raised *on high* her head, and Rome reached with her height[91] to the gods above, both wealth increased and the maddening lust for wealth; and although men possess very much they still desire more. They struggle to acquire, in order that they may lavish; and *then* to obtain again[92] that which they have lavished; and the very changes, *from wealth to poverty*, afford nourishment to their vices. So *with those* whose stomach has swelled with the suffusion of water, the more that water that has been drunk, the more is it thirsted for.[93] Money now is the only thing prized;[94] wealth[95] *alone* gives honours; wealth *gives* friendships: the poor man every where lies *prostrate*. But thou askest me why the omen of the small coin is deemed desirable, and why the ancient pieces of brass[96] are welcome to our hands. In olden times they used to give pieces of brass; at the present day there is a better omen in gold, and the ancient coinage beaten out of the field, yields to the new. Us *deities*, too, though we approve of the temples of ancient fashion, golden ones please right well; that grandeur

[91] *Reached with her height.*]—Ver. 209, 210. These two lines are thus translated by Gower:—

'But when proud fate this place's head had reared,
And Rome's top-gallant near the gods appeared.'

[92] *To obtain again.*]—Ver. 213. This reminds us of the old proverb, which tells greedy people that 'they cannot both eat their cake and have it.'

[93] *Is thirsted for.*]—Ver. 216. The common comparison of the state of the avaricious man to that of a person afflicted with the dropsy.

[94] *Money now is the only thing prized.*]—Ver. 217. 'In pretio pretium est,' equivalent to our common expression, 'Money only makes the man.'

[95] *Wealth.*]—Ver. 217. 'Census' literally means the valuation on oath of the present value of one's possessions for the purposes of taxation—in fact, the Roman return for the income-tax. Hence it came to signify the property itself. Perhaps it might be rendered by 'the reputation of wealth.'

[96] *Ancient pieces of brass.*]—Ver. 220. The ancient pieces of brass were welcome to the hands of Romans, as commemorating the arrival of Saturn in Italy, by the prow of a ship on the reverse of the coin. These pieces were, doubtless, the large and heavy coins of copper, or rather, bronze, and hence termed the as or æs, which originally weighed 1 lb., but were gradually reduced till they scarcely exceeded 1 oz. in weight. The ases of the early kings are supposed to have consisted merely of square ingots of bronze of 1 lb. weight without impress, and Servius Tullius is stated by Pliny, to have first placed the impress of an ox on them. In the early times of the republic, they were coined in a circular form, with the types alluded to by Ovid. The heaviest that have reached us are about 9¼ oz. in weight. These massive coins were distinguished by the Romans from the smaller and more modern money, by the title *æra gravia*, 'heavy

is suited to a divinity. We praise the olden times, but adopt *the manners of* our own day; yet the habits *of either age* are equally worthy[97] to be adopted. He had finished his instructions; then once again, as before, in mild accents I thus addressed the key-bearing god:—"Many things, indeed, I have learned, but why on the brass coin is there stamped on one side the figure of a ship, and on the other, a two-headed *form?*"[98] "Thou mightst," said he, "recognise me in the two-fold form, had not the very length of time worn away the workmanship. The cause of the ship *inscribed* remains *to be told.* In a ship, the scythe-wielding God[99] having first wandered over the whole world, came up the Etrurian river.[1] I remember the reception of Saturn in this land; he had been expelled by Jupiter from the realms of heaven. Thence for a long time did the name of Saturn[2] abide with that nation; the country also was called Latium from the god being there latent. Moreover pious posterity preserved the ship upon the brass coin, attesting the arrival of the god, their guest. I myself inhabited the soil along which, on its left side,[3] glides the most gently flow-

money.' The omen of the *small* coin, is, no doubt, an allusion to the silver and gold coins of a later period; the silver introduced, in 269 B.C., by coined pieces called denarii (from being of the value of ten asses), and the gold, in 209 B.C., in pieces of twenty denarii. It is probable that, after these epochs, omens were sought in preference from coins of the more precious metals.—*See Bohn's Coin Collector's Guide.*

[97] *Equally worthy.*]—Ver. 226. As being the most suitable to the feelings, and the best adapted to the wants and comforts of the people of those respective times.

[98] *A two-headed form.*]—Ver. 230. It has been stated in note 96, when coins with these types were probably first issued. They disappeared altogether towards the end of the republic, some of the last, with the ancient types of the bifrontal head of Janus and the prow of a ship, being those issued by Pompey. In these, one of the profiles of Janus was made to represent Pompey himself, and the other Cneius, his father. Macrobius relates that the boys of ancient Rome played a game similar to our modern toss-halfpenny, crying 'capita aut navim,' 'heads or ship,' just as our boys do 'heads or tails.'—*See Bohn's Coin Collector's Guide.*

[99] *Scythe-wielding.*]—Ver. 234. Saturn is always represented with a scythe in his hand, as emblematical of the ruthless and unsparing power of Time.

[1] *The Etrurian river.*]—Ver. 234. The river Tiber, which flowed with Etruria on its left, and Latium on the right side, into the Etrurian sea.

[2] *The name of Saturn.*]—Ver. 237. 'Saturnia' was one of the old appellations of the Latian nation.

[3] *Along whose left side.*]—Ver. 242. The Etrurian bank of the Tiber, where the Janiculum was situated.

ing wave of the sandy Tiber. Here, where now Rome is, a forest, untouched by the axe, used to flourish, and *this* state so mighty was a *place of* pasturage for a few oxen. My place of retreat was that hill, which this age, paying me all adoration, denominates after my name, and calls it the Janiculum.[4] Then, too, was I reigning, when the earth was fit to receive the gods, and the divinities were interspersed among the abodes of men. Not as yet had mortal crime[5] driven Justice away.[6] She was the last of the deities that left the earth; and instead of fear, a sense of propriety used then without *any other* restraint to govern the people: it was no difficulty to enforce justice among the just. I had no concern with warfare; I used then to have but peace and the thresholds under my protection; and," shewing his key, "these," says he, "are the arms which I *properly* bear." The god had closed his lips; then thus I open mine, my words eliciting those of the divinity—" Since there are so many vaulted archways,[7] why dost thou stand consecrated *by a statue* in one alone,[8] here where

[4] *The Janiculum.*]—Ver. 246. The temple of Janus was built on the 'Janiculum,' one of the seven hills of Rome. In time a small town arose round it, until the whole was included in the immensity of the city of later times. From the dwellings of princes being in the early ages erected on the summit of a hill, which was called the 'arx,' the residence itself subsequently obtained the same title. So, too, the baronial castles of the feudal times were, perched on an eminence generally for the double purpose of overawing the vassals, and being prepared against a surprise by the enemy. In later times the Roman patricians had their palaces on the hills, and when they mingled with the plebeian crowd it was said of them that 'descendebant,' 'they came down.' Thus, Horace Od.—'descendat in campum petitor.' Our word 'descend' has a similar meaning, adapted in a figurative sense from this latter use of the Latin word.

[5] *Mortal crime.*]—Ver. 249. 'Facinus mortale' may either signify 'deadly crime,' or 'the crime of bloodshed,' or 'crime committed by mortals.'

[6] *Driven Justice away.*]—Ver. 249. Her name was also Astræa. Ovid in his Metamorphoses says, 'Ultima cœlestum terras Astræa reliquit,' 'Astræa was the last of the celestial deities to leave the earth.'

[7] *Vaulted archways.*]—Ver. 257. 'Jani,' covered passages, having a look-out on either side, were so called from Janus. The poet asks the deity why he is honoured with a statue in only one 'janus,' or arched temple, when there are so many places in Rome named after him. These passages were always double, for the convenience of people passing both ways.

[8] *In one alone.*]—Ver. 257. According to Varro, this temple was the 'porta Janualis,' or 'gate of Janus,' built by Romulus. Numa placed a statue of Janus in the temple, which was five cubits in height.

thou hast a shrine adjoining to the two market places.[9] He, with his hand stroking the beard that flowed down upon his breast, forthwith related the warfare of the Œbalian Tatius,[10] and how the faithless guard,[11] captivated with the Sabine bracelets, conducted Tatius to the approaches of the lofty citadel. "From that," said he, "there was, as there is now, a steep path by which you descend to the vallies and the market places. And now had he reached the gate[12] whose resisting bolts *Juno* the daughter of Saturn had insidiously removed: when fearing to enter on a contest with a deity so powerful, I slily put in practice the resources of my *peculiar art*.[13] I opened the mouths of the fountains, in which kind of aid I am distinguished, and I showered forth sudden streams of water. But first I mingled sulphur in the hot streamlets, that the boiling flood might obstruct the passage of Tatius. When the useful quality of this stream, after the repulse of the Sabines, was perceived, and the appearance which it formerly had was restored to the place *now* secure *from the enemy*, an altar was erected to me, united with a little chapel: this with its flames consumes the spelt meal with the *salt and* flour cake *of sacrifice*."[14] "But why dost thou lie

[9] *The two market-places.*]—Ver. 258. These were the 'Boarium,' or ox-market, and the 'Piscarium,' or fish-market.

[10] *The Œbalian Tatius.*]—Ver. 260. Œbalus was a Spartan prince, the grandfather of Helen. The Sabines, who are here alluded to, were reputed to have been a Spartan colony. Titus Tatius was the king of the Sabines in their wars with Romulus.

[11] *The faithless guard.*]—Ver. 261. Tarpeia, the daughter of Tarpeius, agreed to betray the Roman citadel (of which her father was the commander) for the golden bracelets worn by the Sabine warriors. When she had fulfilled her promise, she received the just reward of her treachery, for each soldier, as he gave his bracelet, threw also his shield upon her, and she was soon crushed to death by the weight. This circumstance is commemorated on a denarius of the family.

[12] *Reached the gate.*]—Ver. 265. It was the 'Porta viminalis' that Juno on this occasion opened for the admission of the Sabines. It was so called from the quantity of osiers, 'vimina,' that grew in the neighbourhood.

[13] *My peculiar art.*]—Ver. 268. That is, of opening, suited to my guardianship of all entrances and exits. These two lines are translated by Gower:—

'I, loth to thwart it with so high a power,
Did slily help them with a feat of our.'

[14] *Cake of sacrifice.*]—Ver. 276. These were small cakes made in the shape of fingers joined together, and laid in heaps for the purposes of sacrifice, whence the name 'strues,' from 'struo,' 'to build,' or 'pile up.'

concealed[15] in time of peace, and why art thou revealed, when arms are taken up?" There was no delay, the cause *of the circumstance* inquired after was told me in answer. "In order that the means of returning may lie open in readiness for the people when they have gone forth to war, the whole of my gate stands wide open, the bolt being removed. In times of peace I bar my doors, that she may by no means be enabled to depart; and under *the sway of* Cæsar's name long shall I remain shut up." He spoke, and raising his eyes that looked both before and behind, he looked upon whatever there was in the whole world. There was peace: and the Rhine,[16] the occasion of thy triumph, Germanicus, had now surrendered to thee its subservient streams. O Janus, make peace everlasting, and them *to be* the ministers[17] of peace, and grant that the author *of this change* may not abandon his office. But, as I was enabled to learn from the list of the festivals, on this day our forefathers consecrated two temples.[18] The *sacred* Island which the river surrounds with its divided stream, received the son of Phœbus and the nymph Coronis.[19] Jupiter occupies a share; one place received them both, and the temple of the grandson is joined to that of his mighty grandsire.

What forbids me, also, to mention the stars, how each of them rises and sets? That, too, was a part of my promised *undertaking*. Blessed spirits *were they* to whom first it was a care to learn these things, and to ascend to the mansions on high. It is worthy of belief that they raised their heads equally above the vices and the haunts of mortals. Neither lust nor wine enfeebled their exalted

[15] *Lie concealed.*]—Ver. 277. Alluding to the closing of the temple of Janus in time of peace, and the opening of it in time of war.

[16] *The Rhine.*]—Ver. 286. He alludes to the triumph of Germanicus over the Catti, Cherusci, and Angrivarii, A.U.C. 770.

[17] *The ministers.*]—Ver. 287. Tiberius and Germanicus.

[18] *Two temples.*]—Ver. 290. One to Jupiter, consecrated by Caius Servilius, and the other dedicated to Æsculapius, the son of Apollo.

[19] *The nymph Coronis.*]—Ver. 291. Æsculapius was the son of Apollo and Coronis, the daughter of Phlegias and Leucippus. She was slain in a fit of jealousy by Apollo, who gave Æsculapius into the charge of the centaur Chiron; he instructed his charge in the art of medicine, of which he afterwards became the tutelar divinity. In consequence of a plague at Rome, an embassy was sent to Epidaurus, in Peloponnesus, where Æsculapius was worshipped, and one of the serpents sacred to him was brought to Rome, on which the temple mentioned by the poet was built to the god on the 'sacred Isle' in the Tiber.

minds, nor the duties of the Forum, nor the toils of warfare. Nor did giddy ambition, nor glory overspread with artificial glare,[20] nor the craving for vast riches, disquiet them. *It is* they *who* have brought the far distant stars to our eyes, and have subjected the heavens to their intellect. Thus is heaven won, not that Olympus *for that purpose* should bear Ossa,[21] and the peak of Pelion touch the loftiest stars. We, too, under the guidance of these, will apportion out the skies, and will assign their own peculiar days according to the appointed constellations. When, therefore, the third night before the approaching nones shall come, and the ground shall grow damp, besprinkled with the dew of heaven, in vain will the claws of the eight-footed Crab[22] be sought for; he has sunk headlong beneath the western waters. When the nones are just arriving, the showers issuing from the black clouds will give you indications as the Lyre rises.[23]

Add four days passed in regular succession, to the nones, Janus will have to be appeased on the Agonalian day.[24] The aproned priest[25] may perhaps be the origin of the appel-

[20] *Artificial glare.*]—Ver. 303. 'Fucus' is, literally, a marine shrub, or sea-weed, red alkanet, which was used for the purposes of dyeing and painting.

[21] *Should bear Ossa.*]—Ver. 307. Ossa (now Kissova), Pelion (now Plesnid), and Olympus which is still called by its ancient name, were high mountains in Thessaly. He alludes to the attempt by the giants Otus and Ephialtes, sons of Neptune and Iphimedeia, to scale heaven when they were but nine years old, by heaping the mountains one upon the other.

[22] *The eight-footed crab.*]—Ver. 313. Because on the third day of January, at sun-rise, is the acronychal setting of the constellation Cancer, the Crab. In the mythology, it is said to have been placed among the constellations by Juno, after it had been crushed by the foot of Hercules, which it had bitten while the hero was engaged in combat with the Hydra in the Lernæan marsh.

[23] *The Lyre rises.*]—Ver. 316. The cosmical rising of Lyra, usually accompanied with rain. This is feigned to be the lyre on which Orpheus played when he descended to the infernal regions.

[24] *The Agonalian day.*]—Ver. 318. The festival of Janus called 'Agonalia,' or 'Agonia;' the meaning of which name the poet proceeds to describe.

[25] *The aproned priest.*]—Ver. 319. The 'minister' here mentioned was the 'rex sacrorum,' or 'king of the sacrifices,' who was in religious matters the representative of the ancient kings; higher in rank than the 'pontifex maximus,' but inferior in power and influence. His duties were, to perform sacrifice, to propitiate the deities, and to proclaim the festivals. While sacrificing, the priests and their assistants used to wear small aprons.

lation, under the blow of whom the victim falls in honour of the celestial gods; for he, when about to stain with reeking gore the knives already unsheathed, always asks the question, "Do I proceed?"[26] Nor does he proceed unless commanded *so to do*. Some think that the day has the name of Agonal, from the act of driving, because the sheep do not come *of their own free will to the sacrifice*, but are driven.[27] Some think that this festival was called "Agnalia"[28] by the ancients, although by that derivation one letter is removed from its proper place; or is that day thus named from the agony of the sheep,[29] because the victim shudders at the knives perceived *by it* as they lie in the water?[30] Some, too, *think* that the day derived a Grecian epithet from the games[31] that were wont to be celebrated in the time of our forefathers. The ancient dialect, too, called sheep by the name of "Agonia;" and in my opinion the last is the true reason for the name, and to this extent that reason is *ascertained for* certain, that the king of the sacred rites is in duty bound to propitiate the divinities with the mate of the fleece-bearing ewe. That *sacrifice* which has fallen by the right hand of the victor is called the victim:[32] when the hostile troops are driven far away *then the sacrifice* is called the host.[34] In days of old, it was *plain* spelt, and the sparkling grain[35] of

[26] *Do I proceed?*]—Ver. 322. Ago ne. Two Latin words, forming a trisyllable, and signifying 'do I?' or 'am I to proceed?'

[27] *Are driven.*]—Ver. 323. 'Agor' is 'to be driven,' whence this fanciful derivation.

[28] *Agnalia.*]—Ver. 325. From 'Agnus,' 'a lamb,' as sheep were then sacrificed.

[29] *Agony of the sheep.*]—Ver. 327. Ἀγωνία, (agonia), the Greek for 'terror,' whence our word 'agony;' implying pain, and, in this instance, 'extreme horror.'

[30] *In the water.*]—Ver. 327. The knives placed in basins of water, near the altar, for the purposes of ablution.

[31] *From the games.*]—Ver. 330. Ἀγῶνες, 'agones,' is the Greek term for public games or contests.

[32] *Is called the victim.*]—Ver. 335. So called, according to the poet, as being the offering sacrificed by him who is the 'victor,' or conquering party, deriving its name from 'vinco,' 'to conquer.'

[34] *The host.*]—Ver. 336. The sacrifice is so called, according to the poet, when it is offered on the retreat of the enemy; as it would appear, in contradistinction to his death; 'hostis' being the Latin word for 'enemy.'

[35] *Sparkling grain.*]—Ver. 338. Salt was held in high esteem by the ancients. The lares and the salt-cellars were with equal care placed on

unadulterated salt that had efficacy to render the gods propitious to man. Not yet had the stranger ship, impelled through the waters of the ocean, imported the myrrh[36] that is distilled from the bark in tear-like drops. *In those days* neither Euphrates had sent its frankincense,[37] nor India its zedoary,[38] nor were the filaments of the ruddy crocus then known. The altar used to send forth its smoke, contented with the Sabine herbs,[39] and the laurel was burned with no small crackling noise. If there was any one who could add violets to the chaplets wrought from the flowers of the meadow, that person was a rich man. The knife of the present day, which opens the entrails of the stricken bull, had in those times no employment in the sacred rites. Ceres[40] was the first who took pleasure in the blood *of an animal—namely,* the ravenous sow, avenging the injury done to her property by the merited death of the transgressor. For in the early part of the spring she found that the crops of corn, swelling with their young milky juice, were rooted up by the snout of the bristly swine. *From that day* the swine paid the penalty. You, he-goat, warned by her example, wish that you had abstained from the shoot of the vine. A person looking upon him while imprinting his teeth upon the vine would naturally utter some such expression as this, with no silent indignation. '*Well*, gnaw away at the vine, *Master* goat; there will still be *enough juice in it* to be sprinkled upon your horns, when you shall be standing *a victim* at the altar.' Truth attends

their tables. The family salt-cellar was an heir-loom, preserved with the greatest care. Horace, Odes, book 2, Ode 16, mentions the salinum.

[36] *Imported the myrrh.*]—Ver. 339. The myrrh is a shrub that either, with or without an incision in the bark, distils a sweet gum in tear-like drops.

[37] *Frankincense.*]—Ver. 341. This was a perfume which was imported into Europe from Arabia.

[38] *Its zedoary.*]—Ver. 341. 'Costum' was a shrub growing in Palestine and Syria, and prized for its powerful aromatic smell. The Euphrates, running through Mesopotamia and the northern part of Arabia into the Persian Gulf, bore thither for the use of the western world the riches and spices of the east.

[39] *The Sabine herbs.*]—Ver. 343. This was the savin, a herb resembling the cypress. Pliny, Nat. Hist. book 24, mentions the occasional use of it in the place of frankincense.

[40] *Ceres.*]—Ver. 349. For some account of this goddess see note on line 127 of this book.

his words. Bacchus,[41] thy foe given up to thee for punishment, has his horns sprinkled with the outpoured wine.[42] Her guilt was fatal to the sow—fatal, too, was his guilt to the goat. But what *didst thou*, O ox, and what did ye, O gentle sheep, to deserve a like fate?

Aristæus[43] was weeping, because he had seen that his bees, destroyed together with their progeny, had deserted the unfinished honeycombs. Him, then, while grieving, his Cærulean mother[44] with difficulty consoled, and added to what she had said these last words: "Cease thy tears, my son, Proteus[45] will alleviate thy losses, and will teach thee in what manner thou mayst recover what has been lost. That however, he may not deceive thee by his transformations, let strong fetters bind both his hands."[46] The youth comes to the prophet, and seizing the arms relaxed in sleep of the watery sire, binds them together. He, versatile in form, by his peculiar art changes his appearance, but afterwards, overcome by the fetters, he returns to his natural shape, and, raising his countenance all streaming, with his azure-coloured beard, he said, "Dost thou seek to know by what art thou mayst recover thy bees? Bury in the earth the carcase of a slaughtered ox: he, when so buried,

[41] *Bacchus.*]—Ver. 360. The god of wine and revelry. He was the son of Jupiter and Semele.

[42] *The out-poured wine.*]—Ver. 360. Alluding to the pouring the wine between the horns of the victim before it was slain.

[43] *Aristæus.*]—Ver. 363. He was son of Apollo and the nymph Cyrene, and followed the occupation of a shepherd, according to Virgil, who, in the fourth book of his Georgics, relates this story at much greater length, and in more poetical language.

[44] *His Cærulean mother.*]—Ver. 365. Or 'of azure,' or 'light blue colour,' Cyrene being a nymph of the waters; she was daughter of the river Peneius, and is said by Pindar to have given name to the town of Cyrene, in Africa.—Pythia Ode 9.

[45] *Proteus.*]—Ver. 367. He was a deity of the sea, son of Oceanus and Tethys, or, according to some writers, of Neptune and Phœnice. Neptune bestowed on him, as the keeper of the ocean monsters, the gift of prophecy. He resided chiefly in the Carpathian Sea, and on the coast of Egypt. When reposing on the shore, he was much resorted to by persons wishing to test his prophetic powers. Menelaus and Hercules are said to have consulted him.

[46] *Bind both his hands.*]—Ver. 369, 370. Gower translates these lines—

'But bind him sure, in fetters strong, lest he
With his transformed shapes, should coosen thee.'

will supply what thou now askest of me." The shepherd performs his commands. The swarms throng from the putrefying ox. The death of a single being has produced a thousand new lives. Fate, too, demands the sheep. She in her impiety once cropped the sacred plants,[47] which a pious old dame was accustomed to offer to the rustic deities. What remains in safety, when both the sheep that bear the fleece, and the oxen that till the fields, resign their lives upon the altars? Persia propitiates by the *sacrifice of the* horse, Hyperion[48] begirt with rays of light, that no sluggish victim may be offered to the swift god. Because the hind was once slain in honour of the triune Diana[49] in the stead of a virgin,[50] at the present day she is sacrificed though not in the stead of a virgin. I have seen the Sapæans[51] and him who dwells near thy snows, O Hæmus, offer to Trivia the entrails of dogs.

The ass too is slain for the lustful guardian[52] of the fields.

[47] *The sacred plants.*]—Ver. 381. 'Verbenæ' here means the several plants used in sacrifice, such as the laurel, olive, myrtle, cypress, tamarisk, and rose. In the sacred rites they were either used as garlands for the head, or were borne in the hands of suppliants, or were laid on the altars. Some legend is probably here referred to, the particulars of which have not come down to us.

[48] *Hyperion.*]—Ver. 385. A title of the sun among the Greeks. The Persians worshipped him by the name of Mithras. According to some mythologists, Hyperion was the son of Uranus and Terra (heaven and earth), and father of the sun and moon and of Aurora, the goddess of the morning.

[49] *Diana.*]—Ver. 387. See note to line 141, above.

[50] *In the stead of a virgin.*]—Ver. 387. This was Iphigenia, the daughter of Agamemnon and Clytemnestra. The Greeks, when going to Troy, were detained at Aulis by contrary winds. Chalcas declared that this was through the anger of Diana at the loss of a favourite stag, killed by Agamemnon; but that the goddess would be appeased by the death of the daughter of the offender. When about to be sacrificed, she disappeared, and a goat or a hind was substituted for her, though according to some accounts she really was slain.

[51] *The Sapæans.*]—Ver. 389. A people of Thrace, probably visited by the poet when an exile in that country. Dogs were sacrificed to Diana, because by their barking they scared away the spectres which she summoned to earth. These sacrifices took place at Zerinthus, near mount Hæmus, in Thrace.

[52] *Lustful guardian.*]—Ver. 391. Priapus, an obscene god, was the son of Venus and Bacchus (a befitting parentage), and was principally

The reason is indeed one that must cause shame, but quite suited to the character of this divinity. Greece was celebrating the festivals of ivy-crowned Bacchus, which every third winter brings round[53] at the established period. The guardian deities of cool Lycæum[54] came thither, and any one besides that was no enemy to mirth; the Pans, and the youthful troop of Satyrs prone to lust, and the goddesses[55] who inhabit the streams and lonely fields. The aged Silenus[56] too, had arrived upon his ass with bending back, and *Priapus*, who with ruddy aspect scares away the timorous birds. They, having found a grove well suited for their merry carousals, reclined on the couches bestrewed with grass. Bacchus gave the wine; each had brought a chaplet for himself; a rivulet rolled by its waters, to be but sparingly mixed.[57] The Naiad nymphs were there, some with locks dishevelled without the application of the comb, others with their hair arranged both with taste and labour. This one waits upon them with her robe gathered up[58] above the middle of the leg, another exposed as to her breast, with the bosom *of her dress* slashed asunder. This one bares her shoulder, another sweeps her robe along the grass—no sandals confine their delicate feet. On this side some are kindling the gentle flames of desire in the Satyrs,

worshipped at Lampsacus in Mysia, on the Hellespont. He presided over fields and gardens, which he protected from thieves and blight.

[53] *Brings round.*]—Ver. 394. This was the 'Trieterica,' or 'three-year feast.' It was really an annual festival, but was celebrated with greater solemnity every third year, to commemorate the expedition of Bacchus into India. Probably the year alluded to in the poem was the ancient one of four months only.

[54] *Cool Lycæum.*]—Ver. 395. A mountain in Arcadia sacred to Pan and Jupiter. The gods mentioned were the several Pans, fawns, and satyrs, the deities of Arcadia.

[55] *The goddesses.*]—Ver. 398. The Naiads, or water-nymphs.

[56] *Silenus.*]—Ver. 399. He was the foster-father of Bacchus, and, according to Pindar, was born at Malea, in Lesbos. He had a bald head, flat nose, and thick beard. He was the leader of the Satyrs, and was always drunk; yet, singularly enough, he was considered as conspicuous for his wisdom.

[57] *Sparingly mixed.*]—Ver. 404. Moderate drinkers mixed three parts of water with two of wine; but the present company preferred their liquors neat, or nearly so. Perhaps the ladies formed the exception.

[58] *Robe gathered up.*]—Ver. 407. The female tunic reached the ancles; but when expedition was required, it was tucked up as far as the mid-leg.

some in thee who hast thy temples wreathed with pine.⁵⁹ Thee too, Silenus, of lust inextinguishable, they inflame. It is lust alone that precludes thee from being aged. But the ruddy Priapus, the deity and guardian of the gardens, was charmed by Lotis above them all. Her he desires—her he longs after—for her alone he sighs; he signifies his wishes by his nods,⁶⁰ and entreats her by signs. Cold disdain is innate in the fair, and haughtiness accompanies beauty. By her countenance, she despises and she scorns⁶¹ him.

It was night, and, wine producing slumber, their bodies lay overpowered by drowsiness, in various places. Lotis, as she was wearied with sport, lay, the most remote of all, on the grassy earth, beneath the *overshadowing* boughs of a maple. Her lover rises, and, holding his breath, stealthily advances his silent footsteps, treading on tiptoe. When *now* he had reached the sequestered resting place of the nymph, fair as snow, he takes care lest the very drawing of his breath should make a noise. And now was he poising his body on the grass close by her, yet still was she sunk in deep sleep. He is overjoyed, and drawing aside her garment from her feet, began to proceed along the blissful path to the accomplishment of his desires. When, lo! braying with hoarse throat, the ass that bore Silenus sent forth unseasonable sounds. Alarmed, the nymph starts up, and with her hands flings back Priapus, and then flying⁶² arouses the whole grove. The god, already too well prepared for his lustful attempt, was an object of ridicule to all by the light of the moon. The author of the outcry paid the penalty by death, and hence is an acceptable victim to the god of the Hellespont. You, ye birds, charmers of the fields, a race accustomed to the groves, and guiltless, had been as yet unharmed; you, who build your nests, who cherish your eggs

---

⁵⁹ *With pine.*]—Ver. 412. *i. e.* Pan.

⁶⁰ *By his nods.*]—Ver. 417, 418. These lines remind us of those of Milton, in L'Allegro:—

> 'Quips and cranks, and wanton wiles;
> Nods and becks, and wreathed smiles.'

⁶¹ *And sneers.*]—Ver. 420. As we should say in common parlance, 'She turns up her nose at him.'

⁶² *Then flying.*]—Ver. 436. The gods, in compassion for this gross attempt on the nymph, changed her into the lotus tree.

with your plumage, and warble delightful strains from your ready throats. But these things avail you nothing, because you are accused of the power of utterance, and the gods believe that you disclose their purposes. And this charge not entirely groundless; for, as each is most familiar with the gods, at one time, by your wings, at another, by your voices, you give true indications.[62*] The race of the fowls, for so long a time secure, at length came to be slain *in its turn*, and the entrails of the informer against them *then* delighted the gods. For that reason, often is the white ring-dove, the consort, torn from her mate, burned on the glowing hearths. Nor does the defence of the capitol[63] avail, *to prevent* the goose from affording its liver for thy dishes, O dainty daughter of Inachus.[64] On the night *of this day*, the crested bird is slain in honour of the goddess Night,[65] because with watchful throat he calls forth the warm day. In the mean time the Dolphin,[66] a bright constellation, rises over the deep, and puts forth his head from his native waters.

[62*] *True indications.*]—Ver. 447. The poet refers to the omens obtained from the flight and voices of birds.

[63] *Defence of the capitol.*]—Ver. 453. The city of Rome being taken by the Gauls, Marcus Manlius, with a body of men, retired into the capitol, which during the night was attacked by the enemy. Their approach was discovered in time, through the cackling of some geese that were kept in the temple of Juno, and from that time geese were held sacred with the Romans.

[64] *Daughter of Inachus.*]—Ver. 453, 454. Inachis, supposed to have been the same with Io, daughter of Inachus, the river god. From the epicurean taste which she is here represented as indulging, she would probably have been more than usually pleased by a taste of the 'patè de foies gras' of the present day. Gower translates these lines thus,

> 'Nor can the guarded capitol release
> The goose's liver from choice Inach's mess.'

[65] *Goddess Night.*]—Ver. 455. 'Nox,' 'Night,' was one of the most ancient deities, being a daughter of Chaos. By her brother Erebus she produced the Day and the Light. She was the mother of the Fates, Dreams, Discord, Death, Momus, and others, and was worshipped in the temple of Diana at Ephesus.

[66] *The Dolphin.*]—Ver. 457. The cosmic rising of the Dolphin on the 9th of January; being the fifth of the Ides. In Book ii. the poet relates how the Dolphin carried Arion to Tænarus, when the minstrel had been thrown into the sea by the sailors anxious to obtain his wealth. It was also said that the Dolphin was thus honoured for having gained the hand of Amphitrite for Neptune.

The next day marks the winter by a central line,[67] and *the part of it* which will then remain, will be equal to that which is past.

The next dawn,[68] Tithonus having been left by her, shall look upon the pontifical ceremonies of the Arcadian goddess. Thee too, sister of Turnus,[69] the same day received in thy temple, here where the Plain *of Mars* is traversed by the aqueduct of the Virgin. Whence shall I derive the causes and the forms of these sacred rites?[70] Who can guide my sails in the midst of the deep. Instruct me thyself, thou who hast a name derived from song, and favour my undertaking, lest thy glory be lost in uncertainty. Having an origin before that of the moon[71] (if we credit it *when speaking* of itself), the land derives its name from the great Arcas.[72] Here was Evander,[73] who, although on either side of illustrious origin, was more noble in the line of his sacred mother: who, as soon as she had conceived the inspiration of heaven in her soul, used to utter from her unerring lips verses redolent of the divinity. She had told her son that troubles were im-

---

[67] *Central line.*]—Ver. 459. Ovid makes the 10th of January the middle day of winter. Columella makes it the 4th of that month.

[68] *The next dawn.*]—Ver. 461. Aurora was the goddess of the morning, and the daughter of Hyperion, or of Titan. She became enamoured of Tithonus, son of Laomedon, king of Troy, and took him with her to heaven.

[69] *Sister of Turnus.*]—Ver. 463. Juturna was a water nymph, who, according to Virgil, Æneid xii., was beguiled by Jupiter, and by him made a goddess of the streams. Her temple stood in the Campus Martius at Rome. She is again mentioned in the next book.

[70] *These sacred rites.*]—Ver. 465. The Carmentalia, in honour of Carmenta, a goddess of Arcadian origin, called also Nicostrata and Themis. It is said below by the poet, that the name Carmenta was derived from her prophetic powers, 'carmen' being the Latin word for 'prophecy,' which being originally given in verse, the term 'carmen' afterwards became applicable to all kinds of verse. Carmenta had a temple in the forum consecrated to her by the Roman matrons.

[71] *That of the moon.*]—Ver. 469. Indeed all the Arcadians styled themselves προσεληνοί, 'existing before the moon,' or 'Prælunites.' This circumstance is mentioned in the next book.

[72] *Arcas.*]—Ver. 470. Arcas was son of Jupiter and Calisto, and transferred to heaven as a constellation after his death. Arcadia, to which he gave name, was in the centre of Peloponnesus, bounded by Achaia, Messenia, Elis, and Argolis.

[73] *Evander.*]—Ver. 471. He was son of Carmenta, by Mercury, or, according to others, by Echemus.

pending over him and herself, and many things besides, which obtained their fulfilment in the lapse of time. For now the youth exiled with his mother, too true *a prophetess*, leaves Arcadia and his Parrhasian[74] home. To him, as he wept, his mother said, "Stay thy tears, my son, this turn of fortune must be borne by thee with manful spirit. This was thy destiny; it is no guilt of thy own that has exiled thee, but a god; thou hast been banished from thy city by the anger of a divinity. Thou art now enduring, not the penalty of a misdeed, but the wrath of a deity; it is some consolation that guilt does not accompany thy great misfortunes. As the mind of each man is conscious *of good or evil*, so does he conceive within his breast hope or fear, according to his actions. Mourn not as though *thou wert* the first that had suffered such ills; the same storm has borne down many a mighty man. The same did Cadmus[75] suffer, who long ago, when banished from the Tyrian shores, took up his abode, an outcast, on the Aonian soil. The same did Tydeus,[76] the same did Pagasæan Jason[77] suffer; and others besides, whom to enumerate would be a task too tedious. To the brave man every land is a country, as, to the fishes the ocean, and as, to the bird the whole extent of space in the world of air. Nor does bleak winter freeze throughout the whole of the year; to thee too—believe me—the hours of spring will yet come." Evander, with mind emboldened by the words of his parent, cuts the waves with his bark, and reaches Hesperia.[78]

[74] *Parrhasian.*]—Ver. 478. Parrhasia was a town of Arcadia.

[75] *Cadmus.*]—Ver. 490. Son of Agenor, king of Phœnicia. His sister Europa having been carried off by Jupiter, he was sent in search of her, and founded the colony of Bœotia, one of the ancient names of which was Aonia. These lines are thus translated by Gower:—

'This Cadmus, banished from the Tyrian Bay,
Endur'd, then settled in Aonia.'

[76] *Tydeus.*]—Ver. 491. He was son of Œneus, king of Calydon. Having accidentally slain one of his friends, he fled to the court of Adrastus, king of Argos, whose daughter Deiphyle he married.

[77] *Pagasæan Jason.*]—Ver. 491. Pagasæ was a sea-port of Thessaly. Jason was the son of Æson, king of Iolchos, who headed the expedition to Colchis, in pursuit of the golden fleece, which he gained by the aid of Medea.

[78] *Hesperia.*]—Ver. 498. So called from 'Hesperus,' or 'Vesper,' the evening star, as Italy was to the west of Greece, where it first received that appellation. Evander arrived in Italy in the reign of Faunus.

And now, by the advice of the skilled Carmentis, he had directed his bark into the river, and was proceeding against the stream of the Etrurian current. She beholds the bank of the river, to which the fords of Terentus[79] are adjacent, and the cottages scattered over the lonesome districts. And as she was, with her locks all dishevelled, she stood before the poop, and *with* stern *look* withheld the hand of him who was guiding the vessel's course. Then stretching forth her arms towards the right bank afar, she thrice strikes the pine wood deck with frantic foot. Scarcely, *yes*, scarcely, was she restrained by the hand of Evander from springing forward, in her haste to stand upon the shore. "Hail, gods of the regions sought by us," she said, "and thou country that shalt hereafter give new gods to Heaven, and ye rivers and fountains, which this strange land enjoys; ye too, nymphs of the groves, and ye choirs of the Naiads.[80] With favouring omens be ye seen by my son and by me, and may that bank be trodden with an auspicious step. Am I deceived? or shall these hills[81] become a vast city, and shall the rest of the world seek laws from this land? To these mountains *the sway of* the whole earth is promised one day; who could suppose the place to have so high a destiny? And soon shall the Dardanian ships[82] touch at these shores; here too shall a woman be the cause[83] of a fresh war. Pallas,[84] my beloved grandson, why dost thou put on

[79] *Terentus.*]—Ver. 501. This was a place at the end of the Campus Martius, where was a subterranean altar to the infernal deities.

[80] *The Naiads.*]—Ver. 512. The Naiads were deities who presided over rivers, springs, and fountains. They were represented as beauteous damsels, naked to the waist, and reclining on a vase, which was pouring forth a stream of water. Goats and lambs were offered to them, with wine, oil, milk, honey, fruits, and flowers. Gower translates these lines:—

'Ye springs and rivers of this land hospitious,
Ye fairies feat, and water-nymphs delicious.'

[81] *These hills.*]—Ver. 515. Alluding prophetically to the future destinies of Rome. The heights on which it was built were the Palatine, Capitoline, Janiculan, Cælian, Esquiline, Viminal, and Quirinal Hills.

[82] *Dardanian ships.*]—Ver. 519. Trojan. Dardanus was the son of Jupiter and Electra, and was considered as the founder of Troy. She alludes to the arrival of Æneas about sixty years after. His travels and his arrival in Italy, when rendered homeless by the destruction of Troy, form the subject of the Æneid of Virgil.

[83] *A woman be the cause.*]—Ver. 520. Lavinia, the daughter of Latinus, was the cause of the war between Æneas and Turnus. Helen, the wife of Menelaus, had previously been the cause of the Trojan war.

[84] *Pallas.*]—Ver. 521. Son of Evander. He led the auxiliaries which

those fatal arms? *Yet* put them on; thou wilt be slain with no mean avenger *of thy death*. Troy! although conquered, thou shalt conquer, and overthrown, thou shalt rise again;[85] that same ruin shall overwhelm the homes of thy foes.[86] Burn Neptunian Pergamus,[87] ye triumphant flames; is not that heap of ashes more exalted[88] than the whole world? Presently shall pious Æneas bring hither the sacred relics, and his father,[89] a second sacred charge; receive, O Vesta,[90] the gods of Ilium. The time will come, when the same person shall have the charge of thee and of the world *as well*, and thy sacred rites[91] shall be performed by a worshipper, himself a god. In the hands of the Augusti shall remain the guardianship of their native country; it is the decree of heaven that this house should hold the reins of empire. *One* thence *sprung*, the grandson and the son[92] of a god, though he himself

his father supplied to Æneas, and was killed by Turnus, who was slain by Æneas.

[85] *Shalt rise again.*]—Ver. 523. Namely, in Rome, founded by the descendants of thy people.

[86] *Homes of thy foes.*]—Ver. 524. She alludes to the future subjection of the Grecian provinces by Rome.

[87] *Neptunian Pergamus.*]—Ver. 525. Pergamus was properly the Citadel of Troy, but the word is often used by the poets for the entire city. Troy was called 'Neptunian,' because, when banished from Heaven, Neptune, with Apollo, assisted King Laomedon in building it.

[88] *More exalted.*]—Ver. 526. That is to say, 'in its consequences,' if we consider with the poet that the foundation of Rome was owing to the destruction of Troy.

[89] *His father.*]—Ver. 527. Anchises, the father of Æneas, did not, according to Virgil and other writers, reach Italy, but died in Sicily; though Ovid, Cato, Strabo, and Dio Cassius, say the contrary. The relics alluded to, are the images of the Trojan gods, the sacred fire of Vesta, and, according to some writers, the Palladium.

[90] *Receive, O Vesta.*]—Ver. 528. Vesta was the goddess of fire, and had a temple in Rome, which was built by Numa. In her sanctuary was preserved the Palladium of Troy, and a fire kept constantly burning by the Vestal virgins. The goddess received her name from the Greek word ἑστία, a 'hearth.'

[91] *Thy sacred rites.*]—Ver. 530. Julius Cæsar was the 'Pontifex Maximus,' or chief priest, and after his death was deified. Allusion is here made to him, or to the Emperor Augustus, who also received divine honours, and in his lifetime united the imperial with the pontifical office.

[92] *Grandson and the son.*]—Ver. 533. Either one person, Tiberius, the adopted son of the god Augustus, and grandson of the god Julius; or two persons, Tiberius, the son, and Germanicus, the grandson of Augustus.

refuse it, shall bear with godlike mind the burden which his father bore. And as I shall, in times to come, be consecrated in everlasting shrines, so shall Augusta Julia[93] be a new divinity.

When, with such sayings as these she came down to our own times, her prophetic tongue stopped short in the very midst of her accents. Landing from his ship, the exile stood on the Latian herbage; happy the man[94] to whom that country was a place of exile! And no long delay was there; new habitations were erected, and throughout the Ausonian hills there was no one greater than the Arcadian. Lo, the club-bearing hero hither drives the kine of Erythæa,[95] having travelled over the length of the vast world. And now while the Tegeæan[96] house is his place of entertainment, his kine untended wander through the luxuriant fields. It was dawn; startled from his slumber, the Tirynthian[97] guest perceives that

---

Tiberius alone is probably referred to, as he did reign, which Germanicus did not; and we are told that he affected to show great reluctance to assume the reins of government on the death of Augustus.

[93] *Augusta Julia.*]—Ver. 536. This was Livia Drusilla, daughter of L. Drusus Calidanus, and wife of Tiberius Nero, by whom she had Tiberius and Drusus Germanicus. Augustus, in order to marry her, divorced his wife Scribonia, and, on his death, she received the name of Julia by virtue of his will. Though Ovid is here deifying the lady in a spirit of anticipation, and though she survived him several years, it actually was the fact, that she was deified by her grandson Claudius, as Suetonius and Tacitus inform us. She was a woman of bad and unscrupulous character. Gower renders these lines:—

'As sure as altars me perpetually
Shall worship, Julia shall a goddess be.'

[94] *Happy the man.*]—Ver. 540. If, as is generally supposed, these lines were written by Ovid when himself in banishment, this expression perhaps was accompanied by a sigh for his far-distant home.

[95] *Erythæa.*]—Ver. 543. Erythæa was an island near Gades, now Cadiz, in Spain. Geryon, a three-bodied monster, lived there, possessing numerous herds and flocks; Hercules destroyed him, and drove his flocks and herds to Tirynthus.

[96] *Tegeæan*].—Ver. 545. Tegeæa was a city of Arcadia, near the Eurotas. Gower thus translates these lines:—

'And being here entertain'd by King Evander,
His beasts unkept about the plains do wander.'

[97] *Tirynthian.*]—Ver. 547. Hercules was said to have been nursed and brought up at Tirynthus, a town of Argolis, in Peloponnesus.

two bulls are missing from his number. He seeks *them*, and he sees not a trace of the noiseless theft; the fierce Cacus had dragged them backwards into his cave; Cacus,[98] the dread and disgrace of the Aventine forest,[99] no slight curse to both neighbours and travellers. Hideous was the appearance of the creature;[1] his strength was in proportion to his bulk, his body was huge: Mulciber[2] was the sire of this monster, and for his habitation there was a mighty cavern made secret by long passages retreating within, *a den* that could hardly be found by the wild beasts themselves. Human heads and arms hang nailed over the lintels, and the ground is *quite* blanched, frightful with the bones of men. The son of Jove was departing, a part of his oxen having been *thus* carelessly tended by him, when the stolen *animals* uttered a lowing with a hoarse voice. "I accept the recall,"[3] he says; and tracing the sound, the avenger comes through the woods to the accursed cave. The other had obstructed the approach by the barrier of a mountain fragment; hardly could twice five yokes of oxen have moved that mass. The Hero strains with his shoulders, (the heavens, *I should tell you*, had once rested[4] on them),

[98] *Cacus.*]—Ver. 551. Fabled to have been the son of Vulcan and Medusa. According to some accounts, he was a dishonest servant of Evander.

[99] *Aventine forest.*]—Ver. 551. The Aventine was the most extensive of the Roman hills, and was called by that name after an Alban king, who was buried upon it. It was called Murcius, from Murcia, the goddess of sleep, who had a temple there, and Remonius, from Remus, who wished to found the Roman city there.

[1] *Of the creature.*]—Ver. 553. 'Viro' signifies literally, either 'the man,' or the 'hero;' and Cacus, by birth, belonged to the class of heroes or demigods. But inasmuch as he does not seem to have been worthy of the name, according to our conception of its import, and as, by reason of his birth, he could not be called a man, the appellation used in the text seems to be the most appropriate.

[2] *Mulciber.*]—Ver. 554. This was one of the names of Vulcan, derived from 'mulceo,' 'to soften,' because, by his art, he softened iron; being the god of fire and the patron of blacksmiths. He was the son of Juno, and the husband of Venus.

[3] *The recall.*]—Ver. 561. To be called back when setting out on a journey was generally considered a bad omen. Hercules, however, here thought it a good one.

[4] *Had once rested.*]—Ver. 565. He relieved Atlas, who supported the heavens, that he might go and pluck the golden fruit of the Hesperides for him. On his return with the apples, Hercules requested Atlas to hold the load for a moment while he made a pad for his head. Atlas resumed the

and moving it dislodges the mighty weight. As soon as it was uptorn, the crash startled the very sky, and the earth sank down, struck by the weight of the mass. Cacus begins the attack hand to hand, and fiercely maintains the combat with stones and stakes; and when he fails in the use of these resources, with but little courage left, he resorts to the arts of his father, and vomits forth flames from his resounding throat. Often as he blows them forth, you would believe that Typhœus[5] is breathing, and that the rapid flash is hurled from the fires of Ætna. Alcides grapples *with him*, and his trebly knotted club, swung back three or four times, was planted full upon the face[6] of him opposing. He falls, and belches forth smoke mingled with blood; and dying, with his broad chest, he beats the ground. Of those bulls, the conqueror offers one to thee, O Jupiter, and invites Evander and the inhabitants of the country; he builds an altar to himself, which is styled "the Greatest," in the spot[7] where a part of the city has its name derived from an ox.[8] And now the mother of Evander is not silent *on the fact*, that the time is near at hand when the earth shall have sufficiently enjoyed the presence of her own Hercules. But, as in her life she was most pleasing to the gods, so, now herself a goddess, the blessed prophetess possesses this day as her own in the month of Janus.

burden, and Hercules forthwith walked away with the apples. The story bears some allusion, doubtless, to the fact, that Atlas was one of the first to give some knowledge of astronomy, and perhaps geography.

[5] *Typhœus.*]—Ver. 575. A giant called also Typhon, son of Tartarus and Terra. Flames darted from his mouth and eyes, and he had a hundred heads, like those of a dragon. Waging war upon the gods, he so frightened them, that they fled in the shape of various animals. Jupiter at length conquered him by his thunderbolts, and placed him under Ætna, a volcanic mountain of Sicily.

[6] *Upon the face.*]—Ver. 575, 6. Gower renders these lines thus:—

'Alcides drives on, and, with knotty bat,
Three or four times doth dash him o'er the pate.'

[7] '*The Greatest.*']—Ver. 581. This altar, according to Livy, and Dionysius, was built by Evander in honour of Hercules, and not by Hercules himself. According to them, Carmenta suggested the dedication, and the priests who superintended the sacred rites were the Potitii and the Pinarii, two illustrious families of the neighbourhood.

[8] *From an ox.*]—Ver. 582. 'The Forum Boarium,' or ox-market, called so from 'bos,' 'an ox,' and applied to that use on account of the sacrifice there offered by Hercules, as mentioned in the text.

On the Ides, the undefiled priest in the temple of Jupiter, offers on the flames the entrails of a wether; *then* every province was restored to our people,[8] and thy grandsire was called by the title of Augustus. Pass in review the waxen images[9] as they are distributed through the halls of the ennobled; titles so great as his never fell to the lot of any one man. Africa calls her conqueror[10] after herself; another *hero in his title* records the subjection of the Isaurian power,[11] another *the subjection* of the Cretans.[12] The Numidians[13] render one man titled, Messana[14] *makes* another *great in story*—another has derived his distinction from the city of Numantia.[15] Germany gave to Drusus[16] both death and a title. Ah me! how short-lived was

[8] *Restored to our people.*]—Ver. 589. On the Ides of January, B.C. 27, and A.U.C. 726, Augustus offered to resign his power. Being pressed to retain it, he consented, on condition of handing over the tranquil provinces to the people, to retain the unsettled ones and the army, under his entire control. The senate, nominally, at least, took the management of all the tranquil provinces, and to this fact allusion is here made. Octavius on this occasion received the title of Augustus.

[9] *The waxen images.*]—Ver. 591. These waxen images represented those persons who had the privilege of using them. Those who were called 'nobiles,' having filled the office of Consul, Prætor, Censor, or Curule Ædile, had this privilege, which was called 'jus imaginum,' and they were kept with great care by their posterity, and carried before them at their funerals. They were painted busts as far as the shoulders, made in wax; and they were placed in the 'atria,' or halls, carefully enclosed in wooden cases, supplying much the same place as our family pictures. Titles and inscriptions were written below them, describing the honours and achievements of the persons thereby represented.

[10] *Calls her conqueror.*]—Ver. 593. The Romans occasionally took an additional name, 'agnomen,' or 'cognomen,' from some illustrious deed or great event. P. Cornelius Scipio, after his victory over Syphax, king of Numidia, in Africa, received the cognomen of Africanus.

[11] *Isaurian power.*]—Ver. 593. . Publius Servilius, the pro-consul of Asia, conquered the Isaurii, a people near mount Taurus. He received a triumph, and was honoured with the 'agnomen' of Isauricus.

[12] *The Cretans.*]—Ver. 594. Q. Metellus was surnamed Creticus, from the island of Crete, now Candia, which he subdued.

[13] *The Numidians.*]—Ver. 595. Q. Cæcilius Metellus conquered the Numidians, under their king Jugurtha; whence his title ' Numidicus.'

[14] *Messana.*]—Ver. 595. 'Messana,' or 'Messala,' in Sicily, was conquered by Valerius Corvinus Maximus, who assumed the agnomen of 'Messala.'

[15] *Numantia.*]—Ver. 596. A tower in Spain, which, after a fourteen years' war, was destroyed by the Romans under Scipio Æmilianus, thence called Numantinus, A.U.C. 622.

[16] *Drusus.*]—Ver. 597. See note on line 3 above.

that heroic career! Were Cæsar to seek his names from the conquered, he would have to assume as many in number as the vast world contains nations. Some celebrated by one circumstance derive their titles *therefrom,—for instance, the title gained* from a breast-chain[17] won, or the assistance afforded by a raven.[18] O thou entitled 'Great,'[19] thy title is the full measure of thy achievements; but he who overcame thee was too great for any title. And there is no gradation of epithet beyond the Fabii;[20] that house was entitled 'the greatest,' for their services. But yet all these are rendered illustrious by honours *merely* human; he, however, has a title in common with supreme Jove. Our forefathers style the sacred rites 'august;'[21] the temples are called 'august' when consecrated in due form by the hand of the Pontiffs. Augury too is derived from the source of this word,[22] and whatsoever

---

[17] *Breast-chain.*]—Ver. 601. Titus Manlius conquered a gigantic Gaul in single combat, and stripping him of his collar, or breast-chain, 'torques,' obtained the title of Torquatus from the circumstance.

[18] *By a raven.*]—Ver. 602. Marcus Valerius, a military tribune under Camillus, fighting with a champion of the Senones in single combat, was aided by a raven, which, attacking his enemy in the face with beak and claws, enabled him to gain an easy victory. From 'corvus,' 'a raven,' he obtained the surname 'Corvinus.'

[19] *Entitled 'Great.'*]—Ver. 603. Cneius Pompeius, surnamed 'Magnus,' or 'the Great,' from his great successes. He was son of Pompeius Strabo, who was distinguished in the Italic war. He is generally called Pompey the Great, by an adaptation of his name to our ideas of euphony. He was conquered by Cæsar at Pharsalia, and was treacherously slain.

[20] *The Fabii.*]—Ver. 605. Q. Fabius Rutilianus, according to Livy, book ix. c. 46, for his efforts in restoring concord, and lessening the power of the populace during civic elections, received the surname of 'Maximus,' or 'Greatest,' as a benefactor to his country, which name his descendants bore. According to the genealogists, our gracious Queen is a descendant of the Fabii, and, if so, she has, perhaps, a double claim to the name of 'Maxima.' In the next book Ovid mentions the tradition that the Fabii were descended from Hercules.

[21] *August.*]—Ver. 609. He seems to imply that the word 'Augustus' is derived from the same root, 'augurium,' 'an omen,' as though 'consecrated by augury,' or 'omen,' or 'understood by means of the birds.' This name, an epithet of divinity, was considered beyond any human title. The Greeks translated it by σεβάστος from σεβῶ, 'to worship.'

[22] *Source of this word.*]—Ver. 611. The poet seems to mean, that 'augurium' and 'augustus' come from one origin, connected with 'avis,' 'a bird,' and perhaps, 'gero,' 'to bear.' He also appears obscurely to hint,

Jupiter blesses with increase by his aid. May he increase the sway of our chief, may he increase his years; and, Cæsar, long may the chaplet of oak-leaves[23] shade thy doors. The gods being propitious, may the inheritor of a title so illustrious take upon himself the burden of the world with the same auspices that his father did.

When the third Titan[24] shall look back upon the by-gone Ides, there will be a repetition of the sacred rites of the Parrhasian goddess. For in former days, before *the circumstances to which I allude*, covered chariots used to carry the Ausonian matrons; (these, too, I believe to have been named[25] after the parent of Evander.) In after-times this honour being withdrawn from them, each matron formed the determination by no issue to renew the image of her hated lord; and that she might yield no offspring, reckless, with secret blows[26] she was in the habit of loosening from her womb the growing burden. They say that the senate reprimanded the matrons who had dared to perpetrate these inhuman deeds, but that nevertheless they restored the privilege that had been taken from them. And they now order two sets of festivals to be kept in honour of the Tegæan mother,

---

that 'augeo,' 'to increase,' is derived from the same source, perhaps meaning that 'increase' was portended by, and the necessary consequence of, good omens. The 612th line is of somewhat obscure signification.

[23] *Chaplet of oak-leaves.*]—Ver. 614. This was the civic crown, and was presented to him who had saved the life of a Roman citizen. When the senate decreed the title of Augustus to Octavius, they ordered, in their adulation, that a civic crown should be suspended from his house, between two laurel branches which were set on either side of his gate.

[24] *Titan.*]—Ver. 617. An epithet of the sun. The Carmentalia now return, not in honour of Carmenta, but of her two sisters, Porrima and Postverta.

[25] *To have been named.*]—Ver. 620. He suggests a silly derivation of 'carpentum,' 'a chariot,' from the name of Carmenta. The Roman matrons received the privilege of the chariot for their generosity after the capture of the city of Veii, when they contributed their jewels to aid Camillus in performing his vow to Apollo.

[26] *With secret blows.*]—Ver. 622-3. These lines are thus rendered by Gower:—

'And to prevent her embryon, every mother
Forced from her womb by some close means or other.'

both for the boys and the girls.[27] It is not allowed to bring within her holy place any thing made of hide,[28] that substances deprived of life, *by dying a natural death*, may not defile the unpolluted hearth. If you are one who have any taste for ancient ceremonies, stand by the *priest who is* praying; you will then catch names which were unknown to you before.[29] Porrima and Postverta are bein propitiated, either thy sisters, O Mænalian nymph, or companions of thy exile. The one is believed to have sung of that which was long past,[30] the other to have prophecied what would happen hereafter in the revolution of time.

Fair Concord,[31] the succeeding day placed in thee in a snow-white shrine, where elevated Moneta[32] raises her steps on high: now with ease wilt thou look down upon the Latian crowd; now have the august hands *of Cæsar* replaced thee.

Furius, the conqueror of the Etrurian people, vowed the ancient temple, and long since discharged the obligations of his vow. The occasion was, that the commonalty having

---

[27] *Boys and the girls.*]—Ver. 628. By way of expiation for the children of both sexes that had been so made away with.

[28] *Made of hide.*]—Ver. 629. It was forbidden to bring leather articles not only into this temple, but all others. At the same time the rule was confined to the skins of animals which had died a natural death. The priests were allowed to wear leather sandals, made from the hides of beasts that had been killed by them for sacrifice.

[29] *Unknown to you before.*]—Ver. 632. He seems to imply that these deities, Porrima and Postverta, were but little known, and the origin of their worship little enquired into. Porrima is so called only in this place, and by Servius (on the Æneid, Book viii. line 336). Macrobius (Sat. i. 7) calls her 'Antevorta;' and Aulus Gellius (Attic Nights, Book xvi. 6), 'Prosa,' or 'Prorsa.' The name of the first signifies 'turning,' or 'looking before;' of the other, 'looking behind.' Though the poet does not say so, from what we learn from A. Gellius, there is no doubt that they were obstetrical deities, to be invoked against the perils of difficult parturition.

[30] *Long past.*]—Ver. 635. 'Porro' generally signifies 'the future;' but its original meaning might have been ' afar off,' in either sense.

[31] *Fair Concord.*]—Ver. 637-39. He says that on the following day, the 17th of the calends of February, the most ancient of the temples of the goddess of Peace has been vowed by Furius Camillus, the Roman general, when he had conquered the Veienses, a people of Etruria.

[32] *Moneta.*]—Ver. 638. The temple of Juno Moneta stood in the Capitol: a flight of one hundred steps led to it from the temple of Concord. It was the Mint, or place of coinage.

taken up arms, had seceded[33] from the senators, and Rome herself was in dread of her own strength. The late occasion is a more happy[34] one; Germany, venerated chief, extends her dishevelled locks,[35] vanquished under thy auspices. Thence it is that thou hast offered[36] the first fruits of a nation, and hast constructed a temple to the goddess, the peculiar object of thy veneration. This, thy ancestress[37] has endowed both with property and with its altar, the only woman found worthy of the couch of our great Jove.

When this festival shall have passed by, *then*, O Phœbus, Capricorn being left, thou wilt run thy course through the constellation of the youth that carries the water.[38]

When the seventh Orient *sun* from this shall have plunged himself into the waves, then shall no Lyre[39] be glittering through-

---

[33] *Had seceded.*]—Ver. 643. The dissension of the patrician and plebeian orders respecting the election of the consuls ended in the election of one plebeian consul, Lucius Sextus, A.U.C. 328. This arrangement was brought about by Camillus, in his fifth dictatorship.

[34] *A more happy one.*]—Ver. 645. This is a compliment to Tiberius. The first temple was built in consequence of civil commotion; the second on the conquest of Germany.

[35] *Her dishevelled locks.*]—Ver. 646. It was the custom to shave the heads of captives. Ovid may here be speaking figuratively, or perhaps literally. The hair of Germany was much valued by the Roman ladies for making false tresses; and perhaps a supply of hair for the wig-makers was exacted from the conquered people. Gower's translation of these lines is,

'Brave prince, thy thundering knocks
Made Germany cut short her dangling locks.'

[36] *Hast offered.*]—Ver. 647. Tiberius repulsed the Germans, and conquered Illyrium. On his triumph he entertained the people at 1000 tables, and gave to each man 300 sestertii. The poet may here allude to this, or more probably to the offering of the first-fruits of conquest to the deities, and especially to the rebuilding of the temple of Concord by Tiberius.

[37] *Ancestress.*]—Ver. 649. Livia, the mother of Tiberius, and the grandmother of Germanicus.

[38] *That carries the water.*]—Ver. 652. On the 16th of the calends of February the sun leaves the constellation of Capricorn, and enters that of Aquarius, 'the Water-bearer.' Ganymede, the cup-bearer of Jupiter, is said by Ovid to have been translated to this constellation. Gower translates these lines,

'These things thus past, Sol leaving Capricorn,
His race-horse to the water-boy doth turn.'

[39] *No Lyre*]—Ver. 654. On the 10th of the calends of February the Lyre sets heliacally.

out the whole heavens. After the setting of this constellation, at the approach of night, the fire which twinkles[40] in the centre of the lion's breast shall be plunged *into the deep.*

Three or four times had I turned[41] over the calendar that marks out the seasons of observance, and yet no Sementive holiday[42] was found by me; when the Muse (for she perceived my difficulty) says, "This festival is announced by proclamation; why dost thou seek from the calendar to find a moveable feast? And yet, although the day of the festival is unfixed, the season is fixed; it is when the ground is impregnated with the scattered seed. Bedecked with garlands, stand at the well-filled stall, ye oxen; with the warm spring your task shall return. Let the farmer hang on its peg the plough discharged from service;[43] the cold ground shudders at an incision. Do, farmer, give some rest to the earth, now that seed-time is past; give some rest to the men, too, who have tilled the ground. Let the hamlet[44] keep holiday; purify the village, ye swains, and to the hamlet's altars give your yearly cakes.[45] Let Ceres and Tellus, mothers of the fruits, be propitiated with their own corn, and the entrails of a preg-

---

[40] *The fire which twinkles.*]—Ver. 656. The star Regulus, in the constellation Leo, on the ninth of the calends of February, about nightfall, sets acronically. Columella says, it sets on the sixth of the calends of February.

[41] *I turned over.*]—Ver. 657. Literally, 'I rolled over.' If this is to be read literally, it would rather apply to the scroll form of book than the paged book of more recent introduction, and which we have noticed in the note to line 19 above.

[42] *Sementive holiday.*]—Ver. 658. For an account of the 'dies stativæ' and 'conceptivæ,' see the Introduction.

[43] *Discharged from service.*]—Ver. 665. 'Emeritus' is properly applied to the soldier, discharged when the time of military service has expired.

[44] *The hamlet.*]—Ver. 669. 'Pagus.' Servius Tullius divided the Roman territory into 'pagi.' There was in each 'pagus' an altar, on which, during the 'paganalia,' a yearly sacrifice was offered by the 'Pagani,' or people of the 'pagus.' This feast was in honour of the rustic gods, and was instituted by Servius Tullius. As the country people were in general the last to adopt Christianity, the name of 'Pagan' came in time to be equivalent to the term 'heathen.'

[45] *Yearly cakes.*]—Ver. 670. These were called πέλανοι by the Greeks. They were made of eggs, flour, milk, and oil, and were offered by the different families of the 'pagus.' The purification was made by sending the victims round the 'pagus' before they were sacrificed.

nant sow. Ceres and the earth[46] discharge an united duty. The one supplies the origin of the crops, the other the situation. Partners in toil *are they*, by whom antiquity was civilized, and the acorn from the oak-tree was replaced by a more wholesome food. Glut the greedy husbandmen with boundless crops, that they may receive rewards worthy of their tillage. Give ye uninterrupted growth to the tender seed, and let not the shooting blade be withered during the cold snows. While we are sowing, clear the skies with cloudless breezes; when the seed is covered in, besprinkle it with the rain of heaven. And do ye take heed that the birds, a nuisance to the tilled fields, do not in mischievous flocks lay waste the gifts of Ceres. You, too, ye ants, spare the grain when sown; after the harvest there will be a better opportunity for plunder. Meanwhile, let the standing corn spring up free from the leprous mildew, and let not the sickly crop grow wan from the distempered atmosphere; neither let it pine away from meagreness, nor let it, too luxuriant and all run to blade, perish by its own rankness. Let the fields also be clear of darnel that weakens the eyes, and let not the sterile wild oat rise in the cultivated soil. Let the land return, with heavy interest, the produce of the wheat and the barley, and the spelt *destined twice to endure*[47] the fire. These wishes do I *entertain* for you, these wishes entertain for yourselves, ye husbandmen, and may either goddess render these prayers efficient. Wars long engaged mankind; the sword was more handy than the ploughshare, and the ploughing bull gave place to the charger. Then the hoes used to lie idle, the spades were turned into pikes, and from the ponderous harrow the helmet was wrought. Thanks to the gods and to thy house! wars long since bound in chains lie prostrate under our feet. Let the ox come beneath the yoke, and the seed beneath the ploughed soil. Peace nurtures Ceres; Ceres is the nursling of Peace.

But on the day which is the sixth before the approaching

[46] *The earth.*]—Ver. 673. Worshipped by the Romans under the name of 'Tellus,' 'Ops,' 'Tellumo,' and 'Bona Dea,' 'the good goddess.' According to Varro, the Earth was male in producing seed, female in nourishing it. She is sometimes confounded with her partner, Ceres. They are here represented as teaching the aborigines to abandon the acorn for the cultivation of wheat.

[47] *Twice to endure.*]—Ver. 693. The ancients used to parch their corn before they ground it.

calends, their temple was dedicated to the gods, the sons of Leda.[48] The brothers sprung from the race of the gods erected it in honour of the divine brothers, near the lake of Juturna.. My song itself now brings me to the altar of Peace. This will be the second day from the end of the month. Come hither, O Peace, with thy well arranged tresses encircled with Actian boughs,[49] and in thy gentleness take up thy abode through the whole world. While there are no foes, let there be no occasion for triumph; thou shalt be to our chieftains a boast greater than war. Let the soldier bear arms, only for the purpose of putting down the use of arms. By the wildly sounding trumpet let no blast be sounded but that of the pageant. Let all the earth, far and near, dread the descendants of Æneas; and if there shall be any land that dreads not Rome, then let it love her. Throw, ye priests, the incense on the fires lighted in honour of Peace, and let the white victim fall, with stricken forehead. Entreat too, the gods inclining to your hallowed prayers, that the family which gives us peace may equal her in eternal duration. But now the first portion of my task is completed, and together with its month my little book comes to a close.

[48] *Sons of Leda.*]—Ver. 706. Castor and Pollux were the twin sons of Leda by Jupiter. A.U.C. 769, Tiberius built a temple in their honour, in his own name and that of his brother Drusus. The divinities were called 'Dioscuri,' 'sons of Jove.' Their temple was built near lake Juturna and the temple of Vesta.

[49] *Actian boughs.*]—Ver. 711. Augustus gained a great naval victory over Antony and Cleopatra near Actium, a town of Epirus, A.U.C. 723. He soon after closed the temple of Janus, in token of universal peace.

BOOK THE SECOND.

CONTENTS.

The nature of the subject and the dedication, ver. 1—18. Some remarks on the Februa, from which the month derives its name, 19—34. The common opinion on the efficacy of purgations, 35—46. On the ancient place of February among the months, and the change in its position, 47—54. The calends of February distinguished by the dedication of the temple of Juno Sospita; the praises of Cæsar; the ceremony in the grove of the asylum; the sacred rites of Jupiter, 55—70. The cause of tempests at this season, 70—72. The setting of the Lyre and of the Lion midway, 73—78. The setting of the Dolphin and the story of Arion, whose Dolphin is placed among the constellations, 79—118. Augustus styled the father of his country; his great virtues, and a comparison of him with Romulus, 119—144. The rising of Aquarius, and the milder breezes consequent thereon, 145—148. The beginning of spring, 149—152. Arctophylax rises; the story connected with it, 153—192. The sacred rites of Faunus and the slaughter of the Fabii, 193—242. The constellations of the Crow, the Snake, and the Cup rise, and their story is related, 243—266. The rites of the Lupercalia and their origin, with the story of Hercules, Omphale, and Faunus, and the exposure and preservation of Romulus and Remus, 267—452. The changeableness of the weather, 453—456. The entry of the Sun into the Fishes; their story is related, 457—474. The Quirinalia and the deification of Romulus; the festival of Fools and of the goddess Fornax, 475—532. The propitiation of the Manes, 533—570. The sacred rites of Muta or Tacita, 571—616. The Caristia, 617—618. the Terminalia, 639—684. The rape of Lucretia and the expulsion of the kings, 685—852. The return of the swallow, 853—856. The Equiria, 857—864.

THE month of Janus is brought to a close; with my song the year grows apace. As a second month progresses, so let a second book proceed. Now for the first time, elegiac strains, do ye speed onward with more stately sail; you were, I remember, but lately of trifling account.¹ I myself have employed

¹ *Of trifling account.*]—Ver. 4. The Elegiac measure, which Ovid uses in this poem, was usually employed on subjects of a trifling nature. This

you as ready agents in love, when my early youth sported in numbers adapted to it. I *am the same who now* sing of sacred subjects and the days of observance *as they are* marked in the calendar. Who could believe that such could have proved[2] a path to these subjects? This is my line of service; what arms I can, I bear, and my right hand is not destitute of every skill. If javelins are not hurled by me with mighty arm, and if by me the back of the warrior steed is not pressed; if I am not cased in the helmet, nor girded with the sharp sword, (any one, forsooth, may be skilled in such arms as these), still, Cæsar, with zealous breast I trace onwards thy deeds of glory, and proceed on my path through *the recital of* thy titles. Be thou then present, and reward with benign aspect my services, if but for a moment; if thou hast any leisure from thy task of forcing the enemy to *sue for* peace.

Our Roman forefathers called atoning sacrifices by the name of 'Februa;'[3] and even now many traces *of its meaning* confirm this signification of the expression. The Pontiffs ask wool of the king *of the sacrifices* and of the Flamen[4], the name of which in the ancient dialect was 'Februa;' and the purifying substances which the lictor takes for the houses when ascertained *as being impure*, the parched spelt with the grain *of salt*, are called by the same name. This too is the name of the bough, which, lopped from a consecrated tree, covers with its foliage the holy temples of the priests. I myself have seen the Flaminica asking for the 'Februa;' a bough of pine was presented to her making this request for the 'Februa' *by name*. In a

was the character of many of his previous compositions in this kind of verse. Gower translates these lines:—

' Now, Elegies, your sails you 'gin display,
  Methoughts you were but little flags to-day.'

[2] *Such could have proved.*]—Ver. 8. Namely, his 'Amours' and 'the Art of Love,' upon which he had formerly employed the Elegiac measure.

[3] *Februa.*]—Ver. 19. According to Varro (on Rustic Matters, Book 5), this word was of Sabine origin. It probably came from 'ferveo,' 'to be hot,' inasmuch as purification was effected through the medium of heat.

[4] *Flamen.*]—Ver. 21. The 'Pontifex' was a priest who sacrificed to all the gods; the 'Flamen' dedicated his service to but one deity; the 'Flamen Dialis,' or priest of Jupiter, held the highest office among the Flamens. Among other privileges, that of being attended by a lictor was one. The 'Flaminica' was the wife of the Flamen Dialis. Her assistance was essential in the performance of certain sacred duties; and, as the Flamen was restricted to one marriage, if the Flaminica died he was obliged to resign.

word, whatever there is by means of which our breasts are purified, it had with our unshaven ancestors[5] this name. From these circumstances the month derives its name,[6] *either* because the Luperci[7] with thongs of hide, purify all the country, and consider that *rite* an expiation; or because the season is purified, the shades of the dead being appeased when the days devoted to their offerings have passed by. Our ancients believed that purification was efficacious to remove every curse, and every cause of evil. Greece was the originator of the custom; she believes that the guilty, when purified, *forthwith* divest themselves of guilt. Peleus rid of guilt the grandson of Actor,[8] as Acastus by the agency of the Hæmonian[9] waters released Peleus himself from

[5] *Unshaven ancestors.*]—Ver. 30. The Romans did not shave until the year 454 A. U. C., about 300 years before Christ. According to Pliny the Elder, Nat. Hist. p. 59, Ticinius Mena first introduced a barber into Rome. According to others it was Scipio. In the sixth Book of the Fasti, line 264, Ovid calls Numa ' intonsus,' ' unshaven.' Horace calls Cato by the same appellation, Odes, Book 2, ode 16,

[6] *Derives its name.*]—Ver. 31. He says that February is so called from ' Februa,' ' purifying objects,' either because the Luperci purify by their rites in honour of Faunus: or because in this month the graves are purified by the propitiation of the shades of the dead.

[7] *The Luperci.*]—Ver. 31. The Luperci, whose rites are described in the present book, were priests of Pan, and were so called from ' lupus,' a ' wolf,' as Pan was supposed to protect the flocks from wolves. Hence his place of worship was called ' Lupercal,' and his rites were the ' Lupercalia.' They ran through the city naked, with the exception of a girdle of goatskin round the waist; and they carried thongs of the same in their hands, striking whomsoever they met, and in particular married women, who were supposed to be rendered prolific thereby. There were of the Luperci three divisions, two ancient, the Fabiani, and the Quintiliani, and a third in honour of Julius Cæsar. They were not abolished until the time of Anastasius, in the commencement of the sixth century after Christ.

[8] *The grandson of Actor.*]—Ver. 39. Patroclus, son of Menætius, was forced to fly from Opus, where his father reigned, having accidentally slain Chrysonomus, son of Amphidamus, and retired to the court of Peleus, king of Thessaly, and the father of Achilles, where he was kindly entertained. He was slain by Hector in the Trojan war. Peleus was the son of Æacus: he and Telamon having slain Phocus, their half-brother, Peleus fled to Phthia, where he was purified by Eurytion, or by the father of Eurytion. Having in the chase of the Calydonian boar accidentally slain Eurytion, he was purified a second time by Acastus, the king of Iolchos. The poet is mistaken in saying that it was Acastus who absolved Peleus from the murder of Phocus.

[9] *Hæmonian.*]—Ver. 40. So called either from Mount Hæmus, in Thessaly, or from Hæmon. son of Deucalion. The ancients considered sea water more efficacious for this purpose than fresh or spring water.

the blood of Phocus. The too easily persuaded Ægeus[10] assisted with ill-deserved aid the Phasian borne on her harnessed dragons through the air. The son of Amphiaraus[11] said to the Naupactan Acheloüs[12], "absolve me of my guilt." Whereupon he did absolve him of his guilt. Ah! too credulous *mortals*, who imagine that the guilt of bloodshed can be removed by the waters of the stream.

But, however, that thou mayst not be perplexed through ignorance of the ancient arrangement; the month of Janus, as now it is, so formerly it was the first month. *The month that follows that of Janus was by name the last*[13] *of the ancient year; thou also, O Terminus, didst conclude the sacred rites.* For the month of Janus is first, because the gate is at the very entrance; the last month was that which is consecrated to the shades of the dead below. In times after, the Decemvirs[14] are thought to have placed in succession, the periods *before* separated by so long an interval.

[10] *Ægeus.*]—Ver. 41. Ægeus was king of Athens, and son of Pandion. Medea having revenged herself upon Jason by the slaughter of his children, fled in a chariot, drawn by dragons, to the court of Ægeus, whose protection she obtained by promising to instruct him how to raise issue. She is called ' the Phasian,' from Phasis, a river of Colchis, her native country.

[11] *The son of Amphiaraus.*]—Ver. 43. Alcmæon. Amphiaraus, the prophet, concealed himself, in order that he might not accompany the Argive expedition against Thebes, as he knew that he was doomed to perish there. His wife Eriphyle, bribed by Polynices with a golden necklace, betrayed him. On going to the war he charged his son Alcmæon to avenge his death, who, on hearing that his father had fallen, slew his mother, and was purified by Pheggeus in Arcadia, but being still persecuted by the Furies, was purified by the river Acheloüs a second time.

[12] *Acheloüs.*]—Ver. 43. A river of Acarnania, near Mount Pindus, which falls into the gulf of Corinth. Naupactus, now Lepanto, was a town in Ætolia, which derived its name from ship-building there carried on. Gower translates the two following lines:—

' Ah, too, too silly, who imagine water
Can wash away that heavy crime of slaughter.'

[13] *The last.*]—Ver. 49. Ovid is the only author that mentions the fact, that when Numa added the two months to the year, he placed January first and February last, or twelfth, and that as being last or lowest of the months, he dedicated it to the shades below. According to him, the Decemviri transposed its place from after December to after January, from twelfth to second, thus joining the periods that before, counting onwards, had been separated by a long interval.

[14] *The Decemvirs.*]—Ver. 54. Bis quini viri. Literally, ' the twice five

In the beginning of the month, the *temple of the Goddess the Preserver*,[15] adjoining to *that of* the Phrygian Mother, is said to have been enriched by new shrines. You ask, where is now the temple consecrated to the Goddess on those calends? it has perished by length of time. The watchful care of our sacred chief has provided that the other temples should not fall down, tottering with similar ruin; under him the temples feel not the ravages of time; it is not enough *to grant favours to us* mortals, he lays the very Gods under obligations to him. Thou builder of the temples, thou holy restorer of our shrines, may the Deities, I pray, have a reciprocal regard for thee. May the dwellers in heaven grant thee as many years as thou hast bestowed on them, and may they *ever* be the watchful guardians[16] of thy house.

On that day too, the grove of the neighbouring Asylum[17] is resorted to by the crowds, where the Tiber from afar rolls onward to the ocean waters. At the abode of Numa,[18] and *the*

quiries having been made by decree of the senate into the nature of the Grecian laws, and the code of Solon, on the return of the commission in the year B.C. 451. Ten men, called the 'Decemviri,' were chosen, with supreme power to draw up a code of laws, all the other magistrates having abdicated their offices. They were appointed the following year, and were discontinued in consequence of their oppressive conduct and the unjust decision of Appius Claudius, which occasioned the death of Virginia by the hand of her father, to save her from prostitution.

[15] *The Preserver.*]—Ver. 57. It is not known when, or by whom, this temple to Juno 'Sospita,' or 'the Preserver,' was built. It must have stood on the Palatine Hill, as the temple of Cybele, the Phrygian mother was there. 'Sospita' comes from 'sospes,' 'safe,' and that word is derived from 'σώζω,' 'to save.'

[16] *The watchful guardians.*]—Ver. 65. 'Maneant in statione,' literally, 'remain at their post;' a military phrase.

[17] *Asylum.*]—Ver. 67. Romulus constituted an asylum in a grove near the Tiber, as a place of refuge from punishment for guilty persons. He also opened it to the criminals of other states, that he might thereby augment the number of his own citizens. In later times it was walled in. It seems from this passage that it skirted the Capitolium, running down to the banks of the Tiber.

[18] *Abode of Numa.*]—Ver. 69. 'Penetrale' is literally 'the courtyard' or 'hall.' Ovid tells us, in the sixth book, l. 264, that Numa resided in the temple of Vesta. But other writers, with more accuracy, tell us that he only lived near her Temple. It stood opposite the Capitolium. The temple of Jupiter Tonans, 'the Thunderer,' stood on the lowest ridge of the Capitoline Hill, and was built by Augustus. This

temple of the Thunderer, on the Capitoline *Hill*, and on the loftiest height of Jove, a sheep of two years old is slain. Ofttimes the south wind enwrapped in clouds summons together the heavy rains, or the earth is hidden beneath the fallen snow.

When the next day's sun, about to retire into the western waves, removes the jewelled collars from his purple steeds, on the same night many a one, raising his face to the stars, shall say, where, *I wonder*, is to-day *the constellation of* the Lyre,[19] which was shining yesterday? and while he is seeking for the Lyre, he shall observe the back of the Lion as far as his middle[20] suddenly plunged into the flowing waters.

The Dolphin, whom of late you were in the habit of seeing bespangled with stars, on the following night shall pass from our sight. He either was a successful spokesman in loves concealed,[21] or it was he that bore the Lesbian[22] Lyre with its master. What sea has not known, what land does not know of Arion? He with his song used to detain the running streams. Often has the wolf been stayed by his voice, as he was chasing the lamb; oft has the lamb, when fleeing from the ravenous wolf, stopped short *in her flight;* oft have the hounds and the hare reclined beneath the same shade; and the hind has stood still on the mountain crag close to the lioness; without strife the chattering crow has sat in company with the bird of Pallas,[23] and the pigeon has been

must not be confounded with the 'Capitolium,' or more ancient temple of Jupiter Capitolinus. The temple 'of the Thunderer on the Capitoline Hill' seems to be the last, and 'the loftiest height of Jove' appears to refer to the former.

[19] *The Lyre.*]—Ver. 76. The cosmical setting of the Lyre on the night of the second of February.

[20] *As far as his middle.*]—Ver. 77. This must be the hindmost half, as the foremost had already set, Book I, line 591.

[21] *Loves concealed.*]—Ver. 81. The secret love of Neptune for Amphitrite; though, according to some accounts, the god was far too pressing in his attentions to make a favourable impression on the goddess.

[22] *Lesbian.*]—Ver. 82. Arion was a native of Methymna, a town in Lesbos. The Dolphin is said to have landed him on the promontory of Tænarus.

[23] *The bird of Pallas.*]—Ver. 89. The solemn and taciturn owl, which was not likely in general to form any intimate acquaintanceship with the garrulous crow.

coupled with the hawk. Tuneful Arion! Cynthia[24] is said oft-times to have been spell-bound by thy strains as though by those of her brother *Apollo*. The name of Arion had filled the cities of Sicily, and the coast of Ausonia had been charmed by the tones of his lyre. Returning homeward thence Arion embarked, and was bringing with him the treasures thus acquired by his skill. Perchance, hapless one, thou wast in fear of the winds[25] and the waves, but yet did the ocean prove more safe to thee than thy own vessel. For *now* the helmsman stood by him with sword unsheathed, and the rest of the crew conspiring with arms in their hands. What hast thou to do with *that* sword? Sailor, guide the veering bark. These are not the implements that should be grasped by thy fingers. *And now, guessing their purpose*, struck with terror, he says, "I deprecate not death, but let me take my lyre and recall but a few notes." They give him leave, but laugh at this *pretext for* delay. He takes a chaplet which, Phoebus, might grace even thy tresses; he was arrayed *too* in a mantle twice steeped in Tyrian purple.[26] Struck by his thumb the chord returned its usual notes; just as the swan when pierced in his grey temples[27] by the cruel feathered shaft, sings in mournful numbers. Instantly, in his bright array, he leaps forth into the midst of the waves; the azure bark is

[24] *Cynthia.*]—Ver. 91. Diana was thus called from Cynthus, a mountain of Delos, which overshadowed that island, the birth-place of Apollo and Diana. The poet here speaks of her as the moon.

[25] *In fear of the winds.*]—Ver. 97. Implying that he had no suspicion of the quarter in which his danger lay; but Herodotus, who, in his History, book i. cap. 23, gives the story, says that he was apprehensive of danger, and purposely hired a Corinthian vessel.

[26] *Tyrian purple*]—Ver. 107. Vests twice dyed were called 'dibapha,' from the Greek δις, 'twice,' and βάπτω, 'to dip.' The purple dye, for which Tyre was so famous, was obtained from the 'murex,' a kind of shell-fish. Garments dyed therewith were very costly.

[27] *Pierced in his grey temples.*]—Ver. 110. Gower thus translates this and the following lines:—

'He sings in mournful numbers like a swan,
Whose hardened quills have pierced his aged brain-pan,
Then into water thus assured doth skip;
The battered billows all bedash the ship.'

As Travesty nothing could be more successful than this. He seems here, by his translation of 'penna,' to adopt the idea that swans were supposed by the ancients, in their old age, to have their brain pierced by their own feathers. It seems rather to mean 'the feathered arrow.'

splashed by the spray of the water. Then—too wondrous for belief—they tell how the dolphin, with curving back, placed himself beneath his unusual burden. He, as he sits, holds the lyre, and sings in requital for his conveyance, and calms by his strains the ocean waters. The Gods are witnesses of this act of kindness; Jupiter admitted the Dolphin among the Constellations, and desired him to become the owner of nine stars.

Now could I wish that I had a thousand voices, and thy genius, O Mæonian *bard*,[28] by which Achilles[29] has been celebrated. While I am singing in alternating verse[30] those sacred nones, the greatest honour[31] of all is heaped upon my Calendar; my genius fails me, and a subject too great for my strength quite overpowers me. This day must be sung by me in a distinguished strain. Why in my infatuation did I wish to impose on elegiac strains a burden so vast *as this?* This *indeed* were a *proper* subject for heroic metre. Sacred Father of thy country! on thee the people, on thee the senate conferred this title. This *too* we of equestrian rank[32] conferred upon thee. But reality conferred *this title long* previously; and late indeed was it that thou didst receive thy true appellation; long since wast thou the father of the *whole* world. Thou bearest throughout the earth the name that Jupiter bears in the lofty heavens; thou art the father of men, he of the gods. Romulus, thou must give way, *for 'tis* he *who* makes thy walls great by defending them; *while* thou hadst left them *so low as* to be overleapt by Remus. Thee *indeed*, Tatius[33] felt,

[28] *Mæonian bard.*]—Ver. 120. Homer was so called from Mæonia, a mountain in Lydia, at the foot of Mount Tmolus, where he is said to have been born. Others suppose the epithet to have been derived from Mæon, which is said to have been the name of his father.

[29] *Achilles.*]—Ver. 119. It is difficult to say whether Achilles or Hector is the hero of the Iliad, in which they are both celebrated. The latter, at least, is represented as a man of better morals, and of less ungovernable temper, than his antagonist.

[30] *Alternating verse.*]—Ver. 121. His lines are the heroic hexameter, or six-feet line, alternating with the elegiac pentameter, or five-feet line.

[31] *Greatest honour.*]—Ver. 122. Augustus having on this day received the title of 'Pater Patriæ,' or 'Father of his Country,' A.U.C. 758, seven years after his 13th consulate.

[32] *We of equestrian rank*]—Ver. 128. Ovid was of the rank of 'equites,' or knights. The patricians, knights, and plebeians, formed the three classes of the Roman people who were freemen.

[33] *Tatius.*]—Ver. 135. He was the king of the Sabines. Cures and

and humble Cures, and Cænina; *but* under this chief each region[34] of the sun is Roman. Thou didst possess a trifling piece of conquered ground. Over all that is beneath supreme Jove, does Cæsar hold sway. Thou actest the ravisher's part: he bids wives to be virtuous[35] under his rule. Thou shelterest *the guilty* in *the asylum of* the grove; he removes afar all guilt. Violence was thy delight; under Cæsar the laws are in force. Thou hadst the name of Master, he has that of chief citizen.[36] Remus upbraids thee *with murder*; he has forgiven *even* his enemies. Thy sire[37] raised thee to the skies, it is he *who* has raised his father. And now the Idæan youth[38] appears above *the wave* as far as the middle, and pours forth the liquid waters with the commingled nectar.[39] And lo! if any one used to shiver at the northern blast, let him *now* be glad; a milder breeze is coming from the Zephyrs.[40]

Cænina were small towns of Latium, in the neighbourhood of Rome Romulus slew Acron, king of Cænina, and thereby gained the first 'spolia opima.' At Cures Numa was born.

[34] *Each region.*]—Ver. 136. The limits of his empire at his death were, the Atlantic ocean and the Euphrates, on the west and east; the Danube and the Rhine on the north; and the cataracts of the Nile and Mount Atlas on the south; they included nearly all the then known world.

[35] *To be virtuous.*]—Ver. 139. On the absence of their husbands for a certain time, the Roman women were at liberty to marry again. This right degenerated into a source of licentiousness and infidelity, whereupon Augustus by law restricted it. To this, probably, allusion is here made.

[36] *Chief citizen.*]—Ver. 142. The name 'Dominus,' here translated 'master,' comes from 'domo,' 'to govern,' as a master ruled his slaves. According to Suetonius, Augustus would not be called by a title which represented him as the slave-master of the Roman people, and was on one occasion highly offended on being saluted in the theatre by that name. 'Princeps,' the chief,' was the title which the senate conferred on him as being entitled to the first place there.

[37] *Thy sire.*]—Ver. 142. Mars. Julius Cæsar, the father of Augustus by adoption, was deified by him.

[38] *Idæan youth.*]—Ver. 145. The cosmical rising of the constellation Aquarius. Ganymede, son of Tros, king of Troy, while hunting on Mount Ida, was seized by the eagle of Jupiter, and carried to heaven. He took the place of Hebe, as cup-bearer to the gods, and was afterwards enrolled among the signs of the zodiac under the name of 'Aquarius,' the 'water-bearer.'

[39] *Nectar.*]—Ver. 146. Nectar was the peculiar beverage of the gods, as 'ambrosia' was their food.

[40] *Zephyrs.*]—Ver. 148. The zephyr, or Favonius, was the western wind, which announced the opening of spring.

The fifth light-bearing *morn* has raised his glittering beam from the waves of the ocean, and the hours of early spring are at hand; but be not deceived; the cold still remains, yes, *too true*, it remains, and winter while departing has left its deep traces behind.

Be the third night *of the Ides now* arrived, then forthwith you will see that the keeper of the Bear[41] has put forth his two feet. Among the Hamadryads[42] and Diana *the thrower* of the javelin, Callisto was one of the sacred company. Laying her hand on the bow[43] of the Goddess, she says, "Be this bow which I touch the witness of my *vow of* virginity." Cynthia praised her, and said, "*only* keep thy pledged contract, and then thou shalt be the chief of my companions." Had she not been beautiful, she would have kept her compact. She was on her guard against mortals; from Jove *it is that* she incurred her guilt. Having hunted in the woods a thousand beasts of chase, Phœbe was on her return, while the sun was in its midday course, or still further *advanced*. When she reached the *sacred* grove—(the grove was thick with many an holm-oak, and in the midst there was a pond of ice cold water). "In this wood," said she, "maid of Tegeæa,[44] let us bathe." At the untrue name of 'maid' the other blushed. She said the same also to her Nymphs; *whereon* the Nymphs put off their garments. Callisto is ashamed, and gives unhappy proofs of *a purposed* tardiness and delay. She had stripped off her robes; convicted by the size of her person, she is betrayed by the evidence of her burden. To whom, the Goddess, "Forsworn daughter of Lycaon! quit the virgin troop and defile not these chaste waters." Ten times had the moon completed her orb between her horns, *and* she, who had been

---

[41] *Keeper of the Bear.*]—Ver. 153. The achronycal rising of Boötes on the 11th of February. Boötes, or Arctophylax, the Bearward, was the constellation into which Arcas, the son of Jupiter and Callisto, as here mentioned, was changed.

[42] *Hamadryads.*]—Ver. 155. These were nymphs who presided over individual trees, with which they were said to live and die. Their name was derived from the Greek ἅμα, 'together,' and δρῦς, 'an oak.'

[43] *On the bow.*]—Ver. 157. With the ancients it was the usage to touch any thing they swore by. Thus Hannibal touched the altar when he vowed eternal enmity against Rome. See Livy, book 21, c. 1; and Cornelius Nepos, in his Life of Hannibal.

[44] *Maid of Tegeæa.*]—Ver. 167. Callisto being the daughter of Lycaon, king of Arcadia, of which country Tegeæa was a town.

supposed a maid, was now a mother. Offended Juno is filled with rage, and changes the form of the damsel. *Goddess!* what art thou doing? It was with reluctant spirit that she received the embrace of Jupiter. And when she beheld the hideous face of a wild beast in the *former* favourite, "Let Jupiter," says she, "now rush into her embraces." A frightful -she-bear, she roamed along the wild mountains, she who had lately been an object of love to almighty Jove. Just three times five years had the boy, conceived in secret, now passed, when the mother was thrown in the way of her son. Infatuated she stood still, as though she would recognize him, and moaned: that moan was the address of a parent. The boy unknowing would have pierced her with his sharp javelin, had not each been snatched away to the mansions above. As neighbouring Constellations they now shine; the first one is she whom we call the 'Bear;' the 'Bear-ward' has the attitude of one following her behind. Still is the daughter of Saturn incensed, and requests the hoary Tethys[45] not to lave the Mænalian Bear by the contact of the waters.

On the Ides the altars of the rustic Faunus[46] smoke, here where the island breaks the parted waters. This was that day on which, on the plains of Veii, three hundred and six Fabii[47] fell. One house had taken upon itself the strength and burden of the whole city; the hands of one family take up arms volunteered *by them;* each goes forth a high-born soldier from that camp out of which each one was fitted to *go forth* a general. The nearest route is by the right-hand side passage[48] of the gate of Carmenta. Whoever you are, pass

[45] *Tethys.*]—Ver. 191. Tethys was one of the most ancient deities. She was the wife of Oceanus, daughter of Cœlus and Vesta, and the foster-mother of Juno.

[46] *Faunus.*]—Ver. 193. The 'Insula sacra,' on the Tiber, contained the temple of Faunus, as also those of Jupiter and Æsculapius. It was built by the Ædiles, A.U.C. 509.

[47] *Fabii.*]—Ver. 196. Ovid places this event on the 15th of February. Livy, book 6, c. 1, places it on the 18th of July.

[48] *Right-hand side passage.*]—Ver. 201. 'Dextro—Jano.' It has been already mentioned, that the janus was the arched or covered passage of a gateway. Many of those at Rome had two passages for the convenience of people passing each way—similar to the plan of our Thames Tunnel. After this day no one went out by the passage through which the Fabii had passed. The way was called the 'via scelerata,' or 'infelix,' the 'accursed,' or 'unlucky way.'

not through it; it has *an evil* omen. Tradition says, that by that *gate* the three hundred Fabii went forth. The gate is free from blame, but yet it has a *bad* omen. When with rapid step they reached the swiftly rolling Cremera,[49] (it was flowing swollen by the rains of the winter); they pitch their camp on the plain; they themselves, with drawn swords, rush through the Tuscan lines with vigorous onset. Just as when, from the Libyan[50] crag, the lions rush upon the flocks scattered throughout the wide fields. The enemy fly in all directions, and on their backs receive disgraceful wounds; the earth is reddened with Etrurian blood. Once more, and again they fall. When it is not possible for them to conquer in open fight, they prepare a stratagem, and the resources of ambush. There was a plain; hills, and a forest well fitted to harbour the wild beasts of the mountain, shut in the extremities of it. In the midst of this plain they leave a few men, and the herds scattered here and there; the rest of the troops lie hid, concealed in the underwood. Lo! as a torrent, swollen by a deluge of rain, or by the snow which flows melted by the warmth of the Zephyr, is borne over the sown fields and the highways, and no longer, as it was wont, confines its current bounded by the margin of its banks; so do the Fabii fill the valley with their straggling sallies, *and* the few they see they despise; they have no apprehension from any other quarter. Whither rush ye, noble house? It is unsafe to trust a foe, unsuspecting nobles, beware of the weapons of treachery—valour perishes by stratagem; from every part the enemy springs forth into the open plain, and encompasses every side. What can a few brave men do against so many thousands? or what expedient have they that they can avail themselves of in the moment of distress? As the wild boar chased in the Laurentine[51] woods afar scatters with his tusk like the lightning the swift hounds, yet soon he dies himself; so do they perish, *but*

[49] *Cremera.*]—Ver. 205. A Tuscan river, falling into the Tiber a little to the north of Rome, and not far from Veii.

[50] *Libyan.*]—Ver. 209. Mauritania, a district of Libya, in Africa, was remarkable for the fierceness and voracity of its lions.

[51] *Laurentine.*]—Ver. 231. Laurentum was a town of Latium, supposed to be the residence of the ancient kings, Picus, Faunus, and Latinus. Its name was derived from a grove of bay-trees, 'lauri,' between Ostia and Antium. It was remarkable for its breed of boars.

not unavenged; and they deal and suffer wounds with mutual blows.

One day had sent forth to battle all the Fabii; one day cut off those sent, yet it is worthy of belief that the Gods themselves provided that there should survive some seed of the house of Hercules.[52] For a boy of tender years[53] and unserviceable for war alone of the Fabian house had been left behind; doubtless to the end that thou *Fabius* Maximus[54] mightest in future times be born; by whom, through procrastination, the republic might be preserved.

Contiguous in position are three Constellations,[55] the Raven, and the Snake, and the Goblet, that lies between them both. On the Ides they are hidden, they rise on the following night; I will sing why the three are thus connected together.

It happened that Phœbus was preparing a solemn festival for Jupiter (my story shall cause no *very* long delay). "Go, my bird,"[56] said he, "that nothing may retard my rites of duty, and bring a little water from the gushing fountains." The raven lifts with his hooked claws a gilded goblet,[57] and wings on high his aërial route. There stood a fig-tree loaded with fruit, still hard *and unripe*. He tries it with his beak—*the fruit* was not fit to be gathered. Heedless of his commands, he is said to have sat down beneath that tree, until in the slowly passing lapse of time the fruit became sweet. And at last, having satiated his appetite, he seizes in his black claws a long water-snake, and then returns to his master and makes a

---

[52] *Hercules.*]—Ver. 237. It was a tradition, that the Fabii were descended from Hercules, by a daughter of Evander.

[53] *Of tender years.*]—Ver. 239. Niebuhr, in his Roman History, book 2, says that the Fabius who remained at home must have then been a grown man. He gives a political solution of the whole story.

[54] *Fabius Maximus.*]—Ver. 241. From the single survivor sprang Q. Fabius Maximus, who, in the second Punic war, after the defeat of the consul Flaminius at Lake Thrasymenus, was appointed pro-dictator. By counter-marches and ambuscades he harassed and weakened the army of Hannibal, and eventually saved Rome. Hence he was called 'the Delayer,' 'Cunctator.'

[55] *Three Constellations.*]—Ver. 243. He gives the achronycal rising of these three constellations on the 14th of February.

[56] *My bird.*]—Ver. 249. The poets considered the crow sacred to Apollo on account of its supposed efficacy in augury and divination.

[57] *A gilded goblet.*]—Ver. 251-2. Gower translates these lines thus—

' The golden tanker in his claws the crow
   Takes, and through air with waving wings doth row.'

feigned excuse. "This *creature* was the cause of my delay, watching at the running stream; 'tis he that withheld the waters and the fulfilment of my task." Phœbus answers, "Dost thou add to thy fault a lie, and darest thou by thy stories to attempt to impose upon the God of oracles? And now so long as the green fig shall be firm[58] on the tree, be no cooling water drunk by thee from any spring." He spoke, and as a lasting memorial of this ancient affair, the Snake, the Bird, and the Goblet glitter as contiguous Constellations.

The third dawn after the Ides beholds the naked Luperci, and the sacred rites of the two-horned Faunus[59] will proceed. Tell, ye Pierian maids, what is the origin of these rites, and whence derived they reached the abodes of Latium. The ancient Arcadians are said to have worshipped Pan *as* God of cattle; he most *frequents* the Arcadian mountains. Pholoë[60] will attest it, the streams of Stymphalus, and Ladon, which with rapid current flows into the sea, *will* attest it, and the ridges of the forest of Nonacris encircled with groves of pine, and the lofty Cyllene and the snows of Parrhasia. Pan was the guardian of the herd, Pan, the God of the mares; he used to receive offerings for the preservation of the sheep. Evander brought over with him the woodland divinities. Here, where now the City stands, was then *but* the city's site. Thence do we reverence this God, and the rites imported from the Pelasgians.[61] By ancient usage the Flamen Dialis

[58] *Shall be firm.*]—Ver. 263. 'Lactens' is literally 'waxing full of milk.' 'Lac,' 'milk,' was the name given to the juice of the unripe fig, while it is yet in a hard state.

[59] *Faunus.*]—Ver. 267. He was one of the ancient kings of Latium, and being deified, in time became confounded with the Arcadian deity Pan. As Pan was attended by numerous minor Pans, so there were numerous Fauni.

[60] *Pholoë.*]—Ver. 273. 'Pholoë,' and the several places here mentioned, were in Arcadia. Pholoë was a mountain; Stymphalus was the name of a city and a lake there, whence Hercules, as his sixth labour, chased the Stymphalian birds, and slew them. The river Ladon falls into the Alpheus, and not into the sea; it was remarkable for the excellent quality of its water. Nonacris was a town of Arcadia, near which was the river Styx, whose waters were so pestilential that they could be carried in no vessel whatever, except one made of the hoof of a mule. Cyllene was a mountain of Arcadia. Parrhasia was a town of the same country.

[61] *Pelasgians.*]—Ver. 281. The Arcadians were generally deemed to be of the Pelasgian race, who seem to have been the aborigines of Greece.

attended these sacrifices. You ask, then, why they run and why (for thus to run is their practice,) they have their bodies naked, having stripped off their garments. The fleet God himself loves to run at large on the lofty hills, and starts on a sudden the *scared* wild beasts. The God, naked himself, commands his attendants[62] to go naked; for dress was not very convenient for running. The Arcadians are said to have tenanted the earth before the birth of Jupiter, and that nation existed before the moon. Their *mode of* life was like that of the beasts of the field, spent amid no comforts; they were still a multitude unskilled in arts and uncivilized. For habitations, they knew of the boughs of trees alone, for corn the blades of grass; water taken up with their two palms was nectar to them. No steer *then* panted under the crooked plough; no land was *then* under the control of the husbandmen. As yet the use of the horse[63] was not *known;* each one carried himself; the sheep *then* used to go clothed with its own fleece. They dwelt in the open air, and had their bodies naked, taught to endure the heavy showers and the southern blasts. Still do the naked *priests* recall to mind the vestiges of ancient usage,[64] and testify the *humble* resources of olden times. But there is a story told, full of old-fashioned humour, why Faunus has a particular aversion to garments. It chanced that the Tirynthian youth was travelling in the company of his mistress,[65] *Omphale.* Faunus, from a lofty hill-top, saw them both. He saw, and caught the flame—'ye mountain Goddesses,' said he, 'farewell; this *lady* shall hence-

[62] *Commands his attendants.*]—Ver. 287. Gower gives this version,

'The god self-naked, naked makes his frie;
Clothes are a hindrance to agility.'

[63] *Use of the horse.*]—Ver. 297. Bellerophon is said to have been the first to teach mankind the use of the horse.

[64] *Ancient usage.*]—Ver. 301-2. Gower translates these lines,

'Therefore they naked run, in sign and honor
Of hardiness, and that old bare-skinn'd manner.'

[65] *His mistress.*]—Ver. 305. Hercules had been sold by Mercury, to serve as a slave for three years, to Omphale, queen of Lydia or Mæonia, in order that the purchase-money might be paid to Eurytus, as a compensation for the loss of Iphytus, his son, who had been slain by Hercules. That he was taken into the especial favour of Omphale we may perceive from this story.

forth be my love."[66] The Mæonian queen was walking *onward*, distinguished by her gold embroidered vestment, her perfumed tresses flowing over her shoulders. A golden screen repelled the scorching sunbeams, which yet the hands of Hercules, *strong as they were*, supported. And now had she reached the grove of Bacchus, the vineyards of Tmolus, and the dewy Hesperus was running his course on his dusky steed.[67] She enters a grotto whose roof was fretted with porous pebbles, and the natural pumice stone; at its entrance ran a bubbling streamlet. And now while the attendants are preparing the repast, and the wine for them to quaff, she arrays Alcides in her own attire. She gives him her fine wrought gown, dyed with Gætulian purple; she gives him the net-work zone, with which just now she had been girt. The zone is too small for his girth; she unlooses the laces of the gown, that he may get his huge hands through. Her armlets he had *already* broken, not made for such arms as those. His big feet[68] were bursting asunder the scanty ties of her *sandals*. She herself takes the ponderous club, and the spoil of the lion, and his lesser weapons stored in their quiver. In this dress they partake of the repast; in this dress they resign their bodies to sleep, and lie apart upon couches placed closed to one another. The reason was, that they were about to prepare a pious sacrifice to the discoverer of the vine, which they ought to perform in a state of purity[69] when the day had

---

[66] *Be my love.*]—Ver. 307-8. The quaint translation given by Gower of these two lines is,

' He eyes and fries, and "country lasses" cries,
None for my diet; here my Cupid lies.'

[67] *Dusky steed.*]—Ver. 314. He has a dusky steed assigned him, as the sky on his approach becomes darker. For the opposite reason a white horse is assigned to Lucifer, the morning star.

[68] *His big feet.*]—Ver. 324. Gower's version of this line is,

' His huge plaice-foot her pretty sandals rent.'

The Gætulian, or African purple, mentioned a few lines before, was probably of inferior quality. Alcides was one of the epithets of Hercules, from the Greek word ἀλκή, 'strength.'

[69] *In a state of purity.*]—Ver. 330. The sacrifice was to be to Bacchus, god of the vine. Sacrifices to the gods were expected to be performed by the attendant devotees in a state of perfect purity, and uncontaminated by a breach of chastity. Gower's version of this and the preceding line is—

' Because, next day, some rites to Jove's wine son
They should perform, which must be purely done.'

dawned. 'Twas midnight. What does not unscrupulous passion dare? Amid the shades of the night, Faunus comes to the dewy grotto, and when he sees the attendants relaxed with sleep and wine, he conceives hopes that in their master and mistress there is the same drowsiness. He enters, and the daring ravisher wanders to this side and that, and stretches forth his cautious hands and follows *their direction*. *And now* he had come to the bedding of a spread couch which he had found *by groping*, and *as he thought*, was about to be successful in his first venture. When he touched the hide of the tawny lion all shaggy with its coarse hair, he was alarmed and withdrew his hand, and terrified he shuddered with fear; as oft the traveller has withdrawn his startled foot on seeing a serpent. He next feels the soft coverings of the couch which was close by, and is deceived by the false indication. He climbs the bed, and lies down on the side nearest to him. His passions are at the highest pitch—meantime he draws up the bed-clothes from the bottom; the legs *he finds* are all bristling, rough with thick hair. The Tyrinthian hero flings him back[70] with his arm *just as he is* making further attempts; he tumbles from the top of the couch. An uproar is the consequence, the Mæonian *queen* summons her attendants aloud, and calls for lights;[71] the lights being brought, the transaction is discovered. Faunus is groaning aloud, tumbled violently from the lofty couch, and with difficulty he raises his limbs from the hard ground. Both Alcides laughs, and those who see him lie sprawling; the Lydian damsel laughs *too* at her gallant. The God, *thus* deceived through a dress, thence-

[70] *Flings him back.*]—Ver. 349-50. Gower translates this and the following lines—

' Attempting more, Alcides from the couch
Throws him quite off. Down lumps the lustful slouch.
Mæonia at the noise for lights doth cry,
Which, brought there, make a strange discovery.
He, with his fall much bruised, grones and mones,
And, much ado, heaves up his heavy bones.
Alcides laugh'd, and all at that night-rover,
And Omphale laughs at her goodly lover.'

[71] *Calls for lights.*]—Ver. 351. The servants, who slept just outside of the chamber of their master or mistress, usually kept a lamp burning; therefore the light was brought even before Faunus could rise from the floor.

forth hates garments that impose upon the sight, and summons *his officials* to his rites in a state of nakedness. To these causes imported from afar, add, my Muse, the Latin ones, and let my courser *now* pace his *native* dust.

A she-goat being slain, according to custom, to the horny-footed Faunus, a crowd came by invitation to the scanty repast, and while the priests were making ready the entrails transfixed with spits of willow, the sun now reaching his mid course, Romulus and his brother, and the shepherd youth, were exposing their naked bodies to the sun and the *dust of the* plain.[72] They gave exercise to their arms in sport with the boxing-gloves,[73] and the javelin, and the weight of the casting stone. A shepherd from an eminence exclaimed—"Romulus! the robbers are driving away the oxen through the sequestered fields; to the rescue!" 'Twould take too long a time to put on arms; each rushes forth in a different direction: by the spear of Remus the spoil was recovered. As soon as he returned, he takes off from the spits the hissing entrails, and says, "These, in truth, none but a conqueror shall eat." As he says he does, and so *do* the Fabii. Romulus arrives there too late, and sees *nothing but* the board and the picked bones. He smiled, but was annoyed that the Fabii and Remus had been able to gain a victory, and that his own Quinctilii[74] could not. The fame of the transaction still abides *with us*; they *still* run without a garment, and because the result was favourable, it has a lasting celebrity.

Perhaps too, you may ask, why that place is *called* the

---

[72] *The plain.*]—Ver. 366. Probably the 'Campus Martius,' or 'field of Mars,' which was a plain of great extent, near the Tiber, where the Romans used to exercise. It was the private property of the Tarquins, and on their expulsion was consecrated to Mars, as the patron of warlike exercises.

[73] *The boxing-gloves.*]—Ver. 367. This is the nearest translation that can be given to the word 'cæstus,' which were coverings of leather for the hand, with lead or iron sewed on them to render the weight of the blow more effective. On the other hand, with us, the boxing-glove is used for the opposite purpose, to diminish the weight of the blow. The casting-stone was thrown either from the hand or the sling. It does not appear which, in this instance.

[74] *His own Quinctilii.*]—Ver. 378. The Fabii are said to have been the companions of Remus, and the Quinctilii, the associates of Romulus. The Fabii were of Sabine origin, while the Quinctilii were a Roman family.

'Lupercal,' or what reason marks the day with a similar name. The Vestal Ilia[75] had given birth to her heavenly progeny, while her uncle held the sovereign sway. He orders the children to be taken away and to be drowned in the river. What art thou doing? one or other of these will be Romulus *hereafter*. His servants with reluctance perform his cruel commands: they weep and bear the twins to the commanded place. Albula,[76] that stream, whose name, Tiberinus drowned in its waters, changed into *that of* Tiber, by chance was swollen by the floods of winter. Here, where the market-places[77] now are, you might see boats wandering about; where, too, thy valley now lies, O Circus Maximus.[78] When they had come hither, and could advance no further, first one and then the other of them says, "And *see* how like they are! and how lovely is each! yet of the two that one has more life in him. If origin is to be indicated by looks, if the likeness deceives me not, I suspect some God (whom, I know not) to be your father.

[75] *The vestal Ilia.*—Ver. 383. Ilia, or Rhea Silvia, whose story is told more at length in the next book, was the daughter of Numitor, king of Alba Longa. In order that she might not, by becoming a mother, endanger the sovereignty of Amulius, her uncle, who had usurped the throne and banished his brother, he devoted her to the service of Vesta, and, in consequence, to perpetual chastity. Mars having become enamoured of her, she conceived twins by him, whose history is here told, and is repeated in the next book. She was buried alive; the punishment invariably inflicted on Vestal virgins when convicted of a violation of their vow of chastity.

[76] *Albula.*]—Ver. 389. This was anciently the name of the Tiber. 'Albus' is the Latin for 'white,' and the river was so called from the whiteness of its waters. It was called Tiber after Tiberinus Sylvius, the successor of Capetius, king of Alba, and who was drowned in its stream.

[77] *Market-places.*]—Ver. 391. There were two kinds of 'fora' at Rome—the 'forum' for litigation and process at law, and the 'forum,' or 'market-place,' such as the 'forum boarum,' or 'cattle-market;' 'piscarium,' or 'fish-market;' 'olitorium,' or 'herb-market;' 'suarium,' or 'pig-market.'

[78] *O Circus Maximus.*]—Ver. 392. This, 'the Greatest Circus,' was originally built by Tarquinius Priscus, and was situate in a prolonged valley between the Palatine and Aventine Hills. It was a mile in circumference, and received great improvements from Julius Cæsar. It was able to contain at least 150,000 persons; Pliny says 250,000; perhaps the former number when sitting, the latter when standing. There the public games and shews were celebrated, which formed the favourite recreation of the Romans of all classes. It was called 'Maximus,' 'greatest,' because there were several other 'circi' at Rome, as the Circus Flaminius, Circus Vaticanus, and others were built in later times by Nero, Caracalla, and other emperors.

But if any God really was the author of your birth, he would surely bring you aid at so perilous a moment. Your mother for certain would bring you aid, were she not herself in need of help, who in one day has become a mother and has been made childless. Babes! born together, together to die! sink together beneath the waters." He had ceased speaking, and laid them down, *having first taken them* from his bosom. The infants screamed with a similar cry; you would imagine that they were conscious *of their fate*. With tearful cheeks the servants return to their homes. A hollowed ark[78] bears them placed therein on the surface of the stream. Ah! what a weight of destiny did that one slight plank support! The ark driven *by the breeze* into the shady woods settles in the slime as the river subsides by degrees. There was a tree, the remains of it are still in existence; and that which is now called the Ruminal,[79] was once the Romulan fig-tree. Wondrous to relate, a she-wolf that had just brought forth came to the twins thus exposed; who would believe that the wild beast did not hurt the babes? *To do* them no injury is not enough *for her*, she even aids them; and those, whom a she-wolf is nourishing, the hands of a relation could brook to destroy. She stands still, and with her tail she fawns upon her tender fosterlings, and with her tongue forms their two bodies *into shape*. You might know that they were begotten by Mars; they have no fear; they draw her udder, and are nourished by the aid of milk not destined for them *by nature*. She gave a name to the place—the place[80] to the Luperci. The nurse has a high

---

[78] *A hollowed ark.*]—Ver. 407. 'Alveus' is 'a hollow wooden vessel,' or 'a tub.' It may here mean an ark which the servant had provided for the purpose; or more probably the wooden cradle in which the children had been laid, and which, with the view of giving them a chance of safety, he purposely set afloat, instead of drowning them, as he had been ordered.

[79] *Ruminal.*]—Ver. 412. The author supposes this word to be a corruption from 'Romula,' which derivation is unworthy of attention. It is, with much more probability, supposed to have been so named from 'rumis,' or 'ruma,' the ancient name for the breast, from the infants having been there suckled by the wolf. According to some, it took its name from 'rumen,' the 'throat,' because under this tree the cattle used to chew the cud, or ruminate. Tacitus tells us that the tree, in his time, was still standing in the Comitium. Others say that the tree referred to by him was planted by Attius Nævius. Perhaps it was propagated from the one under which the infants were said to have been found.

[80] *The place.*]—Ver. 421. The Lupercal, where Pan was worshipped,

reward for the milk she gave. What prevents that the Luperci should derive their name from the Arcadian mountain? The Lycæan Faunus has his temple in Arcadia. Bride *newly made*, what dost thou await? not by potent herbs, not by prayers, not by the magic incantation—wilt thou become a mother; with patience await the blows of the right hand that fructifies; soon shall thy father-in-law have the wished-for epithet of grandfather.[81] For it was that period, when by a cruel fate the matrons were affording but few pledges of their fruitfulness. "What avails it me," exclaimed Romulus, "to have carried off the Sabine women (this took place while he held the sceptre) if my violence has produced for me, not strength, but *only* war *in return;* it had been better for me to have had no daughters-in-law *at such a price*. At the base of the Esquilian hill, there was a grove, uncut for many a year, *and* called by the name of the mighty Juno. When they came thither, both the matrons and the men with bent knees prostrated themselves in supplication. Then lo! suddenly the tops of the shaken wood trembled, and the Goddess uttered these wondrous words through her sacred grove, "Let a sacred he-goat have access to the Italian matrons." The multitude, alarmed by this ambiguous oracle, was confounded. There was an augur, whose name has been lost in the lengthened lapse of years; he had lately come an exile from the Etrurian soil.[82] He sacrifices a he-goat. The matrons at his bidding submitted their backs to be smitten by the hide that had been cut into thongs. The moon was resuming her new horns

the author here says was so called from 'lupa,' a she-wolf,' and gave its name to the 'Luperci,' the priests of Pan. It was a cave in the Palatine Hill, and is said to have been consecrated to the worship of Pan by Evander. He also suggests that the Lupercal may have been so called from the name 'Lycæus,' which Pan derived from Mount Lycæum, in Arcadia, which name being Λύκαιον, meaning 'of,' or 'infested by wolves,' would be rendered in Latin by 'Lupercum,' a word of similar import. Perhaps the festival was so called from the words 'luo,' to sacrifice or 'expiate,' and 'caper,' a 'he-goat,' as a goat was sacrificed to Pan on this occasion.

[81] *Grandfather.*]—Ver. 427-8. Gower's version of these lines is—

'Take patiently stripes from the fruitful hand;
Thy father then shall be a father grand.'

[82] *The Etrurian soil.*]—Ver. 444. Etruria was the country which supplied Rome both with rites and priests in the earlier ages, and was especially renowned for its skill in the arts of augury and divination.

in her tenth course *from that time*, and suddenly the husband became a father, the wife a mother. Thanks *were given* to Lucina ;[83] this epithet the grove gave to thee, O Goddess ; or *it was* because thou hast *under thy care our* introduction to the light. Spare, I pray, gentle Lucina, the pregnant females, and without pain bring forth from the womb its matured burden.

The next day has *now* dawned ; do thou cease to rely on the winds ; the gales at this season of the year are not to be trusted. The breezes are unsteady ; and for six days the loosened gate of the prison of Æolus[84] *all* unbolted stands wide open.

Now, lightened of his burden, the Waterbearer has sunk on his knee, with his urn obliquely sloped ; be thou, the Fish, the next to receive the heavenly steeds. They say that thou and thy brother[85] (for ye glitter as contiguous constellations) bore on your backs two gods. Once on a time, Dione[86] flying from the frightful Typhon, at that period when Jupiter bore arms in defence of heaven, accompanied by the infant Cupid, came to the Euphrates, and sat on the margin of the river of Palestine.[87] The poplar and the reeds clothed the top of the banks, and the willows afforded a hope that

---

[83] *Lucina.*]—Ver. 449. A title of Diana, as presiding over the birth of mortals, derived from the Latin 'lux,' lucis, 'light,' or from 'lucus,' 'a grove,' the place of her worship, as the poet explains in this and the next line.

[84] *Prison of Æolus.*]—Ver. 456. Æolus was the son of Jupiter and Acesta, or Sergesta, daughter of Hippotas, a Trojan. He was king of Lipara and the adjacent islands (called from him Æolian), near Italy and Sicily. Strongyle, now Stromboli, was one of these. It was a volcanic mountain, and, as it was believed that the inhabitants could tell from its smoke, three days before, what wind would blow, the fable became current that Æolus was the god of the winds, and that he held them imprisoned in his dominions.

[85] *Thy brother.*]—Ver. 458. The one looking towards the north was called 'Boreus,' and was situated under the arm of Andromeda. The one looking towards the south was called 'Notius,' and was below the shoulder of the constellation Equus.

[86] *Dione.*]—Ver. 461. According to Homer, this goddess was the mother of Venus ; but the poet, by here introducing her in company with Cupid, evidently confounds her with that goddess. Typhon, or Typhæus, has been noticed in the note to line 523 of the first book. According to Hyginus, Typhon did present himself, whereon Venus and her son were turned into fishes.

[87] *Palestine.*]—Ver. 464. Palestine was only a small portion of Syria, of which the river Euphrates formed the eastern boundary.

by them they might be concealed. While she is in her place of concealment, the grove roars with the blast; she turns pale with terror, and fancies that the forces of the enemy[88] are at hand. And as she clasps her son to her bosom, she says, "Assist, ye nymphs, and give aid to *us* two Divinities." Immediately, she plunged *into the stream*. Two fishes bore them up; for which they now have Constellations as a merited reward. In consequence, the superstitious Syrians deem it impious to place this kind *of animal* on *their* tables, nor do they profane their lips with fish.[89]

The next day is without any mark of distinction; but the one after it has been consecrated to Quirinus. He who now bears this name was formerly Romulus; either because by the ancient Sabines a spear was called 'curis' (from his spear the warrior God came to the stars), or because the Quirites gave their own name to their king, or because he had joined the Curians[90] to the Roman people. For his father that bears sway over all arms, after he beheld the new walls, and many a war finished by the hand of Romulus, said, "O Jupiter, the Roman power has strength *of its own*, and needs not the service of my offspring. Restore the son to the father; though one is cut off, he that remains shall be to me in place of Remus and himself. Thou didst tell me that there shall be one, whom thou wilt raise to the azure vault of heaven: let the words of Jove be fulfilled." Jupiter nodded assent;

[88] *Forces of the enemy.*]—Ver. 468. 'Hostiles manus' may mean either the troops or forces of the giants, who were aiding their kinsman in the giant war, or 'the hands of her enemy' himself. In the latter case the translation would be, 'fancies that the hands of her enemy are *even now* upon her.'

[89] *Profane their lips.*]—Ver. 473-4. The Syrians had a notion that swelling of the body and ulceration would be the consequence of eating fish, and this was perhaps the true reason of their abstinence from that diet. They offered either fish or representations of them in metal to the goddess, Atergatis, who was their deity corresponding to Venus. Gower thus translates these lines—

'Hence Syrians hate to eat that kind of fishes;
Nor is it fit to make their gods their dishes.'

[90] *The Curians.*]—Ver. 480. When Romulus agreed with Tatius, king of the town of Cures, to incorporate his subjects into the Roman state, it was settled that the Romans should be called 'Curites,' or 'Quirites,' in honour of their new associates, the Curites or Curians, as well as 'Romani,' from the name of Romulus.

at his nod either pole was shaken, and Atlas[91] felt the *pressing* weight of the heavens. There is a place; the people of old called it the fen of Caprea;[92] it chanced that there, O Romulus, thou wast dispensing justice to thy subjects. The sun vanishes, the intervening clouds conceal the sky, and the heavy shower descends with pouring torrents. It thunders, and the heavens are rent asunder with the sent forth lightnings. The people disperse in flight, *the while* the monarch on the steeds of his sire is speeding to the stars. There was mourning, and the senate was under a charge of murder falsely imputed *to it*: and possibly that persuasion might have remained fixed in the minds *of men*. But Julius Proculus[93] was on his way from Alba Longa;[94] the moon was shining, and there was no need of a torch, when, with a sudden peal, the clouds thundered on his left hand. He started back, and his hair stood on an end with terror.[95] Romulus, graceful, and larger than the human size, arrayed too in his kingly robe, seemed to stand before him in the middle of the way, and at the same time to say, "Forbid the Quirites to lament,

---

[91] *Atlas.*]—Ver. 490. He was the son of Jupiter, and was the father of the Pleiädes, who were placed by Jupiter among the constellations. He is also said to have been the father of the Hyades, who received a similar honour. Atlas was the name of a mountain in the country of Mauritania, in Africa, so high that its summit was not visible; hence the fable, that a king of that region supported the heavens. The most probable solution of the fable, is that he was an astronomer of Libya, who frequented that mountain for the purpose of making astronomical observations.

[92] *The fen of Caprea.*]—Ver. 491. This 'fen of Caprea,' or 'Capra,' the 'she-goat,' was a marsh near Rome, in the Campus Martius. Romulus is said to have been promulgating the laws or reviewing his army here when he was translated. Some accounts represent him as having been assassinated while holding the senate in the Temple of Vulcan.

[93] *Julius Proculus.*]—Ver. 499. Dionysius says that he was a citizen of Alba Longa.

[94] *Alba Longa.*]—Ver. 499. This was originally a colony from Lavinium, in Latium, and was founded by Ascanius, the son of Æneas, at the foot of the Alban Mount. It was so named from the discovery in that spot, of a white sow and her litter, as obscurely foretold by Helenus in his prophecy, mentioned in the Æneid, Book 3, l. 389. From its length it was called Longa. It was destroyed, with the exception of its temple, by Tullus Hostilius, who removed its inhabitants to Rome.

[95] *With terror.*]—Ver. 501-2. Gower's translation of this passage is,

'Lo! suddenly the left-hand hedges quake;
He with his hairs turned bolt upright starts back.'

and let them not offend my Godhead with their tears. Let them offer *me* frankincense, and let the pious multitude pay adoration to Quirinus, *their* new *God*, and let them practise my father's arts and warfare." He gave these commands, and vanished into the thin air. Proculus calls the *two* peoples together, and reports to them the words enjoined upon him. A temple is raised to the Divinity; the hill too[96] is named from him, and appointed days[97] bring back the religious services of the *Roman* father.

Why the same day is also called the festival of fools,[98] *now* learn; a reason, trifling indeed, but still appropriate, is suggested. The earth in ancient times had no experienced husbandmen; the toils of war used to weary the active men *of those days*. There was more of *glory* in the *use of the* sword than of the curved plough; neglected by its owner, the fields used to bear but little. Yet did the ancients sow the spelt, and reaped it, and gave the same when cut down, to Ceres as the first-fruits. Taught by experience they exposed it to the flames to be parched, and by their mistakes they suffered many a loss. For sometimes, they used to sweep up smutty ashes instead of grain; sometimes the flames set fire to their cottages. Fornax, the Goddess *of the Kiln*,[99] was deified; pleased with Fornax as a Goddess, the husbandmen pray that she will moderate the heat to the grain *while parching*. Still does the chief Curio[1] appoint the

[96] *The hill too.*]—Ver. 511. The Quirinal hill. But Festus supposes it to have derived its name from the Sabines of the town of Cures, who settled there and on the Capitoline hill. Niebuhr thinks there was a town on it called 'Quirium,' whence the name 'Quirites,' at first peculiar to the Sabine people.

[97] *Appointed days.*]—Ver. 512. The Quirinalia were stativæ, or 'set' festivals.

[98] *The festival of fools.*]—Ver. 513. 'Stultorum festa,' or 'Feriæ.' This was another name of the Quirinalia, because those who from want of time, or being on a journey, or, as the poet says further on, who were unable to learn the time when their own Curia performed the rites, and had not sacrificed with the rest of the people on the Fornacalia, did so on the Quirinalia, which was the last day for that purpose.

[99] *Goddess of the Kiln.*]—Ver. 525. Pliny (Nat. Hist. Book 18) says that Numa deified the goddess Fornax. He says, 'Numa taught his people to propitiate the gods with the produce of the earth, to offer the salt cakes, and to parch the spelt, as when parched it was more wholesome for food. He also instituted the Fornacalia.'

[1] *Curio.*]—Ver. 527. Romulus divided the people into three tribes, and each tribe into ten 'curiæ.' Each 'curia' had a temple of its own for the

festivals of Fornax in form prescribed by law, but offers no sacrifices at a fixed period : and in the Forum, where many a tablet[2] is suspended around, each ward is denoted by a certain mark. The foolish part of the people do not know which is their own ward, but perform a repetition of the sacrifice on the last day.

Honour also is paid to the graves[3] *of the dead.* Appease the spirits of your forefathers, and offer small presents on the pyres that are *long since* cold.[4] The shades of the dead[5] ask but humble offerings : affection rather than a costly gift is pleasing *to them;* Styx below has no greedy Divinities. Enough *for them* is the covering of their tomb overshadowed with the chaplets laid there, and the scattered fruits and the little grain of salt ; and corn soaked in wine, and violets loosened *from the stem;* these *gifts* let a jar contain, left in the middle of the way. I do not forbid more costly offerings, but by these the shade may be appeased ; add prayers and suitable words, the altars being *first* erected. This custom did Æneas, no unsuitable teacher of the duties of affection, introduce into thy

---

performance of the sacred rites, and was presided over by its own 'curio,' so called because he took care of ('curabat') the sacred rites. Over them all presided the 'curio maximus,' or chief curio. Down to A.U.C. 544, he was chosen from the patricians; after that period, from the plebeians.

[2] *Many a tablet.*]—Ver. 529. In the Forum the names of the curiæ were written on tablets, which stated when and where they were about to perform such rites as were not of the class of 'stativæ,' or set feasts, but 'imperativæ,' appointed by order of the Consul, the Prætor, or Pontifex Maximus.

[3] *Paid to the graves.*]—Ver. 533. The 'Feralia,' in honour of the dead, were celebrated on the 19th of February, as it was formerly the last month of the year. Offerings were then made to propitiate the manes or shades of the dead. Festus derives the word from 'fero,' 'to bear,' because they 'bear offerings;' or from 'ferio,' 'to slay,' because sheep were slain for sacrifice. Varro derives it from 'inferi,' 'the inhabitants of the infernal regions,' 'the dead.'

[4] *Long since cold.*]—Ver. 534. Literally, 'extinguished.' The pile, before being lighted, was called 'pyrus;' when lighted for burning the dead, 'rogus;' when extinguished, 'bustum.'

[5] *Shades of the dead.*]—Ver. 535. Literally, 'Manes.' According to some writers, the souls of the good, after death, became ' Lares;' those of the wicked 'Lemures,' or 'Larvæ;' and the 'Manes' were those whose state was as yet uncertain. The name is also applied to the two Genii, Good and Evil, who were supposed ever to attend each individual, and to inhabit his tomb after death. By others the 'Manes' are considered to have been the deities of the infernal regions.

lands, O just Latinus. He used to offer the annual gifts to the Genius of his father: hence did the *adjoining* nations learn the affectionate ceremonial. But at one time, while they were engaged in a lengthened war with contentious arms, they neglected the Parental days.[6] It was not with impunity *that they did so;* for, by reason of that *cause of ill* omen, Rome is said to have felt the heat of the funeral fires in the suburbs.[7] For my part I scarcely believe it, *but* their *dead* forefathers are said to have come forth from their tombs, and to have uttered their complaints in the hours of the still night; and they say that appalling ghosts, a phantom crowd, howled through the streets of the city and the fields of Latium. Afterwards, the omitted honours were paid at the graves, and there came an end of these portentous sights, and of the mortality *as well*. But while these rites are being performed, remain unwedded, ye damsels; let the torch of pine wood await auspicious days. And let not the curved spear[8] part thy virgin ringlets, maiden, who appearest to thy impatient mother *already* of marriageable years. Conceal thy torches, Hymenæus,[9] and remove them afar from *these* dismal fires, the gloomy tombs have other torches than these. Let the Divinities too be concealed,[10] with the doors of their temples closed; be the altars without incense, and let the hearths stand without fire. Now phantom spirits wander abroad, and bodies that have been committed to the tombs; now does the

[6] *Parental days.*]—Ver. 548. So called from 'parens,' 'a parent,' 'ancestor,' or 'relation,' on behalf of the spirits of whom sacrifice was made on these days.

[7] *In the suburbs.*]—Ver. 550. It was forbidden by law to burn the dead within the walls of the city, that the priests might not be defiled by any casual contact with them, and that the houses might not be endangered by the flames of the funeral piles.

[8] *The curved spear.*]—Ver. 560. The hair of the bride was adjusted by the husband into six locks, with the point of a needle made into the shape of a spear, or, as some suppose, with the point of an actual spear. Festus says, that this ceremony was typical of the guardianship of the matrons by 'Juno Curitis,' or Juno 'of the lance.' Perhaps it may have been typical of the dominion intended by the husband to be exercised over his wife.

[9] *Hymenæus.*]—Ver. 561. Hymen, or Hymenæus, was the tutelar deity of marriage. He was son of Bacchus and Venus, or of Apollo and Calliope, Urania, or Clio. By some he is said to have been the son of Magnes.

[10] *Be concealed.*]—Ver. 564. Let the doors be closed, that the deities may not see any inauspicious sights, such as funerals, which were especially objects of aversion to the gods.

ghost feed upon[11] the viands left for it. But yet these rites are to last no longer, than *to allow* that there should remain of the month as many days as my verses have feet.[11*] This day, because *on it* they perform the due offerings *to the dead*, they have called 'the Feralia;' it is the last day for appeasing the shades.

See, an old woman stricken in years, sitting in the midst of the girls, is performing the sacred rites of Tacita,[12] yet she is not quite silent herself:[13] with three fingers she places three cloves of frankincense under the threshold, where the little mouse has made for himself a hidden way: then she binds the enchanted threads with the dark coloured spindle; then she roasts on the fire the sewed-up head of a pilchard[14] which she has first sealed up with pitch, and pierced with a brazen needle. Wine too she drops on it; whatever of the wine is left, she either drinks it herself, or her attendants, yet she herself *takes* the greater part. "We have tied up the tongues of our foes, and the mouths of our enemies," says she, in the act of going out, and *then* the drunken hag goes forth. You will at once ask of me, who is the silent Goddess? learn what is known to me through the men of old times. Jupiter, smitten by an unconquerable passion for Juturna, endured many things

---

[11] *The ghost feed upon.*]—Ver. 566. At this period, viands were placed near the tombs, on which the Manes were supposed to feed. It was supposed that they delighted in blood, and in consequence, animals were frequently slain at the funeral pile.

[11*] *Verses have feet.*]—Ver. 568. There are eleven feet in an Hexameter and Pentameter couplet, and as the Feralia were held on the 12th of the calends of March, there would be only eleven days left in the month; the poet means, that the Feralia must begin and end on the 12th of the calends of March.

[12] *Tacita.*]—Ver. 572. Tacita was also worshipped under the name of Mania or Muta, besides the name Lara, here mentioned. Neapolis, an old commentator on this author, thinks that these rites accompanied the Feralia, as expressive of the maxim, 'De mortuis nil nisi bonum,' 'Be silent over the faults of the dead.' The rites here described are evidently of magical tendency, but are replete with absurdity. Some writers say that Numa worshipped one of the Muses under this name.

[13] *Quite silent herself.*]—Ver. 572. The editor of the Delphin edition most ungallantly remarks on this passage, 'An old woman be silent? She could just as soon hold a red hot coal in her mouth!'

[14] *A pilchard.*]—Ver. 578. The 'mæna' was a small sea-fish of little value, which was eaten salted by the poorer classes. It was perhaps sacrificed to the goddess because its name resembled her name, Mania. Its mouth being sewed up was typical of silence.

that ought not to have been endured by so great a God. At one time she used to lie hid in the wood among the hazel copses, at another time she used to plunge into the kindred streams. He calls together the Nymphs, which then frequented Latium, and utters such words as these in the midst of their company. "This sister of yours is only spiting herself, and shuns that which is for her good, to lock herself in the embrace of the highest God. Consult ye for us both; for that which will be my highest pleasure, the same shall prove the great advantage of your sister. Prevent her, at the very brink, as she flies, in order that she may not plunge her body beneath the waters of the stream." He had said; all the water Nymphs of the Tiber nodded their assent, and those who dwell in thy chambers,[15] O Goddess Ilia. It chanced there was a Naiad Nymph, Lara by name; but her ancient name was the first syllable twice repeated,[16] given to her for her infirmity *of talkativeness*. Many a time had Almo[17] said to her, "Daughter, do hold your tongue;" but she did not hold it. She, soon as she reached the lake of her sister Juturna, says, "Avoid the banks," and repeats the words of Jupiter. She also went to Juno, and expressing pity for *her as* a wife, says, "That husband of thine is *now* smitten by the Naiad Juturna." Jupiter was furious; he deprived her of the tongue which she had used with so little caution, and charged Mercury,[18] "Take her to the shades below; it is a proper place for the silent; a Nymph *she is*, but a Nymph of the infernal lake shall she be." The commands of Jove are *now* being executed; a grove receives them on the road; she is said to have taken the fancy of the God who conducted her. He prepares to offer violence; with her looks in the place of words she intreats him, and in vain with her voiceless mouth does she struggle to speak. She becomes pregnant, and gives birth

---

[15] *Thy chambers.*]—Ver. 598. Ilia, when buried alive on the banks of the Tiber, was fabled to have become wedded to the god of the river.

[16] *Twice repeated.*]—Ver. 599. This name was 'Lala,' from the Greek λαλεῖν, 'to talk,' 'to chatter.' Another of her names was Larunda.

[17] *Almo.*]—Ver. 601. The father of Lara, a rivulet in the Roman territory, running from the Appian way into the Tiber near the city.

[18] *Mercury.*]—Ver. 608. The son of Jupiter and Maia, and the messenger of the gods. His name was probably derived from 'merx,' 'merchandize,' as he was the god of trade and gain. He was represented with winged cap and winged sandals.

to twins, the Lares,[19] who guard the cross ways, and ever keep their watch in our houses.

The kinsfolk, full of affection, have named the next day the "Caristia,"[20] and the company of relations assemble at the family feast. In good truth, it is a pleasant thing to turn our attention from the tombs and our relatives who are dead, to those who survive; and after so many are lost, to see all that remains of our family, and to reckon the degrees of relationship. Let the guiltless come; far, far hence be the unnatural brother, and the mother cruel to her own offspring; *the son* for whom the father is too long-lived, *and* he who counts his mother's years; the cruel mother-in-law, *too*, who hates and oppresses her daughter-in-law. Far hence be the brothers[21] the descendants of Tantalus, and the wife of Jason, and she who gave to the husbandman the parched seed-corn;[22] Progne too, and her sister,[23] and Tereus, cruel to them both; and

---

[19] *The Lares.*]—Ver. 616. These deities were divided into the public and private Lares. The private, or familiars, are by some supposed to have been the same with the 'Manes' or 'shades' of the ancestors of the family occupying the house. The public 'Lares' were, the 'urbani,' presiding over cities; 'rustici,' over the country; 'compitales,' over cross-roads; 'marini,' over the sea. Lar is an Etrurian word, signifying 'lord,' or 'noble.'

[20] *Caristia.*]—Ver. 617. From 'carus,' 'dear,' as these festivals were for the purpose of maintaining family love, and of healing misunderstandings by meeting again.

[21] *The brothers.*]—Ver. 627. Atreus and Thyestes, sons of Pelops and Hippodamia, killed their half-brother Chrysippus. Thyestes having seduced Aërope, the wife of Atreus, sent Pleisthenes, the son of Atreus, whom he had brought up, to murder his father. Atreus, supposing him to be the son of Thyestes, slew him. According to another version of the story, Atreus, feigning a reconciliation, invited Thyestes to his kingdom, and killed and dressed the bodies of Tantalus and Pleisthenes, the sons of Thyestes; and while the latter was enjoying the meal, Atreus had their hands and heads brought in and shown to the father, on which Thyestes fled to the court of Thesprotus. Medea, the wife of Jason, slew her own children.

[22] *The parched seed-corn.*]—Ver. 628. Ino, daughter of Cadmus, married Athamas, who had Phrixus and Helle by a former marriage. These Ino resolved to destroy. She persuaded the women to parch the seed-corn, unknown to their husbands. The crop failing, the oracle at Delphi was consulted how consequent famine might be averted. Ino persuaded the messengers to say that Apollo directed Phrixus to be sacrificed to Jupiter. By celestial interference Phrixus was saved, and Athamas becoming mad, Ino rushed into the sea, and was made a sea-goddess under the name of Leucothea.

[23] *Progne.*]—Ver. 629. Tereus, king of Thrace, married Progne, and at her request went to Athens to bring Philomela to see her sister, and,

whoever increases his wealth by the perpetration of crime. Offer the frankincense to the propitious Gods of the family: Concord is said on this day to be present with extreme benignity; offer, too, a share of the viands, that the presented platter, testimony of the pleasing honour, may feed the well-girt Lares.[24] And now when night, far advanced, shall invite you to balmy slumbers, when ye are about to pray, take wine in abundance in your hand, and say, "Well may it be with us, and well with thee, most excellent Cæsar, father of thy country,"[25] the wine being poured forth *as you repeat* the holy words.

When the night shall have passed away, let the God, who by his landmark divides the fields, be worshipped with the accustomed honours. Terminus,[26] whether thou art a stone, or whether a stock sunk deep in the field by the ancients, yet even in this form thou dost possess divinity. Thee, the two owners *of the fields* crown with chaplets from their opposite sides, and present with two garlands and two cakes. An altar is erected; to this the female peasant herself brings in a broken[27] pan the fire taken from the burning hearths. An old man cuts up the firewood, and piles it on high when chopped, and strives hard to drive the branches into the resisting ground. While he is exciting the kindling blaze with dried bark, a boy[28] stands by and holds in his hands a

having ravished her by the way, he cut out her tongue. Of this Progne was informed by a robe which Philomela sent her, on which was described the conduct of Tereus. Progne, on this, killed Itys, the son of Tereus, and served him up to his father. Tereus would have slain her, but the gods changed him into a hoopoe, Progne into a swallow, and Philomela into a nightingale.

[24] *Well-girt Lares.*]—Ver. 634. The Lares were represented in the Gabinean habit, which covered the left shoulder, leaving the right bare. The 'patella,' or platter, was a broad vessel or dish, used in sacrifices.

[25] *Father of thy country.*]—Ver. 637. The health of Augustus was always given at private and public entertainments, according to a decree of the senate to that effect.

[26] *Terminus.*]—Ver. 641. This god was represented by a stone or stump, and not with human features. Lactantius says he was the stone which Saturn swallowed, mistaking him for Jupiter. His worship was ordained by Numa, and his emblems were crowned with wreaths of flowers on his yearly festivals.

[27] *In a broken.*]—Ver. 645. 'Curta.' It is difficult to say whether the word 'curtus' means, 'broken,' or 'small,' here. Perhaps the former, as being a mark of the poverty of the person sacrificing.

[28] *A boy.*]—Ver. 650. Boys and girls, called 'camilli,' and 'camillæ,'

broad basket. Out of this, when he has thrice thrown the produce of the earth into the midst of the flames, his little daughter offers the sliced honeycombs. Others hold wine; a portion of each thing is thrown into the fire; the crowd, all arrayed in white, look on, and maintain religious silence. The common landmark also is sprinkled with the *blood of a* slain lamb; he makes, too, no complaint when a sucking-pig is offered to him. The neighbours meet in supplication, and they celebrate the feast and sing thy praises, holy Terminus. It is thou that dost set the limits to nations, and cities, and mighty kingdoms; without thee all the country would be steeped in litigation. In thee there is no ambition—by no gold art thou bribed; mayst thou with law and integrity preserve the fields committed to thy care. Hadst thou in times of old marked out the land of Thyrea,[29] *then* three hundred persons would not have been consigned to death, and then, the *name of* Othryades would not have been read on the piled-up armour. Ah! how much of his blood did he expend in his country's cause! What, *too, happened* when the new Capitol was building? *This*, namely; the whole multitude of Divinities withdrew,[30] and gave place to Jupiter. Terminus, as the ancients tell, being *there* found, remained in his shrine, and *still* possesses the temple *in common*

assisted at the Roman sacrifices. They were required to be sound in health, perfect in limb, free born, and with both parents living. Some suppose that they corresponded with the κάδμιλοι of the Curetes and Corybantes, others with Cadmilus, one of the Cabiri of Samothrace. Others again suppose that 'camillus' was merely an old Etrurian word, signifying 'a boy.'

[29] *Thyrea.*]—Ver. 663. Thyrea was a town on the confines of Laconia and Argolis. It was consequently claimed by the people of both countries, and they agreed to decide the claim by the sword. Three hundred men were chosen as champions on each side. Of these only three survived. The two surviving Argives hastened home triumphantly to announce their success; but Othryades, the Spartan leader, who was still living, arose from the ground, and erected a trophy of arms, and, according to Statius, inscribed it with his own name, written in his own blood, in honour of Jupiter Tropœuchus, 'the possessor of trophies;' and then slew himself. Each party claimed the victory, and hostilities being renewed, the Spartans ultimately prevailed. The poet mentions three hundred, but the story is, that six hundred men were engaged in the conflict.

[30] *Divinities withdrew.*]—Ver. 668. They were consulted by Tarquinius Superbus, by auguries, and all but Terminus consented to be removed, which circumstance was regarded as an omen of the future stability of the Roman empire.

with mighty Jove. Now, too, that he may see nothing but the stars above him, the roof of his temple has a little opening. After that circumstance, Terminus, no inconstancy was permitted thee; in whatever situation thou hast been placed, *there* abide, and do not yield one jot to any neighbour asking thee; that thou mayst not appear to favour a mortal rather than Jove. And whether thou shalt be struck by the ploughshares, or whether by the harrows, cry aloud, "This is my field,[31] that is yours." There is a road which leads the citizens to the fields of the Laurentines, realms once sought by the Dardanian chief. On that road, the sixth *mile*-stone from the city is accustomed to witness the sacrifices made to thee, O Terminus, with the entrails of a sheep. To other nations, land has been allotted with *some* fixed limits; the extent of the Roman City and of the earth is the same.

Now must I tell of the banishment[32] of the king *Tarquinius*. From that event the sixth day from the end of the month has derived its name. Tarquinius was the last that held sovereign sway over the Roman people, a wicked man,[33] but brave in arms. Some cities he had taken, others he had rased to the ground, and *Gabii*[34] he had made his own by a disgraceful stratagem. For the youngest of his three *sons*, plainly the offspring[35] of Superbus, came in the silence of the night into the midst of the enemy. *On the moment*, they unsheathed their swords, "Strike," said he, "an unarmed man; this, my brothers[36] and my father Tarquinius would wish; he

[31] *This is my field.*]—Ver. 677-8. Gower translates these lines thus—

'And maugre thou art scratched with rake and plow,
  Cry, this is yours, and this belongs to you.'

[32] *The banishment.*]—Ver. 685. This festival was called the Regifugium, or 'Royal flight.'

[33] *A wicked man.*]—Ver. 688. He had murdered his father-in-law, Servius Tullius, and then usurped his throne. He had been successful against the Volsci, and had taken Suessa Pometia, their principal town.

[34] *Gabii.*]—Ver. 690. This was a town of Latium, nearly half way between Rome and Præneste.

[35] *Plainly the offspring.*]—Ver. 691. Showing himself to be so by his unprincipled conduct. Gower translates this and the following line thus—

'For lo! his young son, and his own son right,
  Came into their foes' garrison by night.'

[36] *My brothers.*]—Ver. 694. Titus and Aruns. Sextus was the youngest. Dionysius, however, makes Sextus to have been the eldest.

who has mangled my back with the cruel lash." That he might be enabled to say this, he had submitted to stripes. It was moonlight, they look upon the youth and sheathe their swords; and, having drawn his dress on one side, they see his back all covered with weals. They go so far as to weep, and they beg that he will superintend the management of the war; he, in his cunning, concurs with *these* unsuspecting men. And now grown powerful, he sends a friend, and asks his father what means he could point out to him for betraying Gabii. There is near at hand a garden well stocked with sweet-scented plants, having its soil divided by a gently murmuring streamlet of water. There Tarquinius receives the secret despatches of his son, and with a staff he knocks off the heads of the tallest lilies. When the messenger returns and mentions *to him* the striking down of the lilies,[37] the son says, "I understand what are the orders of my father." There is no delay; the principal men of the town of Gabii being *first* slain, the walls, deprived of their chiefs, are delivered up. Lo! dreadful to be seen! a serpent issues forth from the midst of the altars, and drags the entrails from the extinguished flames. Phœbus is consulted.[38] An oracular response is returned in these words:—" He shall be the conqueror who first shall kiss his mother." *Then* hastened they each man to kiss[39] his mother, a set who put faith in the Deity whom *really* they did not understand. Brutus[40] was a wise man, who

[37] *The lilies.*]—Ver. 707. Herodotus (book 5. c. 92.) tells us that Thrasybulus, tyrant of Miletus, employed the same mode of giving counsel to Periander of Corinth. Gower translates this and the next line in the following manner:—

'The scout brings word he cropt the highest lilies:
"I know," saith Sextus, " what my father's will is."'

Livy says that the heads of the highest poppies, 'summa papaverum,' were struck off.

[38] *Phœbus is consulted.*]—Ver. 710. Titus and Aruns went to Delphi for this purpose, and at the same time they enquired who should succeed their father as ruler of Rome. The poet does not allude to this query; but to it was given the answer mentioned in the text.

[39] *Each man to kiss.*]—Ver. 715. Dionysius says, that they agreed to conceal the oracle, and that, kissing their parent at the same time, they should reign jointly. Livy states, that they left it to chance, by drawing lots which should salute his parent first.

[40] *Brutus.*]—Ver. 717. His father, M. Junius, and his elder brother,

feigned the part of a fool, in order that he might be in safety from thy machinations, O cruel Superbus! He, falling on his face, kissed his mother earth, while he was supposed to have fallen down by reason of his foot stumbling. In the mean time Ardea[41] is being beleaguered by the standards of Rome, and, under blockade, endures tedious delay. While they are unoccupied, and the enemy fears to join battle, they amuse themselves in camp, *and* the soldier spends his time in idleness. The young Tarquinius entertains his comrades with feasting and wine, and the son of the king says to them, "While this stubborn Ardea detains us by its tedious war, and permits us not to carry back our arms to the Gods of our country, think you, are the partners of our beds faithful to us? and are we objects of reciprocal love to our wives?" They extol, each man his own *wife;* the dispute increases with their earnestness, and both tongue and affection wax warm with much wine. He, to whom Collatia[42] had given an honoured name, rises. "There is no occasion for words," says he; "put faith in facts *alone*. Abundance of the night remains, let us mount our horses, and make for the city."[43] His words meet with their approval, *and* their horses are bridled. These had *now* borne their masters to the end of the journey. Forthwith they repaired to the royal abode; there was no sentinel at the door.[44] Behold! they find the daughter-in-law of the king sitting up and spending the night with wine before her; the chaplets having fallen down[45] on her neck. *Going* thence with

were slain by Tarquin to obtain their wealth. To escape a similar fate, L. J. Brutus counterfeited idiotcy, and was retained by Tarquin in his court for the amusement of his sons.

[41] *Ardea.*]—Ver. 721. A town of Latium, twenty-three miles distant from Rome, so called either from 'ardea,' 'a heron,' from an augury taken therefrom; or from 'ardeo,' 'to be hot,' on account of the extreme heat of the country. Tarquin besieged it, on the pretext that it was conspiring to effect the return of certain Roman exiles.

[42] *Collatia.*]—Ver. 733. A Sabine town, situated on an eminence about four miles to the east of Rome. Tarquinius was called Collatinus, as his father Egerius had been appointed governor of Collatia, when captured by his uncle Tarquinius Priscus.

[43] *For the city.*]—Ver. 735. After that, they would have to ride some miles to Collatia, where the abode of Collatinus was.

[44] *No sentinel at the door.*]—Ver. 738. Meaning that all neglected their duties by reason of the neglect and inebriety of their mistress.

[45] *Having fallen down.*]—Ver. 739. It was not deemed consistent with

rapid pace, Lucretia is visited. She was employed in spinning; before her bed were the work-baskets and the soft wool. By the lamp's dim light her handmaids were spinning their assigned tasks, among whom she thus spoke with gentle voice: —"With all speed there must be sent to your master a cloak[46] made with our hands; now, at this moment, hasten on, my girls. But what *news* have ye heard? for you are in the way of hearing more *than I;* how much of the war do they say still remains? Soon shalt thou be conquered, and fall, vexatious Ardea; thou art resisting better men, while thus compelling our husbands to be from home; only may they return *in safety.* But rash is that husband of mine, and recklessly he rushes on when the sword is drawn. My senses fail me, and I faint, oft as the image of him engaged in battle occurs to my mind; and a chilling coldness pervades my breast." She ends in tears, and drops the tight-drawn threads, and hides her face in her bosom. Even this became her; her tears became a woman so chaste, and her countenance was worthy of, and suited to, her nature. "Lay aside your fears; I am here," said her husband. She revived, and hung, a sweet burden, upon her husband's neck. Meanwhile the royal youth conceives a frantic passion, and, hurried onwards by blind desire, loses all control of himself. Her figure charms him, her complexion, white as snow, her auburn hair, and the grace which atttends her, adorned by no art. Her words charm him, her voice, and her very chastity; and the less hope there is, the more intensely does he desire. And now the bird, the harbinger of dawn, had sent forth his note, when the young men are on their return to the camp. His wonder-stricken feelings are preyed on by the image of her absent, and as he recalls her to his mind, more charms are discovered, and

female delicacy to wear chaplets at all; but it was a plain proof of inebriety when they had fallen from the head on to the neck. It is to be observed, that this demirep had 'merum,' 'pure wine,' and, undiluted, before her.

[46] *A cloak.*]—Ver. 746. By this line we may see that both industry and economy were Lucretia's virtues. The 'lacerna' was a military cloak of thick texture, worn over the 'toga,' or tunic, open in front, and fastened with clasps. Gower thus translates this and the preceding line—

' Maids, you must make (plie, plie your bus'ness faster)
A coat to send in haste unto your master.'

the more they engage him. Thus it was she sat, thus was she attired, thus did she spin the warp, thus lay on her neck her neglected tresses. These were her features, these were her words; this her expression, this her make, this the complexion of her face. As the billow is wont to abate after a great storm, but yet from the wind that has *raged* the waves swell *on;* so, though the presence of her charming form was wanting, the passion *still* remained, which that form when present had inspired. He burns, and, urged on by the goads of unlawful desire, he plans violence and treachery against a bed undeserving of it. "The result is doubtful—we will dare the utmost," said he. "Be it chance, or be it a providence that aids the bold, let him see to it. It was by daring, too, that Gabii we won." Thus having said, he girds his side with his sword, and presses the back of his steed. Collatia receives the youth within her brass-barred portal just as the sun is preparing to hide his disk. An enemy,[47] in the guise of a guest, he enters the house of Collatinus; he is kindly received, *for* he was connected by blood. What ignorance is there in the minds *of mortals!* She, hapless one, unsuspicious of the world, makes ready the entertainment for her enemy. He had *now* finished the repast, *and* slumber demands its hour. It was night, and there were no lights[48] in the whole house. He arises, and draws from its sheath the golden-hilted sword, and he comes to thy chamber, virtuous matron; and when he *now* presses the bed, he says, "*I have* my sword *here* with me, Lucretia; 'tis I, Tarquinius,[49] the son of the king, who address thee." She answers not, for she has no voice, no power of speech, or any sense left in her breast. But she trembles, as when sometime the little lambkin, seized upon after it has left the fold, lies under the wolf, its *deadly* foe. What can she do? Can

---

[47] *An enemy.*]—Ver. 787. The words are, 'Hostis ut hospes,' 'an enemy as a guest.' There is evidently a play upon the similar sound of the two words. Livy also employs the same collocation of these words.

[48] *No lights.*]—Ver. 792. This shews the confidence that Lucretia had in the propriety of her guest's conduct, and her own unsuspecting and innocent nature, as it was generally the custom for a servant near the chamber to keep a lamp burning.

[49] *'Tis I, Tarquinius.*]—Ver. 796. Gower translates this and the preceding line:

' Laid on the bed. Lucretia, no denial;
  Here is my sword; I'm Tarquine of blood royall.'

she resist? A woman, in the contest she will *surely* be overcome. Cry out? But in his right hand there is the sword to slay her. Fly? Her breast is held down by his hands placed on it; a breast now for the first time touched by the hand of a stranger. Her foe, inflamed with passion, urges her with entreaties, with bribes, and with threats. By entreaties, by bribes, by threats, he moves her not. "Thou dost avail nothing," he said; "I will take thy life for the purpose of criminating thee. I, an adulterer, will be the false witness of thy adultery. I will slay the servant, in whose company thou shalt be said to have been detected." The matron yielded, overcome by fear for her good fame. Why, conqueror, dost thou exult? This victory shall prove thy destruction. Ah! what a price did that one night cost to thy sovereignty! And now the day had dawned; she sits with her hair dishevelled, just as a mother is wont to do when about to go to the funeral pile of her son; she summons from the camp her aged father, with her faithful husband; and without any delay they both come. And when they see the state *of her attire*, they ask what is the cause of her mourning, whose obsequies it is that she is preparing, or with what calamity she is afflicted. For a long time she is silent, and, filled with shame, she conceals her face with her dress. Her tears flow like an everspringing stream. On one side, her father, on the other, her husband console her tears, and entreat of her to tell them; and they weep and feel alarm with an undefined dread. Thrice did she attempt to speak, thrice did she fail, and again a fourth time did she attempt it, and even then she raised not her eyes. "Shall I owe this *disgrace* too to Tarquinius? I will speak out," says she; "I, wretched that I am, will speak out my own disgrace." And what she can, she relates. The conclusion remained *untold;* she wept, and the cheeks of the matron were suffused with crimson. Her father and her husband excuse her as the victim of compulsion. "That pardon which ye give," she said, "do I deny to myself." There is no pause: with a poniard that she had concealed she pierces her breast, and, streaming with blood, she falls at her father's feet. And even then, in the moment of death, she uses caution that she may fall in no unseemly manner,—this was her care even as she fell.

Behold! over her body, forgetful of their dignity, lie both her husband and her father, bewailing their common loss. Brutus is there, and now at last by his spirit falsifies[50] his name, and snatches from her dying body the piercing blade; *then* holding the knife dripping with noble blood, with threatening lips he utters these fearless words: "By this noble and chaste blood, I swear to thee, and by thy spirit which shall be to me a deity, that Tarquinius, with his exiled house, shall pay the penalty of this; now long enough has the energy *of my mind* lain concealed." She, as she lay, at this exclamation, turned her eyes, void of the light *of life*, and seemed, by shaking her locks, to express her approval of his words. *This* matron of heroic mind is borne to her burial, and carries with her tears and *popular* indignation. The gash, *all* gaping wide, is exposed to view. Brutus, with loud voice, arouses the Quirites, and recounts the dreadful crimes of the king. Tarquinius flies, with his children.[51] The Consul[52] undertakes the annual jurisdiction. This was the last day of royalty.

Am I deceived, or is the swallow come, the harbinger of spring? and does she fear lest perchance returning winter may retrace his course? Yet ofttimes, Progne, wilt thou complain that thou didst make too great haste, and thy husband Tereus shall be gladdened[53] by *thy shivering in the* cold.

And now two nights of the second month are remaining, and Mars with harnessed chariot drives his swift steeds. The name of Equiria,[54] derived from fact, has adhered *to the games*, which the God himself witnesses on his own plain. Rightly, Gradivus,[55]

---

[50] *Falsifies.*]—Ver. 837. The name Brutus was given to him from his supposed idiotcy. He now shows his real character as a hero, a patriot, and a man of feeling. The father of Lucretia was Spurius Lucretius Tricipitinus.

[51] *With his children.*]—Ver. 851. Titus and Aruns retired with their father to Cære, in Etruria. Sextus returned to Gabii, where he was put to death in return for his treachery and numerous acts of cruelty.

[52] *The Consul.*]—Ver. 851. The kings being expelled A.U.C. 244, two yearly officers, with an equal degree of authority, were appointed, called consuls. Brutus and Collatinus were the first persons named to that office.

[53] *Be gladdened.*]—Ver. 856. On account of his old enmity to Progne. See the note to line 629 of this book.

[54] '*Equiria.*']—Ver. 859. These were chariot races, instituted by Romulus in honour of Mars. They were celebrated on the third of the calends of March, on the Campus Martius; or if that place was flooded, as was sometimes the case at that season, then on a part of the Cælian Hill, called by Catullus 'Campus Minor,' 'the lesser plain.'

[55] *Rightly, Gradivus*]—Ver. 861. Because the poet is about to com-

dost thou come; thy season demands its place, and the month, marked by thy name, is at hand. We have now reached the harbour, our book being concluded with the month; next, it is upon other waters that my bark must sail.

mence the month of March, which was dedicated to him. Mars was called Gradivus from 'gradior,' 'to go,' or 'march' to the battle, or from the Greek word κραδαίνω, 'to shake,' because he shakes the lance; or from 'gramen,' because he was said to have been produced by the agency of a herb through the aid of Flora. According to Servius, in his Commentary on the Æneid, book i., l. 296, he was called Quirinus, when peaceable, but Gradivus, when unappeased; he therefore had two temples, one within the city, as its protector in peace; the other without, on the Appian road, as its defender in war.

BOOK THE THIRD.

CONTENTS.

THE invocation of Mars, ver. 1—8. The history of Romulus and Remus, from their birth to the foundation of the city; the worship of Mars; the origin of the name of March, 9—86. The position of this month in the calendars of other nations, 87—98. The number of the Roman months before the time of Numa, and his addition to that number; the institution of the solar year by Cæsar, 99—104. The Matronalia described; the rape of the Sabine women; the beauties of the spring, 167—258. The origin and festival of the Salii; the descent from heaven of the Ancile, 259—398. The setting of the second Fish, 399—402. The setting of Arctophylax, and the rising of the Vintager, 403—414. The sacred rites of Vesta, and the Pontificate of Augustus, 415—428. The Temple of Vejovis dedicated, 429—448. The neck of Pegasus rises, 449—458. The rising of the Crown, and the story of Theseus and Ariadne, 459—516. The second Equiria, 517—522. The sacred rites of Anna Perenna; the story of Dido and Anna, with the arrival of the latter in Latium; and the secession of the Roman commonalty, 523—696. The death of Julius Cæsar, 697—710. The Scorpion partly sets, 711-712. The origin and description of the Liberalia; the time for assuming the Toga virilis; the praises of Bacchus, 713—790. The procession to the Argei, 791-2. The origin of the Constellation of the Kite, and the battle of the Giants, 793—808. The Quinquatria, or five-day festival of Minerva, 809—850. The sun enters the Ram; the story of Helle and Phryxus, 851—876. The vernal Æquinox, 877-8. The festival of Janus, Health, Concord, and Peace, 879—882. The worship of the Moon on the Aventine Hill, 883.

MARS, thou warlike *God*, awhile laying aside thy shield and spear, approach, and from the helmet's *pressure* liberate thy glossy hair. Perchance thou mayst ask what a poet has to do[1] with Mars; *my answer is*, the month which is *now* being celebrated by me, derives from thee its name. Thou thyself

---

[1] *Has to do.*]—Ver. 3-4. Gower's translation of these lines is—

'Perchance thou'lt say, with Mars, what make the Muses?
This month we sing his name from thee deduces.'

seeest that fierce battles are waged by the hand of Minerva; has she *on that account* less leisure for the liberal arts? After the example of Pallas, do thou take an opportunity for laying aside thy lance; even when unarmed thou wilt find somewhat for thee to do. Then, too, wast thou unarmed when the Roman priestess[2] captivated thee, that thou mightst provide for this city an origin worthy of it. Silvia, the Vestal maid—for what forbids me to commence from that point,—early in the morning, was fetching water *with which* to wash[3] the sacred utensils. She had now reached the bank sloping with a path easy of descent, *and* her earthen pitcher is set down from off her head. Wearied, she has *now* seated herself on the ground, and with her bosom open she admits the breeze, and re-arranges her disordered tresses. While she sits, the shading willows, the songs of the birds, and the gentle murmuring of the stream, invite slumber. Soft sleep stealthily creeps upon her overpowered eyes, and her hand, become powerless, falls from her side. Mars sees her, seeing he desires, desiring he enjoys *her;* and then by his divine power he conceals the stealthy deed. Sleep departs; she lies *there, now* pregnant; for now, founder of the Roman city, thou wast within her womb! She rises languid, nor knows she why *thus* languid she rises; and leaning against a tree, she utters such words as these: " May that prove favourable and fortunate, I pray, which in a vision of my slumbers I have beheld! or was it too distinct for a vision? I was standing near the Ilian fires,[4] when the woollen fillet drop-

[2] *The Roman priestess.*]—Ver. 9. Heinsius suggests 'Trojana,' inasmuch as Rome was not then founded, and she was a native of Alba Longa. The poet, however, may mean to say that in her progeny she became entitled to the epithet 'Romana.' Her name is sometimes Ilia, sometimes Rhea Silvia; in poetry the first is most frequently used. Ovid, however, makes use of both names.

[3] *To wash.*]—Ver. 11—13. One of the duties of the Vestals was to draw water, with which to wash and sprinkle the temple, and cleanse the sacred vessels. Among these were the 'acerra,' or 'thuribulum,' a censer for holding the incense, 'simpulum,' 'capis,' or 'capedo,' 'guttus,' and 'patera,' used in libations; 'ollæ,' pots of various descriptions; the tripods, &c. Gower's version is—

' Now, Sylvia, (here our sail we hoise,) something
To wash i'th' morning went unto the spring.
Now when she came unto the wriggling brook.'

[4] *The Ilian fires.*]—Ver. 29. Having been originally brought from Ilium or Troy by Æneas.

ping from off my hair, fell down[5] before the sacred heath. Thence, wondrous to be seen, two palm-trees shoot up together; of these, one was greater *than the other*, and with its heavy branches it overshadowed the whole earth, and with its new grown foliage reached the highest stars. *And now*, lo! my uncle brandishes the axe[6] against them; I shudder at the recollection, and my heart palpitates with dread. A woodpecker,[7] bird of Mars, and a she-wolf fight in defence of the two trees; by means of these both the palm-trees are preserved in safety." She spoke; and with faltering strength she raised the pitcher; she had filled it while relating her vision. Meantime, as Remus grew, as Quirinus grew, her womb was heavy with the celestial burden. There now remained to the God of light but two signs[8] *for him to traverse* ere the year should take its departure, its course being *duly* performed. Silvia becomes a mother; the images of Vesta[9] are said at that time to have placed their virgin hands before their eyes. Assuredly, the altar of the Goddess trembled as her priestess brought forth, and the flame affrighted sunk back beneath its ashes.[10] When Amulius, the despiser of justice, learned

[5] *Fell down.*]—Ver. 30. The Vestals used to wear on their heads 'infulæ', 'bands,' and 'vittæ,' 'fillets.' As, on the degradation of a Vestal for breaking her vows of virginity, the sacred fillet was removed from her head by the Pontifex Maximus, this dream was ominous of her impending fate. The dream of Astyages, mentioned by Herodotus and Justin, book 1, c. 4, portending the birth of Cyrus, was, in its circumstances, very similar.

[6] *Brandishes the axe.*]—Ver. 35-6. Gower's translation is—

' When lo! my uncle fain would have them cropt,
Smit at the sight, my heart for terror hopt.'

[7] *A woodpecker.*]—Ver. 37. According to Pliny the Elder, this bird received his name, ' picus,' from the father of Faunus, who was so called, and was transformed into that bird by Circe. Plutarch agrees with Ovid in representing that the infants were fed by a wolf and a woodpecker.

[8] *But two signs.*]—Ver. 44. This sentence is a periphrasis for 'ten months.'

[9] *The images of Vesta.*]—Ver. 45. There were no images of this goddess in her temples, and in the sixth book, l. 277, the poet acknowledges his error. She was the guardian of houses, and there were paintings of her usually in every dwelling. On the exterior, however, of her temple at Rome there was a statue of her, which form, together with her symbols, is still to be seen upon some Roman coins.

[10] *Beneath its ashes.*]—Ver. 48. The extinction of the sacred fire was

these things, (for he, victorious, kept possession of the power which he had torn from his brother), he orders the twins to be drowned in the river. The water shrinks back from the crime: the children are left on the dry ground. Who does not know[11] how the infants thrived on the milk of a wild beast, and how, many a time did the woodpecker bear food to them *thus* exposed. I would not pass by thee in silence, Larentia,[12] nurse of so mighty a race, nor would I be silent of thy *humble* circumstances, O poor Faustulus. Thy praises will come when I shall tell of the Larentalia; December, a *month* dear to the Gods of enjoyment,[13] holds these. The sons of Mars had *now* grown up to the age of thrice six years, and the first beard was now appearing beneath their yellow locks. The brothers, the sons of Ilia, were distributing justice, at their request, to all the husbandmen and those who tended the herds. Ofttimes do they come home exulting in the blood of

an event regarded with the greatest horror, as being a presage of great national misfortunes. The Vestal under whose charge the fire was, when it was suffered to go out, was stripped and flogged most severely by the Pontifex Maximus, and the flame was rekindled by the friction of two pieces of wood from the 'felix arbor;' according to some authors, it was rekindled from the rays of the sun by a hollow conical reflector.

[11] *Who does not know.*]—Ver. 53. This story was related in the works of Ennius, one of the olden poets, and it was well known by tradition, and perhaps, in the mouths of the common people, it occupied much the same position as 'the story of King Arthur' or 'the Seven Champions of Christendom' does with us.

[12] *Larentia.*]—Ver. 55. Larentia, or Laurentia, was the wife of Faustulus, and the nurse of Romulus and Remus. Being, as it is supposed, a woman of no good repute, the story is said by some writers to have arisen from that circumstance, that the children were suckled by a wolf; 'lupa' being the Latin for both a 'she-wolf' and a female of unchaste character. The festival of Larentia, the Larentalia, was celebrated in December, though some think that it was in honour of a different person. Faustulus was the shepherd of Amulius.

[13] *The gods of enjoyment.*]—Ver. 58. 'Genii.' The 'Genii' were tutelary deities, each having charge of an individual up to the time of his death. They were supposed to be propitiated with wine and sacrifices, and hence the notion arose that they took pleasure in revelry and feasting. The poet alludes here to the Saturnalia, which took place some days before the Larentalia, and which professedly lasted but three days; but the festival, extending its influence over the remaining part of the month, it naturally imparted a tone of festivity to the Larentalia. At this season all were engaged in mirth and revelry; presents were interchanged, and slaves were, for the time, elevated to a level with their masters.

the plunderers, and bring back into their own fields the oxen that had been carried off. When *now* they learn their origin, the discovery of their father increases their courage, and they feel ashamed to have renown but in a few cottages. And *now* Amulius falls pierced by the sword of Romulus, and the sovereignty is restored to their aged grandsire.[14] City walls are built, which, low as they were, it ill-betimed Remus to leap over them. Now, *in the spot* where lately there had been but forests and the retreats of the cattle, there was a city *sprung up*, when the father of *that* eternal city says, "Ruler of arms, of whose blood I am believed to be born, (and that I may be *with good reason so* believed, I will give sure pledges), from thee do we derive a commencement for the Roman year. Henceforth, let the first month pass on its course called after the name of my sire. His word is ratified, and he calls the month from his father's name; this act of duty is said to have been pleasing to the Divinity.[15] And yet the *Latian* people of ancient times worshipped Mars before all *the Gods;* the warlike multitude had made this *worship* the object of their zealous attention. The people of Cecrops venerate Pallas;[16] Crete, the land of Minos, Diana; the land of Hypsipyle,[17] adores

---

[14] *Aged grandsire*]—Ver. 68. Numitor, the father of Ilia, who had been deposed by Amulius.

[15] *Pleasing to the divinity.*]—Ver. 77-8. Gower's translation of these two lines runs thus—

' His word's made good, this month he thus did call,
And pleas'd his father very well withall.'

[16] *Venerate Pallas.*]—Ver. 81. This was the name under which the Athenians or Cecropidæ worshipped Minerva, the goddess of war and of the fine arts. Cecrops was the first king of the Athenians, and founder of the colony, whence the epithet here given. The people of Crete, now the Isle of Candia, are called ' Minoiän,' from Minos, its king and law-giver, who was promoted to the latter distinction in the Infernal regions. Diana was worshipped by the Cretans under the name of Dictynna, from Mount Dicte, where her sacrifices were performed with great solemnity; or from δικτυς, 'a hunting-net.'

[17] *Land of Hypsipyle.*]—Ver. 82. Lemnos, an island in the Ægean Sea, is thus called from Hypsipyle, daughter of its king, Thoas. The women of Lemnos conspiring to put the men to death, she saved her father, and had him conveyed secretly to Chios. Vulcan having been hurled from heaven by Jupiter, or, as some say, by his mother Juno, on account of his deformity, after a descent of an entire day, alighted in Lemnos. Sparta was a city of Laconia, in Peloponnesus, founded by

Vulcan; Sparta, and Mycenæ the Pelopian city, Juno; the district of Mænalus, the pine-wreathed head of Faunus. Mars was a deserving object of worship to Latium, because he presides over arms: 'twas arms that gave both power and glory to that fierce people. But if you happen to have leisure, examine the Calendars of other states *of Italy;* in these also there will be a month *called* after the name of Mars. It was the third month among the Albans; the fifth with the Falisci; the sixth among thy clans, Hernician land.[18] There is an agreement in the Alban *order of reckoning the* months, with that of the people of Aricia, and the lofty walls built by the hand of Telegonus. The Laurentes reckon this the fifth *month,* the fierce Æquicolus the tenth, the people of Cures the first after the third, and thou, warrior of Pelignum, coincidest with thy ancestors, the Sabines; with each people this God *is* fourth *in the order of the months.* Romulus, that he might surpass all these, in his arrangement at least, dedicated the first month to the author of his birth.

Nor did the ancients have as many Calends[19] as *there* now *are;* their year was shorter by a couple of months. Not yet had Greece, a people more eloquent than brave,[20] imparted to the conquerors the arts of the conquered. The man who fought well, he was acquainted with the arts of Rome; whoever could hurl the javelin, he was eloquent. Who, in

Spartus, grandson of Inachus. Mycenæ was a town of Argos, in Peloponnesus. Pelops never lived there, but it afterwards became one of the principal possessions of his descendants, whence its epithet here.

[18] *Hernician land.*]—Ver. 90. The Hernici occupies a hilly district between the Volsci and the Æqui. Aricia was a town of Latium. Tusculum was situated on a high hill, twelve miles from Rome; it was built by Telegonus, the son of Ulysses and Circe. Laurentium was the capital of Latium. The Æqui or Æquicoli were a people located between the Marsi and the Hernici. The Peligni were a people of Italy, beyond the Marsi, and near the Adriatic Sea. According to Festus they were a colony from Illyria, and not descended from the Sabines, as Ovid here says they were. They were a warlike race, whence the epithet 'miles.' a warrior. Niebuhr, in his Roman History, gives an account of these various nations.

[19] *Calends.*]—Ver. 99. Consequently months, as the 'calendæ' were the first day in every month.

[20] *More eloquent than brave.*]—Ver. 102. He alludes, not to the time when their valour supplied the want of numbers, in their struggles against the Persian power; but to a much later period, when, buried in sloth and effeminacy, they fell an easy prey to the Roman passion for conquest.

those days, had marked the Hyades or the Pleiades, daughters of Atlas, or *had noticed* that there were two poles under the canopy[21] of the heavens? or that there were two Bears,[22] one of which, the Cynosure, was watched by the men of Sidon, while the Grecian bark is observing Helice, *the other?* And *who had remarked* that the signs *of the zodiac*, which the brother traverses in the space of a year, the sister's steeds[23] pass through in a single month? Left to themselves and unwatched, the stars ran their course through the year; but yet it was *universally* agreed that the Gods do exist.[24] They meddled not with the signs that roll along the heavens, but their own *standards*;[25] to lose which was a great crime.[26] These were

[21] *Under the canopy.*]—Ver. 106. 'Sub axe.' Literally 'under the axis,' meaning at the extremities of the imaginary axis on which the earth moves, at which extremities are the Arctic and Antarctic poles.

[22] *Two Bears.*]—Ver. 107. The 'Ursa major' and the 'Ursa minor.' The 'Ursa major,' or 'Greater bear,' was the constellation, whose story is mentioned at length in the second book. It was called also Helice, from the Greek ἑλίσσω, 'to revolve,' because it revolves round the Pole. The lesser bear was also called 'Cynosura,' from κυνος οὐρά, 'dog's tail,' the stars, in their sequence, being fancifully thought to resemble that object. Cynosyra was said to have been a nymph, who nursed Jupiter on Mount Ida, and for that service was raised to the stars. The Phœnicians, who inhabited Sidon, took their observations from this constellation, while the Greeks, for that purpose, used the former.

[23] *The sister's steeds.*]—Ver. 110. The poet means to say, that the sun, 'the brother,' remains for a month in each sign of the Zodiac, while the moon passes through them all in the space of one month.

[24] *That the Gods do exist.*]—Ver. 112. He appears to mean, that, ignorant as they were of astronomical subjects, they were still convinced of the existence of the gods. Burmann and Gierig would read it as though to be translated thus, 'but it was agreed that they [the stars] are gods;' that, in fact, they had come to that opinion about them, but had never noticed them with the ken of the astronomer. The former seems to be most probably the author's meaning.

[25] *But their own standards.*]—Ver. 114. The author here plays upon the different meanings of the word 'signa,' which signifies either 'constellations,' or 'standards,' according to the context. They did not trouble themselves about the 'signa' of the sky, they only moved their own 'signa.' To give effect to his pun, he seems to be guilty of some harshness in speaking of mortals 'moving the constellations.' The expression is, however, not without precedent in other Latin writers.

[26] *A great crime.*]—Ver. 114. For any of the soldiers, and especially the standard bearer, to lose the standard was highly dishonourable, and sometimes it was a capital offence. Among other punishments were, short

of hay *indeed;* but there was as much respect paid to *that* hay as at the present day you see your eagles receive. A long pole used to bear the elevated wisps, from which circumstance the manipular soldier derives his name.[27]

In consequence, those untutored minds, as yet deficient in powers of calculation, observed their five yearly lustra,[28] too short by ten months. When the moon had completed her tenth revolution, it was a year; this number was then in great esteem. Either, because so many are the fingers, by the help of which we are wont to reckon, or because in the tenth month woman brings

commons on barley bread, decimation, being stripped in sight of the whole army, being clad in female vesture, being driven into the enemy's quarters, being left among the baggage with the prisoners, and being severely whipped.

[27] *Derives his name.*]—Ver. 117-18. The author here tells us, that in early times a bundle of hay on the end of a pole served that purpose. The army of Romulus being mostly composed of peasants, this was not at all improbable. To every troop of one hundred men, a 'manipulus,' or wisp of hay (so called from 'manum implere,' to 'fill the hand,' as being 'a handful'), was assigned as a standard, and hence in time the company itself obtained the name of 'manipulus,' and the soldier, a member of it, was called, 'manipularis.' The omen derived from the flight of the eagle was deemed the most auspicious. Hence the figure of that bird was afterwards adopted as the standard in preference to those of other animals, which, before the time of Marius, were sometimes used for that purpose. Gower's version is—

'They hung in bottles on a pole huge tall,
From whence our soldiers by that name we call.'

We may here observe parenthetically, that the expression 'to look for a needle in a bottle of hay,' is still sometimes quoted as a proverb, though few perhaps now know the origin of the term 'bottle.' It comes from an old French word, 'bôstel,' with the 's' silent. From this word, too, is derived the name of an article of female dress, which is worn at the present day, or, if not, was so at a very recent period.

[28] *Five yearly lustra.*]—Ver. 120. As a 'lustrum' consisted of five years, it would in those times contain but fifty months, and be ten months shorter than a modern 'lustrum' of five years of twelve months. For the purposes of revenue, Servius Tullius instituted the 'census' at the end of each five years. When it had been completed, atonement was made for the people by the sacrifice of a sow, a sheep, and a bull, and when this had been done, the people were said to be cleansed, 'lustrari.' This word comes from 'luo,' 'to pay,' because, in those days, the taxes were paid to the censors at these periods; this having been done every fifth year, the word 'lustrum' came into use, as signifying the intermediate space between the five yearly periods.

forth; or because we arrive so far as ten, the number increasing; *and* from that point the commencement of a new reckoning[29] is made. For that reason did Romulus set apart a hundred *men* of equal standing for each of the ten companies,[30] and appointed the ten *companies of* Hastati, and so many men had the Princeps, and so many the Pilanus,[31] and he who served on horse-back as required by law.[32] He also assigned as many subdivisions[33] to the Titian tribe, and to those whom they call the Rhamnes, and to the Luceres. For that reason he observed the usual numbers in the *formation of the* year; during this length of time does the sorrowing wife mourn her husband.

[29] *A new reckoning.*]—Ver. 126. He alludes to the system of decimal notation.

[30] *The ten companies.*]—Ver. 127. That is, one hundred men for each of the ten companies of 'Hastati;' one hundred for each of the ten companies of 'Principes;' and one hundred for each of the ten companies of 'Pilani,' or 'Triarii,' which together formed a legion. The first were the younger soldiers, and formed the front rank, as light-armed troops, armed with 'hastæ,' or lances. The second were men of the middle age, and from that circumstance had their name, as evincing their superiority in strength; these formed the second rank. The third rank was formed of the veterans, who were called from that circumstance 'Triarii,' and from the use of the 'pilum,' or 'javelin,' 'Pilani.' The poet calls them equals, because the three divisions were made according to age.

[31] *The Pilanus.*]—Ver. 129. The word here means the officer commanding the ten centuries of the 'Pilani,' or 'Triarii.'

[32] *Required by law.*]—Ver. 130. In each legion there were three hundred 'equites,' 'knights,' or cavalry. Romulus selected them from the most respectable and deserving of his followers, as his body guard. Those in each legion were divided into ten 'turmæ,' or 'squadrons,' of thirty men each. The meaning of the poet, then, seems to be, that Romulus still kept in mind the number ten, by dividing the 'equites' into ten companies; although they did not consist of one hundred men each. The privileges of the 'equites' were, a horse supplied at the public expense, hence called 'legitimus,' 'required by law;' a gold ring; a separate seat at the public spectacles, and the 'tunica angusticulavia,' a tunic with two narrow purple stripes running from each shoulder down the front to the bottom of the dress. The force of each legion was 3000 foot and 300 horse, besides a still larger number of auxiliaries.

[33] *As many subdivisions.*]—Ver. 131. Romulus divided his subjects into three tribes, and subdivided each of them into ten 'Curiæ.' The Ramnenses were the original Romans, so called, it is supposed, from Romulus; these formed one tribe. The second tribe was that of the Tatienses, or Sabines, so called from Titus Tatius, their king. The third was called the 'Luceres,' either from those vagrants who had taken refuge in the 'lucus,' or grove of the asylum, or because they came from Etruria to aid Romulus, under a 'lucumo,' or noble chieftain, named Hostus Hostilius.

And that you may have no doubt but that the Calends of March were formerly the first *in the year*, you may turn your attention to these proofs. The laurel branch, which has lasted the whole year, is *now* removed by the Flamens, and fresh boughs are raised to the dignity. At this time the gate of the king *of the sacrifices* is green with the tree of Phœbus fixed there; before thy doors, O ancient Court-house,[34] the same thing is done. That Vesta, too, may appear graceful, wreathed with new foliage, the faded laurel is removed from the Ilian hearths. Add *to this*, that in her secret shrine[35] a new fire is said to be *now* kindled, and the flame refreshed receives strength. And the fact is no small proof to me that the years of old commenced from this period, that it was in this month that Anna Perenna[36] began to be worshipped. From this time, too, the ancient honours[37] are said to have been entered upon, up to the period of the war with thee, O perfidious Carthaginian.[38] Lastly, the fifth from this was *the month* Quintilis, and from that point commences *each month*, which has its name from its order. Pompilius, invited to Rome[39] from

---

[34] *Ancient Court-house.*]—Ver. 140. The four 'curiæ' which still survived, out of the thirty originally built by Romulus for the use of the 'curiæ' of the citizens, were distinguished by the title 'veteres.' It is supposed that in lapse of time all the 'curiæ' were used for civil purposes.

[35] *Her secret shrine.*]—Ver. 143. Because, not only was it closed against the male sex, but against all females as well, except the Vestals, or perhaps the chief of the Vestals.

[36] *Anna Perenna.*]—Ver. 146. For her story see line 523 of this Book, where it commences.

[37] *The ancient honours.*]—Ver. 147. The author is guilty of a slight inaccuracy here, as the first Consuls took office on the 23d day of February; and the time fluctuated till A.U.C. 600, the end of the third Punic war, when the calends of January were fixed for that purpose.

[38] *Perfidious Carthaginian.*]—Ver. 148. He alludes to Hannibal, to whom, in common with his countrymen, he was too ready to apply an epithet of abuse. According to the Roman accounts, the people of Carthage were noted for their treachery, whence the term 'Punic faith,' became a by-word for dishonourable conduct. We have no native records of the Carthaginians left, and are consequently ignorant of their opinion of the Romans. Had Hannibal been properly supported, Rome would most probably have fallen, leaving no native records of her existence, and to Carthage alone and its writers would posterity have had to look for the character of its Italian rival.

[39] *Invited to Rome.*]—Ver. 151. Numa was the fourth son of Pomponius, an eminent Sabine. 'Deductus' implies the ceremony with which

the olive-bearing fields, was the first to perceive that two months were wanting; whether so taught by the Samian sage,[40] who considers that we may be born again, or whether by the admonition of his own Egeria. But even then were the divisions of time inaccurate, until amid many others, this too, was a care of Cæsar's.[41] He, *though* a God and the father of such a mighty progeny, did not think this a task too humble for his attention; he wished to know beforehand the heaven that was promised him, and not, when deified, to enter as a stranger into an unknown mansion. He is said, by accurate observations, to have arranged the periods of the sun, in which he should return to his due signs *in rotation*. He added ten times six, and the fourth part of one whole day

he was invited and brought to Rome to reign there. The Sabine land was famous for its olive trees. From his communion with the goddess Egeria, he is said to have obtained an insight, almost supernatural, into things both human and divine.

[40] *The Samian sage.*]—Ver. 153. Pythagoras was born in the isle of Samos, opposite to Ephesus. He was a pupil of the philosopher Pherecydes, of Scyros, and studied philosophy in Egypt and among the Babylonian astrologers. He then travelled into Crete and visited Sparta, to examine the laws of Minos and Lycurgus. He afterwards visited the colony of Magna Græcia, in the south of Italy, and promulgated his doctrines at Crotona, Tarentum, and other towns. Numa is generally supposed not to have been a cotemporary of Pythagoras. Livy says that the philosopher came into Italy in the reign of Servius Tullius, which was 136 years after the elevation of Numa to the throne. Dionysius also says that Numa reigned 120 years before the time of Pythagoras. Plutarch says that Numa received assistance in the compilation of his laws from another Pythagoras, a Spartan, who visited Italy. The chief doctrine of Pythagoras was the 'metempsychosis,' or transmigration of the soul into another body after death. Some of his tenets were similar to those of Numa. They would allow of no images of the deity, whom they considered possible to be comprehended in the mind only. They did not permit blood to enter into their sacrifices, but used only flour and wine for that purpose. It did not require a Pythagoras to show Numa that a year consists of more than ten months, as he might easily perceive that fact from the irregularity with which the seasons would come on, each season in every year being two months earlier than on that preceding.

[41] *A care of Cæsar's.*]—Ver. 186. The year having fallen into great confusion, and the festivals frequently happening at the wrong seasons of the year, Julius Cæsar, then being the Pontifex Maximus, with the aid of Sosigines and Marcus Flavius, altered it so that it might, similarly to the year of the Ægyptians, correspond with the course of the sun. See the 'Introduction.'

to the three hundred and five days. This is the complement of the year. To *each* lustrum there ought to be added one day, which is made up of *these* fractions.[42]

If it be allowed to poets to hear the private intimations of the Deities, as report, at least, thinks they may, tell me why it is, O Gradivus, that while thou art suited to the pursuit of men *only*, the matrons observe thy festival.[43] Thus *said* I, and thus Mavors replied to me, having laid aside his helmet; but there was in his right hand a missile spear. "Now, for the first time, am I a Deity, useful to *the profession of* arms, summoned to the pursuits of peace, and I direct my march to a strange camp. Nor do I repent of my undertaking; on this department, too, I am delighted to dwell; that Minerva may not suppose that she alone can do this. Learn, thou poet engaged upon the Latin days, what thou askest, and mark my words in thy mindful breast. Rome, if thou wouldst but call back to mind her first elements, was small; yet in her *thus* small, was the promise of the present *city*. And now stood raised the walls of defence, too narrow for the future population, but in those days supposed to be too spacious[44] for their own multitude. If thou askest what was the palace of my son; behold *his* house of reeds and straw.[45] On *a bed of* stubble he enjoyed the blessings of calm slumber, and yet from that bed came he to the stars. And already had the Roman a renown greater than his home, *and yet* nor wife, nor father-in-law had he. The rich neighbours had a contempt for poor sons-in-law, and hardly was I believed to be the author of their race. To have dwelt under

[42] *Of these fractions.*]—Ver. 166. The fourth part which he mentions made up a complete day, which was added to every fourth year as an additional day. When he speaks of a lustrum 'here,' he means a full term of four years, and just the commencement of a fifth year, and no more.

[43] *Observe thy festival.*]—Ver. 170. On the calends of March the Matronalia were celebrated by the matrons in honour of Juno, when they sent presents to each other, and received them from their husbands.

[44] *Too spacious.*]—Ver. 181-2. Gower's version is,

'Rome's elements were at the first but small,
Yet has that small great hopes of this great wall.'

[45] *Of reeds and straw.*]—Ver. 184. They still pointed out, in the time of Ovid, a straw-roofed hut on the Palatine hill, which was said to have been the abode of Romulus.

the herdsman's roof, and to have tended oxen, and now to be masters of but a few acres of uncultivated soil, was a reproach to them. The fowls of the air and the wild beasts pair, each of them with its mate; the snake too has its female, from which to propagate its kind. Intermarriages are granted to the remotest tribes; but there was no woman who was willing to marry a man of Rome. I was grieved, and I communicated to thee, O Romulus, thy father's mind. "Cease thy prayers," I said, "what thou dost want, arms will supply. Prepare a festival to Consus.[46] Consus will tell thee the rest that is to be done, on the day on which thou shalt be chaunting the sacred songs to him." The people of Cures[47] grew wroth, and all those whom the same resentment affected. Then, for the first time, did the father-in-law bear arms against his son-in-law. And now nearly all the ravished women were bearing the name of mother as well, and the wars *of states thus* neighbouring were protracted by lengthened duration; the wives met together in an appointed temple, *that* of Juno; among whom my daughter-in-law[48] thus began to speak—"Ye that together with myself have been *thus* carried away, since this character in common we hold, no longer can we with tardiness be dutiful. The lines of battle are formed, but for which side the Gods are to be entreated, choose ye; on one side, the husband, on the other, the father is in arms; we must decide whether we would be widows or orphans. I will

---

[46] *Festival to Consus.*]—Ver. 199. Consus was the god of silence and of secrets. By some he has been confounded with the Roman god Neptune. It is said that the true name of this divinity was not allowed to be divulged, and that his name of 'Consus' was derived from 'conso,' an old form of 'consulo,' 'to give counsel,' such being one of his attributes. He had a subterranean altar in the Circus, uncovered only at the 'Consualia,' and said to have been discovered there by Romulus, having been closed since the time of Evander. The 'Consualia,' or festival of Consus, as appears from the text, was being celebrated when the rape of the Sabine women took place.

[47] *People of Cures.*]—Ver. 201. Namely, the Sabines; but before they took up arms, the Cæninenses, Antemnates, and Crustumini had marched against Rome, to revenge the insult which had been inflicted on them in common with the Sabines. They were, however, repulsed, and then the Sabines took the field, with the result mentioned in the text.

[48] *My daughter-in-law.*]—Ver. 206. This was Hersilia, one of the Sabine women, whom Romulus had married. After her death she was deified and worshipped under the name of Hora, as the goddess of youth,

give you advice, which is both energetic and dutiful." She had *now* given her advice; they obey, and unloose their tresses, and with funereal garb array their sorrowing persons. The lines of battle now stood prepared for the sword and for death, and the clarion was on the point of giving the signal for the combat, when the *women who had been* ravished rush between their fathers and their husbands, and carry in their bosoms their babes, those dear pledges. When they had reached the middle of the plain, with their dishevelled locks they fell upon the earth with bended knee; and as though they had consciousness, the grandchildren, with soothing cry, stretched their little arms towards their grandsires. The child that was able, called on his grandfather then seen for the first time; and he who scarcely was able, was forced *by his mother* to make an effort.[49] The arms and the fury of the warriors fall together, and, their swords *now* laid aside, the fathers-in-law give their hands to their sons-in-law, and receive *theirs in return*. They praise their daughters, and embrace them; and on his buckler the grandsire carries the grandchild; this was a more pleasing use for their shields. From that circumstance the Œbalian mothers hold it no unimportant duty to celebrate my Calends, the day which is first. *Is it not* either because, daring to trust themselves to the drawn swords, they had terminated by their tears the wars of Mars? Or *is it* because by me, with happy results, Ilia became a mother, that the matrons duly observe my sacred rites and my holiday? *And* why *besides*? *It is* because now, at length, the winter, enwrapped in ice, gives way, and the snows disappear, overcome by the warmth of the sun. The foliage that had been shorn by the frost returns to the trees, and the bud full of life sprouts from the tender shoot; the fruitful blade too, which has long lain hid, now finds a hidden path, whereby to raise itself to the breezes *of heaven*. Now is the field teeming; now is the season for breeding the cattle; now does

[49] *To make an effort.*]—Ver. 224. Literally, 'was obliged to be able.' In all probability the meaning is, that the elder children were able to cry out 'ave,' 'grandfather,' and the younger ones were obliged to join in the general clamour, their mothers forcing them. Taubner thinks that the latter were forced by the pinches of their mothers to scream out 'ah! væ!' (something like our 'oh! oh!') which sounding like 'ave,' they were thus compelled perforce to address their grandsires. The suggestion is redolent of more trifling ingenuity than probability.

the bird on the bough prepare a shelter and a home. With reason do the Latian mothers, whose toils and *dearest* longings the bearing of their progeny occupies, observe this prolific season. Add, too, that where, *by his soldiery*, the Roman king was keeping watch and ward, the hill has now the name of Esquiliæ.⁵⁰ There, if I rightly remember, was a temple consecrated to Juno for the public use by the Latian matrons on this day. Why do I delay and burden thy memory with various reasons? See, what thou dost ask is plain before thine eyes; *Juno*, my mother, favours the married women: *hence* the crowd of the matrons resorts to me; this reason so duteous particularly becomes me.

Bring flowers to the Goddess: this Goddess takes delight in blossoming plants; with tender flowrets wreathe your heads. Say ye: "Thou, Lucina, did'st *first* give us the light." 'Say; "Do thou favour the prayers of her who is in travail;" and if any woman is pregnant, let her pray with her tresses untied, that the Goddess may gently facilitate her labour.

Who, now, will tell me why the Salii bear the heavenly arms⁵¹ of Mars, and chaunt Mamurius? Tell me, Nymph, thou that wast wont to minister to the grove and the lake of Diana; Nymph, wife of Numa, come to thy own festival. There is a lake in the valley of Aricia,⁵² inclosed by a dark

---

⁵⁰ *Esquiliæ.*]—Ver. 246. Ovid seems to hint that this name was derived from the 'excubiæ,' or 'watch,' mentioned in the line before; which would seem to be a very far-fetched derivation. Perhaps these watches were set there to keep an eye upon the Sabines, at the time when they had been but newly received into the number of the citizens. According to some authors, this hill derived its name from the word 'excultæ,' 'cultivated,' and was added to the city and brought into cultivation by Servius Tullius. Varro says that the spot had its plural appellation from its consisting of two ridges—the Cispian and the Oppian Hills.

⁵¹ *Heavenly arms.*]—Ver. 259. The 'ancile,' the story of which is told in the text; as also that of the meritorious deeds of Mamurius. The ancilia were borne through the city by the Salii on the calends of March. These were priests of Mars, an order instituted by Numa to keep the sacred shields; they received their name from 'salio,' 'to leap,' or 'dance,' because in the procession round the city they danced with the shields suspended from their necks. Some writers say that they received their name from 'Salius,' an Arcadian, a companion of Æneas, who taught the Italian youths to dance in armour. After the processions had lasted some days, the shields were replaced in the temple of Mars.

⁵² *Valley of Aricia.*]—Ver. 263. Aricia and its grove were situate at the foot of the Alban Mount. Orestes, pursued by the Furies for the

wood, sanctified by ancient religious awe. Here lies concealed Hippolytus,⁵³ torn asunder by the madness of his steeds; for which reason that grove is entered by no horses. *There* the threads⁵⁴ hang down, veiling the long hedge-rows, and many a tablet has been placed to the Goddess *found to be* deserving of it. Ofttimes, the woman having gained her wish,⁵⁵ her forehead wreathed with chaplets, bears *thither* from the city the blazing torches. Those with daring hand and fleet of foot⁵⁶ hold *there* the sway; and each one perishes in succession, after the example he has set. With indistinct

murder of his mother, consulted the oracle at Delphi how he might escape their pursuit; he was ordered to bring away the image of Diana from the Tauric Chersonnesus. Thoas was the king, and by his order all strangers that were caught were immolated. Orestes and his friend, Pylades, were seized and condemned to death; on which, Iphigenia, the sister of Orestes, who was then the priestess of Diana, offered to spare one of them if he would convey letters to Greece for her. A contest of friendship arose as to which should save the other by his death. Pylades at length yielded, and consented to carry the letter, which, he found, was directed to Orestes himself. On this discovery of her brother, Iphigenia joined in their flight, Thoas being first slain; and, according to Ovid and other writers, they brought the image of Diana, and instituted her worship in the Arician grove.

⁵³ *Hippolytus.*]—Ver. 265. He was falsely charged by his step-mother, Phœdra, with a crime, to commit which, she had, without success, solicited him. Theseus, his father, uttering imprecations against him, Neptune sent a sea monster, which frightened the horses of Hippolytus; and they, running away, dashed him against the rocks and killed him. Being restored to life by the art of Æsculapius, he fled to Italy under the name of Virbius, and was sheltered by Diana in the Arician grove.

⁵⁴ *The threads.*]—Ver. 267. The 'licia,' or 'threads,' were used for suspending the gifts and votive offerings of the worshippers. In Catholic countries, and in some parts of England, this practice prevails at the present day, in honour of the patron saint of an adjoining spring or well.

⁵⁵ *Gained her wish.*]—Ver. 269. Women, whose prayers to Diana had been heard, especially in love matters, used to carry lighted torches from the city to the grove of Aricia.

⁶ *Fleet of foot.*]—Ver. 271. To commemorate the flight of Orestes, a runaway slave was always appointed to be her high-priest in the grove of Aricia, who was called 'Rex Nemorensis,' 'the king of the woodland.' The term 'with daring hand' alludes to the fact that the priest might, according to the usual custom, at any time be murdered by another desirous to occupy his place, and hence the necessity arose of his always going armed to protect himself from such attacks. This and the cruelties practised in the worship of the Tauric Diana, perhaps led to the belief that Egeria was identical with the deity.

murmur glides a pebbly stream: ofttimes, but in scanty draughts, have I drunk thence. It is Egeria who supplies the water; a Goddess pleasing to the Muses; she was the wife and the counsellor of Numa. In the first place, it seemed good *to her* that the Quirites, too ready for war, should be softened by justice and the fear of the Gods. For that reason laws were given, that the strongest might not obtain supreme power; and the holy rites delivered *to the people then* began to be religiously observed. Their savage nature is *now* laid aside, right is more powerful than arms, and it is considered disgraceful to engage in civil strife; many a person, but just now violent, is now changed *in character* on seeing the altar, and offers the wine and the salt spelt cake on the glowing hearths. Lo! the father of the Gods is scattering his flashing lightnings through the clouds, and drains the heavens by deluging showers: on no other occasion have the hurled bolts of fire fallen more thickly. The king is alarmed, and terror takes possession of the breasts of the multitude. To him the Goddess *says*: "Be not unreasonably dismayed! the lightning is to be averted by atonement, and the wrath of the angry Jove is *easily* appeased; but Picus and Faunus[57] will be able to reveal the ceremony of expiation, each of them a Divinity of the Roman soil; but they will not inform thee without force: apply chains when thou hast caught them." And thus does she instruct *Numa* by what means they may be taken. There was at the foot of the Aventine *hill*[58] a grove, dark with the shade of the holm-oak, on seeing which you might *readily* say, "*Surely* a Divinity dwells *here!*" In the centre was a grassy plot, and, covered over with green moss, a constant stream of water trickled from the rock. From this stream

---

[57] *Picus and Faunus.*]—Ver. 291. These were ancient deities of Latium. They have been mentioned before, both in the text and in the notes.

[58] *Of the Aventine hill.*]—Ver. 295. This was one of the hills to which Rome extended in the later times. It is supposed that its name was either derived from Aventinus, son of Romulus Silvius, king of Alba Longa, who was buried there, or from 'aves,' 'birds,' which used to flock there. Varro says that it was so called because there was a ferry across the marshes which separated it from the rest of Rome, by which the passengers were carried, 'Advehebantur.' Servius, on the Æneid (Book 7, l. 651), mentions a tradition that it was so called by the Sabines, from 'Avens,' a river in their own territory.

Faunus and Picus were wont generally to drink alone. Hither comes king Numa, and sacrifices a sheep to the fountain; he *then* places for the Gods cups full of fragrant wine; and with his train lies hid, concealing himself in a grotto. The forest Gods come to their accustomed streams, and refresh their parched spirits with copious draughts of wine:[59] sleep is the consequence of their debauch; Numa issues forth from the cool grotto, and puts the hands of them, thus buried in slumber, in tight manacles. When sleep has *now* departed, they strive by struggling to burst the bonds; as they struggle, the more tightly do they hold them. Then Numa *says:* "Gods of the groves, forgive my deed! inasmuch as ye know that impiety is far from my nature; and point out the way in which the lightning may be averted." Thus Numa *spoke*, and thus Faunus replied, shaking his horns:[60] "Thou inquirest on a matter of great difficulty, and which it is against the law of heaven for thee to learn by our instruction; our *privileges as* Deities have their limits. We are the Gods of the country, and have our sway on the lofty mountains; Jove has full power over his own weapons. Of thyself thou wilt not be enabled to bring him down from heaven; but perhaps, by availing thyself of our aid, thou wilt." Faunus had thus spoken: the opinion expressed by Picus is the same. "But take from us these bonds," says Picus; "Jove shall come hither, brought down from his topmost height; the vaporous Styx shall attest my promise." What they do, when released from their bonds, what incantations they repeat, and by what art they bring down Jove from his habitations above, it is not allowed by heaven for man to know; let things permitted be the *only* subjects of my song, and whatever may be repeated by the lips of the poet, without incurring guilt. They bring thee down,[61] O Jupiter, from the skies; in conse-

[59] *Draughts of wine.*]—Ver. 303-4. Gower's version is—

'The wood-gods to their old wont came, the bowls
They turn'd off blithe, and quench'd their thirsty souls.'

[60] *Shaking his horns.*]—Ver. 312. To show that it was a matter not to be settled in a moment, but requiring much deliberation.

[61] *They bring thee down.*]—Ver. 327. It is thought by some that Numa discovered the art of conducting the lightning, and rendering it innocuous in its effects; and the death of Tullus Hostilius, the third king of Rome, is supposed by them to have been owing to his ignorance of the proper mode of conducting the electric fluid.

quence of which posterity still celebrates thee, and names thee Elicius.[62] It is agreed that the tops of the Aventine forest *then* trembled, and the earth yielded beneath the pressure of the weight of Jove. The heart of the king palpitates; from the whole of his breast the blood has fled, and his bristling hair stands on end. When his senses have returned, he says: "O thou, both King and Father of the Gods on high! teach me the assured expiations of *thy* lightnings; if, with guileless hands, I have touched thy altars; if too, my tongue, with *true* piety, asks this which is now entreated of thee." *Jove* nodded assent to his prayer; but, without using any circumlocution, he concealed the truth, and by his equivocal expressions struck the hero with alarm. "Cut off a head," says he. To whom the king *says:* "We will obey: an onion, pulled up in my garden, must be cut off."[63] "Of a man," adds the God. "Yes, the topmost hairs," answers the other. *The God* demands "a life;" to whom Numa *says:* "*Yes*, of a fish." *The God* laughed and said, "See to it then, that with these thou dost propitiate my weapons, O man, not to be repulsed from a conference with the Gods. But to thee, when to-morrow's sun shall have raised his full disk, I will give the sure pledge of empire." He spoke; with loud thunderings he is borne above the trembling firmament, and leaves Numa in the attitude of worship. Joyful he returns, and tells the Quirites what had occurred; credence was given to his words, tardy, and extorted with difficulty. "But surely," says he, "I shall be believed if the result follow my words. See now, hear ye, every one present, what will happen on the morrow. When to-morrow's sun shall have raised his full

[62] *Elicius.*]—Ver. 328. From 'elicio,' to 'entice,' 'allure,' or 'bring out.'

[63] *Must be cut off.*]—Ver. 340. Meaning, 'It must have its "bulb" or "head" taken off.' The conversation seems to have been intended by Jupiter as a test of Numa's ready wit and humane disposition. He bids Numa 'Cut off a head.' Numa says, 'Yes, I will; the head of an onion.' 'Of a man,' says Jupiter. 'Yes, the topmost hair,' says Numa, implying obedience to the original command, as to the cutting off of the head; but dexterously substituting 'capilli,' 'the hair,' for 'caput,' 'the head,' which were often used synonymously. The god, detecting the pun, presses him closer, and demands a life; on which Numa says, 'Yes, you shall have a life, but it must be that of a fish.' Plutarch says the fish was the 'mæna,' a kind of pilchard, which seems to have been a favourite ingredient in the 'materiel' of incantation. See Book 2, l. 578.

disk, Jupiter will give the sure pledge of empire." They retire in doubt; his promise seemed *likely to be of* slow performance, and their belief depends on the approaching day.

The earth was *still* soft, and bedewed with the hoar-frost of the morning; the people are present before the threshold of their king. He comes forth and seats himself in the midst on a throne of maple-wood;[64] around him stand the men in countless numbers, and hold their peace. Phœbus had *now* but risen with his upper edge; their anxious minds are in a state of agitation through hope and fear. He stands, and his head veiled[65] with a snow-white robe, he raises his hands already not unfamiliar *in worship* to the Gods; and thus he speaks —" The time of the promised favour is drawing nigh; confer, O Jupiter, upon thy words the promised fulfilment." While he was speaking, the sun had just raised *from the deep* his entire disk, and from the pole of heaven there came a heavy peal; thrice did the God thunder without a cloud; thrice did he dart his lightnings. Believe what I tell; I speak of things wondrous, but realities. The heavens began to open in the midst; the multitude, with their monarch, cast down their eyes. Behold! there falls a shield, gently poised on the lightsome breeze; a shout from the people ascends to the stars. The king raises the gift from the ground, having first offered a heifer, which had never yielded his neck to be pressed by the yoke. He entitles it 'ancile,' because it is pared away[66] at every point, and whichever way you look at it, every corner is off. Then, mindful that the destiny of empire depends upon this, he forms a plan of much cunning. He orders several[67] to be made, engraved of a

[64] *Throne of maple wood.*]—Ver. 359. The wood of the maple was held by the ancients in the highest esteem, next to that of the cedar, on account of its hardness and the closeness of its grain.

[65] *His head veiled.*]—Ver. 363. The Romans covered their heads when praying or performing any religious rite, in order that nothing of ill omen should present itself to the view of the devotee. See Æneid, book iii. l. 405.

[66] *Because it is pared away.*]—Ver. 375. In the old Latin, 'ancisus,' or 'amcisus,' means 'having the edges cut off.' Ovid means to say, that from this word, the shield received the name of 'ancile.' Its shape, as represented on a gem in the Florentine cabinet, was oblong, each of the two sides receding inwards, with an even curvature, so as to make it broader at the ends than in the middle, and thus it presented a curved edge on every side.

[67] *He orders several.*]—Ver. 381. Ovid says, several. Dionysius says, very many. Other writers say eleven, and that Mamurius made them so

similar shape, that a deception may meet the eyes of those plotting *to steal it*. Mamurius, whether more distinguished for his probity or for his skill as a workman, it is hard for one to say, completed that task. To him the munificent Numa said, " Ask thy own reward for thy work; as my truthfulness is well known, thou shalt ask for nothing in vain." Already had he given to the Salii (from *their* dancing do they derive their name) both arms,[68] and words to be sung to certain measures. Then thus Mamurius *says*, " Let fame be given to me as my reward, and let my name be mentioned at the end of their strain." From that circumstance do the priests pay the reward promised for the ancient workmanship, and call upon Mamurius.[69]

If by any chance you should desire to marry, though both of you should be impatient, postpone it;[70] a short delay has its great advantages. Arms stir up the fight—the fight is unsuited to the *newly* wedded; when arms shall have been laid by, there will be a more suitable omen. On these days, too, ought the wife of the mitred[71] Dialis,

skilfully, that Numa was unable to perceive the difference. Plutarch says that Numa left the work of imitation to be a subject of competition among all the Roman artists. Gower's version of this passage is:—

' Of shields like shap'd he bids to make a dozen,
That so an error might the couzener couzen.'

[68] *Both arms.*]—Ver. 388. The dress of the Salii was an embroidered tunic, with a brazen belt, the ' trabea' and ' apex,' or tufted conical cap; each had a sword by his side, and a spear or staff in his hand. They carried the ' ancilia' in the left hand, or suspended from their shoulders, and, while dancing, struck them with their rods or swords, keeping time with their voices and the movements of the dance. Their verses contained, it is supposed, a kind of rude theogony or history of the Gods, with the exception of Venus, who was omitted from their praises.

[69] *Mamurius.*]—Ver. 392. Some regard this story as utterly fabulous, and Varro believes their mention of 'Veturius Mamurius' to be only an appeal to ' vetus memoria,' ' ancient tradition.'

[70] *Postpone it.*]—Ver. 394. As the ' ancilia,' which were emblems of war, were carried about on the Ides of March, it was not considered auspicious to marry, or to commence a journey, or indeed, any matter of importance on that day.

[1] *Of the mitred.*]—Ver. 397. ' Apicati,' literally wearing the ' apex.' This was a cap worn by the Flamens and the Salii. The name properly belonged to a pointed piece of olive wood, the base whereof was surrounded with wool. This was held on the head by fillets, or by a cap, which was fastened by two bands, called ' apicula,' or ' offendices.' The cap was of

clad in her *flame-coloured* gown, to wear her hair *all* unbraided.

When the third night rising *from the deep* shall have raised its fires, one of the two Fishes will be concealed. For there are two—the one near to the southern, the other to the northern winds; each takes its name from its *neighbouring* wind.

When the bride of Tithonus, with rosy cheeks, shall have begun to shed her dews, and shall urge on the hours of the fifth day, whether that *Constellation is styled* Arctophylax, or whether the lazy Boötes, he shall be plunged in the deep, and shall elude your view.

But not so the Vintager. It is but a trifling delay to relate whence this Constellation derives its origin. Bacchus is said, among the heights of Ismarus, to have loved the long-haired Ampelos,[72] offspring of the Satyrs and of a Nymph. To him he gave, pendant from the foliage of an elm, a vine, which still has its name from that of the youth. While he is heedlessly gathering the blushing grapes on a branch, he falls; him thus lost *to earth*, Bacchus conveys among the stars.

When the sixth Sun from the ocean climbs the steep of Olympus, and on his winged steeds traverses the skies, whoever thou be that art present, and art paying homage to the shrines of hoary Vesta, place both the goblet and the incense on the Ilian hearth. To the countless titles of Cæsar was

---

a conical form, and was generally made of sheep-skin, with the wool on; and from the 'apex,' on its summit, it at last acquired that name also. The Flaminica, or wife of the Flamen Dialis, wore a scarlet or flame-coloured robe, called 'venenatum,' from 'venenum,' 'dye,' and also the 'rica,' or crimson hood, a square cloak, with a border, to which was attached a slip, cut from a 'felix arbor.' On certain days she was not allowed to cut her nails, or comb her hair, to which fact the poet here makes allusion.

[72] *Ampelos.*]—Ver. 409. The story of Ampelos is differently told by other writers. According to them, Ampelos was a youth, the companion of Bacchus. Contrary to the advice of that god, he persisted in sporting with the wild beasts. Ate, the goddess of revenge, persuaded him to torment a bull; and doing so, he provoked the moon, who, in her anger, sent a gad-fly to sting the bull, when Ampelos fell and broke his neck. Bacchus appealed to the 'Parcæ,' or Fates, and Atropos promised to restore Ampelos to him in another form. Forthwith a vine, ἄμπελος, was produced, laden with grapes; Bacchus and the Satyrs discovered the invention of wine, and, in their exultation, became intoxicated. Ismarus was a mountain of Thrace, near the river Hebrus.

added *on this day* the honour which he most desired to merit[73]—that of the Pontificate. Over the eternal fires presides the divinity of the immortal Cæsar; thou *here* beholdest the united pledges of the empire's safety. From the ashes of ancient Troy *came* the most worthy relic, laden with which, Æneas was safe from the foe. A priest descended from Æneas claims an alliance with thy Deity; Vesta, do thou preserve his kindred person.[74] Well do ye thrive, ye fires, which with sacred hand he tends; undying, live on, both *thou sacred flame*, and *thou* Prince, I pray.

There is one distinction for the Nones of March, that on them they believe that the temple of Vejovis, before *you reach* the two groves,[75] was consecrated, when Romulus surrounded the grove with a high stone *wall*. "Hither fly, whoever you are," says he, "and you shall be in safety." Oh! from how low an origin has the Roman grown! How little an object of envy was that ancient multitude!

Lest, however, the strangeness of the name be an obstacle to you in your ignorance, learn who this Deity is, and why he is so called. He is the youthful Jupiter; mark his youthful aspect: mark, too, his hand; it wields no thunder-bolts. The thunder-bolt was assumed by Jupiter after the attempt of the giants to attain to the skies; in early times he was unarmed. Ossa blazed with new flames, and Pelion higher than Ossa, and Olympus rooted in the solid earth. A she goat stands,[76] too, beside him; the nymphs of Crete are said to

[73] *Most desired to merit.*]—Ver. 419. Augustus desired this dignity, that he might appear to stand high in the favour of the gods. He was appointed Pontifex Maximus, A.U.C. 740, in the place of Lepidus. This officer lived in a house at the public expense, called the 'Regia,' or 'palace.' Augustus gave this up, in his Pontificate, to the Vestal Virgins.

[74] *His kindred person.*]—Ver. 426. This passage has puzzled many of the commentators; but it does not appear very clearly where the difficulty lies. The poet repeatedly calls the fire of Vesta the 'Ilian,' or Trojan fires. He also addresses Augustus, the adopted son of Julius Cæsar, as descended from Æneas; and he seems here only to allude to the fact of both being able to trace back their origin to the city of Troy.

[75] *The two groves.*]—Ver. 430. The space between the Arx and the Capitolium, where the Asylum and the temple of Vejovis were, was called, according to Livy, book i. c. viii., and Dionysius, 'Inter duos lucos,' 'Between the two groves.'

[76] *A she goat stands.*]—Ver. 443. This fact goes far to confirm the poet's opinion that 'Vejovis' means 'the young Jove;' as Jupiter in his

have nurtured him; *a she-goat* furnished milk for the infant Jove. Now I am called upon *to explain* the name; the country-women call wheat, which has grown up but indifferently, "vegrandia," and when small *in the grain*, they style it "vesca."[77] If that is the force of the word, "ve," why should I not imagine that the temple of Vejovis is the temple of the little Jupiter?

And now, when the stars shall bespangle the azure sky, look upwards, *and* you shall see the neck of the Gorgon steed.[78] He is believed to have sprung forth, his mane besprinkled with blood, from the teeming neck of the slain Medusa. With him, as he soared above the clouds and beneath the stars, the heavens were as the ground, his wings *were* in place of feet. And now had he taken the strange curb in his fretting mouth, when his lightsome hoof struck forth the Aonian fountains.[79] Now does he enjoy that heaven which

infancy was suckled by the goat Amalthea. He also attempts to prove it from the circumstance, that there Jupiter is represented at a time when he had not yet learned to wield his thunderbolts, and that 've' was an old Latin word, in all cases found to express diminutiveness. Some suppose that 've' is here applied to the name of Jupiter in a bad sense, as 'the evil' or 'the incensed' Jove, on which account his statue was armed with arrows, for the purposes of mischief. Mr. Keightly, in his Mythology of Greece and Italy, thinks that 'Vejovis' and 'Vedius' mean the same deity, their name meaning the 'injurious Jupiter,' and that he was a god of the world below. Vedius, however, would appear to bear the same relation to Pluto, 'Dis,' that Vejovis does to Jupiter, whatever that relation may have been.

[77] '*Vesca.*']—Ver. 446. From 've' 'not,' and 'esca' 'food,' as affording but little nourishment. 'Vegrandis' is, according to the poet's etymology, from 've,' 'not,' 'grandis,' 'large,' or 'of full growth.'

[78] *The Gorgon steed.*]—Ver. 450. The poet describes the Heliacal rising of Pegasus on the nones. He was so called from $\pi\eta\gamma\dot{\eta}$, 'a fountain,' as having been born near the springs of the ocean. Medusa, one of the Gorgon sisters, was pregnant by Neptune, and when Perseus slew her and cut off her head, Pegasus sprung from the blood; hence the poet's expression, 'the teeming neck.' He was tamed and presented to Bellerophon to assist him in the conquest of the Chimæra. Ovid, Metam., 4, 785, says that Perseus was mounted on Pegasus when he slew the sea-monster to which Andromeda was exposed. Minerva, in her vengeance against Medusa, who had been previously remarkable for the beauty of her hair, changed it into serpents, and doomed all who looked on her face to the penalty of being turned into stone. Perseus, with the aid of the gods, destroyed her while sleeping.

[79] *The Aonian fountains.*]—Ver. 456. Pegasus was caught and tamed

formerly he sought by his wings, and he glitters, refulgent with fifteen stars.

Forthwith on the succeeding night you will see the Gnossian crown;[80] by reason of the crime of Theseus[81] was *Ariadne* made a Goddess. Already had the damsel, to her advantage, obtained Bacchus in exchange for her foresworn spouse, she who had given to her ungrateful husband the clue to be retraced. Exulting at the *good* fortune of her marriage, she said, "What was I mourning for, *like* a country lass as I was? It was a good thing for me that he was faithless." In the mean time, Bacchus,[82] with his well-trimmed locks, conquers the Indians,[83] and returns enriched from the Eastern world; among the captive maidens of distinguished beauty, the daughter of the king was too pleasing to Bacchus. His loving wife indulged in weeping, and as she paced the winding shore, with her hair all loose, she uttered such words as these:—"Lo now a second time, ye billows, hear a like complaint! Lo! a second time, ye sands, receive my tears *as they fall*. I used to cry, I remember, 'Foresworn and faithless Theseus!' He is gone; Bacchus now incurs the like guilt. 'Now, too,' will I exclaim, 'let woman put no trust in

---

by Bellerophon, who was thrown off from him by Jupiter, and, falling in Cilicia, was struck with blindness. By striking with his hoof Mount Helicon, in Aonia, a part of Bœotia, the fountain called Hippocrene, ἱπποῦ κρήνη, or 'the horse fountain,' was opened.

[80] *Gnossian crown.*]—Ver. 460. Minos, the father of Ariadne, reigned at Gnossus, in the isle of Crete.

[81] *Theseus.*]—Ver. 460. He was the son of Æthra and Ægeus, and was sent from Athens to Crete, as one of the seven chosen youths to be devoured by the Minotaur. By the aid of Ariadne, he tracked the Labyrinth where the monster had his abode, and slew him. He sailed from Crete with his companions and with Ariadne and seven other damsels; but he cruelly abandoned her to whom he was indebted for his life, on the island of Naxos.

[82] *Bacchus.*]—Ver. 465. Here called 'Liber.' This name was given him either from 'libo,' 'to make a libation,' or from 'libero,' 'to set free,' because he liberates the mind from cares, or from the Greek words λυέιν βαρῆ, 'to loosen the weights,' i. e. of care and despondency. He is called 'Depexus,' 'combed down,' or 'well-trimmed,' in allusion either to his youth or the effeminacy of his character.

[83] *The Indians.*]—Ver. 465. The conquests of Bacchus in the east are said to have extended to the river Ganges. His army consisted of a troop of Bacchanals, his conquests were without blood, and he taught the conquered nations the use of the vine, the art of tilling the earth, and of preparing honey for food. He was accompanied on this expedition by Silenus and Lusus.

man;' change but the name, and my case has been repeated. O, would that my destiny had kept on the course on which it had before commenced, and that now, at this moment, I had been no more! Why, Bacchus, didst thou preserve me when about to die on the lonely sands? I could *then* have ended my sorrows at once. Ah! Bacchus, thou unstable one! *yes*, more unstable even than the leaves that encircle thy temples; Bacchus, known to my sorrow, didst thou dare, by bringing thy paramour before my *very* eyes, to disturb a union *before* so harmonious. Alas! where is thy plighted faith?[34] Where *all* that thou wast wont to swear? Ah! wretched me! How often do I repeat these words. Thou wast wont to blame Theseus, and thou thyself didst use to call him a deceiver; by thy own judgment thou art guilty of a greater crime. May no man know this, and by secret anguish may I be consumed, lest I may be supposed to have deserved to be thus often beguiled. Above all, I would wish it to be concealed from Theseus, lest he should rejoice that thou art a partaker of his guilt. But, I suppose, a paramour of fair complexion[35] was preferred to me, *because* of my swarthy hue; be *then* that colour the lot of my enemy. But what matters that? She is the more pleasing to thee, from this very defect. What art thou doing? She contaminates thy *very* embrace. Bacchus, fulfil thy pledge, and prefer no woman before the love of a wife, *one* who was ever accustomed to love her husband. The horns of a handsome bull captivated my mother; thy horns, me;[86] they commend me; the other was a disgraceful pas-

[34] *Thy plighted faith.*]—Ver. 485-6. Gower's version is—

'Ah! where's thy faith? Those solemn vows indented.
Ah me! how oft have I these dirges vented.'

[35] *Of fair complexion.*—Ver. 493. This is meant ironically, as Bacchus would not be very likely to meet with a 'candida pellex' in his Indian excursion, unless, indeed, he took Georgia or Circassia in his road.

[86] *Thy horns, me.*]—Ver. 500. Bacchus was frequently represented with horns. He seems to have been worshipped by the Thracians and the Phrygians under the name of Sabazius and in the form of an ox.—Keightley's Mythology of Greece and Rome, p. 168. Neptune gave Minos a bull, which, on account of its beauty, he refused to sacrifice to the god. On this, Neptune inspired Pasiphäe, the daughter of Minos, with love for the animal, and the Minotaur, half man and half beast, was the fruit of this passion. Perhaps the truth is, that Pasiphäe had an intrigue with a person named Taurus (which also signifies in Latin 'a bull'), and had twins by him, whom she named Minos and Taurus.

sion. Let not my love prove an injury to me; for, Bacchus, it was no harm to thee that thou thyself didst confess thy love. And, *indeed*, thou dost nothing strange in kindling a flame[87] in me: in fire thou art said to have been born,[88] and from fire to have been snatched, by the hand of thy father. I am she to whom thou wast wont to promise heaven; Ah, me! instead of heaven, what kind of gifts am I *now* receiving?" She had said; for a long time had Bacchus been listening[89] to her words while thus complaining, as by chance he had been following after her. He clasps her in his embraces, and, with kisses, dries away her tears, and he says, "Together, let us seek the heights of heaven;" united to me in wedlock, thou shalt take a united epithet.[90] Henceforth, thy name altered shall be Libera. I will cause, too, that with thee there shall be a memorial of thy crown, which Vulcan gave to Venus, she to thee. He keeps his word, and transforms its nine jewels into stars; by means of nine stars it still glitters in its golden radiance.

When he who bears the purple day upon his rapid car shall have completed six risings, and as many settings of his orb, then shall you behold the second Equiria on the grassy plain which Tiber bounds on its verge with its winding waters.

---

[87] *Kindling a flame.*]—Ver. 503. There is a play here upon the word 'uro,' 'to burn,' which also means, in a figurative sense, 'to inflame with passion.'

[88] *To have been born.*]—Ver. 504. Semele, the mother of Bacchus, at the instigation of Juno, bound Jupiter by an oath to grant her request, and then desired that he would present himself to her, accompanied by his lightnings and celestial effulgence. Unable to endure his presence, she was consumed in the flames, and Bacchus, with whom she was then eight months pregnant, was snatched by the nymph Dirce from the flames, and placed in the thigh of Jupiter until the remaining month was accomplished.

[89] *Was Bacchus listening.*]—Ver. 508-9. Gower's version of these lines is—

'She ended. Bacchus all the while did mind her
Lamenting, as, by chance, he came behind her.
He clips her waste, and tears with kisses dries.'

[90] *A united epithet.*]—Ver. 511. Ovid is the only writer that identifies Ariadne with the goddess 'Libera.' Cicero and other Latin authors make her to be the same with Proserpine. Perhaps she was originally a distinct deity; but, in consequence of the similarity of their offices and of their ceremonials, in lapse of time they became confounded.

But if perchance this shall be covered by the flooding wave, then let the dusty Cælian *plain*[91] receive the steeds.

On the Ides is the mirthful festival of Anna Perenna, not far from thy banks, *thou* Tiber,[92] that flowest from afar. The common people assemble, and carouse scattered in every quarter on the green grass;[93] each with his sweetheart is *there* reclining. Some spend their time in the open air, some pitch their tents; by some a leafy bower is formed of branches. Some, when they have fixed up reeds there in the stead of solid columns, place over them their garments spread out. Yet,[94] with the sun and the wine, do they wax warm; they pray for years as many in number as the cups they quaff, and reckon on as they drink. There you will meet with the man who can drink off the years of Nestor;[95] the woman who be-

---

[91] *Dusty Cælian plain.*]—Ver. 522. We have already observed that when the Tiber overflowed the Campus Martius, the races were run upon a spot which formed part of the Cælian hill. It was originally called 'Querquetulanus,' from its oaks, 'quercus,' with which trees it abounded. Its later name was derived from Cælus Vibennius, an Etrurian, who assisted Romulus against the Sabines, and received this piece of ground as his reward.

[92] *Thou Tiber.*]—Ver. 524. This spot was called the grove of Anna Perenna, and was between the Milvian bridge and the point of confluence of the Tiber and the river Anio. He calls the Tiber, 'advena,' 'stranger,' (here rendered, 'flowing from afar,) because it took its rise in the Apennines, which, at the time when Rome was founded, formed almost the central part of Etruria.

[93] *On the green grass.*]—Ver. 525-6. This festival, in its excess of revelry and many other characteristics, seems to have been a sort of Roman Greenwich Fair. 'Cum pare sua' is literally 'with his equal,' or 'his mate.' It is as likely to mean 'a sweetheart' as 'a wife;' perhaps, from the nature of the carousals, a little more so. Gower translates these two lines thus—

'All sorts together flock; and on the ground
Displaid, each marrow by her make drinks round.'

The word 'marrow' is still used in the north of England, to signify 'an equal,' or 'one of a pair.' 'Make,' is the old form of the word, 'mate.'

[94] *Yet.*]—Ver. 531. That is to say, 'in spite of the exposure of most of them to the open air,' or, as Mr. Stanford suggests, 'notwithstanding the shade they had formed by extending their cloaks upon the upright reeds, and their reclining beneath them.'

[95] *The years of Nestor.*]—Ver. 533. He speaks with a fair allowance of poetic license when he says that some are to be seen who can quaff as many cups (cyathi) as Nestor had years. Nestor was the son of Eleus, and was king of Pylos. He assisted Pirithoüs against

comes *old as* the Sibyl by *the number of* her cups. There, too, they sing whatever snatches they have picked up at the theatres, and move their pliant arms[96] in time to their words. And *now*, having laid aside the bowl, they trip[97] the uncouth dance, and *many* a gaily dressed wench skips about with her locks flowing. When they return *to their seats*, they stagger, and are a gazing sight for the mob, and the multitude that meets them pronounces them to be glorious *souls*. I myself met them lately; the procession seemed to me one that was worthy to be mentioned again. A drunken old hag was dragging after her a drunken old man.[98]

the Centaur, and afterwards shared in the Grecian expedition against Troy. The poets say that he was then in his two hundredth year, as being in the third generation, γένεα. This is an error, as that term signified but thirty years: consequently we may allow him ninety years, which number must have pretty well taken up the day of the drinker. It must, however, be remembered, that the 'cyathus' was a definite measure, being one-twelfth part of a sextarius, which was not quite a pint, and that it was consequently less than one-third of our common gill. Pliny, in his Natural History, Book xiv. c. 22, s. 26, speaks of Novellus Torquatus Mediolanensis, who obtained the cognomen of 'Tricongius,' from his drinking three 'congii' of wine at one sitting. The 'congius' held six 'sextarii,' or nearly six pints. It is a matter in dispute among antiquarians, whether the vessel called 'cyathus' means the cup from which the Romans drank, or the ladle with which the cups were filled from the bowl, corresponding with our punch-ladle, or rather, in capacity, with the toddy-ladles of the Scotch. 'Bibere ad numerum,' 'to drink their number,' would seem most probably to refer to the number of ladlefuls that were placed at one sitting in the drinking-glass, or cup, of each person.

[96] *Move their pliant arms.*]—Ver. 536. In all ages it seems to be a prevalent notion with the unrefined, that the dance cannot be graceful or complete without the continual and independent action of the arms and elbows. As a proof, witness a Highlander dancing a fling, an Irishman a jig, or a Northumbrian peasant a reel.

[97] *They trip.*]—Ver. 539. Gower's version is as follows:

'Bowls set aside, each with his trickt-up lass,
Whose hairs are loosened, trips it on the grass.'

[98] *A drunken old man.*]—Ver. 542. Heinsius, Burmann, and other commentators, think that some lines are wanting after this, as the poet seems by his words to promise a longer story. Burmann supposes that the monkish transcribers omitted them on account of their indelicacy. Why they should all have agreed to make this omission in the numerous manuscripts which still exist, it is difficult to conceive, as no such fastidiousness seems to have actuated them in transcribing the works of Juvenal, Martial, or Ausonius, writers of far more gross diction than Ovid. There appears no occasion for such a supposition, as the sense seems complete without

But as to *the question* who this Goddess is, since there is a wide difference between the accounts, no one of the stories shall be unnoticed according to my purpose. The wretched Dido[99] had been consumed by her love for Æneas; she had been consumed also on the funeral pile which she had built up for her own destruction: her ashes, too, had been collected, and on the marble tablet of her tomb was this brief epitaph, which she herself left when dying:—" Æneas furnished both the cause of death and the weapon; Dido fell by her own hand." Forthwith the Numidians invade the realm, now without a defender. The Moor Iarba possesses himself of the captured palace; and remembering how he had been rejected, he cries, " *Only* see, how I, whom she so often repulsed, am now enjoying the chamber of Elissa!" The Tyrians fly in different directions, wherever each in his wanderings is led, as when at times the bees stray about unsettled, having lost their king. Thrice had the threshing floor received the harvest to be beaten out, and thrice had the must been poured into the hollow vats.[1] Anna is driven from her

having recourse to it. The poet appears to mean, that they put aside their drinking, and stand up, perhaps at some distance, for a dance; that, after the excitement of the dance, combined with the wine, has made them dizzy, they return to their places where they were sitting before, and as they can hardly stand up, their companions call them merry souls. He then seems to say that he was one day walking in this Greenwich Park of Rome, and he perhaps heard some shouting, and saw a crowd. He stopped to see what it was. He found that it was a troop of people running along in company with a drunken old woman, who had hold of a drunken old man (probably her husband), and who from the dance were reeling back to their seats, perhaps within the 'tentoria.' This mob, then, was the 'pompa,' and the richness of the scene—this much ado about nothing—made it 'digna relatu,' 'worthy of mention.' 'Pompa' means literally 'a troop in procession, escorting or attending upon some other person or object,' and he may use it here in an ironical sense.

[99] *Dido.*]—Ver. 545. The story of Dido and Æneas is recounted at length in the Æneid of Virgil, from his kind reception by her in the First Book, to his base betrayal and desertion of her in the Fourth Book. Virgil, however, does not seem to think that by his acts in this matter he at all forfeited his claim to the title of 'pius Æneas.' Elissa was her original name: she was called 'Dido' after her death. In the Punic tongue the latter word signified 'the bold woman.'

[1] *The hollow vats.*]—Ver. 558. 'Lacus' means literally 'ponds,' or 'lakes.' This was the name given to all tubs or casks for liquor, especially the vat into which the wine flowed when pressed. The 'must,' 'mustum,' was the juice of the grape when just pressed out.

home, and weeps as she leaves her sister's walls; *yet* first she performs the funereal offices for her sister. The light ashes soak up the perfumes² mixed with her tears, and receive the locks cut from her head as an offering. Thrice, too, did she say, "Farewell;" thrice did she press the ashes brought close to her lips, and in them her sister seemed to be present. Having found a bark,³ and a companion of her flight, she sails along straight before the wind,⁴ as she looks back upon those walls, the loved work of her sister. Near to the barren Cosyra is the fruitful isle of Melite,⁵ which the billow of the Libyan sea dashes against. For this isle she makes, relying upon her former terms of friendship⁶ with the king; Battus, her friend, abounding in wealth, was the ruler there. After he had learned the misfortunes of each of the two sisters, he says, "This land, such as, small as it is, thou mayst find it to be, is thine." And, in fact, he would, to the very last, have observed the duties of hospitality, had he not feared the great power of Pygmalion.⁷ Twice had the sun revisited his Constellations; the third year was speeding onward, and a new land

² *Soak up the perfumes.*]—Ver. 561. The ancients were accustomed to pour wine and oils of great value on the ashes of the dead. They also cut from the head handfuls of hair, which they threw on the funeral pile.

³ *Having found a bark.*]—Ver. 565. Some accounts state, that Anna was obliged to fly instantly upon her sister's death from the wrath of Iarbas: and that Dido put herself to death to escape his vengeance, excited by her determined refusal of an alliance with him.

⁴ *Straight before the wind.*]—Ver. 565. Or, as the sailors say, 'with the wind right aft.' The 'pes' here mentioned was the 'halser,' or 'rope,' suspended from the lower angles of the sail, by which it might be hauled to the wind, or hauled in or veered out at pleasure. The expression is literally, 'with the halser on a level,' probably with the deck, from which position the wind blowing on either side would cause it to swerve.

⁵ *Melite.*]—Ver. 567. This is the island of Malta, in the Mediterranean. There was also an island of that name in the Adriatic sea, which is now called Melida. Cosyra, now called Gozzo, is a barren, rocky island, between Sicily and the coast of Africa, about seven leagues in length.

⁶ *Terms of friendship.*]—Ver. 569. Melita had been colonized by the Phœnicians. Battus was the son of Polymnestus and Phronime. His name was Aristoteles, but he was called Battus from having an impediment in his speech.

⁷ *Pygmalion.*]—Ver. 574. He was the son of Pygmalius, and brother of Dido and Anna. According to others, he was the son of Belus. He murdered Sichæus, the husband of Dido, to obtain his wealth, on which Dido and Anna fled from Tyre, where he reigned.

must be sought by the exiles. "Thy brother is at hand, and assails us in war," says the king, who detested arms; "we are not prepared for warfare; fly and preserve thyself." At his bidding she flies, and to wind and waves she trusts her bark; her brother was more cruel than any sea. Near to the fishy streams of the craggy Crathis,[8] there is a little spot; the people that inhabit it call it Camere. Thither was her course directed; and *now* she was not further off from it than *the distance which* at nine casts a sling might throw. The sails fall first, and are flapped to and fro by the fitful gale. "Cleave the waters with your oars!" cries the pilot; and while they are preparing to furl their canvass with the twisted tackle, the crooked poop is struck by a violent blast from the south; *the ship* is borne out into the open sea, and the land which they had seen, *now* retreats from their eyes. The billows dash against them, the ocean is upturned from its lowest depths, and the hold of the vessel ships the foaming seas. Skill is baffled by the winds; the steersman now foregoes[9] the use of the helm; but he, as well *as the others*, asks help in prayer. The exile of Phœnicia is tossed over the swelling billows; and with her garments held close she covers her tearful eyes. Then for the first time was Dido pronounced happy by her sister, and whoever *in death* has pressed with his body any spot of land. By a heavy blast, the vessel is dashed upon the Laurentine shore, and all having disembarked *in time*, it perishes, engulfed *in the ocean*.

Already had the pious Æneas been blessed with the throne and the daughter of Latinus, and had blended the two nations.[9*] While along the shore, which he had gained as a dowry, attended by Achates alone, with naked foot[10] he treads the

---

[8] *The craggy Crathis.*]—Ver. 581. This was a river of Magna Græcia, now Calabria. It waters Consentia, now Cozenza, the capital of the Bruttii, and falls into the Gulf of Tarentum. Its present name is 'Crate.' It rises in the crags of the Apennines, hence its epithet here.

[9] *The steersman now foregoes.*]—Ver. 593-4. Gower's translation is,

' Up start the waves, and upside down they wallow:
The leaking keel the foaming streams doth swallow;
Winds non-plus art.'

[9*] *The two nations.*]—Ver. 602. Namely, the Trojans and the Latins, the original inhabitants. How Æneas gained the hand of Lavinia, and conquered Turnus, is the subject of the latter books of the Æneid.

[10] *With naked foot.*]—Ver. 604. This would seem to imply that he was

solitary path, he beholds her as she wanders along, nor can he bring himself to believe that it is Anna. Why should she come to the Latian land? While Æneas *thus debates* within himself, "It is Anna!" cries Achates. At the name she raised her eyes. Whither is she to fly? What is she to do? What chasms of the earth is she to seek? Before her eyes is the fate of her wretched sister. The heroic son of Cytherea divines *her thoughts*, and thus he addresses her in her agitation; he weeps, however, Elissa, at the recollection of thy death. "Anna, by this land I swear, which, formerly thou wast wont to hear, was bestowed on me by a happier destiny, and by the Gods who have accompanied[11] *my wanderings*, lately settled in this their home, that many a time did they chide my loitering. *And* yet did I have no apprehension of her death; that fear was far *from my mind*. Ah, me! more determined was she than could have been possibly imagined. Tell not the tale; I beheld in that breast the wounds that ill beseemed it, when I dared to visit the abodes of Tartarus.[12] But thou, whether thy choice, or whether fortune has driven thee to my shores, do thou avail thyself of the resources of my kingdom; I am *still* mindful that I owe much to thee, and everything to Elissa; on thy own account, on the account of thy sister, shalt thou be dear to me." She believed him as he spoke, for now no other hope remained; and *then* she detailed her wanderings. And when she *now* enters his house, arrayed in her Tyrian attire, Æneas thus begins, *while* the rest are all silent; "Lavinia, my wife, there is a reason, prompted by duty, why I should introduce to thee this lady. When shipwrecked, I partook of her bounty. Sprung from Tyre, she possessed a realm on the Libyan shore; and I beg that as a dear sister thou wilt love her." Lavinia makes every engagement, and hides the causeless wound *of jealousy* in her secret soul, and, *though* indignant, disguises her feelings.

merely sauntering along, and that he was not proceeding on any business of emergency, which might require dispatch and the use of sandals.

[11] *The Gods who have accompanied.*]—Ver. 615. The Penates that he brought with him from Troy.

[12] *The abodes of Tartarus.*]—Ver. 620. His descent to Tartarus, or the infernal regions, and his meeting with the spirit of Dido, are narrated in the sixth Book of the Æneid. Cytherea was an appellation of Venus, the mother of Æneas, from the island of Cythera, on the coast of Laconia which was dedicated to her worship.

And *now*, when she sees many presents made openly before her eyes, and suspects that many, too, are given secretly—and yet it is not certain what she is to do; she hates her to a degree of frenzy, and plans her secret plots, and longs to die, having wreaked her vengeance. It was night; before the bed of her sister, Dido seemed to stand, bloodstained, with her hair dishevelled, and to say, "Fly! pause not! fly from this direful house." Just at the word, the breeze shakes the creaking doors, she leaps from *the bed*, and swiftly she flings herself from a low window upon the plain. Her very fear had made her bold, and clad with her robe untied,[13] she runs, whither by her terrors she is hurried, as the deer when frightened on hearing the wolves. The horned Numicius[14] is believed to have snatched her away in his amorous streams, and to have concealed her in his pools. In the meantime, the Sidonian[15] is sought along the fields with loud shouts; there appear her traces and the marks of her feet. *They had reached the banks of the river;* the impress of her feet was upon them; the conscious river stayed his noiseless stream. She herself appeared to say, "I am a Nymph of the gently flowing Numicius; concealed in the stream with constant tide, I am named Anna Perenna."[16] Forthwith, in their joy they feast in the fields they had wandered over, and they do honour to themselves[17] and to the day with a profusion of wine.

[13] *With her robe untied.*]—Ver. 645-6. Gower's translation is,

'And wing'd with terror in her tuck'd-up coat,
Runs like a roe that hears the wolf's hoarse note.'

[14] *The horned Numicius.*]—Ver. 647. This river was between Laurentum and Lavinium. 'Corniger,' 'horn bearing,' is an epithet frequently given to rivers by the poets, from the windings of their stream, and the roaring of their eddies.

[15] *The Sidonian.*]—Ver. 649. Sidon was a city of Phœnicia, in the neighbourhood of Tyre, and its rival in maritime pursuits. 'Sidonian' here means simply 'Phœnician.'

[16] *Anna Perenna.*]—Ver. 653-4. Gower's translation is,

'She seemed to speak: Numicius nymph, I live here;
Perennall Anne of this Perennall river.'

The poet seems here to imply, that she took her name from 'amnis perennis,' 'the ever-flowing river.'

[17] *Do honour to themselves.*]—Ver. 656. Some commentators would translate 'se' by 'Genium,' 'they honour the festival and their own personal Genius at the same time.' Perhaps it simply means, 'they honour

There are some who look upon this Goddess as the moon, because with her months she fills up the measure of the year; some think her Themis;[18] others the Inachian cow. Thou wilt find, Anna, some *who say* that thou art a Nymph, a daughter of Atlas, and *others who say* that thou didst give to Jove his first food. This story, too, which I am going to relate, has come to my ears, and it is not at variance with probability. The commonalty of olden time, as yet unprotected by their Tribunes, had fled, and taken refuge on the top of the sacred Mount.[19] And now, the provisions which they had brought with them had failed; their bread corn, too, suited to the use of man. There was one Anna, born at Bovillæ,[20] in the vicinity of the city, a poor old woman, but *a person* of great industry. She, having her grey locks bound with a light turban, used to make her country cakes with shaking hand;[21] and so, early in the morning, she used to distribute them smoking hot among the people; to them this supply was welcome. Peace being *now* established at home, they erected a statue to Perenna,[22] because in their state

the day, and pay a compliment to themselves for the pains they have taken in seeking her.'

[18] *Themis.*]—Ver. 658. Hyginus says, that she was the daughter of Æther or Jupiter, and Terra. She had a temple near the river Cephisus, in Bœotia, and she was the instructor of mankind in the principles of piety and justice.

[19] *The sacred Mount.*]—Ver. 664. This was the 'Mons sacer,' to which the commonalty at Rome, at the instigation of Sicinius retired, on their secession from the Patricians, A.U.C. 250. It was beyond the Anio, three miles distant from the city. On this occasion they enforced their right to elect magistrates of their own, whom they called 'Tribuni,' either because elected by the suffrages of the tribes, or selected from the military tribunes. It was on the occasion of this secession that Menenius Agrippa related the now well-known fable of the 'Belly and the Members.'

[20] *Bovillæ.*]—Ver. 667. This was a town of Latium, on the Appian way. It was so called from 'bos,' 'an ox,' which in early times had escaped from an altar on the Alban Mount, and was caught upon the site of the town. He speaks of it as being 'suburbana,' to distinguish it from another town of the same name in Campania, near Sinuessa.

[21] *With shaking hand.*]—Ver. 669-70. Gower translates these lines thus:—

' She in a hood her gray hairs having dress'd,
Made country cymnels with her palsie fist.'

In Shropshire they still make 'simnel cakes.'

[22] *Statue to Perenna.*]—Ver. 673. This account gives but a very silly

of destitution she had brought them relief. Now it remains for me to say, why at *this time* the girls sing indecent songs; for they assemble and repeat by rote indelicate abuse. She had been lately deified; *Mars* Gradivus comes to Anna, and taking her aside, he utters some such words as these:— " Thou art worshipped in my month; I have shared my period of the year with thee; on thy services depends a great hope of mine. I, a warrior myself, am inflamed, consuming with the love of Minerva, the warrior *Goddess;* and long have I cherished this passion. Provide that we, *who are* Deities, similar in our pursuits, should come together; this office befits thee, thou good-natured old lady." He had said; she trifles with the God with a false promise, and in the delays of doubt spins out his silly expectations. As he presses her more frequently, she says *to him*, " I have executed thy instructions, she yielded to my solicitations; but with difficulty has she given her hand." The lover is delighted, and makes ready the bridal chamber; thither is Anna conducted, veiling her face as a bride. Mars, just as he is about to snatch a kiss, suddenly catches sight of Anna's face; first, shame, then rage influences the baffled God. The newly-made Goddess laughs at the lover of his dear Minerva, and there was no circumstance more pleasing to Venus than this. It is by reason of this occurrence that old-fashioned jokes and indelicate sayings are sung, and delight is manifested that she *thus* imposed on the mighty God.

I was on the point of omitting to mention the daggers that pierced our prince, when from her unpolluted shrine thus Vesta spoke:—" Hesitate not to record it—he was my priest;[23] the sacrilegious hands assailed me with their weapons. I myself bore away the hero, and I left but a mere semblance

---

origin to the worship of the Goddess, as he makes her name to be derived from this old woman, either because her name was 'Anna,' or because she was an old woman, 'anus.' The name was most probably derived from 'annus,' 'a year,' for some reason now unknown, and had nothing to do with Dido's sister, whose story, very probably, the poet adapted to his ideas of etymology.

[23] *He was my priest.*]—Ver. 699. Being 'Pontifex Maximus,' it was incumbent on him to take charge of the sacrifices to Vesta. Julius Cæsar was assassinated on the ides of March, A.U.C. 709. The senate decreed that this day should in future be called 'Parricidium,' and that they should hold no sittings on it.

of him; that which fell by the steel was but the phantom of Cæsar. He, indeed, enthroned in heaven, has gone to tenant the halls of Jove, and owns a temple consecrated to him in the great Forum.[24] But every one of those, who, daring this crime, despite of the will of the Gods, assailed the life of a Pontiff, *now* lies *still* in the death so well merited.[25] Witness it, Philippi,[26] and ye, with whose scattered bones the ground is whitened. This was the labour, this was the task of duty, this was the first lesson of Cæsar, in just warfare to avenge his father."

When the next morning shall have refreshed the tender herbage, the Scorpion[27] will be visible in his fore part *only*.

The third day after the Ides is a day universally observed in honour of Bacchus. Bacchus, while I sing thy festival, favour the poet. I will not tell of Semele; to whom had not Jove brought with him his thunderbolts, unarmed he was reckoned *by her* a paltry object; nor will I tell now how the burden of thy mother was matured in thy father's body, in order that thou, a babe, mightst be born in due time. 'Twere tedious to recount the Sithonian[28] and the Scythian triumphs, and the conquests of thy nations, *thou* Indian laden with frankincense. Thou also, unhappy prey of thy Theban mother,[29] shalt remain

[24] *The great Forum.*]—Ver. 704. This was the chief 'Forum' in the city. It was called either 'the Roman,' 'great,' or 'old Forum.' Three years after his death a temple was built here, and consecrated to Cæsar.

[25] *Death so well merited.*]—Ver. 707. History tells us that every person who took any part in the assassination of Julius Cæsar perished within three years after his death.

[26] *Philippi.*]—Ver. 707. This was a city of Macedonia, near the Thracian territory, and close to the Ægean sea. It was formerly called Datos, but king Philip fortifying it, it received its new name from him. Here Brutus and Cassius were defeated by Augustus and Antony, on which Cassius was, at his own request, killed by one of his freedmen, and Brutus fell by his own hand.

[27] *The Scorpion.*]—Ver. 712. On the 17th of the calends of April is the cosmical rising of the middle of the Scorpion. Hyginus tells us that Orion, boasting of his skill as a hunter, Tellus sent a scorpion which killed him by its sting. Jupiter raised the Scorpion among the stars as a reward for the lesson which it had taught to human vanity. At the request of Diana, a like honour was paid to Orion, on the condition that when the Scorpion rose, Orion, as a mark of his fear, should set.

[28] *The Sithonians.*]—Ver. 719. These were a people of Thrace, who, with the Scythians, were subdued by Bacchus.

[29] *Thy Theban mother.*]—Ver. 721. Agave tore in pieces Pentheus,

unmentioned; thou, too, Lycurgus, impelled by madness to assail thy own knee. Behold! 'twould please me much to tell of the Fishes,[30] works of sudden transformation, and the Etrurian miracles; but it is not the province of this *my* poem. The province of this *my* song is *now* to relate the reasons why the mean old woman invites the citizens to her cakes.[31] Before thy birth, O Bacchus, the altars were without sacrifice, and the grass was found on the cold hearths. They tell how, having subdued the Ganges and all the East, thou didst set apart the first fruits for the mighty Jove. Thou wast the first to make offering of cinnamon and frankincense, produce of thy capture, and the roasted entrails of the ox, emblem of thy triumph. From the name of their institutor, the initial offerings take their name[32] of "Libamina" and of "Liba," because from them a part is offered up on the holy hearths. Cakes are offered to the God because he takes delight in sweets; they say that honey, too, was discovered by Bacchus. He was journeying from the sandy Hebrus,[33] attended by the Satyrs (my tale contains no unpleasing humour); and they had now reached Rhodope and the flowery Pangæum. The cymbal-bearing hands of his attendants join in united clash. Behold, winged insects, *till then* unknown, flock together at the tink-

king of Thebes, her son by Echion, because he forbade the celebration of the orgies of Bacchus. Lycurgus, king of Thrace, denied the divinity of Bacchus, and being punished with insanity, killed his wife and child, and cut off his own legs, mistaking them for vine branches. He was murdered by his own subjects, who were forbidden by an oracle to taste wine till he had been despatched. Another account is, that he was slain by panthers sacred to Bacchus.

[30] *To tell of the Fishes.*]—Ver. 723. This story is, that some sailors, finding Bacchus asleep with intoxication, carried him off to sell him as a slave. When sober, he requested them to steer towards the isle of Naxos; which they failing to do, he turned them into dolphins.

[31] *To her cakes.*]—Ver. 726. Varro says that 'the feast of the Liberalia was so called because on that day, throughout the whole city, the priestesses of Bacchus, old women crowned with ivy, sit with their cakes and chafing-dishes, and perform sacrifice for such as will pay them.'

[32] *Take their name.*]—Ver. 733. It is much more likely, as we have before observed, that Bacchus obtained his name of 'Liber,' from 'libo,' in Greek λείβω, 'to pour out,' which is the root of the word 'libamen,' signifying 'that which is poured out in sacrifice.' Ovid is frequently more ingenious than correct in his etymology.

[33] *Hebrus.*]—Ver. 737. This was a river of Thrace, falling into the Ægean sea. Pangæum and Rhodope were mountains of that country.

ling, and on whichever side the brass sends forth its sounds the bees follow. Bacchus collects them as they wander, and shuts them in a hollow tree; and he enjoys the reward of the discovery of honey. Soon as the Satyrs, and *Silenus*, the bald-headed old man, tasted its flavour, they were seeking through the whole grove for the yellow honeycombs. The old man hears the buzzing of a swarm in a decayed elm; he spies, too, the combs, but declares that he has made no such discovery.[34] And as he is lazily lolling on the back of his bending ass, he guides him close to the elm and its hollow bark; he himself, then, stands up above *his ass*, resting on the branchy trunk, and now is *engaged in* greedily seeking the honey hoarded in the trunk. Thousands of hornets fly together, and fix deep their stings in his bare pate, and mark the surface[35] of his countenance. He tumbles headlong, and is struck by the hoof of the ass;[36] and *then* he calls aloud on his companions, and entreats assistance. The Satyrs run to the spot, and laugh at the swollen face of their parent; he limps about from the blow on his knee. The God himself laughs too, and teaches him how to apply mud *to the stings;* he follows his advice, and with mud bedaubs his face. The father enjoys the honey, and with justice do we offer to its discoverer the white honey poured over the warm cake. Why a woman presides over them is not a matter of difficult discovery. It is he who with his wreathed spear arouses the choirs of the women. Why it is an old woman that does this? you ask. It is this period of life which is more addicted to wine, and is fond of the gifts of the loaded vine. *You ask* why she is wreathed with the ivy? The ivy is most

[34] *Declares that he has made no such discovery.*]—Ver. 748. Literally, 'he dissembles,' that is to say, he pretends, either by his words or by his conduct, that he has not found any honey. 'Simulo' is 'to pretend that that is, which is not;' 'dissimulo' is 'to pretend that that is not, which is.' It was not the case that he had made no discovery, but he pretended that such was the fact.

[35] *The surface.*]—Ver. 754. Perhaps 'summa' may here be translated 'the projecting parts' of his countenance, as his nose and long ears.

[36] *The hoof of the ass.*]—Ver. 755—6. Gower's translation is—

'Down tumbles he; his asse about him laid
His heels; there lies he yawling out for aid.
The Satyrs flock and laugh, their sire to see
With face swollen up. He halts on's asse-kick'd knee.'

pleasing to Bacchus, and why this is the case, it will take no length of time to tell. The Nymphs of Nysa,[37] when his stepmother sought the boy, covered his newly-made cradle with this leaf. It remains for me to discover why the gown of freedom[38] is given to the youths upon thy day, fair Bacchus; whether it is that thou thyself always seemest to be *both* a boy and a young man, and thy age is midway between the two; or that because thou art a father, fathers commit their sons, their pledges, to thy care and providence; or that because thou art "Liber," the "vestis libera" [*the dress of freedom*] is assumed under thy patronage, and the course of a life of more liberty *is commenced;* or *perhaps* it is, because, when the ancients cultivated the fields with more attention, and the senator on the farm of his forefathers followed up the business *of agriculture*, and the consul received the fasces *coming* from the crooked plough, and it was no imputation on one's character to have hard-skinned hands, then the rustic population used to come to the games into the city; but that compliment was paid to the Gods, and not to their own private inclination. The discoverer of the grape used to hold the games on his own holiday, which now he holds in common with the torch-bearing Goddess.[39] That therefore the multitude might do

---

[37] *The nymphs of Nysa.*]—Ver. 769. There was a Nysa in Thrace, Bœotia, India, and Arabia. The poet probably means the last, where Bacchus was entrusted to the nymphs, that he might be concealed from the search of Juno, who was wishful, by his death, to avenge herself for the infidelity of Jupiter. Gower thus translates lines 765-6—

'But why old wives? That age most bouzie proves,
And most of all the pleasing vine-juyce loves.'

[38] *The gown of freedom.*]—Ver. 771. The 'toga libera' was one of the titles of the 'toga virilis,' or 'robe of manhood,' which was assumed on the 'Liberalia,' or feast of Bacchus, by the young men who had then arrived at the age of seventeen years, and who then laid aside the 'toga prætexta.' The 'toga' was changed with solemnity, in presence of the Lares, and they then went to the Capitol or some other temple to pray to the gods. It was called 'libera,' because when it was assumed, they were free from the restraint of masters. The similarity between 'liber,' as an epithet of Bacchus, and 'liber,' 'free,' as the poet suggests for his third reason, was perhaps the ground on which this day was chosen for the solemnity.

[39] *The torch-bearing Goddess.*]—Ver. 786. Ceres, who is thus represented in her statues. She carried a torch while seeking her daughter, Proserpine, when she had been carried off by Pluto.

honour to the youth commencing man, the day seemed not unsuitable for conferring the gown *of freedom*. Hither, O Father, mayst thou turn thy head and thy horns with mild intent, and grant to my powers a sail *swelling with the* prosperous *gale*. On this day and the day before, if I remember aright, is the procession to the Argei.[40] What they are, their own history[41] will tell.

The star of the Kite[42] slopes downwards towards the Bear, the daughter of Lycaon; this becomes visible on this night. If you would wish to know what it was that gave heaven to this bird; Saturn had been expelled from his realm by Jove; in his wrath he excites the powerful Titans to arms, and demands that assistance which was due to him from the Fates. There was a bull, a strange monster, born of his mother Earth, a serpent in his hinder parts. Him, by the advice of the three Fates, the fierce Styx had with triple wall shut in the gloomy groves. Whoever should give the entrails of the bull to be consumed by the flames, it was fated that he should be enabled to conquer the eternal Gods. With axe made of adamant, Briareus slays him, and is *now* just on the very point of giving the entrails to the flames. Jupiter commands the birds to snatch them away; the kite brings them to him, and by its services finds its way to the stars.

One day intervenes, and the festival of Minerva takes place, which has its name from the union of five days.[43] The first day is free from blood, and it is not allowable then to contend with the steel; the reason is, that on this day Minerva was

---

[40] *The Argei.*]—Ver. 791. These were certain places in Rome, supposed to have been so called from the burial there of certain Argives who had come over with Hercules. According to Livy, these spots were consecrated by Numa. Some writers think that the Argei was the temple of Castor and Pollux, Spartan divinities.

[41] *Their own history.*]—Ver. 791. Most probably this alludes to some topographical history of the places then extant, and well known to every one at that day.

[42] *The Kite.*]—Ver. 794. On the 16th of the calends of April the Kite rises achronycally. It is not known whence Ovid borrowed this story of the Kite. This constellation, according to Krebs, is not alluded to by any Greek writer on astronomy before the time of Ovid.

[43] *Union of five days.*]—Ver. 810. This was the Quinquatrus, Quinquatres, or Quinquatria, from 'quinque,' 'five,' a festival of Minerva, commencing on the 14th of the calends of April.

born. The next[44] and the three succeeding are celebrated on the sand strewed *in the Amphitheatre; then* the warlike Goddess is delighted with the drawn swords. ⌡ Now, ye youths and tender damsels, celebrate Pallas; he who pays homage to Pallas will be learned. Girls, when you shall have propitiated Pallas, then comb your wool; learn, *by winding,* to take the load off the distaff, when now it is full. She teaches *us* also with shuttle to cross the standing warps, and with the sley she closes the open work. Worship her, thou, whose art it is to remove the stains from the damaged garments; worship her, thou, who preparest the *dyeing* vessels for the fleeces. Nor will any one be able to make neatly the sandals for the foot if Pallas is unpropitious, even though he were more skilful than Tychius;[45] and even if, compared with ancient Epeus, he should excel him in handicraft; *yet* if Pallas is displeased, he will be but a bungler. You, too, who drive away disease by Apollo's art, offer from your fees a few gifts to the Goddess. And do not you, teachers, a set generally robbed of your pay,[46] despise her; she will bring you new pupils: and thou who guidest the graving tool,[47] and thou who dost enamel the slab

[44] *The next.*]—Ver. 813. On the second day of the festival commenced the gladiatorial combats in the amphitheatre, in honour of the goddess. The place where they fought, was called the 'arena,' it being sprinkled with sand or sawdust, to absorb the blood and to prevent slipping. By some the Quinquatria are supposed to have been identical with the Panathenæa, a festival instituted at Athens by Orpheus or Erectheus in honour of Minerva. Similar license is said to have been allowed to the slaves on the Quinquatria to that which prevailed on the Saturnalia, and friends then interchanged presents.

[45] *Tychius.*]—Ver. 824. He was a celebrated artificer of Bœotia, and, according to Homer, the maker of the shield of Ajax; though, as Mr. Stanford remarks, Homer's eulogy of him is only in the character of a cobbler. Epeus was the builder of the wooden horse by means of which Troy was taken.

[46] *Robbed of your pay.*]—Ver. 829. This line has occasioned much perplexity; but it seems to imply pretty clearly that the schoolmaster was an ill-paid drudge, and that he was obliged to look rather to numbers, for a living, than to the individual honesty of his employers. Possibly, like the physicians and barristers of the present day, he was not able to sue for his fees at law; and having to trust solely to the honour of his employers, he not unfrequently, or indeed, very frequently, found that he had built his expectations on the sand. His fee was called the 'Minerval,' and an image of the goddess Minerva stood over the school door.

[47] *The graving-tool.*]—Ver. 831. 'Cœlum.' This was the tool used in carving or graving—a 'burin,' or 'chisel.'

with colours, thou, too, who fashionest the soft stones with skilful hand. She is the Goddess of a thousand crafts; doubtless she is the Goddess of song. If I am deserving, may she be present, a friend to my pursuits.

Where the Cælian Hill slopes from its elevation to the plains, here, where the way is not quite level, but nearly so, you may see a small temple of Minerva "Capta," which the Goddess began to possess on her natal day. The cause of the name is doubtful. We entitle a skilful genius "Capitale,"[48] [shrewd]; she is a Goddess full of genius. Or is it because she is said, without a mother, to have leaped forth with her shield from the crown of her father's head? Or is it because she came to us a captive when Falisci was subdued? And this very fact the ancient records tell. Or is it because she has a law, that thieves who are detected in that place, should suffer capital punishment? From whatever cause thou derivest thy titles, O Pallas, ever do thou hold thy Ægis[49] before our chiefs. The last day of the five, commands us to purify the sounding trumpets,[50] and to sacrifice to the bold Goddess. Now, you can say, having raised your eyes to the sun, "He yesterday weighed down the fleece of the sheep of Phrixus."[51]

By the deceit of the accursed step-mother, the seed-corn

---

[48] *Capitale.*]—Ver. 838-9. We have a vulgar expression somewhat similar to this at the present day. If a person is clever and shrewd, it is common to say of him that 'he has a good head-piece.' So 'capitalis,' from 'caput,' the 'head,' will mean 'with a head, or 'relating to the head.' Gower translates this and the following lines thus—

'The reason's doubtfull: She's the minerall
Of wit, which quick is called capitall.
Or else, because her father's aching head
She, arm'd with shield, sans help of wife, did shed.'

[49] *Ægis.*]—Ver. 848. This was the shield of Minerva, and it was so called because it was covered with a goat skin, αἰγίς, that of the goat Amalthea, that suckled Jupiter. In it too was set the head of the Gorgon Medusa, which turned the beholder into stone.

[50] *The sounding trumpets.*]—Ver. 849. This was the feast of the 'Tubilustrium,' or 'purification of trumpets,' on the 10th of the calends of April. Varro and Festus inform us that the trumpets used in the sacred rites were purified in the 'Atrium Sutorium,' or 'Shoemakers' Hall.' Its locality is not known.

[51] *Phrixus.*]—Ver. 852. The story of Ino, and her device to destroy her step-children, has been in part related in a note to the second Book. The story is here completed. It is again referred to by the Poet.

being parched, the blade had not raised the ear, as it is wont to do. A person is sent to the *oracular*[52] tripod, that he may bring back, by an infallible answer, what remedy the Delphic God gives out for the unproductive soil. He, corrupted too, as well as the seed, brings word, that, by the oracle, the death of Helle and of the youthful Phrixus was required. The citizens, the *unfavourable* season, and Ino, drove the king, while still resisting, to submit to the direful command. And *now*, his sister and Phrixus having their temples wreathed with boughs, stand together before the altar, and bewail their common destiny. Their mother, as by chance she is floating[53] in the air, sees them, and, in dismay, strikes her naked breast with her hand; and then, with clouds in her train, she leaps down into the city of those descended from the dragon,[54] and snatches away her children; and that they may take flight, a ram, most resplendent with gold, is given them. He bears the two through the long channel *of the Hellespont*. The damsel is said to have been holding his horn with a feeble left hand, when from herself she imparts a name[55] to that *tract of* water. Her brother almost perishes together with her, while he is endeavouring to assist her as she falls, and extends afar his outstretched hands. He weeps as though the partner of the twofold danger were lost, not knowing that *now* she was the bride of the azure Deity. Having arrived at the shore, the ram is made a Constellation; but his golden fleece reaches the Colchian palace.[56]

[52] *The oracular tripod.*]—Ver. 855. This was a seat or table with three legs, on which the priestess sat, while delivering the oracles of Apollo in the Delphian temple. Some suppose that it was pierced, and that through it the priestess inhaled certain mephitic fumes, which were productive of a kind of madness or frenzy, which was mistaken for prophetic inspiration.

[53] *She is floating.*]—Ver. 863. 'Pependerat.' 'Floating,' or 'hovering,' is an apt term for 'Nephele,' their mother, who had been changed into a cloud, νεφέλη.

[54] *Descended from the dragon.*]—Ver. 865. Thebes was founded by Cadmus, who killed a dragon, which had slain his companions, and then sowing the teeth, a crop of armed men was raised; these killing each other till their number was reduced to five, with their assistance he built the city, whence the present epithet.

[55] *Imparted a name.*]—Ver. 870. That of Hellespont, 'the sea of Helle.'

[56] *The Colchian palace.*]—Ver. 876. Phrixus bringing the fleece to

When the approaching dawn shall have sent before it three light bearing *days*, you shall have the hours of day equal[57] with those of night. When from this *period* the shepherd shall have four times penned his well-fed kids, four times the grass been white with dew fresh fallen, Janus will require to be adored, and with him mild Concord, and the Health of Rome,[58] and the altar of Peace.

The Moon governs the months; the worship of the Moon on the Aventine Hill[59] terminates the period of this month.

Colchis, Æetes, the king, gave him his daughter, Chalciope, in marriage, and then, to secure possession of the fleece, he put Phryxus to death. To recover it, the Argonautic expedition, under Jason, was formed.

[57] *Hours of day equal.*]—Ver. 878. The vernal equinox on the 8th of the calends of April, or the 25th of March.

[58] *Health of Rome.*]—Ver. 882. 'Salus,' 'Health,' was the daughter of Æsculapius: her temple was built on the Quirinal hill by C. Junius Bubulcus.

[59] *The Aventine hill.*]—Ver. 884. Servius Tullius built a temple in honour of Diana on the Aventine hill.

BOOK THE FOURTH.

CONTENTS.

The invocation of Venus, Ver. 1—18. The noble origin of Germanicus, and his descent from Venus through Æneas; with the reason why April was formerly the second month, 19—60. The different opinions on the origin of the name: the power of Venus, 61—132. The festival of Venus and Fortuna Virilis; Venus Verticordia, 133—162. The setting of the Scorpion, 163-4. The setting of the Pleiades, and their number, 165—178. The Megalesia: the mythological history of the Mother of the Gods, and her arrival at Rome from Phrygia, 179—372. The dedication of the temple to Fortuna Publica: the victory of Cæsar over Juba: the setting of Libra and Orion: the rainy season, 373—388. The games of Ceres, and her praises: the rape of Proserpine, 389—620. The dedication of the temple to Jupiter Victor, and to Liberty, 621—624. The hailstorms, and the victory of Cæsar at Mutina, 625—628. The festival of the Fordicidia, or sacrifice of the pregnant cow: the institution of that ceremonial by Numa, 629—672. Augustus proclaimed Imperator, 673—676. The setting of the Hyades, 677-8. The setting fire to the foxes, in the Circensian games, 679—712. The passing of the Lion from the constellation of the Ram to the Bull, 713—720. The Palilia, or festival of Pales, 721—806. The foundation of the city and the death of Remus, 807—862. The Vinalia: the alliance of Mezentius with Turnus, 863—900. The middle of Spring: the setting of the Ram; the showery season; and the rising of the Dog-star, 901—904. The Robigalia, 905—942. The Floralia; and the reception of Vesta into the Palatium, 943—954.

"Favour *the poet*,"[1] I said, "thou genial mother of the twin loves;"[2] towards the poet, she turned her countenance.

---

[1] *Favour the poet.*]—Ver. 1-2. Gower's whimsical translation is,

> '"Alme, queen of payring love, assist," I cried:
> To me she streight her chearful eye applied.'

[2] *Of the twin loves.*]—Ver. 1. Cicero mentions three Loves or Cupids, (On the Nature of the Gods, Book iii. c. 23,) the first, the son of Diana and Mercury; the second, of Venus and Mercury; and the third, Anteros. Other writers mention two only—the celestial, the son of Jupiter and Venus; and the terrestrial, the son of Nox and Erebus. These are sometimes distingushed as the honourable and the sensual Loves.

"What wilt thou of me?" she said. "Surely thou wast *but just now* in the habit of singing of mightier subjects;[3] hast thou still in thy tender bosom the old wound?[4] *By this time,* Goddess, *I replied,* thou hast heard enough of my wound." She smiled, and immediately in that direction the sky was without a cloud. "Wounded or whole, have I ever been guilty of deserting thy standards?[5] Thou wast ever the *object* of my purpose, *the cause* of my toil. Free from all blame, in my early years, I have sported in scenes that became my age; now a more extensive range[6] is trodden by my steeds. I sing of the festivals with their reasons, as they are extracted from the ancient annals, and of the Constellations as they sink beneath the earth and rise again. I have now arrived at the fourth month, in which *of all* thou art the most extolled. Thou knowest, Venus, that both the poet and the month are devoted to thee." Influenced *by my address,* she lightly touched my temples with a sprig of Cytheræan myrtle,[7] and said, "Accomplish the work which thou hast undertaken." I was sensible of *her power,* and suddenly the *peculiar* reasons for the days *of remark* became evident; Let my bark speed onward while *thus* it may, and while the *favouring* breezes blow. Yet, if any part of my Calendar ought to affect thee, it is in April thou findest that by which thy attention ought to be detained. This month, through an

---

[3] *Mightier subjects.*]—Ver. 3. Namely, the preceding books of the 'Fasti,' which treat of more serious subjects than love, the theme of many of his former poems.

[4] *The old wound.*]—Ver. 4. Alluding to the 'Amores,' one of his previous compositions, in which he had complained of the pains and disappointments attendant on love.

[5] *Deserting thy standards.*]—Ver. 7. This figure is taken from the rigid rules of military discipline among the Romans. The poets were fond of comparing the pains of the lover to the toils of the soldier in active service. Gower thus translates this and the following line—

'Or sound or sore, I ne'er forsook thy tent;
Thou art my daily task, my ornament.'

[6] *A more extensive range.*]—Ver. 10. 'Area.' This figure is derived from the games in the Circus.

[7] *Cytheræan myrtle.*]—Ver. 15. The myrtle was the favourite plant of Venus. Servius (on the Georgics of Virgil, Book ii. l. 64) says, that Venus chose this plant because it flourished near the sea, whence she sprung; and because it was esteemed for its medicinal qualities in female diseases.

illustrious line, descends to thee, and becomes peculiarly thine by the nobility, which is thy lot by adoption. This did our father, offspring of Ilia, perceive, when he planned out the lengthy year, and himself celebrated his ancestors. And as, to fierce Mars he gave the first place in the succession, because he had been the immediate cause of his being; so did he desire that Venus,[8] found in the line of his extraction through many generations, should have the place of the second month. And while seeking the origin of his race, and the generations as they were traced upwards, he went even as far back as to the Gods themselves in the line of his kindred. Could he be ignorant, forsooth, that Dardanus[9] was born of Electra, the daughter of Atlas? And that Electra shared the bed of Jove? His son was Ericthonius; from him Tros sprung: he was the father of Assaracus, Assaracus of Capys. This last begot Anchises, with whom, Venus did not disdain to hold the name of parent in common. Hence was born Æneas; his piety well proved, bore the sacred relics and his father sitting on his shoulders, a second pious charge, through the flames *of Troy*. At length we have arrived at the blessed name of Iülus,[10] from which point the Julian house is connected with its Trojan ancestors.[11] His son was Postumus,[12] who, because he was born in the deep

[8] *Venus.*]—Ver. 27—30. Gower thus renders these lines—

'So Venus many ranks before his mother,
He mistress made of this next following other;
And turning o'er Time's rolls to find the ground
Of his descent, the gods his parents found.'

[9] *Dardanus.*]—Ver. 31. Dardanus was the son of Jupiter and Electra, the daughter of Atlas. He was the founder of Troy, and by his wife Astioche, or Batis, he became the father of Ericthonius. The poet proceeds to recount the ancestry of Æneas from Dardanus, and then the descent of the Alban kings from Æneas down to Romulus.

[10] *Blessed name of Iülus.*]—Ver. 39. Iülus was one of the names of Ascanius, the son of Æneas. He calls that name 'felix,' or 'blessed,' as it was (in a more modern form) the family name of the Julii, of which house Julius Cæsar was by birth a member; and Augustus, Tiberius, and Germanicus became so by adoption.

[11] *Trojan ancestors.*]—Ver. 40. 'Teucros.' This name seems to have been applied to the Trojans almost exclusively by the Latin poets. Homer and the older Greek writers never use it: the later ones but very rarely.

[12] *His son was Postumus.*]—Ver. 41. Or the passage will admit of this translation—'Postumus succeeded him;' for Virgil says that Postumus was the son of Æneas; and Dionysius tells us, that on the death of Æneas,

sylvan shades, was called Silvius, among the Latian nation. And he, Latinus, is thy sire;[13] Alba succeeds Latinus, Epytus succeeds to thy dignity, O Alba. He gave to Capys the revived name of Troy;[14] he, too, became thy grandsire, O Calpetus. And while, in succession to him, Tiberinus was occupying the throne of his father, he is said to have been drowned in the eddy of the Etrurian stream. And yet he had lived *to see* Agrippa, his son, and Remulus,[15] his grandson.

Lavinia, being pregnant, fled into the woods through fear of Iülus, and there produced Postumus, who derived one of his names from his posthumous birth, and his other name (Sylvius) from his birth in the woods.

[13] *Latinus is thy sire.*]—Ver. 43. According to Virgil and other writers, Latinus was the son of Æneas Sylvius, and grandson of Sylvius Posthumus; hence, some writers have concluded that a couplet has been lost here. Livy, Dionysius, and Eusebius have also given lists of the Alban kings, which differ but little from that here given by Ovid. The difference, such as it is, will be seen from a comparison of the following lists.

LIVY.	DIONYSIUS.	EUSEBIUS.	OVID.
Æneas.	Æneas.	Æneas.	Æneas.
Ascanius.	Ascanius.	Ascanius.	Ascanius.
Sylvius.	Sylvius.	Sylvius.	Sylvius.
Æneas.	Æneas Sylvius.	Æneas.	
Latinus.	Latinus Sylvius.	Latinus.	Latinus.
Alba.	Albas Sylvius.	Alba.	Alba.
Atis.	Capetus Sylvius.	Sylvius Athis.	Epitus.
Capys.	Capys Sylvius.	Capys.	Capys.
Capetus.	Calpetus Sylvius.	Calpetus.	Calpetus.
Tiberinus.	Tiberinus Sylvius.	Tiberinus.	Tiberinus.
Agrippa.	Agrippas Sylvius.	Agrippa.	Remulus.
Romulus.	Allades Sylvius.	Remulus.	Agrippa.
Aventinus.	Aventinus Sylvius.	Aventinus.	Aventinus.
Proca.	Procas Sylvius.	Procas.	Proca.
Amulius.	Amulius Sylvius.	Amulius.	Numitor.

Ovid gives a list of the Alban kings in the fourteenth Book of the Metamorphoses, l. 609, where he calls Calpetus, Capetus, and Agrippa by the name of Agrota. This line of the Alban kings is universally considered by historians as a fiction of the later times of the Roman republic. See Niebuhr's Roman History, i. 202.

[14] *Revived name of Troy.*]—Ver. 45. That is, he restored the use of a name or epithet that had been in use at Troy. Capys was the name of the father of Anchises, and of one of the companions of Æneas. Æneid, Book i. l. 183.

[15] *Remulus.*]—Ver. 50. He is called by Livy 'Romulus.' Either name is a diminutive for 'Remus,' or 'Romus.' Ovid, in his Metamorphoses, Book xiv. l. 616, represents him as incurring the vengeance of heaven by imitating lightning, and affecting to be a divinity.

They say that against Remulus the thunderbolts were hurled. After these came Aventinus, from whom the place and the hill, too, derived its name. After him the sovereignty passed to Procas; him Numitor followed, the brother of the cruel Amulius; Ilia and Lausus[16] were the children of Numitor. Lausus falls by his uncle's sword; Ilia is beloved by Mars, and produces thee, Quirinus, with Remus, thy twin-brother. He ever boasted that his lineage was from Mars and Venus, and *well* did he entitle himself to gain credit for the assertion. And, that generations to come might not be ignorant of this, to the Gods of his race he consecrated the months in succession. But I conjecture that the month of Venus received its name '*Aprilis*' from the Greek language;[17] the Goddess obtained her name, '*Aphrodite*,' from the foam of the sea. But you must not wonder that any thing is called by a name from the Grecian tongue; for the Italian land was the Greater Græcia.[18] Evander arrived *there* with a fleet, manned by his fellow countrymen; Alcides, *too*, came *thither;* each of them of Grecian extraction. The Club-bearer, *as* a stranger fed his herd on the pasturage of Aventine, and Albula[19] afforded drink

---

[16] *Lausus.*]—Ver. 54. The brother of Ilia is called Ægestus by Dionysius, and by Plutarch, Ainitus. He was treacherously slain by his uncle while hunting. Plutarch says that Numitor did reign for some time before he was deposed by Amulius.

[17] *From the Greek language.*]—Ver. 61. According to Macrobius, Romulus called the month Aprilis by that name in honour of Venus, who was called by the Greeks 'Aphrodite,' from ἀφρος, 'the foam of the sea.' Ovid prefers this derivation (in flattery to the Julian house) to that from 'aperio,' 'to open,' which has by far the greater probability of being the correct etymology. Scaliger would derive the name of this month from 'aper,' 'a boar,' because that animal was a customary sacrifice at this season.

[18] *The Greater Græcia.*]—Ver. 64. Commentators have been much at a loss to tell why Italy received this name from the Græcian settlers, if it is intended to apply to the whole of Italy, and not the southern part, which in later times was known as Magna Græcia. Mr. Thynne appears to suggest the true reason for the name; because, in fact, the Greeks found Italy a much more spacious country than the limited region which they had left.

[19] *Albula.*]—Ver. 68. This was the early name of the river Tiber. Gower thus renders this and the following line—

> 'That clubbed pilgrime did his club display
> On Aventine, and drank of Albula.'

to a God so mighty. The chief, too, from Neritos[20] *came thither;* the Lestrygonians attest it,[21] and that shore which still bears the name of Circe.[22] And now were the walls of Telegonus[23] erected, and the city of the watery Tibur,[24] which Grecian hands had built. Halesus,[25] too, had arrived, driven away by the death of the son of Atreus, from whom the Faliscan land believes that it received its name.[26] Add Antenor[27] as well, the adviser of peace at Troy, and, Apulian Daunus, thy son-in-law, the grandson of Œneus.[27*] At a later pe-

[20] *Neritos.*]—Ver. 69. Servius tells us that this was a mountain of Ithaca. Virgil (Æneid, Book iii. 1. 270) and Pomponius Mela, the geographer, seem to consider it as a distinct island in the vicinity of Ithaca.

[21] *Attest it.*]—Ver. 69. Attest the arrival of Ulysses in Italy; for, being a race of cannibals, they caught and devoured some of his companions, as we learn in the tenth Book of the Odyssey. They lived in the neighbourhood of Formiæ, in Campania.

[22] *Name of Circe.*]—Ver. 70. This was the promontory of Circæum, in Latium, supposed once to have formed the island of 'Ææa.' Circe inhabited it. She was the daughter of Helius, or the sun, and Persa, and by her magic art changed all intruders upon her island into swine. By the aid of Mercury, Ulysses escaped the exercise of her terrific power upon himself, and obtained the restoration of his companions, who had been transformed by her, to their original form.

[23] *Walls of Telegonus.*]—Ver. 71. Telegonus was the son of Ulysses and Circe. He went to Ithaca to seek his father, and accidentally killed him. On his return to Italy, he founded Tusculum, in Latium, north of Alba Longa.

[24] *Watery Tibur.*]—Ver. 71. This was a town of Latium, on the river Anio, whence its epithet here, 'udi,' 'watery.' It was founded by Tiburnus, Catillus, and Coras, three brothers, who led thither a colony from Argos. Its site is now occupied by the town of Tivoli.

[25] *Halesus.*]—Ver. 73. He is supposed to have been a son of Agamemnon, who conspired with Clytemnestra to slay his father, after whose murder he fled to Italy, where he founded the town of Falisci, and introduced the worship of Juno.

[26] *Received its name.*]—Ver. 74. F and H were sounded by the ancient Digamma, and were therefore confused in sound. According to Cicero and Quintilian, S was changed into R in many instances.

[27] *Antenor.*]—Ver. 75. Antenor, according to Homer, always advocated peaceful measures in the Trojan councils. The Greeks are said to have permitted him to leave Troy with a colony of the Heneti from Asia Minor, on which he came into Italy, and founded Patavium, now Padua. By the Heneti, or Veneti, the city of Venice is supposed to have been founded.

[27*] *Grandson of Œneus.*]—Ver. 75. Diomedes, the grandson of Œneus, king of Ætolia, on his return from Troy, being driven from

riod,[28] and after Antenor, did Æneas bring his Gods from the flames of Troy to our regions. Solymus from Phrygian Ida was one of his companions, from whom the city of Sulmo derives its name. Cold Sulmo,[29] Germanicus, my native place! Ah! wretched me! How distant is it from the Scythian soil! Shall I then, so far?[30]—but suppress thy complaints, my Muse; sacred subjects must not be sung to a desponding lyre. To what point will not envy proceed? There are some, O Venus,[31] who would rob thee of the honour of a month, and who begrudge it thee. For, because the spring at that time is opening every thing, and the contracted ruggedness of the frost is yielding, and the prolific earth is teeming, they say that April is so called from the aperient season; that month, which Venus, having laid her hand upon it, claims as her own. She

his own country by the infidelity and intrigues of his wife, came to Apulia, married the daughter of Daunus, the king, and founded Argyripa, or Argi, in that country.

[28] *At a later period.*]—Ver. 77. Æneas did not arrive in Italy till after the other settlers that have been mentioned. According to Virgil, his wanderings lasted seven years.

[29] *Cold Sulmo.*]—Ver. 81. Solymus was the reputed founder of Sulmo, the birth-place of Ovid, which was a small town of the Peligni, between Aquila and Venafrum. The country of the Peligni was remarkable for its coldness, as is attested by Horace, Odes, Book iii. Ode 19, l. 28. There is something very affecting in the repetition by the exiled poet of the name of his dear Sulmo, his reminding Germanicus that it was his native place, and his allusion to the immense distance that then separated him from it.

[30] *Shall I then, so far?*]—Ver. 83. The poet suddenly checks himself in his complaints. This is a very graceful instance of the figure Aposiopesis; he appears as if about to say, 'Shall I, then, be allowed, so far from my native Sulmo, to draw my last breath?" or to that effect.

[31] *O Venus.*]—Ver. 86. The expressions here used are obviously employed to flatter the ambition of the Julian family to be regarded as the descendants of Venus. Macrobius tells us that both Aphrodite and Venus were names unknown to Rome under the kings; and it is very probable that the name of Venus was introduced at a much later period. Some philologists have supposed her to have been a Syrian goddess, worshipped under the name of Benoth as well as Astarté; and in the books of the Old Testament we more than once find mention made of a place called Succoth Benoth, which is supposed to mean 'the tents of Venus,' as being, perhaps, the especial seat of her worship. If this conjecture is well grounded, the probability is that the Romans received the name of Venus either through their intercourse with Carthage, which was a Phœnician colony, or that it arrived at Rome by the way of Greece and Sicily.

indeed most worthily holds sway over the whole circle *of the year;* she owns a sovereignty inferior to that of no Deity. She rules the heaven, the earth, and the waves that gave her birth; and by the power of her embraces she holds sway over every kind. She it was who created all the Gods; 'twould be a tedious task to enumerate them; she furnished the *primary* causes for the plants and the trees. She it was that brought together the untaught minds of men, and instructed them to unite, each one with his mate. What is it but alluring delights that creates the whole race of the birds of the air? If gentle love is away, then do the flocks refuse to pair. With another male the furious ram fights with his horn, but the forehead of his beloved ewe[32] he is careful not to hurt. The bull, at whom all the pastures and all the wood tremble, follows the heifer, divested of his fierceness. The same influence preserves whatever it is that has life beneath the wide ocean, and it fills the waters with fishes innumerable. It was she that first divested man of his savage habits of life; from her were derived the arts of dress, and the careful attention to the person. The lover is said at first to have chaunted his serenade at the closed doors *of his* mistress throughout the *livelong* night that was denied to him; then, it was an effort of oratory to prevail upon the cruel maid, and each man was eloquent, he *pleading for himself* his own cause. By means of her were a thousand arts first touched upon, and through the desire of pleasing, many things were discovered, which before lay concealed. Can any one be found to dare to deprive this *Goddess* of the privilege of giving her name to the second month?[33] Far from me be such madness. What? Is it *only* because she is every where powerful, and honoured by many a temple, that the Goddess has a peculiar claim to honour in our city? O, man of Rome, it was in defence of thy *ancestral* Troy that Venus was wielding arms, when, mangled by the spear[34] on her

[32] *Beloved ewe.*]—Ver. 101-2. Gower thus renders these two lines—
'The surly ram will with a ram knock horns;
But yet to hurt his lovely ewe he scorns.'

[33] *Second month.*]—Ver. 115. That is to say, the second month in the original year of Romulus.

[34] *Mangled by the spear.*]—Ver. 120. Namely, in the combat between Diomedes and Æneas, where she interfered in favour of her son.—Iliad, Book iii. l. 535.

tender wrist, she lamented aloud. By the decision, too, of a Trojan she overcame two of the daughters of heaven.[35] Ah! would that the defeated Goddesses had failed to remember this! And *doubtless*, she was called the daughter-in-law of Assaracus, that, in fact, in future times the great Cæsar might have ancestors sprung from the line of Iülus, *her descendant*. And no season was there more becoming for Venus than the spring; in spring the earth is beauteous; in spring the soil is unbound: then does the herbage raise its head, having burst the ground; then from the swelling bark does the shoot push forth the bud; and the lovely Venus is deserving of the lovely season, and, as is her wont, she is in close conjunction with her own dear Mars. In spring she bids the curved ships[36] to go on their way along the deep that gave her birth, and no longer to dread the blustering of the winter.

Properly, ye Latian matrons and ye maidens, do ye worship the goddess, and ye who are without the fillets[37] and the garment with lengthened train. Untie the golden necklaces from her neck of marble; remove her jewels: the Goddess must be laved all over.[38] Restore her golden necklaces[39] to her neck when dried: then must other flowers, then must

---

[35] *Daughters of heaven.*]—Ver. 121-2. Gower's version is—

'She put two ladies down (a Trojane judge).
Ah! may those twaine not think of that old grudge.'

This is an allusion to her contest with Juno and Minerva for the golden apple.

[36] *The curved ships.*]—Ver. 131. From the third of the ides of November to the sixth of the ides of March the sea was not deemed navigable. The ships were then laid up on shore. In spring they were launched for the season by the agency of rollers placed under them. To this Horace makes allusion, Odes, Book i. Ode 4, l. 3.

[37] *Without the fillets.*]—Ver. 134. The women of light character at Rome were not allowed to wear the 'vittæ,' or 'fillets,' which were restricted to the priestesses; or the 'stola,' or long garment with a deep 'instita,' or 'flounce,' which was worn by women of character only; on the contrary, they were restricted to wearing the 'toga.'

[38] *Laved all over.*]—Ver. 136. The washings of the statues of the various divinities were common among both the Greeks and the Romans. It is conjectured that only the women of the lowest rank took part in the washing of the Goddess on this occasion.

[39] *Golden necklaces.*]—Ver. 137. 'Redimicula.' This word generally signifies the strings or ribbons which fell on the shoulders from the 'mitra,' or head-dress, and were probably used for the purpose of tying it under the chin. Here, however, it seems to mean 'necklaces.'

a fresh rose be given to her. You *women*, too, she bids to bathe, wearing chaplets of the green myrtle; and why she does so, learn now, *for* a cause exists. All naked, she was drying her dripping tresses on the sea-shore; the Satyrs, a wanton set, beheld the goddess. She perceived it, and concealed her person by an intervening myrtle tree; she was saved by so doing, and she desires you to commemorate *the circumstance*.

Learn now, why ye offer the incense to Fortuna Virilis;[40] in that place which is all moist with the application of warm water. That place beholds you all with your garments *laid* aside, and every imperfection of your naked person is exposed. To conceal these, and to hide them from your husbands, does Fortuna Virilis engage; and this she does, if requested so to do, with the offering of a little frankincense. And be not reluctant to take the poppy bruised with the snow-white milk, and the honey[41] trickling from the squeezed combs. When first Venus was led home by her eager husband, she drank of this; from that time she was a wife. With suppliant words appease her; under her protection abide both beauty, *good* morals, and fair fame. Rome had, in lapse of time, degenerated from the virtue of its ancestors; then, men of the olden time, did ye consult the Cumæan *Sibyl*.[42] She commanded a temple to be erect-

[40] *Fortuna Virilis.*]—Ver. 145. Plutarch, in one instance, says that a temple was erected to the Goddess, Male Fortune, (or rather, Fortune of the Males), by Ancus Martius; in another place he refers the building of it to Servius Tullius, in which statement he is supported by Dionysius. The temple contained a wooden statue of Servius Tullius. Gower thus renders this and the next line—

'Male Fortune, pleas'd with but a little spice,
Hides from your husbands all deformities.'

It must be remembered that Fortuna Virilis was not a God, but a Goddess, to whom were entrusted the fortunes of the male sex.

[41] *And the honey.*]—Ver. 152. A drink made of milk, honey, and bruised poppies, was given to the bride on the day of her nuptials, as we are informed by Pliny, Nat. Hist. Book xix. c. 8. It was called 'cocetum.'

[42] *The Cumæan Sibyl.*]—Ver. 158. Sibylla is a name given by the ancient writers to several mysterious personages of antiquity; Pliny mentions three, Plato one, Ælian four, and Varro ten. The Sibyl alluded to in the text, and mentioned in the third Book, l. 534, with reference to her great age, resided at Cumæ, in Italy. Erythrea was her name, though she is sometimes called Herophile, Daphne, Deiphobe, Manto, &c. Apollo granted her a life to equal in the years of its duration the grains contained in a handful of sand. Forgetting to add to her request the enjoy-

ed[43] to Venus: this being duly performed on that occasion, Venus obtained the name *of "Verticordia,"* from the change of the heart. Ever do thou, most beauteous Goddess, look upon the descendants of Æneas with pleased aspect, and do thou protect so many of thy daughters-in-law.

Whilst I am speaking, the Scorpion, formidable for the sting of his elevated tail, plunges headlong[44] into the green waves.

When the night shall have passed away, and the sky shall first begin to blush, and the birds, touched by the dewdrops, shall complain; and the traveller shall *now* throw aside his half-consumed torch after watching out the night, and the swain shall proceed to his wonted toil; then do the Pleiades begin[45]

---

ment of health and strength, decrepitude and infirmity became her lot as her years advanced. When Æneas requested her aid in his descent to the infernal regions, seven hundred years of her life had elapsed. There was another Sibyl of Cumæa, in Æolia, who is represented as being a different personage from the former. One of the Sibyls offered Tarquinius Priscus, or, as some say, Superbus, nine books for a sum of money; on being twice refused, she each time burned three, and the king then purchased the remaining three for the original price. Pliny (Nat. Hist. Book xiii. c. 13) says there were but three books originally, of which she burned two. They were carefully preserved in the Capitolium, in a stone chest, deposited in a vault underground. They were supposed to shadow forth the destinies of Rome, and were consulted on great emergencies: two men, called the 'Duumviri Sacrorum,' were appointed for that especial purpose.

[43] *To be erected.*]—Ver. 159. In the year A.U.C. 639, in the consulship of Acilius Balbus and Porcius Cato, Elvia, the maiden daughter of Elvius, a man of equestrian rank, was struck with lightning while on horseback, returning with her father to Apulia from the plays at Rome. Her clothes were torn, her tongue forced out, and the trappings of the horse wrenched from his body. On this, the augurs declared that the occurrence portended infamy to the knights and the Vestals of Rome. A female slave gave information that Æmilia, Licinia, and Martia, three Vestals, were carrying on an intrigue with some of the Equites. By the direction of the Sibylline books, two Greeks and two Gauls were buried alive to propitiate some foreign deities, and a statue was erected to Venus Verticordia, 'the changer of hearts,' that she might turn the hearts of the females from iniquity. Sulpicia, the wife of Fulvius Flaccus, was selected, by reason of the purity of her character, to dedicate the statue.

[44] *Plunges headlong.*]—Ver. 164. The cosmical setting of the constellation Scorpio on the calends of April.

[45] *The Pleiades begin.*]—Ver. 169. The heliacal setting of the Pleiades on the fourth day of the nones of April. They were the daughters of Atlas, who was said to support the world on his shoulders; and, as in their setting, the weight of the heavens was supposed to be decreased, they were said thereby to ease his shoulders of a part of his burden.

to relieve the shoulders of their father *Atlas: the Pleiades,* which are wont to be called seven, but which really are but six in number. Either it is because *but* six of them came into the embraces of the Gods; for they say that Sterope shared the bed of Mars; Halcyone, that of Neptune; and you, beautiful Celæno, Maia, Electra, and Taygete, that of Jupiter. Merope, the seventh, was married to a mortal, to thee, O Sisyphus.[46] She repents *of this,* and in solitude lies concealed, through shame of what she did. Or *it is,* because Electra could not endure to look on the ruins of Troy,[47] and placed her hand before her eyes.

Three times let the heavens roll round on their revolving axle; three times let Titan yoke and unyoke his steeds. Forthwith the Berecynthian flute[48] shall blow, together with the crooked horn, and the festival of the Idæan mother shall take place. Her eunuch *priests* shall walk in procession, and shall beat the hollow tambourines, and the cymbals, struck by the cymbals, shall send forth their tinklings. She herself shall be borne, seated on the effeminate shoulders of her companions,[49] carried with loud howlings through the middle of the streets. The theatre is resounding,[50] and the games are now summoning

---

[46] *Sisyphus.*]—Ver. 175. He was the son of Æolus, and the founder of Corinth. He was notorious for his robberies and frauds, and was condemned to roll a stone up a hill in the infernal regions, which, soon as it reached the summit, rolling down again, caused a never-ending toil.

[47] *The ruins of Troy.*]—Ver. 177. She was the mother of Dardanus, the first of the Trojan kings, and hence is supposed to have felt interest in the fate of Troy.

[48] *Berecynthian flute.*]—Ver. 181. Berecynthia was a mountain in Phrygia, sacred to Cybele, whence the present epithet. Midas is said to have invented the flute or pipe here mentioned, which was expanded into a curve all round at the end, for the purpose of emitting a deeper sound. The body of the pipe was usually of box-wood, or of Libyan lotus wood. The end was made of brass or horn. The sacred rites of Cybele were performed on Mount Ida, in Phrygia.

[49] *Her companions.*]—Ver. 185. 'Comitum' is properly used here, as the Goddess was carried by a Phrygian man and woman through the streets. The other names of Cybele, besides 'the Mother,' or 'Parent of the Gods,' were Ops, Rhea, Magna Mater, (or 'the Great Mother,') and Dindymene. It would appear that Rhea was originally a Grecian deity, Ops, an Italian Goddess, and Cybele, a Phrygian divinity, which in time became amalgamated into one object of worship.

[50] *The theatre is resounding.*]—Ver. 187. On the occasion of the Megalesian games, plays were performed in the theatre. The day was

us; attend the spectacle, Quirites, and let the litigious courts be rid of their strife. I wish to ask many a question: but the noise of the clashing brass *quite* frightens me, and the curved lotos pipe with its terrific sound. Send, Cybelean Goddess, thy grand-daughters,[51] skilled in learning, of whom I may inquire what I wish to know. She hears my prayer, and desires them to be present at my request. "Disclose to me, mindful of her command, ye daughters of Helicon, why the great Goddess takes pleasure in a perpetual noise?" Thus I *spoke*. Thus Erato *answered* me (the month of Cytherea fell to her lot, because she bears the name of tender Love[52]), "This oracular answer was returned to Saturn. 'Best of kings, by thy son shalt thou be hurled from thy sovereignty.'" He, fearing his own offspring, devours each of them as each is born, and keeps them, thus swallowed,[53] in his entrails. Often did Rhea complain, so often pregnant, and never yet a mother; and she grieved at her own fruitfulness. Jupiter was born; antiquity obtains credit as a witness of importance; hesitate before questioning the received belief. A stone concealed in a garment lay swallowed in the throat of the God;

'nefastus,' or one on which no work was allowed to be done, which will account for the reference to the Forums. Gower's translation of this and the preceding lines is very quaint—

> 'Thrice more let heaven on constant axles course,
> Let Sol thrice harness and knock off his horse.
> Then straight the Phrygian hornpipe doth resound;
> The Idæan granddame's feast is now renown'd.
> Her eunuchs marching beat their tabrets hollow;
> From brasse knock'd brasse a noise a noise doth follow.
> She, carry'd on her servant's neck, in pride
> About the streets is whooted to, and cri'd.
> Resort, ye nobles; scenes and shews do call:
> Now in the court be there no suits at all.'

[51] *Thy grand-daughters.*]—Ver. 191. The Muses were the daughters of Jupiter; and Cybele, being identified with Rhea, the wife of Chronos, or Saturn, and the mother of Jupiter, they would be her grandchildren. The Goddess derived her name from Mount Cybele, in Phrygia.

[52] *Name of tender Love.*]—Ver. 196. The name of Erato comes from the Greek word ἔρως, 'love.'

[53] *Thus swallowed.*]—Ver. 199-200. Gower's most comical translation is to the following effect—

> 'He, fearing this, devoureth every child
> As it came forth, and in his g—ts it killed.'

thus by the Destinies was the father doomed to be deceived. And now the lofty heights of Ida are resounding with the tinklings, that the babe may cry[54] in safety with his infant voice. Some, with clubs are beating the shields, some, are rattling the empty helmets; in this work are engaged the Curetes and the Corybantes.[55] The truth was concealed from the father; and, as an imitation of what was done in the olden time, the attendants of the Goddess *still* beat the brass and the hoarse sounding hides. Cymbals they strike in place of the helmets, tambourines for the shields; the pipe, just as it did formerly, yielded its Phrygian notes.[56] She had ended; I began, "Why, to her, does the fierce race of the lions afford for the bent yoke their manes, not used to that duty?" I had ended; she *then* began, "Their savage nature is supposed to have been tamed by her: this by her chariot has she attested." "But why is her head adorned with a crown of turrets? Was it she that gave their towers to the earliest cities?" She nodded assent. "Whence arose," said I, "the madness *in her priests* of mutilating their own members?" Soon as I was silent, the maid of Pieria began to speak. "Attis, a Phrygian boy, remarkable for his beauty, in the woods attached the turret-crowned Goddess to him by the ties of a pure love. Him she desired to be devoted to herself, to be the keeper of her temples; and she said, 'See that thou always keep thyself in chastity.' He pledged his faith to her commands, and said, 'If I prove false, may that passion by which I commit the sin be my last.' He sins, and in *his passion for* the Nymph

[54] *The babe may cry.*]—Ver. 207—212. Gower's translation is—

'Long had a tinkling rung in Ida tall,
That so the infant might in safety brall.
The Corybantes and Curetes, some
On ringing helmets, some on bucklers drum.
The child's conceal'd. In signe of this, therefore,
Her followers make their brasse and parchments rore.'

[55] *The Corybantes.*]—Ver. 210. The Curetes were those who, according to the legend, danced the Pyrrhic dance, which was performed in armour around the cradle of Jupiter. They were also called 'Dactyli.' The Corybantes were the priests of Cybele, and were said to have been three in number, Damnameneus, Acmon, and Selmo.

[56] *Phrygian notes.*]—Ver. 214. The Phrygian measure was that used in the musical part of religious ceremonies, and was invented by Marsyas, a Phrygian. We are told by Aristotle that it was deficient in modulation.

Sagaritis he ceases to be that which he was before; on this account the wrath of the Goddess exacts vengeance. She destroys the Nymph by means of wounds inflicted upon a tree; she dies; that tree formed the destiny of the Naiad. He is furious; and believing that the ceiling of his chamber is falling, he takes to flight, and in his course reaches the heights of Dindymus. And at one moment he screams out, 'Away with those torches!' at another, 'Away with the scourges!' Ofttimes he declares that the Goddesses of Palæste[58] are nigh at hand. He mangled his body, too, with a sharp stone, and his long hair was dragged in the foul dust. His cry was, 'Such are my deserts: with my blood I am paying the deserved penalty; perish those which in me have been the sinning parts! perish they!' again said he. He emasculated himself, and in a moment no traces of manhood were left to him. His madness became a precedent, and the effeminate priests *still* mutilate themselves as they toss their hair." In such words, by the eloquent lips of the Aonian Muse, was the cause revealed to me of the madness about which I had made this inquiry. "Guide of my task, tell me this also, I pray; whence was she brought, *when she first arrived here;* or was she always in our City?" "The Mother," said she, "was ever attached to Dindymus, and Cybele, and Ida, pleasant with its fountains, and the realms of Ilium. When Æneas was carrying Troy to the fields of Italy, the Goddess was on the point of following the ships with their sacred freights. But she had perceived, that not as yet was her Divinity invited to Latium by the Destinies, and she had stopped in her native abodes. Afterwards, when Rome, powerful in her resources, beheld five centuries pass over, and raised her head *aloft* from the conquest of the world, the priest examined the words of destiny in the Eubœan prophecies. They say that on examination there were found these words: 'The Mother is far away; I command thee, man of Rome, that thou fetch hither the Mother; when she comes she must be received by the hand of chastity.' The senate is perplexed by the obscure terms of the mysterious oracle as to who the parent is that is away,

---

[58] *Goddesses of Palæste.*]—Ver. 236. From the mention of the torches and whips it is clear that the Furies are meant. They had a temple in Epirus, of which Palæste was one of the principal cities.

or in what spot she must be sought. Pæan[59] is consulted, and he answers, "Send for the Mother of the Gods; she is to be found on the heights of Ida." Men of noble rank[60] are sent on the mission. Attalus was then swaying the sceptre of Phrygia; he refuses their request[61] to the men of Ausonia. Of miracles will I sing; the earth shook with a prolonged murmuring, and thus did the Goddess speak from her shrines: "I myself desired to be sent for. Let there be no delay; send me away, *thus* willing *to depart.* Rome is a place worthy to be the retreat of every Divinity." He, struck with terror at the sound, said, "Depart; thou wilt *still* be ours; Rome traces her ancestry to Phrygian forefathers." Forthwith, axes without number are felling the forests of pine, the same which *Æneas*, the pious Phrygian, had made use of in his flight. A thousand hands unite *in the toil;* and the hollow bark, ornamented with enamelled colours,[62] bears the Mother of the inhabitants of heaven. She is carried in perfect safety over the waters of her son *Neptune*,

[59] *Pæan.*]—Ver. 263. This was an epithet of Apollo, from the Greek παίω, 'to strike,' either in allusion to his having slain the serpent Python, or from the same word in the sense of 'to cure,' from his being the God of medicine.

[60] *Men of noble rank.*]—Ver. 265. They were five in number, according to Livy (Book xxix. c. 11):—M. Valerius Lævinus, of consular rank; M. Cæcilius Metellus, a former prætor; Sulpicius Galba, who had been an Ædile; and Cneius Tremellius Flaccus and M. Valerius Falto. Livy says that Attalus, king of Pergamus, readily consented to the request of the Senate, being in alliance with the Romans against Philip, their common enemy. Attalus was so renowned for his immense wealth, that his name passed into a proverb. Having no male offspring by Berenice, his wife, he bequeathed all his possessions to the Roman people.

[61] *He refuses their request.*]—Ver. 266. Livy says the contrary, and that he forthwith 'gave them the sacred stone, which they said was the mother of the Gods, and bade them carry it to Rome.' Arnobius tells us that this stone was but småll, and could easily be carried by one man; that it was black and tawny in colour, of irregular form, with prominent corners. Mr. Keightley, on very good grounds, as it would appear, considers that it was an aërolithe. Livy says that she was sent for, as the Sibylline books prophecied the invasion of a foreign people, and their repulse from Italy by her assistance, if brought to Rome.

[62] *Enamelled colours.*]—Ver. 275. Perhaps more properly "colours subjected to fire." Pliny (Nat. Hist. Book xxxv. c. 41) says that melted wax mixed with colours was laid on with a brush, and that it was much used for ornamenting ships, as being proof against the action of the sun and salt water.

and she reaches the long straits of the sister of Phryxus;[63] she passes the destructive Rhœtean *Sea*, the shore of Sigæum, Tenedos, and the ancient realms of Eëtion. The Cyclades receive her, Lesbos being left behind, and the spot when the tide breaks on the shallows of Carystum. She passes, too, over the Icarian *Sea*, where Icarus lost his wings that fell off, and he *thereby* gave a name to that extensive tract of water. Then she leaves Crete on her left, on her right, the waters of Pelops; and she comes to Cythera, sacred to Venus. Hence *she* enters the Trinacrian Sea,[64] in which Brontes, Steropes, and Acmonides,[65] are wont to dip the steel when at a white heat: she sails over the sea of Africa, and beholds, over the oars, on the left side, the realms of Sardinia; and *now* she makes Ausonia. She had arrived at Ostia, where the river Tiber empties itself by its two mouths into the deep, and flows in a space of greater extent. All those of the Equestrian order, and the dignified Senate, intermingled with those of Plebeian rank, come to meet her at the mouths of the Etrurian river. Then go forth together both mothers and daughters, and *brides newly become* daughters-in-law, and those who tend the sacred altars in the virgin state. The men weary their labouring arms with the rope tightly stretched; scarcely does the stranger bark make way against the stream. Long time had the land been parched; the drought had burnt up the grass. The keel, overpowered *by the burden of the freight*, rests on

[63] *Sister of Phryxus*.]—Ver. 278. Helle, who gave name to the Hellespont. The places here mentioned in succession are, the Hellespont, the Rhœtean Sea washing Rhœteum and Sigæum, towns of Troy; Tenedos, an island within sight of Troy, famous for its earthenware; Thebes, near Adramyttium, the residence of Eëtion, the father of Andromache; the Cyclades and Lesbos, Islands of the Ægean Sea, near Delos; Caristus, in Eubœa, opposite the isle of Andros; the Icarian Sea, near Samos, into which Icarus fell, when soaring on his wings with his father Dædalus; the isle of Crete, now Candia; the coast of the Peloponnesus; the isle of Cythera, on the coast of Laconia; the Sicilian Sea; the coast of Africa; the island of Sardinia.

[64] *The Trinacrian Sea*.]—Ver. 287. Trinacria was the Grecian name of Sicily, from its three corners or promontories Pachynus, Pelorus, and Lilybæum. Ætna, its volcano, was sacred to Vulcan, and its eruptions were supposed to be caused by the Cyclops working at the forge.

[65] *Acmonides*.]—Ver. 288. Virgil calls him Pyracmon. Brontes is from βρόντη, 'thunder;' Steropes from στερόπη, 'lightning;' and Acmonides from ἄκμων, 'an anvil.'

the shoal covered with mud. Whoever assists at the work is labouring even beyond his strength, and by the sound of his voice[66] gives aid *in keeping time* to the power of his arms. The vessel settles there just like an island, immoveable in the midst of the ocean. Claudia Quinta traced her descent from the noble Clausus;[67] and her beauty was not inferior to her noble birth. Chaste, in truth, was she; but she had not the credit of being so; unjust slander had done her an injury, and she was charged on a false accusation. Her style of dress,[68] and her having appeared in public with her hair fancifully adorned, together with the readiness of her replies to the austerity of old age,[69] had done her this injury. Her mind, conscious of her integrity, laughed to scorn the falsehoods of report; but we are, *all of us*, a set too ready to believe ill. After she had stepped forward from the train of the chaste matrons, she took up with her hands some pure water of the stream, and thrice did she sprinkle her head, and thrice did she raise her hands to the heavens. Those who behold her, think that she is deprived of her senses. And *now*, with bending knee, she fixes her looks on the image of the Goddess, and with her hair all dishevelled[70] she utters these words,

[66] *By the sound of his voice.*]—Ver. 302. This seems to have been, and still is, a habit peculiar to sailors of all ages and all countries. Martial calls the word given to the rowers by the 'pausarius,' or 'hortator' (the 'timekeeper'), 'celeusma,' 'the command,' from the Greek κελεύω, 'to order.' Strabo tells us, that it was dangerous for vessels, when laden, to pass the bar of the Tiber, and that they usually discharged or lightened their cargo at the mouth.

[67] *The noble Clausus.*]—Ver. 305. Atta (or Attus) Clausus migrated from Regillum, a Sabine town, to Rome, where his family was received into the number of the patricians, five years after the expulsion of the Tarquins; and Attus himself was called Appius Claudius. The Claudia here mentioned was the grand-daughter of Appius Claudius Cæcus.

[68] *Her style of dress.*]—Ver. 309-10. Gower's translation is,

'Her habits brave, and music so delicious,
And spruce attire, did make her more suspicious.'

[69] *The austerity of old age.*]—Ver. 310. Perhaps she had been taken to task for her gaiety by her seniors, and had told them to mind their own business, which did not improve their opinion of her.

[70] *Hair all dishevelled.*]—Ver. 318. Ornaments were not permitted to be worn during the performance of religious ceremonies. Our churches at the present day bear no testimony to the continued observance of this regulation.

"Genial *Goddess*, thou fruitful parent of the Gods, receive these the prayers of thy supplicant on this express stipulation. My chastity is impugned. If thou condemnest me, I will confess that I have deserved it. With my death I will pay the penalty, if convicted, a Goddess being my judge. But if guilt is far from me, thou wilt give by the event a pledge of my innocence, and, chaste thyself, thou wilt follow my chaste hands." She said, and with a slight effort she drew the rope. That which I tell of is wondrous; but it is *still* testified by the representations of our stage.[71] The Goddess is moved; she follows her guide, and, by following, bestows on her her testimony of approbation. A shout, the sign of exultation, rises to the sky. They come to the bending of the river; the ancients call that place Ostia,[72] on the Tiber, from which point it takes its course to the left. Night had come; they tie the cable to the trunk of an oak, and after a repast they consign their bodies to gentle slumber. The morning had *now* come; they loosen the cable from the trunk of the oak, but first they offer frankincense on an altar which they had erected; before the poop *of the vessel*, crowned with flowers, they sacrifice a heifer, without spot, that had neither borne the yoke nor been coupled with the bull. There is a spot where the rapid Almo flows into the Tiber, and the lesser stream loses its name in that of the greater. There does the hoary priest, in his purple vestments, lave the lady *Goddess* and her sacred utensils in the waters of the Almo.[73] His attendants raise on high the howl, the maddening pipe is blown, and their effeminate hands strike the *tightened* hides[74] of the oxen. Claudia walks in front, the most distinguished by the joyousness of her countenance, with

[71] *Our stage.*]—Ver. 326. Probably this was one of the stock subjects of the scenic representations in the theatre, on the occasion of the Megalesian games.

[72] *Ostia.*]—Ver. 330. This would seem to be the name of the spot where the river divided itself, at some distance from the sea, and not the town of Ostia at its mouth, which was founded by Ancus Martius, and was celebrated for its salt-pans—'salinæ Ostienses.'

[73] *The waters of the Almo.*]—Ver. 340. It was the yearly custom to wash both the image of the Goddess, and her chariot, in the waters of the Almo.

[74] *The tightened hides.*]—Ver. 341-2. Gower's translation is,

'Her followers hollow. Furious pipes resound;
And velome thumpt t' her eunuch's hands redound.'

difficulty now at last believed to be chaste on the testimony of a Goddess. She herself, seated in a car, is carried through the Capenian gate;[75] the yoked oxen are strewed with flowers newly plucked. Nasica[76] receives her; though at that time the builder of her temple, he has not always continued so. Augustus has now that character; formerly Metellus was its builder." Here Erato stopped. She paused, *to see* if I should make further inquiries. "Tell me," said I, " why *the Goddess* collects a contribution[77] in a few worthless coins?" " *Because*," said she, " the people contributed the brass, of which Metellus formed the shrine; thence is still extant the custom of giving the trifling coin." I inquired why people at that time in particular frequent the banquets, giving them, each in his turn,[78] and spontaneously attend the feasts which are duly proclaimed? " Because," said she, " *as* with good omen did Berecynthia change her abode, *so* by change of place do they seek for a similar omen." I had intended *to ask* why the Megalesian

[75] *The Capenian gate.*]—Ver. 345. The Porta Capena opened out on the Appian Way. The Marcian aqueduct passed over it.

[76] *Nasica.*]—Ver. 347. The sacred image was entrusted to P. Cornelius Scipio Nasica, (the son of Cneius Scipio who had been slain in Spain,) as being the most worthy citizen. He received her at first into his own house, and afterwards she was placed in the temple of Victory, on the Palatine hill. Her temple was contracted for by Scipio, but was not dedicated till thirteen years afterwards, when stage-plays were first acted at the Megalesian games, though both had been introduced into the city before that period. Livy says that the temple was built by the Censors M. Livius and C. Claudius. The latter being the father of the virgin Claudia, Burmann suggests that the reading of the line is, 'Templi pater extitit auctor,' 'Her father founded the temple.' Metellus afterwards repaired it, and Augustus rebuilt it when destroyed by fire.

[77] *Collects a contribution.*]—Ver. 351. During the festival, while the image was being carried through the city, a Phrygian man and woman collected alms in small coins, to defray the expenses of the worship of the Deity. These persons, from this practice, were called by the Greeks μητραγύρται, signifying 'collectors for the mother.' The poet seems to be mistaken in his statement of the reason for the collection.

[78] *Each in his turn.*]—Ver. 353. It was usual at the Megalesia for the principal families to give mutual entertainments, which were duly proclaimed, 'indicta,' and their friends attended without any special invitation, and then gave banquets in return. This was called 'mutitare,' 'to give and take.' The poet very lamely accounts for the custom and the origin of the word, by saying that the Goddess at that season 'changed,' 'mutabat,' her abode.

were the first games[79] in our city, when the Goddess, for she perceived it, said, "It was she that gave birth to the Gods. *The others* gave way to their parent; and their Mother has the first place in the honour that has been given to them."

"Why, then," said I, "do we call those Galli, who have mutilated themselves; inasmuch as the Gallic region is at so great a distance from Phrygia." She said, "Between the green Cybele and the lofty Celænæ[80] there flows a stream with maddening waters, Gallus by name. The person who drinks of it goes mad; depart ye afar thence, you who have a wish for a sound mind; the person who drinks of it goes mad."[81] "Does it not seem a shame," said I, "to place the salad made of herbs[82] on the table of the lady *Goddess?* Or does there exist some peculiar cause *for it?*" "The ancients," she replied, "are said to have used but simple milk, and such herbs as the earth spontaneously produced. The white cheese is mixed up with the bruised herbs, that the ancient Goddess *in them* may recognize the ancient diet."

When the next Pallantias[83] shall have shone, the stars having retreated from the sky, and the moon shall have unyoked her snow-white steeds, that person who shall *then* say, "Once, on

---

[79] *The first games.*]—Ver. 357-8. Gower's version is—

'Why, then, are her games Megalesia,
By Rome kept first? To this my Muse did say.'

[80] *The lofty Celænæ.*]—Ver. 362. This was the name of a mountain and town of Phrygia. near Mount Cybele, and once the chief place of that country. The river Mæander rose on its summit, and the Marsyas in its neighbourhood. Pliny, in his Natural History (book xxxi. c. 2), says, that the waters of the river Gallus were good for persons afflicted with stone, but that taken in excess they produced madness.

[81] *Goes mad.*]—Ver. 365-8. Gower thus translates these lines:—

'It causes madnesse: fly it all in sadnesse,
That love your wits: The water worketh madnesse.
Upon her table 'tis, said I, in season,
To set herb puddings: Is there any reason?'

[82] *The salad made of herbs.*]—Ver. 367. 'Moretum.' This mess, if it can be called a salad, was a mixture of garlic, parsley, rue, coriander, onions, cheese, oil and vinegar. Virgil composed a poem under this name, in praise of the mixture.

[83] *Pallantias.*]—Ver. 373. Aurora is so called from being the cousin of Pallas, who was one of the Titans.

this day, was Public Fortune[84] installed on the hill of Quirinus," will be speaking the truth.

The third day, I remember, was appointed for the games. But as I was a spectator, an old man who sat near me, said, "This was the day on which Cæsar, in the Libyan regions, crushed the traitorous arms of the courageous Juba.[85] Cæsar was my general; under him it is my boast to have served as a Tribune; he was the commander in my time of active service. By war have I obtained the distinction of this seat, by peace hast thou,[86] being invested with office in the number of the twice five men." About to continue the conversation, we were separated by a sudden shower.[87] The vibrating Balance was urging downwards the waters of the sky. But before the last day puts an end to the shows, the sword-girt Orion shall be plunged into the deep.

When the next dawn shall have looked upon victorious Rome, and the stars, put to flight, shall have given place to the

[84] *Public Fortune.*]—Ver. 376. The temple to 'Public Fortune,' or the 'Fortune of the State,' was vowed A.U.C. 549, by the consul Sempronius, on the eve of a battle with Hannibal.

[85] *The traitorous Juba.*]—Ver. 380. After the defeat of Pompey at Pharsalia, Cato and Scipio fled to Juba in Numidia for assistance. Cæsar defeated them with immense slaughter. From his native character as a Numidian, the poet calls him 'perfidus;' or, perhaps, because he resisted Cæsar in his career of conquest. Being defeated at Thapsus, he killed himself, which act, being one highly approved of in the Roman code of morals, would entitle him to the epithet 'magnanimus.'

[86] *By peace hast thou.*]—Ver. 383. There were fourteen rows in the theatre set apart for the Equestrian order, in which the poet might, as a member of that order, have taken his seat. It seems doubtful if the Tribune could have claimed a seat there. But, as a public officer, or rather an officer of the Roman army, he was sitting near Ovid, who was then filling the office of a Decemvir, on a seat most probably reserved for persons bearing office. The Decemviri were appointed by Augustus to assemble the judges, and generally to inspect the management of the courts of law.

[87] *A sudden shower.*]—Ver. 385. The awning over the theatres was only fitted to modify the heat of the rays of the sun, but was not adapted to give shelter against rain. On such occasions the people generally took refuge in the porticoes till the rain was over. The latter part of the speech of the old Tribune is thus translated by Gower:—

> ' I served a Tribune under Cæsar's banner,
> Lord of my actions; which I count my honour.
> My warfare me, this place thy gown gave thee;
> Both raised to the "office of Decemviri." '

Sun, the Circus will be thronged with the procession[86] and the multitude of the Gods; and the first palm shall be contended for by steeds that rival the winds in speed. These are the games of Ceres; there is no need of any explanation of their origin; of themselves, both the office and the merits of the Goddess are plain *to be perceived*. To the first mortals, the green grass, which the earth yielded without the urgent demand of any one, was in the place of the harvest. At one time did they pluck the grass from the green sod; at another time the treetop, with its tender foliage, was their repast. Afterwards, the acorn was produced; well was it with them, now that the acorn was discovered; and the hard oak furnished a sumptuous supply. Ceres was the first to change the acorn for a more nutritious food, by inviting mankind to a better kind of diet. She it was who compelled the bulls to bend their necks to the yoke; then for the first time did the upturned earth see the light of the sun. Brass became valuable; the mass of iron still lay hid; alas! would that it had ever remained concealed. Ceres takes delight in peace; and do you, ye husbandmen, pray that peace may be everlasting, and that our Prince may be immortal. Ye may offer to the Goddess the spelt and the tribute of the crackling grain *of salt*, and the cloves of frankincense, upon her ancient hearths; and if ye shall be without frankincense, then set fire to the unctuous torches. Little offerings are pleasing to the good Ceres, if they are only pure. Ye aproned attendants of the priests, remove the knives afar from the ox—the ox may plough—sacrifice *rather* the idle swine. A neck that is fitted *by nature* for the yoke ought not to be smitten by the axe; let him live *rather*, and many a time may he labour on the hard soil. This opportunity *now* calls upon me to tell of the rape of the Virgin. The greater part of the story you will recal to your memory; on a few points you will require to be informed. The Trinac-

---

[86] *Thronged with the procession.*]—Ver. 391. On the first day of the Ludi Cereales, there was a 'pompa' or procession, from the Capitol, through the Forum, to the Circus Maximus. The officers of state preceded, followed by the men of age for military service on foot and horseback. Then followed the chariots with four, and two horses, and then those with but one horse; musicians and dancers followed, and the procession closed with the images of numerous Gods carried either in chariots or on men's shoulders. The palm-branch was given to the conquerors in the games as the token and prize of victory.

rian land juts out into the vast ocean with three rocks, deriving its name from the position of the spot. *It is* a habitation delightful to Ceres; there possesses she many a city, among which is the fruitful Henna,[89] with its well-tilled soil. Cold Arethusa had invited the matrons of the inhabitants of heaven; the yellow-haired Goddess, too, had come to the sacred banquet. Her daughter, attended as she was by the damsels, her constant companions, was wandering with bare foot along her own meadows. There was a spot at the bottom of a shady vale, watered by the plenteous spray of the stream that falls from a height. There were as many tints there as nature possesses, and the ground was beauteous, decked with flowers of diversified hue. Soon as she beheld this she said, "Come, my companions, and together with me fill your bosoms with the flowers." The worthless prize delights their girlish minds; and, in their earnestness, the toil is not felt. One is filling baskets woven of the pliant osier, another one is loading her lap, another the bosom of her dress loosened *for the purpose*. One is gathering marygolds, to another the beds of violets are an object *of search;* another, with her nail, is cropping the blossom of the poppy. Some thou engagest, O hyacinth,[90] some

[89] *Fruitful Henna.*]—Ver. 422. This town, called also Enna, was, from its central situation, called the 'navel' of Sicily. It had a sacred grove and a temple. Sicily was of proverbial fertility, whence it was considered the chosen abode of Ceres. She had a temple there, founded by Gelon, of Syracuse, containing two images of the divinity, one in marble, the other in brass. Ovid relates this story at some length in the fifth Book of the Metamorphoses. Arethusa was the nymph of a fountain at Syracuse, and is said by some of the poets to have been privy to Pluto's designs against Proserpine. Homer gives Nysa, in Caria, as the scene of her abduction, other authors, Attica, Arcadia, or Crete. Gower's translation of the 419th and 420th lines will oblige us to give a rather Hibernian twang to the end of the first line—

'A land with three rocks crowds into the sea,
From its triangle called Trinacria.'

[90] *Hyacinth.*]—Ver. 439. Hyacinthus, a beauteous youth, having been accidentally slain by Apollo, was changed by the God into a hyacinth, which, according to the exuberant fancy of the poets, bears in its flowers the impress of the letters 'Αι, 'Αι, expressive, in the Greek language, of 'alas! alas!' uttered by Apollo in his grief. The same flower is said to have sprung from the blood of Ajax when he killed himself, bearing the above letters, expressive either of grief, or as denoting the first two letters of the name of Ajax, "Αιας.

thou detainest, O amaranth; some choose the thyme, some the rosemary, and some the melilote; many a rose is gathered, and many a nameless flower is there. She herself is plucking the delicate crocuses and the white lilies. In her eagerness to gather them, the distance is gradually increased, and by chance none of her companions follow their mistress. Her uncle espies her, and having seen her, in haste he bears her away, and on his azure-coloured steed carries her to his own realms. She indeed cries aloud, "Alas! my dearest mother! I am being carried away!" and with her own hand she rends her garments *in despair*. Meantime, a way is opened[91] to Pluto; for his steeds, unused to it, can scarcely endure the light of day. But the company of her companions, their baskets being heaped with flowers, cry aloud, "Come, Persephone, to thy presents." When thus called on, she returns not an answer; they fill the mountains with their wailings, and with sorrowing hand beat their naked bosoms. Ceres was amazed at the lamentation; she had just come to Henna, and straightway she exclaimed, "Woe is me! my daughter, where art thou?" In distraction she is hurried along, just as we are wont to hear that the Thracian Bacchanals,[92] in their raving, go with their hair all dishevelled. As lows the mother when her calf has been torn from her udder, and she seeks for her offspring throughout the wood, even so does the Goddess; she restrains not her wailing, and is swiftly borne on her course; and she begins it from thy plains, O Henna. She finds the marks of the virgin's foot leading thence, and sees where the ground has been imprinted with the well-known pressure. Perhaps that would have been the last day of her wanderings, had not the swine confused the traces which she had discovered. And now in her course she passes the people of Leontium and the streams of Amenanus, and thy banks, grassy Acis. She passes, too, Cyane, and the spring of the

---

[91] *A way is opened.*]—Ver. 449. According to Cicero, the descent was through a lake near the city of Syracuse; but he says that the God had ascended through a vast cavern near Henna.

[92] *Bacchanals.*]—Ver. 458. They are called 'Mænades,' from the Greek μαίνομαι, 'to rave in madness,' as their frantic gestures formed part of their worship. Gower thus translates this and the preceding line,—

'About she hurries, in a dead distraction,
Like shrews of Bacchus in their frantic action.'

gently flowing Anapus, and thee, O Gela, not to be approached by reason of thy eddies. She had *now* left behind Ortygia, and Megara, and Pantagias, and the spot where the ocean receives the waters of Symæthus, and the caves of the Cyclops, burned up by the forges which had been erected there, and the place which has the name of the curved sickle, and Himera, and Didyme, and Agrigentum, and Tauromenus, and Mela, the joyful pasture of the sacred oxen.[93] Hence she goes to Camerina, and Thapsos, and the glens of the Helorus, and the spot where Eryx, ever exposed, lies open to the breeze of the Zephyr. And now had she visited the mountain of Pelorus, and Lilybæum, and Pachynus, the three headlands of her island. Wherever she comes, she fills every place with her pitiable complaints, just as when the bird is bewailing her lost Itys. In turns, she exclaims at one time, "Persephone!" at another, "My daughter!" and, in alternate cries, she calls on her by either appellation. But neither did Persephone hear Ceres, nor the daughter her mother; and, in their turn, each appellation fell dead *on her ear*. And if Ceres saw a shepherd or any one tilling the fields, this was her one speech, "Has any girl passed this way?" And now the world has but one hue, and all things are enwrapped in darkness; *even* the watchful dogs have now ceased their barking. The lofty Ætna lies on the face of the gigantic Typhœus, with whose blazes, emitted by his pantings, the ground is on fire. Then she lights two pines for a torch: from this circumstance, even to this day, the torch is used in the sacred rites of Ceres. There is a cave, rough with the erected piles of the excavated pumice-stone, a place to be approached neither by man nor by wild beast. As soon as she arrives thither, she joins the harnessed dragons to her car, and, untouched by the waters, she traverses the waves of the ocean. She escapes the Syrtes, and thee, O Zanclæan Charybdis,[94] and you, dogs of the daughter

---

[93] *The sacred oxen.*]—Ver. 475-6. Gower thus renders these lines,—

'Then Himere, Didym, Agrigentum, and
Tauromenus: thence to Mela's Holy-ox-land.'

The curved sickle is mentioned a few lines above, in allusion to the old name of Messina, which was Zanclè, meaning, in the Sicilian language, 'a sickle,' from a fancied resemblance to that implement in the form of the spot.

[94] *Charybdis.*]—Ver. 499. This was a violent and dangerous whirlpool

of Nisus, monsters boding shipwreck, and the Adriatic, extending far and wide, and Corinth, situate on two seas; and thus she arrives at thy harbours, land of Attica. Here, for the first time, immersed in sorrow, she took rest on a cold rock,—that rock even to the present day, the people of Cecrops call the Rock of Sorrow.[95] Unshaken in her purpose, she remained unsheltered from the weather for many a day, exposing herself to the rays of the moon and the drenching shower. Each place has its own destiny; where now is Eleusis of Ceres, is said to have been the farm of the old man Celeus.[97] He was carrying home acorns and blackberries shaken down from the bramble thickets, and dry logs for the hearth, to be lighted there. His little daughter was driving homeward two goats from the crag, and his infant son was lying sick in the cradle. "Mother," says the damsel, (the Goddess was moved at the name of mother,) "what art thou doing, *thus* unattended, in these lonely hills?" The old man, too, stops, though heavy is his burden, and begs of her to come under the roof of his cottage, humble though it be. She declines; she had assumed the form of an old woman, and had confined her locks with a turban. When he has renewed his invitation, she then replies, "Unharmed mayst thou be, and a parent mayst thou ever remain. My daughter has been taken away from

in the straits of Messina. Scylla was another whirlpool in its neighbourhood. Scylla, the daughter of Phorcus and Chretheis, was beloved by Glaucus; Circe, in a fit of jealousy, poisoned the stream in which she bathed, on which she became transformed into a monster begirt with barking dogs, and, casting herself into the sea, she was changed into a rock surrounded with a howling whirlpool. The poet here confounds her with Scylla, the daughter of Nisus, king of Crete, who betrayed her father to Minos, by cutting off his lock of purple hair, on which his safety depended. The places previously mentioned are all towns, mountains, or rivers of ancient Sicily.

[95] *The Rock of Sorrow.*]—Ver. 504. This rock, on which the Goddess first seated herself on her arrival in Greece, was called ἀγέλαστος πέτρα, 'the rock of mourning.'

[96] *Eleusis.*]—Ver. 507. Eleusis was a maritime town of Attica, on the western side of the Cephisus. It was so named from Ἐλένσις, 'an arrival,' because Ceres arrived there on her first entrance into Greece. Her worship, attended with the secret and far-famed Eleusinian mysteries, prevailed there.

[97] *Celeus.*]—Ver. 508. Instead of being a poor old man, as here represented, Homer and other writers represent him as being the king of Eleusis, which, in fact, had been built by Ogyges 400 years before this period.

me. Alas! how much happier is thy lot than mine!" She spoke, and a crystal drop, like a tear (for the Gods do not shed tears,[98]) fell upon her bosom made warm *thereby*. Kind in disposition, the damsel and her aged father vied in weeping with her, and these were the words of the good old man, "*I pray* that thy lost daughter whom thou art seeking may return safe to thee; *but* arise, and do not despise the shelter of my humble cottage." To him the Goddess answered, "Lead on, thou knowest the art of persuading me;" and *so saying*, she arises from the rock and follows after the old man. Her guide tells his companion how that his son is ill and enjoys no repose, but is kept awake by his malady. As she is about to enter the humble abode, she gathers the soporiferous poppy from the soil of the field. While she is gathering it, she is said to have tasted it with forgetful palate, and thoughtlessly to have broken her lengthened fast. Inasmuch as she put an end to her fasting in the beginning of the night, those who are initiated[99] choose the time of the stars appearing as the hour for breaking their fast. When she enters the threshold she sees all things pervaded by mourning: there was now no hope of recovery in the child. Having saluted the mother, (her name was Metanira,) she deigns to touch the mouth of the boy with her own. His paleness of colour departs, and sudden vigour waxes strong in his body—such a degree of strength was it that passed from the celestial lips. The whole house is joyful, that is to say, the father, the mother, and the daughter; these three formed the whole household. Presently they serve up the repast, curds dissolved in milk, and apples, and the golden honey in its fresh combs. The genial Ceres fasts, and gives to thee, O boy, poppies, the promoters of sleep, to be drunk infused in warm milk. 'Twas midnight, and there was *now* the stillness of tranquil slumber; she raised Triptolemus[1] in her lap, and thrice

[98] *Do not shed tears.*]—Ver. 521. As the Gods did not live on mortal food, but on ambrosia and nectar, nor shed blood when wounded, but a peculiar fluid, called 'Ichor,' it is not surprising that they did not secrete tears similar to those of mortals.

[99] *Those who are initiated.*]—Ver. 536. 'Mystæ.' Those who were initiated in 'the Eleusinian mysteries' fasted until the evening, in imitation, it was supposed, of the conduct of Ceres on the present occasion.

[1] *Triptolemus.*]—Ver. 550. In the Homeric poem, which has come down to us on this subject, the son of Celeus is called Demophoon, while

with her hand did she stroke him, three verses did she utter, verses not to be repeated by mortal voice; and on the hearth she covered the body of the boy with the live embers, that the fire might purge away that burden, *mortality*, the common lot of man. The mother, unwisely affectionate, is roused from her slumbers, and distracted, she cries out, "What art thou doing?" and snatches his limbs from the fire. To whom the Goddess said, "While *in intention* thou art not, yet *in fact* thou hast proved a cruel *parent;* by the fears of a mother are my gifts rendered worthless. Mortal, indeed, shall he *now* remain, but yet he shall be the first to plough, and to sow, and to bear away the rewards of his labour from the ground that he has tilled." Ceres *thus* speaks, and as she goes forth, she carries a cloud *that envelopes her*, and *now* she betakes herself to her dragon *steeds*,[2] and is borne on her winged chariot. She leaves behind her the unsheltered Sunium, and Piræus[2*] secure with its winding harbour, and the coast which is situate on its right side. Thence she enters on the Ægean sea, in which she beholds all the Cyclades, and she passes over the destructive Ionian and the Icarian sea; through the cities of Asia she seeks the long Hellespont, and soaring on high, she wends her varied way through different spots. For now she is looking down upon the Arabs that collect the frankincense, and now, upon the Indians; afterwards, the Libyan lands, then Meroë, and then the land of Drought[3] is beneath

Apollodorus represents Triptolemus as the elder son. Ovid represents the facts recited as being the occurrences of a single night. Other writers represent Ceres as nightly burning out the gross and mortal parts of the child, and by day restoring the loss, by rubbing in ambrosia, until interrupted by the mother, when she gave up her intention of conferring immortality, but committed to him the guardianship of her mysteries, with a promise of immortal fame.

[2] *Her dragon steeds.*]—Ver. 561-2. Gower thus writes these lines—
'Thus forth she goes, and with a cloud attended,
Her winged-dragon mounted coach ascended.'

[2*] *Sunium and Piræus.*]—Ver. 563. The former was a promontory of Attica; the latter was the sea-port of Athens, consisting of three natural inlets, Piræus, properly so called, Cantharon, and Zea.

[3] *The land of Drought.*]—Ver. 570. This was Æthiopia. Meroë was an island of that country, formed by the Nile. Josephus says that its original name was Saba, but that Cambyses called it Meroë, after his wife or sister who died there. As Mr. Thynne justly remarks, Ovid does not observe any topographical order, but characterises the wildness of the Goddess by the fact of her rushing indiscriminately from place to place.

her. And now she reaches the Hesperian *streams*, the Rhine, the Rhone, and the Po, and thee, O Tiber, destined to be the parent of a mighty stream. Whither am I borne? 'twere an unlimited task to tell the lands that she wandered over—no spot in the world was left unvisited by Ceres. She wanders, too, along the sky, and she addresses those Constellations nearest to the icy Pole, that are exempt from immersion in the watery ocean. "Stars of Parrhasia, for ye are able to know all things, since never do ye set beneath the billows of the sea, discover my daughter Persephone to her wretched mother." She had *thus* said; and thus to her did Helice[4] reply: "The night is free from blame; question the Sun about the stealing of the damsel, who far and wide beholds what is done in the light of the day." The Sun, being visited, says, "Labour not in vain; she whom thou art seeking, now the bride of the brother of Jove, is the mistress of the third empire." Long having complained to herself, she thus addressed the Thunderer, and deep were the traces of grief on her countenance. "If thou bearest in mind by whom Persephone was born to me, she ought to have an equal share of thy regard. Having wandered over the whole world, the lawlessness of the deed alone is discovered by me; the ravisher still holds the reward of his crime. But neither is Persephone deserving of a ravisher for her husband, nor should a son-in-law have been provided for thee and me after such a fashion as this. What greater misfortune could I have endured, as a captive, had Gyges[5] been victorious, than I have now borne, while thou art holding the sceptre of heaven. But let him have carried her away with impunity, and let me bear these things unavenged; *only* let him restore her, and let him make amends for his former deeds by his recent ones." Jupiter mollifies her, and excuses the act on the plea of passion, and says, "He is not a son-in-law for us to be ashamed of. I *myself* am not of more noble birth; my realm is situate in the heavens; one *of my brothers* sways the waters; another the vacant realms of Chaos. But if perchance thy resolution

---

[4] *Helice.*]—Ver. 580. The Constellation of the Greater Bear; see Book iii. ver. 108. Parrhasia was one of the names of Arcadia.

[5] *Gyges.*]—Ver. 593. He was one of the hundred-handed giants who warred with Jupiter for the dominion of the heavens, being the brother of Briareus.

is unchangeable, and it is thy determination to dissolve the bonds of wedlock when once united, this *that thou desirest* we will assay, if it is the fact that she has continued fasting;[6] if not, the wife of the monarch of the infernal regions she shall be. The *God*, bearer of the Caduceus, departs to Tartarus, having assumed his wings, and, returning sooner than is hoped for, reports the ascertained result of his visit. "The damsel that has been carried off," says he, "has broken her fast with three of the grains which the pomegranate conceals beneath its thin rind." The wretched mother grieved, in no less degree than if her daughter had that moment been carried away, and scarcely, by the lapse of time, did she recover. And thus did she say: "The heavens are not to be inhabited by me: command that I, as well, may receive admittance into the valley of Tænarus."[7] And she would have done so, had not Jupiter made the stipulation that Persephone should be for twice three months *in each year* in heaven. Then, at length, did Ceres recover her *former* looks and her spirits, and placed upon her locks the garlands of wheat. Plenteously, too, did the harvest spring up in the fields, whose produce had been interrupted, and hardly did the threshing floor suffice to hold the stores

---

[6] *Continued fasting.*]—Ver. 603. The poets in general represent it as a rule that no one could return from Erebus who had once eaten there. In the Homeric Hymn, Pluto purposely induces Proserpine to eat the pomegranate grains, that he may avail himself of this law. Gower gives a quaint translation of this and the nine succeeding lines:—

' We'll try this means; sh' is thine, if meat sh' abstein;
If not, sh' must th' infernall bride remain.
Caduceus sails to Styx on nimble wings,
And quick as thought eye-witness'd tidings brings.
She had her stomach staid with kernels three
Of th' apple pluck'd from the pomegranate tree.
She mourns as much as if herself had now
Been forc'd away, and scarce could grief outgrow:
And there she cries, Your heaven to me is hatefull;
Let me go to live in Tartary more gratefull.'

The inhabitants of the Tartary of our day would not feel flattered by this adaptation of the name of their country, if they heard it.

[7] *The valley of Tænarus.*]—Ver. 612. Tænarus was a promontory of Laconia, now Cape Matapan. In a vale, or in its vicinity, was a cave, sacred to Neptune, which was said to be the entrance to the infernal regions, through which Hercules dragged Cerberus to the upper world. 'Chaos,' is used, a few lines preceding, by poetical license, to signify 'the infernal regions.'

piled up *there*. Things which are white are befitting Ceres: on the feast of Ceres put on white garments; at this season the wearing of woollen robes of dark colour is not allowed.

Jupiter, surnamed Victor,[8] takes to himself the Ides of April; on this day was a temple dedicated to him. On this day, too, if I mistake not, did Liberty, most worthy of our race, begin to possess her own mansions.

On the following day, do thou, sailor, repair to safe harbours; a gale, mingled with hail, will come from the west. In good truth, be this as it may, it is the fact, that on this day, in such a storm, did Cæsar and his troops conquer the arms of the enemy at Mutina.[9] When now the third day of the Ides *of the month* of Venus shall have dawned, perform the sacrifice with a cow that is pregnant. A cow, that is bearing and with young, is called "forda,"[10] from "fero," [to bear]; from this word, too, it is believed that the fœtus derives its name. Now are the cattle pregnant; the earth is teeming with the seed; to the pregnant earth a pregnant victim is offered. Some are slain in *the Capitol*, the heights of Jove. The court-houses[11] receive thrice ten heifers, and become wet, besprinkled with the streams of blood. But when the attendants of the priests have snatched the calves from the womb, and have consigned the entrails, when cut out, to the smoking altars, she who is by birth the oldest of the

---

[8] *Victor.*]—Ver. 621. In a war with the Samnites, A.U.C. 457, Q. Fabius Maximus vowed to erect a temple to Jupiter Victor. The temple of Liberty was dedicated on Mount Aventine, in the second Punic war, by the father of the Gracchi. It was repaired A.U.C. 559, by the Censors, and rebuilt by Asinius Pollio, in the reign of Augustus. To this last circumstance the poet seems here to refer.

[9] *Mutina.*]—Ver. 627. The battle of Mutina was fought against Antony by the Consuls Hirtius and Pansa, and the proprætor Octavianus (afterwards Augustus Cæsar), A.U.C. 710, and ended in the defeat of Antony. The two Consuls died of their wounds, and Augustus was thereby enabled to appropriate the glory of the victory to himself. The poet, in his flattery, would seem to imply that the hailstorm was of Augustus's own special brewing for the occasion.

[10] *Is called 'forda.'*]—Ver. 630. Varro, on Rustic Matters, Book ii. c. 5, calls this word 'horda,' and the festival 'Hordicidia,' or 'Hordicalia;' originating in the digamma, the H and the F of the ancients often betokened convertible sounds.

[11] *The court-houses.*]—Ver. 635. 'Curia.' The singular is here used for the plural. One cow was sacrificed in the 'curia,' or 'court-house,' of each of the thirty 'curiæ.'

Vestal Virgins burns the calves with fire, that, on the festival of Pales, those ashes may purify the people. When Numa was king, the crops not repaying the labour *expended on them*, the wishes of the disappointed husbandman remained ungratified. For, at one time, the year was suffering from drought through the cold northern blasts, at another time the soil became too luxuriant from constant showers. Often did the corn disappoint the owner, while in the *rising* blade, and the barren wild oat stood on the soil choked up *with* it. The cattle, *too*, before their time, used to yield immature births, and oft did the lamb, at its yeaning, prove the death of the ewe. There stood an ancient grove, which had for many a year remained inviolate by the axe, left as sacred to the Mænalian deity. He used to give responses in the stilly night[12] to the soul when at rest; here does the King Numa offer two sheep in sacrifice. The first is offered to Faunus, the next to gentle Sleep; the fleece of each is spread upon the hard ground. Twice is his unshorn head sprinkled with water of the fountain; twice does he wreathe his temples with the beechen bough. The joys of love are forbidden; it is not allowed to place animal food on the table, and no ring is left upon the finger. Clad in a coarse garment, he places the fresh fleeces upon his person, having worshipped the Deity in an address in the form prescribed. In the meantime the night comes, her gentle brow crowned with the poppy, and, with her, escorts the shadowy dreams. Faunus comes, and with his hard foot pressing the fleeces of the sheep, he utters such words as these from the right side of the couch:[13] "O king, thou must appease the earth by the sacrifice of two cows; let the death of one yield two lives to the sacrifice." His rest is broken by terror; Numa ponders over his vision, and reflects within himself on these dark sayings and the hidden injunctions. His wife, to the grove most dear, relieves him in his perplexity, and says, "Thou art asked for the entrails of a preg-

---

[12] *In the stilly night.*]—Ver. 651. The peculiar name of the sleep of divination or prophecy with the Romans was 'incubatio,' and among the Greeks, ἐνκοίμησις. It is possible that from this superstition may be derived the not uncommon saying among us, 'I will sleep on it,' used by a person who intends to give a matter all due consideration.

[13] *Right side of the couch.*]—Ver. 664. This boded an auspicious visit of the Deity.

nant cow." The entrails of a pregnant cow are offered, a year more happy ensues, and the earth and the cattle bring forth their increase. This day, too, did Venus once command to press on its course with greater haste, and downwards she urged the steeds of the heavens; that, with the utmost speed, on the following day, success in war might confer the title of empire[14] on the young Augustus.

But now, when the fourth light-bearing *day* looks back on the by-gone Ides, on this night do the Hyades visit Doris.[15]

When the third moon shall have dawned, after the departure of the Hyades, the Circus shall receive the steeds started from the goal.[16] I must teach the reason why the she-foxes let go, have their tails burning with fire-brands[17] fastened to them. Cold was the land at Carseoli,[18] and not fit for the production of the olive, but a soil naturally fertile in corn. By this way, was I journeying to *the land of* the Peligni, the country of my birth, small, but ever watered by the constant rains. I entered the well-known abode of an old friend of mine; Phœbus

---

[14] *The title of empire.*]—Ver. 676. On the 16th of the Calends of May, A.U.C. 724, Augustus Cæsar was first saluted by the senate with the title of 'Imperator,' on account of his victories. This honour, according to Tacitus and Dio Cassius, was conferred on him twenty-one times. It appears to have been distinguished from the word 'imperator,' signifying 'emperor,' by being placed after the name of the person, whereas the title of the emperor was placed before it. The nearest English translation of the word seems to have been ' successful leader.'

[15] *Hyades visit Doris.*]—Ver. 679. On the 15th of the Calends of May, the Hyades set acronychally. Doris was the daughter of Oceanus, the wife of Nereus, and the mother of the Nereides; her name is here used to signify ' the sea.'

[16] *The steeds started from the goal.*]—Ver. 680. 'Carcere partitos.' The 'carcer' was the place where the horses stood, with a cord stretched before them, on the dropping of which they started. 'Partitus' means literally 'divided,' that is 'from the course,' by the cord just mentioned.

[17] *Burning with fire-brands.*]—Ver. 681-2. Gower thus renders these lines,—

' Here let one tell, why foxes on the rails
 Run loose with fire-links at their backs and tails.'

[18] *Carseoli.*]—Ver. 683. This was a town of the Æqui, situate near the river Anio. Ovid seems to relate a custom that prevailed at Rome, and which had been borrowed from a rustic ceremony at Carseoli, of which he here narrates the origin. The reader cannot fail to call to mind how the idea of doing mischief to his enemies by a similar contrivance came to the mind of the unfortunate but wrong-headed Nazarite, Samson.

had already taken the yoke from off his exhausted steeds.[19] He was wont to tell me many other things, and this story as well, by which my present work might be furnished *with information*. "In this plain," said he, pointing to the plain, "a frugal peasant woman, with her hardy husband, used to own a little bit of land. He used to work it himself, whether there was occasion for the use of the plough, or the curved sickle, or the spade. She sometimes used to sweep out the cottage supported on the buttress,[20] and sometimes used to set the eggs to be hatched by the plumage of the parent bird; or *now* she is collecting the green mallows, or the white mushroom, or makes warm their humble hearth with the cheerful fire. And yet she *finds time and* employs her arms at the web constantly plied *by her*, and *thereby*, she prepares a defence against the menaces of the winter. She had a son, sportive in the dawn of life; he had added two years to two 'lustra.' He catches a fox in a sloping corner at the end of the willow grove: she had carried off many a bird from their poultry yard.[21] He wraps the captive in stubble and hay, and sets fire to her; she escapes from his hands, as he is applying the fire. Wherever she flies, she sets in a blaze the fields, *at that time* clothed with the harvest; the breeze gave strength to the all-consuming flames. The occurrence has *long since* passed away: the recollection of it *still* remains; for, even to this day, does the law of Carseoli forbid a she-fox when caught to be suffered to live; and that this tribe may atone for their fault, they are set on fire on the festival of Ceres, and perish in the

---

[19] *His exhausted steeds.*—Ver. 687-8. Gower's translation is curious,—

'Into an old acquaintance-house I turned,
Just as Sol's coach-horse had their day's task journeyed.'

Does he mean to say that his old acquaintance and 'Sol's coach-horse' had journeyed together, or that the house and the coach-horse had travelled in company? It is not clear why he limits the sun to one horse on this day.

[20] *On the buttress.*]—Ver. 695. 'Tibicine.' This was a prop or buttress placed at the side of a house to prevent it from falling. It evidently implies here the decayed and humble nature of the building.

[21] *Their poultry-yard.*]—Ver. 704. 'Cohortis.' Cato tells us that the cohors was round, and, from what Varro says, it appears to have been covered over. On Rustic Affairs, Book iii., c. 3, s. 6,—' There were two ('cohortes,' or) receptacles for poultry; one level with the ground, where cocks and hens were fed; the other aloft, in which pigeons inhabited turrets or the tops of a house.' Perhaps the turrets and the house were mimic ones, such as may be seen at the present day in fancifully built dovecotes.

very manner in which the one that I have mentioned destroyed the standing corn.

When next the saffron-coloured mother of Memnon shall have come, upon her rosy-coloured steeds, to visit the broad earth, then passes away the light of the sun from the leader of the wool-bearing flock, him who betrayed Helle. As he departs, a larger *animal*,[22] *oft used as a* victim, is at hand. Whether it be a cow or a bull it is not easy to know; the fore parts appear, the hinder parts are concealed. But whether this Constellation is a bull or whether a cow, against the will of Juno,[23] it enjoys the reward of love.

The night has passed away, and morning dawns. I am called to the Palilia;[24] and I am not called in vain, if genial Pales favours *me*. Genial Pales, do thou favour the poet who celebrates thy shepherd rites; if with pious attention I describe thy festival. Many a time, in truth, have I carried in my full hand the ashes of the calf and the bean stalks, the holy purgatives. Often, in truth, have I leaped over the fires placed in three rows, and the dripping bough of laurel[25] has flung the

[22] *A larger animal.*]—Ver. 716. As Mr. Keightley justly observes, this is a bad periphrasis, as being very awkwardly worded. He says, that now the sun leaves the Constellation of the Ram, but enters that of a larger animal, in common use as a victim, namely, the Bull.

[23] *Against the will of Juno.*]—Ver. 720. Whether it was the bull which carried off Europa, or the cow into which Io had been changed, it was, by reason of the infidelity of Jupiter, equally an object of aversion to Juno. The fore part only of this Constellation is represented in the signs of the Zodiac when depicted.

[24] *The Palilia.*]—Ver. 721. On the 11th of the calends of May, the anniversary of the foundation of the city, the festival of Pales, the Goddess of the shepherds, was held. Some writers considered Pales as being originally a male deity, the servant and bailiff of Jupiter. The festival is also by some authors called 'Parilia,' as being from 'pario,' 'to bring forth.'

[25] *Bough of laurel.*]—Ver. 728. The olive, laurel, rosemary, or pine, were usually employed to disperse the lustral water. Gower thus translates this and the three preceding lines,—

'I oft calves' ashes and bean-straws have held,
With burn'd purgations in a hand well fill'd;
Oft ore the bone-fires have I tane three hops,
And dew'd myself with holy-water-drops.'

These rites doubtlessly originated in the universally received notion of the purifying power of fire. Dionysius says, that while building the city, Romulus had fires kindled, and made his people jump through them for the purposes of expiation.

sprinkled waters. *Lo!* the Goddess has been moved, and she grants success to my undertaking. My bark leaves the dock, my sails now have favoring breezes. Proceed, you multitude, and take the fumigation from the Vestal altar—Vesta will grant it; by the gift of Vesta you will be cleansed. The blood of a horse[26] will be the fumigation, and the ashes of a calf; and the third ingredient will be the stripped stalk of the hard bean. Shepherd, purify the full sheep at the beginning of twilight; let the water first sprinkle them, and let the broom, made of twigs, sweep the ground. Let the sheepfolds, too, be decorated with leaves and branches fastened up, and let the long garland shade the ornamented doors. Let a blue smoke arise from the native sulphur, and let the ewe bleat aloud while rubbed with the brimstone as it smokes. Burn, too, rosemary, and the pitch tree, and the Sabine herbs, and let the burnt laurel crackle in the midst of the hearth. Let the basket of millet accompany the cakes of millet; this rustic Goddess takes especial pleasure in this kind of food. Bring on, too, the banquet and the milk-pail, peculiarly her own; and when the banquet has been removed, appease Pales, the inhabitant of the woods, with warm milk, and say, "Protect thou, alike, the cattle and those who tend the cattle, and let all harm fly afar, repelled from my stalls. Whether I have fed them on holy ground, or whether I have seated myself beneath a sacred tree, or whether any ewe of mine, unknown to me, has browsed on the grass growing over the graves, or whether I have trespassed on a grove forbidden *to be entered*, or whether the Nymphs have been scared away by my gaze, or whether the God, half goat *in form*, or whether my knife has despoiled a sacred grove of its shady bough, from which, the bundle of leaves has been given by me to my ailing ewe, do thou grant pardon to my error; nor be it a cause of

---

[26] *The blood of a horse.*]—Ver. 733. The ashes of the calf had been reserved as a 'februa,' or purgative, from the Fordicidia, mentioned before in line 639. Festus tells us that the horse, whose blood was most probably now used, was slain in October. 'A horse, called the "equus October," or "October horse," was slain in the month of October on the Campus Martius, in honour of Mars, the tail of which, streaming with blood, was carried with all possible speed to the "Regia."' This 'Regia,' or 'palace,' was most probably the temple of Vesta, and the blood was preserved there to be used with the ashes of the calf and the bean-stalks on the Palilia.

evil to me, if, while the hail was pouring down, I have sheltered my flock within the rustic fane; nor be it a cause of harm to me that I have disturbed the waters of the ponds. Pardon me, ye Nymphs, if *at any time* the motion of the hoof has rendered turbid the streams. Do thou, Goddess, for me, appease the fountains and the Deities of the fountains; do thou *propitiate* the Gods that are dispersed throughout all the groves. Far be it from us to look upon the Dryades, or to behold the bathing places of Diana,[27] or Faunus, while at midday he treads the fields. Drive disease afar; let both men and flocks enjoy the blessing of health; let, too, the dogs enjoy health, that watchful race. Let me not drive home my sheep fewer than they were in the morning; nor let me grieve as I bring home the fleeces which *alone* I have recovered from the wolf. Let evil hunger be afar; let grass and leaves be in abundance, and water, both to lave the limbs and *to serve* for the purpose of drinking. May it be my lot to press the full udders; may my cheeses bring me money home, and may the twigs, as they lie far apart *in the sieve,* give a passage to the liquid whey; may the ram prove a good tup, may his mate return the seed when conceived, and may there be many a lamb in my sheep-folds: may wool, too, be produced that will hurt none of my damsels, soft, and suited to even the tenderest hands. Let that happen which I pray for, and may we, at the close of the year, offer cakes of goodly size to Pales, the mistress of the shepherds. With these words must the Goddess be propitiated: turning to the east do you repeat these words three times, and in the running stream thoroughly wash your hands. Then you may drink the snow-white milk and the purple must, with the milk-bowl[28] set on in the place of

[27] *Bathing places of Diana.*]—Ver. 761. It was a belief that those who had the misfortune to come where the Nymphs or Goddesses of the fountains were bathing were immediately deprived of their reason. Gower thus translates this and the next line,—

'Nor nymphs, nor Cynthia, in her cistern play,
Let us not see, nor Pan in fields all day.'

[28] *With the milk bowl.*]—Ver. 779. Camella. This was a wooden bowl used in the country. It is by some supposed to have been so called from the Greek κάμπτω, 'to bend,' as being of a curved form, either on the top or on the sides. The 'sapa,' which is here rendered 'must,' as there is no word in English adapted to its meaning, really was the must

the goblet; and afterwards with active foot fling your strong limbs across the burning heaps of the crackling stubble. The ceremonial has *now* been told *by me;* the origin of that custom still remains for me *to mention.* The great number *of the causes alleged* makes me doubtful, and delays my undertaking. Devouring flame is the purifier of all things, and melts the dross from out of the metals, therefore is it used for purifying the ewes with the leader *of the flock.* Or is it, because there are two opposing principles in all things, fire and water, the discordant Deities, that our forefathers united these elements, and deemed it to be fitting to touch the body with the fire and the sprinkled water? or is it, because in these is the origin of life; the exile has lost[29] *his right to enjoy* these; by these the bride is wedded;[30] that these two things they think of primary importance? For my part I hardly believe it. Some there are, who think that Phaëton[31] is represented, and the deluging waters of Deucalion. Some, too, say that while the shepherds were rubbing stone against stone, a spark suddenly leaped forth. The first indeed was lost; *but* the second was caught on some straw. The fire of Pales has this for its alleged cause; or did the piety of Æneas rather give rise to this custom, to whom, when conquered, the fire gave a

or new wine, boiled down to one-third of its original quantity. This is Pliny's account. Varro says that it was boiled down to one-half, which Pliny, however, calls 'defrutum.' The mixture of milk and 'sapa,' Festus calls 'burranica potio,' 'red drink,' probably from the Greek word πυρρὸς, 'red.'

[29] *The exile has lost.*]—Ver. 791. Banishment, as a punishment, was not known to the Romans, but the same effect was produced by the interdiction of fire and water; by reason whereof, for the purpose of supporting life, a man was obliged to leave his country.

[30] *Bride is wedded.*]—Ver. 792. Fire and water were placed at the door by which the newly-married pair entered, and were touched by the bride and her husband on entering.

[31] *Phaëton.*]—Ver. 793. He was the son of Apollo and Clymene; being taunted with not being really the offspring of the sun, he requested the loan of his father's chariot for one day, which being unwillingly granted, he lost his control over the horses, and, to prevent a general conflagration, Jupiter struck him to earth with his lightnings. Deucalion was the son of Prometheus; when Jupiter sent a deluge to destroy mankind, he and his wife Pyrrha took refuge on Mount Parnassus, or, according to Hyginus, on Mount Ætna, and escaping, re-peopled the earth by throwing stones behind them, of which, those thrown by Deucalion became men, those by his wife, women.

harmless passage? This, however, is nearer to probability, that when Rome was built, the Lares were ordered to be transferred to new abodes, and that when changing their home they set fire to their rustic habitations and the cottage now no longer to be used; and that through the flames leaped the cattle and the swains, as is still done upon thy natal day, O Rome. The very occasion itself calls for an account of its origin from the poet. The beginning of the City we have now arrived at; be thou present, great Quirinus, at the recital of thy deeds. Now had the brother of Numitor paid the penalty, and all the shepherd people were under *the government of* the two chieftains. They agreed to call together the shepherds, and to build a city; a question of doubt arises, which of the two should lay the foundations. "There is no need," said Romulus, "of any dispute. Great is the truthfulness of birds; let us make trial of *the omen of* the birds." The thing *proposed* pleases; the one goes among the crags of the woody Palatine, the other in the morning ascends the heights of the Aventine. Remus sees six birds in succession, his brother twelve; they abide by their agreement; and Romulus has the direction of the city. A suitable day is chosen, on which he may trace out *the plan for* the walls with the plough. The festival of Pales was at hand; from that time the work is commenced upon. A trench is dug[32] down to the firm clay; fruits are thrown into the bottom of it, and some earth fetched from the neighbouring soil. The trench is filled again with the earth, and, when filled, an altar is built over it; and the hearth, but newly erected, is graced with the kindled fire. After that, pressing the tail of the plough, he traces out the walls with a furrow; a white cow with a snow-white bull bears the yoke. These were the words of the king: "Do thou, Jupiter, aid me as I found this city; and Mavors my father and mother Vesta, and all other, ye Deities, whom it is a religious duty to invoke, attend; let this work of mine rise under your auspices. Long may be its duration, may its sway be that of an all-ruling land; and under it may

[32] *A trench is dug.*]—Ver. 821. The ceremony here mentioned was performed according to the ritual prescribed by the superstitions of Etruria. This trench or pit was filled up again, and it must not be confounded with the furrow made by the plough. It was called 'mundus,' and was supposed to form a passage to the infernal regions.

be both the rising and the setting of the day." Thus he prayed; Jupiter gave an omen by a peal of thunder on the left hand, and from the heavens on the left the lightnings were hurled. Rejoicing in the omen, the citizens laid the foundations, and in a short space of time there stood the new wall. Celer urged on the work, whom Romulus himself had called, and had said to him, "Celer, be this the task of thy care, that no one pass over the walls or the furrow that has been made with the plough: him who dares to do so, put to death." Remus, in ignorance of this, begins to scoff at walls so lowly, and to say, "Shall the people receive any protection from these?" And without pausing, he leaps over them. Celer strikes him down[33] with a pick-axe for his daring; streaming with blood he presses the hard ground. When the King is informed of this, he swallows down the tears that inwardly arise, and keeps his sorrow shut up within his breast. He is unwilling openly to weep, and is careful to set an example of fortitude, and "With like results," says he, "may the foe pass over my walls." Yet he performs his obsequies; he *then* is no longer able to restrain his tears, and the affliction which he had concealed becomes manifest. He imprints the last kisses on him laid out on the bier, and he cries, "Farewell, my brother! snatched from me by no will of mine." And *then* he anointed the corpse about to be committed to the flames; what he did, the same did Faustulus and Acca with her sad locks dishevelled. Then did the Quirites (though not yet become entitled to that name) bewail the youth; and the last fire was applied amid laments to the funeral pile.[34] A city arises, (who then could have believed this tale from any one?) destined *one day* to place her conquering foot upon *all* lands. Mayst thou hold sway over the universe, and mayst thou ever be under the rule of mighty Cæsar; still continue to have more and more chiefs

[33] *Strikes him down.*]—Ver. 843. Eusebius says that Remus was killed by Fabius, an officer under Romulus. Other writers represent that he was killed by Romulus himself, while some say that he was slain in a popular tumult.

[34] *The funeral pile.*]—Ver. 856. Remus was buried in a spot called Remuria, on the Palatine Hill, where he had taken his augury. It is said that there was a dispute among the citizens whether the city should be called Roma, Rema, or Remura. The Romans were not called by the name of Quirites till after they had been united with the Sabines.

of that name, and oft as, in the subdued world, thou shalt stand erect, may all realms be lower than thy shoulders.

Pales has been sung by me. I, too, shall now sing of the Vinalia:[35] but between the two *festivals* one day intervenes. Do, ye damsels of the town, worship the deity of Venus; very favourable is Venus to the gains of the prostitutes.[36] Pray, with an offering of frankincense, for beauty and the public favour: pray for the arts of allurement, and for words well suited to merriment: offer to your mistress the pleasing spearmint, with her own myrtle, and the chaplets of bulrushes woven with the enwreathed roses. Now it is proper that the temple adjoining to the Collinian gate should be resorted to. From the hill of Sicily[37] does it derive its name. And when

[35] *The Vinalia.*]—Ver. 863. There has been considerable discussion among the critics whether this festival was celebrated in honour of Jupiter or Venus alone. The truth seems to be that it was in honour of both Deities, as Plutarch says (Rom. Quest. 45), that wine was on this day poured forth in honour of Venus, whence the festival received the name of Veneralia, and among the Greeks of ἀφροδίσια. Ovid, too, says (in lines 898-9) that Jupiter claims it as his festival. Varro says that the Vinalia was celebrated in honour of Jupiter, and not Venus. But there was a festival called the 'Vinalia rustica,' or 'rural Vinalia,' celebrated on the 19th of August, and it is of that that Varro, in all probability, speaks. Ovid may have possibly confused the characteristics of the two festivals. The Vinalia were so called from 'vinum,' 'wine.'

[36] *Gains of prostitutes.*]—Ver. 866. 'Professarum.' When a woman at Rome intended to adopt the calling of a prostitute, she professed, or declared, her intention of so doing before the ædiles. She was then entered among the 'Togatæ,' or wearers of the 'toga,' and was no longer allowed to wear the 'stola,' or long robe of the matrons, and became exempt from the laws against adultery. Females of patrician and equestrian rank were not allowed to enter in the ranks of the 'Professæ,' even if they had the inclination to attain a distinction of so unenviable a nature. This method of enrolment and supervision, as business-like as it is unbecoming, prevails in France, Belgium, and other countries on the continent even to the present day.

[37] *The hill of Sicily.*]—Ver. 872. That is, Mount Eryx, from which Venus derived her epithet of 'Erycina.' The temple at the Collinian gate was dedicated A.U.C. 571. Syracuse was not taken by M. Claudius Marcellus till thirty-one years afterwards; so that the poet is guilty of an anachronism in attributing the dedication to that event. But there was another temple to Venus Erycina, built on the Capitoline Hill by the direction of the Sibylline books, three years after the taking of Syracuse; and it is most probably to that, that the poet intended to make allusion. Mount Eryx was near Drepanum, on the west coast of Sicily. On it, there was a splendid temple of Venus, the foundation of which was attributed to Æneas and his followers.

Claudius[38] gained possession of the Syracuse of Arethusa, thee too, O Eryx, he conquered in war. Venus was transferred thence, according to the verse of the long-lived Sibyl, and preferred to be worshipped in the city of her descendants. Why, then, they call the feast of Venus by the name of Vinalia, you *now* ask; and why that day is sacred to Jove? There was a war to decide *the question* whether Turnus or Æneas should be the son-in-law of the Latian Amata.[39] Turnus solicited the aid of Etruria. Mezentius was famed, and fierce when *once* he had taken up arms: mighty as he was on horseback,[40] even mightier was he on foot. Him, the Rutulians and Turnus endeavoured to unite to their side. On the other hand, thus the Etrurian chieftain replied: "My bravery costs me no small price, I call these scars of mine to witness; this armour, too, which oft have I had sprinkled with my own blood. Do thou who seekest my aid divide with me the next new wine from thy vats—no *very* great reward. I delay not to give my aid. For you it is to pay; to conquer is my part. How would Æneas wish that this price had been refused to me?" The Rutulians assented: Mezentius puts on his armour; Æneas arms too, and addresses Jove *in prayer*: "The vintage of my foe has been promised to the Etrurian king, O Jove! Thou shalt quaff the new wine from the branch of the Latian vine!" The better vow prevails; the huge Mezentius falls, and beats the ground with his scornful breast; autumn arrives, stained with the trodden grapes; the wine owed to him is given to Jupiter, well deserving of it. Hence the day is called Vinalia. Jupiter claims it as his own,

---

[38] *Claudius.*]—Ver. 874. M. Claudius Marcellus was the first Roman general that defeated Hannibal. He besieged Syracuse, in Sicily, and took it while the inhabitants were celebrating the festival of Diana in the night time. Again engaging with Hannibal, he was killed in an ambuscade in his sixtieth year, and his fifth consulship. He was the third person who governed the 'Spolia Opima,' having, after the first Punic war, defeated the Gauls, and slain, with his own hand, their king Viridomarus, A.U.C. 530.

[39] *The Latian Amata.*]—Ver. 879. She was the wife of Latinus, king of Latium, and the mother of Lavinia, whom Æneas married after his conquest of Turnus. This war, including the alliance of Turnus and Mezentius, the King of Etruria, and the death of them both, forms the subject of the last six books of the Æneid of Virgil.

[40] *On horseback.*]—Ver. 882. The passage, 'Et vel equo magnus, vel pede major erat,' will either admit of the translation above given, or it may mean 'powerful was he in horse, and still more so in foot.'

and takes pleasure in its being in the number of his festivals.

When April shall have but six days to remain, the season of the spring will be in the midst of its course; and in vain will you look for the Ram of Helle, daughter of Athamas; the rains now show themselves; the Dog, too, rises.[41] On this day, as I was returning to Rome from Nomentum,[42] a procession, all arrayed in white, met me in the middle of the way. The Flamen was going to the sacred grove of the ancient *Goddess* Rubigo,[43] about to offer in the flames the entrails of a dog and those of a sheep. Forthwith I approached him, that I might not be unacquainted with this ceremonial: and thy Flamen, O Quirinus, gave utterance to these words: " Corroding[44] Robigo, do thou spare the blade of the corn, and let the smooth top quiver on the surface of the ground. Do thou permit the crops, nourished by the favoring seasons of the heavens, to grow apace until they are ready for the sickle. Thy power is not harmless *in its exercise*. The grain which thou hast marked as thine own, the sorrowing husbandman

---

[41] *The Dog, too, rises.*]—Ver. 904. This is not the fact, as the Constellation Canis sets on the 7th of the Calends of May. One Manuscript reads, 'Occidit atque Canis,' 'And the Dog sets,' which would be correct. On this day was the acronychal setting of the Ram.

[42] *Nomentum.*]—Ver. 905. This was a town of the Sabine country, to the east of Rome; the road to it lay through the Viminal gate.

[43] *Ancient Goddess Rubigo.*]—Ver. 907. Rubigo, or Robigo, was a Goddess, whose name signifies 'rust,' or 'mildew.' Her festival was the 'Robigalia,' here mentioned. It was celebrated by Numa, to propitiate her at this season in favour of the growing crops, to ensure their protection against blight, smut, and mildew. Some writers call the Divinity, Robigus, making him a God. The temple was in the Via Nomentana, near the Porta Catularia. Gower thus renders this and the following line:—

> ' A flamen into Rust's old grove did hie,
> The entrails of a dog and sheep to frie.'

Festus says, that at the 'Porta Catularia,' or 'Dog's Gate,' (through which the Nomentan road ran), 'they used to propitiate the Dog-star, which is injurious to corn, with the sacrifice of rusty-coloured or tawny dogs, in order that the corn might ripen free from disease.' He, perhaps means to say that at the setting of the Dog-star this sacrifice took place, as in another passage he himself tells us that the sacrifice was made to the God Robigus.

[44] *Corroding.*]—Ver. 911. 'Robigo,' mildew, or properly meal-dew, infects corn in the shape of a red powder, of a glutinous nature, which, eating into it, gives it a rough, leprous appearance.

reckons in the number of the lost. Not so injurious to the corn are the winds or the showers; nor is it so pallid when consumed by the frost, rigid as marble, as, when with his warmth, the sun makes hot the moistened stalks; in such case, dread Goddess, is thy wrath exercised. Spare, I pray thee, and keep thy rough hands from the crops; injure not our fields: to possess the power of inflicting injury is enough: seize not in thy embrace the tender crops, but rather the hard iron, and do thou first destroy that which has the power of destroying others. More to our benefit wilt thou corrode the swords and the hurtful weapons; them we want not: the world is at peace. Let the rakes and the hardy mattocks, and the crooked ploughshare, the implements of the country, be furbished: let rust stain arms; and let some one as he strives to draw his sword from the scabbard, find that it has become fast by the lapse of time. But hurt not the corn, and let the husbandman be ever enabled to pay his vows to thee, keeping thyself afar." He had spoken; in his right hand hung a towel, with a loose nap, and there was a censer of frankincense, with a bowl of wine. The frankincense and wine he placed on the altars, and the vitals of a sheep; the filty entrails, too (of this I was a witness), of an unclean dog. Then the Flamen says to me, "You ask," *for, in fact,* I had asked, "why so strange a victim is offered in sacrifice? understand the reason; there is a Dog;[45] they call him the Icarian, and as his Constellation rises, the parched earth is athirst, and the corn is burnt up. Instead of the dog of the Constellation, this dog is placed on the altar, and it has no other reason than its name why it should *thus* be put to death?"

When the sister of Titan, having left the brother of the Phrygian Assaracus,[46] has thrice raised[47] her beams over the

[45] *There is a dog.*]—Ver. 939. Icarus, the father of Erigone, being slain by some intoxicated shepherds, his dog Mæra, returning home, drew his daughter by her robe to where her father lay. She died of grief, and the dog perished of hunger. In compassion, Bacchus raised him to the skies, calling Icarius by the name of Boötes, Erigone the Virgin, and Mæra, Canicula, 'the Dog-star,' or Procyon.

[46] *Brother of the Phrygian Assaracus.*]—Ver. 943. The poet alludes to Tithonus, the husband of Aurora, but by mistake he has put Assaracus in the place of Priam, as Priam was the brother of Tithonus, and Assaracus was their great uncle.

[47] *Has thrice raised.*]—Ver. 944. The Floralia began on the fourth of the Calends of May.

boundless world, the Goddess comes, wreathed with the variegated chaplets of a thousand flowers: the stage, *then*, admits the practice of a looser merriment. The festival of Flora ends on the Calends of May; then will I return to it: at this time a greater work engages me.

Vesta claims a day; *on this day* Vesta was received within a kindred threshold.[48] Thus did the just Senators appoint. Phœbus[49] has a part; to Vesta was yielded a second part. What remains from them, *Augustus* himself possesses. Last *for ever*, ye laurels of the Palatium,[50] and *long* may the house stand, its front garlanded with oak. Three everlasting Gods does *this* one *house* contain.

[48] *A kindred threshold.*]—Ver. 949. The Pontifex Maximus being required to live in a public building, and Augustus filling that office, he gave a part of the Palatium, where he resided, to the service of the Goddess, and on this day, by a decree of the Senate, her sacred fire was removed thither. The threshold is called kindred, in the same sense in which we have before seen the poet, in his flattery, finding some affinity between Vesta, a Trojan deity, and the Julii (among whom Augustus was adopted) descended from Æneas.

[49] *Phœbus.*]—Ver. 951. A temple was dedicated to Apollo by Augustus, probably on this day, on the Palatine Hill. It contained a public library, where the poets used to recite their compositions, and where the works of the Roman authors were preserved.

[50] *The Palatium.*]—Ver. 953. The poet alludes to the civic crown of oak-leaves, which, as has been before stated, the Senate ordered to be suspended before the palace of Augustus between two branches of laurel, symbolical of the preservation of the lives of the people by Augustus, and of his triumphs over his enemies.

BOOK THE FIFTH.

CONTENTS.

The three conflicting opinions on the origin of the name of the month of May, Ver. 1—110. The rising of the Constellation of the Goat, and its history, 111—128. The Lares Præstites, and the erection of their altar, 129—146. The temple of Bona Dea, 147—158. The wind Argestes, and the rising of the Hyades, with their history, 159—182. The Floral games, their origin, and the worship of the Goddess Flora, at Rome, with the story of the birth of Mars, 183—371. The rising of the Constellation of the Centaur, and the story of Charon, 379—414. The rising of the Lyre and the Scorpion, 415—418. The nocturnal celebration of the Lemuria, and the burial of Remus, 419—492. The setting of Orion, his birth and translation to heaven, 493—544. The temple of Mars Ultor; the slaughter of Crassus; and the recovery from the Parthians of the Roman standards, 545—598. The rising of the Pleiades, and the beginning of summer, 599—602. The rising of the Constellation of the Bull, with its origin, 603—620. Figures made of rushes are thrown in the river Tiber; the arrival of Hercules in Latium, 621—662. The hymn to Mercury; his festival; the tradesman's prayer to him, 663—692. The Sun enters the Constellation Gemini; its origin; the combat of Castor and Pollux with Lynceus, 693—720. The Agonalia repeated; the setting of the Dog Star, 721—724. The Tubilustria, or purification of the trumpets, 725, 726. The four initials in the Calendar, 727, 728. The temple of Fortuna Publica, 729—732. The setting of Boötes, and the rising of the Hyades, 733—734.

You inquire for what reason I suppose that its name was given to the month of May. *My answer is*, the cause has not been quite clearly ascertained by me.[1] Just as the traveller comes to a stand, and, in his uncertainty, knows not which way to go when he sees a road in every direction; so,

---

[1] *Ascertained by me.*]—Ver. 1, 2. Gower thus translates these lines,—

'You ask me whence this month is called May.
I know not well what reason down to lay.'

because it is in my power to assign different reasons, I know not in which direction to turn, and the very abundance of them is a difficulty *to me*. Tell me, ye who hold possession of the springs of Aganippian Hippocrene,² the pleasing track of the steed of Medusa.³ The Goddesses differed *on the point*. Polyhymnia⁴ begins, the first of them *to speak;* the others keep silence, and mark her sayings in their minds. After the state of Chaos, when first the three elements⁵ were given to the world, and the whole universe receded into new forms, the earth, by its own weight, tended downwards, and drew after it the seas; whereas its lightness buoyed up the æther to the highest position. Thou too, O Sun, together with the stars, weighed down by no gravity, and you, ye steeds of the Moon, sprung forth in a direction upward. But neither did the earth for any length of time yield to the heaven, nor the rest of the stars to the sun; there was an equality of honour among them. Ofttimes did any one of the lower class of the Deities dare to sit on the throne, which thou, O Saturn, was wont to occupy: *then* any stranger God reclined side by side with Ocean, and Tethys was received many a time in the lowest place;⁶ until, *at length,* Honour and Reverence, with

---

² *Aganippian Hippocrene.*]—Ver. 7. The author seems here to confuse the streams of Aganippe and Hippocrene, which were distinct fountains near Mount Helicon, in Bœotia. Pausanias tells us that Aganippe was on the left of the ascent to the grove of the Muses, on Mount Helicon, and that Hippocrene was situate twenty stadia beyond the grove. As the poet distinguishes them in the fifth Book of his Metamorphoses, l. 132, we may presume that he here gives the epithet to the one from the other, on account of their contiguity.

³ *Steed of Medusa.*]—Ver. 8. Pegasus; who was fabled to have sprung from the blood of Medusa, when slain by Perseus. These fountains were said to have sprung from the ground when struck by the hoof of Pegasus.

⁴ *Polyhymnia.*]—Ver. 9. She was the muse of lyric poetry. All the Greek poets call her Πολύμνια, or 'Polumnia,' meaning 'she of the many songs.' Ovid and Horace introduce the additional letters into her name.

⁵ *The three elements.*]—Ver. 11. In the first Book, l. 103, and in the Metamorphoses, he mentions four elements. Here he looks upon æther and air as together constituting but one element.

⁶ *The lowest place.* Ver. 21, 22. Gower thus renders these lines,—

'Each noteless deity would by Ocean old
Sit cheek by joul. Oft Tethys was controll'd.'

Allusion is here made to the seats, or rather the couches, on which the

mild aspect, placed their bodies on the *nuptial* couch, sanctioned by the laws. Hence did Majesty spring, she who rules the universe, and of full growth was she on the very day on which she was produced. She delayed not; she took her seat on high in the midst of Olympus, resplendent with gold, and conspicuous with purple plaited robe. Together with her sit Modesty and Awe; you might behold every Deity assuming an aspect in conformity with hers. Forthwith respect for high rank take possession of their minds; dignity is *now* valued, and each is no longer occupied by self-complaisance. This state of things remained in heaven for many years, until, by the decree of the Fates, the oldest of the Gods was removed from the topmost place *of heaven*. The Earth brought forth her savage offspring, huge monsters, giants, who would dare to attempt an entrance into the palace of Jove. A thousand hands she gave to them, and serpents in place of legs; and she said, "Take up your arms against the great Gods." These were preparing to pile up the mountains to the highest stars, and to provoke the mighty Jupiter to battle. Jove, hurling his thunderbolts from the heights of heaven, overturned the vast piles on those who had formed them.[7] Defended by these arms the Majesty of the Gods still remains, and *from that time* abides in security. Next to Jove she sits; she is his most trusty guardian, and without violence she secures the sceptre to his sway. She came on earth, too; Romulus and Numa[8] worshipped her; afterwards the others,

ancients reclined, when taking their meals. The lowest was esteemed the least honourable place.

[7] *Those who had formed them.*]—Ver. 41, 42. The poet here refers to the war of the giants against the Gods of heaven. This story has been thought by some to have been the corruption of a tradition of the fall of the angels from their blessed state; by others, it is supposed to bear reference to the heaping pile upon pile in the construction of the tower of Babel. Gower thus translates these lines,—

'He from his tower discharged his thunder straight,
And on th' invaders' pates whelm'd that vast weight.'

[8] *Romulus and Numa.*]—Ver. 48. The poet means merely to assign as the first reason for the name of May, 'Maius,' that it was derived from this goddess, 'Majestas,' whose name in the early days of the Latin tongue would be spelt and written 'Maiestas.' The beauty of the story is worthy of far more commendation than the ingenuity of the suggestion founded on it.

each in his own day. She invests fathers and mothers with dutiful respect; she is the companion of boys and maidens. She adds dignity to the fasces when granted, and to the curule *chair of* ivory; she triumphs, standing aloft,[9] the horses wreathed with garlands." Polyhymnia had ended her words; Clio and Thalia, skilled at the sounding lyre, approved of what she said. Urania[10] took up *the discourse;* all kept silence, and no voice, save hers, could be heard. In days of yore, great was the respect of the hoary head, and the wrinkles of old age were honoured. The youths undertook the toils of Mars and the undaunted warfare; and in defence of their Gods, they remained at their posts. That age, which was feebler in strength and useless in bearing arms, often by its counsel assisted its country. Nor then was the Senate-house open *to a citizen* but in his latter years, and the Senate was the placid synonyme of old age. The old man gave ordinances to the people, and by definite laws the age was fixed at which *this* honour should be obtained. In those days *the old man* walked between the youths,[11] they not denying him *the honour;* and if he had but one companion, he took the inner place. Who *in those days*, in the presence of an old man, would dare to utter words worthy of a blush? Old age conferred the right to reprimand. Romulus saw this, and he called the selected persons, 'Fathers.' To these was referred the government of the new-built city. From this circumstance I am inclined *to think* that the elders gave their name to May, and consulted the honour of their old age. It is possible, too, that Numitor may have said, "Grant, Romulus, this month to the aged," and that the grandson did not refuse his grandsire.

[9] *Standing aloft.*]—Ver. 52. The meaning is, that she attends the general in his triumph, when he stands aloft in his chariot drawn by horses crowned with garlands.

[10] *Urania.*]—Ver. 55. Clio presided over history; Thalia was the patroness of comedy; and Urania was the muse of astronomy. She gives it as her opinion that as June was so called from the 'juniores,' the younger men, so May received its name from the 'majores,' or 'maiores,' the aged.

[11] *Between the youths.*]—Ver. 67. The middle was deemed the most honourable place in walking, the persons on either side being said 'claudere latera,' 'to shut in the sides.' Maturity of years was at an early period considered as an indispensable qualification for office. By the law of Villius, the age for the Quæstorship was 31; for the Ædileship, 37; the Prætorship, 40; and the Consulship, 43 years.

June, too, is at hand, so called from the name of the Juniors, the successor *of this month*, and no small guarantee for the honours of the month before it." Then did Calliope, first of her party,[12] thus begin, her careless tresses wreathed in ivy, " In former times, Ocean had wedded Tethys,[13] daughter of Titan, who encircles the earth whichever way it extends, with her flowing waters. Pleïone, born of this marriage, is united to Atlas, supporter of the skies, and becomes the mother of the Pleiädes. Of these, Maia is said to have surpassed her sisters in beauty, and to have been embraced by the mighty Jove. She brought forth on the brow of Cyllene, clad with the cypress, him who with his winged feet cleaves through the æthereal path. Him the Arcadians, and the rapidly flowing Ladon, and the mighty Mænalus duly worship, a land believed to be more ancient[14] than the moon. Evander, an exile from Arcadia, had come to the fields of Latium, and had brought the Gods which he had placed *on board his ships.* Here, where now is Rome, the capital of the world, there were then but trees and grass, and a few sheep, and a cottage here and there. When they had come hither, " Stop," cried his prophetic mother, " for this spot of country shall *one day* be the site of an empire."[15] The Nonacrian hero obeys his mother and prophetess, and, a stranger, he paused on a foreign soil. Many sacred rites indeed did she teach these nations, but first the ceremonial of the horned Faunus and of the God of the winged foot.[16] Faunus, half-goat in form, thou

---

[12] *Calliope, first of her party.*]—Ver. 80. Calliope, or Calliopea, was the muse that presided over epic poetry. The mention here made, of her beginning, as the first of her party, may either mean that she began to speak, the first of those that were of the opinion expressed by her, or that she was the first of those who had not yet spoken, to break silence.

[13] *Had wedded Tethys.*]—Ver. 81. Ocean was the brother of Tethys, and they were of the Titan race. Pleïone was their daughter, who married Atlas, son of her uncle Iapetus, and brought forth the Pleiädes, on Mount Cylene. Maia was one of them, and she bore Mercury to Jupiter.

[14] *To be more ancient.*]—Ver. 90. See note to Book i. line 469, on the antiquity of the Arcadians.

[15] *Site of an empire.*]—Ver. 95, 96. Gower thus renders these lines;

' Here sailing, Hold, his learned mother cried;
For on those fields a kingdom's plat I've spied.'

[16] *God of the winged foot.*]—Ver. 99, 100. Gower gives this translation of these lines;—

' He taught these nations many services,
Both horn-hoofed Pans, and winged Mercuries.'

art worshipped by the aproned Luperci, at the time when the hides cut *in thongs* purify the thronged ways. But to *this* month hast thou given the name of thy mother, thou inventor of the curved lyre, patron of the thieves.[17] And this was not thy first act of duty; thou art believed to have given to the lyre the seven strings, *as being* the number of the Pleiädes." She, too, had ended, and was applauded by the voice of her sisters. What am I to do? Each part of the choir has the same *weight with me*. Let the favours of the Piërian train be equally bestowed on me, and let no one of them be praised by me more or less *than her sisters*.

From Jove let my work commence. On the first night is to be seen the star[18] that tended the cradle of Jove. The rainy Constellation of the Olenian she-goat[19] rises; she enjoys heaven as the reward of the milk which she afforded. The Naiad Amalthea, noble on the Cretan Ida, is said to have concealed Jupiter in the woods. To her belonged a beautiful goat, the dam of two kids, with horns towering, and bending over her back, and with an udder, such as *by right* the nurse

[17] *Patron of the thieves.*]—Ver. 103, 104. The poet gives, as the third origin of the title of the month, the name of Maia, the mother of Mercury, who (through the medium of his son Evander) called it 'Maius,' in honour of her. Gower thus renders these and the two following lines—

'But witty shirking Mercury who framed
The harp, this month from his fair mother named.
Nor was 't his first good deed, for he made even
His harp-strings number with the Pleiads seven.'

[18] *To be seen the star.*]—Ver. 112. On the Calends of May is the heliacal rising of the star 'Capella,' 'the She-goat.' It is on the right shoulder of Heniochus, 'the Charioteer,' a Constellation on the north side of the Milky Way.

[19] *The Olenian she-goat.*]—Ver. 113. Olenus was a town of Achaia, in the Peloponnesus, situated on the river Melas. There was also a town in Bœotia of that name. Lactantius tells us that Jupiter was nursed by Amalthea and Melissa, daughters of Melisseus, king of Crete, upon goats' milk and honey. Amalthea, the daughter of Olenus, is said by some writers, among others by Musæus, as quoted by Eratosthenes, to have owned the goat that is mentioned in the text, and to have given Jupiter to be suckled by it when he was delivered to her from Rhea by the hands of Themis. According to other accounts, the names of the daughters of Melisseus were Adrastea and Ida, who committed the infant to be suckled by the goat Amalthea. Who can look for uniformity in a story whose very existence depended on the fertility of the imagination? Ovid does not say, or even seem to imply, that the name of the goat was Amalthea.

of Jove ought to have. She gave milk to the God; but against a tree she broke her horn, and *thus* was mutilated of half of her beauty. This the Nymph took up, and wreathed it with fresh gathered herbs, and then raised it, filled with fruits, to the mouth of Jupiter. He, when he held the sovereignty of heaven, and sat on the throne of his father, and when there was no one greater than the unconquered Jove, changed his nurse, and her fruit-bearing horn into Constellations, which *last* still retains the name of its owner.

The Calends of May beheld the altar erected to the guardian Lares,[20] and the little statues of the Gods. These Curius[21] vowed; but the great length of time is *fast* destroying them, and extreme age is wearing away[22] the stone. However, the cause of the title which is applied to them is, that they stand in guard over all things kept in safety under their eyes. They stand in guard over us, too, and they guard the fortifications of the city; they are *ever* at hand, and are giving us their assistance. But before their feet there used to stand a dog, hewn out of the same stone. What was the reason of its *so* standing with the Lar? *It is, because* each of them guards the house; each, too, is faithful to his owner. The cross roads[23] are

[20] *Guardian Lares.*]—Ver. 130. On the Calends of May, public sacrifice was offered to the Lares. Augustus directed them to be publicly worshipped twice in the year.

[21] *Curius.*]—Ver. 131. Manius Curius Dentatus held the consulship with P. Cornelius Rufinus. He enabled the Romans to withstand Pyrrhus, and triumphed over the Samnites. When their ambassadors came with the intention of bribing him, they found him at work in his field, and in answer to their solicitations, he told them that he would rather be the ruler of the rich than be rich himself, and that invincible in the field, he could not be conquered by money. He was not, however, the first to introduce the worship of the Lares into Rome, as Varro tells us that Titus Tatius, the Sabine, raised a shrine to the Lares; and Dionysius says, that Servius Tullius first instituted the Compitalia.

[22] *Is wearing away.*]—Ver. 131. The poet says that Curius erected a statue to the 'Lares Præstites,' or 'Protectors,' and that it represented them (probably in their usual loose Gabinian garb) with a dog, the emblem of watchfulness, at their feet; but he says that from length of time (the lapse of about 400 years) the statues had gone to decay.

[23] *The cross roads.*]—Ver. 140. The Lares were, perhaps, originally only represented by the statues mentioned in the text, and the shrine of Tatius. But at the time when the poet wrote, we learn from the Scholiast on Horace, Sat. book ii. Sat. 3. l. 281, that Augustus had set up

pleasing to the God; pleasing, too, to the dog.[24] Both the Lar and the tribe of Diana scare away the thieves; both the Lares and the dogs keep their watch throughout *the night*. I was inquiring after the statues of the twin-brother Gods that had fallen down under the power of lengthened years. A thousand Lares does our city contain, and the Genius of the chief,[25] who confided them *to our care;* and to the three Deities do the streets pay homage. Whither am I hurried away? The month of August will give me a right opportunity for this strain, meanwhile the good Goddess[26] must be sung by me.

Lares, or Penates, at the 'Compita,' which were places where two or more roads met, and that he instituted an order of priests to attend to their worship, taken from the Libertini, and called Augustales. This accounts for the 'mille,' or thousand Lares mentioned in the text below. Varro says that there were 265 stations for the Lares at the corners of the streets at Rome. Probably, this custom first suggested the idea of setting up the images of the Virgin and Saints at the corners of the streets, which are still to be seen in Catholic countries at the present day.

[24] *Pleasing, too, to the dog.*]—Ver. 140. Probably, because the offals of the neighbouring houses were thrown there. As, in towns, the idlers of the human race generally select the corner of a street for the purposes of gossip and warming their hands in their pockets, surely the canine race may be allowed at a humble distance to follow their example in choosing such a locality, especially when for a much more legitimate and practical purpose—that of satisfying their hunger. Dogs were sacred to Diana, as the Goddess of the chase. This and the previous line are thus translated by Gower—

'Both lov'd of masters, both the house defend;
Both god and dog the three leet ways do tend.'

[25] *Genius of the chief.*]—Ver. 145. This is an allusion to the image of Augustus, which, by his order, was erected at the corners of the streets, in company with the Lares or Penates. Some have supposed that Mercury, the father of the Lares, is here signified, but the expression ' qui tradidit illos,' ' who confided them,' seems especially to point to Augustus.

[26] *The good Goddess.*]—Ver. 148. According to Macrobius, ' Bona Dea,' ' the good Goddess,' was Fauna, or Fatua, the daughter of Faunus, who was so modest that she never left the woman's apartment, and never set eyes on a man, or was seen by one, and her name was never mentioned in public. Other accounts make her the wife of Faunus, who flogged her to death for drunkenness, while others make her a Phrygian, the mother of Midas. Others take her for either Ops, Juno, Maia, Cybele, or Tellus. Men were forbidden to enter her temple, or to be present at her sacrifices, which were performed by the women in secret. It was her rites that Clodius profaned by his presence in disguise, when enamoured of Pompeia, the second wife of Julius Cæsar, who was one of the priestesses of the Goddess.

There is a natural rock; the reality of the fact gave its name to the place. They call it "The Crags;" it is a large part of the hill. On this spot[27] had Remus stood, to no purpose, at the time when you, ye birds of the Palatine, gave the commencing sovereignty to his brother. There did the Senators erect, on the gently sloping hill, the temple that utterly abhors the gaze of males. The heiress of the ancient name of the Clausi[28] dedicated this; one who never submitted her virgin person to the embrace of man. Livia restored it, that she might not fail to imitate her husband, and that in every point she might follow in his footsteps.

When the next *dawn*, the daughter of Hyperion, raises on the steeds of the morning her rosy light, the stars being driven away, the cold north-western wind[29] will gently bend the tops of the ears of corn, and the white canvass will be set from the Calabrian waves; and soon as the darkening twilight ushers in the night, no one of all the train of the Hyades[30] lies concealed. The face of the Bull glitters, radiant

[27] *On this spot.*]—Ver. 150. That is, the Aventine Hill, or Mount; on which was located the temple of 'Bona Dea,' which the poet proceeds to mention.

[28] *Name of the Clausi.*]—Ver. 155. This was probably Claudia Quinta, mentioned in the fourth book, l. 305; and the more so, as the poet does not think it necessary here to mention her name, which, if he had not already given it, he would most probably now have done. The temple of Bona Dea was built by this lady, and was restored by Livia, the wife of Augustus.

[29] *North-western wind.*]—Ver. 161. Argestes. This wind was fabled to be the son of Aurora, and was called by the Greeks 'Iapyx.' It was a favourable wind for persons sailing from Calabria, in the south of Italy, for Greece; the passage to which country was usually taken from Brundisium, a city on the Calabrian coast.

[30] *The Hyades.*]—Ver. 164. The poet says that the Hyades rise acronychally on the sixth of the Nones of May; whereas Pliny (Nat. Hist. Book xviii. c. 66) says that they rise cosmically on that day. Some authorities, differing from Ovid, say that these stars were originally Nymphs of Dodona in Epirus, and the nurses of Bacchus; and that, dreading the resentment of Juno, they were translated by Jupiter to the skies. Three derivations of this name are mentioned by ancient writers; the first from ὕειν, pronounced by the Latins, hyein, ' to rain;' the second, from the Greek letter Ψ, 'upsilon,' which the Constellation was thought to resemble in figure; and the third, from ὕς, 'a pig,' for some fanciful reason unknown to us. Cicero says that his own countrymen, supposing this to have been the origin of the name, thence called the Constellation by the name of 'Suculæ,' ' the little pigs,' derived from the Latin word ' sus,' ' a pig:' he adopts the first derivation. On the Nature of the Gods, Book ii. c. 43.

with seven flaming stars, which the Grecian mariner calls Hyades, from rain. Some think that they nursed Bacchus; some have supposed that they were the granddaughters of Tethys and of old Ocean. Not as yet was Atlas standing, bearing on his shoulders the burden of Olympus, when Hyas was born, distinguished for his beauty. Him and the Nymphs, did Æthra, daughter of Ocean, bring forth with timely throes; but Hyas was the elder born. While the down *of his cheek* is still young, with the net beset with variegated feathers,[31] he scares the timid deer; and the hare proves to him an abundant prey. But when his manliness ripened with his years, he dared to attack even the wild boars and the shaggy beasts of prey; and now while he was seeking the lair and the cubs of a lioness that had just brought forth, he himself became the bloodstained prey of the Libyan wild beast. His mother and his sorrowing sisters bewailed Hyas; Atlas too, destined to support with his neck the burden of the skies, *bewailed him.* Yet were both of the parents surpassed by the affection of the sisters; that *affection* raised them to the sky; Hyas gave them their name.

"Come hither, thou mother of the flowers, to be honoured by mirthful sports; in a former month I had deferred the recital of what related to thee. In April thou dost begin; thou passest on to the days of May. The one month at its departure receives thee; the other as it comes. Since the limits of the *two* months are thine, and make place for thee, either this one or that is suitable for thy praises. In this month, end *the games* of the Circus,[32] and the award of the prizes with the applause of the theatres: with this performance of the Circus let my strain proceed. Teach me thyself who *thou* art. The opinions of men are fallible; thou wilt be the best instructor as to thine own name." Thus I spoke; thus replied the Goddess to my request; while she was speaking, she breathed forth the vernal roses from her mouth. "I, who now am called Flora, was

[31] *Variegated feathers.*]—Ver. 173. 'Formidine.' The 'formido' was a toil, or net, covered with feathers of different colours, for the purpose of scaring birds and wild beasts. According to some authors, Hyas met his death by the sting of an adder.

[32] *The Circus.*]—Ver. 189. This was the Circus of Flora, in the sixth region of the city. The Floralia commenced on the 28th of April, and finished on the 3rd of May.

once called Chloris.³³ The Greek spelling of my name became corrupted by the Latin pronunciation. I was Chloris, a Nymph of the blessed plains, where, as thou hast heard, was formerly the abode of the blessed men. How great was my beauty it is irksome to one of my modesty to tell; but it procured a God as a son-in-law for my mother. 'Twas spring; I was roaming about: Zephyrus beheld me. I walked on; he followed me: I fled; he proved the stronger. Boreas³⁴ too had given to his brother a full precedent for violence, when he dared to bear off his prize from the house of Erectheus. Yet he made amends for his violence by giving me the name of wife, and in my married state I have no ground for complaint. I enjoy perpetual spring; *to me* the year is always most beauteous; the tree always bears its foliage; the earth its herbage. A fruitful garden in the fields of my dowry is mine; the breeze cherishes it; it is irrigated by a spring of trickling water. This my husband has filled with flowers of the choicest kinds, and he says, 'Do thou, Goddess, rule the empire of the flowers.' Ofttimes have I desired to reckon the tints as they were arranged, and I could not: their multitude exceeded all number. When first the dewy rime has been dashed from the leaves, and the variegated flowers warm in the beams of the sun, the Seasons³⁵ arrayed in painted robes as-

³³ *Chloris.*]—Ver. 194. This name is derived from the Greek adjective χλωρὸς, 'green,' and similarly, the word Flora is from 'flores,' 'flowers.' Though they are kindred terms, it could only arise from the exuberance of the poet's fancy to imagine that one word was a corruption of the other. There is little doubt that the story of Chloris, now lost to us, was a fiction of purely Greek origin; and that Flora was essentially an Italian deity. She was worshipped by the Sabines, and Titus Tatius erected a temple to her in Rome. Lactantius and Plutarch tell a very business-like and matter-of-fact story that she was a courtezan, who left her wealth to the Roman people, on the condition that her birth-day should be always celebrated by a festival, to be called the 'Floralia,' and that the Senate, out of shame, took upon themselves to feign that she was the Goddess of Flowers.

³⁴ *Boreas.*]—Ver. 203. This was the name of the north wind. He was fabled to have carried off Orithyia, the daughter of Erectheus, as she was dancing on the banks of the Ilissus. Mr. Keightley justly observes, that the name of Orithyia, signifying in Greek 'mountain rusher,' was a very good name for the spouse of the north wind.

³⁵ *The Seasons.*]—Ver. 217. They were the daughters of Jupiter and Themis, and were represented in embroidered robes. The Charites, or Graces, were also the children of Jupiter, and three in number, Aglaia, Thalia, and Euphrosyne. Some say that they were the daughters of Bac-

semble, and gather my presents into their light baskets. Forthwith, *to them* are added the Graces, and they plait the chaplets, and the garlands, *destined* to bind their heavenly locks. I was the first to spread the new seed throughout the unlimited nations; before then the earth was of but one tint. I was the first to create the flower of the Therapnæan[36] blood, and the complaint still remains that is written on its leaf. Thou too, Narcissus,[37] hast a name throughout the cultivated gardens—unhappy *in thy fate*, that thou didst not in thy own person form two individuals! Why should I tell of Crocus[38] or Attis, or the son of Cinyras,[39] from whose blood by my art their fame arises *in the shape of a flower?* Mars,[40] too, if thou art ignorant of the fact, was born by my art: that Jove may still remain in ignorance of it is my constant prayer. The sacred Juno, when, without a mother, Minerva was born, was grieved that Jupiter had not needed her aid. She was on her way, that she might complain to Ocean of the deeds of her husband; wearied with her toil, she stopped at my doors.[41] Soon as I saw her, I said, 'Daughter of Saturn, what has

chus and Venus; very unlikely parties, one would think, to be the full sisters of Priapus. In early days they were represented clothed, in later times naked. The Spartans reckoned but two, Clita and Phœna.

[36] *Therapnæan.*]—Ver. 223. Therapnæ was a town of Laconia. Hyacinthus was born at Amyclæ, in its vicinity. Reference has been made to him in a former page.

[37] *Narcissus.*]—Ver. 225. He was the son of the river Cephisus, and the nymph Liriope. While he was at a fountain he became enamoured of his own person, and pined away into the flower that still bears his name.

[38] *Crocus.*]—Ver. 227. He was enamoured of the nymph Smilax, and pined away into the flower that bears his name, while the Nymph was converted into a yew tree. Attis has been already mentioned (see book ii. l. 223.) Arnobius says that the violet sprang from his blood.

[39] *The son of Cinyras.*]—Ver. 227. Adonis was the son of Cinyras, king of Cyprus, by his daughter Myrrha, or, according to others, he was the son of Thoas and Myrrha. Hesiod makes him the son of Phœnix and Alphesibæa. Being killed by a wild boar, he was changed by Venus into an anemone. He was worshipped in Syria under the name of Thammuz, to which worship allusion is several times made in the writings of the prophets in the Old Testament.

[40] *Mars.*]—Ver. 229. Ovid is the only ancient writer that narrates this story of the birth of Mars by the aid of Flora.

[41] *Stopped at my doors.*]—Ver. 233-4. Gower thus renders these lines—

> Comes to old Ocean for to make her mone,
> And at our gate quite tired sits her down.'

brought thee here?' She tells me the place to which she is going: she adds, too, the reason. I consoled her with words of friendship. 'My care,' said she, 'cannot be alleviated by words. If Jove has become a father, having neglected the instrumentality of his wife, and if he in his own person possesses the title of both *husband and wife*, why should I despair of becoming a mother without the aid of my husband, and, keeping myself chaste, of bringing forth, untouched by any man? All the drugs in the wide world I will try. I will search both the seas and the abysses of Tartarus.'[42] She was in the middle of her speech:[43] I appeared to have the look of one in consideration. 'Thou seemest, Nymph,' she said, 'to have some influence *in such matters*.' Thrice did I intend to promise her my assistance—thrice was my tongue stayed. The wrath of Supreme Jove was the cause of my alarm. 'Give me, I pray, thy aid,' she said; 'my adviser shall not be disclosed:' and she *then* calls to witness the Deity of the Stygian stream. 'What thou seekest,' said I, 'a flower sent to me from the Olenian fields will give to thee; the one in my garden is the only plant. He who made me a present of it said, 'Touch, with this, a sterile cow; she shall become a dam.' I touched one; forthwith she did become a dam. Straightway, with my thumb, I plucked the flower as it adhered *to the stem;* she was touched *by me;* and when touched, she conceived in her womb. And now, pregnant, she enters Thrace and the regions on the left of the Propontis.[44]

[42] *Abysses of Tartarus.*]—Ver. 243-4. Gower renders these lines in the following quaint manner;—

'All charms and mixtures, both in land and seas,
I'll search and trie, and grope the Stygian lees.'

[43] *She was in the middle of her speech.*]—Ver. 245. 'Vox erat in cursu.' Literally, 'her voice was in the course.' It is absolutely the fact, that one critic takes the meaning of this to be, 'Juno spoke as she ran.' Well may Mr. Keightley express his astonishment. In such case we must suppose Flora to be 'keeping pace' with her, to listen to her story; which Juno could not, in civility, have permitted, especially as she was a very punctilious deity.

[44] *Propontis.*]—Ver. 257. This sea, which is now called the Sea of Marmora, was so called from being πρὸ, 'before,' the Euxine, or Black Sea. It was a part of the eastern boundary of Thrace, where Mars was especially venerated, on account of the hardy and warlike character of the people.

She gains her wish, and Mars is born. He, mindful that by means of me he had received his birth, said, 'Do thou occupy a place, too, in the city of Romulus.' Perhaps thou mayst imagine that my sway is only over the delicate chaplets; but my divine power extends to the fields *as well*. If the cornfields have blossomed well, then will the threshing floor be rich; if the vineyards have blossomed well, there will be *plenteous* wine; if the olives have blossomed well, most shining *with oil* will the year prove; the pomes as well enjoy the increase of this season. When the blossom has once been injured, the vetches and the beans perish, and thy lentiles, O Nile, river that flowest from afar. The wine, too, carefully stowed away in the spacious cellars, flowers,⁴⁵ and the scum covers the surface of the casks. Honey, too, is my province. I invite the winged insects that will yield the honey, to the violet, the cytisus, and the hoary thyme. The same thing do I when the spirits abound in the years of youth, and the body is *now* in strength." As she said these things I regarded her with silent astonishment. But she said, "Thou hast the privilege of learning, if there be any thing that thou seekest to know." "Tell me, O Goddess," I answered, "what was the origin of the games." Scarcely had I fully concluded, when she answered me. The other appliances of luxury were not yet in full operation: the man who was rich possessed either cattle or a wide tract of land. From this circumstance, too, it was that the rich man was called "locuples,"⁴⁶ and that money had the name of "pecunia." But now *at length* each was acquiring wealth by forbidden

---

⁴⁵ *In the cellars flowers.*]—Ver. 270. The poet is considered to be going rather too far here, when he places the scum of wine under the care of Vesta, because, when it rises, the wine is said 'florere,' 'to flower,' by virtue of a figurative adaptation of the word. The term is generally supposed to apply merely to the scum or effervescence of new wine. Might it not possibly apply to the mouldiness that would supervene upon that scum if left long standing, and which we know to be a vegetable subtance, or 'lichen?'

⁴⁶ *Was called 'locuples.'*]—Ver. 281. That is to say, the man who had much land was 'loci plenus,' 'full of land.' 'Pecunia,' 'money,' according to the poet, derives its name from 'pecus, 'cattle,' because originally the greatest part of a person's wealth consisted of cattle and flocks; as in those times cattle formed the most convenient medium of exchange, money, as its substitute, received its appellation from it. The first money that was used had figures of cattle stamped upon it; and, according to some, it was made out of the hides of cattle in a tanned state.

means. It had become a custom to depasture the lands of the people;[47] and long was that permitted, and there was no penalty *for so doing*. The people kept their public places in the guardianship of no one: and to pasture on his own private property was *deemed* the act of a simpleton. Such irregularities as these were reported to the Ædiles, the Publicii:[48] spirit before was wanting in *these* men. The people took cognizance of the matter: the offenders suffered the penalty of a fine; to its guardians the care of the public was a theme of praise. In part, the price was granted to me; and with great applause did the *Ædiles*, victorious *in the contest*, institute new games. With the *other* part they made, by contract, the carriage-road,[49] which then was a steep precipice; now it is a useful way, and they style it the Publician. I had *before* supposed that annual spectacles were instituted; she told me, not so, and added to her expressions these words: " Honour influences us too: in festivals and altars do we take pleasure, and we that inhabit the heavens are an ambitious set. Often, by his sin, has some mortal made the Gods enraged, and the victim has been a soothing sacrifice for his

[47] *The lands of the people.*]—Ver. 283. These lands were called 'pascua,' and a rent was paid for the liberty of grazing thereon, which went into the public funds, and was called 'scriptura,' as Mr. Thynne suggests, probably as being paid for the permission to enter one's name in the roll of those admitted to the advantage. The poet tells us that this payment was evaded to a great extent, till the Ædiles put a stop to the practice, who, then, no longer allowed interest or favour to screen those guilty of these malpractices.

[48] *The Publicii.*]—Ver. 288. These were Lucius and Marcius Publicius Malleolus, who were Ædiles of the people, A.U.C. 513. By the Licinian law no one person was allowed to stint more than 100 head of cattle or 500 sheep on the public pastures. Besides instituting the Floral games, a temple, which is not mentioned by the poet, was built in honour of Flora, out of the fines; this was afterwards repaired by Tiberius, as we learn from Tacitus, Annals, Book ii. c. 49.

[49] *The carriage road.*]—Ver. 293. 'Locant,' ' they let out to contract.' Varro and Festus confirm this account. Festus says, ' they made a road so that carriages could come up the Aventine hill to Velia:' Velia being one part, perhaps the highest, of the hill. Gower thus renders the four lines beginning from line 283,—

> ' The custom was to feed the people's commons
> Without controlment; they long time were no man's.
> Some law the people did their commons keep,
> He was a churl that by himself fed sheep.'

crimes. Ofttimes have I seen Jove,⁵⁰ when he was just about to hurl his thunderbolts, withhold his hand on the offering of some frankincense. But if we are slighted, the wrong is atoned for with weighty penalties, and our wrath proceeds beyond moderate bounds. Look at the grandson of Thestius;⁵¹ with flames, at a far distance, did he burn: the reason was, because the altar of Diana was without its fire. Look at the descendant of Tantalus;⁵² the same Goddess withheld from him the power of setting sail. A Virgin *indeed* she is, and *yet* twice has she avenged her altars when subjected to a slight. Hapless Hippolytus, thou couldst wish that thou hadst paid homage to Dione, when thou wast torn in pieces by thy frightened steeds. 'Twere a tedious task to recount the slights that have been chastised by calamity. Me, too, the Roman fathers neglected. What could I do? By what means could I give symptoms of my displeasure? What penalty could I inflict for this my disgrace? My wonted duties were forgotten by me in my sorrow. No longer I guarded the fields: no longer was the fruitful garden valued by me. The lilies faded; you might see the violets parched; and the filaments of the ruddy crocus become flaccid. Many a time did Zephyrus say to me, 'Do not, thyself, destroy thy own dowry.' Worthless to me was my dowry. The olive trees were in bloom; the wanton blasts nipped them. The corn-fields were in blossom; the corn was injured by hailstorms. The vine as yet gives a ground for hope; the heaven blackens in the quarter of the south wind, and the leaves are

⁵⁰ *Have I seen Jove.*]—Ver. 300-1. Gower's version of these lines runs thus,—

'Oft have I seen Jove hurling his fire storm,
At sight of incense hold his threat'ning arm.'

⁵¹ *Grandson of Thestius.*]—Ver. 305. Meleager, son of Æneus and Althea, daughter of Thestius. His mother, on his birth, was informed by the Fates that he would live till a log of wood, then burning on the fire, was consumed. On this, she removed it, and carefully preserved it. Meleager killed the Calydonian boar sent by Diana in revenge for the neglect of her worship; and he gave its skin to Atalanta, who had first wounded it. His mother's brothers attempting to deprive her of it, Meleager slew them; on which, in revenge, his mother threw the log on the fire, and he expired, when the flames, thus at a distance from him, had burnt out. Althea killed herself through grief.

⁵² *Descendant of Tantalus.*]—Ver. 307. Agamemnon; descended from Tantalus, through his son, Pelops. See Book i. l. 387.

stripped off by the sudden shower. I did not wish all this to happen, for I am not cruel in my wrath; but I took no care to repel *the evil*. The Senators assembled;[53] and if the year should blossom well, they vowed to my Godhead an annual festival. I assented to the vow. Lænas, the Consul, with his colleague Posthumius, in discharge of their promise, instituted in my honour these games." I was preparing to inquire why there was in these games a greater license,[54] and more freedom in merriment. But it occurred to me that she was no austere Deity, and that she had functions suited for the enjoyment of pleasure. Her temples are entirely surrounded with the wreaths of flowers[55] sewed together, and the gorgeous board is concealed by the roses showered down upon it. The drunken reveller dances with his hair wreathed with the bark of the linden-tree, and scarcely knowing what he does, is whirled along by the influence of the wine. In his drunken fit, *the lover* sings at the cruel threshold of his beauteous mistress; his perfumed locks support the delicate garlands. No grave matters are transacted with a brow enriched with the garland: and limpid water is not the beverage of those wreathed with flowers. As long as thou wast mixed, Ach-

[53] *The Senators assembled.*]—Ver. 327. In the consulship of L. Posthumius Albinus and M. Popilius Lænas, A.U.C. 580, directions were given that the Floral games should be celebrated annually.

[54] *A greater license.*]—Ver. 331. The greatest license was permitted at these games; and to the sound of music, lewd women danced in a state of nudity. The story is told, that when Cato of Utica once appeared at the games, the spectators would not call on the dancers to strip, being overawed by his presence, on which he retired, that he might not interfere with their amusement, and was loudly applauded for so doing. This would appear very like an encouragement of the practice on his part; and he, probably, did not think of the maxim, as good in ethics as it is in law,— 'Qui facit per alium, facit per se.'

[55] *Wreaths of flowers.*]—Ver. 335. The poet here describes, not the Floral games, but the gaiety of life that the Goddess was wont to promote. This and the next seven lines are thus translated by Gower—

'Brows are embroidered with spruce garlands sew'd,
And tables cover'd with fresh roses strew'd.
The bouzy guest, deck'd with a film flower crown,
In drunken garb there dances up and down:
And's head with oyl and flow'rs and wine well-lin'd,
He catches sings at's sweet-heart's door unkind.
Crown'd temples meddle with no serious matter;
Nor are flow'rs us'd in drinking of fair water.'

loüs,[56] with the juice of no clusters, there was no pleasure in assuming the rose. Bacchus loves the flowers; you may know that the garland is pleasing to Bacchus, from the Constellation of Ariadne. A merry stage becomes this Goddess; she is not, believe me, she is not to be reckoned in the number of the tragic Goddesses.[57] And why the multitude of the courtezans throng to these games, the reason, when sought for, is not difficult to be ascertained. She is none of the morose ones, nor is she one of the great boasters: she wishes that her festival should be open to the Plebeian multitude. She teaches us, too, to make use of the beauty of our youth, while it is still in bloom; and that the thorn is slighted when the roses have faded. But why, whereas white garments are worn on the festival of Ceres, is this Goddess gay with habits of various colours? Is it because the harvest grows white with its ripened ears, but every hue and tint is to be found in flowers?" She nodded her assent, and, as she shook her hair, the flowers fell, just as the rose, when dropped, is wont to fall[58] on the *festive* board. There still remained the torches,[59] the origin of which was concealed from me; when thus she removed my uncertainty. "It is either because the fields are

[56] *Thou wast mixt, Acheloüs.*]—Ver. 343. It seems to have been a general notion with the Latin poets that the waters of the Acheloüs were the first that were used for the purpose of tempering wine. Virgil (Georgics, Book i. l. 9) speaks of mixing the waters of the Acheloüs with the juice of the newly-discovered grape. Hyginus, Fable 274, tells us that Cerasus, the Ætolian, was one of the first who taught men to mix water with their wine, and recommended them to use the waters of the river Acheloüs for that purpose.

[57] *Tragic Goddesses.*]—Ver. 348. 'Cothurnatas.' Literally, 'buskined Goddesses.' The 'cothurnus' was a high shoe or buskin, worn by actors in tragedy, with the view of thereby rendering the figure more stately and elevated. Its introduction on the stage is sometimes ascribed to Sophocles, but more generally to Æschylus. This appellation was often given to Diana and Minerva.

[58] *Is wont to fall.*]—Ver. 360. Allusion is here made to the custom at the feasts of the ancients of showering down flowers, and especially roses, from the ceiling. At their potations, garlands of roses were often hung from the ceiling; from this circumstance, whatever secrets were imparted in the freedom of postprandial conversation, were said to be 'sub rosa,' 'under the rose,' and it was considered a breach of good faith and of politeness to divulge anything that might transpire upon such occasions.

[59] *The torches.*]—Ver. 361. Torches were used at the Floralia, as the rites were protracted to a very late hour of the night.

resplendent with purple flowers, that lights appear to be becoming to my festival, or because neither the flower nor flame is of a dull colour, and the brightness of each attracts our attention, or because the licence of the night is suited to my pleasures. The third reason is derived from fact. "There is still a little matter," I said, "about which it remains for me to inquire, if I may be allowed." She said, "I permit thee." "Why, in honour of thee, are the feeble roes and the timid hares[60] enclosed in the net in place of the Libyan lionesses?" She replied that the woods were not her domain, but the gardens and the fields not to be approached by the savage beast of prey. She had concluded her speech; and she vanished into empty air. A sweet perfume remained; you might know that she was a Goddess. That the song of Naso may flourish throughout all times, diffuse, I pray, O Goddess, thy gifts in my breast.

On the night before the fourth *from the Calends*, shall Chiron[61] raise his star, half-man, and half-formed of the body of a yellow steed. Pelion is a mountain of Hæmonia, facing the south; its summit is green with pine; the oak covers the other part. The son of Phillyra inhabited it. The cave is still extant in the ancient rock which they say was the abode of the worthy old man. He is believed to have occupied with the strains of the lyre those hands that were destined in future times to effect the death of Hector. Alcides had come, a part of his task performed, and now almost the last[62]

---

[60] *The timid hares.*]—Ver. 372. The animals that were generally hunted in the Circus were of the fiercer kind; but at the Floralia, deer and hares were brought in nets, and let loose then for the purpose of chasing them. Very probably, one reason for then hunting the hare was, the fact that these animals are very destructive to flowers, and have an especial liking for pinks and carnations.

[61] *Chiron.*]—Ver. 379. On the 5th of the Nones of May, the Centaur rises. Chiron was the son of Saturn and Phillyra, and was celebrated for his skill in medicines. He was a Centaur, half-man and half-horse, and was the great grandfather of Achilles, whom he educated. He was also said to have nursed Æsculapius. Hercules conquered Troy in the reign of King Laomedon; Achilles slew Hector, its bulwark, in the Trojan war. Ovid seems to have derived this story from Homer's Iliad, the Argonautic poem of Orpheus and Callimachus.

[62] *Almost the last.*]—Ver. 388. Apollodorus says, that so far from its being at the time of almost the last of the labours of Hercules, this accident happened to Chiron when he was engaged on his fourth task. Pliny

of the labours enjoined on him, remained for the hero. You might see the two destined for the destruction of Troy, by chance, standing together. On the one side was the boy, the son of Æacus; on the other side was the son of Jove. The hero, the son of Phillyra, receives the youth with hospitality, and asks him the cause of his coming; the other one informs him. Meanwhile he examines his club and the spoil of the lion, and he says, "Hero worthy of these arms, and arms worthy of the hero!" Nor could the hands of Achilles refrain from daring to touch the hide bristling with its shaggy hair. While the old man is handling the arrows, tipped with poison, one falls, and the barb is fixed in his left foot. Chiron groans aloud, and draws the steel from the wound; Alcides weeps, and so does the Hæmonian boy. Yet he himself prepares the herbs collected on the hills of Pagasæ, and soothes the wounds with various remedies. The eating venom was too powerful for a remedy, and the pestilence was entirely absorbed in his bones and throughout his whole body. The blood of the Hydra of Lerna mingling with the blood of the Centaur gave no time for aid. Achilles stood bedewed with tears, as though before his father; thus was Pelias to be mourned had he *then* died. Often did he chafe the hands of the patient with his affectionate hands: the teacher then received the advantages of that disposition of which he had had the training. Often did he kiss him; often, too, did he say to him as he lay, "Live on, I pray; leave me not, my dear father!" The ninth day had come, when thou, most righteous Chiron, hadst thy body girt with twice seven stars.

Him the curving Lyre[63] would desire to follow; but not yet is the path in readiness; the third night will be a suitable time. At the hour, when on the morrow, we say, that now the Nones are dawning, the Scorpion shall be marked in the sky from its middle.

When thrice from this time the Star of the Evening shall have raised his beauteous disk, and thrice the conquered stars shall have made way for the Sun, then will be the rites of your

(Nat. Hist. book xxv. c. 6) says that Chiron recovered by the application of the herb centaury, which received its appellation from the Centaur.

[63] *The curving Lyre.*]—Ver. 415. On the 3d of the Nones of May, the Lyre rises acronychally. On the day before the Nones, half of the Scorpion sets cosmically.

ancient ceremonial, feast of the Lemures; this feast will present the offerings to the silent shades.[64] Their year was shorter, and not as yet had they been taught to employ, for purification, the affectionate Februa, and not *yet* wast thou the leader of the months, O Janus! thou of the double form. Yet already did they offer their peculiar gifts to the ashes of the dead, and the grandson performed the rites at the tomb of his buried grandsire. The month was called Maius, from the name of the "majores," [their ancestors,] which even now retains a part of the ancient custom. When midnight now is come, and affords silence for sleep, and ye dogs, and birds with your various tints, are still; at that hour rises the person who bears in mind the ancient ceremonial, and stands in awe of the Gods; his two feet have no sandals[65] on them, and he makes a noise with his fingers clasped in each other with his thumb in the middle,[66] for fear lest the aërial spectre should meet him if silent. After he has washed his hands clean in the water of the spring, he turns round, and first he takes up the black beans;[67] with his face turned away, he flings them;

[64] *The silent shades.*]—Ver. 422. 'Tacitis Manibus.' Literally, 'the silent Manes.' As Mr. Keightley observes, the Manes were, according to this description of them, what we term, disturbed spirits.

[65] *Have no sandals.*]—Ver. 432. On performing magical incantations, it was always deemed necessary to have the feet bare for that purpose.

[66] *His thumb in the middle.*]—Ver. 433. There is some difficulty in understanding from the context how the sound here described was to be produced. Neapolis thinks it means merely a snapping of the thumb and finger. Mr. Thynne and Mr. Stanford seem to be of the same opinion. Mr. Keightley thinks that it may have been done by locking the fingers in one another, whereby the thumbs were joined in the middle, and then making a noise by bringing the hands smartly together. If 'medius pollex' here means the middle finger, a signification which Ovid gives elsewhere to 'pollex,' then it may mean that he closes the fingers in the fist of the left hand, and makes a snapping noise on them thus joined, with the middle finger of the right, which is very easily done, by smartly striking the space between two adjoining fingers.

[67] *The black beans.*]—Ver. 431—6. Gower gives the following translation of these lines—

'The rite-rememb'ring, ghost-abhorring sunne,
Arises gently, and no shoes puts on;
Then points with his clos'd fingers, and his thumb
Put in the midst, lest ghosts should near him come;
Then in spring-water he his hands doth cleanse,
But first doth roll about his mouth blue beans.'

We are told by Festus, that the bean was particularly used in the rites

but while he flings them, he says "I offer these; with these beans do I ransom myself and mine." Nine times does he say this, and looks not behind him.[68] The ghost is believed to gather them, and to follow behind if no one is looking on. A second time he touches the water and tinkles the copper of Temesa,[69] and begs the ghost to leave his house. When nine times he has repeated, "Shades of my father! depart," he looks back, and believes that his rites are duly performed. Whence the day was called, or what is the origin of the name, is unknown to me; from some God it must be learned. Thou son of the Pleiad, worthy of veneration from thy potent wand, do thou instruct me; ofttimes has the palace of the Stygian Jove been visited by thee. The wand-bearing *God* comes at my prayer. Hear *now* the reason of the name; the reason was learned from the God himself. When Romulus consigned to the tomb the remains of his brother, and the obsequies of Remus, unhappily too active, were duly performed, woe-stricken Faustulus, and Acca with her dishevelled locks, were sprinkling his burnt bones with their tears. Afterwards, in their sorrow, they returned home, about the beginning of twilight, and threw themselves down to rest on their couch, hard as it was. The blood-stained ghost of Remus seemed to be standing by the bed, and, with a subdued gibbering, to utter these words, "Behold me, the half, the equal part, of all your prayers! Behold of what nature I *now* am! and of what nature but a little while ago I was! I, who so short a

performed to the ghosts or Lemures, and at the Parentalia; and that the Flamen Dialis was forbidden, not only to eat that pulse, but even to name it, because it was dedicated to the dead. Pythagoras forbade his disciples to eat this pulse, as it was supposed that the souls of men in the first stage of the metempsychosis were transferred into the interior of the bean. This fiction, which perhaps was the key to some more mysterious doctrine, was probably borrowed by him from the priests of Egypt.

[68] *Looks not behind him.*]—Ver. 439. Mr. Keightley justly remarks, that this superstition reminds one of that of sowing the hemp-seed on All-hallows Eve, and refers to Burns's Hallowe'en, st. 16-20. The nine times, as mentioned, was perhaps of magic efficacy, for Virgil, Ecl. viii. l. 75, tells us that the Gods take pleasure in uneven numbers. So with us, the vulgar notion is, that there is 'luck in odd numbers.'

[69] *Copper of Temesa.*]—Ver. 441. Temesa, called also Tempsa by the Latins, was a town of Bruttium, in Calabria. There was also a place in the isle of Cyprus called Temesa, or Temsa, famous for its copper mines.

time since, if I had obtained the omens conferring on me the sovereign sway, might have been the chief among my people. Even now have I glided from the flames of the funeral pile, and am a phantom of air.[70] This shape is all that is left of that which was Remus. Alas! where is Mars, my father? If ye did but speak the truth, and if it was he that gave to us, when outcasts, the udder of the wild beasts. Me has the rash hand of a fellow citizen destroyed—me, the very man whom a she-wolf preserved—of the two, how much the more humane was she. Ah, cruel Celer, mayst thou yield up thy remorseless soul through wounds, and mayst thou pass under the earth all stained with gore, as I have done. My brother willed not this; his brotherly affection is equal to my own. 'Twas all he could do; he expended his tears on my doom. Entreat him by those tears, by the nourishment you afforded him, to appoint a day to be celebrated in my honour." As he gives them these commands, they long to embrace him, and extend their arms: the gliding phantom escapes their hands as they grasp at him. As the ghost in its flight deprived them of their slumber, they both of them reported to the king the words of his brother. Romulus obeyed, and he called that day on which the prescribed rites are performed in favour of the buried dead, "Remuria." The harsh letter[71] which was the first in the entire name, in lapse of time was changed into one of softer articulation. Afterwards, they called the ghosts of the silent shades the "Lemures:" this was the meaning of the word; this the import of the expression. Yet, on those days, the ancients shut their temples as you now see them shut at the festival of the Feralia. That time, too, was not auspicious for the marriage torches of the widow or of the virgin. She who married *then* did not long remain[72] *a*

[70] *A phantom of air.*]—Ver. 463-4. Gower thus renders these lines—
  'Now is your Remus but a dream of air,
    A fitting relique of the piles impair.'

[71] *The harsh letter.*]—Ver. 481. He says that the feast in honour of the shade of Remus was originally called, Remuria, but that in lapse of time the first letter was changed into the letter L, and that eventually all spirits of the dead obtained the appellation of 'Lemures,'—a very improbable story.

[72] *Did not long remain.*]—Ver. 488. He means to say that such wives, either by their shrewishness, or for worse reasons, soon create a necessity for a divorce on the part of their husbands.

wife. For this reason, too, if proverbs have any weight with you, the common people say that "bad prove the wives that are married in May."

But these three festivals, I should observe, are at the same season, but continued on no one of the days *intervening*[73] between them. On the middle one of these days if you seek for the Bœotian Orion,[74] you will be disappointed. The origin of this Constellation must *now* be sung by me. Jupiter and his brother, who rules over the wide ocean, together with Mercury, were on their travels. It was the hour when ploughs turned over on the yoke are carried homeward, and the lamb drinks the milk of the ewe as it downward presses the udder. By chance, the old man, Hyrieus, the cultivator of a scanty farm, catches sight of them while he is standing before his humble cottage, and thus he accosts them,—"Long is the road, and but little of the day now remains; my door, too, is *ever* open to the stranger." He adds looks to his words *which fully confirm* them: they comply with his invitation, and conceal their divine nature. They come beneath the roof of the old man, soiled with the blackening smoke; there is a little fire remaining[75] in the log that had been laid on the day before. He, himself, on his knees, kindles the blaze with his breath, and *then* brings out and breaks up the split firewood. The pipkins stand *on the table;* the smaller of them contains beans; the other herbs; and each of them, covered with its lid, sends forth its steam. While there is a a pause, he presents with his shaking right hand the blushing wine. The God of the Ocean receives the first cup. When he has drunk off the contents, he says, "Pour out some more, that Jupiter, in his turn, may drink." At hearing the name of Jupiter, the man turns pale. As soon as his self-posses-

---

[73] *Days intervening.*]—Ver. 492. The Lemuria were held on three alternate days, the 7th, 5th, and 3rd of the Ides of May, answering to May 9th, 11th, and 13th.

[74] *Orion.*]—Ver. 493. The Constellation of Orion sets on the 5th of the Ides of May. Hesiod says that he was the son of Neptune by Euryale, daughter of Minos. Pindar makes the Isle of Chios to have been his birth-place, and not Bœotia.

[75] *A little fire remaining.*]—Ver. 506. Allusion is here made to the block which was kept on the hearth smouldering from day to day, to be in readiness for cooking the principal meal of the day, for which service only, fire would probably be required by poor people, in a warm climate.

sion returns, he sacrifices the ox, the tiller of his humble farm, roasting him on a large fire, and he draws the wine which he had racked in his early years,[76] when stored in a smoky cask. He admits of no delay; *now* they reclined on couches that concealed under the linen cover the sedge of the river, and even with that addition, by no means lofty ones. Now was the board graced with viands,[77] and with the wine placed upon it. The bowl was of red clay; the cups of beech wood. These were the words of Jove,—"If thy inclination leads thee to desire anything, wish for it: thou shalt receive anything." These were the words of the mild old man,—"I once had a dear wife, known as the choice of my early youth. You ask where she is now: the urn covers her. To her did I swear this, having called yourselves as witnesses of my vow, thou alone shalt enjoy wedlock with me. I swore it, and keep my oath; but now I have desires that are not compatible with each other; I do not wish to be a husband; but I desire to be a father." They assented *to his desire;* they all stood round the hide of the bull. Modesty forbids me to tell the rest. Then did they cover the soaking hide with earth heaped upon it. And now ten months had passed, and a boy was born; him Hirieus calls Urion, because he was thus begotten; the first letter has *now* lost the ancient sound. He had grown to a huge size; the Goddess of Delos took him as her companion; he was the protector and the attendant of the Goddess. His unguarded words excited the anger of the Gods. "There is no wild beast," said he, "that I am unable to conquer." The earth sent a scorpion;[78] it attempted

[76] *In his early years.*]—Ver. 517-18. Gower thus renders these lines—

'Then broach'd a hogshead of his special sack,
Which in his young days he himself did make.'

The 'amphoræ,' or 'cadi,' 'casks,' were exposed purposely to the action of smoke, as it was supposed to mellow the wine.

[77] *Graced with viands.*]—Ver. 521-2. Gower thus renders these lines—

'Now braves his board with dainty cakes and liquors,
In earthen dishes, and in beech-tree beakers.'

[78] *A scorpion.*]—Ver. 541. Horace does not represent him as being killed by the sting of a scorpion, but as being slain by the shafts of Diana, when he had made an attempt on her chastity. Other writers, however, with Ovid, represent him as the favourite and protector of that Goddess, and like her, excelling in the chase.

to fasten its crooked claws in the Goddess, the mother of the twins; Orion opposed it. Latona added him to the number of the radiant stars, and said, "Enjoy the reward of thy deserts."

But why do both Orion and the other stars hasten to leave the sky? and why does Night contract her path? Why, more swiftly than usual, does the fair day raise its beams from the watery deep, the morning star preceding? Am I mistaken? or do arms now clash? I am not deceived: it was the clash of arms. Mars is approaching,[79] and, as he comes, he gives the indications of war. The Avenger himself comes down from heaven to his own honours, and to the temple conspicuous in the Forum of Augustus. Mighty is the God, and so is the work; in no other fashion ought Mars to have his habitation in the city of his offspring. These shrines are worthy of the trophies won from the giants; it becomes Gradivus from this spot to give an impulse to the cruel warfare; whether it be that any one shall assail us from the eastern world, or whether, under the western Sun, the enemy will have to be subdued. He, all-powerful in arms, surveys the pinnacles of the highest part of the building, and considers it right that the unconquered Gods should possess its summit. He surveys, on the portals, the weapons of various forms,[80] and the arms of the world conquered by his own soldiers. On one side, he beholds Æneas laden with the burden of affection, and so many progenitors of the noble house of Iülus: on another side he beholds the son of Ilia[81] bearing on his shoulders the armour of the chieftain, and their illustrious deeds *written on the base* beneath the heroes ranged in order. He sees, too, the temple adorned

[79] *Mars is approaching.*]—Ver. 550. On the 4th of the Ides there were sports in the Circus in honour of Mars Ultor, or 'the Avenger.' At the battle of Philippi, Augustus had vowed a temple to Mars. When peace was restored, he built the Augustan Forum, at an immense expense, and there erected a temple to Mars, of surpassing magnificence. On the 4th of the Ides of May he consecrated it.

[80] *The weapons of various forms.*]—Ver. 561. Suetonius tells us, that on the building of this temple the successful generals of the time were ordered to erect their trophies therein; and Pliny (Nat. Hist. Book xxxv. c. 10) says that Augustus erected in his own Forum (probably in the temple of Mars) two pictures, representing a battle and a triumph.

[81] *The son of Ilia.*]—Ver. 565. Romulus; bearing the 'spolia opima,' the armour of Acron, king of the Cæninenses, whom he had slain with his own hand.

with the name of Augustus; and as he reads the name of Cæsar, the work appears still greater. This, when a young man, he had vowed, at the time when he took up the arms of duty; from such acts as these ought a Prince to commence *his career of command*. He, stretching forth his hands, as, on one side, stood his avenging army, on the other, the conspirators, thus spake:—" If the father of warfare, and the priestess of Vesta, are the founders of my race, and I am preparing to avenge either of these Divinities, do thou, Mars, come hither and satiate thy sword in the accursed blood, and let thy favour abide by the better cause. Thou shalt receive a temple, and when I am victorious 'The Avenger' shall be thy title." He had uttered his vow, and returned, exulting, from the routed foe. Nor is it enough for Mars once to have merited this epithet: he pursues the standards detained in the hands of the Parthian. This was a nation protected both by their plains, their horses, and their arrows, and inaccessible from the rivers that surrounded them. The slaughter of the Crassi[82] had given daring to the nation, when soldier, general, and standards were lost together. The Parthian was in possession of the Roman standards, the token of honour in warfare; and an enemy was the bearer of the Roman eagle. And still would that disgrace have been remaining, had not the empire of Ausonia been protected by the valiant armies of Cæsar.[83] 'Twas he, that removed the ancient stains, and the disgrace of so long duration; the standards, when recovered, recognized their friends. What, then, thou *Parthian*, availed thee the arrows wont to be discharged behind *thy back?* What, thy *inaccessible* places? What, the management of thy fleet steed? Parthian! thou restorest the eagles! thy conquered bows,[84] too, thou ex-

[82] *The Crassi.*]—Ver. 583. Both M. Licinius Crassus, the father, and his son, P. L. Crassus, with eleven Roman legions, were cut to pieces by the Parthians on this occasion. Flaccus (Book iii. c. 2.) says, that at the time of his surprise 'he was gaping after,' 'inhiabat,' the Parthian gold. It is said that the Parthians, in ridicule of his known weakness, cut off his head, and poured melted gold down his throat.

[83] *Arms of Cæsar.*]—Ver. 588. Phraates, the Parthian leader, had agreed to restore to Cæsar the standards which his countrymen had taken from Crassus, and afterwards from Antony; but he hesitated to fulfil his engagement until he heard that Augustus was preparing an expedition to enforce compliance with his demand.

[84] *Thy conquered bows.*]—Ver. 593. Some of the Roman coins of this

tendest! Now, not any pledges of our disgrace hast thou. Well was the temple and the name given to the Deity who twice avenged us, and the deserved honour acquits us of the obligation undertaken by our vows. Celebrate, ye Quirites, these solemn games in the Circus; the theatre does not seem to be befitting the God of valour.

When one night shall be remaining before the Ides, you shall see all the Pleiades,[85] and the whole company of the sisters. At that time, according to no mean authority, as I think, the summer commences, and the season of the mild spring comes to a close.

The day before the Ides shows the Bull[86] raising his face bespangled with stars; a well-known story is attached to this Constellation. Jupiter, in the form of a bull, offered his back to the Tyrian maid,[87] and bore horns on an assumed forehead. She, with her right hand, held by his mane, and with her left she held her dress; and her very alarm was a source of additional grace. The breeze swells her flowing robes; her auburn hair floats along the wind. In such guise, Sidonian maid, it was befitting that Jove should behold thee. Full oft did she raise her maiden feet from the water of the ocean, and dread the splash of the dashing wave; often did the God purposely sink deeper in the waves, that she might the more tightly cling to his neck. The shore *now* reached, Jove stood without horns, and from a bull was changed into a God. The bull enters the heavens; thee, maid of Sidon, Jupiter embraces, and a third part of the earth bears thy name. Others have said that this Constellation is the cow of Pharos,[88] which, from a human being, was made a cow, from a cow, a Goddess.

period are still in existence, which represent a Parthian on his bended knee, extending towards Augustus the standards, and a bow and arrows.

[85] *All the Pleiades.*]—Ver. 599. On the 3rd of the Ides of May, the Pleiades rise acronychally, and the summer begins. The ancients generally regulated their agricultural operations by the rising and setting of the Pleiades.

[86] *Shows the Bull.*]—Ver. 603. On the day before the Ides, the 14th of May, the head of the Bull rises cosmically.

[87] *The Tyrian maid.*]—Ver. 605-6. Europa, the daughter of Agenor, king of Phœnicia. The following is Gower's comical translation of these lines,—

'Once Jove, well horn'd and turned to a bull,
Pack'd up the Tyrian virgin by the gull.'

[88] *The cow of Pharos.*]—Ver. 619. Io, or Isis; thus called from Pharos, an island of Egypt, at the mouth of the river Nile.

On this day, too, the *Vestal* virgin is wont to throw from the oak-built bridge the images of the ancient men, platted in rushes.[89] He who has formed a belief that aged men, after their sixtieth year, were put to death *by them*, charged our ancestors with *wanton* cruelty.[90] The tradition is an old one: at the time when this was called the Saturnian land, these were the words of the prophetic God :—"Ye nations, throw two bodies in sacrifice to the sickle-bearing aged *God*, to be caught by the Etrurian stream." Until the Tirynthian came to these fields, each year was the cruel sacrifice performed with the Leucadian rites.[91] *They say that* he *was the first·* to throw into the stream citizens made of bundles of straw; and that, after the example of Hercules, fictitious bodies are still *so* thrown. Some think that, with the view that they alone might enjoy the right of suffrage, the youths did fling[92] from the bridges the infirm old

---

[89] *Platted in rushes.*]—Ver. 622. On the Ides of May, or, as Ovid seems to say, on the day before, the Vestals, attended by the Pontifices and Prætors, used to throw from the Sublician bridge thirty images of old men, stuffed with bulrushes. These were called Argei; and the poet proceeds to inquire into the origin of a custom so remarkable. The Sublician bridge, from which they were thrown, was so called from the 'sublicæ,' or piles on which it was built: it was the original bridge of Rome, and, from its having been the duty of the priests to keep it in repair, they received the name of 'pontifex,' or 'bridge-maker,' which is the literal signification of the word. It was rebuilt of stone by Æmilius Lepidus.

[90] *With wanton cruelty.*]—Ver. 624. The poet rejects the first opinion, that it was done to commemorate a time when the ancient Romans used to throw the aged men into the Tiber and drown them.

[91] *With the Leucadian rites.*]—Ver. 630. The poet says that the second opinion on its origin was, that it commemorated a time when human sacrifices were offered at Rome. Leucas, now Santa Maura, was anciently a peninsula of Acarnania; now it is an island. The custom alluded to was that of throwing a criminal, on the festival of Apollo, from the heights into the sea, wings and a multitude of birds being first attached to him to break his fall. Persons in small boats waited below to catch him in his descent, and to carry him beyond the bounds of the country. This comparatively merciful dealing with a criminal would hardly justify the poet in applying the epithet 'Leucadian,' to the horrid custom of human sacrifice. Perhaps it ought to be translated rigidly 'after the Leucadian manner,' in allusion merely to the 'mode' of treatment in both cases; throwing from a height being the method adopted, though with intentions, and probably, results, of so different a nature. Disappointed lovers and persons in distress used to throw themselves from the Leucadian rock, whence it obtained the name of 'the Lover's Leap.'

[92] *The youths did fling.*]—Ver. 634. The poet here states the third

men. Tiber, teach me the truth; thy bank is of higher antiquity than the City; thou hast the opportunity of well knowing the origin of the ceremony. Tiber raises his head crowned with reeds from the midst of his channel, and in such accents opens his hoarse mouth:—"I have beheld this place, a lonely piece of pasture land, without walls; each of my banks used to feed the straggling cattle; and I, that Tiber which all nations now know and hold in dread, then was an object, even to the flocks, unworthy of notice. The name of Arcadian Evander is ofttimes mentioned to thee; he, as a stranger, dashed my waters with his oars. There came, too, Alcides, attended by a Grecian multitude. Then, if I remember *aright*, Albula was my name. The hero of Pallantium[93] receives the youth with hospitality, and the punishment which was his due falls at length upon Cacus. The conqueror departs, and with him carries away the kine, the booty of Erythea; but his followers refuse to proceed any further; a great part of them had come having left Argos behind; in these mountains they establish their hopes and their home. Yet many a time are they influenced by sweet love of their father-land, and as he dies, oft does some one of them enjoin this slight task—"Throw my body into the Tiber, that, carried by the waves of the river, I, become lifeless dust, may go to the Inachian shore."[94] The care of *providing* such a tomb as he enjoined displeases his heir; the corpse of the stranger is buried in Ausonian ground; a rush-made image is thrown into the Tiber instead of the

opinion. Festus explains this story on the ground of a singular misconception; that the aged men being free from the burden of public duties, but still retaining their right of voting, the younger ones became jealous of their retention of this right, and that, on their going over the 'pons,' or 'plank,' to record their votes, the young men used to cry out, 'that they ought to be thrown from the 'pons,' (which word also means 'a bridge'), or, in other words, that they ought to lose the right of voting. The poet seems to say that the young men actually had the ill manners to push the older ones off the 'pontes.' If so, it is a very early specimen of an election row.

[93] *The hero of Pallantium.*—Ver. 647. Pallantium, a town of Arcadia, was the native place of Evander. The arrival of Evander and Hercules in Italy are referred to in the first Book.

[94] *The Inachian shore.*]—Ver. 656. The Inachus was a river of Argos. The only ground on which the story is based seems to be the similarity of the name, 'Argei,' by which these images were called, and the name of the Argives in their own language, Ἀργεῖοι.

master *of the family*, that over the wide seas it may return to a Grecian home." Thus much *he said;* when he descended into his grottoes, dripping from the natural rock, you, ye lightly flowing streams, withheld your current.

Illustrious grandson of Atlas! come hither. Thou whom once, on the Arcadian mountains, one of the Pleiades brought forth to Jove: thou minister of peace and war to the Gods above, and the Gods below: thou who wendest thy way with winged foot;[95] thou exulting in the touch of the Lyre; exulting, too, in the Palæstra shining *with oil*,[96] under the patronage of whom the tongue learned to speak with elegance! On the Ides did their fathers erect for thee a temple looking towards the Circus. From that time is this a day devoted to thee. Whoever make a business of selling their wares, having first offered thee the frankincense, beg of thee that thou wilt grant them profit. The fountain of Mercury[97] is near the Capenian gate: if we may believe those who have experienced it, it has a divine efficacy. Hither comes the tradesman, having a girdle[98] round his robes, and, in a state of

---

[95] *With winged foot.*]—Ver. 663—6. Gower thus renders these lines,—

' Brave lad of Atlas, whom of Joviall seed
Fair Maia on th' Arcadian hill did breed:
Thou wing-foot arbiter between the gods
Of heaven and hell, in friendship and at ods.'

On the Ides of May, A.U.C. 497, a temple was dedicated to Mercury, as the patron of traders, near the Circus Maximus. His name, no doubt, came from the Latin word ' merx,' ' merchandize;' and when, in later times, he was identified with the Grecian deity, Hermes, he received the office of that deity as herald or messenger of the Gods, and the giver of eloquence.

[96] *The Palæstra shining with oil.*]—Ver. 667. ' Palæstra' was a general term for all athletic exercises, such as wrestling, running, and boxing; before commencing which, the persons contending used to anoint themselves with oil. Mercury was the patron of these exercises; probably, because they required both agility and cunning for the purpose of excelling in the art of self-defence, which qualifications were eminently two of the characteristics of Mercury.

[97] *The fountain of Mercury.*]—Ver. 673. This fountain or well is not mentioned in any other passage now existing of the ancient authors.

[98] *Having a girdle.*]—Ver. 675. It was customary with the tradesmen in those times to have a girdle round the waist, from which they suspended their purse; sometimes, too, they used the folds of the girdle for the purpose of depositing their money therein. This custom must have considerably promoted the interests of the pickpockets at Rome.

purity, he draws some of the water, to carry it away in a perfumed urn; in this a laurel branch is dipped, and with the wet laurel are sprinkled all the things which are intended to change owners. He sprinkles his own hair, too, with the dripping bough, and runs through his prayers in a voice accustomed to deceive."[99] "Wash away the perjuries of past time," says he: "wash away my lying words of the past day, whether I have made thee to attest for me, or whether I have invoked the great Godhead of Jove, whom I did not intend to listen to me. Or if I have knowingly deceived any other of the Gods, or any Goddess, let the swift breezes bear away my wicked speeches. Let there be no trace left of my perjuries on the morrow, and let not the Gods care whatever I may choose to say. Do but give me profits; give me the delight that rises from gain, and grant that it may be lucrative to me to impose on my customers." From on high, Mercury laughs at his worshipper while making such requests as these, remembering that once on a time he himself stole the Ortygian kine.[1]

But explain to me, I pray, who am making far more becoming requests, from what time the Sun passes into *the Constellation of* the Twins? His answer was, "When thou shalt see days remain of the month as many as were the exploits of the labours of Hercules." "Tell me," I said, "the origin of this Constellation?" The God, with eloquent lips, explained the cause:—"The brothers, the sons of Tyndarus, had borne off Phœbe,

[99] *Accustomed to deceive.*]—Ver. 681. The character of the trader was held in bad repute at Rome, and no citizen who prided himself upon his own respectability would be employed in commerce. From this ban being put upon trade, it is not surprising that it fell into the hands of such characters as the one mentioned in the text. Gower thus translates lines 685-690 :—

> 'What power soever broker to my lie
> I've made, now let them vanish all and die.
> Wink thou at all my slie deceits to-day,
> Let not the Gods take notice what I say.
> Afford me gains, and joy that my desire
> Of gain is fed, and that I've gull'd the buyer.'

[1] *The Ortygian kine.*]—Ver. 692. Ortygia was the ancient name of the Isle of Delos. The allusion in the text is to the theft by Mercury of the cattle of Admetus, king of Thessaly, which were tended by Apollo, who was born in Delos. Ortygia was also the name also of a small island near Sicily, and was one of the epithets of Ephesus, in Ionia.

and the sister of Phœbe;[2] the one of them was a horseman, the other skilled as a pugilist. Idas and his brother prepare for war, and seek to recover those betrothed to them, being both of them affianced to be sons-in-law of Leucippus. Love persuades these to recover the damsels, the others, to refuse *to* give them up; and from the same motive each one of them fights. The Œbalian brothers[3] were fully able to escape their pursuers by flight; but it seemed a disgrace to conquer only by speed in flight. There is a spot, destitute of trees, suited as a fitting ground for a combat. There had they taken their stand; Aphidna[4] was the name of the place. Castor having his breast pierced by the sword of Lyncæus, lay stretched on the earth by an unexpected wound. The avenging Pollux is at hand, and pierces Lyncæus with his spear, in the spot, where the neck at its termination joins the shoulders. Idas was rushing on him, and hardly by the lightning of Jove was he repelled, and they say that his weapon was not *even* wrenched from his right hand by the bolt. And now, Pollux, the lofty heaven was open to thee, when thou saidst, 'Hear my words, my father! That heaven which *as of right* thou grantest to me alone, divide between us two; half will *then* be more valuable to me than the whole of the gift.' He spoke, and ransomed his brother by an alternate change of place;[5] the pair form a Constellation serviceable to the tossed bark." Let him return to *the month of* Janus,[6] who asks what are the Agonia? which, however, occupy this period as well in the Calendar.

[2] *The sister of Phœbe.*]—Ver. 699. Her name was Elaïra, Ilaïra, or Hilayra. She and her sister Phœbe, the daughter of Leucippus, were betrothed to their cousins Idas and Lynceus, the sons of Aphareus. The Tyndaridæ, who were also their cousins, carried the damsels off in the manner stated in the text.

[3] *The Œbalian brothers.*]—Ver. 705. Castor and Pollux are thus styled, either because they were Laconians, who were also called Œbalians, or because Œbalus was their grandfather.

[4] *Aphidna.*]—Ver. 708. This was a Demus, or small district of Laconia. Theocritus (Idyll. 25) and Pindar (Nem. ode 10) represent this combat as taking place at the tomb of Aphareus, in Messenia.

[5] *Change of place.*]—Ver. 719-20. The following is Gower's rather incomprehensible translation of these lines:—

'Then to his brother he divides his charge,
A welcome couple to a vexed barge.'

[6] *The month of Janus.*]—Ver. 721. See book i. line 317. On the 12th of the Calends of June the Agonia were repeated. On the 11th the Dog-star sets; for as such is the fact, and as 'exit' can be so trans-

On the night succeeding this day, the Dog of Erigone departs. In another place, the origin of this sign is explained.

The next day is that of Vulcan: they call it Tubilustria. The trumpets[7] which he makes are purified as sacred.

Then comes the place for the four initials,[8] which being read in order, either the custom of the sacrifices, or the flight of the king *of the sacrifices*, is meant *thereby*.

Nor do I pass by thee, Public Fortune,[9] of the *all*-powerful nation; to whom on the following day a temple was given.

When Amphitrite, abounding in waves, shall have received this day, thou shalt behold the beak of the russet bird[10] so pleasing to Jove. The coming dawn removes Boötes *from our sight*, and, on the succeeding day, the Constellation of Hyas[11] will be *risen*.

lated with propriety, it does not seem to be just to the poet to force him to misrepresent an astronomical fact, when, in all probability, he had not even inadvertently been guilty of an error. As to the Dog-star, see book iv. l. 936.

[7] *The trumpets.*]—Ver. 726. On the 11th of the Calends of June the Tubilustria were repeated. See book iii. l. 849.

[8] *The place for the four initials.*]—Ver. 727. It appears that the ninth day of the Calends of June, in the Roman Calendar, was marked with the four initials, Q. R. C. F. Varro tells us that they stood for ' quando rex comitiavit fas,' the time 'when the king (of the sacrifices) informs the people, in full assembly, of the days that are auspicious (fasti) and inauspicious (nefasti).'. Others think that they may signify 'quando rex comitio fugit,' 'when the king (of the sacrifices) flies from the people assembled' Plutarch tells us that the priest, or 'rex sacrificulus,' attended some religious ceremonies at the ' comitium ' or assembly, at the termination of which he formally ran out of the building, probably to signify the fact that he was debarred by his sacred duties from taking part in any civil matters. To the latter solution, the 'flight of the king' mentioned by the poet most probably bears reference; whatever the ceremonial may have been, on this day it seems to have taken place.

[9] *Public Fortune.*]—Ver. 730. On the eighth of the Calends of June, the temple of Fortuna Publica was dedicated. Some commentators think that this was the temple dedicated to Fortuna Primigenia by Servius Tullius. Mr. Thynne thinks that they were different temples, and that the temple of Fortuna Publica was on the Capitolium, while that of Fortuna Primigenia was on the Quirinal.

[10] *The russet bird.*]—Ver. 732. On the evening of the 8th of the Calends of June, the eagle (Aquila) rises. The eagle was the attendant bird of Jupiter. Hor. B. iv. Od. iv. 1. Ministrum fulminis alitem.

[11] *The Constellation of Hyas.*]—Ver. 734. On the 7th of the Calends of June, Boötes sets heliacally, and on the 6th of the Calends, the Hyades rise in the same manner.

BOOK THE SIXTH.

CONTENTS.

The three opinions on the origin of the name of the month of June, Ver. 1—100. The Goddess Carna, her attributes, and her sacred rites, 101—182. The temple of Juno Moneta; and the punishment of Manlius, 183—190. The temple of Mars before the Capenian Gate; the temple of Tempest; the rising of the Constellation of the Eagle, 191-196. The rising of the Hyades, 197, 198. The temple of Bellona, (on mentioning which, allusion is made to Appius), 199—208. The temple of Hercules Custos, in the Circus Flaminius, 209—212. Mention is made of Sancus, Fidius, or Semo, a Sabine Deity, 213—218. The early part of June inauspicious for marriage, 219—234. The setting of Arctophylax; the games of the Fishermen on the Campus Martius, 235—240. The temple of the Mind, 241—248. The Vestalia, with some account of Vesta and her worship, (in which the poet introduces the story of the attempt of Priapus on the chastity of the Goddess; a description of the sphere of Archimedes; and the origin of the altar to Jupiter Pistor, with the history of the Palladium), 249—460. The surname of Callaicus given to Brutus; Crassus conquered by the Parthians, 461—468. The rising of the Dolphin, 469—472. The temple of Matuta, and the Matralia celebrated in her honour, 473—562. The death of Rutilius and Didius in battle, 563—568. The temple of Fortune erected by Servius Tullius; the murder of Tullius by the agency of his daughter; his miraculous birth, 569—636. The temple dedicated to Concord by Livia, 637—648. The temple of Jupiter and the lesser Quinquatrus; the departure of the pipers from Rome, and their return; the invention of the flute, and the punishment of Marsyas, 649—710. The rising of the Hyades; the cleansing of the temple of Vesta, 711—714. The rising of Favonius, 715, 716. The rising of Orion; the triumph of Posthumus Tubertus over the Volsci and the Æqui, 717—724. The Lion enters the Constellation of the Crab; the worship of Pallas on Mount Aventine, 725—728. The temple of Summanus, 729—732. The rising of Ophiuchus; the death of Hippolytus, 733—762. The defeat and death of Caius Flaminius at Lake Thrasymenus, 763—768. The conquest of Syphax and the death of Hasdrubal, 769, 770. The rites of Fors Fortuna, the Goddess of chance, with a reference to Servius Tullius, 771—784.

The rising of Orion, 785—790. The temple of the Lares and of Jupiter Stator, 791—794. The temple of Quirinus, 795, 796. The temple of Hercules and the Muses; the praises of Marcia, 797—812.

THIS month, too, has varying causes *assigned* for its name; all of these being stated, you shall choose for yourself those which you approve of. Of realities will I sing; but some there will be to say that I have invented fictions, and to believe that divine beings never were seen by mortals. There is a Deity within us; under his influence we glow *with inspiration;* this poetic fervour contains the impregnating particles of the mind of the Divinity. To me, especially, it is allowed to see the countenances of the Gods, both because I am a poet, and because of sacred matters do I sing. There is a grove densely shaded with trees, a spot sequestered from every sound, did it not re-echo with the murmurs of a stream.[1] Here was I engaged in inquiring what could be the origin of this month which I had commenced upon, and I was in deep thought upon this name. Lo! I beheld Goddesses; not those whom the instructor on agriculture had seen while he was tending the sheep of Ascra;[2] nor yet those whom the son of Priam compared in the vales of Ida abounding in rills; yet there was one of them; *yes,* there was one of them, *she who is* the sister of her husband; 'twas she, I recognized her, who stands on the heights[3] which belong to Jove. I was struck with awe, and by my speechless pallor, I was betraying my feelings, when the Goddess herself removed those alarms which she had caused, for she said, "O poet, compiler of the Roman year, thou who hast attempted to treat of mighty subjects in humble strains, thou hast earned for thyself the privilege of beholding a Divinity of heaven when it pleased thee to compile their festivals in poetic numbers. But that thou mayst not remain ignorant, and be influenced by a vulgar error, June, *I tell thee,*

---

[1] *Murmurs of a stream.*]—Ver. 9, 10. Gower thus translates these lines—

'There is a tree-thronged grave, reserv'd from all
Shape of a sound, unlesse some water-fall.'

[2] *Sheep of Ascra.*]—Ver. 14. Ascra was a town near Mount Helicon, in Bœotia, of which place the poet Hesiod is said to have been a native. In his poem, entitled 'the Works and Days,' Hesiod treats of rustic matters, and invokes the nine Muses as his guides.

[3] *On the heights.*]—Ver. 18. The temple of Juno was on the right of that of Jupiter, on the Capitoline Hill.

derives its name from mine. 'Tis something to be the bride of Jove, to be the sister of Jove; I hesitate *to decide* whether I should take the more pride in him as a brother or as a husband. If birth is regarded, 'twas I that first made Saturn a parent; I was the earliest offspring of Saturn. From my father, was Rome once called the land of Saturn; for him, this land was the next *abode* after heaven. If marriage is held in respect, *then* I am called the spouse of the Thunderer, and my temple is adjoining to Tarpeian Jove. Was a concubine able[4] to give her name to the month of May, and shall this honour be grudged to me? Why, then, am I styled the queen, the mistress of the Goddesses, or why in my right hand have they placed the sceptre of gold? Shall the days *united* constitute the month, and shall I from them be called Lucina,[5] and yet shall I receive no renown from a month *named after* me? In such case, may I repent that, in good faith, I laid aside my wrath against the descendants of Electra and the house of Dardanus. Twofold was the cause of my wrath; I grieved when Ganymede was borne away; my beauty, too, was surpassed in the judgment of him of Ida. May I repent that I do not *still* encourage the towers of Carthage, since there are my arms, and there is my chariot. *Then* may I repent that I subjected Sparta and Argos, and my own Mycenæ, and the ancient Samos to the sway of Latium. Add, too, the ancient Tatius, and Falisci, worshippers of Juno, whom I brooked to see succumb to the men of Rome. But may I have no cause for repentance, for no nation is dearer to me. Here may I still be worshipped; here may I share the temples with my Jove. Mars himself said to me, 'To thee do I entrust these walls; in the city of thy grandson, *Romulus*, shalt thou hold sway.' His words are verified; at a hundred altars am I worshipped, and the honour *of giving name to* this month is not of less value to me than any other *mark of respect*. Nor is it Rome only that pays me this honour; the neighbours of the City show me the same mark of respect. Examine the Calendar,

---

[4] *A concubine able.*]—Ver. 35. The Pleiad Maia, the mother of Mercury. See Book v. l. 85. Gower thus renders this line and the following one—

'Could May, that strumpet, have a month's renown?
What? And shall any dare deny me one?'

[5] *Lucina.*]—Ver. 39. For the origin of this name, see Book ii. l. 449.

which Aricia, the city of the grove, and the people of Laurentum, and my own Lanuvium⁶ have; there is the month Junonius to be found. Look at Tiber and the walls sacred to the Goddess of Præneste; *there* wilt thou read of a *portion of* time called after the name of Juno. And yet it was not Romulus that founded these; whereas Rome was the city of my own grandson." Juno had ceased. I looked behind me; *there* stood the wife of Hercules, and on her features were the indications of grief. " I will not," said she, " if my mother bids⁷ me quit heaven entirely, stay *there* against the will of my parent. And now I enter into no contest on the name of this month. In soothing accents I address thee, and I almost act the part of a suppliant; and though the matter is my right, I would prefer obtaining it by entreaty; and perhaps thou thyself mayst favour my cause. My mother has gained possession of the Capitol glittering with gold, in her temple there erected; and, as is her due, she shares the high places with Jupiter. But all the glory belongs to me that is *derived* from the origin of *the name of* this month; this is the only point of honour about which I feel any anxiety. What matter so weighty *is it*, if thou, man of Rome, didst give the honour of this month to the wife of Hercules, and if posterity conforms to it? This land, too, owes me something on account of my illustrious husband. Hither did he drive his captured kine; here Cacus, making but a poor defence with his flames and the gifts of his father, stained with his blood the ground of the Aventine. To more recent transactions I am now called; according to their years, did Romulus arrange the people and divide them into two classes; the one is more ready to deliberate, the other to fight; those of the one age recommend

⁶ *Lanuvium.*]—Ver. 60. At Lanuvium there was a temple and grove dedicated to Juno Sospita. At Præneste, also, there was a temple of that Goddess. On ancient coins, she is sometimes called Juno Sispita.

⁷ *If my mother bids.*]—Ver. 67, 68. Gower thus quaintly renders these lines—

'Should my dear mother bid me pack away
From heaven, saith she, in heaven I would not stay.'

Hebe was the daughter of Jupiter and Juno, and the wife of Hercules; she was the cup-bearer of the Gods, and was the Goddess of Youth. Juno having asserted that the month of June was so named after her, Hebe, who, as the Goddess of Youth, was called ' Juventas' by the Romans, now asserts that the name is derived from ' juvenis,' ' young.'

the warfare, those of the other, wage *the fight*. Thus did he appoint, and with the same mark did he distinguish the months—June is the month of the juniors; the month that precedes it, that of the aged." She said, and with the keenness of contention they would have entered on the discussion, and in their anger would the ties of affection have been lost sight of, *when* Concord came, her long tresses wreathed with the laurel of Apollo, the Deity and the object of our peaceful chief. When she told how that Tatius and the brave Quirinus, and the two kingdoms, together with their subjects, had united, and that fathers-in-law and sons-in-law were received under one common roof, "from the junction [8] of these *nations*," says she, "does the month of June derive its name." The causes of the three have been stated; but pardon me, ye Goddesses, it is a matter not to be decided by my arbitration. Depart, equal *in your claims*, as far as I am concerned. Through one who gave a judgment on beauty, did Pergamus fall; two Goddesses are more potent to injure than one is to aid.[9]

The first day is dedicated to thee, O Carna.[10] She is the Goddess of the hinge; by her power she opens what is shut, and shuts what is open. Whence she derives the power that has been given to her, is a tale rendered obscure by lapse of time; but by my verse you shall be informed *thereon*. The ancient grove of Helernus is near the *stream* of the Tiber; even now do the Pontiffs bear thither the sacrifice. From him was born a Nymph (the men of the olden time called her

---

[8] *From the junction.*]—Ver. 96. The Goddess Concord suggests that the month of June received its name from 'jungo,' 'to join;' in commemoration of the union of the Romans with the Sabine people; this was a reason very appropriately urged by that Goddess.

[9] *One is to aid.*]—Ver. 99, 100. Gower thus renders these lines—

'I leave you even. Troy ru'd th' award of Paris,
One cannot make so much as two will marre us.'

[10] *O Carna.*]—Ver. 101. On the Calends of June, the festival of this Deity was celebrated. Cyprian, Augustine, and Tertullian call her 'Carda,' or Cardea: they unite with her Forculus and Liminius, the Gods of the door and the hreshold, and derive her name from 'cardo,' a hinge.' Macrobius (Sat. Book i. ch. 12) seems to imply that her name was derived from 'carnis,' 'flesh,' and says that she was the guardian of the heart and the vital parts of the human body. They were very probably different Deities. Junius Brutus, on the expulsion of the Tarquinii, established the worship of Carna on the Cælian hill.

Cranè); ofttimes was she wooed by many a suitor, but in vain. It was her wont to haunt the fields, and to chase the beasts of prey with her javelin, and to spread her knotty toils along the hollow dell. A quiver she did not wear; yet did people believe that she was the sister of Phœbus; and she was not one, O Phœbus, that might cause thee shame. If any of the young men addressed to her words of love, forthwith she uttered this reply, "This place has too much of light, and of the blushes that attend on the light: if you lead to the caves that are more sequestered, I follow." The credulous *lover* goes before her; she, having arrived at the bushes, stops short, and lies concealed, and is nowhere to be found. Janus had beheld her, and captivated with desire for her thus seen, he employed tender words in addressing the cruel *Nymph*. The Nymph, in her usual manner, desires a more retired grot to be sought, and follows as though accompanying him, and *then* deserts him as he leads the way. Foolish one! Janus sees what is done behind his back; nothing dost thou avail; lo! he is *now* looking behind him upon thy hiding place. "Lo! nothing dost thou avail," I said, *and truly*; for *now*, as thou art concealing thyself under the crag, he clasps thee in his embrace;[11] and, having realized his hopes, he says, "In return for this embrace of mine, take unto thyself the government of the hinge; take this as the price of thy lost virginity." Thus saying, he gave her a wand ('twas a white one), by which she might be enabled to drive afar from doors *all* evil mischiefs. There are ravenous fowls; not those which used to rob the

---

[11] *In his embrace.*]—Ver. 125. Neapolis, one of the commentators of the seventeenth century, thus expresses himself on this story of Janus. 'Oho! can this be the Janus that Augustine speaks of, when he says, " nothing occurs to me disparaging to the character of Janus; perhaps he was one that lived a life of innocence far removed from crime and wickedness?"' Mr. Keightley justly remarks that this tale must have escaped the knowledge or the memory of the zealous father. Gower thus renders this and the following lines—

> ' She, as she us'd, bids him walk to a cave;
> And as she follow'd, him the slip she gave.
> Fool! 'tis in vain: for Janus sees thy scout;
> He sees behind him; and will find thee out.
> He sayes the same; and as thou close wert laid,
> He clip'd thee close.'

mouth of Phineus[12] at the board, but thence do they derive their origin. Large are their heads, fixed is their gaze, for plunder are their beaks adapted; on their wings is a greyish colour, crooked talons are on their claws.[13] By night they fly, and they seek the children unprotected by the nurse, and pollute their bodies, dragged from their cradles. With their beaks they are said to tear the entrails of the sucklings, and they have their maws distended with the blood which they have swallowed. "Striges," are they called; and the origin of this name is, the fact, that they are wont to screech in the dismal night. Whether it is that these birds are produced by nature, or that they are created by the agency of charms, and the magic song of the Marsi[14] transforms hags into birds; they came to the chamber of Procas;[15] Procas, born there *but* five days before, becomes the new-born prey of the birds; and with greedy

[12] *Phineus.*]—Ver. 131. The Harpies were winged monsters, which were sent by Juno to pollute the food of Phineus, and thereby to avenge his cruelty towards his sons Plexippus and Pandion, in putting out their eyes on a false accusation. Caläis and Zethes afterwards delivered him from their persecution. Hesiod says they were two in number, Aëllo and Ocypete, and Apollodorus says they were the offspring of Thaumas and Electra, and represents them as snatching away the food of the Argonauts. Virgil says that they had the face of women, wings, and hooked talons, and were foul and disgusting objects.

[13] *On their claws.*]—Ver. 133, 134. Gower thus renders these lines—

'Great heads; glore eyes; hook beaks upon their jaws;
Their feathers gray; huge tallons on their claws.'

Mr. Stanford informs us that the description here given agrees closely with that of the 'vespertilio vampyrus' of Linnæus; a species of bat, with large canine teeth, sharp black beak, the claws very strong, and hooked. They inhabit Guinea, Madagascar, and all the islands thence to the remotest in the Indian Ocean. Buffon supposes that they were not unknown to the ancients, and that they gave rise to the fiction of the Harpies. Linnæus calls this species of bat, the vampyre, conjecturing it to be the kind which draws blood from any creature it may find asleep. The name 'strix' is derived from the Greek στρίζω, 'to screech.'

[14] *The Marsi.*]—Ver. 142. 'Striges,' the plural of 'strix,' also signified 'hags,' or 'witches,' from a belief that they had the power of assuming this form at night: reference is made in the text to this belief. The Marsi were a people of Italy, celebrated for their skill in sorcery; and were supposed to be descended from Marsus, the son of Circe, the enchantress.

[15] *Procas.*]—Ver. 143. He was one of the kings of Alba Longa, and is found in the list given in the note to Book iv. l. 52.

tongues they suck the breast of the infant; the hapless child screams, and *thereby* summons aid. Frightened by the cries of her young charge, the nurse runs to him and finds his cheeks mangled by their hard claws. What was she to do? The hue of his face was that which is wont to be on the latest leaves, which the winter, just arrived, has seared. She came to Cranè, and told her of the matter. She said, "Lay aside thy fear; safe and sound shall be thy charge!" She had *now* come to the cradle: the father and mother were weeping. "Stay your tears," said she; "I myself will find a remedy!" Forthwith, thrice in due order, she touches the lintels with a branch of the arbutus; thrice, with the same branch, does she mark the threshold. The entrance she sprinkles with water, but which water contains a drug, and she holds the raw entrails of a two-year-old sow; and thus she says,—" Ye birds of the night, spare the vitals of the child! for a little babe a little victim falls; take ye heart for heart, I pray—vitals for vitals! this life we give to you in the stead of a better one." When thus she presented the offering, cut in pieces, she lays it in the open air, and forbids those who are present at the rites to look back upon it. The wand, too, of Janus, made of the white thorn,[16] was placed *in the spot* where the narrow window gave light to the chamber: after that, it is said that the birds no more polluted the cradle, and the complexion which he formerly had, returned to the child.

You ask why fat bacon is tasted on these Calends, and beans[17] are mixed with the boiled spelt? She is a Goddess of ancient days, and she still diets on the food that in olden time she used *to receive*, and she does not in a spirit of luxury ask for the dainties of foreign lands. In that day, uncaught by that people, swam the fish; and the oysters[18] were safe in

[16] *Made of the white thorn.*]—Ver. 165. The wood of this tree was supposed to avert the evil effects of drugs and enchantments, to repel ghosts, and to heal wounds inflicted by the sting or bite of serpents.

[17] *And beans.*]—Ver. 170. Those who are fond of the dish of beans and bacon little imagine that they are indulging in a purely classical taste, and that, unwittingly, they are, to some extent, votaries of the Goddess Carna.

[18] *And the oysters.*]—Ver. 173. The man who was to be the first to eat an oyster had not then appeared; a feat which, in the opinion of some, required a very considerable amount of courage. So fond did the Romans become of this fish, that their emperors were supplied from the

their shells. Latium had not become acquainted with *the* fowl, which rich Ionia[19] produces, nor that which delights in the blood of the Pygmies. *Then*, beyond its plumage, there was nothing to please in the peacock; nor had *any* land sent its animals encaged, which before were beasts of chase. Swine *then* were valuable; by killing a sow they honoured their festivals. The land *then* produced but beans and the hard-grained spelt. Whoever eats these two things mingled, on the Calends of the sixth *month*, they say that his stomach can receive no harm.

On the loftiest height *of the Capitol*, tradition says that a temple was built to Juno Moneta, according to thy vow, O Camillus! Before, it had been the house of Manlius,[20] who formerly repulsed the arms of Gaul from Capitoline Jove. How gracefully—great Gods! had he fallen in that fight, the defender of thy throne, O Jove, *who sittest* on high! He lived, that he might die, condemned for aspiring to regal power. The credit of doing this, did protracted old age give to him.

The same day is a festival of Mars;[21] whom the Capenian gate beholds, outside the walls, situated close to the covered way.

beds at Rutupium, in Kent, near the modern Sandwich, which were celebrated for the delicate flavour of the oysters found there.

[19] *Ionia.*]—Ver. 175. The bird here mentioned was the 'Attagen,' similar to our woodcock, the best flavoured of which came from Ionia. The Pigmies were a fabulous people of Thrace, who were but a foot and a half in height, and against whom the cranes are fabled to have waged continual warfare.

[20] *Manlius.*]—Ver. 185. Marcus Manlius was the first to drive the Gauls from the battlements of Rome when they were entering the Capitol in the night, and, by raising the alarm, to save that last hope of the City. In remembrance of this, he received the surname of Capitolinus. Being of a turbulent disposition, he became an object of dislike to the Patricians, and was finally thrown from the Tarpeian rock, on the charge of aspiring to the sovereign power at Rome. Gower thus renders this and the following line, little suspecting, perhaps, the anachronism that he was committing,—

'There Manlius' house once stood; who did remove
The Frenchmen's troops from Capitolian Jove.'

[21] *Festival of Mars.*]—Ver. 191. On the Calends of June a sacrifice was offered to Mars, outside of the Capenian gate. It is not clear whether the temple of Mars here mentioned was on the Appian road, or had a way leading to it from the Appian road, which began at the Capenian gate. Perhaps the 'Tecta via' was a covered way or arcade leading up to it. Commentators are at a loss for the signification here of the word 'tecta.'

Thee too, O Tempest,[22] we acknowledge to have deserved a shrine, at the time when our fleet was almost overwhelmed by the waves of Corsica. These memorials raised by men are exposed to our view. If you inquire as to the stars; at that time rises the bird of Jove[23] with its crooked beak.

The next day summons the Hyades, the horns on the forehead[24] of the bull: and the earth is soaked with copious showers.

When twice the Moon has come, and Phœbus has twice repeated his rising, and twice the standing corn has been rendered moist by the descent of the dew upon it; on this day Bellona[25] is said to have been enshrined in the Etrurian war; she, auspicious, ever favours Latium. Appius was the builder: he, who, when peace was refused to Pyrrhus,[26] saw clearly in his mind: *though*, as to his eyes, he was blind. A small open space[27] before the temple looks forth on the highest

---

Mr. Stanford suggests 'paved' as the meaning, a term especially applicable to the Appian way, which was so firmly paved with flint and cement that portions of it are still entire after a lapse of above two thousand years.

[22] *Tempest.*]—Ver. 193. L. Scipio, the Consul, having conquered the island of Corsica, built a temple to the deity 'Tempestas,' A.U.C. 495, in gratitude for his escape from a violent tempest while engaged in his descent upon that island.

[23] *The bird of Jove.*]—Ver. 196. On the evening of the Calends of June, the Constellation Aquila rises.

[24] *The horns on the forehead.*]—Ver. 197. The Hyades are so called, as they are situated in the forehead of the Constellation Taurus. On the fourth of the Nones of June, the Hyades rise heliacally, accompanied with rain.

[25] *Bellona.*]—Ver. 201. A temple to Bellona, the Goddess of War, was raised by Appius Claudius, during a battle in the Etrurian war, A.U.C. 458, and in this temple, which was near the Carmental gate, he erected the statues of his ancestors. Here the Senate gave audience to such foreign ambassadors as, from political motives, were not admitted into the city.

[26] *Refused to Pyrrhus.*]—Ver. 203. When the Senate were inclining to make peace with Pyrrhus, the king of Epirus, and to allow him to retain possession of his Italian conquests, Appius, who was then blind, had himself conveyed to the Senate-house in a litter, to dissuade them from adopting that step.

[27] *A small open space.*]—Ver. 205. Before the temple of Bellona was a small open space, which reached to the upper part of the Flaminian Circus. Here was a small column, and on proclaiming war against the enemy, the Fecialis (who combined in his person the character of priest

part of the Circus. There stands a column, small *indeed*, but of no small fame. From this spot, is wont to be hurled by the hand, the spear, the herald of war, when it seems good that arms should be taken up against the monarch and against the nations.

The other part of the Circus is secure under the guardianship of Hercules,[28] which honour, through the prophecy of the Eubœan *Sibyl*, that God possesses. The season of the dedication is the light-bearing *day*, which is before the Nones. If you ask what is the inscription, *it is*, "Sylla[29] sanctioned the building."

I was inquiring whether I should attribute the Nones to Sancus, or to Fidius, or to thee, O Father Semo?[30] when Sancus said to me, "To whichever of them thou shalt assign it, I shall *still* hold the honour. I bear these three names; 'twas thus that Cures willed." Him then, the ancient Sabines presented with a temple, and enshrined him on the Quirinal hill.

I have a daughter[31] (and long, I pray, may she survive my years), as long as she is in comfort I shall ever be happy. When I was wishful to bestow her on a son-in-law, I inquired what period was proper for the nuptial torch, and what *time* should be shunned. Then June was pointed out to me as

and herald) threw a spear over the column into a field adjoining, called the 'Ager Hostilis,' to signifying the commencement of hostilities. In the early days of Rome, when the hostile states were close at hand, the Fecialis used to throw the spear into the enemy's territories.

[28] *Hercules.*]—Ver. 209. It is doubtful whether there was one temple to Hercules, or two, in the Flaminian Circus. Neapolis thinks there were two; the one mentioned in the text, and another erected by Fulvius Nobilior, and repaired by Philippus, as stated in line 802 of this Book.

[29] *Sylla.*]—Ver. 212. Sylla, in his Censorship, approved, 'probavit,' this temple of Hercules. The Censors had the charge of the public buildings and temples, superintended their erection, and inspected and sanctioned them when built. Sylla regarded Hercules with especial veneration, as, to that Deity he imputed his political success and the immensity of the wealth that he had acquired.

[30] *O Father Semo.*]—Ver. 214. This deity was named Sancus or Sangus, Sanctus, Fidius or Dius Fidius, and Semo, and is generally supposed to have been the Sabine Hercules. St. Augustine says that Sancus was one of the kings of the Sabines, whom they had deified.

[31] *A daughter.*]—Ver. 220. The very little that has come down to us concerning the daughter of the poet will be found mentioned in the life of Ovid, sketched in the Introduction.

being, after the sacred Ides,[32] lucky for brides, and lucky for their husbands. The first part of this month was found to be ill-suited for nuptials; for thus did the holy wife of the *Flamen* Dialis say to me, " Until the gently flowing Tiber[33] shall have borne on his yellow waters, to the deep, the cleansings from *the shrine of* Ilian Vesta, it is not lawful for me to comb, with the box-wood, my shorn locks, nor to pare my nails with the knife, nor to approach my husband's bed; although he is the priest of Jove, *and* although to me he has been given by an eternal compact. Be not thou in any haste; thy daughter will marry more auspiciously when *the shrine of* Vesta, *Goddess* of the *Holy* Fire, shall be graced with a cleansed floor.

The third Moon[34] after the Nones is said to remove Lycaon, and the Bear has no more cause of alarm behind her. I remember that it is at that time, O rolling Tiber, that I beheld thy games upon the sward of the Campus *Martius*. This is a holiday to those who drag the dripping nets, and who bait with tiny morsels the hooked brass.[35]

The Mind[36] too is deified. We see shrines to the Mind, that were voted through fear of thy war, treacherous Carthaginian, Carthaginian, thou hadst renewed the war, and all, in dismay at

[32] *After the sacred Ides.*]—Ver. 223. It was not lucky to marry before the Ides of June; all the rest of the month was auspicious for that purpose.

[33] *The gently flowing Tiber.*]—Ver. 227. Festus and Varro tell us that the garbage and cleansings of this temple were deposited in a place near the Capitoline hill; and, most probably, (notwithstanding what the poet here says), they are correct in the assertion. It is hard to believe that the Romans treated their Tiber as badly as we do our Thames. Gower thus renders this and the preceding line,—

> ' Till gilded Tiber all the soil and trash
> Of Vesta's temple into sea doth wash.'

[34] *The third Moon.*]—On the 7th of the Ides of June, Arctophylax or Boötes sets in the morning. Lycaon is here put for Arcas, who was the grandson of Lycaon. See Book ii. l. 153.

[35] *The hooked brass.*]—Ver. 239, 240. Gower thus renders these lines,—

> ' This is the fisherman's feast day, who tangle
> Fish in their nets, with those who use the angle.'

[36] *The Mind.*]—Ver. 241. This temple is supposed to have been dedicated shortly after the defeat of the Roman army at Lake Thrasymenus, and the death of the Consul C. Flaminius, by the direction of the Sibylline books.

the death of the Consul, stood in dread of the Moorish arms.[37] Terror had banished hope; when the Senate made a vow to the Mind, and forthwith, more auspicious[38] did she become. That day, on which the vow was performed for the Goddess, sees the approach of the Ides in six days *from it*.

Vesta,[39] bestow on us thy favour! Now do we open our lips in honour of thee, if it is lawful to do honour to thy sacrifices. I was totally wrapt in my prayer; I became sensible of the presence of the celestial Divinity, and the joyous ground reflected back the purple light. As for me, I saw thee not, O Goddess—farewell to the fictions of the poets—by *the eyes of* man thou wast not possible to be seen. But those things which I had not known, and as to which I was *hitherto* kept in *entire* ignorance, were known to me without the instruction of any one. They say that Rome had kept the festivals of Pales, four times ten in number, when the guardian of the *sacred* flame was received into her temple. *This was* the act of *that* peaceful king, than whom, no one more piously disposed, did the land of the Sabines *ever* bear. *The shrines* which you now see roofed with brass, then you might see covered with straw, and their walls were woven of the pliant osier. This little spot, which now supports the hall of Vesta, was in those days the vast palace of the unshaven Numa. Yet the shape of the temple which now remains is said to have been anciently *the same:* and there exists a reason for its figure worthy of our approval. Vesta is the same Divinity as the Earth; the never-sleeping fire belongs to each. The Earth and the *Vestal* fire represent their respective positions.[40]

[37] *The Moorish arms.*]—Ver. 244. Livy tells us that there were Moors in the army of Hannibal; but the poet most probably here employs the term to signify Africans generally.

[38] *More auspicious.*]—Ver. 246. This is said in reference to the able conduct of Q. Fabius Maximus, surnamed 'Cunctator,' 'the delayer,' who, by his masterly conduct, rescued Rome and Italy from the subjugation so lately threatened by Hannibal.

[39] *Vesta.*]—Ver. 249. On the 5th of the Ides the Vestalia were celebrated.

[40] *Respective positions.*]—Ver. 268. He seems to mean, that the temple of Vesta being round, and the Vestal fire being in the midst of it, the fire was symbolical of the position which the earth was then supposed to occupy in the middle of the system. In the 267th line he says that Vesta and the Earth are the same; but in line 290 he says that Vesta is the same as fire; and in other instances he seems to be guilty of a similar confusion of ideas. Perhaps Vesta may have been originally considered as the

The Earth, like a ball[41] *in shape*, upheld by no support, hangs, a mass, weighty as it is, in the surrounding air. Its very roundness keeps *this* orb well poised, and there are no angles in it to press upon the parts *external to it*; and since it has been placed in the very middle of the universe, and is touching no one side more or less *than the other*, were it not round, then it would come nearer to one part *than the other*, and the universe would no *longer* have the earth as a weight in the middle of it. *And, by way of illustration*, there stands a globe in the citadel of Syracuse, suspended in the air,[42] confined *within a limited space*, a little model of the boundless system; and as far as the earth is distant from the top, so far is it from the bottom; the roundness of its form produces this result. Similar is the form of the temple: in it, there is no projecting angle—a dome protects it from the showers of rain.

You ask why the Goddess is worshipped by virgin attendants? On this subject, too, I shall discover suitable reasons. They say that Juno and Ceres were born of the seed of Saturn, from Ops; Vesta was the third. The two *former* were wedded; both are stated to have become mothers; one of the three remained without knowing man: what wonder is there if a

phlogiston, or natural heat which pervades the earth, and by degrees she may thus have become confounded with the earth itself. This is the more probable, as Vesta is sometimes styled the soul of the earth. However the point may be settled, this and the previous line are full of difficulties, and are not very easily rendered intelligible.

[41] *Like a ball.*]—Ver. 269. This and the next five lines are wanting in all the MSS. but seven, and are considered by Gierig to be spurious, though it is difficult to conceive for what reason, as they are intelligible, and bear no marks of corrupt Latinity. Mr. Keightley, however, agrees with Gierig's opinion.

[42] *In the air.*]—Ver. 277. Mr. Keightley suggests, that 'in aëre clauso' may mean, 'shut up in a glass-case.' The words may probably have that meaning, and the suggestion is ingenious. They would not appear, however, of necessity, to mean anything more than that the model stood under cover, and not in the open air; the air being not 'apertum,' or 'open,' but 'clausum,' 'shut up,'—perhaps by four walls, and certainly by the 'tholus,' or dome, for a roof. 'Polus' seems to mean 'the system,' which was probably represented on an exterior surface, within which the earth hung (perhaps by a thread, or fine cord, in its centre) in the middle, and consequently, as the poet says, on all sides equi-distant from the surrounding system. The citadel of Syracuse was called Achradina; and there, according to Athenæus, this model was kept.

virgin, pleased with a virgin attendant, admits chaste hands *alone to* her sacrifices. And consider Vesta nothing else than the living flame; you see that no bodies are produced by flame. In truth, then, she is a virgin, who neither yields nor receives the principles of conception, and who has *like* companions of her virgin state. Long did I, in my simplicity, imagine that there were statues of Vesta, but I afterwards ascertained that there were none under her concave dome. The fire that has never been extinguished lies hidden in that temple. Neither Vesta nor fire has any likeness. By its own strength does the earth rest: from standing by her own strength is she named Vesta;[43] and similar may be the origin of her Græcian appellation; but the hearth derives its name ["focus"] from the flames, and because it cherishes[44] all things: it formerly stood in the porch of the houses. From this I think *that spot* is called the " Vestibule." It is from that circumstance that we say in prayer, "O Vesta, thou who dost inhabit the foremost place." Before the hearths, it was the custom formerly to sit together on long benches,[45] and to believe that the Gods were *there* at the board. Now, too, when sacred rites are performed to the ancient Vacuna,[46] they stand and sit before the hearths of Vacuna. To our years has come down a relic of the ancient custom; a clean platter bears the food sent as a present offered to Vesta. Behold! the loaves of

[43] *Is she named Vesta.*]—Ver. 299. The poet here says, that the name of Vesta is derived from the two words 'vi stare,' 'to stand by (her own) strength.' In this he is wrong, as the word is derived from the Greek name of the Goddess, Ἑστία, which also signifies 'a hearth,' and comes from the Greek verb ἵστημι, 'to stand.'

[44] *It cherishes.*]—Ver. 301. He says that 'focus' is derived from the verb 'foveo,' 'to cherish,' or 'warm;' because the hearth, by the aid of flame sends forth heat.

[45] *Long benches.*]—Ver. 305. The poet refers to early times, when people sat on benches to take their meals, before the custom of reclining on couches, on those occasions, had been introduced from the East. He means to say, that as they sat near the fire, they considered Vesta (who was represented by it) and the Lares, or Penates (whose shrine was close by), were joining in the meal.

[46] *Ancient Vacuna.*]—Ver. 307. She was the Goddess of Leisure and Indolence, and is supposed to have been a Sabine deity. By some, she is identified with Diana, Ceres, or Venus; and by others with Minerva, or Victory. The husbandmen worshipped her, after the gathering in of the harvest, that they might, through her favour, obtain a winter of repose.

bread hang down from the asses bedecked with garlands, and the wreaths of flowers cover the rough mill-stones. In former times the peasants were wont to parch their spelt only in ovens; and *hence* the Goddess of the kiln[47] has her own rites. The hearth itself used to bake the bread placed beneath the ashes, and broken tiles were strewed along the warm floor. From that circumstance, does the baker reverence the hearth, and *Vesta*, the mistress of the hearths, and the same does the ass, which turns round the mill-stones rough as the pumice. Shall I pass it by, or shall I tell thy disgrace, ruddy Priapus?[48] It is a short story, but full of fun. Cybele, with her brow crowned with turrets, invites to her feast the eternal Gods. She invites, too, the Satyrs and the Nymphs, Deities of the country. Silenus comes, *too*, though no one had invited him. It is not lawful, 'twere tedious, too, to relate the banquet of the Gods; a sleepless night is spent over copious draughts of wine. Some are carelessly wandering in the vales of the shady Ida; some are lying down, and resting their limbs on the soft herbage. Some are disporting:[49] upon some, Sleep lays her hand: some join hands, and then with active foot they beat the ground. Vesta is lying down, and, free from fear, she enjoys quiet repose, supporting her head, reclining just as it was, on a tuft of grass. But the ruddy keeper of the gardens is *now* chasing both Nymphs and Goddesses, and turns his wandering steps, first in this direction, then in that. He spies Vesta, too; whether he took her for a Nymph, or whether he knew that she was Vesta, is a matter of doubt; he himself declares that he did not know her. He conceives impure hopes, and stealthily attempts to approach her, and with a palpitating heart he advances on tiptoe. By chance the old

---

[47] *The Goddess of the kiln.*]—Ver. 314. For an account of the rites of the Goddess Fornax, see Book ii. l. 525.

[48] *Priapus.*]—Ver. 319. This story is so like that of the nymph Lotis, Book i. l. 391, that it is difficult to imagine why the poet should repeat it; except that it is here introduced in connexion with Vesta.

[49] *Are disporting.*]—Ver. 329, 330. Gower thus renders these lines—

'Some sport, some snort; some arm-in-arm a round
Do make, and nimbly trip it on the ground.'

Lines 233, 234 he renders thus—

'But tawny Priap up and down there traces,
And peers on all the Goddesses and lasses.'

man Silenus had left the ass on which he had rode, near the bank of a gently murmuring stream. The God of the extended Hellespont is about to commence his project, when, with an unseasonable noise, the ass brays aloud. Alarmed at this harsh sound, the Goddess arises. All the company run to the same spot: he escapes through their indignant hands. Lampsacus[50] is wont to sacrifice this animal to Priapus: aptly, *too*, do we consign to the flames the entrails of the tell-tale ass. Him dost thou, O grateful Goddess, adorn with necklaces made of loaves:[51] *at that time, too*, the mill-stones, in idleness, cease their grating noise. I will tell what means the altar of Jupiter Pistor,[52] on the height of the Thunderer, more glorious in its renown than in its actual value. The Capitol, beleaguered, was pressed hard by the savage Gauls: the extreme length of the siege had caused a famine. Jupiter having called the Gods to his royal throne, says to Mars, "Do thou begin." Forthwith he answers, "Is it unknown *to thee*, forsooth, what is the *present* fortune of my people; and does this pang of my soul need the voice of complaint? If, however, thou requirest that I should, in a word, relate their woes in conjunction with their disgrace; Rome *now* lies at the foot of an Alpine foe. Is this the city, O Jupiter, to which had been promised the sovereignty of the world? Is it this that thou wast to impose as a ruler upon the earth? Already has she crushed the people in her vicinity, and the arms of Etruria. In their *full* career were our hopes; now, from her very home, has she been expelled. We have seen the veterans graced by many a triumph, adorned with their embroidered garments,

---

[50] *Lampsacus.*]—Ver. 345, 346. These lines are considered to be spurious by Heinsius and other commentators. The following is Gower's quaint translation of them:—

'The Lampsacenes to him the asse do kill;
This tell-tale's g—ts are fitly broiled still.'

[51] *Necklaces made of loaves.*]—Ver. 347. He says, that in gratitude for the service done by the ass to Vesta on this occasion, it was the custom, at her festival, to give that animal a day of rest, and a necklace made of loaves. It is not clear whether the necklace was formed of one entire loaf, baked in the form of a ring, or whether it was made of a number of small cakes or loaves strung together.

[52] *Jupiter Pistor.*]—Ver. 350. Literally, 'Jupiter the Baker.' This God is mentioned only by this author and Lactantius.

fall *under the slaughtering hand*, in the halls[53] bedecked with **brass**. We have seen the pledges of the Ilian Vesta[54] transferred from their abode *to another retreat;* clearly, they believe that some Gods[55] do exist. But if they only took notice that the spot where ye *Gods* inhabit on the *Capitoline* heights, and so many of your mansions are invested in blockade; *if so, I say*, they would surely know that there no *longer* exists any benefit in their worship of the Gods, and that the frankincense offered with the anxious hand is lost. Oh! would that an opportunity for the fight were given to them! Let them take arms; and if they cannot conquer, *why* let them perish. Now destitute of food, and dreading an inglorious death, a rabble of barbarians is beleaguering them, cooped up on their own hill. Then Venus, and Quirinus graced with his staff[56] and his kingly robe, and Vesta, pleaded many things in behalf of their Latium. Jupiter said, in reply, "All *of us* are concerned *in common* for these walls, and conquered Gaul shall suffer retribution. Do thou, Vesta, but effect, that of those provisions which are scarce, there should be thought to be a superabundance, and desert not thy own abode. Whatever unground grain there is, let the hollow machine[57] bruise it, and, kneaded with the hand, let the hearth harden it upon the fire." He had given his commands, and the Virgin, the daughter of Saturn, assents to the orders of her brother.

---

[53] *In the halls.*]—Ver. 363. Florus tells us, that on the irruption of the Gauls, the Senators devoted themselves to the Manes, in the Forum, and then retired to their houses, there to await their fate. Plutarch and Livy inform us that they were slain in the Forum.

[54] *The Ilian Vesta.*]—Ver. 365. The sacred fire, and other holy things in the temple of Vesta, were conveyed from Rome to Cære, a town of Etruria, where those who fled with them were hospitably entertained. The people of Cære received the freedom of the city of Rome by way of recompense for their pious hospitality.

[55] *That some Gods.*]—Ver. 366. The meaning of this somewhat obscure passage seems to be—Although the Romans find themselves deserted by us, yet from the care which they still take of the sacred things of Vesta, it is clear that they believe in her existence at least.

[56] *With his staff.*]—Ver. 375. 'Lituus' properly means a staff with a curved top, used by the augurs in pointing to the heavens, the form of which is still retained in the crosier of the bishops.

[57] *The hollow machine.*]—Ver. 381. The mill is so called here, probably from the circumstance that the lower stone was somewhat hollowed, whence it was called 'catillus,' which properly signifies 'a dish.'

'Twas now the hour of midnight: toil had brought sleep to the chiefs. Jupiter chides them, and, with his holy lips, he signifies to them his wishes: " Rise ye, and, from the topmost towers, hurl down into the midst of the enemy that succour which least of all ye prefer to resign." Sleep departs, and, in agitation, by reason of these strange dark sayings, they make inquiries what succour it is that they would be unwilling, and *yet* that they are ordered to resign? Lo! it seems *to them* that it is bread. They hurl down the gifts of Ceres; thrown down, they rattle over helmets and long bucklers. All hope that they could be overcome through famine, deserts *the enemy*. The foe being repulsed, a marble altar is erected to Jupiter Pistor.

It chanced that I was returning from the festival of Vesta, by that way by which the new street is now joined to the Roman Forum. I saw a matron coming along down it with bare feet; I was surprised, and, in silence, I made a pause. An old woman who lived near the place perceived *my astonishment*, and, requesting me to be seated, she addressed me, shaking her *palsied* head, in a tremulous voice:—" This place, where now are the markets, *formerly* fenny marshes covered; a ditch was *here* swimming with water, from the overflowing of the river. That spot formed the Curtian lake[58] which now supports the altars on dry ground; 'tis now dry ground, but once it was a lake. In the spot where the Velabra[59] are *now*

---

[58] *The Curtian lake.*]—Ver. 403. In early times, the valleys between the hills of Rome were often rendered swampy, and almost impassable, through the frequent inundations of the Tiber. The spot called the 'Curtius Lacus' received its name from some heroic act there performed by a soldier named Curtius; but there are doubts as to the period when that name was first given. Some suppose that it was so called from Marcus Curtius, who there exhibited his heroism by leaping into the yawning gulf, a self-devoted sacrifice for the benefit of his country; while others understand it to refer to Mettus Curtius, a Sabine soldier, who withstood the Romans on this spot, and lost his horse in the marsh. It retained the name 'Lacus,' for centuries after it had been drained, and had 'supported the altars on dry ground.'

[59] *The Velabra.*]—Ver. 405. The 'Via Nova,' or 'New way,' led from the streets called 'Velabra' into the interior part of Rome. The greater, and the less 'Velabrum,' lay between the Palatine and Capitoline hills: oil, fruits, and other commodities were there sold in booths, or under awnings. Varro says that these streets received their name from the verb 'veho,' 'to carry,' because in early times that part was traversed in boats; which mode of carriage also was called 'Velatura.'

wont to lead the processions into the Circus, nought was there *then* but willows and dense reeds. Ofttimes does the reveller sing, as he is returning *homeward* through the waters of the suburbs, and passes his drunken jokes upon the sailors. Not yet had *the God*, he who adapts himself to various forms, received a name from the turning aside of the river.[60] Here, too, there was a sacred grove, dense with bulrushes and reeds, and a marsh not to be approached with covered feet. The standing waters have been drained off; its own bank confines the stream, and now the ground is dry; yet still is the custom kept up." She had told me the cause. "Farewell, most worthy dame," said I; "tranquil be the remainder of thy days."[61] The rest *that I shall tell*, I learned long since in the days of my childhood; but it must not on that account be passed over by me. Ilus,[62] the descendant of Dardanus, had just built his new walls: the wealthy Ilus still held the sovereignty of Asia. The heavenly statue of the armed Minerva[63] is believed to have fallen on the heights of the city of Ilus: to see it was my

[60] *Turning aside of the river.*]—Ver. 410. On this spot, in a street called the Etrurian Street, there was a statue of Vortumnus, or Vertumnus, a God of Etruria. He received this name from having, on an inundation, changed the course of the river; 'Verto' signifying 'to turn.' The poet makes allusion to the variety of forms which were assumed by Vertumnus while wooing the nymph Pomona, which story he relates in the 14th book of the Metamorphoses, l. 637. According to some, he was the God of the autumnal fruits; and, according to others, of merchandize; while others suppose him to have been the God who presided over the thoughts of mankind, and thus account for the fickleness and versatility which were his characteristics.

[61] *Remainder of thy days.*]—Ver. 415, 416. Gower gives the following quaint translation of these lines:—

'She ended. Farewell, good old soul, said I;
Maist thou spend all thy old dayes merrily.'

[62] *Ilus.*]—Ver. 420. He was the great grandson of Dardanus, and built a considerable part of the city of Troy.

[63] *The armed Minerva.*]—Ver. 421. This statue was called the 'Palladium.' It was supposed to have fallen from Heaven, and being deposited in Troy, was brought thence to Italy, as the poet here says, either by Æneas, Diomedes, or Ulysses; though the credit of having so done is distinctly given by most writers to Æneas. By some it is described as a wooden statue of the Goddess, about three cubits high, holding in her right hand a pike, and in her left a distaff; by others it is said to have been made of the bones of Pelops. It was deposited near the sacred fire, in the temple of Vesta, at Rome.

care. I saw the temple and the spot: they are still left to *Troy; but* Rome has *the image of* Pallas. Smintheus[64] is consulted, and in the gloom of a shady grove he utters these words, with a voice that never deceives :—"Preserve the Goddess that comes from the skies, and ye will preserve your city: with herself, she will transfer the empire of the place." Ilus preserves her, and keeps her shut up in the heights of his citadel, and the care of her descends to his son Laomedon. Badly guarded was she under Priam; thus wished she *that it should be*, from the time when her beauty was impugned by the judgment *of his son*. Either the descendant of Adrastus,[65] or Ulysses, skilled in theft, or else the pious Æneas, is said to have carried her away: the perpetrator of the deed is unknown; the image itself is Roman; Vesta protects her, because she watches all things with her unceasing light. Oh! how great was the dread of the Senators, at the time when *the temple of* Vesta was burned, and *she* herself was almost overwhelmed by her own ruins! The sacred fires were burning with the accursed ones; and the sacrilegious flames were mingling with the pious. Her priestesses, astounded, were weeping with dishevelled locks: their very fear had deprived their bodies of strength. Metellus flies forward into the midst, and, with a loud voice, he cries, "Haste to the rescue! tears afford no help. Remove the pledges of destiny with your virgin hands! By the hand, and not by vows, must they be rescued. Woe is me! Do ye hesitate?"[66] says he. He saw that they were hesitating, and that in their dismay they had fallen down on their knees. He takes up some water, and, raising his hands, he says, "Forgive me, ye holy things! Though a man, I will enter the shrines which ought not by man to be entered. If this be a crime, then full upon me fall the penalty of my sin, and at the cost of my life let Rome be redeemed." He

[64] *Smintheus.*]—Ver. 425. This was an epithet of Apollo, derived either from 'Sminthus,' a village near Troy, or from 'Sminthus,' or 'Sminthea,' the Phrygian name for a mouse or rat; which, at the intercession of his priest Chryses, when his gardens and orchards were much infested by them, he had driven away and extirpated.

[65] *Descendant of Adrastus.*]—Ver. 433. Diomedes, the son of Tydeus by Deiphyle, the daughter of Adrastus, King of Argos.

[66] *Do ye hesitate?*]—Ver. 447, 448. Gower thus renders these lines:—

'O heavens! D'ye stand? Them in a stam he sees,
And in amazement fall'n upon their knees.'

said, and he burst in. The Goddess, carried off, approved of the deed; and by the devotedness of her Priest[67] was she saved. Now, happily do ye glow, ye sacred fires, under Cæsar. Now the fire both is, and will be, upon Ilian shrines; and while he is our chief, no priestess will be told of as having defiled her fillets, or will be buried alive in the earth. Thus perishes the unchaste one,[68] inasmuch as she against whom she has sinned is heaped upon her; for the Earth and Vesta are the same deity.

On this day did Brutus gain a surname from the Callaican foe,[69] and stain with blood the Spanish soil. Sometimes, forsooth, is sorrow mixed with rejoicings; lest the festal day should delight the people to their very hearts' *content, and leave nothing for them to desire.* Crassus, near the Euphrates, lost his eagles, his son, and his soldiers; and, last of all, was himself consigned to death. "Parthian! why dost thou exult?" said the Goddess. "*Those* standards thou shalt restore, and there shall be an avenger to take satisfaction for the death of Crassus." But as soon as the violets are taken off from the long-eared asses, and the rough millstones grind the grain of Ceres, the mariner, sitting in his bark, says, "We shall see the Dolphin,[70] when the damp night, having chased away the day, shall have set in."

Now, Phrygian Tithonus, thou complainest that thou art deserted by thy bride, and the watchful light-bearing *star of the morn* comes forth from the eastern waves. Go *in procession,* good matrons,—the Matralia is your festival,—and offer the yellow cakes to the Theban Goddess.[71] There is an open space ad-

[67] *Devotedness of her Priest.*]—Ver. 454. Metellus lost his sight in the flames: in consequence of which he was allowed to come to the Senate-house in a chariot (an honour never before bestowed on any one), and a statue was erected to him in the Capitol.

[68] *The unchaste one.*]—Ver. 459. Allusion is here made to the punishment of being buried alive, which was awarded to the Vestal who was found guilty of a violation of her vows of chastity.

[69] *Callaican foe.*]—Ver. 461. On the day of the Vestalia, D. Junius Brutus overcame the Callaici, a people of the north-west of Spain, whose chief city was Calle, now Oporto, on the river Durius, now Douro.

[70] *The Dolphin.*]—Ver. 471. On the 4th of the Ides of June, the day after the Vestalia, the Dolphin rises in the evening. The termination of the festival is signified by the garlands being taken off the asses, and their being set to work again at turning the mill-stones.

[71] *Theban Goddess.*]—Ver. 476. The Goddess Mater Matuta is here identified by the poet with Ino, daughter of Cadmus, the founder of

joining to the bridges and the great Circus, which derives its name from an ox placed *there*. Here, on this morn, they say that the sceptred hands of Servius gave a temple[72] to Mother Matuta. *As to* what Goddess she is, why she keeps hand-maidens afar from the thresholds of her temple (for she does keep them away), and why she requires the toasted cakes, Bacchus, with thy hair crowned with clusters and wreathed with ivy, if this family be thine, do thou guide the course of my bark. Through Jove's compliance *with her request*, Semele had been consumed; Ino received thee, O child, and carefully reared thee with her best attention. Juno was enraged, because she was bringing up the child that was snatched from *the womb of* a concubine of Jove. But, *in good truth*, he was the offspring of her sister.[73] On this account, Athamas is haunted by the Furies and by false imaginings, and thou diest, infant Learchus, by the hand of thy father. The sorrowing mother had now buried the corpse of Learchus, and had performed all the rites due to the dismal pile. She, too, bounds forward just as she is, with her locks torn in funereal woe, and snatches thee, Melicerta, from thy cradle. There is a spot[74] contracted within a narrow compass,—two seas it dashes back, and one tract of land is beaten by two tides. Thither she comes, embracing her son in her maniac arms, and plunges him, along with herself, from the high summit *of the cliff* into the deep. Unharmed, Panope[75] and her hundred sisters receive them, and

Thebes, who was deified under the name of Leucothea. Reference has been already made to the story of Ino and Melicerta, and Helle and Phryxus, in Book ii. l. 628, and Book iii. l. 859.

[72] *Gave a temple.*]—Ver. 480. The poet says that Servius Tullius built the temple of Mater Matuta, in the Forum Boarium, or Ox Market, which was near the Palatine bridge and the Circus Maximus. There was a brazen statue of a bull in this market-place.

[73] *Offspring of her sister.*]—Ver. 487, 488. Gower thus renders these lines:—

'Vex'd Juno swell'd, that she, the strumpet gone,
Should nurse her brat; yet 'twas her sister's sonne.'

[74] *There is a spot.*]—Ver. 495. The poet here describes the Isthmus of Corinth, whence Ino plunged into the sea. It was very narrow, the space between the Ægean and Ionian seas not being more than about six miles in width.

[75] *Panope.*]—Ver. 499. She was the daughter of Nereus and Doris, and sister of the Nereids.

with a gently gliding pace they bear them through their realms. Not yet does Leucothoë—not yet does that boy Palæmon[76] possess the mouth of Tiber, abounding with its eddies. There was a sacred grove: whether it is called the Grove of Semele, or of Stimula,[77] is a matter of doubt; they say that the Bacchanals[78] of Ausonia inhabited it. Of these, Ino enquires what nation that is? She hears that they are Arcadians, and that Evander wields the sceptre of the place. Concealing her divinity, Juno, the daughter of Saturn, insidiously urges on the Latian Bacchanals by deceiving words:— "O, *people*—too credulous,[79] and utterly mad! This stranger comes, no friend to our choirs. By fraud she seeks and endeavours to become acquainted with the ceremonial of our rites; she has *with her* a pledge by which she can pay the penalty." Hardly has she ceased; the Bacchanals fill the air with their howlings, their locks streaming down their shoulders; they lay hands upon her, and strive to tear away the babe; she invokes those Gods whom, as yet, *a stranger*, she knows not. "Ye Gods, and ye men of this place, assist a mother in her distress!" Her cries re-echo among the neighbouring crags of the Aventine. The hero of Œta[80] had *just* driven to the bank *of the river* his Iberian cows; he hears *her*, and in haste pursues his way towards the sounds. At the approach of Hercules, those who, but a moment before, were preparing to offer violence, turn their cowardly backs

[76] *Palæmon.*]—Ver. 501. As Ino, when deified, received the names of Leucothoë and Matuta, so was Melicerta called by the Greeks, Palæmon, by the Latins, Portunus.

[77] *Stimula.*]—Ver. 503. There was a Goddess of this name, in whose grove the orgies of Bacchus were celebrated, until they were discontinued by order of the Senate, on account of the gross irregularities discovered to have been committed there.

[78] *The Bacchanals.*]—Ver. 504. Literally, the 'Mænades,' or 'frantic' votaries of Bacchus.

[79] *Too credulous.*]—Ver. 509, 510. Gower gives the following translation of these lines:—

'O simple souls! O senselesse folk and blind!
D'ye take this vagrant huzzie for your friend?'

[80] *The hero of Œta.*]—Ver. 519. Hercules is so called here prolepterally, or by anticipation, because he ordered his body to be burned, after his decease, on Mount Œta, in Thessaly. At the period mentioned in the text, he was driving the oxen which he had taken from Geryon, King of Iberia, or Spain.

in womanish flight. He says, "What seekest thou in this spot, aunt of Bacchus?" for he had recognized her: "Does the same Deity that *harasses* me, harass thee also?" Partly she informs him;[81] as to some part *of her story*, the presence of her son is a check *upon her*, and she is ashamed that in her frenzy she has resorted to crime. Fame, swift as she is, flies about with flapping wings; and ofttimes, Ino, is thy name on her lips. As the guest of Carmentis, thou art said to have entered a faithful abode, and to have broken thy protracted fast. The priestess of Tegeæa[82] is said to have given to thee cakes hastily made with her own hand, and baked upon a hurried hearth. And *so* at the present day, on the festival of the Matralia, are cakes pleasing to her; this rustic courtesy was more pleasing than all *the appliances of* art. "Now," she says, "do thou, a prophetess, unseal the decrees of destiny as thou mayst be pleased; add this *favour*, I pray, to thy hospitable reception of me." But little delay is there: the prophetess receives the *inspiration of the* Deities of the heavens, and becomes filled with the God throughout her entire soul. On a sudden, scarcely could you recognize her, so much more holy, and so much more stately did she seem than the moment before. "Tidings of joy will I sing; rejoice, Ino, that thou hast ended thy toils," she said, "and ever be present, propitious to this nation! A Deity of the ocean shalt thou be: the deep, too, shall receive thy son; amid our seas take ye *both* another name. Leucothoë shalt thou be called by the Greeks; Matuta by our nation; thy son shall have universal sway over the harbours.[83] Him whom we shall call Portunus, his own tongue shall call Palæmon. Go ye *both*, I pray, propitious

---

[81] *She informs him.*]—Ver. 525, 526. Gower thus renders these lines—

'Part tells she; part the presence of her sonne
    Withheld. She's sham'd for those mad tricks were done.'

[82] *Priestess of Tegeæa.*]—Ver. 531—534. The following is Gower's translation—

'The holy woman made a fire in hast,
    And bak'd a bisket for her quick repast.
    Hence in her matrals bake they biskets dry;
    No art pleas'd her like that tight houswifry.'

[83] *Over the harbours.*]—Ver. 546. The poet here implies that Melicerta received his name 'Portunus' from the harbours, 'portus,' which he was to take under his protection.

to *these* our lands." They nodded their assent. Truth attended her promise: they ended their labours: they changed their names: the one is a God, the other a Goddess. You enquire why she forbids the handmaids to approach; she hates *them,* and if she permits me, I will sing the origin of her hate. Daughter of Cadmus,[84] one of thy female servants was wont ofttimes to submit to the embraces of thy husband. The faithless Athamas wooed her by stealth. From her he learned that grain subjected to the fire was given out to the husbandmen. *The queen* herself denied that she did *this,* but rumour has given reception *to the story;* this is the reason why this class of servants are objects of her hatred. But let not the fond mother offer up to her, prayers for her own family; she herself seems to have been *but* an unhappy parent. With more fortunate results, ye will entrust to her the offspring of another; she was more beneficial to Bacchus than she was to her own children. It is reported that this *Goddess* said to thee, O Rutilius,[85] "Whither dost thou hasten on my festival? A Consul, thou shalt fall, by the hand of the Marsian foe." The event accorded with her words; and the empurpled stream of Tolenus ran with his waters mingled with gore. The next year came: on the same morn[86] the slaughter of Didius[87] redoubled the success of the foe. The same day[88] is thine, O Fortune;[89]

[84] *Daughter of Cadmus.*]—Ver. 553. This appears to be a very absurd story. Plutarch tells us that a female servant used to be admitted into her temple, but only for the purpose of being soundly flogged by the matrons. He adds, that no Ætolian was admitted into the temple of Leucothea at Chronea, as the favorite of Athamas was an Ætolian by birth.

[85] *Rutilius.*]—Ver. 563. On the day of the Matralia, in the Marsian or Social war, the Consul P. Rutilius Lupus was slain near the Tolenus, a river flowing from the Marsian into the Sabine territory.

[86] *On the same morn.*]—Ver. 567. 'Pallantide.' Literally, 'the kinswoman of Pallas;' an epithet of Aurora, the Goddess of the Morning, who was the cousin of Pallas, one of the Titans.

[87] *Didius.*]—Ver. 568. Appian informs us that Didius was Prætor during the Marsian or Social war; but we have no record of his defeat and death, which are probably here referred to.

[88] *The same day.*]—Ver. 569, 570. Gower thus quaintly translates these lines—

'Thine, Fortune, is this day, this place, this founder.
But who's that statue wrapt up in a gown there?'

In good truth, the translator was not a respecter even of rhyme on all occasions!

[89] *O Fortune.*]—Ver. 569. On the same day with the temple of

the same the builder; *the same* the site. But who is this that lies hid beneath the garments⁹⁰ covering him? It is Servius: for this much is agreed upon; but various reasons are assigned for his concealment, and they leave me uncertain in my own mind. While the Goddess timidly confesses her stolen loves, and blushes that she, a daughter of heaven, had submitted to the embrace of a mortal, for she was inflamed *with love*, being seized with a violent passion for the king, and in the case of this man alone she proved herself not blind.—By night she was wont to enter his abode through a little window, from which circumstance the gate bears the name of Fenestella.⁹¹ Now is she ashamed, and she covers with a veil those beloved features, and the face of the king is hidden by many a gown. Or is it rather the truth, that after the death of Tullius the people were shocked by the death of their peaceful chief? No bounds were then set *to their grief;* at sight of his statue their sorrow increased, until they concealed it by putting gowns over it. The third reason must be sung by me in a wider space; yet shall I keep my steeds within the narrowest limits as I drive. Tullia having effected her marriage, the wages of iniquity, was wont to urge her lord with these words: " What boots it that we are equally matched *in guilt*, thou, with the murder of my sister, and I, *with the blood* of thy brother, if now a life of piety contents us? My husband and thy wife should both have lived, if we were to dare no greater crime *than this?* The life and the kingdom of my father I present to thee as my dowry; if thou art a man, go and exact the benefits of my dower, that I tell thee of. Crime is worthy of a king; slay thy father-in-law, and seize the throne, and do thou stain *both* our hands with my father's blood." Goaded on by such words, he, a private person, had *now* taken his seat on the lofty throne: in amazement, the multitude takes to arms.

Matuta, by the same person, Servius Tullius, and in the same place, the Forum Boarium, or ox-market, the temple of Fortuna Virilis was dedicated.

⁹⁰ *Beneath the garments.*]—Ver. 570. We are told by Dionysius that this statue was of wood gilt, and that two togas were thrown over it. Varro speaks of the statue thus covered, as though it had been that of the Goddess herself.

⁹¹ *Fenestella.*]—Ver. 578. He tells us that the Goddess Fortuna used to pay her nightly visits to Servius through a window, and that, in commemoration thereof, one of the gates of the city was called ' Porta Fenestella,' from the word ' fenestra,' ' a window.'

Bloodshed and slaughter are the consequence, and feeble age is overpowered. The son-in-law, *Tarquinius* Superbus, wields the sceptre that he has won from his father-in-law. *The king* himself, slain at the foot of the Esquiliæ, where his palace was, fell, weltering in his blood, on the hard ground. His daughter, about to enter the home of her father, was passing in her chariot, lofty and impudent, through the middle of the street. The charioteer, soon as he beheld the body, bursting into tears, stopped short; with such words as these did she reproach him: "Are you going on?[92] or are you awaiting the bitter reward of your affection? Drive, I tell you, the wheels over his very face, whether they will go or not." A sure evidence of this deed, from her the street was called "The Accursed,"[93] and that transaction is thereby impressed with a lasting mark. Yet, after this, she dared to touch the temple that was the memorial of her father: wonders, truly, but still facts, do I relate. There was a statue, the resemblance of Tullius, sitting on a throne; this is said, with its hands, to have covered its eyes; and a voice was heard, "Cover ye my countenance, that it behold not the impious face of my daughter." He was covered with the garment presented to him; Fortune forbade it to be removed, and thus from her temple did she speak: "That day, on which, with unveiled features, Servius shall first be uncovered, shall be the first of the departure from shame." Forbear, ye matrons, to touch the forbidden garments; it is enough to utter prayers with the voice of worship; and may he who was the seventh king[94] in our city, ever keep his head concealed in the Roman garb. This temple was burned by fire; yet did the flames spare that statue; Mulciber himself gave his aid to his son. For Vulcan was the Father of Tullius; Ocrisia was his mother, a woman of Corniculum,[95] remarkable for her beauty. Her,

[92] *Going on.*]—Ver. 607, 608. Gower thus translates these lines—

'Drive on, or I'll pay you for your foolish zeal;
Run o'er, I say, his carkasse with the wheel.'

[93] *Accursed.*]—Ver. 609. Dionysius says, that before this tragic occurrence, that street or road was called 'the Happy;' Livy calls it the 'Virbian,' and Festus 'the Orbian way.'

[94] *The seventh king.*]—Ver. 624. That is to say, by reckoning, as one of the kings, Titus Tatius the Sabine, who reigned jointly with Romulus.

[95] *Corniculum.*]—Ver. 628. This was a town in the Latian territory, which was taken by the Romans, on which occasion Ocrisia, the mother of Servius Tullius, became a captive.

Tanaquil, having duly performed the sacred rites, ordered, in company with herself, to pour the wine on the decorated altar. Here among the ashes either was, or seemed to be, a form of obscene shape; but such it really was. Being ordered so to do, the captive submits to its embraces; conceived by her, Servius has the origin of his birth from heaven. His father afforded the proof, at the time when he touched his head with the gleaming fire, and a flame, rising to a point, blazed upon his locks.

Thee, too, O Concord,[96] does Livia enshrine in a gorgeous temple, thee, whom she bestowed upon her beloved husband. But know, generations to come, that where the portico of Livia now is, *once* stood the building of an immense house. One house was the work of a whole city; and it occupied a space, a smaller than which many towns contain within their walls. This was levelled with the ground, under no accusation of one aiming at sovereign power, but because, by its gorgeousness, it was deemed injurious *to public virtue*. Cæsar had the moral courage to level so vast a pile of buildings; and himself, the heir to it, to lose so much property of his own. Thus is his Censorship discharged, and thus is an example given; when the assertor *of morality* himself practises that which he enjoins on others.

There is no mark of distinction on the succeeding day which I am able to mention.

On the Ides a temple was given to unconquered Jove. And now I am commanded to tell you of the lesser Quinquatrus;[97] Minerva, *thou* with thy auburn locks, assist my un-

---

[96] *O Concord.*]—Ver. 637. On the 3rd of the Ides of June, Livia dedicated a temple to Concord, in token of the harmony which had always subsisted between her and her husband Augustus. It was near the 'Liviæ Porticus,' which was built on the site of the former palace of Vedius Pollio. This he had bequeathed to Augustus; but it was of such immense extent, and its splendour was supposed to furnish so bad a precedent, that Augustus ordered it to be razed to the ground.

[97] *Quinquatrus.*]—Ver. 651. On the Ides of June a temple had been dedicated to Jupiter; and on that day the Lesser Quinquatrus or Quinquatria were celebrated. It is doubtful whether 'Invictus,' 'unconquered,' is here a mere supplementary epithet of Jupiter, or whether the temple had been dedicated to him with that 'cognomen' or 'surname.' No other writer mentions any such 'cognomen.' The greater 'quinquatria' were on the 14th of the Calends of April. They are described in Book iii. l. 809. Gower thus renders the two preceding lines—

'Two following days are blank. To Jove invicted
Upon the Ides a chapell was addicted.'

dertaking. Why does the strolling piper[98] rove about all the city? What mean the masks, what the long flowing hair? Thus I *spoke*. Thus said Tritonia, having laid aside her lance (would that I could repeat *exactly* the words of the learned Goddess): "In the times of your forefathers of old, the piper was much employed, and was always held in high estimation. The piper used to sound his notes in the temples, and at the games; at the sorrowful funerals the piper used to sound. His toil was then sweetened by reward; but a time followed,[99] which suddenly put an end to the employment of the Grecian art.[1] Add, too, *the fact*, that the Ædile had ordered that there should be but ten musicians who should attend the funeral procession. They quit the city in *self-imposed* exile, and they retire to Tibur. The hollow pipe is missed on the stage, it is missed at the altars; no dirge *now* escorts the last obsequies. A certain man, *himself* worthy of any rank, had been a slave at Tibur,[2] but after a length of time he had become free. He prepares a repast at his farm, and invites the musical band; they assemble at the festive banquet. 'Twas now night, and their sight and their eyes and their souls were drenched with wine, when a messenger came with a speech previously arranged, and thus he

[98] *The strolling piper.*]—Ver. 653, 654. Gower gives the following translation—

' Why do the waits walk all about the town?
Why do they mask disguis'd? What means the gown?'

[99] *A time followed.*]—Ver. 661. The time which the poet here refers to was when Appius Claudius was Censor, A.U.C. 443, by whom the pipers, or flute-players, were prohibited from eating in the temple of Jupiter. He had previously restricted the number of them which should accompany funerals to ten.

[1] *Grecian art.*]—Ver. 662. Ovid is here mistaken in ascribing the invention of the flute or fife to Greece. The Romans received the use of the flute from Asia; whereas the 'Cithara,' or lyre, was the national music of Greece. Most of the MSS. read 'gratæ,' which would, if adopted, alter the passage to the ' pleasing art,' which, most probably, is the correct reading. It must, however, be remembered, that the poet is here consistent with the sequel, in which he ascribes the invention of the 'Tibia' to Minerva or Pallas, who was originally a Grecian deity.

[2] *At Tibur.*]—Ver. 669, 670. Livy says that the stratagem here related was practised by the Government of Tibur, at the request of envoys sent thither from Rome. Gower thus renders these lines:—

' At Tybur liv'd a libertine, in's 'art
A long time free, and one of great desert.'

said: 'Why delayest thou to put an end to the banquet? the giver of thy freedom[3] is at hand. There is no delay;[4] the guests move their limbs staggering under the strong wine; their stumbling feet now stand, now give way. But the master *of the house* said, 'Depart ye,' and lifted them into a cart as they yet lingered; with broad hurdles was the cart fenced round.[5] The late hour, the jolting, and the wine, all bring on sleep, and the drunken crew think that they are going back to Tibur. And now, *the cart* had entered the Roman city through the Esquiliæ, and in the morning it was standing in the middle of the Forum. Plautius, that he may deceive the Senate both as to their appearance and numbers, orders their faces to be covered with masks. He also puts among them others, and, that the *band of* female musicians may increase this multitude, he orders them to go in long garments, that so those who had returned might be thoroughly concealed, lest, by chance, they should be remarked to have come back contrary to the commands[6] of his colleague. The thing was

[3] *Thy freedom.*]—Ver. 676. 'Vindicta' is, literally, the rod which the Victor laid on the head of the slave about to receive his freedom.

[4] *There is no delay.*]—Ver. 677—682. The following is Gower's comical translation of these lines :—

'Away all staggering hastily do pack:
Their legs unruly large indentures make.
Away, the master cry'd: and as they slack'd,
Into a matted waggon all he pack'd.
Time, wine, and motion sleep provok'd. They thought,
All fox'd, the cart had them to Tybur brought.'

Of course the indentures made by their legs were bipartite.

[5] *Fenced round.*]—Ver. 680. Varro says that a 'plaustrum' was an open cart; and it seems to be the opinion of Neapolis, a very intelligent commentator, that the 'sirpea' was a hurdle fence round the cart, and not an awning over it. At the present day, carts are sometimes to be seen in the country, fitted up in this way for the safe conveyance of pigs and sheep. The object of putting up the hurdles in the cart was clearly to prevent the pipers from recognizing the face of the country, if any of them should chance to wake, and thus prematurely discover the trick that was being played on them.

Contrary to the commands.]—Ver. 690. Though the pipers had voluntarily withdrawn from Rome, it is not unlikely that Claudius and the senators had determined that they should not return, after having once abandoned their home and their duties as citizens. On the other hand, it seems that C. Plautius, the other censor and the colleague of Appius, adopted the views of those who wished for their return, and having succeeded in his stratagem, used his best endeavours to conceal it from his colleague and the Senate.

approved of; and *ever since* it has been allowed *by usage* to wear strange dresses on the Ides, and to chant merry sayings to the old-fashioned airs.' When she had given me this information, I said, 'It still remains for me to learn why that day is called Quinquatrus?' 'March,' says she, 'keeps a festival of mine by that name, and this kind of people are in the number of my inventions. I was the first to cause the long pipe to give forth its sounds, the box-wood having been *first* bored in a few holes. The melody pleased me; *but* in the clear waters that reflected my face, I saw the swelling out of my virgin cheeks.' 'The art is not worth the penalty to me,' I cried; 'farewell! my pipe.' The *river's* bank received it as I threw it away. A Satyr[7] having found it, is at first struck with wonder, and knows not its use; but he perceives that when blown into it emits a sound; and at one moment, he lets forth the air with his fingers, at another, he stops it. And now among the Nymphs he is vain of his *new-found* art. He challenged even Phœbus; Phœbus being victor, he was hung up; *and* his mangled limbs were stripped of their skin. Yet I am the inventress and the originator of this melody; this is the reason why that branch of art observes my *festive* days."

The third day[8] shall come, on which thou, Thyene of Dodona, shalt stand conspicuous on the forehead of the Bull of Agenor's *daughter*. This is the day on which thou, O Tiber, dost roll to the deep, along thy Etrurian streams, the cleansings *of the shrine* of Vesta.

If there is any dependence at all on the winds, ye mariners, spread your canvass to Zephyrus: to-morrow he shall come propitious, over your waves.

But when the parent of the Heliades[9] shall have plunged his

---

[7] *A Satyr.*]—Ver. 703. This was Marsyas, who, in his exultation, challenged Apollo to a musical contest. The God being successful, flayed his antagonist alive; and the tears which were shed by the rural Deities on his death, formed the river of Phrygia, known by his name.

[8] *The third day.*]—Ver. 711. On the 17th of the Calends of July the Hyades rise acronychally. Thyene was the name of one of them. As to the cleansing of the temple of Vesta, see line 287 of this Book.

[9] *Heliades.*]—Ver. 717. Literally, 'the daughters of the sun.' They were the sisters of Phaëton. Hyrieus is mentioned in the 5th Book, l. 499. He was the father of Orion, which Constellation rises acronychally on the 15th of the Calends of July.

beams in the waves, and the bright stars shall gird the two extremities of the skies, the son of Hyrieus shall raise from the ground his strong shoulders; on the succeeding night, the Dolphin will be visible. In truth, he once had seen the Volsci and the Æqui routed on thy plains, O land of Algidus; from which circumstance, Tubertus Posthumus,[10] thou wast carried, renowned by a triumph over thy neighbouring foes, by snow-white steeds.

Now six days and as many more of the month are remaining; and to this number add one day. The sun leaves Gemini,[11] and the sign of the Crab grows ruddy *with his light: on this day* Pallas began to be worshipped on the heights of the Aventine.

Now, Laomedon, thy daughter-in-law[12] rises, and rising, dispels the night, and the damp rime departs from the meadows: *then* a temple is said to have been given to Summanus,[13] whoever he may chance to be, at that season when thou, O Pyrrhus, wast an object of dread to the Romans.

When Galatea[14] shall have received her, too, in the waves of her sire, and the earth shall be full of rest, undisturbed with care; then rises from the earth the youth who was smitten by the weapons of his grandsire, and extends his hands, wreathed with two snakes. Well known is the passion of Phædra—well known the injustice of Theseus: he, in his credulity, devoted to destruction his own son. The youth who, not with impunity, adhered to virtue, is on his way to Træzene; a bull

---

[10] *Tubertus Posthumus.*]—Ver. 724-5. In his Dictatorship, he triumphed after defeating the Volsci and Æqui at Algidus, a town of Latium. Gower gives the following version of these lines:—

'Whose starres the Volsci and the Equi saw
Yerwhile expell'd the plains of Algida.'

[11] *Leaves Gemini.*]—Ver. 727. On the 13th of the Calends of July, the sun enters Cancer, the Crab; on which day a temple was dedicated to Minerva on the Aventine Hill.

[12] *Thy daughter-in-law.*]—Ver. 729. Aurora was fabled to be married to Tithonus, the son of Laomedon.

[13] *Summanus.*]—Ver. 731. The poet does not seem to know what Deity is meant by this name. He is generally supposed to have been the same with Pluto, and to have received this name as being 'summus manium,' 'the chief of the spirits.' Varro says that the worship of this Deity was instituted by Tatius, the Sabine.

[14] *Galatea.*]—Ver. 733. On the night of the 13th of the Calends of July the Constellation Ophiuchus rises. Galatea was a sea-nymph, one of the daughters of Nereus and Doris.

cleaves with his breast the opposing waters; the startled horses are frightened; and, in vain held in, they drag their master over the crags and hard rocks. Hippolytus fell from his chariot, and was hurried along by the draggling reins, with his body all torn; and he yielded up his life, to the great indignation of Diana. "There is no cause for thy sorrow," says the son of Coronis,[15] "for I will restore life to the virtuous youth, without a wound *being left on him*, and his sad destiny shall give way to my art." Forthwith he brings out the herbs from his ivory cabinet; they had formerly benefited the manes of Glaucus:[16] *'twas* at that time when the augur stooped to the examination of herbs, and the snake experienced the *benefit of the* remedy that was given by a snake. Thrice did he touch his breast; thrice did he repeat the healing charms; the other raised from the ground his head, as it lay *there*. A sacred grove, and Dictymna, in the recesses of her retreat, shelters him: he is Virbius, in the lake of Aricia.[17] But Clymenus and Clotho take it amiss; the one, that her threads are unspun, the other, that the privileges of his kingdom are violated. Jupiter, taking alarm at the precedent, aimed his bolt against him, who applied the aid of an art too profound. Phœbus, thou didst complain. He is a God; be appeased with thy sire: for thy sake, he himself does that very thing which he forbids to be done!

I would not wish thee, Cæsar, to move thy standards, though to victory thou shouldst hasten, if the auspices forbid. Flaminius, and the shores of Thrasymenus,[18] can attest to thee that the just Gods give many intimations by birds. If thou en-

---

[15] *Son of Coronis.*]—Ver. 746. Æsculapius was the son of Apollo and Coronis, and was raised to the Constellations under the name of Ophiuchus, the Serpent Bearer, in allusion to his strangling the serpent which Juno had placed in his cradle.

[16] *Glaucus.*]—Ver. 750. He was the son of Minos, and was restored to life by Æsculapius. It is said that while Æsculapius was considering how he might effect that object, a serpent came in his way, which he killed, on which another serpent brought a herb in his mouth, and having touched the head of the dead one, restored him to life. With this herb Æsculapius effected his most wonderful cures.

[17] *Lake of Aricia.*]—Ver. 756. See Book iii. l. 263. Clymenus, in the next line, is an epithet of Pluto.

[18] *Thrasymenus.*]—Ver. 765. On the 9th of the Calends of July, the Consul Q. Flaminius was defeated and slain at Lake Thrasymenus, having fought contrary to the warnings of the auspices.

quirest the season of rashness, *on which occurred* the ancient defeat, it was the eighth day from the end of the month.

More fortunate is the next day. Masinissa [19] *then* conquers Syphax, and by his own weapons does Hasdrubal [20] himself fall. Time rolls on, and with noiseless years do we reach old age: the days flee away with no rein to check them. How quickly have arrived the honours of the Goddess of Chance; [21] after some days, June will be no more. Go, ye Quirites, and joyfully throng to the bold Goddess; on the banks of the Tiber she possesses *an abode*, the gift of a king. Some of you, go on foot; some run down [22] *the stream*, too, in the rapid skiff; and be not ashamed to return home intoxicated. Ye boats, crowned *with garlands*, bring the jovial troops of youths, and let plenty of wine be drunk in the midst of your voyage! The commonalty worship her, because he who built *this temple* is said to have been one of the commonalty, and, from an humble rank, to have wielded the sceptre. She is also suited for slaves; because Tullius, born of a bond-woman, erected the neighbouring temple to the fickle Goddess.

[19] *Masinissa.*]—Ver. 769. On the 8th of the Calends of July, Syphax, king of Numidia, was defeated by Caius Lælius and Masinissa, king of the Massyli. Cyrta, his capital, was captured, and his wife and family were made prisoners.

[20] *Hasdrubal.*]—Ver. 770. The brother of Hannibal is probably here meant. He was defeated by the Roman Consuls, M. Livius Salinator and C. Claudius Nero, in a battle on the banks of the Metaurus. There was also another Hasdrubal, who was an ally of Syphax. By ' his own weapons' an ambuscade is most probably meant.

[21] *The Goddess of Chance.*]—Ver. 773. It is not improbable that ' Fortuna Fortis' here means the same Goddess that is mentioned in Book iv. l. 145, as ' Fortuna Virilis,' or ' manly Fortune.' Mr. Keightley suggests that this appellation was probably given from a misapprehension of the meaning of ' Fortis.' That word appears to be the genitive singular of the substantive ' fors,' ' chance,' and not of the adjective ' fortis,' ' brave,' or ' manly;' as a substitute for which latter word, very possibly by mistake, the epithet ' virilis' may have originated.

[22] *Run down.*]—Ver. 777. It is a matter of dispute on which side of the river stood the temple of Fors Fortuna. The meaning of ' decurrite' throws no light upon it, for we may with equal propriety speak of running down with the tide, or running down the river, whether we intend to land on the opposite side, or on the same side as that on which we embarked. By the mention of the wine we may conclude that the Romans had their pic-nics as well as ourselves, and that this is one more illustration of the truth of the adage, that ' there is nothing new under the sun.'

Lo! some one returning from the temple in the suburbs, far from sober,[23] utters to the stars some such words as these: "Now is thy belt concealed; and perhaps to-morrow it will be concealed; afterwards, Orion,[24] it will be visible to me." Were he not intoxicated, he would say, as well, that the *summer* solstice would come on the same day.

The *next* day arriving, the Lares received their temple; here, where many a chaplet[25] is wrought by a skilful hand; *Jupiter* Stator has the same time *as the anniversary* of *his* temple, which Romulus formerly built on the front of the Palatine Hill.

As many days remain of the month as the Fates have names, *on the day*, when there was a temple, O Quirinus,[26] erected in honour of *thee in* thy kingly robe. To-morrow[27] is the natal day for the Calends of Julius: Piërian maidens![28] put the conclusion to my undertaking. "Tell me, ye Piërian maids! who

[23] *Far from sober.*]—Ver. 785-90. Gower thus renders these lines—

'Lo! now in troops scarce sober home they walk,
When some starre-peeper with the starres doth talk.
Your belt, Sir Orion, now you will not shew it;
Nor yet to-morrow; but e'er long we'll view it.
But, were his brain not pickled, he would say,
The Summer solstice is upon that day.'

[24] *Orion.*]—Ver. 788. On the 6th of the Calends of July the Belt of Orion rises heliacally. On the same day (the 26th of June), the poet tells us, is the Summer solstice.

[25] *Many a chaplet.*]—Ver. 792. It appears from this, that in the neighbourhood of the temple of Jupiter Stator was the shop of some famous seller of garlands. On the 5th of the Calends of July the temple of the Lares in the Forum, and that of Jupiter Stator vowed by Romulus, were dedicated.

[26] *Quirinus.*]—Ver. 796. On the 4th of the Calends of July was the dedication of the temple built to Romulus, or Quirinus, on the Quirinal hill.

[27] *To-morrow.*]—Ver. 797. This line is merely a circumlocution for 'this is the last day of June,' as the Calends of July were the first day of that month. Julius Cæsar was born in the month of July, whence it received its name.

[28] *Piërian maidens.*]—Ver. 798. These were the Muses: their statues were placed in a temple of Hercules, built by M. Fulvius Nobilior, in the Circus Flaminius. It was repaired by Marcius Philippus, who married the maternal aunt of Augustus, and, by her, was the father of Marcia, who is mentioned in the 802nd line. She clandestinely married Fabius Maximus; on his discovery of the marriage, Augustus expressed great displeasure, on which the unhappy husband, after censuring his wife, put an end to his own existence.

placed you next to him, to whom, *Juno,* his conquered stepmother, offered her reluctant hands?" Thus I said; thus Clio answered—"Thou beholdest a memorial of the illustrious Philippus, from whom the chaste Marcia derives her birth. Marcia, a name derived from the religious Marcus, in whom her beauty is equal with her noble birth; in her, too, her, beauty is equal to, and in accordance with her spirit. In her, are birth, beauty, and genius, united; nor should'st thou think it so mean a thing that I praise her beauty; in this respect, too, am I wont to praise the great Goddesses. The aunt of Cæsar was once the bride *of this noble.* O thou glory; thou woman worthy of that sacred house!" Thus Clio sang; her learned sisters gave their assent; Alcides, too, nodded his assent, and struck his lyre.[29]

If the new year[30] shall commence to be reckoned from the sacred rites of Janus, *the month* Quintilis will be so called by a wrong appellation. If you begin your Calends from the month of March, as they *formerly* were, then the months, taken in their order, will be consistent *with their appellations.*

[29] *Struck his lyre.*]—Ver. 811-12. Gower translates these lines—

'The learned nine applaud what Clio sang;
Alcides nodded, and the harp cried twang.'

Thus Gower concludes his work with a translation fully as comical, and as nearly allied to the burlesque, as any of those most amusing versions which have been from time to time presented to the reader.

[30] *If the new year.*]—Ver. 813. The translation of these lines is added, because they are found in some of the MSS. of this poem. They are, however, generally considered to be spurious; but if genuine, they must have formed the commencement of a seventh Book of the Fasti; see the remarks in the Life of the poet, in the Introduction.

END OF THE FASTI.

THE TRISTIA;

OR,

LAMENT OF OVID.

BOOK THE FIRST.

ELEGY I.

The poet, in exile at Tomi, addresses his book, and recommends it, as it is about to visit the city of Rome, to appear there in the garb of an exile, telling it what answer to give to those who shall make inquiries after him. He also says what it is to plead by way of excuse, if his verses should appear inferior to his former productions. He tells it to avoid the royal abode, whence the lightnings had proceeded by which he had been prostrated.

Without me, little book, you will visit the *Roman* City, whither it is not allowed your master to go; but I do not envy *your fortune.* Go on your way, but unadorned, just as becomes *the book of* an exile; put on the *fitting* garb, unhappy one, of this season. Let not the hyacinth[1] array you in its purple tints; that is not a colour suitable for mourning. Let not your title be inscribed in vermilion,[2] nor let your leaves *be prepared* with the oil of the cedar; and do not wear whitened

---

[1] *The hyacinth.*]—Ver. 5. 'Vaccinium' is by some writers considered to mean the hyacinth; but it is really a matter of doubt to what plant this name was given; some suppose it to have been the garden 'larkspur.'

[2] *In vermilion.*]—Ver. 7. It has been before remarked that the ancients adorned their manuscripts with various colours, among which vermilion was conspicuous. Pliny tells us that they steeped their books in the oil or juice of cedar, to preserve them from decay, and to impart to them a pleasant smell. This oil was especially useful in averting the attacks of insects, and gave the paper a yellow colour

extremities³ with a blackened page. Let these appliances be the ornaments of *more* fortunate books: it befits you to keep your fate in remembrance. And let not the two sides *of your leaves* be polished with the brittle pumice,⁴ so that you may appear, *as you ought*, all rough with your dishevelled hair. And be not ashamed of your blots: he who beholds them will be sensible that they were caused by my tears. Go, *my* book, and in my words salute *those* pleasing spots; *for*, in the only method that is allowed me, I will assuredly reach them. If there shall be any one there not forgetful of me, as in *so great* a multitude *is not unlikely;* if there shall be any one who, by chance, may inquire what has become of me; you will say that I am *still* living: you will say, too, that my state is but an unhappy one; and that the very life that I have I receive as a favour from the God.⁵ And you will present yourself, in silence, to be read by any one making further enquiries, lest perchance you may utter what may not be to my advantage.

The reader, put in mind, will at once recall to memory the charges against me; and by the mouth of the public shall I be condemned. But beware that you say nought in my defence, although you will be carped at with *reproachful* speeches. The cause that is not a good one will be made worse by your support. You will find the person, who will sigh in regret that I was snatched away, and who will not read these

---

³ *Whitened extremities.*]—Ver. 8. 'Cornua.' This word literally means 'horns.' The paper or parchment which formed a book was joined together so as to form one sheet; when finished, it was rolled on a staff, and was called 'volumen,' from 'volvo,' 'to roll.' The staff on which it was rolled was fastened to it at the top, and the two projecting ends of it were often capped with balls or bosses, which were of various colours and patterns, and had the name of 'cornua.' Ovid bids the 'cornua' of this work not to be white, but rather to assume an aspect of sorrow.

⁴ *Brittle pumice.*]—Ver. 11. Only one side of the paper or parchment was written on, and that was first rubbed smooth with pumice-stone, that the pen of the writer might run freely, and not be impeded by hairs or other foreign substances. The pumice of the isles of Melos and Scyros and of Lipara was the most esteemed. Lightness and whiteness were the two most desirable qualities in pumice.

⁵ *A favour from the God.*]—Ver. 20. We find the poet throughout addressing Augustus as a Divinity; this, when suffering in exile the effects of his anger, he could hardly have omitted to do, as extreme adulation of Augustus and his family was one of the fashionable failings of the day.

verses of *mine* with unmoistened cheeks; who also, in silence, that no mischievous person may overhear him, will breathe a wish that, Cæsar *once* appeased, my punishment may be lighter. Whoever he may be, that wishes the Gods to be softened against wretched me,—that he may never be unfortunate is my prayer. And what he wishes, may the same be accomplished; may the wrath of the Prince, *once* assuaged, grant me leave to die in the home of my fathers.

Perhaps, my book, you will be blamed for having obeyed my commands, and you will be said to be inferior to my *usual* reputation for genius. As it is the duty of a judge to consider facts, so *ought he to take into consideration* the circumstances. *In your case*, when the circumstances are inquired into, you will be safe. When composed by a spirit at rest, verses flow easily; *but* my days are overclouded by sudden misfortunes. Verses require both retirement and ease for their writer: the sea, the winds, and the cruel storm, are tossing me[6] to and fro. All alarm ought to be afar from *him who is composing* verses; I, wretched man that I am, each moment, think that a sword is about to be plunged into my throat. A considerate judge will even wonder at this performance of mine; and such as they are, he will read my compositions with indulgence. Give me Homer[7] *himself in my place*, and *then* look round upon my calamities: all his genius would vanish amid misfortunes so great.

Lastly, my book, remember to go regardless of your reputation; and let it be no cause of shame to you, when read, to have displeased *your reader*. Fortune does not show herself so favouring to me, that any care needs be taken by you of your fame. So long as I was in prosperity, I was influenced by the love of glory, and ardent was my desire of acquiring reputation. If I do not now abhor *all* verses, and that pursuit which proved my ruin, let that be enough; for thus was my exile caused by my genius.[8] But go: go instead of me; and

[6] *Are tossing me.*]—Ver. 42. This Elegy either was written by Ovid while going to his place of banishment, and when out at sea; or, by a poetical license, he supposes such to have been the case.

[7] *Homer.*]—Ver. 47. Literally, 'Mæonides.' He was so called either from 'Mæonia,' or Lydia, in Asia Minor, which was the place of his birth; or, according to some writers, from Mæon, which was the name of his father.

[8] *By my genius.*]—Ver. 56. He alludes to his having been banished from Rome, ostensibly for having written the 'Art of Love;' though he

do you, to whom it is allowed, behold *the city of* Rome. Oh! that the Gods would grant, that, this moment I could be my book! And do not, because you come from afar into the great City, suppose that you come unknown to *its* people. Although you want a superscription, you will be recognized by your very colour; should you wish to conceal *the fact*, it is clear that you belong to me. But enter by stealth, lest verses of mine should prove an injury to you; they are not now loaded with *public* favour, as once they were. If there be any one who thinks that because you are mine you ought not to be read, and throws you from his bosom, say to him, "Look at my title: I am not the instructor in love; that work has already paid the penalty that it deserved."

Perhaps you may expect that I should order you, *thus* sent, to ascend to the lofty palace, and the home of Cæsar. May that august spot and its Gods[9] pardon me; from those heights, descended the bolt on this *my devoted* head. I remember, indeed, that there are in those abodes Deities, full of mercy; but still do I fear those Gods who have wrought my ruin. The dove is startled at the slightest flutter of *its* wing, when once she has been wounded, *thou* hawk, by thy talons. The lamb, too, dares not stray afar from the sheep-folds, if by chance it has *once* been seized by the teeth of the ravening wolf. Were Phaëton *now* living, he would shun the skies; and he would be unwilling to touch the *very* horses which, in his folly, he wished for. And so do I, who have experienced them, confess that I dread the weapons of Jove. When it thunders, I imagine that it is I who am sought by the fires *of heaven*. Each person in the Grecian fleet that has escaped Caphareus,[10] always makes all sail away from

frequently reveals the fact that his offence really was the possession of some secret relative to the family of Augustus, which had accidentally come to his knowledge. He nowhere reveals what that secret was, and only persists in declaring throughout his 'Lament,' that criminality of intention was no part of his fault.

[9] *And its Gods.*]—Ver. 71. Under this title he intends to include not only Augustus, but Tiberius, Germanicus, and Drusus.

[10] *Caphareus.*]—Ver. 83. This was a promontory of the island of Eubœa. Nauplius, the king of the island, to avenge the death of his son, Palamedes, who had been put to death by the Greeks, when they were returning from Troy, caused lighted torches to be exhibited on this promontory; supposing that a harbour was at hand, many of the ships made for land, and suffered shipwreck in consequence, amid the rocks with which Caphareus is girt.

the Eubœan waves. My little bark, too, once struck by the o'erwhelming storm, dreads to approach the spot on which it has been shattered! Therefore, beloved book *of mine*, look around you with timorous feelings, and let it satisfy you to be perused by the middle classes. While Icarus was soaring on high, with wings too weak, he gave a name to the Icarian waves. And yet is a matter of difficulty to say whether you should make use of your oars or of the breezes:[11] circumstances and opportunity will give you fitting advice. If you can be presented when he is at leisure; if you shall see any thing favourable; if his wrath shall have spent its strength; if there shall be any one to present you hesitating and fearing to approach him, and to say first a few words in your favour; *then* do you approach *his presence*. May you arrive there at a fortunate hour, more fortunate yourself than *me*, your master, and may you diminish my calamities. For either no one, or he only, who has inflicted on me the wound, is able to remove it, after the example of Achilles.[12] Only take care that you do not injure me, while you are intending to serve me: for my hope is less strong than the apprehensions of my mind. Beware, too, that the wrath which was lulled be not excited, and that it do not again burst forth; and that you become not a second cause of disgrace *to me*.

And when *now* you shall have been received back again into my closet, and shall have reached the hollow book-case,[13] your *destined* home, there will you see your brothers arranged in order, whom the same anxiety has composed in its hours of watching. The remaining portion will openly show their titles exposed *to view;* and will bear their own names on their undis-

---

[11] *Oars or of the breezes.*]—Ver. 91. This is a metaphorical expression, signifying that he was doubtful whether his recall might be hastened by his own efforts as a rower, or rather by watching for the breezes, the blowing of which would be indicated by the returning favour of Augustus.

[12] *Example of Achilles.*]—Ver. 100. Achilles wounded Telephus, the son of Hercules, with his lance; and afterwards, being reconciled to him, he healed him by an application of the rust of the same weapon.

[13] *Hollow bookcase.*]—Ver. 106. 'Scrinium' was the name of a box, or case for books, among the Romans. The smaller sort of these boxes were called 'capsæ,' and the larger ones 'scrinia.' They were made of beech wood, and were of cylindrical form, almost exactly resembling the common band-box of the present day. The books when rolled up were placed perpendicularly in the 'scrinium' or 'capsa.'

guised front. You will see three hiding apart,[14] in a dark corner. 'Tis these, too, that teach, what no one is ignorant of, how to love. Do you at least shun these, or even, if you shall have boldness enough, call them so many *parricides*, *like* Œdipus and Telegonus.[15] And of the three, I warn you, if you have any regard for your parent, bestow not your love on any one, even if he himself shall instruct *you in so doing*. There are, too, thrice five volumes on the change of the *human* shape, verses that were lately rescued from my funereal obsequies:[16] to these I bid you say, that the aspect of my *altered* fortune may be reckoned in the number of the forms that have been changed. For, on a sudden, it has been rendered unlike to what it was before; and, now a source of sorrow, 'twas once full of joy. If you ask me; I had some further commands to give you; but I fear to be the cause of delay that may retard you. And if, my book, you were to convey every thing that occurs to me, a heavy burden would you become to him who is to carry you. Long is the way; make speed. *Meanwhile*, the extremity of the earth will be my habitation—a region far removed from my *native* land.

ELEGY II.

THE poet, setting out on his exile by the order of Augustus, is overtaken by a storm at sea: he prays the Gods to show him mercy, and not to combine with Cæsar in his destruction. He cites many reasons for the extension of their beneficence to him. He then describes the tempest, and prays the Deities for his safe arrival at Tomi.

GODS of the sea and skies (for what resource have I but prayers?) abstain from rending asunder the joints of our shattered bark; and second not, I pray, the wrath of the mighty Cæsar. Ofttimes, as one God harasses us, does another Deity

[14] *Three hiding apart.*]—Ver. 111. These were the three 'volumina,' or books of his 'Art of Love;' the ostensible causes of his banishment.
[15] *Telegonus.*]—Ver. 113. Œdipus unknowingly killed his father Laius, and Telegonus, the son of Ulysses and Circe, slew his father by mistake.
[16] *Funereal obsequies.*]—Ver. 118. He refers to the fact that before leaving Rome for his place of exile, he placed on the fire his fifteen books of the Metamorphoses; and this fire, lighted at the period of his downfall, he poetically alludes to as his funeral pile, or rather that of his fortunes. The Metamorphoses were, however, saved to posterity, through the medium of duplicates which were in the hands of his friends.

bring us assistance. Mulciber was arrayed against Troy; Apollo was for Troy; Venus was friendly to the Trojans; Pallas hostile. The daughter of Saturn, more favourable to Turnus, hated Æneas; yet was he safe under the tutelage of Venus. Ofttimes did the fierce Neptune attack Ulysses; as oft did Minerva rescue him from her uncle. And what forbids, far inferior though I be to these, that a Deity should aid me, when a Deity is enraged? Wretched man that I am; in vain I waste my unavailing words: the heavy billows dash against my very lips as I speak. The raging South wind, too, sweeps away my words, and does not allow my prayers to reach the Gods to whom they are addressed. The same winds, for the reason that I may not be afflicted on one point only, bear away the sails and my prayers, whither I know not.

Ah, wretched me! What mountains of water are heaped aloft! You would think that this very instant they would reach the highest stars. What abysses yawn as the sea recedes! You would suppose that this very instant they would extend to black Tartarus. On whichever side you look, there is nothing but sea and sky; the one swelling with billows, the other lowering with clouds. Between the two, the winds rage in fearful hurricane. The waves of the ocean know not which master to obey. For at one moment, Eurus gathers strength from the glowing East, at another instant comes Zephyrus, sent from the evening West. At one time, the icy Boreas comes raging from the dry North; at another, the South wind wages battle with adverse front. The steersman is at fault: and he knows not what to avoid, or what course to take. Skill itself is at a loss amid these multiplied evils.

In truth, we are on the verge of destruction, and there is no hope of safety, but a fallacious one; as I speak, the sea dashes o'er my face. The waves will overwhelm this breath of mine, and in my throat, as it utters vain entreaties, shall I receive the waters that are to bring my doom.

But *meantime*, my affectionate wife is bewailing nothing else but that I am an exile: this one *portion* alone of my misery does she know and lament. She is not aware how my body is tossed on the boundless ocean; she knows not that I am driven *to and fro* by the winds; she knows not that death is impending o'er me. 'Tis well, ye Gods, that I suffered her not to embark with me: so that death might not have to be twice endured by wretched me! But now, although I perish, since she is safe from danger, doubtless I shall still survive in *her*, one half *of myself*.

Ah, wretched me! how the clouds glisten with the instantaneous flash. How dreadful the peal that re-echoes from the sky of heaven. The timbers of our sides are struck by the waves, with blows no lighter than *when* the tremendous charge of the balista[17] beats against the walls. The wave that now is coming on, o'ertops all the others; 'tis the one that comes after the ninth and before the eleventh.[18]

I fear not death; 'tis the dreadful kind of death; take away the shipwreck; *then* death will be a gain to me. 'Tis something for one, either dying a natural death,[19] or by the sword, to lay his breathless corpse in the firm ground, and to impart his wishes to his kindred, and to hope for a sepulchre, and not to be food for the fishes of the sea.

Suppose that I am worthy of such a death as this; I am not the only person that is carried here. Why does my punishment involve the innocent?

Oh, ye Gods above, and ye azure Deities, in whose tutelage is the ocean! Do you, each of your number, desist from your threatenings. Suffer, that, in my wretchedness, I may take to the appointed destination that life which the most lenient wrath of Cæsar has granted me. If you wish me to endure a punishment which I have merited, *still*, in my own thinking, my fault is not deserving of death. If Cæsar had wished now to send me to the Stygian waves, in that, he had not needed your aid. He has a power over my life, amenable to the envy of none;[20] and that which he has given, when he shall please, he will take away. Only do you, ye Gods, whom I assuredly think that I have injured by no misdeeds, be content with my *present* misfortunes.

[17] *Charge of the balista.*]—Ver. 48. The 'balista' was an engine of war, used by the ancients for the purpose of discharging stones against the higher part of the walls of besieged places, while the catapulta was directed against the lower. The charge of the 'balista' varied from two pounds in weight to three hundred weight.

[18] *Before the eleventh.*]—Ver. 50. It was a common belief among the ancients that every tenth wave exceeded the others in violence.

[19] *A natural death.*]—Ver. 53. 'Fato suo.' Literally, 'according to one's fate,' or 'destiny.'

[20] *The envy of none.*]—Ver. 67. 'Invidiosa' means either 'envious,' or 'causing envy,' according to the context.

And yet, even if you all wished to preserve unhappy me, it is not possible that one who is utterly undone can be in safety. Although the sea be calmed, and I avail myself of favouring winds; although you should spare me: shall I, any the less, be an exile? I am not ploughing the wide ocean for the exchange of my merchandize, greedy of acquiring wealth without limit. I seek not Athens, which once, when studious, I sought: *I seek not* the cities of Asia, nor spots which once I visited. Nor yet *do I wish*, that carried to the famed city of Alexander,[21] I should behold thy luxuries, thou revelling Nilus. The object, for which I desire favouring winds (who could credit it?) is the Sarmatian land, to which my prayers *now* tend. I am bound to reach the barbarous shores of Pontus, situate on the left hand; and what I lament is, that my flight from my country is so tardy. In my prayers do I make my travel of short duration, that I may see the people of Tomi situate in some obscure corner of the globe. If so it is, that you favour me, restrain the waves *thus* overwhelming, and let your powers be propitious to my bark: if rather you hate me, bring me to the appointed land. A part of my punishment is in the situation *of the spot*. What do I here? Speed on my canvass, ye raging winds. Why do my sails *e'en* look on the Italian shores? Cæsar willed this not to be: why do ye detain him, whom Cæsar drives afar? Let the Pontic land behold my face. He both orders this, and I am deserving of it; and I deem it neither just nor righteous for those accusations to be defended, on which he has condemned me. But if the deeds of mortals never escape the Gods, you are aware that *wilful* crime is no part of my fault. So it was: and ye know it. If my ignorance has carried me away, and if my mind was foolish, but not imbued with crime; if though but *one* of the least, I have been devoted to that house; if the public edicts of Augustus have been sufficient for me *for my own guidance*: if, in this Prince, I have pronounced the age to be blessed: and if, in my reverence, I have offered frankincense for Cæsar and the Cæsars:[22] if such

[21] *City of Alexander.*]—Ver. 79. This was the city of Alexandria, in Egypt, which was founded by Alexander the Great. For luxury and dissolute manners, it occupied much the same rank, in the time of Ovid, that Paris does at the present day.

[22] *The Cæsars.*]—Ver. 104. These would be, perhaps, Caius and Julius, the grandsons of Augustus; and Tiberius, who was adopted by Augustus after their death, together with his son Drusus, and Germanicus, his nephew and adopted son.

have been my feelings: then pardon me, ye Gods; but if not, *then* let the wave, falling from on high, overwhelm my head.

Am I deceived? Or are the clouds, pregnant *with storms*, beginning to disappear, and does the wrath of the sea *now* changed *in aspect*, diminish? This is no chance; but when invoked on these terms, you, whom it is not possible to deceive, bring me this assistance.

ELEGY III.

THE poet describes his consternation when first he was exiled by the order of Cæsar; and how he spent his last night at Rome. He depicts the affliction of his wife, and of his household, on that occasion.

WHEN the most sad remembrance recurs to me of that night, which was my last in the City—when I recal that night, in which I left so much that was dear to me—even now does the tear start from my eyes.

Now was the day near at hand, on which Cæsar had ordered me to depart from the limits of *even* the extremity of Ausonia: neither my feelings nor the time *allowed*, were well adapted for me, to make my preparations; my senses had become by protracted delay. I paid no regard to *procuring* attendants,[23] nor to making choice of a companion, nor to *providing* clothes or means suitable for an exile. I was astounded, just as when a man, struck by the bolts of Jove, lives on, and himself is unconscious that he lives.

But when grief itself removed this cloud from my mind, and my senses at last regained their strength, about to depart, for the last time I addressed my sorrowing friends, who, out of *so* many, were only one or two *in number*. My affectionate wife, bitterly weeping, herself clung to me weeping; as the shower *of tears* flowed down her cheeks, undeserving *of sorrow*. My daughter was far distant from me, in the Libyan regions; nor could she be informed of my fate. On whichever side you might look, grief and tears re-echoed *within the house:* there was the semblance of a funeral, not cele-

---

[23] *Attendants.*]—Ver. 9. For the purpose of accompanying him to his place of banishment. He seems not to have been fortunate in his choice when it was made; as he was in constant peril, he tells us elsewhere, from the treachery of those who accompanied him.

brated in silence. Both wife and husband, and my servants, too, were lamenting at my obsequies; and in the house, every corner had its *share of tears*. If, in a small matter, I may make use of great examples, such was the appearance of Troy when it was taken.

And now the voices of men and *the baying* of dogs were lulled, and the Moon on high was guiding the steeds of the night. Looking up to her, and from her, turning my eyes to the Capitol, which, in vain, was adjacent[24] to my house, I said, —" Ye Deities that inhabit these neighbouring abodes, and ye temples, never again to be beheld by these eyes; and ye Gods, whom the lofty city of Quirinus contains, that must be left by me, be ye bade adieu by me for ever! and although 'tis but late after my wounds that I assume my shield, yet do ye divest this my exiled state of hatred *against me;* and tell that heaven-born person what error it was that deceived me: lest, instead of a fault, he may think it was a crime *on my part;* so that, what you are aware of, of that same the author of my punishment may be sensible. I can *still* be not unhappy, *that* Divinity once being appeased."

With these prayers did I address the Gods above; with more *entreaties* did my wife, as the sobs broke her sentences in the midst; she even, prostrated before the household Gods with her hair dishevelled, touched the extinguished hearths with trembling lips, and many words did she pour forth to the Penates, *now* alienated, to be of no avail for her lamented husband.

And now, the advanced night refused *any* time for delay, and the Parrhasian Bear[25] was turning from the *North* Pole. What could I do? I was detained by affectionate love for my country; but that was the last night *before* my prescribed banishment. Ah! how often did I say, as any one put me in mind,—" Why dost thou hurry me? Consider both whither thou art hastening me, and whence!" Ah! how often did I falsely say, that I had *fixed on* a certain hour, which was suited

[24] *In vain was adjacent.*]—Ver. 30. He implies that his house was near the Capitol to no purpose, as the Deities who were there residing, did not extend their benign influence to one who was so very contiguous to them.

[25] *The Parrhasian Bear.*]—Ver. 48. This was Callisto, whose story has been related in the second Book of the Fasti. Parrhasia was in Arcadia, of which country she was a native; hence her present epithet

s

for *commencing* my destined journey. Thrice did I touch the threshold; thrice was I called back, and my lingering foot itself proved indulgent to my feelings: often, having bade farewell, did I again give utterance to many a word, and, as if *now* departing, I gave the last kiss. Oft did I give the same injunctions, and I became my own deceiver, looking back with my eyes upon my dear pledges.[26] At last I said,—" Why do I hasten? It is Scythia to which I am banished—Rome must be left by me: either way my delay is justified; my wife, while living, is for ever denied to me still in life; my home, too, and the dear members of my faithful household; the companions, too, whom I loved with the attachment of a brother— hearts that, alas! were linked to me in an affection worthy of Theseus.[27] While *yet* I may, I will embrace them; perhaps, never again shall I be allowed *to do so*. The moment that is conceded to me, is so much gained." I delay no *longer;* I leave the words of my discourse but half finished, while embracing each that is dearest to my heart.

While thus I was speaking, and we were in tears, the Lightbearing *star* had risen in its effulgence in the lofty heavens —a star full of woe for us. I was *then* torn away, just as though I was leaving my limbs; and one part of me seemed to be dissevered from its trunk. So did Priam grieve at the time, when the horse, changing to the contrary *of its supposed purpose*, held *within it* those who were to avenge the treason.[28] Then, indeed, arose the sobs and the lamentations of my family, and their sorrowing hands beat their bared bosoms; *and* then my wife, clinging to my shoulders as I departed, mingled

[26] *Dear pledges.*]—Ver. 60. It is pretty clear from his writings, that Ovid had no children at the time of his banishment, except one daughter, who was then absent in Africa. Reference is most probably here made to her children, who perhaps had been left in their grandfather's house during the absence of their mother.

[27] *Theseus.*]—Ver. 66. He refers to the friendship of Theseus and Pirithoüs, which was celebrated in ancient story.

[28] *Avenge the treason.*]—Ver. 75, 76. This perhaps refers to the treason of which Paris had been guilty in seducing the wife of Menelaus, his entertainer, and thus violating the laws of honour and hospitality. The wooden horse 'changed to the contrary,' when, instead of producing advantage to the city of Troy as had been anticipated on its admission, it introduced the enemy, who was to destroy it. Heinsius suspects that these two lines are not genuine, which, from their very vague and ambiguous meaning, seems likely to be the case.

these sad words with her tears,—"Thou can'st not be torn *from me*: together, alas!—together with thee will I also go." She said,—"Thee will I follow; and I, an exile, will be the wife of an exile. For me, too, has this journey been destined; and me do the remotest lands receive: I shall prove but a slight burden, to add to the flying bark. The wrath of Cæsar bids thee depart from thy country—affection *bids* me *do the same!* This duty shall be *in place of* Cæsar to me." Such attempts as these did she make; thus, too, had she pressed *me* before; and scarcely did she yield, overcome by *a sense of* my advantage.

I go forth (that, indeed, was to be borne *to the grave*, with no funereal rites!) all neglected, with my hair hanging about my unshaven face. She—overwhelmed with sorrow—is said, a faintness coming over her, to have fallen down lifeless in the midst of the house; and when she rose again, with her hair soiled with the foul dust, and lifted her limbs from the cold ground, *they say* that she bewailed her household Gods, that moment left destitute, and many a time called on the name of her husband, *just* torn away *from her;* and *they say* that she grieved no less than if she had seen the erected pile receive the body of our daughter, or my own; and that she wished to die, and in death to put an end to her sufferings; but that, from regard for me, she did not terminate *her life*.

May she live on; and, since the Fates have thus decreed, may she live ever to relieve me, *far*, far away, by her aid.

ELEGY IV.

He describes a tempest which arose in the Ionian sea during his voyage; and he depicts the despair of the crew.

The guardian of the Erymanthian Bear[29] is immersed in the ocean, and, by the influence of her Constellation, arouses the waves, while I am ploughing the Ionian sea by no inclination of my own; but apprehension *itself* forces me to be bold. Ah, wretched me! by how tremendous a gale is the sea aroused, and *how* the sand seethes again as it is ploughed up

[29] *Erymanthian Bear.*]—Ver. 1. Callisto is here called Erymanthian, from Erymanthus, a mountain of Arcadia.

from the lowest depths. The waves, no lower than a mountain, are hurled over the prow and the curving poop, and dash against the resemblances of the Deities.[30] The pinewood texture creaks; the rigging, with loud noise, is beaten to and fro; and the very ship groans responsively to my woes. The sailor, betraying his fear by the paleness of an ice-cold chill, now passively follows his bark o'ercome *by the storm*, and guides it not by his skill. Just as the driver, failing in his strength, loosens the useless reins on a horse of unbending neck, so do I behold our charioteer set the sails of the ship, not in the direction that he desires, but whither the raging current of the sea is driving us; and, unless Æolus sends breezes from another quarter, I shall be carried to lands now forbidden to be approached *by me*. For Illyria, being descried afar to the left, the forbidden *shores of* Italy are beheld by me. May the wind, I pray, cease to blow towards the forbidden regions, and, together with me, may it obey the great Deity. While I am speaking, and am, at the same moment, both longing and fearing to be hurried back again, with what tremendous force does the wave lash upon our sides! Spare me, ye Deities of the azure ocean, spare me; let it be enough that Jove is incensed[31] with me: save my wearied life from a cruel death, if, *indeed*, one who is already undone can *possibly* be saved from perishing.

ELEGY V.

The poet extols the constancy of his friend, who in adversity had not abandoned him. He says that but few out of so many of his acquaintances had thus deserved his esteem. He also exhorts his friend to remain firm in his attachment, and not to stand in fear of the resentment of Augustus.

Oh thou! that must be recorded as second to none of my companions; oh thou! to whom especially my lot seemed to be

[30] *Resemblances of the Deities.*]—Ver. 8. On the 'puppis,' or 'poop,' there was usually a statue of one or more Deities, the guardians of the ship. From these, or from the 'insigne,' or 'figure head,' which was placed at the bow, the vessel had its name.

[31] *Jove is incensed.*]—Ver. 26. In an excess of the all-prevailing adulation of the time, he does not content himself with calling Augustus a God, but he very frequently calls him either Jupiter, or the equal of Jupiter.

his own; thou, most beloved friend, who first of all didst dare to cheer me, when overwhelmed, by thy words; thou who didst give me the kind advice to live, when desire of death was existing in my wretched heart! Thou knowest well whom I am addressing by allusions and not by name; and thy kind attention is not forgotten by thee,[32] my friend. These things will ever remain impressed upon my very innermost marrow; and I shall ever be indebted to thee for this life *of mine*. My breath shall go forth to vanish in the vacant air, and shall leave my bones upon the heated pile, before forgetfulness of thy deserts comes o'er my mind; only by dint of length of time may that affection fade *from my* memory. May the Gods be propitious to thee; may they also grant thee a fate that needs the assistance of no one, and *quite* unlike to mine. But if this ship were not now being borne on by favouring breezes, perhaps *the extent of* that friendship would have remained unknown to me. Pirithoüs would not have experienced Theseus as being so much his friend, had he not descended, while yet living, to the infernal streams. Thy *persecuting* Furies, sad Orestes, caused *Pylades*, the Phocian, to be an example of true friendship. Had not Euryalus fallen, *when* fighting against Rutulian foes, no praise would there have been for Nisus, sprung from Hyrtacus.

Just as the yellow gold is beheld in the flames, so is fidelity to be tested in the season of distress. While Fortune aids us, and smiles with serene countenance, all good attends undiminished wealth. But soon as peals the thunder, all fly afar, and by none is he recognized, who, the moment before, was surrounded with troops of acquaintances. And this fact, long since gathered *by me* from the instances of those of olden times, is now known to be true, from my own misfortunes. Out of so many friends, scarcely are two or three of you now remaining to me. The rest of the crowd belonged to Fortune, not to me. Do you, then, the more, O ye few, aid my broken fortunes, and afford a saving shore for my shipwreck. And be not too much alarmed with an ill-grounded dread, fearing lest the Divinity should be offended at this your affection. Ofttimes,

[32] *Not forgotten by thee.*]—Ver. 8. He means to say that, without mentioning his friend's name, he will, when he mentions the circumstances attending his acts of kindness, easily recall them to his mind, and know to whom Ovid alludes.

even in adverse warfare, has he praised fidelity; Cæsar loves it in his friends, and in his foe he approves of it. My case is a still better one, as I have not favoured adverse arms; but by my sincerity[33] have I earned my exile. Therefore, I entreat you, watch over my misfortunes, if by any means the wrath of the Divinity can be assuaged.

Should any one wish to know of all my woes, he would be asking more than possibility allows of. Evils have I endured, as many as there are shining stars in the heavens, and as many as the little particles which the dry dust contains. Many woes, too, have I endured, great beyond credibility; such as, though they *really* have befallen me, would not receive implicit credence. A certain portion,[34] too, it is fitting should perish together with me; and would that it may be concealed, while I strive to hide it. Had I a voice that could never grow weak; had I a breast stronger than brass; had I many mouths, together with many tongues; not even on that account would I include every subject in my words; the *very* extent of the topic exhausting my strength.

Ye learned poets, write of my woes, instead of the chief from Neritos;[35] far more evils have I endured than he of Neritos. He, for many a year, wandered in a limited space between the settlements of Dulichium and those of Troy. Me, Fortune has borne to the Getic and Sarmatian shores, having traversed distant seas through all the ranges of the seasons.[36] He had a faithful band, and faithful friends had he; me banished, have my companions deserted. He, exulting and a conqueror, sought his country; I, overpowered and an exile, fly from my country. Neither Dulichium, nor Ithaca nor Samè[37] is my

[33] *My sincerity.*]—Ver. 42. He seems here to allude to the real ground of his banishment, and to imply that excess of sincerity or frankness had been the cause of his ruin. Perhaps he had spoken his mind too freely on some of the family matters of the emperor, which had accidentally come to his knowledge.

[34] *A certain portion.*]—Ver. 51. That is, the secret connected with the family of Augustus, which he was in possession of, and which he nowhere discloses.

[35] *Neritos.*]—Ver. 57. "He of Neritos" here means Ulysses. Dulichium was an island in the vicinity of Ithaca.

[36] *The ranges of the seasons.*]—Ver. 61. This seems here to be the only assignable meaning to 'distantia sideribus notis,' which means literally, 'distant under the known Constellations.'

[37] *Samè.*]—Ver. 67. This was an island of the Ionian sea, and it

home (places from which it was no great punishment to be far away); but Rome, the seat of empire and of the Gods, which from her seven hills looks round on the whole earth, *is my home.* Hardy was his body, and able to endure toil; my powers are *but* weakly and enfeebled.[38] He was continually engaged in savage warfare; I have been accustomed to the pursuits of refinement. A God has crushed me, there being none to alleviate my woes; to him, the warrior Goddess brought assistance. And whereas he who holds sway over the billowy waves is inferior to Jove; 'twas the wrath of Neptune that pursued him; Jove's anger presses upon me. Besides, the greater part of his labours is fictitious; in my misfortunes, no fabulous story is told. In fine, still[39] did he arrive at his desired home; and *still* did he reach the fields which long he sought. But by me must the land of my fathers be left for ever, unless the wrath of the incensed Deity become appeased.

ELEGY VI.

The poet praises the fidelity and attention of his wife, because, when some were endeavouring to obtain his property, she preserved it, by her own firmness and the assistance of his friends. In return for her virtues, he promises her immortality in his poems.

Not so much was Lydè[40] beloved by the poet of Claros; not so much was Battis adored by him of Cos,[41] as you, my wife, are endeared to my heart, worthy of a husband, less unhappy,

formed part of the realms subject to Ulysses. Its present name is Cephalonia.

[38] *Enfeebled.*]—Ver. 72. 'Ingenuæ,' properly means 'free-born;' hence the word came to signify 'weak,' or 'feeble,' because, in general, the free-born could not endure fatigue so well as the slave, who was born to labour.

[39] *Still did he.*]—Ver. 81. That is to say, 'In spite of all his misfortunes, he returned home, which at present is not my happy lot.'

[40] *Lydè.*]—Ver. 1. Lydè was the mistress of Callimachus, a Greek poet, who wrote in praise of her beauty.

[41] *Him of Cos.*]—Ver. 2. Philetas, a native of Cos, who lived in the time of Alexander the Great, in his verse celebrated his mistress, Battis. He is said to have been of so slight a figure, that he was obliged to attach weights of lead to his person, to avoid being blown away by the wind.

though not a kinder one. By you, as though a beam for my support, was my fall upheld; if still I am anything, 'tis all of your giving. 'Tis you that are the cause that I am not become a prey, and am not despoiled by those who have sought the remnants of my shipwreck. As, when hunger stimulates him, the wolf, ravenous and greedy of blood, surprises the unguarded sheepfold; or, as the hungry vulture looks around if he can see any carcase uncovered by the earth—so a certain perfidious wretch, treacherous in my sore adversity, would have fallen on my property, if you had suffered him. Him did your firmness displace, *aided* by strenuous friends, to whom no sufficient thanks can be returned by me. Therefore are you approved of by the testimony of one as wretched as he is honest; if only that witness has any weight. In fidelity neither is the wife of Hector your superior, nor Laodamia,[42] *who followed as* a companion in death to her husband. Had it been your lot to gain the Mæonian Homer as your poet, the glory of Penelope had been inferior to yours. Whether is it to yourself you owe it, that you became virtuous by the tuition of no instructress, and that virtue was granted you at the moment of your birth? or is it that the princely woman,[43] venerated by you all your life, has instructed you by the example of a good wife, and, by long practice, has made you like herself?—if it may be allowed me to compare mighty subjects with those of humble nature. Ah me! that my verses have no great weight, and that my praises are inferior to your deserts! If even there was formerly some native vigour in me, it has all departed, extintinguished by my prolonged miseries; you ought to have place the first of all among the pious women of story; you ought to be conspicuous, the first of all, for the goodness of your disposition. Yet, so far as any praises of mine shall avail, to all future time shall you live in my verse.

[42] *Laodamia.*]—Ver. 20. She was the wife of Protesilaüs, who was the first person slain in the Trojan war. Her grief at his death was so extreme, that she refused to survive him.

[43] *The princely woman.*]—Ver. 25. Livia, the wife of Augustus, to whose family the wife of Ovid seems to have been probably attached in some capacity.

ELEGY VII.

The poet requests his friend, when he looks on his likeness engraved on a ring, to think of him in his exile, and to remove the wreath of ivy which he wears, as that only belongs to a fortunate poet. Instead of looking at his likeness, he requests his friends to read the fifteen books of his Metamorphoses, of which he hears that several copies are still in existence, though when about to leave Rome he had committed the original to the flames. He requests that six verses, which he inserts. should be written at the beginning of that work, in which the reader is informed that it was published in an unfinished state, by reason of the suddenness of his misfortune.

If there is any one of you who has a likeness of me in a portrait, take off from my locks the ivy, the garland of Bacchus. Those happy tokens befit only the joyful poet; the garland is not befitting my circumstances. Thou dost not confess it, but thou knowest that this is addressed to thee, thou who dost carry me to and fro on thy finger, and who having set my likeness in the yellow gold, beholdest the beloved features of the exile, so far as it is now possible to do. Oft as thou dost look upon them, perhaps it may occur to thee to say, "How far away from us is our friend Naso!" Pleasing is thy affection; but a more faithful likeness are my verses, which, such as they are, I bid thee read; verses that celebrate the changed forms of men; a work that the wretched exile of its master cut short. These, at my departure, like a good many more of my works, did I myself, in my sorrow, throw into the flames with my own hand. As the daughter of Thestius[44] is said to have burnt her son by means of the brand, and to have proved a better sister than mother, so did I place the innocent books, my offspring, on the blazing pile, to perish with myself. 'Twas either because I held in abhorrence the Muses, as being the causes of my condemnation; or because my poem was still imperfect, and in an unpolished state. But since these have not been utterly destroyed, but are in existence (I believe that they were written out in several copies), I now pray that they may still exist, and delight the leisure of the reader, not idly spent, and may put him in remembrance of me.

[44] *The daughter of Thestius.*]—Ver. 18. Althea, the mother of Meleager, who caused his death, in revenge for that of her brothers, who were slain by him.

But it is not possible that they can be read with patience by any one, if he shall be ignorant that the finishing hand was not *put* to them. That work *of mine* was snatched from the anvil in the midst, and the concluding polish[45] was wanting to my lines. Pardon, too, in place of praise, do I crave; abundantly shall I be praised, reader, if I shall not cause you disgust. Insert, too, these six lines at the beginning of the little book, if thou shalt deem them worthy to be prefixed. "Whoever thou art, that art touching these volumes, deprived of their parent, let at least some spot be granted to them in thy City. And, the more to ensure thy favour, 'tis not by himself that they have been made public, but they have been snatched, as it were, from the funeral *pile* of their master. Whatever faults, therefore, the rugged verse in them shall chance to have, these should I have corrected, had it been allowed me so to do."

ELEGY VIII.

THE poet complains of the faithlessness and desertion of his familiar friend at the moment of his ruin and banishment. He entreats him to resume his friendship, that he may be enabled to substitute praise for censure.

THE deep rivers shall flow back again to their sources from the sea, and the sun shall repass his course, having turned his steeds. The earth shall bear stars, the heavens shall be cleft by the plough; the waves shall send forth flames, and the fire shall produce water. All things shall proceed contrary to the laws of nature, and no part of the system shall hold on its usual course. All things shall now come to pass which I was wont to call impossible; and there is nothing which is not worthy of belief. This is my prophecy; because by him have I been deceived, whom I expected to aid me in my wretchedness.

Has so great forgetfulness of me, deceiver, taken possession of thee? Was it so great a disgrace to approach one in

---

[45] *The concluding polish.*]—Ver. 30. 'Ultima lima' is literally the 'last file.' He alludes to the fact, that the Metamorphoses were in an incomplete state when he committed them to the flames; and that, though rescued from destruction, he had not made any alteration in the work, or had in any way amended it.

distress? Wouldst thou neither look upon nor console me, lying prostrate, oh cruel *man?* Wouldst thou not attend my funeral rites? Is the holy and venerated name of friendship trodden by thee under foot as a worthless thing? What *so great matter* was it for thee to visit thy companion, prostrated by an affliction so heavy, and to alleviate it by a share of thy discourse? and if not to shed a tear at my misfortunes, yet, *at least*, to utter a few words of complaint in feigned sorrow? at least, too, to bid me farewell, which even strangers do? and to imitate the language of the many, and the expression of public *sorrow? Was it not thy duty* on the last day, and while it was allowed thee, to behold, for the last time, my tearful face, never to be beheld again? and to give and receive, with like voice, the farewell, never again to be repeated during all my life? This even those did that were united to me in no intimacy, and they shed tears, the evidence of their feelings. Why was it? even had I not been bound by intimacy and the *most* stringent reasons, and the attachment that grows in length of time; Why? even if thou hadst not known so much of my moments of relaxation and of my serious hours, and if I had not known so much of thy moments of relaxation and of thy serious hours; Why? even if thou hadst been only known to me at Rome, thou who wast so often invited *by me* to every kind of place; have all these things fled as unavailing, amid the blasts of the ocean? Are all these things borne away, sunk amid the streams of Lethe?

I do not believe that thou wast born in the gentle *clime of the* City of Quirinus, a City never to be paced again by my foot; but *rather* amid rocks, which this coast of Pontus, lying to the left,[46] claims as its own, and amid the savage steeps of Scythia and of Sarmatia. Round thy heart, too, are veins made of flint, and the ore of iron possesses thy hardened breast. The nurse, also, which once gave thee her full breast, to be drawn by thy tender mouth, was a tigress, otherwise thou wouldst have thought my loss less a matter of indifference to thee than thou now dost, and thou wouldst not now be convicted by me of hardness of heart. But since this, too, is

---

[46] *Lying to the left.*]—Ver. 39. This epithet is given to the region of Pontus, as lying to the left hand of a person proceeding thither by sea from Rome, or the countries lying to the south of it.

added to my destined evils, that my recent life should miss its wonted harmony of *friendship*, do thou cause me not to bear in remembrance this lapse of thine, *but rather* that, with the same lips with which I complain, I should also proclaim thy affection.

ELEGY IX.

THE poet complains that the vulgar wait on fortune, and that a man has friends in prosperity, but is deserted in adversity; and he says that the truth of this had been bitterly experienced by him; that before he was banished by Augustus, he had many acquaintances; but after his sudden downfall, he found no one to come to his succour, although the good feeling of Cæsar would not have forbidden it, inasmuch as, even in the case of an enemy, he would approve of fidelity in friendship. He congratulates his friend on the renown that his genius and attainments have acquired for him, and he contrasts his graver pursuits, and their reward, with the evil consequences of his own indiscreet compositions.

MAY it be granted thee to arrive at the limit of life free from misfortune, thou who readest this work with no unfriendly feeling towards me. And would that these prayers of mine may be of avail for thee, which have not moved the cruel Deities in my behalf. So long as thou shalt be fortunate, thou wilt number many friends; if the weather becomes o'ercast, thou wilt be alone. Thou seeest how the pigeons resort to the whitened roofs, and how the begrimed turret receives no bird. The ants never proceed to empty granaries; no friend will attend the ruin of the wealthy. And just as the shadow accompanies those who walk in the rays of the sun, but flies when he lies hid o'erwhelmed with clouds, e'en so does the crowd follow the brightness of Fortune, and departs, soon as it is obscured by night coming on. It is my prayer that this may always appear a fiction to thee, but that it is the truth must be confessed by my experience. While I stood erect, a house, well known, but, of no pretensions, entertained a circle sufficiently large. But, soon as *that house* was shaken, all dreaded the crash, and, in their caution, joined the common flight. And I am not surprised if they do fear the ruthless thunderbolts, by whose fires they see each nearest object blasted. But yet in an enemy hated ever so much, Cæsar approves of him that adheres as a friend in adversity; and he is not wont to be angered (indeed, no one is more lenient than he) if a person loves him still in his affliction, whom he has loved before. Thoas himself is said to have approved of Pylades, when he learned the story of the friend of Argive Orestes. The faithful ties that existed between the son of Actor[47] and the great Achilles used to be praised by the lips of Hector. They say that the God of Tartarus grieved that the affectionate Theseus had attended his friend to the shades below. 'Tis worthy, Turnus, of belief, that thou didst bedew thy cheeks with tears when the attachment of Nisus and Euryalus was related to thee. Towards the wretched, there is a duty, *which, even* by an enemy is praised. Ah, me! how few are moved by these words of mine! Such are my circumstances, such is the downfall of my fortunes, that no limit ought to be set to anguish.

But my heart, though filled with sadness at my own lot, is made joyful at thy advancement. I foresaw, dearest *friend*, that this would come to pass, while a gentler breeze was still speeding on thy bark. If there is any value in good morals, or in a life free from stain, no one will be more deserving of esteem than thee; or if any one has raised himself through the liberal arts; through thy eloquence, every cause becomes a good one. Influenced by these *considerations*, I forthwith said to thee, "a wide field, my friend, awaits thy endowments." Not the entrails of sheep, not the thunders on my left, or the voice or the wing[48] of some bird observed by me told me this. Reason is my augury, and my estimate of the future; from this did I predict, and *from facts* did I derive this knowledge. And since *now* it is verified, with all my heart do I congratulate myself and thee that thy genius did not escape me. But would that mine had lain concealed in the deepest shades! It were my interest that fame had not attended my productions. And as, eloquent *man*, serious studies promote thy welfare, so have those of no like character been my ruin. And yet my life is well known to thee; thou knowest that the morals of the author refrained from the pursuits *therein de-*

[47] *The son of Actor.*]—Ver. 29. This was Patroclus, the bosom friend of Achilles. He was slain by Hector, and his death was avenged by Achilles.

[48] *Voice or the wing.*]—Ver. 50. He says that he did not learn this by the aid of augury, either by observing the flight of the 'præpetes,' or listening to the voice of the 'oscines.'

dicted. Thou knowest that the poem was sportively composed by me long ago, when a youth; and that those lines, although worthy of no encouragement, are yet but *so many* sportive trifles. Therefore, as I think that my sins can by no plea be defended, so do I believe that they may yet be palliated. So far as thou canst, excuse me; and forsake not the cause of thy friend. Mayst thou always proceed well in the steps in which thou hast commenced *to go.*

ELEGY X.

OVID here eulogises the ship on board of which he embarked in the Gulf of Corinth. He then describes his voyage, and the places which he touched at. He prays that he may arrive in safety at Tomi, and on his safe arrival he promises to sacrifice a lamb to Minerva. He also prays to Castor and Pollux to look upon his bark with favour.

THE yellow-haired Minerva has the guardianship[49] of my bark, and long may she hold it, I pray; from the helmet, too, painted therein, does it take its name. Is there need for spreading sail? She runs well at the very slightest breeze; are the oars to be plied? with them she hastens on her way. Nor is she contented to surpass her companions in the swiftness of her course; she overtakes the vessels that have gone out *of harbour* ever so long before. She makes head against the seas; she bears up against the waves that assail her, *rolling* from afar; and, *when* struck by the raging billows, she springs no leak. She, first known to me at Cenchreæ, of Corinth,[50] abides as the faithful leader and companion of my flight. And, throughout so many casualties, and through so many seas lashed by the hostile gales, under the tutelage of Pallas, is she safe and sound. Now, too, I pray, may she cleave her way in safety along the straits of the extended Pontus; and may she enter the waves of the Getic shore, whither she is steering.

[49] *The guardianship.*]—Ver. 1. He means to say, that Minerva was the tutelar deity of the ship, whose statue was placed on the poop; but that it took its name from the helmet which was painted on the 'insigne,' or 'figure-head,' on the prow.

[50] *Cenchreæ of Corinth.*]—Ver. 9. Corinth, being situated on an isthmus between the Ægean and Ionian seas, had two harbours, Lecheæ on the one side, and Cenchreæ on the other. From the latter, the poet set sail for the Hellespont.

After she had brought me to the sea of the Æolian Helle, and proceeded on her long voyage between the narrow limits, we bent our course to the left, and from the city of Hector we came to thy harbours, land of Imbros. Then, after having made the shores of Zerynthus with a gentle breeze, the weary bark touched at the Thracian Samos. From this spot to Tempyra is but a short passage for the traveller; up to this point did she accompany her master; but I preferred to travel by land over the Bistonian plains. Again she sailed over the waters of the Hellespont; and steered for Dardania, that bears the name of its founder, and thee, Lampsacus, safe under the care of thy rustic God, and where the sea divides Sestos from the city of Abydos, by means of the straits *named after* the virgin that was so badly carried;[51] and thence, Cyzicus, situated on the shores of Propontis, the renowned work of the Hæmonian nation; and where the coasts of Byzantium skirt the entrance of Pontus; (this spot is a vast inlet to two seas). May she pass these spots, I pray; and, impelled by the fresh south winds, may she bravely pass the moving isles of Cyanea;[52] and may she steer her way along the Thynnian bays; and thence impelled past the city of Apollo,[53] may she pass on her course the walls of Anchialus. Thence may she pass the harbours of Mesembria and Odessus, and the towers, Bacchus, that are called after thy name, and *where* they say that those sprung from the city of Alcathoüs[54] re-established their exiled homes in these parts. Thence may she arrive in safety at the city sprung from Miletus,[55] whither the wrath of the offended God has driven me.

[51] *So badly carried.*]—Ver. 27. Because she fell off as the ram was carrying her, and, from her accident, gave the name of Hellespont to that tract of water.

[52] *Isles of Cyanea.*]—Ver. 34. These were also called the Symplegades, or 'floating islands.' They were two rocks at the mouth of the Euxine sea, and were fabled to shift their position. One very simple explanation of the story is, that, standing opposite to them, they appeared to be two in number, but looking at them obliquely they seemed to be but one.

[53] *City of Apollo.*]—Ver. 35. This was Apollonia, a city on the shores of Pontus.

[54] *Alcathoüs.*]—Ver. 39. He was a son of Pelops, and reigned over Megara, in Greece. His subjects were said to have founded the city of Callatia, on the Getic coast.

[55] *City sprung from Miletus.*]—Ver. 41. Namely, Tomi, his destined place of banishment, which he tells us, elsewhere, was founded by a colony from Miletus, in Asia Minor.

If she arrives thither, a lamb shall be slain to Minerva, meriting it; a larger sacrifice does not suit my circumstances.

Do you also, ye brothers, sons of Tyndarus, whom this island holds in veneration, be present with your favouring protection, on my two-fold journey. For the one ship is preparing to steer her course through the straits of the Symplegades, while the other[56] is about to cleave the Bistonian waters. Grant ye, that when we are going on our way to different points, the one may have favouring breezes, and the other may have them not less favourable.

ELEGY XI.

Ovid excuses himself, if there should appear in his verses any marks of haste or inelegance; and he attributes them to the tempests and the ocean, amid whose conflicts he says that they were composed.

EVERY letter that has been read by thee in the whole of this book was composed by me at the time of an anxious voyage. Either the Adriatic sea beheld me writing it in the midst of its waves, while I was shivering in the month of December; or, after I had passed on my route the Isthmus of the two Seas,[57] and another ship was taken for my voyage. I *verily* believe that the Ægean Cyclades were astounded that I could compose verses amid the jarring tumults of the ocean. I myself am now surprised, that, amid such billowy conflicts both of my spirit and of the sea, my genius did not vanish. Whether insensibility or madness is the *proper* name for this anxious feeling, my intellect was entirely upheld by this pursuit. Ofttimes was I tossed, full of apprehension, under the influence of the stormy *Constellation of the* Kids; often was the sea threatening under the Constellation of Sterope,[58] the keeper, too, of

---

[56] *While the other.*]—Ver. 48. He speaks metaphorically of himself and his intended passage by land over the Bistonian plains, having disembarked, while the ship pursued her course (probably carrying his baggage) to Tomi.

[57] *Of the two Seas.*]—Ver. 5. The isthmus of Corinth, between the Ægean and the Ionian seas.

[58] *Constellation of Sterope.*]—Ver. 14. She was one of the Pleiades, the name of one being here substituted for all, which is also frequently done by the poet, when speaking of the Muses or the Furies.

the Erymanthian bear made the day o'ercast; or the South wind had heaped the raging torrents on the Hyades. Often did she ship a sea; yet still, with trembling hand, did I compose my verses, such as they are. Now, the rigging rattles, blown out by the North wind, and the curving wave rises like a hill *aloft*. The helmsman himself, raising his hands to the stars, forgetful of his art, implores aid in his prayers. Whichever way I look, there is nothing but the form of death, which, with anxious mind, I fear, and, as I fear, I pray. If I gain my port, by that very port I shall be frightened; the shore has more horrors for me than the hostile waves. For by the deceit both of men and of the ocean am I buffeted, and the sword and the wave give me double grounds for fear. I fear lest the one, through shedding my blood, should hope for my spoil, and lest the other should wish to have the credit of my death. The part on my left hand is a barbarous *region*, surrounded by greedy rapine; a *region* which bloodshed, slaughter, and wars are always in possession of. And, although the sea be agitated by the wintry storms, yet is my breast more agitated than the sea itself.

Therefore thou oughtst, candid reader, the more to pardon these *lines*, if they are, as *really* they are, inferior to thy expectation. These I write not, as once *I did*, amid my gardens, nor dost thou, my wonted little couch, *now* receive my body. I am tossed on the unruly deep on a wintry day, and my very paper is dashed o'er by the azure waves. The boisterous storm battles and rages because I dare to write, while it hurls its cruel threats. Let the storm prove stronger than man. Yet, at the same instant, I pray that I may put an end to my lines, it, to its *threats*.

BOOK THE SECOND.

Ovid entreats Augustus, if he will not permit his return, at least to grant him a safer and more civilized place for his exile. He declares that he will try whether verses, which have caused his disgrace, will not now obtain a mitigation of his punishment, just as the spear of Achilles both wounded Telephus and healed him. In a lengthened argumentative poem, he endeavours to appease Cæsar, showing that he had written many things in his praise. He enumerates a vast number of poets who never received any punishment whatever, although they had published works of either a loose or a slanderous character.

What have I to do with you, ye little books?—an unhappy pursuit *of mine*, who, in my misery, am undone by my own genius. Why do I turn again to the Muses but just condemned—the grounds of my accusation? Is it too little, but once to have been found deserving of punishment? My verses have been the cause that both men and women desired to know me, by reason of my ill-omened fate. My verses have been the cause that Cæsar formed his estimation of me and my morals, from my Art *of Love*, seen by him after *a lengthened* lapse of time. Take from me my productions—you will *then* remove, too, the disgrace of my life; I owe to my verses, as the result *of them*, that I am a criminal. This is the reward that I have received for my pains and my labours, the result of my watchings: my punishment was the discovery of my ingenuity.

Had I been wise, I ought, by rights, to have hated the learned sisters—Deities, the destruction of their devotee! But now, so great is the madness that accompanies my disease, that again (sad fate!) I turn my steps to the rocks on which I have struck: the conquered gladiator, forsooth, is seeking once more the arena, and the wrecked ship is returning to the boisterous waves.

Perhaps, as once, in the case of him who held sway o'er

the realms of Teuthrantus,[1] so to me, the same object shall give the wound and the remedy; and the Muse, who has excited it, shall assuage the anger that has been provoked: verses often propitiate the great Gods. Cæsar, too, himself ordered the matrons and the brides of Ausonia to repeat verses in honour of Ops, crowned with turrets;[2] he had ordered them also to be repeated in honour of Phœbus, at the time when he appointed the games, which one age beholds but once.[3] After these precedents, O most merciful Cæsar, I pray that thy anger may be appeased by my productions. It is justified, indeed, and I will not deny that I have been deserving of it: *all* shame has not, to that degree, fled from my face; but, had I not sinned, what had there been for thee to pardon? My fate has given thee the opportunity for mercy. If, ofttimes as mortals sin, Jove were to hurl his lightnings, in a little time he would be disarmed: when he has thundered, and has alarmed the earth with his peal, he makes the air clear by dispersing the showers; justly, therefore, is he called both the Father and the Ruler of the Gods; justly has the capacious universe nothing superior to Jove. Do thou as well, since thou art styled the Ruler of thy country, and its Father, follow the example of the God that has the same title. And thus thou dost; and, than thee, no one could, with greater moderation, hold the reins of government. Pardon hast thou often granted to the conquered party, which, if victorious, it would not have granted to thee; I have seen many even exalted with riches and honours, who had taken up arms against thy person. The *same* day which ended the warfare, ended with thee the angry feelings of warfare; and either

---

[1] *The realms of Teuthrantus.*]—Ver. 19. The kingdom of Mysia, a country of Asia Minor, is thus called from Teuthrantus, its king, who, having no male issue, married his daughter Argiope to Telephus, the son of Hercules, and made him heir to his kingdom.

[2] *Ops crowned with turrets.*]—Ver. 24. This was one of the names of Cybele, Rhea, or Bona Dea, who was generally thus represented.

[3] *Beholds but once.*]—Ver. 26. He alludes to the Secular games, which were celebrated every 110 years, and which were held in the reign of Augustus, A.U.C. 736. They were first instituted by Valerius Publicola, the Consul, after the expulsion of the kings, according to Festus and Censorinus; though the occasion of their first institution is generally considered very doubtful. Before they commenced, heralds were sent to invite the people to a spectacle which no one of them had ever beheld, and which no one would ever behold again.

side, at the same moment, bore offerings to the temples; and, as thy soldiers rejoice that they have subdued the enemy, so has the enemy reason to rejoice that he is subdued.

My cause is a better one; who am neither said to have taken up arms against thee, nor to have followed the fortunes of thy enemies. By the sea, by the land, by the third Deities,[4] do I swear, by thee *too*, a Divinity present and visible to us; that this spirit *of mine* prayed for thy welfare, and that I, in mind, the only way I could be so, was devoted to thee. I wished that, late *in life*, thou mightst attain the stars of the heavens; and I was an humble fraction of a multitude that prayed the same. For thee, with pious feelings, have I offered the frankincense; and with all the rest, I myself, as one, have seconded the prayers of the public with my own. Why shall I make mention of those books as well, my causes of offence, which, in a thousand places, are filled with thy name? Examine my larger work, which as yet I have left incomplete, about bodies changed into incredible forms. There wilt thou find the commendations of thy name; *there* wilt thou find many a pledge of my affection. Thy glory is not enhanced by verse, nor has it any means of increasing, so as to become greater. The glory of Jove is transcendent; yet he is pleased that his deeds should be recounted, and that he himself should be the subject of poetry; and when the battles of the Giant warfare are related, it is worthy of belief that he takes a pleasure in his own praises. Others celebrate thee with as loud a voice as is befitting, and sing thy praises with a more fertile genius; but yet, as a God *is moved* by the streaming blood of a hundred bulls, so is he influenced by the least offering of frankincense.

Ah! cruel was he, and too inhuman a foe to me, whoever it was that read to thee my love tales! for fear lest verses in my books, so full of respect to thee, might possibly be read under *the influence of* a judgment more favourable. But who, when thou art offended, could prove a friend to me? Hardly, under such circumstances, was I other than an enemy to myself? When the shaken house began to sink, all the weight rested upon the part that subsided; all sides open wide when Fortune has made the breach; buildings themselves fall down through their own weight. And thus the hatred of mankind has been the

---

[4] *By the third Deities.*]—Ver. 53. Those of the heavens; or, possibly of the infernal regions; a Euphemism being employed, to avoid the mention of their names.

result of my verses: and, where it ought, the multitude has followed thy looks.

But, as I remember, thou didst approve of my life and manners, as I passed by thee *in review*, on the horse[5] which thou hadst given me. And if this is of no avail, and no favour is shown to my probity, still, *in that position*, I gave no ground for crimination. The fortunes of the accused[6] were not ill entrusted to me, and the litigation that was to be taken cognizance of by the hundred men; on private matters, too, did I arbitrate as a judge, without any cause of accusation, and even the party that was defeated bore witness to my uprightness. Wretched me! I had been able, had not late events redounded to my injury, to be safe on thy judgment, not once only *expressed in my favour*. 'Tis recent matters that have proved my ruin; and one tempest engulfs in the ocean the bark that has been so oft unscathed. Nor was it any little portion of the sea that injured me; but all the waves, and Ocean himself, o'erwhelmed my head.

Why was I the witness of anything?[7] Why did I render my *very* eyes criminal? Why was I unadvisedly made acquainted with the error? Actæon beheld Diana without her garments, unconsciously: not the less was he a prey to her hounds. In dealing with the Gods above, even accident, *forsooth*, must be atoned for; and chance receives no pardon when a Deity is affronted: for, on that same day on which my unfortunate mistake removed me *from my home*, a family, humble indeed, but without a stain, was ruined.

---

[5] *In review on the horse.*]—Ver. 90. The inspection of the Equestrian order originally belonged to the Censors; but that office having been abolished, Augustus substituted in its place the 'præfectura morum,' which office he took on himself. Suetonius tells us that he frequently reviewed the troops of Equites, and restored the disused 'transvectio Equitum,' which was a solemn procession of the body on horseback, and in martial array, on the Ides of July. It appears from the present passage, and the information given us by Suetonius, that the 'recognitio,' or review, which was formerly held by the Censor, was connected by Augustus with the 'transvectio,' or procession, and held at the same time.

[6] *Fortunes of the accused.*]—Ver. 93. He alludes to the fact of his having held office as one of the 'centumviri,' or 'hundred men.' Their number was really 105, being elected, three from each of the 35 tribes; their duty was to assist the Prætor in questions of property between individuals.

[7] *Witness of any thing.*]—Ver. 103. He here alludes to his having accidentally been witness to that fact, connected with the family of Augustus, the seeing, or speaking of which, was the real cause of his exile.

Humble, however, though it be, in the days of my father it may be said to have been illustrious, and in point of nobility inferior to none; it was remarkable for neither its wealth nor its poverty; whence, rendered conspicuous by neither *extreme*, it holds its Equestrian rank. Be it, however, that my family is humble, either in the point of riches or of origin, assuredly it is not rendered obscure by my talents. Although I may seem to have used them too frivolously, still I have derived *thence* great fame through the whole earth. The class of the learned knows of Naso, and ventures to reckon him among those men that it is not ashamed of.

This house, then, beloved by the Muses, falls ruined through but one error, though that was no slight one; and it has so fallen, that it can rise again, if only the wrath of the offended Cæsar should be mitigated, whose clemency, in the case of my punishment, has been so extreme, that it is less severe than I had apprehended. My life was granted me, and thy anger stopped short of death, Prince, that hast *thus* used thy power with moderation. There still remains to me, as thou didst not take it away, my paternal property, as though the gift of my life was too small. Thou didst not condemn my deeds by the decree of the Senate, nor was my banishment pronounced by a commissioned judge.[8] Censuring me in words of sadness (as becomes a Prince), thou thyself hast avenged, as is proper, my offence against thee. Add, too, that the edict, although terrible and threatening, was still full of mercy in the designation of the punishment; for in it I am called not an "exile," but merely one "removed,"[9] and but few words are employed in *pronouncing* my destiny. There is, in truth, no punishment more weighty to a man of principle, and who retains his senses, than

---

[8] *Commissioned judge.*]—Ver. 132. The 'judices selecti' were selected by the city Prætor, according to the Lex Aurelia, from the three classes of the Senators, the Equites, and the Tribuni Ærarii. From these classes a body of 350, or, according to some writers, 450 men was selected, and from these, the numbers of 'judices' requisite for the trial of each particular case was chosen by lot.

[9] *One removed.*]—Ver. 137. This is the only translation that can be given for the word 'relegatus,' which, while it implied removal from one's country, did not necessarily imply any thing more, such as loss of civic rights and of property, which were the consequences of 'exilium.' 'Relegatio' was of two kinds; the less severe only forbade residence in some particular place, while the other kind confined the person condemned to it to one spot, and no other. The latter was the fate of the poet.

to have displeased so great a personage. But *even* a Divinity is wont sometimes to be pacified; the day is wont to proceed in its brightness when the clouds are dispersed. I have beheld the elm, laden with the leafy vines, which had been struck by the dreadful lightnings of Jove. Though thou thyself forbid me to hope, yet hope I will; and this alone can I do, *even* against thy commands.

Great is the hope that I entertain, when I consider thee, O most merciful Prince! When I reflect upon my lot, my hope vanishes. But as, when the winds ruffle the sea, their rage is not equal, nor their blasts always the same, but sometimes they are lulled, and with intermissions they are at rest, and you would suppose that they had rid themselves of their violence; so do my apprehensions depart, return, and fluctuate, and both give and deny me the hope of appeasing thee.

By the Gods above, then, who both can and will give thee length of days, if only they are attached to the Roman name; by thy country, which is safe and free from cares, with thee for its Parent, of which but lately I formed a part, as one of its people; so may the love of the grateful City, thy due, of which, both for thy deeds and for thy disposition, thou art *so* deserving, attend thee. May Livia, who was deserving of none but thee for her husband, with thee, complete the number of her years as thy companion. Were she not in existence, a single life would *then* befit thee; for no one would there be, *worthy* for thee to be her husband. And while thus thou dost flourish, may thy son flourish too; and may he, one day, full of years, rule this empire, in company with thee, more aged *than himself*. And may thy grandsons,[10] *that* youthful Constellation, follow in the steps of thee, and of their father, as *already* they do. May Victory also, always attached to thy camp, show herself ever nigh at hand, and may she attend the well-known standards: may she, too, o'ershadow with her wings the Ausonian chieftain, and may she place the laurel wreaths on his beauteous locks. By him thou wagest the war, in his person dost thou now fight; to him dost thou entrust thy mighty destinies, and thy Gods. In one half of thyself dost thou *here* present look upon this City; in the other half, thou art far

---

[10] *Thy grandsons.*]—Ver. 167. This is in allusion to Drusus, the son of Tiberius, himself the adopted son of Augustus; and Germanicus, the nephew of Tiberius, who had adopted him, in accordance with the commands of Augustus.

away, and art carrying on the dreadful warfare. E'en so may he return to thee a conqueror from a subdued enemy, and may he be resplendent aloft, with his steeds decked with *triumphal* garlands.

Spare me, I pray, and lay aside thy bolts, those cruel weapons—weapons, alas! but too well known to me! Spare me, Father of thy country! and do not, in forgetfulness of this title, deprive me of the hope of appeasing thee one day. But I pray not to return; although 'tis worthy of belief that the great Gods have often granted *favours* greater than those that have been asked for. If thou wouldst grant a more tolerable place for my exile, and at a less distance, then in a great degree would my punishment be alleviated. I am enduring the greatest agony, thrust forth in the midst of our enemies; and no one is there in banishment at a greater distance from his country.

Sent, in solitude, as far as the mouth of the sevenfold Danube, I am oppressed with cold under the icy sky of the Parrhasian virgin. The Iazyges and the Colchians, and the Meterean race[11] and the Getæ are scarcely divided *from me* by the waters of the Danube between us; and where others have been banished by thee for a cause more weighty, a more distant land has been assigned to no one *of them* than *has been* to myself. Nothing is there beyond this *region*, but cold and the foe, and the wave of the sea which unites in firm ice. Thus far is the Roman portion of the left side of the Euxine; the Basternæ[12] and the Sauromatæ occupy our neighbourhood. This land is the remotest under Ausonian sway, and is hardly situate within the limits of thy empire. A suppliant, I entreat thee to send me hence to a place of safety, that quiet may not be withheld from me as well as my country; that I may not have to dread the nations from which the Ister is no good defence,

---

[11] *The Meterean race.*]—Ver. 191. The Iazyges were a people of Sarmatia. The Colchians here referred to were probably a colony founded by the people of Colchis who pursued Medea, but being unable to overtake her, settled in the vicinity of Tomi. The Metereans, or, more probably, the Neureans, which is supposed to be the correct reading, were a nation living near the vicinity of the river Borysthenes, now the Dnieper. The Getæ lived in the country lying to the east of Pontus.

[12] *The Basternæ.*]—Ver. 198. This nation lived near the Danube. Tacitus calls them the Peucini, and is in doubt whether to number them among the tribes of Germany or of Sarmatia. The name 'Sarmatian,' was applied in general to all the tribes living in the neighbourhood of the Borysthenes.

and that, a citizen of thine, I may not be captured by the enemy. Justice forbids that any one born of Latian blood should endure the fetters of the barbarian, while the Cæsars are in safety.

Although two charges, my verses and my mistake, wrought my ruin, yet the guilt of this latter action must be suppressed in silence by me. For I am unworthy, *even by the allusion*, to renew thy wound, O Cæsar, whom it is far too much to have offended even once.

The other part remains *to be spoken of*, in which, impeached on a base accusation, I am convicted as the teacher of foul adultery. It is possible, then, that the minds of the Gods can sometimes be deceived; and are *not* many things too humble for thy observation? Just as there is not time for Jove to attend to trifling matters while he looks at the same moment upon the Deities and the heavens on high, so, while thou art looking around upon the earth, that depends upon thee, things of less consequence escape thy consideration. Wouldst thou deign forsooth, O Prince, abandoning thy high position, to read verses composed in the unequal measure?[13] It is no weight *so trifling* of the Roman name, that presses upon thee, and no burden so light is supported by thy shoulders that thou couldst occupy thy godlike majesty with my silly trifles, and examine with thine own eyes my idle productions. At one moment, Pannonia, at another, the Illyrian region, is to be subdued by thee; and now the Rhætian and the Thracian arms give grounds for apprehension. At another time, the Armenian sues for peace; and now the Parthian horseman, with trembling hand, holds out *to thee* the bow and the captured standards. At another time, Germany feels that thou hast grown young again in thy offspring, and in the place of the great Cæsar, *another* Cæsar conducts the war. In fine, what never happened before, in the case of so great a whole, there is no part of thy empire that is insecure; the City also, the care of thy laws, and attention to the *public* morals, which thou wishest to resemble thy own, fatigue thee. That leisure, which thou affordest to nations, falls not to thy lot, and with many, thou art waging war destructive of repose.

Ought I, then, to be surprised if, *oppressed* by the weight of

---

[13] *The unequal measure.*]—Ver. 220. Namely, Elegiac verse, which consists of an Hexameter, or six feet line, alternately with a Pentameter, or line of five feet.

matters so important, thou hast never perused these pastimes of mine? But if (and would it had been so!) thou hadst perchance had leisure, thou wouldst in reading it have found nothing criminal in my Art *of Love*. I confess that these are not writings *suited* to a grave brow, and are not worthy to be read by a Prince so great; but they are not, on that account, contrary to the precepts of the laws; and they are for the edifying of the Roman women. That thou mayst not doubt to whom I address my writings, one little book of the three has these four lines:—

"Be ye afar, *ye with* the little fillets *on your hair*, the mark of chastity; and thou long flounce,[14] which concealest the middle of the foot; we will sing nought but what is lawful, and thefts allowable; and in my song there shall be nothing that is criminal." And have I not scrupulously removed from this Art *of Love* those whom the lengthened gown, and the assumption of the fillet, forbid to be brought in contact *with it?*

But still,[15] the matron may make use of the arts that belong to others; and even though she be not taught, she has the means of gaining *information*. Let the matron, then, read nothing at all, because, from every poem she can receive instruction how to misbehave. Whatever she glances upon, if she is at all inclined to sin,[16] thence will she adapt her morals to crime. Let her take up the Annals;[17] nothing is more uninviting than them: yet, in truth, *there* will she read how Ilia became a mother. Let her take up *the book* in which the "ancestress of the line of Æneas" comes first;[18] she will find how the genial Venus be-

[14] *Long flounce.*]—Ver. 248. The Roman matrons wore a broad flounce with wide folds, sewed to the bottom of the dress, and reaching to the instep. The use of it was indicative of regard to modesty and propriety of manners.

[15] *But still.*]—Ver. 253. He implies that Augustus is making this objection, which he endeavours to answer, though, we must confess, not very successfully.

[16] *Inclined to sin.*]—Ver. 257. Or, in Pope's words, more famed than gallant, 'is at heart a rake.'

[17] *The Annals.*]—Ver. 259. These, containing nothing beyond a mere table of events connected with the Roman people, written in ancient and uncouth language, would not be very likely to attract the attention of one in search of love stories. Yet even these, he says, to the impure in mind, would be not quite unproductive of nurture for the prurience of their thoughts.

[18] *Æneas comes first.*]—Ver. 261. Some suppose that he here alludes to the Æneid of Virgil. That does not appear to be the fact. He rather

came the ancestress of those descendants. I will descend lower (if only I may be allowed to proceed in order), to show that every kind of poetry can injure the mind. Yet, for that reason, every book should not be condemned. That thing is of no use which is not able to hurt as well. What is there more useful than fire? Yet, if any one endeavours to burn a house, it is with fire that he provides his rash hands. The healing art sometimes takes away health, at other times, bestows it; and it shows what herb is wholesome, and what is injurious. Both the cut-throat and the wary traveller is ready girt with the sword; but the one *plans* treachery, the other carries a protection for himself. Eloquence is taught to plead the cause of the innocent; *yet* it protects the guilty, and presses hard on the guiltless.

So, then, it will be clear, that my verses, if they are read in a proper spirit, can injure no one. But whoever it is that derives any idea of viciousness from them, he is in the wrong, and detracts too much from the credit of my writings. Suppose, however, that I confess it: the games[19] as well afford incentives to vice. Order, *then*, the whole of the theatres to be swept away, which have given to many a one an opportunity for wickedness, when the sand of Mars is besprinkled on the hard ground. Let the Circus be abolished: the licence of the Circus is unsafe; here sits the girl by the side of some strange man. Why are any porticos left open, when some women walk in them, that their lovers may meet them there? What spot is there more venerable than the temples? If any woman has a turn for criminal pursuits, let her avoid these as well. When she shall be standing in the temple of Jove, there, in his temple, will it occur to her how many were made mothers by that God. It will occur to her, who pays respect to the neighbouring temple of Juno, how that Goddess was vexed by many a concubine. On beholding Pallas, she will enquire why the Virgin brought up Ericthonius, who derived his being from a criminal attempt. *Suppose* she enters the temple of mighty Mars, thy own gift, there, before his

---

alludes to the poem of Lucretius, which commences with the very words here used by him, 'Æneadum genitrix,' and in which the poet expatiates largely upon the attributes of Venus, or the creative power, a subject which the Æneid does not profess to treat of.

[19] *The games.*]—Ver. 280. He alludes to the extreme licentiousness of the theatrical representations, which were sanctioned by law.

doors, stands Venus, in conjunction with *Mars*, the Avenger. Sitting in the temple of Isis, she will ask why the daughter of Saturn drove her over the Ionian and the Bosphorean seas. In the case of Venus, Anchises; in that of Diana, the Latmian hero;[20] and in the case of Ceres, Jasius,[21] will have to be made mention of. All these are able to lead perverted minds astray, and yet they are all standing safe on their sites. But the first page warns the virtuous matrons away from the Art *of Love*, written for the wanton only. Whoever breaks in by force, where the priest does not allow her to go, forthwith, on that account is she accused of a crime that is forbidden. But it is not a crime to peruse wanton poems, although females of virtue may there read many things not to be put in practice. Ofttimes does the matron of severe aspect[22] look upon the females naked, and practising each kind of indelicate posture. The eyes of the Vestals behold the persons of the wanton, nor has that been any ground for punishment by their master.

But why is there in my poetry an excess of wantonness? or why does my book persuade any one to love? That it is nothing less than a sin, and a manifest fault, must be confessed. I grieve for *thus perverting* my talents and my judgment. Why was not rather that Troy, which fell by the weapons of Argos, harassed once again in my verses? Why was I silent about Thebes, and the mutual slaughter of the brothers?[23] and the seven gates, each of them under its chief? Warlike Rome, too, was not sparing of material for me; it is a labour of affection to recite the exploits of one's country. Lastly, Cæsar, inasmuch as thou hast filled all places with thy glorious deeds, one portion *selected* from many might have been sung by me; as the brilliant rays of the sun attract the eyes, so might thy deeds have attracted my feelings.

[20] *The Latmian hero.*]—Ver. 299. Endymion, who was beloved by Diana, is thus called, from Latmus, a mountain of Caria.

[21] *Jasius.*]—Ver. 300. He was the son of Jupiter and Electra, and the brother of Dardanus and Armonia, the wife of Cadmus. By his wife Cybele he was the father of Corybantus. The story was, that Plutus was the fruit of an adulterous intrigue between Ceres and Jasius, who was struck by the thunderbolts of Jove for his audacity.

[22] *Severe aspect.*]—Ver. 311. It is hardly credible that matrons of character can have been the willing spectators of the obscene representations of the Floralia, to which allusion is here made.

[23] *The brothers.*]—Ver. 319. He alludes to Eteocles and Polynices, the sons of Œdipus, who slew each other in single combat.

Unjustly am I accused. A humble field is tended by me; the other were a work requiring great fertility *of invention*. If, perchance, one ventures to sport on a little pond in a small boat, that is no reason for trusting one's-self on the ocean. Perhaps (and of that I am doubtful) I am well enough suited for trifling compositions, and am adapted for slight productions; but if thou shouldst order me to sing of the Giants subdued by the bolts of Jove, the weight would exceed my strength for the attempt. It belongs to a mind richly endowed to treat of the mighty deeds of Cæsar, lest the work be overpowered by its subject. And yet I made the attempt; but I seemed to be detracting *from thy* fame, and unrighteously to be a detriment to thy virtues. Again I resorted to my lighter labours, my youthful compositions: and with a fictitious passion was my breast smitten. I wish, indeed, that I had not; but my destiny drew me on, and I exercised my ingenuity to my own destruction. Oh! wretched being that I am, that ever I received instruction! that my parents taught me, and that any letter ever arrested my eyes! This wantonness rendered me hateful to thee, by reason of *my books on* the Art *of Love*, which thou didst suppose had been aimed against ties forbidden *to their influence*. But, under my instruction, the matrons did not learn furtive loves; for no one is able to teach that of which he knows but little. I have so composed my love tales and my light poems, that no *evil* story *ever* wounded my reputation. There is no husband of the middle class that is in doubt whether he himself is *really* a father through any fault of mine. Believe me, my morals are far different from *those of* my poem; my life is one of decency: my Muse is a sportive one.

A great part, also, of my labours, that is untrue and fictitious, has allowed itself more license than *ever* its author did. My book, too, is no index of my mind, but is an honourable amusement, that presents many things in apt expression for tickling the ear. *If thus judged,* Accius[24] would be a savage; Terence would be a glutton;[25] those who sing of fierce wars must needs be *ever* embroiled.

[24] *Accius.*]—Ver. 359. He was one of the older Roman poets, who wrote several tragedies, besides translating some of those of Sophocles into the Latin language. His tragedies were written in rugged and uncouth language, and this, together with the humble subjects they treated of, would form a ground for the epithet suggested by the poet.

[25] *A glutton.*]—Ver. 359. Terence, the Roman comic writer, was par-

In fine, I am not the only one who has sung of voluptuous amours; *yet* I am the only one that has received punishment for his love compositions. What precepts did the Teian muse[26] of *Anacreon,* the Lyric old *bard,* give, except how to unite love with abundance of wine? What did Lesbian Sappho[27] do, but teach the girls how to love? And yet Sappho was safe, and he was unharmed. And to thee, descendant of Battus,[28] it was no injury that thou thyself didst often confess thy gaieties to the reader. There is no play of the pleasing Menander[29] without an amour, and yet he is accustomed to be read by youths and virgins. The Iliad itself, what is it but *the case of* a base adulteress, about whom there was a strife between the lover and the husband? What *happens* in it before the flame *conceived* for Chryseis? and how did the ravished damsel cause anger between the chieftains? Or what is the Odyssey, but *the case of* one woman, sought, while her husband is away, by a host of suitors, to gratify their passion? Who but the Mæonian *bard* tells the story of Venus and Mars fastened together, and their two persons caught in a polluted bed? Whence should we learn, but from the showing of great Homer, how two Goddesses[30] fell in love with their guest? Tragedy surpasses every style of composition in seriousness; this as well, always has love for its subject. For what was there in *the case of* Hippolytus, but the flame of his blinded step-mother? By the love of her own brother is Canace celebrated. What *besides?* Did not the son of

---

ticularly successful in depicting parasites, gluttons, and selfish young men devoted solely to their own pleasures.

[26] *The Teian Muse.*]—Ver. 364. Anacreon, a Grecian lyric poet, was a native of Teos, a city of Ionia, in Asia. Some of his poems have survived to our times.

[27] *Lesbian Sappho.*]—Ver. 366. Sappho was a writer of love songs of a licentious character. She was a native of Lesbos, an island in the Ægean sea.

[28] *Descendant of Battus.*]—Ver. 367. He alludes to the poet Callimachus, who was descended from Battus, the founder of Cyrene. He sung the praises of his mistress, Lyde.

[29] *Menander.*]—Ver. 369. He was an Athenian comic poet of eminence. His works are lost, with the exception of some fragments; but Terence is supposed to have borrowed largely from them.

[30] *Two Goddesses.*]—Ver. 380. Calypso and Circe, who, as Homer tells, successively fell in love with Ulysses.

Tantalus, with his ivory limb, carry her of Pisa[31] with Phrygian steeds, while Love gave speed to his chariot. Grief, caused by blighted love, made the mother stain the steel with her children's blood. Love suddenly changed the king and his concubine into birds, and her who, even now, a mother, laments her Itys. If a wicked brother had not loved Aërope,[32] we should not read of the horses of the Sun turning back. The impious Scylla, too, would not have obtained the buskin of tragedy,[33] had not love cut off the locks of her father. You who read of Electra and of Orestes, deprived of reason, read, too, of the crime of Ægisthus, and of the daughter of Tyndarus. And what shall I say of the grim subduer of the Chimæra, whose death a deceitful hostess[34] was nearly causing? Why should I mention Hermione? Why the virgin daughter of Schœneus?[35] And why thee, priestess of Phœbus, loved by the Prince of Mycenæ? Why mention Danaë and her daughter-in-law,[36] and the mother of Lyæus?[37] And why, Hæmon, and her, for whom[38] two nights were united? Why

[31] *Her of Pisa.*]—Ver. 386. Pelops, the son of Tantalus, having conquered Œnomaus, carried off his daughter, Hippodamia, from Pisa, a city of Arcadia, and made her his wife. His steeds were Psilla and Harpina, which he brought from Phrygia.

[32] *Aërope.*]—Ver. 391. She was the wife of Atreus, and was guilty of incest with her brother Thyestes.

[33] *The buskin of tragedy.*]—Ver 393. The 'cothurnus,' or buskin, was worn by the performers of tragedy, to render the person taller, and more august in appearance. Hence, the expression is often used to denote a lofty and florid style of composition.

[34] *A deceitful hostess.*]—Ver. 398. Sthenobœa, the wife of Prœtus, being unable to captivate Bellerophon, brought a false accusation against him, and he only escaped through the known purity of his character.

[35] *Daughter of Schœneus.*]—Ver. 399. Atalanta was the daughter of Schœneus, King of the Isle of Scyros. Hermione was the daughter of Menelaus and Helen, and was betrothed to Orestes, the son of Agamemnon.

[36] *Daughter-in-law.*]—Ver. 401. Andromeda, who was the wife of Perseus, the son of Danaë.

[37] *Mother of Lyæus.*]—Ver. 401. This was Semele, the mother of Lyæus, or Bacchus. Hæmon was the lover of Antigone, and when she was put to death by the order of Creon, he stabbed himself at her tomb.

[38] *Her for whom.*]—Ver. 402. He here alludes to Alcmena, the wife of Amphitryon, who was the mother of Hercules by Jupiter. When the God was enjoying her society, he is said to have united two successive nights. Admetus was the son-in-law of Pelias, having married his daughter Alcestis.

the son-in-law of Pelias? Why Theseus? And why *Protesilaüs*, him who was the first of the Greeks to touch the Trojan ground? To these be added Iole,[39] and the mother of Pyrrhus; the wife of Hercules as well, Hylas,[40] and the Trojan boy. Time would fail me, should I recount the loves of Tragedy, and scarcely would the whole of my book contain the bare names.

Tragedy, too, is distorted by obscene jokes, and contains many expressions which violate decency. It is no reproach, too, to the author, who, in his verses, has represented Achilles as in love, and stopping short in his warlike deeds. Aristides connected with his name the crimes of Miletus; and yet Aristides was not banished from his city. Nor yet was Eubius, the compiler of impure stories, who described how abortions are produced. Nor was he exiled who lately composed the Sybaritic poem; nor yet those who have not kept silence on their own intrigues. These are even mingled with the memorials of the learned, and by the munificence of our Princes are they made public.

And not only by foreign armour shall I be defended; the Roman writings as well have many a wanton passage. As the grave Ennius sang of Mars with his own mouth, Ennius excelling in talent, *yet* rude in his management *of it*; as Lucretius, *too*, explains the principles of blazing fire, and prophesies that the threefold work will *one day* perish,[41] so, too, many a time, was his sweetheart, whose fictitious name was Lesbia, sung of by the wanton Catullus.[42] And, not content with that, he published many of his amours, in which he himself confessed his own adultery. Equal, too, *in degree*, and like *in character*, was the licen-

---

[39] *Iole.*]—Ver. 405. She was the daughter of Eurytus, King of Œchalia, and eloped with Hercules after he had slain her father. Deidamia, the daughter of Lycomedes, King of Scyros, was the mother of Pyrrhus by Achilles.

[40] *Hylas.*]—Ver 406. He was a boy beloved by Hercules; being lost by him in Ionia, he was supposed to have been changed into a fountain.

[41] *Will one day perish.*]—Ver. 426. The object of the writings of Lucretius is to prove that the world is not eternal, but that matter must perish. By the 'threefold work,' he means the earth, the sea, and the heavens.

[42] *Catullus.*]—Ver. 427. Catullus was a Roman poet, some of whose writings have come down to our time. He celebrates his mistress, whose real name was Clodia, under the epithet of Lesbia.

tiousness of the little Calvus,⁴³ who revealed his stolen caresses in various songs. Why shall I mention the poems of Ticida⁴⁴ and of Memmius, with whom names cannot be found for their subjects, or decency for their names, *when found*. Cinna, too, is the companion of these, and Anser, more lascivious *even* than Cinna, and the sportive work of Cornificius, and the similar one of Cato. Those, too, of whose books, she who before was concealed under the name of Perilla, is the subject, called by her own name of Metella. He as well, who brought *the ship* Argo⁴⁵ into the Phasian waters, was not able to be silent upon the stealthy joys of his intrigues. No less impure are the verses of Hortensius, nor less impure are those of Servius. Who could hesitate to follow the example of names so great? Sisenna translated Aristides; and yet it did him no harm to insert wanton jests in his history. It was no disgrace, too, to Gallus to sing of Lycoris, but *it was*, for him not to have held his tongue, when he had taken too much wine.⁴⁶

Tibullus⁴⁷ thinks it is a difficult thing to believe *a woman* on her oath, and similarly with regard to the denials she makes about herself to her husband. He confesses, too, that he has taught her how to deceive her protector: and he says that he, to his sorrow, has been injured through his own precepts. He says that he has many a time squeezed a hand, on the pre-

---

⁴³ *The little Calvus.*]—Ver. 431. Calvus was a Roman poet and orator, who contested the palm of eloquence with Cicero. He was the friend of Catullus, and was very short in stature, whence his present epithet.

⁴⁴ *Ticida.*]—Ver. 433. He was a Roman poet, who wrote Elegiac verses in praise of his mistress Metella, under the assumed name of Perilla. Memmius, Cinna, Anser, Cornificius, and Cato were, all of them, writers of a similar character.

⁴⁵ *The ship Argo.*]—Ver. 439. Varro Attacinus, a Roman poet, wrote in praise of Leucadia, his mistress. He wrote a poem on the Argonautic expedition, in imitation of that of Apollonius Rhodius.

⁴⁶ *Too much wine.*]—Ver. 446. Gallus, a Roman poet, having been entrusted with certain secrets of the Emperor Augustus, betrayed them in his moments of inebriety, and was, in consequence, punished with exile and confiscation of his property. He composed five books in praise of a damsel, named Lycoris. Sisenna, above mentioned, was a learned orator and historian of Rome.

⁴⁷ *Tibullus.*]—Ver 447. Tibullus was a Roman poet of considerable merit. Ovid alludes to the fact of his having written of his mistress, Delia, to the following effect:—'She denies many a thing; but 'tis difficult to believe her; for even about me does she make denials to her husband.'

text as though he was praising the jewel or the signet *of its owner*. And, as he tells, many a time has he conversed with his fingers and with signs, and drawn the silent hints on the surface of the table. He teaches, too, by means of what extracts the paleness may be removed from the features, which is usually caused by the pressure of a kiss. Besides, he asks the too careless husband even to watch him, that the *wife* may have the less chance of sinning. He knows at whom the dog is barking, while he is walking up and down alone; *and* why he spits so many times, *as a signal*, before the closed doors. And many a precept does he give for such *guilty* thefts; he teaches, too, by what means wives may systematically deceive their husbands. And yet this was no injury to him; Tibullus is read, and amuses, and was already well known when thou wast made Prince. Thou wilt find, too, the same precepts in the pleasing Propertius;[48] and yet he was not punished with the slightest disgrace.

Of these I was the successor, since honour bids me not mention *many* excellent names of persons now living. I was not afraid, I confess, that in the track where so many ships had gone, one would be wrecked, when the rest were all saved.

The skill has been described by some, which is *requisite* for playing at games of hazard,[49] and this sin against our ancestors is no small crime. They teach what is the value of the throws on the dice; how you may make the most at a throw, or how

---

[48] *Propertius.*]—Ver. 465. He was the most graceful of all the Roman writers of Elegiac measure; but, like those before mentioned, amatory subjects were his principal theme.

[49] *Games of hazard.*]—Ver. 471. 'Alea' seems to have been a term applied to all games involving hazard, and depending on chance. The 'talus' was originally the knuckle-bone of a sheep or goat. These were imitated, for the purposes of gaming, in ivory, gold, silver, bronze, glass, and agate. They were played with by women, boys, and old men. They were originally used without marks, and, being thrown in the air, were caught on the back of the hand. In later times they were used in games of chance, and for that purpose bore numbers. They had four flat faces and two curved ones. On the flat faces were fourteen points; the numbers on the opposite sides being ace and six, and three and four. Four 'tali' were generally used, and they were thrown from a dice-box, which was called 'fritillus,' 'turricula,' 'pyrgus,' or 'phimus.' The ace, which was called 'unio,' was the most unlucky number; and, while 'Venus' was the highest cast of a set of four 'tali,' 'canis' was the name of the worst throw. Games of chance were forbidden in the early times of the Roman Republic; and the character of a gamester was held in extreme contempt.

you may escape the losing numbers; how many numbers the *gamester's* cube⁵⁰ has; in what manner it is proper to throw when the wanting number⁵¹ is called, and in what manner to move the throws; how, too, the man of the opposite colour proceeds onward in a straight line, when the piece is lost that lies in the middle between two enemies; how *the player* may understand when rather to follow, and how to recall *his piece* when advanced; that, as it retreats in safety, it may not *again* advance unprotected. There is a little board, provided with three pebbles, on which, to bring one's own *men* in a straight line gives the victory. And other games there are (I will not now recount them all), which are wont to waste a valuable thing, *namely*, our time. And see *how* another sings of the shape and the throw of the ball;⁵² another teaches the art of swimming; another of *bowling* the hoop.⁵³ The art of dyeing in colours has been taught by others; and another *writer* has laid down the law for feasting and good fellowship. Another one points out the clay from which cups are made, and he informs us what kind of vessel is fit for the flowing wine. Such *sportive trifles*

⁵⁰ *The gamester's cube.*]—Ver. 475. 'Tessera' received its name probably from the Greek word τἰσσαρες, 'four.' They resembled the cubes or dice of the present day, and were used in sets of four.

⁵¹ *The wanting number.*]—Ver. 475. This seems to be the meaning of the word 'distanti,' which has caused considerable doubt among the commentators. The player, in his anxiety, seems in those days, as now, to have called for the desired number. The poet appears to allude to some cheating directions given by the writer, used to obtain favourable casts by due management of the dice, in throwing them. The game of 'duodecim scripta,' or 'twelve points,' was played with 'calculi,' or 'lapilli,' 'counters,' of different colours, which were moved, according to the throws of the dice, perhaps in a manner not unlike our game of backgammon; the meaning of the passage is, however, involved in considerable obscurity.

⁵² *The ball.*]—Ver. 485. Games with the 'pila,' or 'ball,' were those played with the 'pila trigonalis;' so called, probably, from the players standing in a triangle; the 'follis' was a large ball inflated, and used for football; 'paganica' was a similar one, but harder, being stuffed with feathers, and was used by the rustics. 'Harpastum' was a small ball used by the Greeks, and was scrambled for as soon as it came to the ground.

⁵³ *The hoop.*]—Ver. 486. The hoop of the Roman boys was a bronze ring, which sometimes had bells attached to it. It was impelled by means of a metal hook attached to a wooden handle, similar to that in use at the present day. The game was borrowed by the Romans from the Greeks, and was one of the exercises of the Gymnasium.

as these are composed in the month of smoky December, *and* no one has received injury from having composed them.

Deceived by these *considerations*, I have made my verses the reverse of sad; but a sad retribution has been the result of my jests. In fact, I see not one out of so many writers, of whom his Muse has been the ruin; I am the *only* one *to be* found. But, suppose I had written Mimes,[54] with their obscene jokes, which are always amenable to the charge of containing a love story? In these, constantly does the spruce adulterer strut about; and the cunning wife plays tricks upon her booby husband. The marriageable virgin, the matron, the husband, the boy, are *all* spectators of these: and a great part of the Senate is there. And it is not enough for the ears to be polluted with filthy language: the eye is accustomed to put up with many indecent sights. When the lover has outwitted the husband by any new device, they clap aloud, and the victory is granted him with great applause. The less its utility, the more lucrative is the stage to the poet, and the Prætor buys[55] abuses of such enormity at no small cost. Examine, Augustus, the expenses of thy games; many such as these wilt thou find that have been bought for thee at a heavy price. At these thou hast been a spectator, and hast many a time given them for a spectacle, so kindly disposed in every way is thy Majesty. With thy own eyes, too, which all the world follows, sitting at thy ease, thou hast looked upon the adulteries of the stage. If it is allowable to write Mimes, that imitate vicious actions, a less punishment is *surely* due to my case. Do their boards[56] ensure safety for this kind of composition, and is the stage privileged to allow

[54] *Mimes.*]—Ver. 497. The Roman Mimes were either parodies and burlesques of serious circumstances, or imitations of indecent and obscene occurrences. They differed from Comedy, in consisting more of gestures and mimicry than of spoken dialogue, which was interspersed in various parts of the representation, while the action continued uninterruptedly from the beginning to the end of the piece. They were originally exhibited at funerals, when one or more persons in burlesque represented the life of the deceased person. They were afterwards performed in the public theatres, as well as in private houses. Decius Laberius, and Publius Syrus, were the most distinguished writers of them.

[55] *The Prætor buys.*]—Ver. 508. It was the duty of the Prætor, or the Ædiles, to provide mimes and plays at the public expense, for representation at the games and festivals. The Andria of Terence was acted at the Megalesian games.

[56] *Their boards.*]—Ver. 517. 'Sua pulpita.' The 'pulpitum' means

in its Mimes whatever it pleases? My songs, as well, have many a time been represented in the dance;[57] many a time have they arrested thy attention.

As in truth, in thy abode the ancient figures of heroes are resplendent, painted by the artist's hand; so, in a certain spot *there*, there is a little picture, which shows the variety of postures and figures which belong to Venus. And as the son of Telamon sits, expressing his anger in his countenance, and the barbarous mother [58] is conceiving crime in her very eyes; so dripping Venus is wringing her wet hair with her fingers, and seems but now covered with the waters that gave her birth.

Others recite warfare, armed with its blood-stained weapons; some, too, sing the exploits of thy family, some thy own. Penurious nature confined me within narrow limits, and gave but little strength to my genius. And yet he *who was* the fortunate author of thy Æneid introduced his arms and his hero[59] to a Tyrian intrigue: and no subject is more read of, throughout the whole work, than love united by unlawful ties. The same *poet* had before, when a youth, sportively related in his verse the soft flames of Phillis and of Amaryllis. I, long since, erred by one composition; a fault that is not recent endures a punishment inflicted thus late. I had already published my poems, when of Equestrian *rank*, so many times, according to my privilege, in review, I passed thee unmolested, who, *at the very time*, was the inquirer into criminal charges. *Is it*, then, *possible that* the writings which, in my want of prudence, I supposed would not injure me when young, have now been my ruin in my old age? This late vengeance for a work written so long since, is superfluous, and the punishment is far removed from the time when it was merited.

That thou mayst not, however, suppose that all my works

---

that part of the stage which was nearest to the orchestra, and where the actors stood when they were addressing the audience.

[57] *In the dance.*]—Ver. 519. Love scenes, taken from the mythology, were acted in pantomimic dance, to the recitation of words written by the poets of the day. This text was called the 'canticum,' and was frequently written in the Greek tongue. Ovid here shows that he had been the composer of 'cantica' for the public amusement.

[58] *The barbarous mother.*]—Ver. 526. Medea, who slew her children in revenge against Jason. Her story has been already referred to in the Notes.

[59] *Arms and his hero.*]—Ver. 534. He here alludes to the commencing lines of the Æneid of Virgil, 'Arma virumque cano.'

are *thus* loose, I have often fitted ample sails[60] to my bark; I have written the books of six *months'* Fasti, and *themselves* as many *in number* :[61] and each book comes to an end with its month. My fate interrupted that work; that work, too, dedicated under thy name, Cæsar, and consecrated to thee. I have produced also a poem of kings[62] for the tragic buskin; and *that* buskin employs such expressions as, in its gravity, it ought to use. The transformation, too, of bodies into new shapes has been sung of by me, although a finishing hand has been wanting to the work. And I wish that thou wouldst relieve thy mind but a little of its anger, and order, at thy leisure, a few *lines* of this work to be read to thee. A few *lines*, in which, commencing from the earliest origin of the world, I have brought the work down, Cæsar, to thy times: thou wouldst then behold how much spirit thou thyself hast given me, and with what devotion of mind I sing of thee and thine.

No one have I pulled to pieces in spiteful verses, nor does my poetry contain a charge against any one. In my innocence, I have abstained from witticisms steeped in gall; not a letter is there tainted with a venomous sarcasm. Among so many thousands of our people, so many thousands of our writings, I am the only one whose own Muse[63] has been his ruin. I do not suppose, then, that any Roman will rejoice at my misfortunes, but *rather*, that many have taken them to heart. It transcends my belief, that any one could trample on me, when prostrate, if any regard has been had to my innocence.

On these and other *considerations*, I entreat that thy divine Majesty may be moved, O Father, O thou care and salvation of thy country. I *pray* not to return to Ausonia, except, perhaps, at a future day, when thou shalt be prevailed on, by the lengthened duration of my punishment. I pray for a safer place of exile, and one a little less disturbed, that my punishment may be commensurate with my transgression.

[60] *Fitted ample sails.*]—Ver. 548. He alludes to his Metamorphoses, which he composed in the Hexameter, or Heroic measure; and to his Fasti, which treat of more serious subjects.

[61] *Many in number.*]—Ver. 549. This possibly is the proper translation of a line which has caused much trouble to commentators. In the life of the poet prefixed to the work, will be found some remarks on this line, and its possible meaning.

[62] *A poem of kings.*]—Ver. 553. He here speaks of the tragedy of Medea, which he composed, but which has not come down to us.

[63] *Whose own Muse.*]—Ver. 568. Literally, 'my own Calliope,' the name of one Muse being used instead of them all.

BOOK THE THIRD.

ELEGY I.

The Poet sends his book to Rome, in neglected and sordid attire, and represents it as wandering through various parts of the city, and praying Augustus to pardon the Poet, pining in exile. When it finds that it is rejected by all, it requests the hands of the Plebeians to receive it, and afford it a place of shelter.

I, the book of a trembling exile, sent *hither*, am come to this City; give me a soothing hand in my weariness, friendly reader; fear not that by chance I should prove a disgrace to thee; there is no line in this sheet that gives precepts for love. The fortune of my master is not of that kind that he ought, in his wretchedness, to gloss it over with any jesting. That work, too, which once, to his cost, he sportively composed in his youthful years, he now, too late, alas! condemns and abhors. Look at my contents: thou wilt see nothing here but what is sorrowful, in verses befitted to their circumstances. That my limping verses[1] halt in each alternate line, either the nature of the measure, or the length of my journey, is the cause. I am neither yellow with cedar *oil*, nor smoothed with the pumice stone; 'tis because I was ashamed to be more gay than my master. *The reason* why my smeared letters have blots scattered over them is, that the poet himself has disfigured the work with his tears. If, perchance, anything shall appear not to be expressed in the Latin idiom, the land in which he wrote *me* was a barbarous one. Tell me, my readers, if it is not a trouble *to you*, whither I must go, and what abodes in this City I, a stranger book, must seek.

---

[1] *My limping verses.*]—Ver. 11. Alluding to the alternating measure of the Hexameter and Pentameter lines. The remark is but a poor attempt at wit.

When I had stealthily said thus much with a stammering tongue, there was hardly *even* one person who would show me the way. "May the Gods[2] grant thee what they have not given my parent, to be able to live at thy ease in thy own country. Lead on, I pray, for I follow; although, weary, I am come by land and sea from a distant region." He obeyed *my request*, and conducting me, he said, "This is the Forum of Cæsar; this is the way which derives its name from the Sacred rites.[3] This is the shrine of Vesta, which contains the Palladium and the *eternal* fire; this was the little palace of the ancient Numa." Then, bearing to the right, he said, "That is the gate of the Palatium; this is Jupiter Stator's *temple*: on this spot was Rome first founded." While I was admiring each object, I beheld a portal gorgeous with shining arms, and a habitation worthy of a Deity. "Is this the house of Jove?" said I, for a wreath of oak-leaves caused a presentiment in my mind for taking it to be such. When I learned who was its owner, I said, "I am not deceived, and it is true that this is the house of the great Jove. But why is the gate wreathed with the laurel fastened to it, and why does the overshadowing tree surround the doors of majesty? Is it because this one house has deserved everlasting triumphs? or is it because it has been ever beloved by the Leucadian God?[4] Is it that it is festive itself, or because it makes everything joyful? or is that an emblem of the peace which it has bestowed on all lands? As the laurel is always green, and is not plucked with withering leaves; has that *house*, in like manner, perpetual glory? The cause of the wreath *thus* placed above, testified by an inscription, declares that the citizens were saved by his aid. Add, most excellent Father, one citizen to the number of the saved; one who, banished afar, lies prostrate in the remotest regions. In him, not criminality, but his own inadvertence, gave occasion for that punishment, which he confesses himself

---

[2] *May the Gods.*]—Ver. 23. These are supposed to be the words of the Book to the person who has pointed out to it the way.

[3] *The Sacred rites.*]—Ver. 25. The 'via Sacra' received that name from the treaty being there concluded between Romulus and Tatius, which was attended by the performance of sacrifice.

[4] *The Leucadian God.*]—Ver. 42. Apollo is so called, from a promontory in the isle of Leucadia, where Augustus consecrated a temple to him, after the battle of Actium.

to have deserved. Wretched me; I both dread the place, and I venerate its master, and the writing on me shakes with tremulous fear. Dost thou perceive how my paper becomes white with a pallid colour? Dost thou behold how my alternating feet tremble? That thou, house of Cæsar, one day appeased by my parent, mayst always be seen under the same masters, is my prayer."

Thence, in similar manner, I was led by lofty steps to the white temple, situate on high, of *Apollo* the unshorn God; where the descendants of Belus[5] and their barbarous father, with his drawn sword, stand as statues, alternately with the columns of foreign *marble; and where*, those things which the ancients and the moderns have conceived in their learned breasts, are made public for the inspection of readers.[6] I sought my brothers, those, forsooth, excepted, whom my parent would fain wish he had never begotten. As I was seeking them in vain, the keeper appointed over that place ordered me to leave the holy spot.

I turned my steps to another temple, adjoining to the neighbouring theatre; this, too, was not allowed to be approached by my feet. Liberty did not permit me to touch her halls, which, first of all, were thrown open[7] for the reception of learned works. The destinies of my wretched author extend to his progeny, and we, his children, suffer the exile which he himself has endured. Perhaps Cæsar, prevailed upon in length of time, will one day be less severe with us and with him. Ye Gods, I pray, and *thou* Cæsar too, (indeed, to the rest I direct not my entreaties), listen, most powerful God, to my prayers. Meanwhile, since a public place has been denied me, let it be allowed me to lurk in some private spot. And do you, hands of the Plebeians, if it is permitted, receive my verses, ashamed through the disgrace of their rejection.

[5] *Descendants of Belus.*]—Ver. 62. The Danaides are so called, as Belus was the father of Danaus, of whom they were the daughters.

[6] *Inspection of readers.*]—Ver. 64. He alludes to the Library which Augustus had founded on the Palatine hill, in a wing of his palace, and from which the works of Ovid were excluded.

[7] *Thrown open.*]—Ver. 71. Asinius Pollio founded the Temple of Liberty, and in it established the first public library at Rome.

ELEGY II.

The Poet laments his destiny, which has compelled him in exile to visit the Scythian regions, and he complains that neither Apollo nor the Muses aided him, who was their priest. He says, that his life is spent in tears and lamentation, and entreats the Gods to permit him to die.

Was it then ordained, by my destiny, that I should visit Scythia and the land which lies under the Lycaonian pole? And did not you, Piërian maids, nor thou, son of Latona, a learned body, give aid to your priest? Is it of no avail to me, that I sportively composed without any real ground of offence, and that my Muse was more wanton than my mode of life? But Pontus, pinched with perpetual frost, confines me, after I have undergone many a danger, by sea and by land. I, who avoided business, and was born to careless ease, who formerly was delicate, and unable to endure fatigue, am now suffering in the extreme: and yet neither could seas without harbours, nor varied modes of travel, put an end to me. My mind bore up, too, under my misfortunes; for, from it, my body derived strength, and endured things almost beyond endurance.

But while I was tossed to and fro by wind and waves, occupation beguiled my cares and the sadness of my heart. When my wanderings were concluded, and the fatigue of travelling had ceased, and the land of my exile was reached by me, *then* my only pleasure was in weeping, and a shower flowed from my eyes, not less than the stream from the wintry snows. The Roman City and my home recur to me, and longing for *my former* haunts, and whatever remains connected with me in that City, *now* lost *to me*. Ah, wretched me! that so oft the gate of my tomb should have been knocked at, and yet at no time opened! Why did I escape so many weapons, and why did no storm, when so often threatening, overwhelm my wretched head?

Ye Gods, whom I experience as too constant in your hostility, whom one Divinity has as partners in his wrath, urge on, I pray, my lingering destiny, and forbid the gates of death to be longer closed to me.

ELEGY III.

Ovid, writing to his wife, from his place of exile, excuses himself, because the letter is written in handwriting not his own. He says that it is a matter of necessity, on account of the ill health with which he is afflicted; and he then enlarges upon his miseries. Of all these, he says that the greatest is, to be debarred from her society. He gives directions for his bones to be carried to Rome in a little urn, and composes an Epitaph to be inscribed thereon.

If, perchance, you are wondering why this letter of mine is written by the hand of another, 'tis *because* I was ill. Ill, *too*, at the very extremity of an unknown region, and almost in doubt of my life. What, do you suppose, are my feelings, now placed here in this dreadful country, between the Sauromatæ and the Getæ? I can neither endure the open air, nor can I accustom myself to the water here; and the country itself is repulsive to I know not what degree. My habitation is not sufficiently convenient; the food here is unsuited for an invalid, and there is no one to relieve disease by the art of Apollo. There is no friend nigh to console me, no one to beguile my moments with his conversation, as they slowly creep along. I am lying here worn out, among the remotest tribes and regions; and whatever is at a distance, now recurs to me, thus indisposed. And though all things so recur; yet you, my wife, are chief of all, and occupy more than your *equal* share in my heart. I address you far away; my voice names you only; no night, no day comes to me without you. They even say, that I speak so wildly, that your name is *ever* on my wandering lips. If at any time, my mouth being closed, my voice fails me, scarcely to be restored by pouring wine *down my throat*, any one should tell me that his mistress is come, I should arise *at once*, and the hope of *seeing* you would be a source of strength *to me*.

I am then in doubts as to my life; are you, perchance, forgetful of me, there, *at a distance*, passing a happy life? You are not doing so, I affirm it; I am sure, O dearest one! that without me life is only passed in sadness by you.

If, however, my fate has completed the number of years which it was destined to complete, and the end of my life is so very near at hand, how grand a thing was it, ye great Gods, to spare a man on the point of death! at least, I might have received sepulture in my native land. Either my punishment might have been delayed to the moment of my death, or an accelerated end might have forestalled my exile. Unscathed, I might but lately have well left this world in happiness; *but* now, my life has been granted me, that I might die an exile.

Shall I then depart, so far away in unknown regions? and will death be embittered by the very spot? Will my body not waste away on my wonted couch? will there be no one to lament me at my sepulture? and will not a few moments be added to my life, as the tears of my wife fall upon my face? And shall I give no *last* injunctions? And shall no friendly hand close my failing eyes, amid the sobs attending my last moments? But shall barbarian earth cover this head, unlamented, without funereal rites, and without the honour of a tomb?

And will you not, when you hear of it, be afflicted to the greatest degree; and will you not beat your faithful bosom with a trembling hand? And will you not, as you vainly stretch your arms in this direction, call upon the departed name of your wretched husband? Yet desist from tearing your cheeks, and rend not your hair. I shall not then, my life,[8] have been torn from you for the first time. When I left my country, fancy that then I died; that was the first and the more grievous death to me. Now, if you but could, (but you cannot), rejoice, best of wives, that my many troubles are ended in death. As far as you can, diminish your griefs, by enduring them with a courageous heart, evils against which you have already had your mind too well prepared. And oh! that my soul would perish with my body, and that no part of me would escape the consuming pile! For if my immortal spirit soars aloft into the vacant air, and the words of the Samian sage[9] are true, a Roman *shade* will be wandering amid Sarmatian ghosts, and will ever be a stranger amid uncivilized spirits.

Yet do you cause my bones to be brought back in a little urn, *and* thus I shall not be an exile, even when dead. No one forbids thee. The Theban sister placed her slain brother in the tomb, *even* when the king forbade it.[10] And do you mingle

---

[8] *My life.*]—Ver. 52. 'Lux mea,' is literally, 'my light;' it may be translated 'my life,' or 'my angel.'

[9] *The Samian sage.*]—Ver. 62. Namely, Pythagoras, who was a native of Samos, and taught the doctrine of the immortality of the soul, and of its inhabiting various bodies in succession.

[10] *When the king forbade it.*]—Ver. 68. Antigone, in spite of the orders of Creon, buried the body of her brother, Eteocles, and was put to death for this act of affection.

them with leaves and powdered amomum,[11] and place them, when inurned, in the ground near the City. And cut an inscription in large characters on the marble of my tomb, which the traveller may read with glancing eye:—"I who lie here, the poet Naso, the sportive composer of tender loves, was undone through my own genius. And let it not be a hardship for thee, the passer-by, who has felt what is love, to say, 'May the bones of Naso repose *here* in peace.'"

This is enough for my inscription; for, indeed, my books are greater and more lasting memorials of me. And these, I trust, although they have injured him, will give fame and lasting years to the author. But do you perform the funereal rites for me when dead, and offer chaplets wet with your tears. Although the fire shall have changed my body into ashes, yet the sad dust will be sensible of your pious affection.

Fain would I write more; but my voice, weary with speaking, and my parched tongue, deny me strength to dictate. Receive the farewell uttered by me, perhaps for the last time, and which applies not to the lot of him who sends it you.

ELEGY IV.

The Poet advises his dearest friend, whom he is afraid to name, to avoid the abodes of the great, and the society of the powerful; and says, that though they have it in their power to help others, they give no assistance, but rather cause injury. He then extols the constancy of his friend, which has never flagged in the time of adversity; and recounting the miseries of his exile, he entreats his friends to give him all the assistance in their power.

Oh thou! always beloved by me, but *especially* tried in adversity, after my fortunes were ruined; if thou puttest any faith in a man taught by experience, live for thyself, and keep at a distance from the names of the great. Live for thyself, and, so far as thou canst, avoid splendour. It is from a resplendent heaven that the ruthless lightning descends. For although the powerful alone are able to aid, if one of them can do thee harm, he would not choose rather to do *thee* a service. The sail-

---

[11] *Amomum.*]—Ver. 69. This was a small shrub found in Armenia, with fruit like a cluster of grapes, and leaves like the white vine, of which the Romans made a fragrant ointment. It was used in the process of embalming; the word 'mummy' is a corruption of 'amomum.'

yard, hanging low, escapes the wintry storms, and wide sails cause more fear than small ones. Thou beholdest how light cork floats on the surface of the water, whereas the heavy weight sinks, together *with itself*, the net attached *thereto*. If I, *now* the adviser, had *only* been formerly advised of these things, I, perhaps, should *now* have been in the City in which I ought to be. While I lived in intimacy with thee, while a gentle breeze was bearing me on, this bark of mine ran through still waters. The man that falls on smooth ground (scarcely, however, does such a thing happen), falls so, that when he has touched the ground, he can rise again; but the wretched Elpenor,[12] falling from the top of the house, met his king as a miserable phantom. Why did it happen that Dædalus waved his wings in safety, whereas Icarus impressed the boundless waters with his name? It is because the latter soared aloft, and the former *flew* at a more humble distance. And yet did not they each of them have wings for himself?

Believe me, he who has the good fortune to escape notice lives the happiest life, and every one ought to live within his means. Eumedes[13] would not have been deprived of his son if, in his folly, he had not hankered after the horses of Achilles. And Merops[14] would not have seen his son in flames, and his daughters *changed* into trees, had he, *as being* his father, owned Phaëton. Do thou, too, always shun what is too lofty, and, remembering my determination, gather in thy sails. For thou deservest to pass along the course of life without a stumbling foot, and to enjoy a happier lot. That I should entertain these wishes for thee, thou deservest for thy kind affection, and thy fidelity that will adhere to me at all times. I beheld thee, bewailing my destiny, with such a countenance as may be supposed to have been presented by my own visage. I beheld thy tears

---

[12] *Elpenor.*]—Ver. 19. When Ulysses and his companions were fleeing from the realms of Circe, Elpenor, who was intoxicated, fell from a height and broke his neck.

[13] *Eumedes.*]—Ver. 27. Dolon, the son of Eumedes, having stipulated that he should receive the horses of Achilles as his reward, went as a spy into the Grecian camp, where he was slain by Diomedes and Ulysses.

[14] *And Merops.*]—Ver. 30. He was the husband of Clymene, who, by Apollo, became the mother of Phaëton. The meaning is, that if Phaëton had been contented to be owned by Merops as his son, he would not have been tempted to guide the chariot of Apollo, and so might have avoided his unhappy fate.

as they fell over my face; at the time that I drank in thy words breathing constancy. And now thou defendest thy distant friend with energy, and dost alleviate evils that can hardly be alleviated in any degree. Live on, without envy; pass in obscurity thy tranquil years, and attach thy equals to thyself in friendship. Love, too, the name of thy own Naso, the only *part of him* which is not yet exiled. The Scythian Pontus confines the rest *of him*. The land nearest to the Constellation of the Erymanthian She-bear, pinched with hard frosts, confines me. Bosphorus and Tanais, and the swamps of Scythia, and a few *other* names of a region almost unknown, are beyond. Further than these, there is nothing but uninhabitable cold. Alas! how near to me is the end of the earth! But my country is afar; afar my dearest wife; and whatever, besides these two, was delightful to me. Yet so are they afar from me, that, in my mind, those can all be seen whom, bodily, it is not possible to touch. Before my eyes, flit my home, the City, and the aspect of the *various* spots; and *then* follows, in order, everything as it happens in its appropriate place. The form of my wife, as though she were present, is before my eyes. She both increases my misfortunes and she alleviates them. She increases them, because she is absent; she alleviates them, by shewing her affection; and she bears with firmness the burden that is imposed on her.

You, too, my friends, remain attached to my heart; you, whom I long to mention, each by name. But cautious fear restrains this act of duty, and I believe that you would prefer not to be inserted in my lines. Once you were anxious for it; and it was as good as a pleasing mark of distinction, for your names to be read in my compositions. But, as now it is a matter of doubt, I will address each one in my own thoughts, and to none *of you* will I be a cause of apprehension. My verses, shall betray my concealed friends by no hint; if any one has been attached to me in secret, let him *still* be attached. But know that although I am removed to a distant land, you are always present to my thoughts. So far as each of you can, do alleviate my misfortunes in some degree and refuse not a faithful hand to me, *thus* prostrate. May Fortune be ever propitious to you; and may you never, experiencing a similar lot, have to implore the aid *of others*.

ELEGY V.

Ovid praises the constancy of his friend, which he had experienced in adversity, and declares that the remembrance of it will never be effaced from his memory. He confesses that he entertains some slight hopes, that Augustus will one day be pacified, and make his exile more endurable.

The extent of my acquaintanceship with thee was not great, so that thou mightst have concealed it without any difficulty, hadst thou not united me to thyself in closer ties, while my bark, perchance, sped on with favouring gales. When I fell, and all fled through fear of my wreck, and turned their backs upon my acquaintanceship, thou didst dare to touch a body struck by the bolts of Jove, and to enter the threshold of a woe-stricken house. And that, thou, a recent *acquaintance*, and known by no prolonged intimacy, didst do, which scarcely two or three of my old *friends did* for wretched me. I beheld thy alarmed countenance, and I marked what I saw. *I beheld* thy face bedewed with tears, and more pale than my own; and, seeing thy tears as they fell at each word, I drank in those tears with my face, those words with my ears. I felt, too, thy arms, as they hung around my sorrowing neck, and thy kisses, mingled with the sound of thy sobs. By thy efforts, too, Carus, in my absence, am I defended. Thou knowest that Carus is *put* in the stead of thy real name. I receive, besides, many tokens of thy evident kindness, that will never be effaced from my heart. May the Gods grant thee power ever to defend thy friends, *and* mayst thou assist them on a more fortunate occasion.

But if, in the mean time, thou makest inquiry what I, a ruined man, am doing in these parts, (and I may suppose that thou dost make the inquiry), I am influenced by a slight hope (and do not thou deprive me of it) that the offended Majesty of the God can be appeased. Whether I am rash in my expectations, or whether it is possible to attain that object, do thou prove to me, I pray, that what I desire is possible. And, whatever eloquence of language thou possessest, employ it for the purpose of showing that my wishes may possibly attain success. For the greater any one is, the more placable is he in his anger, and a noble disposition easily receives an impression. It is sufficient for the noble-hearted lion to have brought the body to the ground; the contest is ended when the enemy lies prostrate. But the wolf and the disgusting bears attack *even* the dying, and *so does* each wild beast that is inferior in nobleness *of blood*. What have we greater at Troy than the brave Achilles? He was not proof against the tears of the Dardanian old man.[15] Porus,[16] and the ceremonial of the celebrated funeral, show how great was the clemency of the Emathian general. And not to mention *cases where* the wrath of mortals has been turned into milder feelings; he who once was her enemy, is *now* the son-in-law of Juno. Besides, it is impossible that I can despair of some favour, as the cause of my punishment is not one deserving of death. The life of Cæsar, which is a life belonging to the *whole* world, has not been attempted by me, endeavouring to spread universal ruin. I have said nothing, nor has my tongue uttered threats; and no profane words have been let slip, in excess of wine. I am punished, because my unguarded eyes were witnesses of a sin; and my crime is, that I had eyes. For my part, I cannot entirely defend my fault; but mistake embraces a part of my accusation. A hope therefore remains, that that will cause him to moderate my punishment, on the terms of a change of the place *of my exile*. I pray that the brilliant Light-bearing *star*, the forerunner of the beauteous Sun, may bring on that day, pressing onward his steed.

ELEGY VI.

The Poet praises the constancy of his friend, and says, that even if he wished, he is not able to conceal it; and that if he had applied to him for advice, he might still have been in safety. He entreats him to pacify Augustus, that he may obtain a change of his place of exile, and he asserts that he has been guilty of no criminality.

Thou neither desirest, my dearest *friend*, nor canst thou, shouldst thou perchance desire it, conceal the ties of our friendship. For so long as it was permitted me, no one was

[15] *Dardanian old man.*]—Ver. 38. This was Priam, on the occasion of his begging the body of Hector from Achilles.

[16] *Porus.*]—Ver. 39. Porus was a prince of India, who was conquered by Alexander the Great. The latter, in admiration of his courage, bestowed on him a larger kingdom than that of which he had previously deprived him. The same conqueror honoured the body of Darius, his adversary, with a gorgeous funeral. Emathia was the ancient name of Macedonia, of which country Alexander was the king.

dearer to me than thee, nor was any one in all the City more intimate with thee than myself; and that was so well proved to the public, that our friendship was almost better known, than thou and I *were*, ourselves. The kindness that exists in thy mind towards thy friends, is known to the man whom thou makest thy friend. Thou wast wont to conceal nothing, so that I was not conscious of it; and thou didst impart many things to be concealed in my breast. Thou, too, wast the only one to whom I used to tell whatever secrets I had, except that one which has proved my ruin. Hadst thou known that, as well, thou wouldst have been blessed with thy friend in safety, and I should have been saved, my friend, by thy advice. But, doubtless, my destinies dragged me onwards to destruction, *and* closed every avenue to my own benefit.

However, whether by caution I could have avoided this misfortune, or whether no reasoning is able to control destiny, still do thou, most closely united to me by lengthened intimacy, and *thyself* almost the greatest object of my regrets, keep me in remembrance; and, if favour has given thee any influence, make use of it, I pray, in my behalf; so that the anger of the offended Deity may be less violent, and my punishment may be lessened by a change of locality. And this *I ask thee*, since there is no criminality in my heart, and mistake holds the chief place in my offence. It is no light matter, nor is it safe to say, by what accident my eyes became acquainted with so shocking a disaster. My mind, too, shudders at that time, as though at its own wounds, and by the recollection, my grief itself is renewed. Whatever can be productive of such disgrace, is proper to be concealed in the obscurity of the night. I will, then, mention nothing, except that I offended; but that from that fault no advantage was sought to be gained by me; and that my offence ought rather to be styled foolishness, if you would give a thing its proper name. And if this is not the truth, seek some other place, where I may be still more distant, and let this region be but a city suburb *in comparison to it.*

ELEGY VII.

The Poet, writing to a young lady named Perilla, says that, badly as he has been treated by them, he is still devoting himself to the Muses; and he exhorts her by similar pursuits to aspire to immortality. He tells her that her native grace and beauty will depart in old age, but that the endowments of the intellect are immortal.

My letter, now you are finished, go forthwith, the faithful messenger of my words, to salute Perilla.[17] You will either find her sitting with her charming mother, or among her books and her Muses. Whatever she shall be doing, she will leave it, when she knows that you have come; there will be no delay; she will ask why you have come, and what I am doing? You will say that I am living; but in such a way that I would prefer not to be living; *and you will say*, that my woes have not been alleviated in such a length of time; that I have returned to the Muses, though they have proved my ruin, and that I am fitting my words to alternate measures. Do you say, too, "Why dost thou apply thyself to ordinary pursuits, and why dost thou compose learned poems *in Greek*, and after a manner not that of thy country? For nature, with the Destinies, has granted thee chaste manners, and rare endowments and genius." I was the first that led *thy genius* to the Pegasian streams, lest the spring of gushing water should unfortunately be wasted. I was the first to perceive it in thy tender years, *when yet* a girl; and, as is seen, I was the guide and the companion of this tendency. Therefore, if the same fires *still* dwell in thy breast, the Lesbian *Sappho* will be the only poetess to excel thy works. But I fear that my fortune may now retard thee, and that thy spirit may flag after my downfall. While there was the opportunity, often *didst thou read* thy own works to me; often did I read mine to thee. I either gave my attention to the verses thou hadst just composed, or when thou

---

[17] *Perilla.*]—Ver. 1. Some commentators have supposed that Perilla was the daughter of Ovid. There does not appear any indication of such a fact in this Elegy; and he seems rather to speak of her in terms of admiration than of the affection of a parent for his daughter. He would hardly be content with a mere allusion to his wife, as being her 'dulcis mater,' and then saying no more about her. The name of his daughter is nowhere to be found.

hadst neglected to do so, I was the cause of a blush.¹⁸ **Perhaps, after *my* example, because my books injured me, thou, too, hast** traced retribution in my punishment. Lay aside thy fears, Perilla; only let no woman be led astray, or learn from thy writings how to love.

Lay aside, then, most learned *girl, all* grounds for slothfulness, and return to the liberal arts and to thy pursuits. That beautiful form will be spoiled by length of years, and the wrinkle of age will be on thy antiquated brow. Withering old age, too, which comes with noiseless step, will lay his hand on thy good looks. And when any one shall say, "She *once* was a beauty," thou wilt grieve and wilt complain that thy mirror is deceitful. Thy means are *but* moderate, although thou art most deserving of great *wealth;* but fancy that thy means are equal *in amount* to immense riches. For, in good truth, Fortune both gives to whom she pleases, and takes away again; and he is Irus¹⁹ on a sudden, who was Crœsus the moment before. Why should I enter into details? We have nothing that is not perishable except the blessings of the heart and of the intellect. Behold how I am deprived of my country, yourselves, and my home, and *how* everything has been torn from me that could be taken away; and yet I have my genius as my companion and source of enjoyment; over this, Cæsar could hold no sway. Let who pleases put an end to my life with the cruel sword, yet when I am dead, my fame will survive me, and, so long as victorious Rome, sprung from Mars, shall look down from the hills on the whole earth subdued, my writings will be read. And do thou too, whom may a happier result of thy studies await, so far as thou canst, avoid extinction in time to come.

ELEGY VIII.

He says that his longing to revisit his country and his friends is so great, that he wishes he could find some instantaneous means of transporting himself thither. He speaks of the wretchedness of his exile, and prays that Cæsar may one day modify his anger, and assign him a more endurable place of banishment.

At this instant could I wish to ascend the chariot of Triptolemus, who planted the unknown seed in the ground then

---

¹⁸ *Cause of a blush.*]—Ver. 26. Probably, by reason of his blaming her for her idleness, and her neglect of the Muses.

¹⁹ *Irus.*]—Ver. 42. He was a beggar of Ithaca, and a dependant of the suitors of Penelope. Ulysses slew him with a blow of his fist. His name

unused *to it*. At this moment could I wish to harness the dragon-steeds of Medea, which she had, Corinth, at her flight from thy citadel. At this moment could I wish to assume the waving wings, either thine, O Perseus, or thine, O Dædalus; that, the thin air yielding to my flight, I might on a sudden behold the delightful soil of my *native* land, and the face of my deserted home, and my companions that *still* remember me, and, chief of all, the dear features of my wife.

Fool! why, with thy childish desires, dost thou vainly hanker after that which no day brings thee, or will bring thee? If this must ever be thy ardent desire, pray to the divine power of Augustus, and address in prayer that God, whose *wrath* thou hast experienced: he is able to give thee both the wings and the swift chariot. Should he grant thy return, at once thou wilt be fitted with wings.

Should I pray for these things, (and more I cannot pray for,) I fear that my prayers would be too exorbitant. Perhaps, at a future day, when his anger shall have expended itself, this *favour* will have to be asked by me with anxious mind; meantime, what is less *than that, but* equal to an ample boon *to me*, would that he would order me to depart from this region to any other place: neither the climate, nor the water, nor the soil, nor the air agrees *with me*, and a perpetual weakness pervades my body. Whether it is that the contagion of a diseased mind affects my limbs, or whether the cause of my illness lies in the situation of the place: soon as I arrived in Pontus, sleeplessness distressed me; my leanness scarcely kept my bones covered, and food became repulsive to my palate. That hue which exists in leaves smitten with the first cold in autumn, *and* which the fresh-come winter has nipped, the same do my limbs present. I obtain relief by no medicines, and some occasion for complaining misery is never wanting.

I am not more healthy in my mind than in my body; both of them are equally affected with infirmity, and twofold ills do I endure. The *hideous* aspect of my fate haunts me, and stands before my eyes to be scanned, just as if it were a body that could be seen. When I look on the spot, the manners of

afterwards became a proverbial expression for a beggar. Crœsus was the rich king of Lydia, who was conquered by Cyrus the Great. His wealth was so enormous that his name passed into a proverb, meaning the very converse of that of Irus.

the people, their dress, and their language, and it occurs to me what I am, and what I have been, so great is my desire for death that I complain of the wrath of Cæsar, because he did not avenge his grievances with the sword; but since he has once satisfied his hatred by legal means,[20] may my exile, I *pray*, become more tolerable by a change of situation.

ELEGY IX.

He shows that the Grecians founded cities on the Getic shores, and informs us that they gave its name to the city of Tomi.

Here too, then, do Grecian cities exist: who could have believed it! *here*, among the names of savage barbarism. Hither, too, have come the colonists sent from Miletus, and among the Getæ have they founded Grecian homes. But the ancient name of this spot, and *one*, older than the city built *here*, was clearly derived from the murder of Absyrtus.[21]

For the impious Medea, flying from her deserted father in a ship which, made by the care of the warlike Minerva, was the first to speed through waves *which* before *were* untried, is said to have plied her oars in these fords. Soon as the sentinel beheld *her father* from the lofty hill,—"A stranger comes from Colchis," he cries; "I recognize the sails." While the Minyans are hastening, while the rope is being loosened from the quay, while the anchor, drawn up, follows their swift hands, the Colchian dame, conscious of her crimes, beats her bosom; she who had dared, and who was to dare, many impious deeds with her own hand. Although abundance of audacity remains in her spirit, paleness is impressed on the astonished features of the virgin. When, therefore, she beholds afar the approaching sails, she says, "We are overtaken; and my father must be delayed by some stratagem." While she is considering what to do, while she turns her eyes on every side, by chance she fixes them, as they turn towards her

---

[20] *By legal means.*]—Ver. 41. That is, by punishing him according to the laws, and not by taking vengeance with the sword, after the fashion of tyrants.

[21] *Absyrtus.*]—Ver. 6. He was the son of Æetes, and the brother of Medea. His death by the hand of his sister is here related by the poet. He says that Tomi was so called, because there he was cut into pieces by Medea; thus deriving the name of the place from the Greek τέμνω, 'to cut.'

brother. When his presence occurs to her, "we are the conquerors," says she; "he, by his death, shall be productive of my safety." On the instant, with the cruel sword, she pierces his innocent side, he not suspecting it, and fearing no such *fate;* and she tears him in pieces, and scatters his limbs, torn asunder, about the fields, so as to be found in many places; and that her father may not be ignorant *of it,* she exposes on a lofty rock both the pallid hands and the head dripping with blood, in order that her parent may be arrested in his course by a new sorrow, and that he may be delayed on his sad road, while he is gathering up the lifeless limbs.

Thence was this place called Tomi; because in it the sister is said to have cut to pieces the limbs of her brother.

ELEGY X.

THE Poet describes the miseries of his exile, and, among other things, he says, that the frost is so intense, that the river and the sea, and even the fish, are frozen; and that when that is the case, the Scythian foe, which excels in cavalry and archers, is able to pass the river Danube, and lay waste the country, and lead the inhabitants into captivity.

IF any one, yonder, remembers the banished Naso, and if, without me, my name still survives in the City, let him know that I am living in the midst of barbarism, exposed under stars that never set in the ocean. The Sauromatæ, a savage race, the Bessi and the Getæ surround me, names how unworthy of my genius *to mention!* yet, while the air is mild, we are defended by the intervening Danube; while it flows, it repels invasion by its waves. But when dire winter has put forth his rugged face, and the earth has become white with ice, hard as marble; when Boreas is at liberty, and snow has been sent *upon the regions* under the Bear; then it is true that these nations are distressed by a shivering climate. The snow lies *deep;* and as it lies, neither sun nor rains melt it; Boreas hardens it, and makes it endure for ever: hence, when the former *ice* has not yet melted, fresh succeeds, and in many a place it is wont to last for two years.

So great is the strength of the North wind, *when* aroused, that it levels high towers with the ground, and carries off roofs borne away: *the inhabitants* poorly defend themselves from the cold by skins and sewn trowsers; and of the whole body, the face is the only part exposed. Often, the hair, as it is moved, rattles with the pendant icicle, and the white beard shines with the ice that has formed upon it. Liquid wine becomes solid, preserving the form of the vessel: they do not quaff draughts of liquor, but pieces *which are* presented.

Why shall I mention how the frozen rivers become hard, and how brittle water is dug out of the streams. The Danube itself, which, no narrower than the river that bears the papyrus, mingles, through many mouths with the vast ocean, freezes as the winds harden its azure streams, and it rolls to the sea with covered waters; where ships had gone, they now walk on foot; and the hoof of the horse strikes the waters hardened by freezing. Sarmatian oxen drag the uncouth waggons along unwonted bridges, as the waters roll beneath; indeed, I shall scarcely be believed; but inasmuch as there is no profit in untruths, an eye-witness ought to receive full confidence. I have seen the vast sea frozen with ice, and a slippery crust covered over the unmoved waters. To have seen it is not enough: I have trod upon the hardened ocean, and the surface of the water was under my foot, not wetted *by it*. If, Leander, in days of old thou hadst had such a sea, thy death would not have been a charge *laid against* the narrow stream.[22] At that time, too, the curved dolphins cannot raise themselves to the air; the severity of the winter hinders them striving *to do so;* and, although Boreas resounds with agitated wings, there is not a wave on the sea *then* blocked up. The ships stand, hemmed in by the frost, as though by marble, and no oar can cleave the stiffened water.

I have seen fish remain bound fast in ice, and even then *some* part of them retained life; whether, therefore, the severe power of the mighty Boreas congeals the waters of the sea, or those flowing in the river, immediately, the Danube being made level by the drying Northern blasts, the barbarous enemy is carried over on his swift steed: an enemy, strong in horses, and in the arrow that flies from afar, depopulates the neighbouring region far and wide. Some take to flight, and no one *being left* to protect the fields, the unguarded property becomes a prey; *such as* cattle, and the creaking waggons, the little trea-

---

[22] *The narrow stream.*]—Ver. 41. He alludes to the Hellespont, which was not more than a mile in width, from Sestos to Abydos, between which towns Leander was in the habit of swimming to visit his mistress, Hero.

sures of the country, and the riches besides that the poor inhabitant possesses; some are driven along as captives, with their arms fastened behind their backs, looking back in vain upon their fields and their homes; some die in torments, pierced by barbed arrows, for on the winged steel there is a poison, in which it has been dipped. What they cannot carry with themselves, or lead away, they destroy, and the flames of the enemy consume the unoffending cottages; even when there is peace, they cause alarm from the apprehension of war, and no one ploughs the ground with the pressed ploughshare.

This spot either beholds the enemy, or is *always* in dread of *a foe* which it does not behold; the earth deserted, becomes worthless, left *untilled* in ruinous neglect. Here the luscious grape does not lie concealed under the shade of the foliage, and the fermenting new wine does not fill the deep vats; the country does not bear fruit, and Acontius would have nothing *here* on which to write a line to his mistress. You may behold naked plains without trees—without leaves; places, alas! not to be visited by a fortunate man! Since, then, the extensive globe is so wide, has this land been discovered for the purpose of my punishment?

ELEGY XI.

THE Poet, without mentioning the name, charges some cruel person, that he insults his misfortunes while thus confined in Scythia, and deprived of home and every comfort; and he tells him that it is the greatest disgrace to press hard on a man who is already prostrate. He reminds him of the story of Phalaris, and the punishment of him who contrived the destruction of others; and then recommends him to keep in mind the fluctuating fate of man, and no longer to bear his faults in remembrance, but rather to let his wounds heal with time; and he ends by telling him that his wretchedness cannot possibly be exceeded.

IF thou art one, unfeeling *man*, to insult my misfortunes, and endlessly, in thy cruelty, to persecute me with accusations, *surely* thou wast born of a rock, and nourished with the milk of savage beasts; I should say, too, that flint fills thy breast. What further lengths remain, to which thy anger can proceed? or what dost thou see to be wanting to my misery? A barbarous region, the inhospitable shores of Pontus, and the Mænalian she-bear, with her *attendant* Boreas, behold me. I have no intercourse in language with *this* savage nation; all places *for me* are filled with anxious apprehensions. As the fleeing stag, when caught by the greedy bears, or as the lamb, when surrounded by the mountain wolves, trembles, so am I filled with dread; hemmed in on every side by warlike tribes, while the enemy almost pierces my side. Suppose it were a trifling punishment to be deprived of my dear wife, my country, and my pledges *of affection;* suppose I suffered no misfortune, but barely the wrath of Cæsar—is the bare wrath of Cæsar too light a misfortune to me? And yet there is one who can handle again my bleeding wounds; and who can open his eloquent lips against my morals? On an easy subject every one can be eloquent; and but little strength is required to break what is *already* bruised. It is *true* courage to overthrow towns and standing walls: 'tis only cowards that destroy what is *already* prostrate. I am not what *once* I was. Why dost thou trample on an empty shadow? Why with stones dost thou press upon my ashes and my tomb? 'Twas Hector *himself*, at the time when he fought in battle; but he who was fastened to the Hæmonian horses was not Hector: remember, too, that I am not the person whom thou didst formerly know—the phantom only of that person is left. Why, insulter, dost thou persecute a phantom with reproachful words? Cease, I pray, to harass the *mere* ghost of myself.

Suppose all my crimes to exist; let there be nothing in them which thou mayst suppose to be rather *the result of* error than *of* criminality. Lo! as an exile, I pay the penalty—*a penalty* both dreadful in the banishment *itself*, and in the place of banishment; glut thy anger, *then!*

My lot might appear worthy of tears, even to an executioner; yet, in thy sole judgment, 'tis not sufficiently dreadful: thou art more cruel than the savage Busiris,[23]—more cruel than he who heated the fictitious bull by the slow fire, than *he, too,* who is said to have given the bull to the Sicilian tyrant,[24] and

---

[23] *Busiris.*]—Ver. 39. He was a cruel king of Egypt, who sacrificed strangers to Jupiter, and, at length, was slain by Hercules.

[24] *The Sicilian tyrant.*]—Ver. 41. Phalaris, the king of Agrigentum, who, being of a cruel disposition, received as a present from Perillus, a brazen bull, with the suggestion mentioned by the Poet; and who tried, with retributive justice, the first experiment with it on the inventor, as related in the text.

by his words to have recommended his invention. "O king!" *says he,* "there is utility in this gift, and that greater than would appear: not only is the appearance of my work worthy of approval. Dost thou see, on the right hand, this side of the bull that can be opened? Here the person must be inclosed, whom thou wouldst put to death. Forthwith, when he is inclosed, burn him with a slow fire: he will roar out, and it will be *exactly* the voice of a real bull. To recompense one present with another, give me, I pray, in return for this invention, a reward worthy of my ingenuity!" He had spoken; but Phalaris said, "Wonderful inventor of punishment! be thou at once the first to make trial of thy work!" There was no delay; dreadfully roasted on the fires, *his own* invention, he gave a specimen of the cries of suffering with shrieking voice.

What have I to do with the Sicilians, among the Scythians and the Getæ? Whoever thou art, my complaint reverts to thee. That thou mayst be able, too, to satiate thy thirst with my blood, and that thou mayst experience as much pleasure with greedy heart as thou mayst wish; so many evils have I suffered by land and by sea, in my journey, that I could think that even thou, on hearing them, wouldst grieve. Believe me, were Ulysses compared with me, the wrath of Neptune is less than that of Augustus. Therefore, whoever thou art, refrain from opening my wounds afresh, and take off thy hands from my painful sores; and, that oblivion may take possession of the story of my fault, permit my destiny to heal my scars. Keeping, too, the lot of man in thy recollection, which raises and crushes the same persons, do thou stand in awe of the chances of uncertainty; and since, what I never supposed could happen, thou hast so much anxiety about my affairs, thou hast no reason to be alarmed. My fate is a most wretched one. The wrath of Cæsar brings with it every woe. That this might be the better proved, and I might not be thought to deceive thee in this, I could wish that thou thyself wouldst make trial of my punishment.

ELEGY XII.

He says that the winter is past, and that spring has arrived. He then compares its delights in Pontus with those of other countries. He says that the seas have become navigable, and that, should any sailor arrive from civilized lands, he will go to meet him, and learn the recent triumphs of Cæsar. Should any one be enabled to give him the desired information, he says that he will entertain him as his guest; and he concludes by praying that his abode in the Scythian regions may not be lasting, but that his stay there may be only temporary, and that, at a future day, he may return to his country.

Now the Zephyrs moderate the cold; and, the year *now* finished, this Mæotian winter has seemed *to me* more protracted than any former ones; *and now, the Ram,* which did not safely carry Helle *when* placed on him, makes the length of the days equal with that of the nights. Now the boys and the sportive lasses are gathering the violet, which the ground in the country bears, no one planting them. The meadows, too, become clad with flowers of various tints, and the prattling birds revel with their untaught throats; the swallow, that she may avoid the crime of her cruel ancestress, makes her nest and her little home under the rafters; the blade, which has lain hid, covered in the ridges devoted to Ceres, puts forth its tender top from the warmed earth; and in whatever region the vine exists, the bud is pushed forth from the shoot: but from the Getic shores the vine is far distant. In whatever region any tree exists, the branch begins to swell on the tree; but trees are far removed from the Getic land. *At Rome* there, *it is* now a time of enjoyment, and the garrulous warfare of the wordy Forum gives place[25] to the games, as they succeed in order. Now the horse is employed, now they sport with light arms; now the ball *is tossed,* and now the hoop is rolled with its whirling circle; now, when the youths have been besprinkled with the flowing oil, they bathe their wearied limbs in the Virgin's aqueduct. The stage is frequented, and the applause waxes loud with divided opinions; and the three theatres now resound, in place of the three Forums.

Oh four times, *aye,* immeasurably blest is he who is allowed to enjoy *the delights of* the City, not forbidden *to him!* but by

---

[25] *Forum gives place.*]—Ver. 18. The days on which the public games were celebrated were 'nefasti,' and, on them, the courts of law were closed.

me is beheld snow melted by the vernal sun, and water which can hardly be dug out of the hardened stream. The sea is not now congealed with ice, and no longer, as before, does the Sauromatian herdsman drive the creaking waggon over the Danube; a few ships, too, will be beginning to sail this way, and the stranger bark will be on the Pontic shore. I will be careful to meet the sailor, and having saluted him, I will enquire why he comes? who *he is?* and from what country? Wonderful, indeed, *will it be,* if he has not merely ploughed in safety the neighbouring waters from some adjacent place. Few are the sailors that cross so large a tract of sea from Italy; few are they that come to these shores, destitute of harbours; yet, whether he knows how to speak in the Greek, or whether in the Latin language, assuredly on the latter account will he be more pleasing. It is possible, also, that one may have directed his course hither, with a steady South wind from the mouth of the straits *of the Hellespont,* and from the waves of the prolonged Propontis: whoever he is, he can tell the news with in faithful narrative, and it may be a portion of, and a substitute for, the topics of the day. I pray that he may be able to tell me the triumphs of Cæsar that he has heard of, and of the vows that have been fulfilled for Latian Jove; and that thou at length, rebellious Germany! hast laid thy weeping head beneath the feet of the great General. He who brings me this news, of things which I shall grieve not to have seen—the same shall forthwith be a guest at my home.

Ah, me! and is the home of Naso in the Scythian land? and does punishment give me a place of its own for my home? May the Gods grant that Cæsar make this but a temporary shelter in my disgrace, and not my *lasting* abode and my home!

ELEGY XIII.

His birthday having arrived, he pronounces it to be needless, as it comes in a place where it is not possible for him to perform the customary solemnities; he tells it to return no more, so long as he shall remain in the Scythian regions.

BEHOLD, my birth-day comes round at its *usual* time; needless, *indeed,* for of what use to me was it to be born? Why, in thy cruelty, didst thou come, an addition to the wretched years of the exile? Thou oughtst *rather* to have put an end to them.

If thou hadst had any care of me, or had there been any shame in thee, thou wouldst not have accompanied me beyond my country. In the place where first I was unfortunately known to thee as an infant, in that same thou wouldst have tried to be my last. Thou, too, in thy sorrow, wouldst have said farewell (as said my friends) in the City, when now about to be left by me.

What hast thou in common with Pontus? Has the wrath of Cæsar sent thee as well, to the extreme region of the freezing climates? Dost thou expect, forsooth, the honour of thy wonted tribute, *and* that the white robe[26] should hang from my shoulders? that the smoking altar should be girt with flowery chaplets? that the morsel of frankincense should crackle in the flames? that I should offer the sacrificial cakes to mark the day of my birth? and that I should give utterance to auspicious prayers, my lips uttering words of good omen? I am not so situated; and my circumstances are not such that I can be joyful at thy arrival. A funereal altar, wreathed with the mournful cypress, and flames prepared on the erected pile, befit me. I choose not to offer the frankincense that fails to conciliate the Gods; and words of good omen occur not *to me*, amid evils so great. If, however, any thing can be gained by me on this day, I pray thee never to return in these regions, so long as Pontus, almost the remotest spot in the earth, and wrongly called by the name of Euxinus,[27] retains me.

ELEGY XIV.

He praises the constancy and fidelity of a friend who is collecting his works, and entreats him, to the best of his ability, to keep alive his name in the City. He tells him that his Metamorphoses have been published in an uncorrected state; and he concludes by alleging, that allowance ought to be made for whatever he composed in Scythia during the time of his exile.

Thou worshipper, and holy guardian of learned men, my

[26] *The white robe.*]—Ver. 14. On the celebration of birth days the white robe was assumed as being an emblem of purity and happiness, and of good omen in its hue.

[27] *Euxinus.*]—Ver. 28. This name is derived from the Greek Εὔξεινος, 'hospitable,' or 'friendly to strangers.' The Poet implies, that, from its stormy character, and the barrenness of the neighbouring regions, it ought to have been called ἄξενος, or 'Axenus,' 'inhospitable,' which, indeed, was its ancient name.

friend, who art ever the favourer of my talents; and dost thou not, as once thou wast wont to honour me in my prosperity, now too, have a care that I seem not wholly lost? Art thou compiling my poems, those Arts alone being excepted[28] which have brought ruin on their composer? Do so, I pray, thou admirer of the modern poets, and to the best of thy power retain my body in the City. Exile has been awarded to me; exile has not been awarded to my books, which have done nothing to deserve the punishment of their master. Often is the banished father an exile in most distant lands; yet it is allowed the children of the exile to remain in the City. After the example of Pallas, verses have been born of me without a mother. These are my own offspring, and *my own* progeny. These I commend to thy care: the more they are deprived of their parent, the greater will be the burden to thee, their protector. Three have been born to me that have followed my *unhappy* example; remember to make the rest of them thy care in the eyes of men. There are also thrice five volumes on the changes of figure, poems that were snatched from the funeral pile of their master. That work might have gained a surer reputation from my correcting hand, had not my ruin happened first. Now, uncorrected, it has come into the presence of the public—if, indeed, anything of mine is still before the public.

Add to my works, this composition, such as it is, which comes sent to thee from a distant region; and when any one reads it (should any one do so), let him first consider under what circumstances, and in what place it was written. He will be considerate to writings whose time *of composition* he will know was a *time of* exile, and *which were written in* a barbarous clime. And, amid so many misfortunes, he will be surprised that I was capable of framing any poem with my trembling hand. Misery has ruined my powers, the fountain of which even before was not prolific, and the vein *but* unproductive. But, such as it was, it has disappeared, for want of exercise, and, dried up, it has perished by lengthened stagnation. Here is no abundance of books, by which I might be both invited and instructed: instead of books, there is the sound of the bow and of armour. There is no one in this region, should I recite my verses, whose ear I could engage so

---

[28] *Those Arts alone being excepted.*]—Ver. 6. He means his three books on the Art of Love the ostensible cause of his misfortunes.

as to understand me. There is no spot for me to retire to: the guard of the city walls, and the closed gate, keep off the Getic foe. Many a time do I enquire about some word, name, or place, and there is no one to inform me. Often (I am ashamed to own it) words fail me, when endeavouring to say something; and I have forgotten how to speak.

I am almost stunned with the Thracian and the Scythian jargon on every side; and I seem as though I could write in Getic measures. Believe me, I am afraid lest Pontic words should be mixed with Latin ones, and thou shouldst read them in my writings. Deign, then, to grant pardon to my book, such as it is, and excuse it, on the ground of my *wretched* lot.

BOOK THE FOURTH.

ELEGY I.

He says that his works must be excused, if they are found to be of inferior character; since he writes them in exile, not for the sake of glory, but only that he may solace his griefs, and lull the recollection of them. He then enumerates the afflictions which he endures in the Scythian region.

If there are any blemishes in my books, as there will be, excuse them, reader, on account of the time of their composition. I am an exile; and repose, not fame, is my object: that my mind may not dwell too intently on my misfortunes. This, too, is the reason why the miner sings chained with the fetter,[1] when he lightens his heavy labour with his untaught numbers; and why *the man* sings, who strives, as he bends forward on the oozy sand, while he drags the slow barge against the tide; *and why he, too,* who brings together his pliant oars to his breast, moves his arms to time, as he strikes the water. When the weary shepherd leans on his staff, or sits on the rock, he soothes his sheep with the song of his reed pipe. The labour of the handmaid is cheered and beguiled as she sings, and while, as she sings, she draws out her allotted task *in spinning*. Even Achilles, in his sadness, is said to have lessened his sorrows with the Hæmonian lyre, when the Lyrnessian[2] damsel had been taken from him. Or-

---

[1] *Chained with the fetter.*]—Ver. 5. The word 'fossor' literally means 'a digger;' but, by the mention of the fetter, it would seem that the punishment of malefactors is here referred to; very probably they were employed in the mines and public works of the state. It is certain that slaves were employed in the mines belonging to the Republic.

[2] *The Lyrnessian damsel.*]—Ver. 15. Briseis is so called, from Lyrnessus, a town near Troy. She was taken from Achilles by Agamemnon, when he had lost Chryseis, whom the Gods ordered to be restored to her

pheus was in sorrow, having twice lost his wife, when he attracted the woods and the hard rocks with his song.

Me also, did the Muse comfort, as I sought the appointed spot in Pontus; she was the only companion of my exile. She alone fears neither the treachery of man, nor the sword of the enemy, nor the sea, nor the winds, nor a state of barbarism. She knows, too, when I was undone, what error it was that deceived me, and she knows that there was mistake, and not criminality, in what I did. In good truth, for the very reason that she before proved my injury, she is now propitious to me. She has been condemned for a common crime, in conjunction with me. Would that, for my part, I had never employed my hand in the rites of the Piërian maids, since *that sacrifice* was to prove my ruin.

But what shall I do now? The very potency of the Sisters retains me, and, in my madness, I, ruined by poesy, am still in love with poesy. Thus was the newly-found lotus, when tasted by the palate of him of Dulichium, grateful in flavour to him whom it injured.[3] The lover is generally sensible of his losses; yet he persists in them, and he follows after the *very* cause of his error.

Me too, my books delight, although they have injured me, and the very weapon that has caused my wounds, I love. Perhaps this attachment may appear to be a madness, but this madness has some advantages. It precludes my mind from always brooding over my woes, and makes me forgetful of my present misfortunes. And just as the Bacchanal, when wounded, feels not the wound while, in her delirium, she howls along the steeps of Edonis;[4] so, when my breast waxes warm, aroused by the verdant Thyrsus, its spirits are superior to mortal woe. They are sensible neither of exile, nor of the shores of the Scythian ocean, nor do they feel that the Deities are incensed. Just as though I had quaffed the cup from the soporific Lethe, does my sense of adversity become blunted. With justice, then, do I venerate the Deities that

father. Hæmonia was the ancient name of Thessaly, of which country Achilles was a native.

[3] *It injured.*]—Ver. 32. Homer tells us that the companions of Ulysses found the flavour of the lotus so delightful that they forgot their country, and it was with the greatest difficulty that Ulysses could persuade them to embark, and leave the shores of the Lotophagi.

[4] *Edonis.*]—Ver. 42. This was a mountain in that part of Macedonia which bordered upon Thrace.

alleviate my woes, companions from Helicon of my anxious flight; and who have deigned to attend my steps, partly by sea and partly by land, both on board and on shore. May these, at least, I pray, be propitious to me; for the rest of the Gods make common cause with Cæsar, and they load me with as many troubles as the shore has sands, as the sea has fishes, and as the fishes have spawn. You will sooner *be able to* number the flowers in spring, the ears of corn in summer, the fruit in autumn, and the snow in winter, than the evils which I endured, while, driven over the face of the world, I sought, in my wretchedness, the shores on the left side of the Euxine sea. Nor yet, when I had arrived, was the allotted number of my woes more endurable; hither, too, did my destinies track my steps. Here, too, do I recognize the threads *of fate* allotted me at my birth, threads made for me with blackened wool. And, not to speak of treachery, and my life being in danger, things true, indeed, but too extraordinary for implicit belief; how sad a thing is it for one, who was always in favour with his fellow-citizens, to be *living* among the Bessi and the Getæ! How sad a thing is it for one's life to be protected by gate and walls, and to be hardly in safety through the resources of one's place of abode! When young, I avoided the fierce conflicts of warfare, and I touched not arms but with sportive hand. Now, in my old age, I *gird* my side with the sword, my left arm with the shield, and I place my white locks under the helmet. For when the watchman from his tower gives the signal of some rising, forthwith I take up arms with nervous hand. A savage enemy, that has bows and arrows tipped with venom, surveys the fortifications on his panting steed. And, just as the ravening wolf drags and carries along some sheep, which has not hidden itself in the fold, over corn-fields and through woods, so, if the barbarian foe finds any one in the fields that has not yet betaken himself within the protection of the gates, he carries him off. The person so taken, either follows them, and has chains thrown over his neck, or is killed with a weapon dipped in poison.

Here am I placed, a newly-come denizen of an anxious abode. Alas! too long is the duration of my existence! And yet, *even* amid so many woes, the Muse, a sojourner, endures to return to her numbers and to her former devotions. But there is no one to whom to recite my verses, and none to listen with their ears to Latin words. I myself (what else can I do?) both write and read for myself; and my writings are reviewed by my own judgment *alone*. Yet many a time have I said, on whose account do I labour at these pursuits? Will the Sauromatæ and the Getæ read my writings? Many a time, as I was writing, the tears have trickled down, and the writing has been moistened with my weeping. My mind, too, is as sensitive to its old wounds as though they were fresh; and showers of sorrowful tears fall upon my bosom. When I call to mind what I am and what I was, my fortune thus changed, and reflect whither and from what quarter my destiny hurries me; many a time, in my desperation, angered at my ruinous studies, has my hand thrown my lines upon the hearth, there to be consumed. And since, out of *so* many, only a few are remaining, do, whoever thou art, read them with indulgence; and do, as Rome is forbidden to me, take it in good part that my poetry is not any better than my *present* circumstances.

ELEGY II.

THE news has reached the poet that Tiberius has commenced his expedition against Germany. He says that, perhaps, at the moment of his writing, victory has been obtained, and that though corporeally he cannot be present at the triumph, yet mentally he can behold the pageant. He concludes by saying, that, should any one bring him an account of the triumph, he will receive the news with extreme delight, and will lay aside his own private sorrows in his love for the public welfare.

BY this, fierce Germany, like the rest of the earth being overcome, thou mayst have bent the knee to the Cæsars. Perhaps, too, the lofty Palatium is being decorated with wreaths, and the frankincense is crackling in the blaze, and *by its smoke* is obscuring the day; the white victim, struck on its neck with the planted axe, is dyeing the ground with its crimson blood; and each of the Cæsars is preparing, as conqueror, to offer the promised gifts in the temples of the favouring Gods; the young men, too, who are growing up under the name of Cæsar, that that house may ever rule over the earth; and Livia, with her good daughters-in-law, *destined* often to present them, is presenting gifts for her son returned in safety,[5]

---

[5] *Son returned in safety.*]—Ver. 12. Tiberius; who is here supposed to have returned victorious from his German expedition. The daughters-in-law

and the matrons as well, and those who, free from imputation, preserve in perpetual virginity the chaste altars. The common people, too, in its veneration, and with the people *so* revering, the Senate, is rejoicing; and the Knights, of whom but lately I formed a small fraction.

Driven far away, I share not in the public joy, and but little of the news travels thus far. The whole of the people, then, *of the City*, will be able to be spectators of the triumphs, and will read of[6] captured cities with the titles of their kings; and will behold monarchs, bearing the fetters of the captive, going before the horses wreathed with garlands; and will see the countenances of some changed with their fortunes, those of others still firm, and forgetful of their condition. Some of them will be enquiring the reasons, and the circumstances, and their names; some will be telling, although they themselves know little *about it*. He who is resplendent on high in Sidonian purple, was the leader in the war; he is next to *our* general. He, who is now fixing his sorrowful looks on the ground, bore not that countenance while he was in arms. That one in his pride, and who still sends burning glances from his indignant eyes, was the instigator and the adviser of the war. The one who covers his squalid face with his dishevelled locks, in his perfidy, hemmed our troops in an ambuscade. They say that by the priest that follows, the bodies of the captives were many a time offered up to the unpropitious Deity. This lake, these mountains, this number of fortresses, these many rivers, were all filled with slaughter, and were streaming with blood. Drusus, who was the excellent son of a worthy sire, once earned a title in these lands. Rhine, having broken his horns, and vainly concealing himself in his sedge, will be discoloured by his own blood. See too, Germany is borne along with dishevelled hair, and sits in sadness at the feet of the invincible chief; extending her courageous neck to the Roman axe, she is now bearing fetters on the hand with which she wielded arms.

Duly, Cæsar, art thou borne *towering* above these in thy

here mentioned were probably Agrippina, the daughter of Julia and Agrippa, and who was the wife of Germanicus; and Livia, the sister of Germanicus, who was the wife of Drusus, the son of Tiberius.

[6] *Will read of.*]—Ver. 20. Not only were the captives led in the triumphal procession, but models and paintings of the captured places were also exhibited, with their titles written over them.

victorious chariot, arrayed in purple, in the presence of thy people; whichever way thou shalt turn, thou shalt receive applause from the hands of thy subjects, as the strewed flowers on every side cover the way. The soldier will have his brow girt with the laurel of Phœbus, and will sing, "Io Triumphe,"[7] with loud voice. Thou wilt see the horses of the chariot often stop, through the sound and the applause, and the noise of the musicians. Thence thou wilt go to the heights *of the Capitol*, and to the temples that listened to thy vows; and the promised laurel branch will be given to Jove, who deserves it.

I, removed afar, so far as I can, shall mentally behold these things, for *my mind* has the privilege of *resorting to* a spot forbidden to me. In freedom it ranges at large over unbounded regions; with swift flight it attains to the Heavens. It directs my eyes to the very midst of the City, and allows them not to be deprived of a blessing so great. It will find out the way, too, to behold the ivory chariot;[8] and thus, doubtless, for a moment, shall I be in my father-land.

But the people, *supremely* blest, will see the pageant in its reality, and the joyous crowd will be there with its Prince. By hearsay only will this enjoyment be experienced by me, thus giving range to fancy, and removed afar. There will, too, be scarcely one, sent afar from Latium to a distant clime, to tell me, anxious *to hear it*, this news. Even *then*, he will tell me of the triumph when it is long since past and grown old; but at whatever time I shall hear of it, I shall rejoice. *When that* day shall come, I will lay aside my griefs, and the cause of the public will rise superior to my private *sorrows*.

[7] *Io Triumphe.*]—Ver. 51. 'Io,' or 'Io Triumphe,' was especially the cry of exultation used by the troops, following their general, on the occasion of his triumph. It was used in much the same spirit as our 'Huzza,' and the German 'Hoch,' at the present day.

[8] *The ivory chariot.*]—Ver. 63. The 'quadriga,' or four-horsed chariot, was used by the Roman generals in their triumphs. The body was cylindrical, and enriched with gold and ivory, and the utmost skill and elegance were lavished upon the workmanship. The car was elevated, so that the person triumphing was the most conspicuous object in the procession. The triumphal chariot had no pole, the horses being led by men stationed at their heads.

ELEGY III.

THE Poet entreats the Constellations of the Greater and the Less Bear to look upon the Roman City, and tell him whether or not his wife keeps him in remembrance. He then blames himself for doubting his wife's constancy; and he launches forth in her praises, and grieves that, through him, she passes a life of sorrow. He exhorts her to remain firm in her constancy.

YE Bears, both the Greater and the Less, of which the one guides the Grecian, the other the *Sidonian ship, and both *are* untouched by the waves; since, situate in the lofty sky, ye survey all things, and set not in the Western wave; and your circuit, in its circumference, embracing the topmost height of heaven, is free from contact with *the horizon of* the earth. Cast a look, I beseech you, on those walls which Remus, son of Ilia, is said once lucklessly to have overleapt; turn your shining eyes on my wife, and tell me whether she keeps me in her memory or not. Alas! why do I inquire what is too well known? Why fluctuate my hopes, mingled with doubting apprehensions? Believe that that which thou wishest *to be true,* is *true;* cease to fear for what is secure; and have a certain assurance of undoubted constancy. And that which the stars set in the sky are unable to tell thee, do thou repeat to thyself, with voice that will not deceive; *say* that she who is thy greatest care keeps thee in her memory, and, so far as she is able, retains thy name in her mind. She clings to *the recollection of* thy features as though thou were present; and, far away, she loves thee, if only she lives.

And does not, *at times,* when her afflicted mind has been overcome with virtuous grief, soft slumber depart from her anxious breast? Then do your woes recur to you, *my wife,* when my couch and my *wonted* place affect you, and allow you not to be forgetful of me. Anxieties arise, and the night appears without an end; and the wearied bones of your restless body are sore.

For my part, I doubt not, that these and other *like* things happen; that your love of me gives proof of its pure sorrow, and that you are not less distressed than when *Andromache,* the Theban matron, beheld the blood-stained Hector dragged along by the Thessalian chariot. Yet what to pray I know not; and I am unable to say what are the feelings I would wish you to have. Are you sad? I am grieved to be the cause of your sorrow. Are you not *sad?* Would that you were worthy of the husband lost *to you.*

But grieve at your loss, my dearest wife, and pass a life embittered by my woes. Weep for my afflictions; there is a certain pleasure in weeping. Tears both satisfy sorrow and give vent to it. And, oh! that not my life, but my death were mourned by you; and that by my death you had been left in solitude! That this spirit, by your aid, had mingled with the air of my father-land! That the tears of affection had bedewed my breast! That your hands had closed my eyes, looking on my native sky at the last moment! That my ashes had rested, laid in the tomb of my forefathers! That the same earth had held me that was touched by my body at my birth! And, lastly, that as I had lived, so I had died without stain! Now, through my disgrace, my *very* life is a source of shame.

Ah! wretched am I, if you think it a disgrace to be known as my wife! Wretched am I, if you are now ashamed of being mine! Where are those times *gone*, when you were wont to take a pride in your husband, and not to conceal his name? Where are those times *gone* (unless, perchance, you desire to forget them), when it pleased you, as I remember, both to be called mine and to be mine? As became a virtuous woman, I *then* was pleasing to you in all of my qualities; *and* the esteem of yourself, who loved me, added much *in my favour* to what was true. No other man was there whom you would prefer (so great a prize did I seem to you), or whom you would rather have made your husband. And now be not ashamed that you are my wife; your shame, and not your grief, ought to be laid aside.

When the rash Capaneus fell by a sudden stroke, do you read that Evadne blushed for her husband? Not because the King *of heaven* subdued the flames of the world with his bolts, wast thou, Phaëton, thyself to be disavowed by thy relations? Semele was not disowned by her father Cadmus, because, through her ambition, she met her death by her entreaties. And do not, because I have been struck by the cruel bolts of Jove, let the crimson blush arise on your placid face; but rather arouse yourself to the care of defending me, and prove yourself the *very* pattern of a good wife for me: and adorn with your virtues your state of sorrow. Let glory, *so* difficult of attainment, mount the steep path. Who would have known of Hector, had Troy been flourishing? A path has been laid open for fortitude, through the midst of sorrows. Thy art, Tiphys, is thrown away, if there are no storms on the ocean; if men are *always* in health, thy skill, Phœbus, is worthless. The virtue which, in prosperity, is concealed and lies unknown, makes its appearance and is proved in adversity. My fate gives you an opportunity for fame, and your piety has *a height* to which to raise its head aloft. Use, then, this opportunity, and trust in reliance on its advantages. Behold! a wide field lies open for your fame.

ELEGY IV.

The Poet extols the virtues of his friend, and recounts his own hardships in exile at Tomi; he beseeches him, while he conceals his name, to ask Augustus to grant him a more desirable place of exile; and he says, that so great is the clemency of the Emperor, that he is sure that he will readily grant his request. He relates how Orestes fled with his sister from the cruelties of the neighbouring region; and how the statue of Diana was taken by them to a more happy clime.

Oh thou! who, whilst ennobled by the names of thy ancestors, excellest thy high birth in the nobleness of thy manners: in whose mind exists the reflection of thy father's integrity, *but in such degree* that that integrity is not without its proper strength; whose gift is eloquence in thy native language, so great, that there was none superior to it at the Latian bar. Far from my wishes, thou art described by signs, employed in place of thy name. Pardon for this the extent of thy fame. In nothing have I erred; it is thy good deeds that betray thee; if thou art seen to be what thou *really* art, then is my fault absolved. And do not suppose that esteem shown for thee in my verses could hurt thee, under a Prince so just. The Father of his country himself (who more observant of the laws than he?) endures often to be mentioned in my poetry. And Cæsar cannot prevent it, because he belongs to the public; and a part is he, that belongs to us, of the common welfare. Jupiter proffers his own majesty to the scope of the poet's genius, and allows himself to be sung by the lips of all. Thy case is safe in the precedents of two of the Gods above; of these, the one is seen, and the other is believed to be a God.

Though I ought not, yet will I cling to this error *of mine:* my writings are not subject to thy control. The injury arising from my addressing thee is nothing new; for oft, while I was yet safe, had I conversed with thee.

Therefore thou mayst have the less apprehension that I should cause thy disgrace by being a friend of thine: I, the origin *of it*, can bear the blame, if there is any. For thy father was always respected by me from my earliest years (at least conceal not that fact): he used to praise my talents (this, *perhaps*, you can remember); *yes*, even more than I deserved, in my opinion; and he used to tell about my verses in that voice in which some part of his high nobility of descent was *conspicuous*. It was not thee, then, but thy father, that was imposed upon, for it was his house that gave me a reception. And yet, believe me, there was no deceit; but in all my actions, if the last is excepted, my life cannot be impugned. Thou wouldst deny, too, that this fault, through which I was undone, was a crime, if the lengthened detail of so great a misfortune were known to thee. Either timidity or mistake, *say* rather mistake, proved my downfall. Ah, suffer me to lose the recollection of my fate, and let me not, by handling them, burst open my wounds not yet closed; scarcely will rest itself be of any avail to them. Although, therefore, I am justly punished, yet all criminality and all *bad* intention were no part of my error. And of that the God is sensible; for which reason, I have neither been deprived of life, nor does any other person possess my property taken from me. Perhaps (should he live) he will one day put an end to this banishment, when his wrath shall have become moderated. Now, my entreaty is, that he will order me to go hence: if my desire is not wanting in becoming moderation. I pray for a more civilized place of exile, and one a little nearer *to Rome*, and a spot which is at a greater distance from a savage enemy. And so great is the clemency of Augustus, that if any one asked him this for me, perhaps he would grant it.

The cold shores of the Euxine Pontus confine me; by the ancients it was called Axenus. For its seas are ruffled by no moderate breezes; and *there* no stranger ship enters a quiet harbour. Around are tribes which seek their prey through bloodshed, and the land has no fewer sources of alarm than the faithless waves. Those whom thou hearest of as revelling in the blood of human beings, are situate almost under the sky of the same star. And not far from me is the place where the Tauric altar of the quivered Goddess is fed with dreadful slaughter. These regions formed once, as they tell, the realms of Thoas—*realms* not hateful to the wicked, nor desirable for the good. Here the virgin descendant of Pelops, the hind having been substituted *for her*, presided over the rites of the Goddess, such as they were. After Orestes, (whether more pious or wicked, is a matter of doubt,) driven by his *avenging* Furies, had come here, and his companion; from Phocis, a pattern of true friendship, they who were two in body and one in mind: forthwith they were led in bonds to the altar of Trivia, which stood, all bloodstained, before the twofold doors. Neither did his own fate affect the one or the other of them; each was in affliction, on account of the other's death. And now, with drawn sword, the 'priestess had taken her station, and a barbarian fillet had girded the Grecian locks; when Iphigenia, in the course of conversation, recognised her brother, and gave him embraces in place of death. She joyfully transported the statue of the Goddess, who holds cruel rites in abhorrence, from those regions into more happy *climes*.

This region, then, the most remote part of the vast world, from which both Gods and men have taken their flight, is neighbouring to me. Close to my country are these deadly rites, if, indeed, a land of barbarians can be the country of Naso. Would that those winds, by which Orestes was borne away, would bear back my sails, as well, the Divinity being appeased.

ELEGY V.

The Poet praises the constancy of his friend, and requests him never to fail in his friendly offices, and to speak in his favour to Augustus. He shows that, by length of time, all things, except his own woes, become more endurable; and concludes, by wishing that every worldly happiness may be the lot of his friend.

O THOU, especially allotted to me by destiny among my beloved companions, the only altar[9] that I have found in my calamities;

[9] *The only altar.*]—Ver. 2. With the ancients, all altars to the Deities were places of refuge; hence the present complimentary allusion. The supplicant was considered to place himself under the protection of the Deity to whom the altar was consecrated, and, under such circumstances, violence offered to the person so flying for refuge, even if a criminal, or a runaway slave, was looked upon as an act of sacrilege.

through whose discourse, this spirit of mine, about to perish, resumed life, just as the watchful flame waxes strong by the infusion *of oil, the invention* of Pallas;[10] thou, who didst not fear to open thy friendly doors, a refuge to my bark when struck by the lightnings; through the aid of whose fortune I should not have found myself in want, had Cæsar *even* deprived me of my patrimonial property. While my feelings are carrying me away, forgetful of present circumstances, how very nearly did thy name escape me. Yet thou dost recognize thyself; and, moved by the desire of applause, thou wouldst wish to say openly, " It is I." Truly would I, if thou wouldst allow me, be ready to give thee glory, and to commend thy remarkable constancy to Fame. But I fear lest I should injure thee by my grateful strains, and lest an honour paid to thee at a not fitting season, should be to thy prejudice. What thou mayst do in safety, rejoice in thy heart that I remember thee, and that thou keepest me in thy memory. And, as thou art doing, strive with all thy oars to bear me aid, until a more gentle breeze arise, the God being propitiated. Do thou defend that person who can be saved by the aid of none, if he who has overwhelmed him on the Stygian wave should not give him his assistance. Do thou, also, what seldom *happens*, show thyself with constancy ready for every duty of a friendship not to be shaken.

Then may thy good fortune have everlasting increase; then mayst thou never stand in need of aid thyself, and mayst thou always help thy friends. May thy wife share with her husband in lasting felicity, and may but few complaints occur in your married life. And may *thy brother*, thy companion in blood, always love thee with that affection with which his attached brother loved Castor. May the youth, thy son, be like to thee, and, by his manners, may every one recognize that he is thy son. May thy daughter make thee a father-in-law, by *lighting* her marriage torch, and may she speedily confer the name of grandsire on thee while yet a young man.

[10] *Invention of Pallas.*]—Ver. 4. 'Pallade,' literally the name of the Goddess, is here used to signify 'oil,' as Minerva, or Pallas, was the discoverer of the olive, from which it was extracted.

ELEGY VI.

Ovid here enlarges upon the effect of length of time, and says, that though by its efficacy all difficulties are surmounted, yet that his miseries experience no mitigation, but rather an increase. He complains of his protracted wretchedness, and describes its effects upon his health; and concludes, by hoping that death will bring a speedy termination to his woes.

In time, the bull becomes accustomed to the plough that tills the fields, and yields his neck to be pressed by the curving yoke. In time, the spirited horse obeys the flowing reins, and, with quiet mouth, receives the hard bit. In time, the anger of the Punic lions is assuaged, and the fierceness which once was, exists in their nature no longer. The Indian beast,[11] too, which obeys the commands of its master, overcome in time, submits to servitude. Length of time, too, causes that the grape swells out on the spreading clusters, and that the berries can scarcely contain the juice that they hold within. Time, too, pushes forth the seed into the whitening ears of corn; and makes the apple to be not of a sour flavour. 'Tis this that blunts the edge of the plough that renews the land; 'tis this that wears the hard flint and the adamant. This, too, by degrees, mitigates raging anger; this lessens sadness and elevates the sorrowing heart. Length of time, then, as it glides on with silent foot, is able to lessen everything except my cares.

Since I have been deprived of my country, twice has the threshing floor been beaten with the corn; twice has the grape, pressed with the bare foot,[12] been burst asunder. And yet, in so long a space *of time*, patience has not been acquired; and my mind retains its sensitiveness to its recent woes. In fact, the oxen, even when old, fly from the curving yoke; and the horse that has been broken in, often struggles against the bit. My present sorrow is even more bitter than it once was; for though it be similar to its *former* self, it has waxed stronger, and increases as time wears on. My woes, too, were

---

[11] *The Indian beast.*]—Ver. 7, 8. He alludes to the elephant, which in time is taught even to kneel, in obedience to the command of his master.

[12] *With the bare feet.*]—Ver. 20. The practice of crushing the grape by the pressure of the bare foot, prevails in the wine-growing countries of the south of Europe at the present day.

not so well known to me *once* as they now are; but the better I become acquainted with them, the more heavily do they press upon me. This, too, is not the least *evil*, for one to bring fresh strength *to their endurance*, and not to become utterly spent beforehand by the passing sorrows. A fresh wrestler on the yellow sand is stronger than he whose arms are wearied *with exercise* for a length of time. The gladiator that comes fresh, is better in shining arms than he whose arms are red, stained with his own blood. The ship, but lately built, bears well the impetuous storm; the old one is battered to pieces by ever so slight a gale. I, too, at first endured my sufferings with patience, and, by length of time, my evils have become multiplied.

Believe me, I despair, and, judging from my body, so far as I can form an opinion, but few days will be added to my sorrows. For I have neither the strength nor the colour that I used to have, and scarcely have I a thin covering of skin for my bones. But my mind is more diseased than my sickening body, and it stands eternally gazing upon its afflictions. No sight is there here of the City; my companions, my delight, are afar, and my wife, than whom nothing is dearer *to me*, is far distant. There is here a Scythian multitude, and crowds of the Getæ wearing trowsers; and so, both what I see, and what I cannot see, are a cause of misery to me. Yet one hope there is, which consoles me amid these things; that, through my death, these woes will not last long.

ELEGY VII.

THE Poet expresses his surprise, that, now two years have elapsed, he has received no letter from his friend, especially after he has heard from some with whom he was not so intimately acquainted. He adds, that he would rather believe any thing than that his friend had not written to him; and he concludes that his letter must have miscarried. He tells him to write again and again, that he may not always have to suggest these excuses for him.

TWICE has the Sun visited me after the frosts of icy winter, and twice, passing through *the Constellation of* the Fish, has he run his course. In so long a time, why did not thy right hand employ itself on some lines *to me*, however few? Why has thy affection grown tardy, while those have written to me with whom I had but little acquaintanceship? Why, often as

I untied the fastenings of any packet, have I been hoping that it enclosed thy name? Oh, that the Gods may grant that a letter has often been written by thy right hand, but that out of so many not one has reached me! What I pray I am sure is the case. I will sooner believe that the face of Medusa, the Gorgon, is surrounded by locks formed of serpents; that there are dogs beneath the stomach of the virgin *Scylla;* that there is a Chimæra, which amid her flames divides the form of the lioness from that of the dreadful dragon; that there are quadrupeds that have their breasts joined to the breasts of human beings; that a man exists with three bodies, and a dog with three bodies; that the Sphinx exists, the Harpies, and the Giants with serpents for their feet; that Gyges, with his hundred hands, and the man half a bull exist.[13] I will believe all these things sooner, my dearest friend, than I will believe that thou, changed, hast ceased to care for me. Innumerable mountains and roads, and rivers and plains, and no little of the ocean, lie between thee and me. The letter which has been often sent by thee, may, for a thousand reasons, never have reached my hands. Yet overcome these thousand reasons by writing repeatedly: that I may not, my friend, always have to be excusing thee to myself.

ELEGY VIII.

He complains that now, in his fiftieth year, he is becoming hoary with age, in a wretched spot, at a time when he ought to have been enjoying the pleasures of home, and the society of his wife and friends. He says, that if his destiny had been foretold by the Delphic oracle, or by Dodona, he could not have credited them, and should have accused them of falsehood. He shows that there is nothing strong enough to be able to resist the divine will and power, and he concludes by advising others to take a lesson from his misfortunes, and to deserve the esteem of Augustus, whose power is equal to that of the immortal Gods.

Now do my years assume the hue of the feathers of the swan, and hoary age tints my black locks. Now hours of weakness are coming on, and old age more desirous of repose;

---

[13] *Half a bull exist.*]—Ver. 18. He alludes to the Minotaur, half a man and half a bull, the fruit of the intrigue of Pasiphaë with the Bull. The quadrupeds mentioned by the poet are the Centaurs. The man with three bodies was Geryon, or Herilus, mentioned by Virgil. The dog with three bodies was Cerberus. All of these are mentioned in fabulous story.

and now it is a matter of difficulty to support myself in my weakness. Now was the time *that I ought* to live, having put an end to my toils, while no cares were harassing me; to enjoy, too, that repose which was ever pleasing to my mind, and to be at ease amid my own pursuits; to live in my humble home, and in my dwelling-place of old, and amid my patrimonial fields, which now are deprived of their master. *Now I ought* to be growing aged, *free* from care, in the bosom of my wife, among my dear grandchildren, and in my native land.

My youth once hoped that this would come to pass; *and then* I was worthy thus to spend these *latter* years. Otherwise did it seem to the Gods, who have exposed me in the Sarmatian regions, tossed to and fro by sea and by land. The shattered ships are taken into the excavated docks, that they may not go to pieces at hazard in the midst of the waves. The steed, worn out, crops the grass in the meadows, that he may not stumble, and *thereby* disgrace the many victories that he has won. The soldier, when, through length of years, he is no longer useful enough *for war*, puts away the arms which he has borne, at the home of his youth. So, too, as old age slowly creeping on, diminished my strength, it was time for me, as well, to be presented with my discharge.[14] It was time for me neither to be breathing a foreign atmosphere, nor to be quenching my parching thirst at a Getic spring, but *rather*, to be at one time retiring at my leisure to the gardens which I possessed,[15] at another, enjoying the intercourse of men and *the pleasures of* the City.

Thus, in my former days, with a mind having no presage of the future, used I to desire to spend my old age in calm repose. The Fates refused it; who, though they granted me an early life full of delights, are now rendering my latter days wretched. And now, having passed fifty years without any stain, I am afflicted in the decline of my life. Not far from the goal,[16] at which I seemed almost

[14] *Presented with my discharge.*]—Ver. 24. Literally, 'rude donari' means, 'to be presented with a rod.' The 'rudis' was a 'rod,' or 'foil,' with which soldiers or gladiators fought for exercise and sport. Such a rod was given to gladiators when, for their merit, they were discharged from fighting in the arena. Hence, figuratively, the term came to signify 'to receive an honourable discharge,' or, 'to be released from one's duties.'

[15] *Gardens which I possessed.*]—Ver. 27. He alludes to his patrimonial possessions at Sulmo, in the Apennines, the place of his birth.

[16] *The goal.*]—Ver. 35. The 'Meta' was a pyramidal column at each

to have arrived, a dreadful crash befel my chariot. Did I, in my madness, compel him to be angered against me, than whom the unbounded earth contains no one more full of mercy? And was that very clemency overpowered by *the magnitude of my faults?* And still was life not denied to my errors? A life to be spent afar from my country, under the Northern pole, where the land extends on the left of the Euxine *sea*. Had Delphi and Dodona itself foretold me this, either place would have appeared untruthful to me. There is nothing strong enough, even though it be riveted with adamant, to be able to endure the impetuous bolt of Jove. Nothing is there so lofty, and that soars so high above dangers, that it is not lower than the Deity, and submissive *to his will*. For although a part of my sorrows was earned by *my own* fault, yet the wrath of the God awarded the greater share of my downfall, *for the better manifestation of his power.*

But be ye instructed, too, by my misfortunes, to deserve favour at the hands of one who is equal to the Gods above.

ELEGY IX.

The Poet threatens his enemy that he will attack him in his writings, if he does not desist from his hostility.

If it is allowed me, and if thou sufferest me *to do so*, I will be silent on thy name and thy misdeeds; thy actions shall be given to the waters of Lethe, and my forgiveness will be obtained by thy entreaties, *even thus* late. Only take care that it is clear that thou hast repented. Only remember to condemn thy own conduct, and to show a desire to cleanse thy life of these moments devoted to the Furies.[17] But if not, and if thy breast is still burning with hatred *against me*, my sad state of misery will assume the arms that have been forced upon it. Although, as I have been, I am sent to the extremity of the earth; still even, thus far, shall my anger

---

end of the Roman Circus, round which the horses and chariots turned seven times. Hence it came, figuratively, to mean, any fixed term or limit, to which to look forward. The goal here alluded to by the poet was the ease and quiet retirement of old age.

[17] *The Furies.*]—Ver. 6. Literally, 'to Tisiphone,' the name of one Fury being used for all.

stretch forth its hands. Cæsar, if thou knowest it not, has left to me all my rights *as a citizen*, and my sole punishment is to be deprived of my country. From him, too, if he only lives, do I hope for *a return to* my country. Often does the oak thrive *again*, that has been struck by the bolts of Jove. In fact, if I have no means of vengeance, the Piërian maids will give me strength, and weapons of their making. Although I am living removed afar, amid the Scythian regions, and although the Constellations that avoid contact with the waves are close to my eyes, yet my commendations will travel through nations innumerable, and my complaints will become known as far as the earth extends. Whatever I shall give utterance to, will travel from the East to the West, and the climes of the morn will be conscious of the voice from Hesperia. Beyond the land, beyond the wide waves, shall I be heard, and great will be the echo of my laments. Nor will thy own age only be acquainted with thy guilt; thou wilt be a disgrace to late posterity.

I am now summoned to the combat, but not yet have I assumed my horns,[18] *my weapons of defence;* and I would rather that there was no cause for assuming them. The Circus is as yet in quietude; but the fierce bull is already spurning the sand, and is beating the ground with hostile hoof. Even this is more than I wished *to say*. Sound the retreat, my Muse, while yet it is allowed this man to conceal his name.

ELEGY X.

He gives an account of his life and his family, after saying when and where he was born. He describes the miseries of his exile, and says that the Muses are his only consolation and delight.

That thou mayst know, Posterity, *the man* whose works thou art reading, understand that I am he who sportively sang of voluptuous love.

Sulmo is my native place, which, abounding in its cold streams, is distant ninety miles from the *Roman* City. Here was I born, and (that you may know the date) at the

[18] *My horns.*]—Ver. 18. He is here comparing himself to a bull about to be baited in the Circus, which was one of the favorite sports of the Romans. As in Spain, at the present day, the bull was irritated by objects of a red colour being placed before his eyes, especially straw figures of men, clothed in that colour.

time when two Consuls fell with a similar death. If that is anything, I am heir to an hereditary *Equestrian* rank, *descended* from my ancestors; and I was not created a Knight merely through the chance of riches. I was not the eldest son; I was born after my brother, whose birth was thrice four months before *mine*. The same light-bearing *day* was the birthday of us both; one day was honoured by two sacrificial cakes. This day is one of the five festival days of the armed Minerva, *the one* that is wont to be the first stained[19] with *gladiatorial* blood. When young, we were attentively educated, and, through the care of our father, we resorted to men in the *Roman* City distinguished in the arts. My brother had a turn for eloquence from his earliest years, born, *as it were*, to the vigorous warfare of the wordy Forum. But, while yet a boy, the rites of the heaven-born maids delighted me, and imperceptibly the Muse attracted me to her vocation. Many a time did my father say, "Why are you striving at a worthless pursuit? *Even* the Mæonian bard himself left no wealth." I was influenced by his words; and having entirely deserted Helicon, I endeavoured to write words disengaged from *poetic* measures. Spontaneously, my lines ran according to befitting numbers, and whatever I tried to express, the same was poetry.

In the mean time, as years rolled on with silent pace, the gown of freedom[20] was assumed by my brother and myself. The purple with the broad hem[21] was put on our shoulders, and the attachment which before existed still remained. And now my brother had lived twice ten years, when he died; and then was I first deprived of one half of myself. I enjoyed, too, the first

[19] *The first stained.*]—Ver. 14. This was the second day of the Quinquatrus, or Quinquatria, the five day festival of Minerva, and the first of the gladiatorial shows on that occasion. The birth-day of Ovid was, therefore, on the 13th of the Calends of April, or the 20th of March. For a full account of the Quinquatria, see the third book of the 'Fasti.'

[20] *The gown of freedom.*]—Ver. 28. This was the 'toga virilis,' or 'manly robe,' which was generally assumed by the young men in their seventeenth year. Full reference has already been made to the mode of its assumption, in the notes.

[21] *The broad hem.*]—Ver. 29. From Dr. Smith's Dictionary of Greek and Roman Antiquities, we learn, that Augustus formed a select class of 'equites,' or 'knights,' who possessed the property of a senator, and the former requirement of free birth up to the grandfather. He permitted this class to wear the 'latus clavus,' or 'broad hem,' and distinguished them by the title 'illustres,' 'insignes,' and 'splendidi.'

honours that belong to a tender age, and once I formed one of the Triumviri. The Senate-house still remained; the breadth of my *distinctive* hem was still restricted:[22] that was a burden too onerous for my shoulders. My body was not fitted for labour, my mind could not endure fatigue, and I was one who shunned the anxieties of ambition. The Aonian sisters, too, persuaded me to seek a repose free from care, that had been always courted by my inclination.

I loved and I honoured the poets of those days; and as many bards as there were, I thought them to be so many Gods. Macer,[23] when stricken in years, many a time repeated to me his *poem on* birds, and each serpent that is deadly, each herb that is curative. Many a time was Propertius wont to repeat to me his love songs; he was united to me by the ties of friendship. Ponticus,[24] famous in heroic measure; Bassus, too, famed in Iambics, were delightful members of my circle. Horace, too, with his varied numbers, used to captivate my ears, while he sang his beauteous strains to his Ausonian lyre. I only saw Virgil; and bitter destiny[25] did not grant time for my friendship to Tibullus. He was thy successor, Gallus; Propertius was his. In order of time, I was the fourth of them; as I honoured my seniors, so did those who were younger, honour me; and my poetic talents were not long in becoming known. When first I recited my juvenile poems before the people, my beard had been shaved but once or twice. Corinna[26] (so called by a fictitious name), the subject

[22] *Was still restricted.*]—Ver. 35. This expression seems contradictory to the words found in line 29, if we give them the meaning which Dr. Smith has, as quoted in the last note, given to them. It would not, however, be at all discrepant with the suggestion which is made in the Introductory Life of the poet, that the children of the knights were, up to a certain age, graced with the laticlave, as being candidates for senatorial rank.

[23] *Macer.*]—Ver. 44. Æmilius Macer, a Roman poet, was a native of Verona; he wrote a poem on plants, serpents, and birds; and, according to Eusebius, he died in Asia. He was a friend of Virgil and Ovid; of whom he was the senior.

[24] *Ponticus.*]—Ver. 47. He wrote a poem on the Theban war, which Ovid compares with the writings of Homer. Of the poet Bassus, no particulars have come down to us. Propertius merely mentions him as being a poet.

[25] *Bitter destiny.*]—Ver. 52. Because the poet, Tibullus, died prematurely, at a youthful age.

[26] *Corinna.*]—Ver. 60. It is most likely that this character is quite

of song throughout the whole City, had imparted a stimulus to my genius.

Much did I write, but what I considered faulty, I myself committed to the all-correcting flames. At the time, too, when I was banished, I burnt some things that would have afforded amusement, being enraged both with my pursuits and with my verses.

My heart was tender, and not proof against the darts of Cupid, and a slight cause could *easily* affect it. And yet, though this was my nature, and I caught fire with the slightest flame, there never was any *scandalous* story *attached* to my name. While yet but almost a boy, a wife was given me, neither worthy of me, nor good for anything; she was married to me but a very short time.[27] A wife succeeded her, who, though without any fault, was not destined long to be united to me. My last, who remained with me up to my later years, has endured to be the wife of a banished man. My daughter, who twice bore children in her early youth, but not by the same husband, made me a grandfather.

And now my father had completed his allotted time, and to nine "lustra" had added nine other "lustra."[28] I bewailed him in no other degree than he would have bewailed me, if carried off. I performed the prescribed funereal rites for my mother, immediately after him. Happy were they both, and timely in their burial, that they died before the day of my punishment! Fortunate, too, am I, that I am wretched when they no longer live, and that they had no misery on my account! But yet, if anything remains to the dead besides their name, and if the unsubstantial ghost survives the erected pile, if the news about me reaches you, shades of my parents, and if my offences are *taken cognizance* of in the Stygian hall of judgment; understand, I pray (and you I may not deceive), that error was the cause of my prescribed exile, and not criminality.

This is enough for the shades below. I turn to you, studious minds, who enquire into the events of my life.

ideal, originating solely in the imagination of the poet. Some have suggested that she represented the daughter; others, the granddaughter of Augustus; but without the slightest ground of probability.

[27] *A very short time.*]—Ver. 70. She may have soon died; but the probability is that he speedily divorced her; and perhaps the same was the case with his second wife.

[28] '*Lustra.*']—Ver. 78. 'A lustrum,' consisting of five years; the poet's father would consequently be ninety years old at the time of his decease.

Hoary age had now come upon me, the years of my prime having fled, and had tinted *with its hue* my hair, *now grown* ancient. And *now*, since the hour of my birth the victorious steed, crowned with the olive of Pisa,[29] had ten times carried away the prize; when the anger of the offended Prince commanded me to seek the people of Tomi, situate on the left side of the Euxine *sea*. The cause of my ruin, which is too well known to all, needs not to be pointed out by my testimony. Why should I make mention of the wickedness of my attendants, and how my servants injured me?[30] Many things did I endure, not less afflicting than my exile. My spirit disdained to succumb to misfortune, and showed itself unconquered, using its *native* energy. Forgetting, too, the arts of peace, and how my life was passed in tranquillity, I took up arms for the occasion[31] with hand unused *to them*. I endured as many dangers, both by land and sea, as there are stars between the pole that is concealed, and the one that is seen. At last, the Sarmatian shore, that is adjoining to the quivered Getæ, was touched by me, tossed about in wanderings *so* protracted. Here do I, though on every side I am stunned by the neighbouring warfare, alleviate my sad lot, so far as I am able, by my poesy. And, though there is no one to whose ear I can repeat it, yet in this way do I consume and beguile my time.

Thanks then to thee, my Muse, that I *still* live, and bear up against my heavy calamities, and that the irksomeness of a life of anxiety does not take possession of me. For it is thou that affordest me a solace, thou art a rest for my cares, a cure for my woes; thou art my leader, thou art my companion; 'tis

---

[29] *Olive of Pisa.*]—Ver. 95. The victors at the Olympic games, which were celebrated near Pisa, in Elis of the Peloponnesus, were crowned with olive.

[30] *Servants injured me.*]—Ver. 101. The attendants of his journey, here mentioned, were, probably, those deputed by Augustus to escort him to the place of his destination. According to his account, they seem to have conspired with his servants to increase his miseries on his journey to his place of exile.

[31] *Arms for the occasion.*]—Ver. 106. He seems here to allude to patience and resignation, as these were the only arms which could avail him during his voyage to his destination. If we are to translate the words literally, they would appear to imply that he considered himself in danger of his life during the voyage, and that he was forced to use weapons in self-defence, which fact, however, we do not find mentioned elsewhere in his writings.

thou, that sendest me *afar* from the Danube, and that givest me a place in the midst of Helicon. Thou hast given to me (what rarely happens) that distinguished name while yet living, which Fame is wont to give after death. Envy, who disparages what is present, has never fastened on any work of mine with her unjust tooth. For, although my age has produced great poets, Fame has not been unkind to my talents. And though I prefer many to myself, I am said to be not inferior to them; and my works are much read throughout the whole world. If, then, the prophecies of poets contain any truth, though I'should die at once, I shall not be thine, O Earth. Whether through kindly feeling, or whether, through my verses, I have gained this celebrity of my own right, candid reader, I return thee thanks.

BOOK THE FIFTH.

ELEGY I.

Ovid, sending this last book of his Lament to Rome, requests his friends to receive it in addition to the four that he has sent before. He says, that under the sad circumstances in which he is placed, he cannot possibly write on any other than melancholy topics; but that if he is restored to his native land, he will write on pleasing and lively subjects. He concludes by craving pardon, should his lines prove not to the taste of the reader.

ADD this little book too, my friend, to those that have before been sent by me from the Getic shore: this, too, will be just such as the fortunes of the poet are. You will find nothing cheerful throughout my whole song. As my state is a mournful one, so are my verses mournful, the writing befitting its master. Unharmed and joyful, I have composed playful and juvenile strains; but now I repent that I composed them. When I fell, I assumed the heralding of my sudden fall; and I myself am the originator of my own subject. Just as the bird of Caÿster[1] is said, as he lies on its banks, to lament his death with his dying voice, so do I, expelled afar into the Sarmatian regions, cause my funereal rites not to pass by in silence. If any one seeks for love tales and wanton lines, I warn him beforehand never to read these compositions. Gallus will be better suited to him, and Propertius with his pleasing language; Tibullus, *too*, a mind full of elegance, will be more adapted *to him*. Would that I was not one of that number! Ah, wretched me! why did my Muse ever become

---

[1] *The bird of Caÿster.*]—Ver. 11. Caÿster was a river of Asia, not far from Ephesus. Swans were very numerous on its banks, and they were supposed to sing melodiously just before their death.

thus sportive? But I have paid the penalty, and the trifler with quivered Cupid is now far away in the regions of the Scythian Danube. For the future, I turn my attention to verses for the public perusal, and I have commanded them to be careful of their reputation; but yet, if any one of you should ask the reason why I sing so many mournful *lines:* many a mournful woe have I endured. I compose not these lines through my inventive powers, or my skill; my matter is ingeniously furnished by my own sorrows. How small a part of my fortunes is *described* in my lines! Happy the man, who suffers *evils* that he can number! As many as the shrubs which the woods contain, as many as the grains of sand which the yellow Tiber holds, as many as the tender blades of grass which the field of Mars bears, so many evils have I endured, for which there is no cure, no repose, but in *indulging* my poetic vein, and in the solace of the Muses.

"What limit, Naso," you will say, "is there to be to your tearful ditties?" The same, *I say*, that will terminate this fate of mine; this supplies me with complaints from an abundant source; and these words are not mine, but those of my destiny. But if you were to restore to me my country, with my dear wife, then my features would be joyous, and I should be what once I was. Were the wrath of the invincible Cæsar, against me, mitigated, then should I give thee lines full of gladness; but no more should my writings be sportive, as once they were; let them indulge but once in that mischief. I would sing that which *Augustus* himself would approve; if, only a part of my punishment being alleviated, I could escape from barbarism and the savage Getæ. In the meanwhile, what employment but a mournful one can my writings have? That is the pipe that befits my funereal obsequies.

"But," you will say, "you could have better borne your evils in silence, and have quietly concealed your woes!" *In this* you are requiring that no groans should be consequent upon my torture, and are forbidding me to weep, after receiving a severe wound. Phalaris himself allowed him *who was inclosed* in the brass of Perillus to utter his shrieks, and to lament, through the mouth of the bull. Achilles was not offended by the tears of Priam; *whereas* you, more cruel than *any* enemy, forbid my tears. When the progeny of Latona made Niobe childless, they still did not command her to keep her cheeks untouched by tears.

'Tis something to alleviate a deadly evil, by giving utterance *to sorrow;* 'tis this that makes Progne and Halcyone[2] always complaining; this was the reason why *Philoctetes,* the son of Pæas, in the cold cavern, wearied the Lemnian rocks with his voice. Grief repressed chokes *one;* it agitates internally, and is compelled to redouble its intensity. Grant me pardon rather, or lay aside all my works; if, reader, that hurts you which is my delight. But they cannot hurt you: my writings were never injurious to any one but their author.

They are but poor, I confess. Who compels you to take them up; or who forbids you, when disappointed, to put them down? I do not correct them, but *I wish* them to be read as being composed here: they are not more uncouth than the place *of their origin;* and Rome ought not to form comparisons of me with her own poets. Among the Sauromatæ I shall pass for talented. Lastly, no glory is sought by me, nor that Fame which is wont to stimulate the genius. I desire my mind not to be consumed by everlasting cares, which still break in, and go where they are forbidden *to go.* I have said why I write: you ask why I send these works; *it is, that* I wish to be among you, in some measure at least.

ELEGY II.

WRITING to his wife, he says that he is well in health, but that his grief is still as intense as when he was first banished by Augustus. He expatiates upon the innumerable misfortunes which surround him on every side. He entreats her to apply to the Emperor in his behalf, as the cause for his punishment was not of a serious nature, and the clemency of Cæsar is known to be extreme; and he says, that in this spirit of mercy is centred his only hope of a mitigation of his punishment.

AND do you grow pale when a fresh letter arrives from Pontus; and is it unfolded by you with a tremulous hand? Lay aside your apprehensions: I am well, and my body, which formerly was weakly, and unable to endure fatigue, is recruited, and, tossed about, has become hardy by length of habit. Or is it

---

[2] *Halcyone.*]—Ver. 60. She was the daughter of Æolus and Ægiale, and the wife of Ceyx, on hearing of whose death, she threw herself into the sea. The Gods, in their compassion, changed them both into kingfishers.

rather that I have no leisure to be ill? Yet my spirit is prostrated by weakness, and has acquired no strength by lapse of time; and the condition of my mind remains the same as it was before. The wounds, which I supposed would close in length of time, and at their proper season, pain me as though this moment inflicted; in truth, length of years is good for little mishaps, *but* in lapse of time, evils are added to heavy calamities. For almost ten whole years did the son of Pæas endure the pestilential venom yielded by the puffing serpent. Telephus would have died, consumed with lasting disease, if the hand that did the injury had not brought the remedy. I hope, since I have committed no crime, that he who has caused my wounds will be ready to assuage them thus made; and now at length, satisfied with a part of my penalty, may he take a little drop of water from the full ocean. However much he may take off, much of what is bitter will remain; and a part of my banishment will, *in its intensity*, be equal to the whole. As many as the shells which the sea shore contains, as many as the flowers which the pleasant rose-beds bear, as many as the grains which the drowsy poppy holds, as many as the wild beasts which the wood nourishes, as many as the fishes that swim in the waves, as many as the birds that beat the thin atmosphere with their wings, by so many adversities am I overwhelmed. Should I endeavour to enumerate them, I might *as well* attempt to tell the number of the waves of the Icarian Sea. To pass over in silence the casualties of my journey, the bitter dangers of the ocean, and the hands that were arrayed against my life: a barbarous country, one the most distant in the great earth, *now* confines me, a place beset with savage enemies *on every side*.

Hence I should be transferred (for my crime is not a capital one), if you had the care for me which you ought to have. That God, on whom the Roman empire justly relies, when a conqueror, was often merciful towards his enemy. Why do you hesitate? Why fear, when there is no danger? go and ask *him*. The vast earth contains nothing more full of clemency than Cæsar.

Ah, wretched me! What shall I do if those dearest to me forsake me? Do you, too, withdraw your neck from the yoke *now* broken? No anchor now holds my bark. He may look to it: I myself, hated as I am, will fly for refuge to the sacred altar: the altar removes the hands of none. Behold! at a distance I address the Deity that is present; if it is allowed man to be able to commune with Jove.

Thou ruler of the empire, in whose safety it is evident that all the Gods have a care for Ausonia. Thou Glory, thou resemblance of the country that flourishes through thee, O thou that art not less *in value* than the world that thou dost govern; mayst thou live on earth, may the heavens long spare thy presence there! far distant be the time for thee to go to the stars, which have been promised thee! Pardon me, I pray, and remove but the least portion of thy lightnings: what shall *then* remain will be a sufficient punishment. Thy anger, indeed, has been moderated, and thou hast granted *me* my life: I am neither deprived of the rights nor the name of a citizen. My property has not been granted to others; nor am I styled an exile in the words of thy edict. All these things I dreaded, because I seemed to deserve them; but thy anger was more moderate than my offence. Thou hast ordered me to go in banishment to the fields of Pontus, and to cleave the Scythian seas in the fleeing ship. By thy command, I came to the unsightly shores of the Euxine Sea. This land is situated under the icy pole. Not so much does the climate annoy me, never free from cold, and the ground ever parched up with hoar frost; and the barbarous tongue that is ignorant of the Latin language, and *the fact* that the Greek dialect has been overpowered by the Getic pronunciation; as, that I am hemmed in, beset on every side by the neighbouring hosts; and a narrow wall scarcely renders me safe from the enemy. Yet there is peace sometimes, *but* never any confidence in that peace; *and* so the place is at one time experiencing war, at another, it is standing in dread of it.

So that I be only removed hence, let either Zanclæan Charybdis devour me, and by its waters send me to Styx, or let me patiently be consumed in the flames of glowing Ætna; or let me be thrown in the deep waters of the Leucadian God. What is required, is punishment, and I refuse not to be wretched; but I entreat that I may be wretched with a little more safety *to myself*.

ELEGY III.

He laments that he cannot be at Rome to assist at the celebration of the festival of Bacchus by the poets, as had been his former custom. He expresses surprise that Bacchus should have thus neglected one of his devotees, and concludes by praying him, and his companions the poets, to entreat Cæsar to permit his return.

This is the day, Bacchus, on which the poets are wont to celebrate thee, if I am not deceived in the time; and *now* they bind their temples with the fragrant wreaths, and sing thy praises over thy wine. Among them, as I remember, while my destiny permitted it, I was one by no means hated by thee. The Sarmatian region, neighbouring to the ferocious Getæ, now confines me, placed beneath the stars of the Cynosurian Bear. I, who in former days passed a life of ease, and freedom from labour, amid my *poetic* studies, and in the company of the Muses, am now, far from my country, surrounded on every side by the Getic arms, having first endured many fatigues on the sea, many by land: whether 'twas chance, or whether the anger of the Gods, that caused me this, or whether my destiny was lowering at my birth; still thou oughtst, by thy divine power, to have defended one of the sacred cultivators of the ivy. Is it, that everything which the Sisters, the mistresses of Fate, have pronounced, ceases to be under the influence of a Deity? Thou thyself, too, for thy deserts, hast been carried to the heights of heaven, a way to which was made by no small exertion. Thy native land was not inhabited by thee; but thou didst come even as far as the snowy Strymon,[3] and the Getan devoted to Mars; to Persia, too, and the Ganges spreading with its broad stream, and the waters which the swarthy Indian drinks. In truth, the Destinies, spinning the threads of Fate, twice pronounced this doom for thee, twice born.[4] If I am allowed to follow the example of the Gods, a rigid and a hard lot in life harasses me too. Not less heavily did I fall, than he whom Jupiter drove with his bolt from Thebes, while

---

[3] *The snowy Strymon.*]—Ver. 22. The Strymon was a river which, taking its rise in Mount Hæmus, separated Thrace from Macedonia.

[4] *Thee twice born.*]—Ver. 26. Because he was first taken from the womb of Semele, and, being enclosed in the thigh of Jupiter, was produced from it, when he had arrived at the completion of the usual period of gestation.

boasting aloud. But thou, when thou hast heard of the poet struck by the lightnings, mayst condole with him from the recollection of thy mother. And thou mayst, when looking upon the poets *assembled* around thy sacrifice, say, "I know not which worshipper of mine it is that is absent."

Give me thy aid, good Bacchus; let the vine weigh down the lofty elm, and let the grape be full of the wine inclosed in it. Let the active youthful troop of the Satyrs, with the Bacchanals, accompany thee, and be not thou silent amid the stunning noise. And may the bones of Lycurgus wielding the axe be but lightly covered, and may the impious shade of Pentheus not escape punishment. May the Cretan crown of thy spouse shine for ever in the heavens, and surpass *in radiance* the neighbouring Constellations.

Come hither, most beauteous *God*, and alleviate my woes, remembering that I am one of thy number. There exists an intercourse among the Gods: do try, Bacchus, to soften the divine power of Cæsar by thy divine influence.

You too, *ye* poets, a holy band, sharers in my pursuits; do ye, each of you, after making a libation of wine, prefer a like petition. And may some one of you, when the name of Naso is mentioned, set down the cup that has been mingled with his tears: and remembering me, when he looks round upon the rest, may he say, "Where is Naso, *who was* but lately a member of our society?" And thus *be it;* if by my uprightness I have deserved your esteem; and if not a line *of your works* was ever injured by my criticism. If, *too*, at the same time that I pay due veneration to the writings of the men of old, I am of opinion that the recent *compositions* are not inferior to them. Then, may you *continue to* compose your verses under the auspices of Apollo; *and*, so far as you can, keep up my name among you.

ELEGY IV.

He represents his letter as announcing its arrival at Rome, and extolling the constancy of his friend, to whom it was sent. He entreats him always to continue his friendship and support.

I, A LETTER from Naso, have come from the Euxine *Sea*, wearied with the ocean, wearied too with my journey. He, with tears, said to me, "Do you, to whom it is permitted, visit Rome; how much preferable, alas! is your fate to my own!" In tears, too, did he write me; and the signet with which I was sealed was not first put to his mouth,[5] but to his moistened cheeks. If any one desires to know the cause of his sorrow, he is requiring the Sun to be pointed out to him. He neither sees leaves in the woods, nor the tender grass on the wide meadow, nor water in the flowing stream. He will wonder why Priam grieved, when Hector was snatched *from him;* or why Philoctetes wept, when stung by the serpent. Oh! that the Gods would grant that *my master's* state were such that no cause for grief were to be lamented. Yet, as he ought *to do*, he bears his bitter sorrows with patience, and refuses not the bridle like an unbroken horse. Nor yet does he expect that the wrath of the Deity will be lasting, as he is conscious that criminality was no part of his fault. He often mentions how great is the clemency of the God; and is wont to reckon himself as an illustration of it. For he says that it is through the favour of that God that he still possesses his patrimonial property, and the name of a citizen, and, in fine, that he still lives.

But thee, O friend beloved more than all, if thou believest me, he always retains in his entire heart. He calls thee his son of Menætius, thee his companion of Orestes, thee his son of Ægeus, thee his own Euryalus. He longs not more for his own country, and the many other things of which, with his country, he finds himself deprived, than *for a sight of* thy features, and thy eyes, thou, *that art* 'sweeter to him than the honey which the Attic bee lays up in the combs!

Many a time with tears, does he remember that day, which he grieves was not anticipated by his death. And while others fled the contact of his sudden downfall, and were unwilling to approach the threshold of a stricken house; he bears in mind that thou, with a few more (if any one calls two or three a few), remained faithful to him. Although struck with amazement, he was sensible of every thing, *and saw* that thou didst grieve at his sorrows not less than himself. He is wont to recall *to memory* thy words, thy features, thy lamentations, and how that with thy tears thou didst bedew his bosom; *he remembers* the aid that thou didst give him, the comfort with which thou didst console thy friend, when thou thyself shouldst

---

[5] *To his mouth.*]—Ver. 5. By this remark we see that in those days, as with us now, they were in the habit of moistening the seal before they applied it to the wax.

have been consoled. For these things he declares that he will prove grateful and affectionate, whether he beholds the *light of* day, or is buried in the ground. By his own head, and by thine, was he wont to swear: *thine* which, I know, is not less dear to him than his own. May abundance of thanks be given in return for services so many and so great; he will not allow thy oxen to plough the *barren* sea-shore.[6] Only, do constantly defend the exile. What he, who knows thee well, asks not, *that* do I myself entreat *thee*.

ELEGY V.

He prepares to celebrate the birthday of his wife, on whose behalf he prays for every blessing, and extols the day that brought into the world one so deserving of admiration for every virtue. And, though she deserves a better fate, he entreats her to endure her sufferings with equanimity, as virtue becomes the most conspicuous when suffering adversity. He entreats the Gods, that, if they refuse to pardon him, they will spare his wife, who has been guilty of no crime.

The yearly birthday demands the wonted honour for its mistress: turn, my hands, to the rites of affection. Thus, perhaps, in former days, the hero, son of Laërtes, celebrated the festive day of his wife at the extremity of the earth. Let an auspicious tongue be used, forgetting my protracted woes: it, I doubt, has quite forgotten by this, how to utter words of happiness. Let, too, the white dress be assumed, (not according in its hue with my lot,) which is put on by me *but* once a year. Let the altar, too, be erected, green with the grassy turf; and let the wreath, bound *to it*, veil the warm hearth. Boy, give me the frankincense, that makes the strong flame, and wine to hiss when poured on the flame *lighted* by affection. Dearest natal day! Although we are far distant, I wish thee to come hither in white array, and unlike to mine. And if any direful calamity impended on thy mistress, let her have suffered it for all *future* time in my misfortunes. And let the bark, which has lately been more than shattered by a dreadful storm, for the future, speed onward through the sea in safety.

---

[6] *Barren sea-shore.*]—Ver. 48. By this remark he means that he will not show himself devoid of gratitude, and of a desire to make a due return for his kindness.

May she enjoy her home, *the society of* her daughter, and her country; let it suffice for her to be torn from me only. And since she is not blessed in her beloved husband, let the other portion of her life be without a cloud of sorrow. May she live, and may she love her husband far away, since this she is obliged to do; and may she fill her destined years, but after a prolonged life. I would add mine as well; but I am afraid, lest the contact of my destiny should taint the years that she is passing.

There is nothing sure to mortals. Who could have supposed that it would come to pass, that I should be celebrating these rites in the midst of the Getæ? But see how the breeze wafts the smoke, arising from the frankincense, towards the regions of Italy, and the lands on my right hand. There is sense, then, in the clouds which the fire raises; almost every thing else refuses *to second* my purpose. Designedly, when the common rites were being performed on the altar, for the brothers who perished by each other's hand, did the black ashes, at variance, divide themselves into two parts, as though at their command. This I remember, I was wont formerly to say, could not happen; and, in my opinion, the son of Battus spoke not the truth. Now, I believe it all: when thou, conscious smoke, fliest from the North, and takest the direction of Ausonia. This, then, is the day; and had this not risen, no festival would there have been to be seen by me. This *day* gave birth to virtues equal to *those of* the heroines, of whom Eëtion and Icarius[7] were the fathers. *Then* was chastity, morality, honesty, and fidelity brought forth: but on this day joyousness was not produced: but toil, and care, and a destiny unsuited to her virtues, and just complaints of a union almost widowed.

In truth, probity, harassed by adversity, furnishes a subject for praise in its day of sorrow. Had the hardy Ulysses seen nothing of adversity, Penelope would have been happy, but unknown to fame. If the hero *Capaneus* had victoriously penetrated to the citadel of Echion,[8] perhaps her

[7] *Eëtion and Icarius.*]—Ver. 44. Eëtion was the father of Andromache, the wife of Hector; and Icarius was the father of Penelope, the wife of Ulysses; both of them, women celebrated for their virtues.

[8] *Citadel of Echion.*]—Ver. 53. This was Thebes, in Bœotia. Echion assisted Cadmus in building it. Capaneus was struck with lightning, when uttering threats against the city.

own land would scarcely have known of Evadne. When so many daughters of Pelias were born, why is *but* one famous? It is because she only was married to an unfortunate husband. Make it so that another should be the first to touch the Trojan sands; there would then be nothing for Laodamia to be mentioned for. And your affection would have remained unknown, as I should have preferred, if favouring breezes had filled my sails.

And yet, O ye Gods, and thou, Cæsar, to be added to the number of the Gods, but at a far distant period, when thy life has equalled in number the Pylian days *of Nestor;* spare, not me, who confess that I have deserved punishment, but her, who sorrows when she is deserving of no sadness.

ELEGY VI.

He complains that he is deserted by his friend; and entreats him to maintain that friendly feeling which had formerly existed between them.

And dost thou, too, once the safeguard of my fortunes, who wast my refuge and my haven, dost thou even throw aside the cause of thy acknowledged friend; dost thou so soon dismiss the affectionate obligations of duty? I am a burden, I confess; but if thou wast about to lay that *burden* down in adversity, it should not have been taken up *by thee.* Dost thou desert the ship, Palinurus, in the midst of the waves? Fly not, and let not thy confidence be less than thy skill. Did the inconstancy of the faithful Automedon desert the steeds of Achilles during the fierce battle? Did not Podalirius[9] afford the promised aid of the medical art to the invalid whom he had once received? The stranger is turned out with more disgrace *to the host,* than *is the case if he* is not *first* received. Let the altar which has been afforded me, stand firm for my right hand.

At first, thou didst defend nothing but myself alone; do thou now defend both me and the opinion thou hadst formed of me; if only there is no new fault in me, and if my *alleged* crimes have not suddenly wrought a change in thy confidence. May this breath, which I draw with difficulty in the Scythian air, first leave my limbs (as I wish it

---

[9] *Podalirius.*]—Ver. 11. He was a son of Æsculapius, and with his whether Machaon, accompanied the Grecian army to the Trojan war, brore they acquired great celebrity by their skill in the healing art.

may) before thy heart be wounded by any fault of mine, and before I deservedly appear worthless to thee. I am not so entirely crushed by my adverse destiny, that my mind, as well, is affected by my prolonged misfortunes. Imagine it affected, however: how often, dost thou suppose, that the son of Agamemnon uttered harsh words against Pylades? and it is not very unlikely that he may have even struck his friend; yet not a whit the less did he remain firm in his dutiful attentions. This is the only thing in common with the wretched and the happy, that devotedness is wont to be shown towards them both. Room is made both for the blind, and for those whom the prætextal robe[10] and the rod of command, together with their orders, causes to be dreaded. If thou dost not consider me, yet thou oughtst to be considerate to my lot; anger has no grounds *for its existence*, in my case. Choose the least, *yes*, the very least, of my afflictions; it will be *far* greater than what thou dost imagine it to be. As many as the reeds with which the wet ditches are filled, as many as the bees which the flowery Hybla holds, as many as the ants which are wont to carry the grains which they have found, by the narrow path to their subterranean granaries, so numerous do the multitudes of my countless evils throng around me. Believe me, my complaints come short of the truth. He who is not contented with these, would pour sand on the sea shore, ears of corn amid the standing crop, and water in the waves. Restrain, then, thy unreasonable fears, and do not forsake my sails, in the midst of the ocean.

ELEGY VII.

Ovid tells his friend, who inquires what he is doing in Scythia, that he lives a life of misery. He describes the manners of the inhabitants of Tomi, and says that he beguiles his griefs by writing poetry, and that, amid his compositions alone, he is able to forget his misfortunes.

THE letter which thou readest, comes to thee from that land, where the wide Danube is added to the waters of the ocean.

[10] *The prætextal robe.*]—Ver. 31. The 'toga prætexta' had a broad purple border. It was worn by the Consuls and other magistrates, not only of Rome, but of the colonies, and the 'municipia,' and by the priests and other persons when engaged in celebrating sacred rites. The 'rod of

If life, with pleasing health, is thy lot, one part of my destiny is still propitious.

Doubtless, my dearest friend, as thou alwayst dost, thou inquirest what I am doing? although thou mightst know that, even if I were silent upon it. I am wretched; this is the limited substance of my woes; and whoever shall live, having offended Cæsar, will be so.

Hast thou a wish to learn what is the race in the region of Tomi, and among what manners I am living?

Although this spot is divided among the Greeks and the Getæ, it follows rather the *customs of the* Getæ, who have been but half subdued. A greater multitude of the Sarmatian and of the Getic nations comes and goes along its roads on horseback. Among them there is no one who does not carry a bow-case,[11] a bow, and arrows livid with the venom of serpents. Their voice is wild, their countenance savage, the very resemblance of Mars; neither their hair nor their beard is shorn by any hand. Their right hand is not slow to give a wound with the implanted knife, which every one of these barbarians wears, fastened to his side. Thy poet, alas! my friend, lives in the midst of these, forgetful of his gentle loves; these he beholds, to these he listens. And may he live, but not die among them! And still may his ghost be far away from these baleful regions!

Thou writest, my friend, that my verses are danced to in the crowded theatre, and that applause is given to my lines. I, indeed, have done nothing for the theatres, and thou thyself knowest it, and my Muse never was ambitious of applause *on the stage*. But whatever precludes forgetfulness of me, and brings the name of me, in banishment, into the mouths *of the people*, is far from displeasing. And yet sometimes I curse my verses and my Piërian mistresses, when I recollect the injury they have done me; and, after I have cursed them to the utmost, still I cannot exist without them, and I attach myself to the arms that are stained with the blood of my wounds.

command,' 'virga imperiosa,' here mentioned, was probably the rod with which the Lictor was wont to summon people to move aside, as the Consul or other magistrate was passing.

[11] *A bow case.*]—Ver. 15. This is the usual meaning of the word 'corytos,' though, perhaps, it may here mean a case in which both the bow and arrows were kept, which was frequently used by the Eastern nations, and sometimes by the Greeks and Romans.

The Grecian bark, which has just been shattered by the Euboean waves, dares to cleave the waters of Caphareus. But yet I have no anxiety to be praised, and I have no care for future glory, which had, more to my comfort, better been obscured. I occupy my mind with my pursuits, and I beguile my sorrows; I try, too, thereby to deceive my cares. What should I do, in preference, alone on these solitary shores? or what occupation wouldst thou rather that I should endeavour to seek? If I look at the place, it is odious; and there cannot, in all the world, be one more wretched than it. If *I look at* the men: the men are hardly worthy of that name, and they have more savage ferocity than wolves. They regard not laws, but right yields to might, and justice, overcome, lies prostrate under the warlike sword. They poorly repel the cold, with skins and flowing trowsers; and their faces are rough, covered with long hair. Vestiges of the Greek language are remaining, in a few words: this, too, has become barbarous, through the Getic pronunciation. There is no one among this people who can by chance translate into Latin, words in general use. I, *who am* a poet of Rome (pardon me, ye Muses), am compelled to say many things in the Sarmatian language. I am ashamed, I confess it; *for* now, from long disuse, scarcely do the Latin expressions occur to me; and I have no doubt but that there are no few barbarisms in this little work. That is not the fault of the man, but of the place. But, that I may not lose *all* acquaintance with the Ausonian tongue, and my voice become dumb in its native language, I talk to myself, and I run over the unaccustomed words, and repeat the unfortunate exponents[12] of my pursuits. Thus I occupy my mind and my hours; and *thus* I take myself away, and remove myself from the contemplation of my woes. I seek in my verse forgetfulness of my miseries; if by my pursuits I obtain that reward, it is enough.

[12] *Unfortunate exponents.*]—Ver. 64. He either means words or lines; because, either through speaking without due precaution, or, at least, ostensibly through his poetical effusions, he was sentenced to banishment.

ELEGY VIII.

He recommends an enemy, who insults him, to remember the fickleness of fortune, and to cease to exult at his downfall; and he tells him, that it may possibly be his fortune to be permitted to return, and see his antagonist exiled, for some offence of greater magnitude.

Although prostrate, not so low have I fallen, that I am beneath even thee, than whom nothing can be lower. What is it that excites thy anger against me, thou wretch? Or why dost thou insult my misfortunes, which thou thyself mayst have to endure? Do not my miseries, at which *even* wild beasts might weep, render thee gentle and lenient towards me, thus lying prostrate? And dost thou stand in no fear of the divine power of Fortune, standing on the unsteady wheel,[12*] and of the Goddess that abhors boastful words? Ah! the Rhamnusian avenger[13] will exact a befitting punishment! Why dost thou crush my destiny with thy foot placed upon it? I myself have beheld a shipwreck, and men drowned in the sea; and I said, never were the waves more justly avenging. He who once denied a worthless morsel of food to the destitute, is now fed upon the bread of charity. Fleeting Fortune wanders with doubting steps, and remains in no one place for certain, and to be relied upon. At one moment, she abides *in a place* full of joy; at another, she assumes an austere countenance; and only in her *very* fickleness is she constant. My fortunes, too, have had their bloom, but that bloom was *but* fleeting, and my *brilliant* flame arose but from stubble, and was of short duration.

But that thou mayst not relish thy savage joy with all thy soul, *I tell thee*, my hope of appeasing the Divinity is not quite extinguished. Both because I committed a fault which fell short of criminality; and though my error is not unaccompanied with shame, it is not attended with hatred: and because the vast earth, from the rising of the sun to his setting, contains nothing more full of clemency, than he, to whom it pays obe-

---

[12*] *On the unsteady wheel.*]—Ver. 7. The Goddess Fortuna was represented as standing on a wheel, the attitude being indicative of her unsteadiness and inconstancy.

[13] *The Rhamnusian avenger.*]—Ver. 9. Nemesis, the Goddess of justice and retribution, was thus called, from Rhamnus, one of the boroughs of Attica, where she had a temple.

dience. Truly, as he is not to be subdued by force by any one, in the same degree he has a heart that is tender to humble entreaties. *And from him*, after the example of the Gods, to whom he is *one day* to be added, I shall obtain many other requests, with a remission of my punishment.

If thou wast to count the fine days and the cloudy ones, throughout the year, thou wouldst find that the day has oftener been bright. Therefore, that thou mayst not exult too much in my downfall, consider that even I may one day be restored *to my* country. Consider that it may happen, that, the Prince being appeased, thou in thy sadness mayst behold my features in the midst of the City, and I may behold thee exiled for a more weighty reason. This is my next prayer after my former one.[14]

ELEGY IX.

He praises the constancy of his friend, and says, that it is through his beneficence that he exists, and he expresses his gratitude for it. He says that he would willingly make public his extreme kindness, if he would allow his name to be mentioned in his writings.

Oh! if thou wouldst but permit thy name to be placed in my verse, how often wouldst thou be inserted there! Remembering thy deserts, I would sing of thee alone; and in my books not a page should swell without thee. It should be known throughout all the City, how much I am indebted to thee: if indeed, an exile, my works are read in the City *now* lost to me. The present age should know of this kindness, a future age *should know it;* if only my writings shall reach an age of antiquity. The learned reader should not fail to extol thee: this honour should await thee, for being the preserver of the poet. The chief gift is that of Cæsar, that I breathe the air; next after the great God, thanks must be given to thee. 'Twas he that granted me life; of that which he granted, thou art the protector; and thou causest me to be able to enjoy the gif which I have received *from him.*

While the greater part of my acquaintances were dismayed

---

[14] *After my former one.*]—Ver. 38. His first prayer is, that he may return to his country: his next wish is, that exile for a graver offence may be the lot of his enemy.

at my calamities, and some, too, wished to be thought to be horrified, and from a lofty hill looked down upon my shipwreck, and yet extended no hand *to me*, as I swam through the surging waters ; thou wast the only one to recall me, half dead, from the Stygian waves. This, too, is thine, that I have the power to be grateful. May the Gods, together with Cæsar, ever shew themselves friendly to thee : my prayers cannot extend further.

My care, if thou wouldst permit, would insert these things in my ingenious books, to be seen in the broad light *of day*. Even now, my Muse, although she has been bid to keep silence, scarcely restrains herself from naming thee, *thus* unwilling. And as the strong leash with difficulty withholds the struggling hound, when he has found the traces of the deer; and just as the high-mettled steed, now with his foot, now with his forehead, beats at the doors of the starting-place, not yet opened,[15] so does my Muse, bound and restrained by the injunction imposed *on her*, desire to recount the praises of this name, forbidden *to be uttered*. But that thou mayst not receive injury from the affection of a grateful friend, cease to fear, I will obey thy commands. But *yet* I would not obey, didst thou not believe that I keep in memory *thy kindness*. I will be grateful, a thing which thy words do not forbid. And while I shall look on the light of the sun, (a short time may it be !) this spirit will be devoted to thy service.

ELEGY X.

THE Poet says, that the three years which he has passed in Pontus, have appeared to him to be ten, from the wretched nature of the place, which he then proceeds to describe.

SINCE I have been in Pontus, thrice has the Ister frozen and thrice has the wave of the Euxine sea become hardened. But, to myself, I seem now to have been absent from my country as many years as Dardanian Troy was exposed to the Grecian foe. The time passes so slowly, you would think it to be

---

[15] *Not yet opened.*]—Ver. 29. The 'carceres' were vaults at the end of the race-course, closed by gates of open wood-work, which, on the signal being given, were simultaneously opened by the aid of men and ropes, and the chariots came forth, ready for starting. The number of 'carceres' on a course are supposed to have varied from eight to twelve.

standing still; and with *but* slow steps the year performs its course. The *summer* solstice diminishes not my nights, and midwinter does not make my days shorter. In good truth, the nature of things, in my case, has become *quite* altered, and renders every thing protracted along with my woes. Do the usual periods *really* perform their wonted courses, and is it rather that *this* period of my life is unendurable? *Me,* whom the shores confine, false in their name of Euxine, and the land of the Scythian, near the Scythian seas, truly sinister *in name and in character.*

Innumerable tribes around are threatening cruel warfare; *tribes* which deem it a disgrace not to live by rapine. Outside, nothing is safe; the hill is but poorly defended by small fortifications, and the resources of the place. When you would least expect it, the enemy, in a dense mass, like birds, is flying down upon you, and, before he is well seen, is driving off his prey. Often do we pick up in the midst of the streets their dangerous arrows, that have come within the fortifications, when the gates have been shut. There are few, therefore, that dare to live out in the country; and they, wretched people, plough with one hand, and hold their arms with the other. Covered with a helmet, the shepherd plays on his oaten pipe, joined with pitch; and, instead of the wolf, the timid sheep are in dread of war. By the aid of the citadel, we are hardly defended; and even within, a multitude of the barbarians, mixed with the Greeks, causes apprehension. *It is,* because the barbarians live together with us, no distinction *being made;* and they occupy the greater portion of the houses. Even if you did not fear them, you would be disgusted, on seeing their foreheads covered with skins and long hair. Even those, who are supposed to derive their origin from the Grecian city, the Persian trowsers cover, instead of the dress of their country. They enjoy the intercourse of a common language; by gestures, anything must be signified to me. Here it is I who am the barbarian, because by no one am I understood; the stupid Getæ laugh at Latin words. Many a time, before my face, do they speak ill of me in safety, and perhaps are reproaching me with my banishment; and as often as by signs I assent or dissent when they are speaking, just as it happens, they *always* suppose something to my disadvantage.[16] Besides, iniquitous retaliation is dealt with

[16] *To my disadvantage.*]—Ver. 42. He seems to imply, that whether

the cruel sword, and wounds are often inflicted in the middle of the court of justice. Oh, cruel Lachesis, who hast not given a shorter thread of life to one who has a star so disastrous.

I lament, my friends, both that I am deprived of the light of my country and of yourselves, and that I am *here*, in the Scythian land. Either is a heavy punishment: yet I deserved to be expelled from the City; *though*, perhaps, I did not deserve to be in such a place. Ah! what, in my madness, am I saying? I deserved to lose even my life, when I offended the majesty of Cæsar.

ELEGY XI.

He laments that his wife has been reproached and insulted, as being the wife of an exile. He exhorts her to endure her misfortunes with patience; and says, that Augustus did not pronounce him an exile, but only ordered his withdrawal from his native country.

YOUR letter made the complaint that some fellow reproachfully called you the wife of an exile. I was grieved at it; not so much because my fate received blame, as I have now accustomed myself to bear my misery with fortitude; as because I am a source of disgrace to one to whom I would far from wish to be so, and because I think that you have felt ashamed at my misfortunes. Bear up and endure it; you endured a much greater misfortune, when the anger of the Prince snatched me away from you.

Yet he is deceived, in whose allegations I am called an exile. A milder punishment was the consequence of my fault. My greatest punishment is, that I gave offence to *the Prince* himself: and I would prefer that the hour of my death had come before that. Yet my ship was shattered, not wrecked or sunk; and although she is not in harbour, yet she still keeps above *water*. He has not deprived me of life or property, or the rights of a citizen; all which I deserved to lose, through my fault. But, because crime was not added to that error *of mine*, he gave no order, but that I should leave the home of my fathers. And as it is to others, whose numbers cannot be counted, so was the might of Cæsar lenient towards me. He himself, in my case, uses the title of "one removed," not of "an exile;" my case is established by *the words of* its own judge.

he assents or dissents, they are always suspicious of his motives, and are determined never to put a just and fair construction on his words.

With justice, then, do my verses, Cæsar, such as they are, celebrate thy praises, with all my energies. Justly do I entreat the Gods still to keep the threshold of heaven closed against thee, and to desire thee to be a God, *but* not in their company.[17] The public desires the same thing; but just as the rivers, so the stream of the little brook is wont to run into the vast ocean.

And do thou, by whose lips I am styled an exile, cease to aggravate my lot, by the imposition of a false name.

ELEGY XII.

THE Poet answers a friend, that had exhorted him to compose a fresh work, and he gives his reasons for not doing so. He confesses that he cannot restrain himself from composing something at times, but he says that he makes it a practice to burn his compositions.

THOU writest, that I ought to while away my wretched hours in study, that my talents may not decay in disgraceful sloth. What thou advisest, my friend, is a difficult matter, because versifying is a cheerful occupation, and requires to have the mind at ease. My fortunes are buffeted by adverse storms; and no lot can be more sad than my own. Thou art requiring that Priam should be merry on the death of his children, and that the bereft Niobe should lead the festive dance. Whether does it appear that I ought to be engaged in weeping or in study, *thus* ordered to go in solitude among the most distant Getæ? Even if thou shouldst give me a breast supported by stout courage, such as Fame says there was in him accused by Anytus;[18] *even then*, would wisdom lie prostrate, crushed under the weight of so great a downfall. The anger of a God is too strong for human endurance. The old man that was called wise by Apollo, would have been able to write no works under such a calamity. Although forgetfulness of my country should come *on me*, forgetfulness of yourselves should come, although every recollection of my offence should be able to depart; still

---

[17] *Not in their company.*]—Ver. 26. That is to say, may they leave you on earth, to enjoy your honours as a God, and not receive you in the skies till a period far distant hence.

[18] *Anytus.*]—Ver. 12. Anytus, Melitus, and Lycon, were the accusers of Socrates, the greatest of the ancient philosophers. By the oracle of Apollo, he was pronounced to be the wisest of men.

does very fear forbid me to perform a duty that needs tranquillity. A place confines me, girt around by foes innumerable. Besides, my invention is grown dull, injured by long-continued rust; and it is far smaller than it once was. The fertile field, if it is not renewed by the constant plough, will contain nothing but grass and thorns. *The steed*, which has been long standing *in the stable*, will run badly, and will be the last among the horses issuing from the starting-place. If any bark has been for a long time out of the accustomed water, it becomes changed to crumbling rottenness, and gapes wide with leaks. I despair that I, too, humble though I was even before, can become equal to what I formerly was. The lengthened endurance of fatigues has crushed my powers, and a large portion of my former vigour is lost. Yet many a time, as now, has the writing-tablet been taken up by me; and I have essayed to arrange the words in their *proper* feet: either no verses have been composed by me, or such as thou seeest; worthy of the circumstances of their master, worthy of the locality.

Lastly, fame gives no little energy to the mind, and the love of praise renders the genius prolific. Formerly, I was attracted by the splendour of praise and celebrity, while *yet* a favouring breeze bore on my sail yards. Things go not now so well with me, for glory to be a care to me; if it be allowed me, I wish to be known to no one.

Dost thou persuade me to write, that because my verses have before turned out so well,[19] I should follow up my successes? With your leave, may I be allowed to say it, ye Nine Sisters, you are the principal cause of my banishment; and as the designer of the brazen bull paid the just penalty, so do I myself pay the penalty of my own pursuits.

Nothing more ought I to have to do with verses; but, when shipwrecked, I ought, by rights, to avoid all parts of the ocean. But, no doubt, if, in my madness, I should try again my fatal pursuits, this place will afford[20] me opportunities for *making* my verses. Here, there are no books, no person to give me his attention, or to know what is the meaning of my words. Every spot is full of barbarism and of a savage jargon; all

---

[19] *Turned out so well.*]—Ver. 43. He says this ironically, implying that his poetical pursuits had turned out anything but to his advantage.

[20] *This place will afford.*]—Ver. 52. This is also said ironically, as in the next line he says that there is nothing there to encourage him to continue his poetical labours.

things are filled with the misery of the Getic babble. I seem to myself by this to have forgot my Latin; I have now learned to speak the Getic and the Sarmatian languages.

Nor yet, to confess the truth to thee, can my Muse be restrained from composing poetry. I write, and I burn my books when they are written: a little ashes are the result of my labour. I cannot, and I do not wish to compose any more verses; for that reason, are my labours thrown in the fire. No produce of my invention has come among you, unless snatched from the flames by chance, or by stealth. And so do I wish that my Art *of Love* had been turned to ashes, which ruined its master, when he apprehended no such *a calamity*.

ELEGY XIII.

He exhorts his friend, as he has given him many proofs of his affection, not to deny him the pleasure of his letters. He says, that if he will only comply with this request, he will leave nothing that can possibly be demanded of his friendship.

HEALTH does thy Naso send thee from the Getic *shore*, if any one can send the thing which he himself is in want of. For I, in ill health, have contracted an infection from my mind in my body, that no part of me may be free and undisturbed by pain. For many days I have been tormented with pains in my side, which, *as well*, the winter injured with its immoderate cold. But yet, if thou art well, *then*, in some degree, I am well: because it was by thy shoulders that my downfall was upheld.

Since thou hast afforded me *these* large pledges of affection, and since, through all vicissitudes, thou defendest this person *of mine;* thou dost wrong, in that thy letters console me but so seldom: and thou performest the duties of affection, I own, unless thou refusest me thy correspondence. Correct this, I pray; shouldst thou correct this only, there will be no blemish in thy faultless person. I would accuse thee more at length; might it not happen, perchance, that the letter did not reach me, and yet that it might have been sent. May the Gods grant, that my complaint is groundless, and that I wrongly supposed that thou didst not remember me. It is clear that that is the fact, which I pray: for it is not possible for me to believe that the strength of thy mind is liable to change. Let the white wormwood first be wanting in the freezing Pontus, and let Trinacrian Hybla[21] be without its sweet thyme, before any one can prove that thou art forgetful of thy friend. The threads of my destiny are not so black *as that*.

But do thou, that thou mayst also be enabled to repel the charge of a fault wrongfully alleged, take care lest thou appear to be what thou art not. And as we were wont to spend much of our time in conversation, the day not sufficing for our discourse ; so let our letters carry to and fro our silent words ; and let the paper perform the duty of our tongues.

And that I may not appear too distrustful that this shall come to pass, and that it may suffice to have put thee in mind in a few lines, receive that word with which a letter ever closes, and *a wish* that thy lot may be different from mine. Farewell.

ELEGY XIV.

He promises his wife immortality in his writings, and tells her that there are many who, though they may deem her wretched, will still consider her fortunate, and envy her lot. He exhorts her to remain constant to him, and to give no room for aspersions on her fidelity. He shows, by citing examples, that constancy of wives to their husbands has been considered a marked theme for praise in all ages, and among all nations.

O wife, dearer to me than myself, you yourself behold what lasting fame my books have conferred on you. Fortune will be at liberty to detract much from the author, but by my talents you will become illustrious. So long as my works shall be read, together will your praises be read : and you cannot entirely cease to exist at the mournful pile. And though you may appear deserving of compassion, on account of the downfall of your husband, some you will find, to wish to be what you are ; to call you happy, and to envy you, although you share my miseries. In giving you riches, I could not have given you more ; the ghost of the rich man will take nothing

---

[21] *Trinacrian Hybla.*]—Ver. 22. Hybla was a mountain of Trinacria, or Sicily. It was famous for its bees, whose honey was rendered of the finest quality by the wild thyme with which its sides were covered.

to the shades below. I have presented you with the gift of a lasting name, and you have that, than which I could have presented you with nothing greater.

Besides, as you are the sole guardian of my property, to you falls no slight amount of honour. Inasmuch as my voice is never silent about you, you ought to be proud, too, of the *good* opinion of your husband.

Be it your care, that no one may say that it is rashly pronounced: and regard both me and your own constant fidelity. For your merit, while I was fortunate, remained without any evil charge, and, unblamed, received the praises of all; it has not been unequal to itself in this my term of calamity. Here may your virtues erect a glorious fabric.

'Tis easy to be virtuous, when that which may forbid virtue, is afar off; and when a wife has nothing to obstruct her in *the path of* duty. When the God has sent his thunders, not to hide one's self from the storm, that is affection, that is conjugal love. Rare, indeed, is that virtue, which Fortune does not influence; which stands with a firm foot, when she flies. But if any virtue was *ever* the reward of its own deserts[22] sought by it, and showed itself erect in disastrous circumstances; though you should reckon the occasions, yet it is forgotten in no lapse of ages, and all places admire it, wherever the surface of the earth extends.

Do you observe how the fidelity of Penelope has remained, a subject of praise, an immortal name for lengthened ages? Do you see how the wives of Admetus, and of Hector, are celebrated in song, and how the daughter of Iphis[23] dared to ascend the lighted pile? How, too, the wife, she of Phylax,[24] lives in fame, whose husband with active foot trod on

[22] *Reward of its own merits.*]—Ver. 31, 32. This seems to approximate, probably, to the sense intended to be conveyed by these lines; but the reading is so corrupt and confused, that it can hardly be said for certain, whether he is speaking of a virtue, or of a woman, or what he really intends to say.

[23] *Daughter of Iphis.*]—Ver. 38. This was Evadne, the wife of Capaneus, who, in her excess of grief, threw herself on the funeral pile of her husband.

[24] *She of Phylax.*]—Ver. 39. Laodamia, the wife of Protesilaüs, is here alluded to. Phylax was a town of Phthiotis, in Thessaly, of which Protesilaüs was the king. Phylax was also the name of the father of Iphiclus, who was the father of Protesilaüs. Laodamia refused to live any longer, on hearing of the death of her husband, who was killed immediately on his landing on the Trojan shore.

the Trojan soil. I require not Death, but love and constancy. Fame is not to be sought by you by an arduous path. But do not suppose that I recommend these things to your notice, because you do them not; I hoist my sails, although the ship speeds on with its oars. He who exhorts you to do, what you are already doing, praises you by his exhortations, and by his advice shows his approval of your actions.

END OF THE TRISTIA.

THE PONTIC EPISTLES OF OVID.

BOOK THE FIRST.

EPISTLE I.—TO BRUTUS.

He entreats his friend Brutus to give his books a kind reception, especially as his works share his disgrace; and he then states what forms the subject of his Pontic Epistles.

NASO, now *become* an old inhabitant of the region of Tomi, sends thee this work from the Getic shores. If thou hast leisure, Brutus, receive with hospitality these little books, coming from afar, and put them in any place thou mayst please, so that it be some place. They dare not approach the public buildings, lest their author should have *already* closed the path against them in that direction. Ah! how often have I said, "assuredly ye teach no bad precepts; go on your way; that spot is open for verses that are pure." And yet they go not; but, as thou seeest, they think it safer to lie concealed, in a private abode. Dost thou enquire where thou mayst place them, no one being offended? That spot is vacant for thee, where the Arts *of Love* used to stand. Perhaps thou mayst ask, on this their sudden arrival, why they have come? Receive them, whatever the reason is, so that it is not Love. Thou wilt find, although its title is not redolent of woe, that this work is not less sorrowful than the one I produced before. They are similar in subject, *but* there is a difference in the title, and *each* letter shows to whom it is sent, the name no *longer* being concealed. You, *my friends*, do not desire this, but you are not able to prevent it; and the dutiful Muse approaches those who are unwilling *to receive her*. However that is, add *these lines* to my works. There is nothing to hinder the progeny of an exile from enjoying *a life in* the City, if they observe the laws. There is no reason for fear. The writings of *even* Antonius are read, and the learned Brutus[1] publicly occupies the book-case. I am not so insane as to compare myself with names so great; but yet I never bore blood-stained arms against the Deities. In fine, not one of my books fails to do honour to Cæsar, although he wishes it not. Shouldst thou hesitate as to me; admit the panegyrics of the Divinities, and receive my poem, omitting my name. The branch of the peaceful olive has its influence in warfare; will it avail *my books* nothing, to mention the *very* Founder of Peace? When the neck of Æneas was placed beneath his parent, the flame itself is said to have made a way for the hero. This book bears *the name of* the descendant of Æneas; and shall not every path be open to it? The latter, too, is the Father of his country; the former *was the father* of *Æneas* himself *only*. Who is there so rash, that he would compel him that shakes the tinkling sistrum of Pharos[2] to depart from his threshold? When the piper is playing on the crooked horn, before the Mother of the Gods, who can refuse the brass pieces of trifling coin? We know that no such thing *as this* is done by the order of Diana; yet the soothsayer has *thence* the means of making a livelihood. The heavenly influence of the Gods above acts upon our feelings; and it is no disgrace to be beguiled into such a belief. Behold! instead

---

[1] *The learned Brutus.*]—Ver. 24. Brutus, who was one of the murderers of Julius Cæsar, was a man of great genius and learning. He wrote a work 'On Virtue,' which has been praised by Cicero, Seneca, and Plutarch. He was also the author of some poems, some of which, however, according to Pliny the Younger, were of a very loose character.

[2] *Sistrum of Pharos.*]—Ver. 38. The 'sistrum' was a mystical musical instrument, used by the ancient Egyptians (whence the present epithet 'Pharia') in their ceremonies, and especially in the worship of Isis. It was shaken with the hand, and emitted a tinkling sound. Plutarch tells us that the shaking of its four cross bars was supposed to represent the agitation of the four elements, earth, air, fire, and water; and that the cat, which was usually sculptured at the end of it, represented the moon. Apuleius says that these instruments were sometimes made of silver, and even of gold. The 'sistrum' was introduced into Italy, with the worship of Isis, shortly before the Christian era. It is used in Nubia and Abyssinia at the present day. The word is sometimes used by Latin authors, to denote simply 'a child's rattle.'

of the sistrum, and the *pierced* holes of the Phrygian boxwood, I bear the sacred names of the family of Iülus. I both prophecy, and I instruct; make way for him that bears the sacred things; not for myself, but for the great God, it is asked. But do not suppose that, either because I have deserved, or have experienced the anger of the Prince, he is unwilling that he should be worshipped by me. I have beheld one who confessed that he had offended the Divinity of Isis, clothed in linen,³ sitting before the altars of Isis; another, deprived of his sight for a fault like his, was crying, in the middle of the road, that he had deserved it. The inhabitants of heaven rejoice that such public declarations are made, that they may prove by testimony how great is the extent of their power. Often do they mitigate the punishment, and restore the sight that has been taken away, when they see that *a man* has truly repented of his error. Great, oh! great is my penitence (if credence can be given to any of the wretched); and I am agonized by my fault! Though my exile afflicts me, my error afflicts me still more; and to endure punishment is less grievous than to have been deserving of it. Even should the Gods, among whom *Augustus* himself is most conspicuous, show favour to me, the punishment, *indeed*, may be removed, but the fault will last for ever. Death, assuredly, will cause me to be no *longer* an exile, when it shall have come; but death will not, as well, make me not to have committed a sin. It is not, then, to be wondered at, if my mind, wasting away, melts like the water that trickles from the snow. It is consumed, like a ship infected with the hidden wood-worm; *and* as the wave of the salt sea hollows out the rocks; as the iron, when thrown by, is corroded by the scaly rust; as the book that has been shut up is gnawed by the bite of the moth; so does my heart feel the eternal remorse of its cares, to be everlastingly affected thereby. These stings will not leave my mind sooner than my life; and he that grieves, will cease to exist, before his grief *will cease.*

If the Gods above, in whose power all things are, believe me in this, perhaps I shall be deemed worthy of a little favour; and I shall be transferred to a spot, free from the Scythian bow. Of shameless face should I be, if I prayed for more than that.

---

³ *Clothed in linen.*]—Ver. 51. Isis is thus called, as it was requisite that, in her worship, her priests and devotees should be arrayed in linen garments.

EPISTLE II.—TO MAXIMUS.

He commences by extolling the family of Fabius; and he beseeches his attention, while he is making his request. He then laments his cruel fate, and sets forth his numerous woes, his dangers from the enemy, the natives of the country, and the effect which his misfortunes have produced on his mind and body. He says that he trusts in the clemency of Cæsar for a change in the place of his exile; and he entreats Maximus to make this request alone of Augustus in his favour.

Maximus, thou who fillest the measure of a name so great,[4] and dost amplify thy descent by the nobleness of thy mind; that thou, *especially* mightst be born, although three hundred fell, yet one day did not carry off all the Fabii. Perhaps thou mayst ask, by whom this letter is sent; and thou mayst wish to be informed, who it is that is addressing thee. Ah me! what shall I do? I fear, lest, when thou shalt read my name, thou mayst read the rest, unfavourably disposed and with alienated feelings. If any one shall see this; I will dare to confess that I have written to thee, and that I have lamented over my own woes. Let him see it, I will dare to confess that I have written to thee, and to publish the extent of my transgression. *And,* though I acknowledge that I deserve a greater punishment, I can scarcely have to endure a penalty more weighty.

I live in the midst of foes, and among dangers; as though, together with my country, peace had been torn away from me: These *foes,* that they may effect a twofold cause for death in the cruel wound, dip all their darts in the venom of the viper. Provided with these, the horseman surveys the fortifications, just like a wolf prowling round the sheep in their fold. Their light bow, when once stretched with the horse-hair cord, always remains with its string unrelaxed. The houses bristle as though pallisaded with the arrows fixed there, and the gate, with its strong lock, is hardly able to keep out the warfare. Add too, the appearance of the place, gladdened with neither

---

[4] *A name so great.*]—Ver. 1. This may allude either to the other name of Maximus, which was Fabius, the cognomen of one of the most illustrious of the Roman families, and of which he was a member; or it may bear reference to the literal meaning of the name 'Maximus,' which signifies 'the greatest;' whereby the poet intends to compliment him on the possession of each virtue in the highest degree.

leaves nor trees; and *the fact*, that one sluggish winter is *ever* joined to another. Here is a fourth winter, wearing me out, as I struggle against the cold, and the arrows, and my destiny. My tears are without an end, except when senselessness has checked them; and a torpor like death takes possession of my heart. Happy was Niobe, though she beheld the deaths of so many, when, changed into stone, she lost *all* sense of her misfortunes! Happy too, were ye, whose mouths, when calling on your brother, the poplar covered[5] with its new-made bark! I am one, who can be turned into no wood; I am one, who in vain desire to become a stone. Even if Medusa herself were to come before my eyes, *yet* would even Medusa lose her power.

I live, so as never to be free from a feeling of sadness: and by length of time my punishment becomes more severe. So, the liver of Tityus, unconsumed and ever growing again, wastes not, that it may be devoured many times over.

But, I suppose,[6] when rest comes, and sleep, the universal remedy for care, the night passes, free from the usual woes. Visions *then* alarm me, that pourtray my real misfortunes, and my senses are *ever* awake to my sorrows. Either, I seem to be flying from the Sarmatian arrows, or to be placing my captive hands in the cruel fetters; or, when I am beguiled by the outline of a happier dream, I behold the lost home of my native land: and at one time, I am conversing at length with you, my friends, whom I esteemed, at another, with my dear wife. *And* thus, when a short-lived and imaginary pleasure has been experienced, this state of mine becomes worse, from the *very* recollection of happiness. Whether, therefore, the day looks upon wretched me, or whether the horses of the frosty night are urged on; my heart melts away with everlasting cares, just as new wax is wont *to do*, on the application of fire. Often do I pray for death, often too, do I avert it by prayer, in order that the Sarmatian soil may not cover my bones. When it occurs *to me* how great is the clemency of Augustus, I trust that a share of repose may be granted to my shipwreck.

[5] *The poplar covered.*]—Ver. 34. The sisters of Phaëton are fabled, after his death, to have pined away with grief, and to have been changed into poplars, or, according to Virgil, into alders.

[6] *But, I suppose.*]—Ver. 43. This is said ironically, and is supposed to be uttered by some one who is expostulating with him.

When I see how obdurate is my destiny, I despair; and fleeting hope fails, overcome by great alarm. And yet I neither hope nor pray for any thing more, than that I may leave this country, *even if* changed for a worse. Either it is this, or nothing, that thy credit *at Court* may with propriety endeavour to obtain for me, without compromising thy moderation. Maximus, thou *embodied* eloquence of the Roman language, undertake the kind defence of a difficult case. 'Tis a bad one, I confess; but, thou being my defender, it shall become a good one. Only do utter soothing words, on account of my wretched exile; for Cæsar does not know, although a God knows every thing, in what state is this remote region. The weighty avocations of business occupy that Divinity: this care is too trifling for a heaven-born mind. He has no leisure to inquire in what region the people of Tomi are situate, a spot scarce known to the neighbouring Getæ; or what the Sauromatæ are doing, or what the savage Iazyges, and the Tauric land, beloved by the Goddess *carried off* by Orestes: or what other nations, when the Danube has frozen, pass on their swift horses over the hardened surface of the river. The greatest part of *these* men care not for thee, most beauteous Rome, and fear not the arms of the Ausonian soldiers. Their bows, their full quivers, and their horses, equal to the longest distances, give them courage; *the fact* too, that they have long learned to endure thirst and hunger; and that the enemy that follows will be deprived of water. The anger of the merciful Deity would not have sent me to that spot, if these things had been sufficiently known to him. It delights him not that I, or that any Roman, should be destroyed by the enemy; and me, to whom he himself has granted life, the least of all. He was unwilling, though he had the power, to injure me with the slightest nod; there is no need of any Getæ for the purpose of my death.

Besides, he has found that I have done nothing why I should suffer death; and he may be less hostile *against me* than he has been. He has done nothing, too, but what I myself have forced him to do; his anger has even been almost more moderate than my offence. May the Gods therefore, of whom he is the most merciful, grant that the genial earth may produce nothing greater than Cæsar; that long in his charge may be the public burden of the State; and that, descending, it may pass into the hands of that family. But, do thou, open thy lips in behalf of my tears before a judge so lenient, as even I have experienced him to be. Make no request that it may go well with me, but that my woes may continue in a place of safety; that my exile may be spent at a distance from a cruel enemy; and that the life which the favouring Deities have granted me, the disgusting Getan may not deprive me of, with his drawn sword. Lastly, that if I die, my bones may be laid in a more peaceful spot, and may not be covered with Scythian soil; that the hoof of the Bistonian horse may not crush my ashes half unburied (as, forsooth, befits an exile); and that if, after death, there is any perception, no Sarmatian ghost may alarm my shade. These things, Maximus, when heard, could affect the feelings of Cæsar; if first they could influence thine. Let thy voice, I entreat thee, which is wont to aid the trembling accused, soothe the ears of Augustus in my behalf: and do thou, with the wonted blandness of thy learned tongue, soften the heart of him who is to be reckoned equal with the Gods. Neither Theromedon,[7] nor cruel Atreus,[8] will have to be entreated by thee, nor he that made human beings food for his mares;[9] but a Prince, slow to punish, quick to reward, and who grieves, as often as he is forced to be severe: one who ever conquers, that he may spare the conquered, and who has shut up civil warfare with everlasting locks. One who prevents many *a crime* by the dread of punishment, but few by punishment *itself;* and who hurls but few bolts, *and those* with a repugnant hand. Therefore, sent as my pleader before ears so lenient, do thou entreat that the place of my banishment may be nearer to my country. I am one, who held thee in esteem, *and* whom the festive table used to see among thy guests. I am he who led Hymenæus before thy *marriage* torches, and repeated verses[10] worthy of a happy

[7] *Theromedon.*]—Ver. 121. He was a cruel king of Scythia, who fed his lions upon human bodies.

[8] *Cruel Atreus.*]—Ver. 121. He killed the children of Thyestes, and served them up to him at a banquet. Reference has been previously made to this fable.

[9] *Food for his mares.*]—Ver. 122. He alludes to Diomedes, the barbarous king of Thrace, who fed his mares upon the bodies of strangers found within his kingdom. He was slain by Hercules, who caused him to be eaten by his mares.

[10] *And repeated verses.*]—Ver. 134. He means by this, that he wrote the

union; whose works, as I remember, thou wast wont to praise, with the exception of those that brought ruin on their master; *and* to whom, admiring *them*, thou wast wont sometimes to read thy writings. I am he, to whom a bride was given, from out of thy family. Martia esteems her, and from her earliest youth has always reckoned her, *much* beloved, in the number of her companions. Formerly, the maternal aunt of Cæsar had her among her own companions; if a person is to be esteemed according to their opinion, she is virtuous. Claudia,[11] herself superior to her own character, would not have stood in need of the Divine aid, had they praised her. I, too, spent my former years without a stain: the last portion of my life must be omitted. But, to keep silence about myself, my wife is thy charge; without impeachment of thy honour, thou canst not treat her with neglect. To thy family she flies for aid: your altars does she embrace. Every one, properly, resorts to the Gods that have been worshipped by him: and, weeping, she entreats that, Cæsar *once* appeased by thy supplications, the tomb of her husband may be nearer *to his country*.

EPISTLE III.—TO RUFINUS.

Ovid declares that he has received much pleasure from his friend's letters; and that he has conceived fresh hopes since he has read them; but he says, that, consoling as they are, they cannot dispel his grief; and he gives his reasons for saying so. He recounts the instances of those who have endured exile with fortitude; but he says they did so, because they were not removed far from their native land. He confesses, however, that if the wounds of his spirit were capable of being healed, it would be by his friend's kind advice and eloquent language; and declares that he considers his kind attentions as a great boon.

Thy *friend* Naso, Rufinus, sends thee this salutation; if he, who is in misery, can be owned as the friend of any one. The consolation that has been lately given by thee to my disturbed spirit, has afforded both aid and hope, amid my woes. As

---

Epithalamium, or nuptial song, on the occasion of the marriage of Maximus. The name of Hymenæus, the God of Marriage, is here used to signify the Epithalamium.

[11] *Claudia.*]—Ver. 144. This is the Vestal virgin, whose miraculous deliverance from the imputation of unchastity is recounted at length in the fourth Book of the 'Fasti.'

the hero, the son of Pæas, through the skill of Machaon experienced the aid of medicine in the cure of his wound; so I, prostrate in mind, and wounded with a cruel blow, began, at thy exhortation, to take courage. And when now failing, I revived at thy words, as the pulse is wont to return on wine being administered.[12] But yet thy eloquence did not put forth powers so great, that my heart was *entirely* healed by thy words. However much thou mayst subtract from the floods of my cares; that which will remain, will be no less than that which is removed. In length of time, perhaps, the scar will be covered over; wounds, while yet raw, shudder at the application of the hand. It is not always within the physician's power, that the invalid should recover: sometimes disease is more powerful than the experience of art. Thou seeest, how blood discharged from the tender lungs leads by a sure path to the Stygian streams. Should even he of Epidaurus himself apply the sacred herbs, by no skill *of his* will he heal the wounds of the heart. The medical art is at a loss how to remove the swelling gout, and gives no aid in cases of hydrophobia. Grief, too, is sometimes curable by no skill; or, even if it is, by length of time must it be alleviated. After thy advice had strengthened my prostrate spirit, and the armour of thy mind had been assumed by me, again did longing for my country, more powerful than all reasoning, destroy the work which thy writings had formed. Whether thou wouldst have it called affectionate or womanish: I confess that the heart of wretched me is *but* tender. The wisdom of him of Ithaca is undoubted; and yet he longed to be able to behold the smoke of his paternal hearths. The land of our birth impels us, influenced by an extraordinary attraction, and allows us not to be forgetful of it. What is there better than Rome? What is there more intolerable than the Scythian frosts? Yet, hither does the barbarian flee from that City. Although the daughter of Pandion[13] is safe, when shut in a cage; *yet* she struggles to regain her woods. The oxen seek their wonted pastures, the lions their wonted caves, and their fierceness

---

[12] *Being administered,*]—Ver. 10. 'Infuso;' literally, 'poured in;' meaning, 'on wine being poured down the throat.'

[13] *Daughter of Pandion.*]—Ver. 39. He alludes to Philomela, who was changed into a nightingale; a bird which never becomes reconciled to the cruel confinement of a cage.

hinders them not *from doing so*. *And* yet thou believest that the torments of exile can be removed from my heart by thy consolations. Make yourselves to be not so worthy to be loved by me, that it may be a lighter misfortune to be deprived of such.

But, I suppose, now that I am driven from the land of my birth, it has still fallen to my lot to be in a place fit for man. I lie here, deserted, amid the sands of a far distant region, where the hidden earth supports eternal snows. Here the land produces neither the pome, nor the sweet grape; willows flourish not on the bank, nor oaks on the mountain. And praise not the sea any more than the land: the ocean, deprived of *the heat of* the sun is ever unsettled through the raging of the winds. Whichever way you look, plains extend without a cultivator; and vast fields, to which there is no one to lay claim. A foe is at hand, to be dreaded, both on the right side and the left; and either direction brings its alarms through fear of our neighbours. One side is to be made to feel the Bistonian lances; the other, the javelins hurled by the Sarmatian hand. Come now, and recount to me the examples of men of ancient times, who have endured misfortunes with fortitude. Admire, too, the firmness of the magnanimous Rutilius,[14] who accepted not the liberty of returning, that was granted him. Smyrna received that heroic man, not Pontus, and the land of an enemy; Smyrna, not less desirable than hardly any other place. The Cynic of Sinope[15] did not grieve that he was far from his country; for he chose, land of Attica, thy abodes. The son of Neocles,[16] who crushed the Persian arms in warfare,

[14] *Rutilius.*]—Ver. 63. Publius Rutilius was a man of great integrity and learning, who having, during his Quæstorship, rectified considerable abuses, drew upon himself the enmity of the Equestrian order. Being wrongfully accused of malpractices, he was exiled. When Sylla's cause was victorious, he had permission to return; but he declined to live at Rome, even under a former imputation of dishonesty; and he spent his latter years at Smyrna, in Asia Minor, where he died.

[15] *The Cynic of Sinope.*]—Ver. 67. Diogenes, the Cynic philosopher, was the son of Icesius, and was a native of Sinope, a town of Paphlagonia, in Asia Minor. Coming to Athens, he became a disciple of Antisthenes, the philosopher, who founded the sect of the Cynics. These philosophers professed to reject the amenities of life, and to live conformably to nature; a doctrine which Diogenes, in some instances, carried to the extent of neglecting common decency.

[16] *The son of Neocles.*]—Ver. 69. Themistocles, the Athenian general,

experienced his first banishment in the city of Argos. Aristides,[17] when driven from his country, fled to Lacedæmon; between the *two*, it is a matter of doubt which was preferable. Patroclus, when a youth, being guilty of homicide, left Opus, and arrived in the land of Thessaly, as the guest of Achilles. *Jason*, under whose guidance the sacred bark sped onwards to the Colchian waves, went as an exile, from Hæmonia, to the spring of Pirene. Cadmus, the son of Agenor, left the walls of Sidon, that he might found his city on a preferable site. Tydeus came to Adrastus, expelled from Calydon; and the land pleasing to Venus[18] received Teucer. Why shall I make mention of the forefathers of the Roman race, among whom Tybur[19] was the remotest spot for the exile? Should I detail all of them, to no one, in all ages, has a place been assigned so far from his country as this, or more dreadful *than it.* Therefore, the more readily should thy wisdom find a pardon for me in my sorrow, who profit but so little by thy exhortations. And yet I do not deny, that if my wounds were capable of closing, they could close under thy advice. But I fear lest thou shouldst strive in vain to save me, and lest, weak and past all recovery, I can derive no benefit from the application of thy aid. And I say this, not because I have any greater foresight, but *because* I am better known to myself than to my physician. But, though so it is, thy good wishes have come as a great boon to me, and are gratefully accepted.

was the son of Neocles. The Athenians, with their usual ingratitude, unmindful of his great services in withstanding the Persian power, banished him several times. On the first occasion of his banishment, he retired to Argos.

[17] *Aristides.*]—Ver. 71. He was an Athenian, the son of Lysimachus. He was the rival of Themistocles, and, for his virtues, received the epithet of 'the Just.' Being banished, he fled to Sparta, which being, at that time, the rival of Athens, as the poet says, it is doubtful whether he made a change for the worse.

[18] *Land pleasing to Venus.*]—Ver. 80. The island of Cyprus, where that Goddess was especially worshipped. Teucer, being expelled after the Trojan war, by his father Telamon from his own country, retired to Cyprus, and there founded a city, which he called Salamis after his native place.

[19] *Tybur.*]—Ver. 82. Tybur was eighteen miles from Rome. Of course, in the earliest days of Rome, exiles could not be driven away any further than its very limited boundaries would admit of.

EPISTLE IV.—TO HIS WIFE.

He says that his hair has become grey, and his body weak, and that the cause is twofold, old age, and incessant grief. He then compares the voyage of Jason, who came to that region, with his own exile, and shows that his troubles are far greater than those of Jason. He prays for a return to his country, to enjoy the society of his wife, and to evince his gratitude to the family of Cæsar.

My declining years are now besprinkled with grey hairs; and the wrinkle of old age now seams my countenance; now vigour and strength are growing languid in my exhausted frame; and those amusements which delighted me when a a youth, delight *me* no longer. If you were to behold me on a sudden, you would not recognize me, so great has been the decline of my age. I confess that length of years causes this; but there is, too, another cause; anxiety of mind, and eternal care. For, were any one to distribute my woes through a length of years, (believe me,) I should be older than Nestor of Pylos. You see how, in the rugged fields, *hard* work weakens the strong bodies of the oxen; and what is stronger than an ox? The soil which has never been accustomed to rest in the repose of the fallow, wearied with continually producing, grows old. If a horse shall be always engaging in the contests of the Circus, without the intermission of any of the races, he will die. Although a ship be strong, she will go to pieces at sea, if she is never dry, and free from the action of the flowing water. An endless series of troubles wears me away, too, and, before my time, forces me to be an old man. Repose gives nourishment to the body; the mind, too, is refreshed by it: on the other hand, immoderate care consumes them both.

See, what fame the son of Æson will gain from latest posterity, because he came to these regions. But his labours were both lighter, and less than mine; if only, illustrious names do not smother the truth. He set out for Pontus, being sent by Pelias, who was hardly to be dreaded within the limits of Thessaly. The wrath of Cæsar has caused my afflictions; him, at whom both sides of the earth tremble, from the rising of the sun to its setting. Hæmonia is nearer to the baleful Pontus than Rome *is*, and he travelled a less distance than I *did*. He had for his companions, the chief men of the Grecian land; whereas, all deserted me on my banishment. I ploughed the vast ocean on a frail bit of timber; the ship that bore the son of Æson was strong. Tiphys,[20] too, was not my pilot, and the son of Agenor did not instruct me what course to follow, and what to avoid. Royal Juno, with Pallas, protected him; no Divinities have defended my person. The furtive arts of Cupid aided him; *arts*, which I wish that Love had not learned from me. He returned home; I shall die in these lands, if the heavy wrath of the offended God shall be lasting. My burden, most faithful wife, is a harder one than that which the son of Æson bore. You, too, whom I left *still* young at my departure from the City, I can believe to have grown old under my calamities. Oh, grant it, ye Gods, that I may be enabled to see you, *even if* such, and to give the joyous kiss on each cheek in its turn; and to embrace your emaciated body in my arms, and to say, "'twas anxiety, on my account, that caused this thinness;" and, weeping, to recount in person my sorrows to you in tears, and *thus* enjoy a conversation that I had never hoped for; and to offer the due frankincense, with grateful hand, to the Cæsars, and to the wife that is worthy of a Cæsar, Deities in real truth!

Oh, that the mother of Memnon,[21] *that* Prince being softened, would with her rosy lips, speedily call forth that day.

EPISTLE V.—TO MAXIMUS.

He requests Maximus not to be surprised, if his verses are neglected and repulsive from their want of polish; but he says, that his mind is so overwhelmed by his misfortunes, that his abilities have suffered decay in length of time. He then explains why he continues to write, in spite of the injury which his verses have done him; and he tells the reason why he is not anxious to make them remarkable for their elegance.

Naso, once not the last among thy friends, entreats thee, Maximus, to read his words. In these, cease to look for my *former* ability, that thou mayst not seem to be ignorant of my

[20] *Tiphys.*]—Ver. 37. He was the pilot of the Argo, which conveyed Jason and his companions, on their expedition to recover the golden fleece. Phineus, the son of Agenor, instructed Jason how to steer clear of the Cyanean rocks.

[21] *Mother of Memnon.*]—Ver. 57. Aurora was the mother, and Tithonus the father, of Memnon, who, being born in Æthiopia, was of a swarthy or black colour. He assisted the Trojans in the Trojan war, and was killed by Achilles.

exile. Thou seeest how ease enervates the slothful body; how water contracts a taint, if it is not stirred. If ever I had any facility in composing verses, it *now* fails me, and has been diminished by listless sloth. These words too, which ye read, (if you will believe me, Maximus), I write, put together with difficulty, and with a reluctant hand. It delights me not to give the bent of my mind to such pursuits, and the Muse, *though* invited, comes not among the savage Getæ. Yet, as thou seeest, I struggle to compose a line; but it is not less harsh than is my destiny. When I read it over again, I am ashamed that I wrote it: because I see many things that are deserving to be erased, even in the opinion of myself who have composed them. And yet I correct them not: this were a greater labour than to write *them*, and the mind that is sick, is able to endure no hardship. Should I, forsooth, begin to use polished language with more attention, and should I repeat every word according to rule? Does Fortune torment me too little, unless the Nile is in confluence with the Hebrus, and unless Athos adds his leaves to the Alps? We must make allowance for the mind that bears the wound of sorrow; let the oxen withdraw their galled necks from the burden.

But I suppose, *forsooth*, profit is the result, the justest stimulant of labour; and the earth returns the seed sown with bounteous interest. Up to this moment (even should you review my whole career), no work of mine has been of any advantage to me, and I *only* wish no one *of them* had done me an injury. Dost thou, then, wonder why I write? I wonder as well; and I often ask myself, what I shall get by it. Does the multitude say truly, that poets are insane; and am I the greatest illustration of this saying? I, who, when I have been so often deceived in a barren soil, persist in sowing my seed in unproductive ground. In truth, each one is attached to his own pursuit; and it is pleasant to spend our time in one's usual occupations. The wounded gladiator curses the combat, and *yet* the same man, forgetful of his former wound, resumes arms. The shipwrecked person says that he will have nothing to do with the waves of the sea; soon he is plying the oars, in the water, in which but just now, he was swimming. So am I constantly following a useless pursuit; and I seek again those Goddesses, to whom I wish I had not devoted myself. What am I to do in preference? I am not one to indulge in listless sloth: time unemployed is considered death by me. I take no pleasure in wearing myself out till dawn, with excess of wine; and alluring games of hazard do not occupy my shaking hands. When I have devoted the hours to sleep which the body demands, after I am awake, how shall I dispose of the long hours? Forgetting the manners of my country, shall I learn to stretch the Sarmatian bow; and shall I be allured by the *peculiar* art of this place? My strength too forbids me to follow this pursuit; and my mind is stronger than my thin body. When you have well considered what I am to do; there is nothing more useful than these pursuits, which have no utility. From them I gain forgetfulness of my calamity; if my field yields this for its harvest, it is enough. Glory stimulates you, *ye poets;* keep your attention fixed on the Piërian choirs, that your poems, when recited, may meet with approval. It is enough for me to compose anything that occurs without an effort: and no necessity exists for extreme labour. Why should I polish my lines with anxious care? Ought I to fear, lest the Getan should not approve of them? Perhaps I may be acting rashly, *in so doing,* but I boast that the Danube possesses no genius superior to my own. It is enough, if in this land, where I must live, I attain to being a poet among the savage Getæ. Of what use is it to reach distant regions by my fame? Let that place, which Fortune has given, be Rome *for me.* With this for her theatre, is my Muse content. This have I deserved; this have the great Gods willed. Besides, I do not think that there is any way hence to that spot for my works, *a spot*, at which Boreas arrives with flagging wing. We are in quite a different climate; and the Bear, which is afar from the City of Quirinus, looks down on the hairy Getæ close at hand. Through so great a tract of land, so many seas, I could hardly believe that any exponent of my pursuits could make its way. Suppose *my works* to be read, and, what is surprising, suppose they give pleasure: assuredly that thing will avail the author nothing. Of what use is it to thee, if thou art praised when situate in the hot Syene,[22] or where the Indian waves surround Taprobane?[23] Do

[22] *Syene.*]—Ver. 79. Syene was a city of Egypt, on the confines of Æthiopia, where the heat would naturally be intense.

[23] *Taprobane.*]—Ver. 80. This was the Roman name of the island, which at the present day is called Ceylon. It was but very little known

you wish to go further? If the far distant Constellations of the Pleiädes please thee, what benefit dost thou derive from that? But I do not reach there, with my homely writings: with their master, his glory has fled from the City. And ye, to whom I have been dead, from the time when my fame was entombed, I suppose you have kept *a rigid* silence upon my death up to the present moment.

EPISTLE VI.—TO GRÆCINUS.

The Poet laments that Græcinus was not near at the time when he was banished by Augustus; and he expresses a belief that, on hearing of it, his friend was much affected by his misfortunes. He entreats him to afford him the pleasure of his conversation at least by letter; and requests him not to inquire the cause of his exile, that his wounds may not bleed afresh. He says that he has not lost all hope of returning; and that he still confides in the clemency of Cæsar, and trusts thereby to regain his favour. He ends by expecting every impossible thing to happen, before he finds himself deserted by his old and attached friend, Græcinus.

And was not thy heart sad, when *first* thou heardst of my calamities? (for *then* a distant land withheld thee). Although, Græcinus, thou shouldst hide it, and hesitate to confess it, if I know thee well, I am sure thou wast sad. Unamiable insensibility does not befit those manners *of thine*, nor is it less at variance with thy pursuits. By the liberal arts, to which thou payest the greatest attention, the heart is made tender, and harshness is dispelled; and there is no one who embraces them with more sincerity than thyself, so far as duty and the avocations of war permit.

Assuredly, at the first moment that I could be sensible of what I was (for, in my stupor, for a long time I had no understanding), I felt that this, too, was a part of my destiny, that thou, my friend, who couldst have been a great protection to me, shouldst be at a distance. With thee, the solace of a dejected spirit was wanting; and a great part, as well, of my mind and of my faculties. But now, grant me this aid from afar, which alone remains, and cheer my heart by thy converse: *a heart* (if thou wouldst put any trust in a friend that speaks no un-

---

to the Romans in the days of Ovid; but in the time of the later emperors it became somewhat better known.

truth), that ought rather to be called unwise, than wicked. It is neither a slight matter, nor a safe one, to write what was the cause of my offence: my wounds will not endure handling. Do not inquire, how they have come to be inflicted on me; if thou wishest the wounds to close, disturb them not.

Whatever it is, though not a crime, yet it must be called a fault; or is it that every fault, committed against the great Gods, is a crime? Some hope then, Græcinus, is still left to my spirit, of a mitigation of my punishment. *Hope* was the only Goddess, that, when the Deities fled from the wicked earth, alone remained on the soil *so* hateful to the Gods. She causes even the miner, bound with the fetter, to live on, and to expect that his legs will be liberated from the iron. She causes the shipwrecked *sailor* to extend his arms in the midst of the waves, when he beholds no land on any side. Many a time has the skilful care of the physicians given a person up; and yet, as his pulse has failed, hope has not deserted him. Those shut up in prison are said to hope for safety; and *the criminal*, as he hangs on the cross,[24] breathes his prayers. How many, when they have fastened their necks with the noose, has that Goddess forbidden to die by the fate they had purposed! Me too, endeavouring to end my griefs by the sword, she prevented, and restrained me by laying her hand *upon me*. "What art thou doing?" said she. "Tears are needed, not blood; by means of them, often is the wrath of the Prince wont to be assuaged." Although then it is not the due of my deserts, yet there is great room for hope, in the clemency of the God. Do thou entreat him, Græcinus, not to be inexorable against me; and contribute thy words towards *the attainment of* my wishes. May I lie entombed amid the sands of Tomi, if I do not believe that thou wishest the same in my

---

[24] *On the cross.*]—Ver. 38. This instrument of capital punishment was used by the Romans and Carthaginians. It was usually in shape like the letter T or X, but there were other forms of it also. The first was the most common sort: the stem being a little elongated above the point of intersection by the transverse beam; and on a cross of this kind, according to the unanimous testimony of the Fathers of the Church, Our Saviour suffered. The punishment was usually inflicted on slaves, and the commonest malefactors. The condemned, as we are informed by Plutarch, carried his own cross, and, being first stripped of his clothes, was either nailed or bound to it, and, in the latter case, was left to die of hunger. The body was usually left on the cross after death

behalf; for first would the pigeons begin to avoid the turrets, the wild beasts their dens, the sheep their pastures, the didapper the waves, before Græcinus would show himself unkind to his old friend. Everything has not been so far reversed *as that*, by my destiny.

EPISTLE VII.—TO MESSALINUS.

In this Epistle, he reminds Messalinus of his former acquaintanceship with him, and of his intimacy with his father and brother. He then enlarges on the punishment which has been inflicted on him by the hand of Augustus, and gives his reasons why he ought not to be disowned on that account. He concludes, by declaring the affection he has ever felt towards the house of Messalinus.

The letter, Messalinus, which thou art reading, has, in the place of words, brought thee *my* salutation, even from among the savage Getæ. Does the region reveal who the writer is? or is it unknown to thee, unless thou readest my name, that it is I, Naso, who write these words? Who of thy friends lies prostrate, far removed in a distant region, except myself, who pray *ever* to be thy friend? *Oh!* that the Gods would wish that all who esteem and love thee, should gain no knowledge of this race. It is enough for me, to be living among ice and the Scythian arrows; if a kind of death is to be considered life. Let the earth with its wars, or the climate with its cold, be distressing me, and let the fierce Getan be striking me with his arms, and the storm with its hail. Let a region confine me that is prolific neither in pomes nor in grapes; and of which no side is free from the enemy. Let the rest of the multitude of thy friends be in safety, among whom I was a small fraction, like one out of a great number. Ah, wretched me! if thou art offended by these words; and if thou denyest that I was *ever*, in any degree, thy friend. Suppose that to be the truth, thou oughtst to forgive me thus guilty of a falsehood: my praise subtracts nothing from thy fame. Who is there, if the Cæsars are known *to him*, that does not pretend that he is a friend *of theirs?* Pardon me, if I confess it; thou shalt be my Cæsar. But I rush not in where I may not tread; and it is enough, if thou dost not deny that thy hall was *once* open to me. And although I had no further *intimacy* with thee *than this;* thou art now saluted by one mouth less than formerly thou wast; but thy father did not deny that I was his friend, the encourager, the cause, and the *very* light of my pursuits. To him I gave both my tears, as my last gift at his death, and my verses for recitation in the middle of the Forum. Besides, thou hast a brother, united to thee in an affection as strong as that between the sons of Atreus and the offspring of Tyndarus. He rejected me, neither as a companion, nor as a friend; if thou art of opinion that these *avowals* will not do him any injury; but, if thou dost not *think so*, I will confess that in this respect, also, I have been untruthful. Sooner *than that*, may the whole of thy house be shut against me. But there is no necessity for it to be shut, for there is no power that has the means of preventing a friend from doing wrong. And although, much as I could wish that my fault could be denied, no one is ignorant that I was not guilty of a sin. And, unless some part of my offence had been excusable, 'twould have been but a light penalty to be removed *from my country*. But Cæsar himself, who perceives everything, saw that my offence might be construed to be thoughtlessness; and, so far as I permitted him, and so far as the matter allowed of, he showed himself merciful; and he used the flames of his lightnings with moderation. He took not away my life, nor my property, nor *even* the possibility of my return; if only his wrath can be moderated by your entreaties, *my friends*.

But heavy was my fall; and what is there surprising, if one who has been struck by Jupiter, has no slight wound? Even when Achilles spared to exert his strength, the spear of the son of Pelias, when hurled, gave heavy blows. Since, therefore, the sentence of the avenger was favourable to me, there is no reason why thy gate should deny acquaintance with me. It was attended, I confess, less often than it ought to have been; but this, too, I believe, was the effect of my destiny. And yet no other one was more sensible of my respect; and whether in this place, or in that, I was ever under the protection of thy family. Such is thy affection, that, even if he did not cultivate thy friendship, the friend of thy brother has some claim upon thee; and is it not thy own good fortune, as gratitude is ever the result of kindness, now to have made thyself deserving of it? And if thou allowest me to persuade thee what to desire, pray the Gods that thou mayst give, rather than exchange for a requital.

And so thou art wont to do, and, so far as I can remember, thou wast wont to be the originator of kindnesses shown to many.[25] Give me, Messalinus, whatever place thou mayst please, so that I be a portion not alienated from thy house; and, if thou dost not grieve that Naso has endured misfortunes, since he appears to have deserved them, still grieve that he has been deserving of them.

EPISTLE VIII.—TO SEVERUS.

He shows his friend how he is surrounded with enemies, and amid eternal warfare, at a time when he feels the pangs of regret for his friends, his wife, his daughter, and his country. He expresses his sorrow at not having the opportunity of giving his time to agricultural pursuits, such as ploughing and sowing; but he says that such a thing is impossible, as the city of Tomi is ever surrounded with multitudes of the enemy. He congratulates Severus on his prosperity; and entreats him to request Augustus to grant him some other place of banishment.

Receive, Severus, thou great portion of my life, the salutation sent from Naso, beloved by thee. But ask not what I am doing: if I should recount everything, thou wouldst weep. Let it be enough, if the sum of my misfortunes is known to thee.

Destitute of peace, I am living in eternal warfare, the quivered Getan provoking the cruel strife. Out of so many banished, I am the only one that is a soldier, as well as an exile; all the rest *of the exiles* are in safety, but I do not envy *their lot*. And that thou mayst the more readily accord pardon to my writings, thou wilt read these lines composed *by me*, in readiness for military duty.

There stands an ancient city, near the bank of the Danube, that bears two names,[26] scarcely accessible, from its fortifications and the position of the place. The Caspian Ægypsus (if we believe them, *when* speaking of themselves) founded it, and

---

[25] *Kindnesses shown to many.*]—Ver. 66. This is clearly the meaning of the passage; but there must either be a corrupt reading here, or Ovid must have forgotten his Latinity among the Getæ. 'Causa,' instead of 'causam,' would be correct Latin, though it would not suit the measure.

[26] *That bears two names.*]—Ver. 11. The Danube was called by that name, from its source to the city of Axium; and thence, to the sea, it was known by the name of Ister.

called it after his own name. The savage Getan took it, the Odrysii being massacred in a sudden incursion, and *then* he waged war against its king. He, mindful of his high birth, which he enhances by his courage, *immediately* presents himself, surrounded with soldiers innumerable; and he does not withdraw, before, through the well-deserved slaughter of the aggressors, he, in his excess of vengeance, himself becomes the aggressor. O king, the most valiant in *this* our age, may it be granted thee, ever to wield the sceptre with an honoured hand. May Rome, too, the offspring of Mars, and the great Cæsar, grant thee their approval, a thing still more desirable; what greater boon *than this* could I pray for thee?

But, not forgetful whence I have digressed, my dear companion, I complain that cruel warfare is added to my calamities. The rising Pleiad has brought on four autumns, since, driven into these Stygian regions, I have been deprived of thee. But do not suppose that Naso regrets the conveniences of a city life; and yet he does regret them. For at one moment I recall to mind you, my much-loved friends; at another time, my daughter, with my dear wife, recurs to me: and *then*, from my house I turn to the spots of the beauteous City: and my mind, with its eye, surveys them all. Now the markets, now the temples, now the theatres paved with marble, and now all the porticos recur to me, with their level ground.[27] Now the grass of the plain that looks on the beauteous gardens, and the standing waters of the Euripus,[28] and the aqueduct of the Virgin, *recur to me.*

But, I suppose, the delights of the City have been thus torn from wretched me, that, at least, I may be allowed, in some de-

---

[27] *With their level ground.*]—Ver. 36. The porticos which were attached to the temples and public edifices, as well as to the houses of the great, served both for the purposes of ornament and utility, as they afforded to persons, wishful to take exercise, a retreat from the rain and the rays of the sun. For this reason, care was taken that the ground should be made level, by being paved.

[28] *Waters of the Euripus.*]—Ver. 38. The Euripus was properly the sound or strait between Euboea and Boeotia, now called the straits of Negropont. From the resemblance, aqueducts, canals, ditches, and water-passages were called by that name. There were several canals or pieces of standing water in the Circus Maximus. The aqueduct of the Virgin is said to have been so called, because when water was being sought, a little girl was the first to point out the spring.

gree, to enjoy the pleasures of the country. My spirit longs not for the fields that it has lost, and the rural retreats to be beheld on the Pelignian soil; nor yet for the gardens, situate on the pine-bearing hills, which the Clodian way, at its junction with the Flaminian, looks upon. For another, whom, I know not, have I cultivated them; in them I was wont to conduct the fountain streams to my plantations, and I repent it not. There too, if they are *still* alive, are apples, once planted with my hand, but not destined to be gathered by it as well. In exchange for the loss of these things, would that some piece of land, at least, had fallen to my lot to cultivate in my exile. I myself could wish, were it only allowed me, *to feed* my she-goats balancing on the edge of the crag, and, leaning on my staff, to feed my sheep. I myself, did not my heart continually dwell on my wonted cares, could lead the oxen that till the land under the curving yoke. I could learn the words that the Getan bullocks understand, and I could apply to them the wonted threats *of the ploughman*. I myself, guiding the handle of the pressed plough, with my hand could try to scatter the seed in the ground that has been turned up. I would not hesitate to cleanse the field with the long hoe, and to supply the water, for the thirsting garden to drink up. But in what quarter am I to find this, between whom and the foe, the fortifications and the closed gate form but a scanty interval? But for thee, (and with all my heart do I rejoice at it) the Goddesses of Destiny have spun strong threads. At one moment, the Field *of Mars* receives thee; at another, the portico, with its dark shade; at another, the Forum, to which thou givest but little of thy time. And now Umbria[29] recalls thee; and the Appian way takes thee, going towards the fields of Alba with swift wheel. Perhaps here thou mayst wish that Cæsar would check his deserved anger; and that thy country residence might be my hospitable retreat. Oh! my friend, 'tis too much, what thou dost wish for; request something more moderate, and take in the sails of thy desires. Would that a land were granted me nearer *to my country*, and subject to no warfare; then would a great part be subtracted from my woes.

[29] *Umbria.*]—Ver. 67. This was a district between the Sabines and the country of Etruria, where the country residence of Severus was situate.

EPISTLE IX.—TO MAXIMUS.

THE poet having been informed by Maximus of the death of his friend Celsus (through whose intercession he had hoped that Maximus would interest himself in soliciting a reversal of his sentence), declares that he has moistened the letter of Maximus with his tears; and that nothing more grievous has befallen him, since he arrived in Pontus. He enlarges upon his friendship both with Maximus and Celsus. He declares his wish, in some manner, to celebrate his funereal rites, which, however, he can only do with his verses: and he concludes, by entreating Maximus to look upon him as dead, and to show him a similar degree of attention.

THY letter, which came to me, speaking of the loss of Celsus,[30] was immediately moistened with my tears; and, what I ought not to say, and I did not think possible to happen, thy letter was read by unwilling eyes. Nothing has come to my ears more distressing, since I have been in Pontus; and may it *long* be so, I pray. His countenance *ever* remains before my eyes, as though he were present; and affection makes the dead still to live. My mind often recalls his playful remarks, when stripped of gravity; and often *recalls* his performance of the serious *duties of life* with sincere fidelity.

But no occasion recurs to me more frequently than that, which I wish had been the last moment of my life; when my house coming down suddenly, fell in ruins with a tremendous crash upon the head of its master. He was present with me, Maximus, when a great part deserted me; and he proved himself no hanger-on upon Fortune. I beheld him, weeping at my downfall, in no other manner, than if his brother was about to be placed on the burning pile. He remained *fastened* in my embrace, and consoled me, as I lay prostrate, and even mingled his own tears with mine. Oh! how often did he, *at that moment*, the repulsive defender of my hated life, restrain my hands prepared for my own destruction! Oh! how often did he say, "The anger of the Gods is capable of being appeased; live on, and do not deny that possibly thou mayst receive pardon." Yet these were his most remarkable words, "Consider how much assistance Maximus ought to afford thee! Maximus will apply himself to the task, and, such is his affec-

---

[20] *Celsus.*]—Ver. 1. Aulus Cornelius Celsus was a Roman physician of great learning and ability. His works on medicine have come down to us. He wrote also on Rhetoric and the Military Art.

tion, he will ask that the anger of Cæsar be not lasting for ever. Together with his brothers, he will use his energies and try every resource, that thy griefs may be alleviated." These words diminished in me the hatred of my wretched existence; and be it thy care, Maximus, that they prove not to have been unfounded. Hither, too, he used to swear to me that he would come, if only thou didst grant him permission to undertake so long a voyage. For he esteemed thy family with no less veneration, than that with which thou thyself dost worship the Gods that rule the earth. Believe me, although thou deservedly hast many friends; out of so many he was inferior to none: if only, it is not riches, nor the illustrious names of ancestors, but probity and talent that make men great. Justly then do I shed the tear for Celsus removed from us, which he gave for me still living, *at the time* when I was banished. Deservedly do I afford these lines, that attest thy rare virtues; *in order*, Celsus, that posterity may read of thy name. This is what I am able to send thee from the Getic regions; in this place, this is the only thing that 'tis certain is my own.

I could not attend thy funeral, nor anoint thy body; and from thy pile I am separated by the distance of the whole earth. Maximus, who was able, and whom, when alive, thou didst esteem as a Divinity, performed every duty for thee. He performed thy sepulchral rites, and gave thee a funeral of great pomp; he, too, poured the amomum on thy cold breast. He, weeping, mingled the ointment with his gushing tears, and buried thy bones, laid at rest in the neighbouring ground. And since he gives their due to his friends when dead, he is at liberty to reckon me in the number of them.

EPISTLE X.—TO FLACCUS.

OVID details the languid state of his body, and the causes of his illness; and he entreats Flaccus and his brother to give him their assistance, and to endeavour to moderate the wrath of Augustus against him.

FLACCUS, the exile Naso sends thee health; if any one can send the thing which he himself is in want of. For lasting grief does not allow a body diseased by grievous cares to retain its strength. And yet no pain is there; I am not parched by panting fever, and my pulse beats with its usual tenor. My appetite is blunted; food set before me creates loathing; and I complain when the hour comes for my hated repast. Set before me whatever the sea, whatever the land, whatever the air produces; there will be nothing there, to create an appetite in me. Were *Hebe*, the active damsel, with her beauteous hand to present to me nectar and ambrosia, the drink and the food of the Gods, yet the taste of them would not sharpen my dulled palate; and the weight would rest long on my inactive stomach. This, though it is most true, I dare not write to any one; lest they should style my malady *mere* affectation. Such is my state, forsooth, such is the aspect of my fortunes, that there can be room even for affectation! I wish such affectation as this, to be the lot of the man, if such there is, who fears lest the wrath of Cæsar against me should be mitigated. That sleep, too, which, to a weakly body, is aliment, affords no nourishment by its virtues to my emaciated frame. But I keep awake, and for ever do my griefs abstain from sleep; matter for which the *very* place itself affords me. Scarcely, then, couldst thou recognize my features, if seen; and thou wouldst ask whither the colour has gone, that formerly existed. But little nourishment comes into my wasted limbs; and my members are paler than new wax. These maladies I have not contracted through excess of wine; thou knowest how almost water alone is drunk by me. I am not stuffed with food: and were I affected with a desire for it, there is no abundance in the Getic regions.

The injurious pleasures of Venus take not away my strength: she is not wont to approach my bed of sorrow. The water and the climate are injurious to me; and, a cause still more powerful than these, the anxiety of mind that is ever present with me. And hadst thou not, together with thy brother, like to thee, alleviated this, scarcely could my sorrowing mind have borne its weight of sadness. You *two* are *as* a hospitable shore for my frail skiff, and you give me that aid which many refuse. Give it me always, I pray, because I shall always stand in need of it: as long as the divine Majesty of Cæsar shall be offended with me. And do you, both, humbly entreat your Gods, that he may moderate, not that he may put an end to, the anger that I have merited.

BOOK THE SECOND.

EPISTLE I.—TO GERMANICUS CÆSAR.

THE Poet says, that the fame of the triumph of Tiberius Cæsar has reached even Scythia, and that it has afforded him much delight; he then describes the procession; and praising the clemency which Cæsar has shown, in sparing the lives of the enemies whom he had taken in battle, he concludes that he himself has a greater right to expect it. He prays that the Gods will grant length of days to Tiberius.

EVEN thus far has the fame of the triumph of Cæsar arrived, whither the languid breeze of the wearied South wind comes with difficulty. I thought that there could be nothing pleasing to me in the regions of Scythia; the place is less hateful to me now, than it was before. The cloud of my cares being dispelled, I have, at length, seen a little clear sky: and *thus* I have deceived my destiny. Even if Cæsar should wish that no joys should fall to my lot, he may still be desirous that this one *pleasure* should be granted to every man. The Gods also command sorrow to be laid aside on their festivals, that they may be worshipped by all with cheerful veneration. In fine, what it is undoubted madness to dare to confess; even should he forbid it, I shall experience pleasure on this occasion. Often as Jupiter refreshes the fields with nourishing showers, the clinging burr is wont to spring up, mixed with the corn. I too, a useless weed, feel the effects of the bounteous Divinity; and often am I refreshed with unintentional benefits. The joys that pervade the mind of Cæsar are *made* my own, to the best of my ability: that house has nothing that belongs to itself alone. Fame, I return thee thanks; by means of whom the procession of triumph[1] has been beheld by me, though shut

---

[1] *Procession of triumph.*]—Ver. 19. It has been supposed by some commentators that he here refers to the ovation of Tiberius after his defeat

up in the midst of the Getæ. Under thy instruction I learned that nations innumerable had lately assembled, to behold the features of their Prince; and that Rome, which embraces the immense world within her extensive walls, scarcely found room for their entertainment. 'Twas thou that didst tell me, how, after the lowering South wind for many a day before had poured down its constant showers, the Sun shone forth brilliantly with his heavenly refulgence, the day being in accordance with the countenances of the people; and how *that* the Conqueror, with the great honour of his eulogies, had distributed the prizes of war among the heroes bepraised *by him; and how that*, when about to assume the embroidered garments, the insignia of glory, he first placed the frankincense on the hallowed altars; and *how* that he piously propitiated Justice, *the peculiar Deity* of his parent; she who ever holds a temple in his breast: and *how* that wherever he proceeded, a happy omen was given in shouts of applause, and the stones turned red with the dew-besprinkled roses. *How* that, next in order, along with the conquered men, the cities of the barbarians were carried, imitating in silver the real walls: and *how* that rivers and mountains, and meadows among lofty woods, and *various* arms were mingled with their weapons in *trophy* piles. And *how* that the roof of the Roman Forum was gilded by the triumphal gold, which the Sun shone upon. And *how* that as many chiefs bore chains fastened to their captive necks, as were almost sufficient to compose *an army* of the enemy. Of these, the greatest part received life and pardon; among whom was Bato, the head and the very existence of the war. Why should I deny that the wrath of the Divinity may possibly be mitigated against me, when I behold how the Gods are merciful to their enemies? The same report, Germanicus, brought the news to me, how that cities had passed in the procession under the title of thy name:[2] and *how* that

of the Pannonians; but it is much more likely that the victory of Tiberius over the Illyrians, which happened in the year preceding the death of Augustus, is here celebrated; as this seems to be the period at which this book was composed. Messalinus, to whom the next letter is addressed, was one of the lieutenants of Tiberius on this occasion, and, with him, partook of the honour of the triumph.

[2] *Under the title of thy name.*]—Ver. 50. Models of the captured cities were carried in the procession; over them was a label or superscription, bearing the name of the general by whom each place had been taken.

they were not secure against thee, either in the thickness of the walls, or in the arms *with which they were defended*, or 'n the natural advantages of their situation.

May the Gods grant thee length of years! *All* other *blessings* from thy own self thou wilt derive, let only length of time be granted for thy virtue. That which I pray, will come to pass; the prophecies of the Poets have some value; for the God gave an auspicious sign as I breathed the wish. Thee too, will Rome behold, in her joy, ascending as a conqueror to the Tarpeian heights, thy horses wreathed with garlands: the Father will behold the ripening honours of his son, experiencing that joy, which he himself has afforded by his own *glories*. Thou *that art* the first of our youths, both in war and in peace, mark the words that have just been spoken by me, as I uttered my prophecy to thee. Perhaps I shall recount this triumph as well in my verses, if my life shall only bear up against my woes: if I myself shall not have first dyed the Scythian arrows *with my blood*, and the savage Getan shall not have first struck off this head *of mine* with his sword. And if, while I am still living, the laurel shall be granted thee in the temples, thou wilt pronounce that my presage was doubly true.[3]

EPISTLE II.—TO MESSALINUS.

He entreats him to receive this letter, coming from the shores of the Euxine, with the same countenance that he was wont formerly to show to himself. He also requests him, when he has read the writer's name, not to refuse to read the whole Epistle; as he has not been guilty of such crimes as to forbid his lines to be read by him. He entreats him, on many considerations, at a fitting time, to entreat Augustus in his behalf; but he requests him only to do so, if he shall feel convinced that no injurious results will be the consequence.

Naso, the admirer of thy family from his earliest years, *now* banished to the shores on the left of the Euxine *sea*, sends thee, Messalinus, this salutation, from among the savage Getæ, which he was accustomed to give thee personally. Wretched am I, if, when thou readest my name, thy countenance is not the same as *once* it was, and if thou hesitatest to read the rest to the end. Read them through, and do not banish my

---

[3] *Doubly true.*]—Ver. 68. True, both as to his having gained a triumph, and as to the poet being alive to witness it.

words, as well as myself: it is allowed my verses to be in your City. I never conceived *the thought* that the brilliant stars could be touched by my hand, if Ossa could *only* bear Pelion. I have not, following the mad expedition of Enceladus, wielded arms against the Gods, the rulers of the earth. No Deities have been struck by any weapon of mine, as was done by the rash right hand of the son of Tydeus. My fault was a heavy one, but such as could ruin myself only; and no greater heinousness has it attained. I can be called nothing else than imprudent and timid; these are the two real characteristics of my mind. I acknowledge, indeed, that, with justice, thou dost not lend an easy ear to my entreaties, after the merited wrath of Cæsar. And such is thy affection to all who bear the name of Iülus, that thou considerest thyself to be offended, when any one of them is offended. But even shouldst thou bear arms, and shouldst thou threaten cruel wounds, still thou wilt not cause me to be in dread of thee. The Trojan ship received the Grecian Achæmenides;[4] and the spear of the son of Pelias bore aid to the Mysian chief. Sometimes the violator of the temple flies for refuge to the altar, and dreads not to implore the aid of the offended Deity. Some one, perhaps, may say that this is not safe; I confess it; but my bark is not sailing in smooth water. Let others seek safety. The most wretched Fate affords its security; for there is no fear of worse mishaps. The man that is hurried on by his destinies, what but his destinies should he entreat? Often does the prickly thorn produce the sweet rose; he that is carried along by the foaming tide, extends his arms towards the crag, and catches at the brambles and the hard rock; the bird that is in dread of the hawk, with trembling wings dares to come, in its weariness, to the breast of man; the hind that in its terror, is flying from the savage dogs, hesitates not to trust itself to the neighbouring house. Grant, I pray thee, most kind friend, access to my tears; and shut not the obdurate door to my kind words. And, do thou kindly carry these words of mine to the Deities of Rome, venerated by thee not less than the Thunderer of the Tarpeian. As my

[4] *Achæmenides.*]—Ver. 25. He was one of the companions of Ulysses, who was left on shore, in Sicily, when Ulysses fled thence. Virgil and Ovid [Metamorphoses, Book xiv.] relate how Æneas discovered him there, and rescued him from the danger of falling into the hands of the Cyclop, Polyphemus.

ambassador, undertake *to plead* the cause of *this* my request: although, under my name, no cause is *really* good. Now, nearly entombed, now assuredly cold *as death*, with difficulty shall I be saved by thee, if I am saved at all. On this occasion, the favour which the esteem of the immortal Prince bestows upon thee, may make an effort in behalf of my ruined fortunes. On this occasion, that brilliancy of speech, which is peculiar to the members of thy family, with which thou wast wont to aid the trembling accused, may be employed by thee. For in thee still lives the tongue of thy eloquent parent; and that point *of excellence* has found its own heir.

I intreat not that *tongue* to attempt to defend me; the cause of a criminal that has made a confession cannot be defended. Yet consider whether thou canst palliate my misdeed under the name of error, or whether it is better not to enter upon that point. The kind of wound is such, that as it admits of no cure, I consider it safer for it not to be handled. Be silent, *thou* tongue *of mine;* not another word must be said. I could wish myself to cover these ashes of mine. Take care, then, to speak in such a manner as if no mistake beguiled me, that I may enjoy that life which he has granted me. And when he shall be calm, and shall have laid aside that countenance, which agitates by its influence[5] both the earth and the empire, entreat him not to allow me to become an humble prey to the Getæ, and to grant me a quiet spot for my wretched exile.

The time is propitious for thy entreaties; he himself is prosperous, and sees, O Rome, thy resources prospering, which he has created. His wife, in happiness, preserves her nuptial couch[6] *with chastity:* his son is extending the sway of Ausonia. Germanicus himself is exceeding his years in his spirit, and the *natural* vigour of Drusus is not less than his great-

---

[5] *By its influence.*]—Ver. 66. 'Secum;' literally, 'with itself;' meaning that the earth enjoys repose, or is distracted with trouble, according as the countenance of Augustus is indicative of a corresponding state of things.

[6] *Her nuptial couch.*]—Ver. 71. 'Pulvinaria.' These were stuffed cushions, which were used on the couches on which the statues of the Deities reposed at the 'Lectisternia,' which were celebrated in their respective temples. By the use of this term, a compliment is intended to be conveyed to the elevated position enjoyed by Livia.

ness of soul. In addition to this, his daughters-in-law, and his affectionate granddaughters, and the children of his grandsons, and the other members of the house of Augustus, are flourishing. Add, too, that the Pæonians[7] have just now afforded a triumph, and that the arms of the mountainous Dalmatia have been reduced to tranquillity. Illyria, too, throwing away her arms, has not disdained to bear the foot of Cæsar, *impressed* on her servile head. He himself, conspicuous in his chariot, with a mild countenance, has had his temples wreathed with *laurel, the produce of* the virgin beloved by Phœbus. Him, as he went along, together with yourselves, his affectionate offspring attended—*an offspring* worthy of their parent, and of the titles that have been given to them: *an offspring* like to the brothers, whom, as they occcupy the neighbouring temple, the God Julius beholds[8] from his lofty shrine. Messalinus does not deny, that to thee, to whom all things ought to give place, the first rank in happiness belongs. Whoever comes next after these, he enters into the contest of love *for the Cæsars;* thou, *Messalinus,* in this respect, shalt be the inferior of no mortal. Him dost thou venerate, by whose means, before the *fitting* age, the laurel, deservedly decreed to thee who merited it, descended upon thy honoured locks. Happy *were they,* to whom it was allowed to behold these triumphs, and to enjoy a sight of the face of a Prince that is the equal of the Gods. But by me, instead of the face of Cæsar, the *country of the* Sauromatæ must be beheld, a land devoid of peace, and water bound up in ice. But if thou hearest this, and if my voice reaches even so far; let thy favour be kindly *employed,* for a change of the place *of my exile.* This does thy father ask, who was venerated by me from my earliest years, if *indeed* that eloquent shade still enjoys any perception. This, too, does thy brother ask; although, perchance, he apprehends that thy care of saving me may be

[7] *The Pæonians.*]—Ver. 139. These were a people of Mysia, neighbouring to the Illyrians and Pannonians. In mentioning these, and Dalmatia and Illyria, he alludes to the successes that Tiberius had lately gained in Illyria.

[8] *The God Julius beholds.*]—Ver. 86. This either means that the statue of Julius Cæsar was placed in a temple (perhaps that of Venus, which he had founded), looking down upon the temple of Castor and Pollux; or it refers to his Equestrian statue, which was near the threshold of that temple.

to thy injury. All thy family asks this; and thou thyself canst not deny it, that I was in the number of thy friends. With the exception of my Art *of Love*, often wast thou the approver of my talents, which I have *since* found that I employed to bad purpose. And to thy family, no cause for shame can my life afford, if only my last fault is excepted. May, then, the fortunes of thy family *ever* flourish, and may the Gods above, and the Cæsars, have a care for thee; supplicate the Divinity that is merciful, but that is deservedly offended with me, to remove me from the barbarism of this Scythian spot. 'Tis difficult, I confess; but courage seeks obstacles; and so much the greater will be my gratitude for thy deserts. And yet neither any Ætnæan Polyphemus in his vast cavern, nor any Antiphates,[9] will be hearing thy words: but a parent, gentle and lenient, and *ever* ready to pardon; one who often thunders, without *hurling* his fiery bolts: one who, when he has come to a sad decision, himself too becomes sad; and to whom it is almost a punishment to inflict punishment. Yet his clemency has been overcome by my fault, and his anger has been forced to have recourse to his power.

And, since I am removed from my native land by the distance of the whole earth, and I have not the liberty to throw myself at the feet of the Deities themselves; do thou, as the priest, bear these requests *of mine* to the Gods above, whom thou dost adore; and to my words, add thy own entreaties *as well*. However, try these means only, if thou shalt be of opinion that they will not prove injurious. Pardon *my timidity; once* shipwrecked, I am in dread of the whole ocean.

EPISTLE III.—TO MAXIMUS.

THE Poet extols the fidelity and constancy shown by Maximus towards him in his adversity; and he says, that he was not, like the multitude, led by motives of interest, but by those of honour and virtue. He entreats him to persist in his attachment, and to give him all the aid in his power.

MAXIMUS, thou, who by thy illustrious virtues, dost equal thy name, and dost not suffer the gifts of thy intellect to be

---

[9] *Antiphates.*]—Ver. 116. He was the king of the Læstrygons, who were cannibals; they are mentioned in the Odyssey, and by Ovid in the 14th Book of the Metamorphoses.

eclipsed by thy nobleness of birth; honoured by me, even to the latest moment of my life, (for in what does this state differ from death?) Thou dost a thing, in not turning thy back upon thy friend in his affliction, than which there is nothing more uncommon in *this* thy age. It is a shocking thing, indeed, to be owned, but, if we must only confess the truth, the multitude esteems friendship according to interest. It is first, a care what is expedient, before what is honourable; and attachment both stands and falls with *a man's* fortunes. Among many thousands, thou wouldst not easily find one, to believe that virtue is its own reward. Its own comeliness, if there is no reward for a virtuous action, does not influence them, and they are sorry to be honest for no recompense. There is nothing dear *to them*, but that which is for their advantage. Go, *now, and* deprive the greedy mind of the hope of profit, *and* not one will be found, *to practise virtue for nothing*. But now-a-days every one loves his own interest, and he reckons, on his anxious fingers, what may turn out useful to himself. The once venerated name of Friendship is prostituted, and she sits like a harlot, *to be bought* at a price. The more, then, do I admire thee, that thou, as well, art not contaminated by the blemish of the universal vice, as though by a rushing torrent. No one *now*, is beloved, but *the man*, to whom Fortune is favourable: soon as she thunders, she chases away all that are near.

See my own case; I was once surrounded with no few friends, while the favouring breeze swelled my sails; soon as the raging billows were aroused by the boisterous wind, I was left, in the midst of the waves, in a shattered bark: and while the rest were unwilling to appear even to have known me, barely two or three *of you* gave aid to me, *thus* prostrate. Of them, thou wast the chief; and thou wast deserving not to be the follower *of others*, but the originator; not to seek an example, but to give *one*. Virtue and attachment, lend their aid to thee, deriving no profit from thy actions, except *the fact*, that thou hast not acted amiss. In thy judgment, virtue requires no reward, and is to be sought for her own sake, unaccompanied by external benefits. Thou thinkest it a disgrace for a friend to be repulsed, because he is in misery; and for him cease to belong to thee, because he is unfortunate. It is more merciful to place the hands under the wearied chin of the swimmer, than to overwhelm his head in the flowing waters. See, what the grandson of Æacus[10] did for his friend, after his death; and consider, that this life *of mine* is as bad as death.

Theseus accompanied Pirithoüs to the Stygian waves. In what degree does my fate differ from the Stygian streams! The youth from Phocis attended Orestes in his madness; my error, also, has no little amount of insanity. Do thou, too, accept these praises of the illustrious heroes; and, as thou art wont to do, give thy aid, so far as thou canst, to me *thus* ruined. If I know thee aright; if thou art now also what formerly thou wast wont to be, and if thy spirit has not failed thee; the more fiercely Fortune rages, the more strongly dost thou resist; and, as befits thee, thou takest care, that she shall not overcome thee. An enemy that fights well, causes thee, too, to fight well; so that the same cause works both for my advantage and my disadvantage. In truth, inestimable youth, thou thinkest it not worthy of thee, to become the attendant on *Fortune*, the Goddess that stands upon the wheel. Thou art steadfast, and inasmuch as they are not such as thou couldst wish, thou guidest the sails, such as they are, of my shattered bark. And so greatly have its ruins been shaken, as to have been deemed on the point of falling; *but* they still stand, supported by thy shoulders. At first indeed, thy wrath was just, and not any lighter than his, who was deservedly offended with me: and thou wast wont to swear that the same grief which affected the heart of the great Cæsar, was forthwith thine own. But, when the cause of my downfall was heard of by thee, thou art reported to have grieved much at my faults. Then, for the first time, did thy letters begin to console me; and to afford a hope that the offended God could be propitiated. Then, the constancy of thy continued friendship, which commenced with me before thy birth,[11] moved thee *in my favour;* both because, whereas thou didst become so to others, to me thou wast born a friend; and because, in the cradle, I gave thee the first kisses. And, whereas, thy family was ever revered by me, from my tenderest years, now in my

---

[10] *The grandson of Æacus.*]—Ver. 41. Achilles; who avenged the death of his friend Patroclus, by resuming the arms which he had laid aside, and slaying Hector.

[11] *Before thy birth.*]—Ver. 70. He alludes to his former intimacy with the father of Maximus.

old age, I am compelled to become a burden to thee. 'Twas thy father, *the embodiment of* an eloquence in the Latian language, that was not less, in degree, than the nobleness of his birth, that first urged me to dare to trust my verses to Fame; he was the guide of my genius. I assert, too, that thy brother cannot recollect at what time he first enjoyed my friendship. But, thee, before all, did I so embrace, that thou, alone, mightst be my comfort in any calamity. The extreme shores of Italy[12] saw me together with thee, and received the tears that fell down my sorrowing cheeks; *at the time*, when, as thou didst enquire whether the news was true, which an evil report of my error had circulated, I was hesitating, in doubt whether to confess, in doubt whether to deny, while alarm showed the marks of fear; and, just like the snow, which the watery South wind melts, the starting tear was trickling down my affrighted cheeks. Calling these things, then, to memory; and because thou seeest that the charges against me can be veiled under the forgiveness of a first error; thou regardest thy former friend amid the wreck of his fortunes; and thou soothest my wounds with thy consolations. In return for this, if I might be allowed to form a wish, I would pray a thousand blessings for thee, so well deserving of them.

But, if wishes entertained by thee, are alone granted me, then I will pray that Cæsar and thy mother too, may live long in health. This is the request, that I remember thou wast wont first to make of the Gods, when thou didst sacrifice upon the altars, rich with frankincense.

EPISTLE IV.—TO ATTICUS.

He calls to recollection his ancient friendship with Atticus, and the pleasant hours they had spent together; he tells him that he is persuaded of the continuance of his attachment, although he is far distant, and entreats him to continue his friendship towards him.

Receive the converse of Naso from the freezing Danube, Atticus, in my estimation one not to be doubted. And dost thou still bear in memory thy unhappy friend? or is weakened affection deserting its post? The Gods are not so far

---

[12] *Extreme shores of Italy.*]—Ver. 84. He alludes very probably to Brundisium, to which place Maximus had perhaps accompanied him when embarking for his place of banishment.

hostile to me that I could believe it, or suppose it possible that thou dost not now remember me. Before my eyes thy form stands, and is ever there; and mentally, I seem to behold thy features. I call to recollection many an hour of seriousness that has been spent by me together with thee; and no few occasions that have been devoted to pleasing sportiveness. Often did the hours seem too short-lived for our prolonged conversation; often was the day shorter than was my discourse. Often did my verses, but just composed, come to thy ears, and my new-born Muse was submitted to thy judgment. What thou wast wont to praise, I used to think would please the public; that was the delightful reward of my recent labours. And as my book was corrected by the criticism of my friend, many a time was an erasure made at thy suggestion.

Together did the market-places behold us, and every portico, the streets, and the curving theatres, our seats being next to each other. In fact, dearest *friend*, as great was the affection between us, as between the grandson of Æacus and the grandson of Actor. I could not believe, even shouldst thou drink the cup of Lethe, that banishes care, that these things could fade from thy memory. Sooner shall the long days arrive under the Constellation of midwinter, and the nights of the *summer* solstice shall be more tardy than those of winter; Babylon shall experience no heat, Pontus no cold, and the marigold shall surpass the roses of Pæstum in fragrance; than forgetfulness of my fortunes shall overtake thee. Not to that extent is no part of my destiny happy. But be it thy care that this confidence be not pronounced unfounded, and *called* a silly credulity: defend, too, thy old friend with firm constancy, so far as thou canst, and so *far* as I shall be no burden *to thee*.

EPISTLE V.—TO SALANUS.

He acknowledges his gratitude to Salanus, in return for the sorrow he manifested on his banishment, although they were not intimately acquainted; and returns him thanks for the praises he had bestowed on his verses. He requests him, if his book on the Triumph of Tiberius should come under his notice, to favour it with his protection; and concludes, by enlarging upon the natural ties that exist between persons devoted to the different branches of literature.

I Naso, have *here* sent to *my friend* Salanus my words formed into unequal numbers, prefacing them with my salutation. I desire it may obtain its fulfilment; and that it may realize its *good* omen by facts, I pray that this may be read by thee, my friend, in good health. Thy sincerity, a thing almost extinct in these days, requires me to form such wishes. For, although I was known to thee by but a slight acquaintanceship, thou art said to have lamented over my banishment; and when thou didst read my verses, sent from the far distant Pontus, thy kindness defended them, such as they were. Thou, too, didst wish that the wrath of the favoured Cæsar against me, would be but short-lived; and, did he know it, he himself would allow of such a wish. Of thy own natural excellence, hast thou conceived wishes so kind; and not the less pleasing are they to me, on that account.

And 'tis worthy of belief, most learned one, that thou art the more moved by my misfortunes, through the nature of this place. In the whole world (believe me) thou couldst scarcely find a spot which, less than this, enjoys Peace, the gift of Augustus. But here thou readest verses composed amid direful battles, and, as thou readest, thou approvest of them with favouring lips. Thou praisest, too, my genius, which flows with but an humble stream, and of a brook thou makest great rivers. This approval is, indeed, pleasing to my spirit; although thou canst hardly suppose that the wretched can be productive of pleasure for themselves. But as long as I attempt verses upon humble subjects, my ability is equal to my scanty matter. Lately, when the fame of the great triumph reached here, I dared to commence upon a work of so great importance. The magnitude and the splendour of the subject overwhelmed me, while thus daring; and I was unable to endure the burden of my enterprize. There, will be found duteous attention *on my part*, for thee to praise; *all* the rest is deficient, being weakened by the subject-matter. And if, perchance, my book has come to thy ears, I request that it may experience thy protection. Let regard for me be added *as* some small obligation by thee, who would have done this, even if I myself had not entreated thee. It is not I that deserve the praise, but 'tis thy heart, more unspotted than milk, and than the untrodden snow. Thou admirest others, when thou thyself art the object of admiration; neither thy learning nor thy eloquence can be concealed. The Prince of the youths,[13] to whom Germany gives a name, is wont to have thee, as a companion in his studies. Thou, his companion of old, thou, united to him from his earliest years, delightest him by thy genius, that equals thy virtues. As thou declaimest, the inspiration immediately rises in him: and he has thee to elicit his words by thy own. When thou hast ceased, and the lips of men are at rest, and *when thus* shut they have no long time been silent; the youth arises that is worthy of the surname of Iülus, just as the light-bearing *star* arises from out of the Eastern wave. And while he silently stands, his carriage and his aspect are those of a man of eloquence, and his becoming dress creates the expectation of a graceful delivery. Then, when delay is put an end to, and his heavenly mouth is opened, you could swear that in this manner the Gods above are wont to speak; and you would say, "This is eloquence befitting a Prince, so much nobleness is there in his language." Although thou art *thus* pleasing to him, and touchest the stars with thy head, thou still thinkest that the writings of the exiled Poet are worthy to be had. In truth, there is a certain alliance between kindred spirits, and each one cherishes the ties of his own pursuit. The rustic loves the husbandman; the soldier him that wages the cruel war; the helmsman the pilot of the veering ship. Thou too, lover of study, art influenced with a love for the Piërian maids, and, thou dost, O man of genius, feel sympathy for my genius. Our occupations are different; but they arise from the same source, and each of us is the cultivator of a liberal art. For the thyrsus[14] has been wielded by thee, the laurel by me; but enthusiasm ought to belong to us both. And as thy eloquence gives vigour to my numbers; so from us *poets* comes the *requisite* polish for thy language.

With reason, then, dost thou think that verses are on the confines of thy pursuits, and that the ties of communion in study ought to be defended. In return for this, I pray that he, with whose acquaintanceship thou art honoured, may remain

---

[13] *Prince of the youths.*]—Ver. 41. Germanicus.

[14] *The thyrsus.*]—Ver. 67. This was a staff surrounded with leaves of the vine and the ivy, which the Bacchanals waved when performing the rites of Bacchus. It was deemed the emblem of eloquence; the laurel was the characteristic of poetic excellence.

thy friend to the last moments of thy life; and that he may succeed to guide the reins of the world, that belong to thee, *Augustus:* a thing which the prayers of the public also entreat.

EPISTLE VI.—TO GRÆCINUS.

He entreats Græcinus not to censure his fault, which he has already admitted, since what has been done cannot be undone. He entreats him, rather to aid him in his misfortunes, than to persist in condemnation of him; at the same time, he acknowledges, with gratitude, the kind sympathy that he has manifested towards him.

THE sorrowing Naso, who formerly was wont, personally with his voice, *to do so,* salutes Græcinus from the Euxine waves. This is the voice of the exile. *This* letter finds me a tongue, and were I not allowed to write, I should be dumb. Thou blamest, as thou oughtst, the offence of thy foolish companion; and thou teachest me to endure woes inferior to my deserts. Thou utterest a rebuke against my fault, true *indeed,* but tardy. Cease harsh expressions, to a criminal who has made his confession. So long as I was able to pass by Ceraunia[15] with a steady sail, I was to be advised how to avoid the dangerous rocks. Of what use is it to me now, when my shipwreck has happened, to learn what course my bark ought to steer? Rather extend thy arms, to be grasped by the weary swimmer, and think it no trouble to place thy hands under my chin. And so thou dost, and so, I pray, continue to do. May thy mother and thy wife, may thy brother and all thy family be prospering. And—what thou art wont to pray in thy spirit, and ever with thy voice—mayst thou, in all thy actions, meet with the approval of the Cæsars. 'Twould be a disgrace for thee to have given no aid, in any degree, to thy old friend, in his afflicted circumstances. 'Tis a disgrace to turn back again, and not to stand with a firm attitude;[16] 'tis a disgrace to desert the ship in distress; 'tis a disgrace to follow chance, and to yield to fortune, and to deny that a person is one's

---

[15] *Ceraunia.*]—Ver. 9. These, which are also sometimes called Acroceraunia, were high rocks, which formed a very dangerous promontory of Epirus.

[16] *With a firm attitude.*]—Ver. 21. 'Passu,' literally, 'step;' but, 'to stand with firm step,' in our language, would be amenable to the charge of being paradoxical.

friend, unless he is prosperous. Not so lived the sons of Strophius and of Agamemnon; such were not the ties of the son of Ægeus and Pirithoüs. These a past age has admired, *and* a succeeding age will admire; in their applause, whole theatres re-echo.

Thou too, art worthy, having served thy friend in his adversity, to reckon thy name among heroes so great Thou art worthy *of it:* and since thou deservest praise for thy attachment, my gratitude for thy affection shall not prove dumb. Believe me (if my verses shall not perish), thou shalt be often on the lips of posterity. Only do, Græcinus, remain constant to me, *thus* ruined; and let that warmth *of feeling* endure for many a day. Although thou dost grant this, still do I use my oars[17] in the breeze. There is no harm in giving spur to a horse *even* at full speed.

EPISTLE VII.—TO ATTICUS.

AFTER saluting his friend, he inquires what he is doing, and whether he retains his former affection for him; he complains of his sad fortune, and laments his innumerable woes. He says, that amid so many evils, hope is his only consolation; and entreats him to adhere to his determination, not to abandon his friend.

THIS letter of mine, Atticus, sent from amid the half-subdued Getæ, first bids thee to be saluted; next follows the pleasure of hearing what thou art doing; and if, whatever thou art doing, thou still hast regard for me. I doubt not but thou hast; but the very dread of evils often compels me to entertain unnecessary fears. Pardon me, I pray, and forgive my excess of apprehension: the shipwrecked man dreads the waves, even when calm. The fish that has once been hurt by the lurking hook, thinks that the barbed brass is concealed in every morsel; oft does the lamb fly from the dog, seen afar, and believes it to be the wolf, and unknowingly, shuns its own protector; the wounded limb shudders at even a gentle touch; and the unsubstantial shadow strikes alarm in the apprehensive. So I, pierced with the cruel darts of Fortune, con-

---

[17] *Use my oars.*]—Ver. 37. His meaning is, that although his friend Græcinus entertains the kindest feelings, and proffers his assistance to the best of his ability, his request that he will continue to do so ought to do him no more injury than if he were to use his oars when a favourable breeze was blowing.

ceive in my breast nothing but sadness. Now I feel assured that my destiny, preserving the course it had commenced, will always pursue the paths to which it has accustomed itself. *I think* that the Gods keep watch, that nothing may turn out to my advantage; and I hardly think that Fortune can be deceived; she has a determination to ruin me, and she who was once wont to be fickle, is now constant and well-assured in her hostility. Believe me, if I am known to thee to be of truthful speech, no deceit can there be in my misfortunes. Sooner wilt thou reckon the ears of the Cinyphian[18] standing corn, and with how many sprigs of thyme the lofty Hybla is blooming; *sooner* wilt thou ascertain for certain, how many birds are soaring in the air on the wing, and how many fishes are swimming in the sea, than the amount of my troubles can be reckoned, which I have endured by land and by sea. There is no nation, in all the world, more savage than the Getæ, and yet even these have lamented over my calamities. Did I attempt to enumerate them to thee, in exact lines, 'twould be a long Iliad on my destinies. I fear not, then, because I suppose thee to give grounds for fear, whose love has afforded me a thousand pledges; but, because every one in misery is *but* a timid creature, and because for a long time the door has been shut against my happiness. Sorrow has now become a habit with me; as rocks are hollowed out by the constant contact of the falling water, so am I wounded by the lasting blows of Fortune; and scarcely can a fresh wound find on me any spot *unharmed*. Not more is the plough consumed by continual use; not more has the Appian *way* been worn by the curving wheels, than my heart has been overpowered by its series of ills; and nothing have I found to give me relief.

Glory has been attained by many through the liberal arts; I myself have been undone by my own endowments. My former life is without fault, and has been spent without a blemish; *yet* that gave me no aid in my distress. Many a time is a serious fault pardoned at the entreaties of one's friends: in my behalf all influence was dumb. In adverse circumstances, to be present is of use to others; this tremendous storm has overwhelmed

---

[18] *Cinyphian.*]—Ver. 25. This epithet signifies 'Libyan;' as the Cinyps was a river of that region, running through a tract of country which was extremely prolific in corn. Libya was frequently styled 'the granary of Rome.'

this head *of mine* in *my* absence. Who has not dreaded even the silent wrath of Cæsar? Harsh expressions have formed an addition to my punishment. Banishment is *sometimes* made more tolerable by its season; I, cast upon the ocean, have been exposed to Arcturus, and the threats of the Pleiädes. Ships are wont often to experience a calm winter; to the bark of the Ithacan the waves were not more boisterous. The faithful attachment of one's companions *would* have been able to alleviate evils of such magnitude; a perfidious set were enriched by my spoils. The place makes exile more endurable; no land, more repulsive than this, lies extended beneath the two poles. 'Tis something to be near the confines of one's country; a most remote region, the end of the earth, confines me. Thy laurels, *too*, Cæsar, ensure peace to the exiled; the Pontic land lies exposed to the neighbouring foe. 'Tis pleasant to pass one's time in the cultivation of the land; the barbarian enemy allows not the ground to be turned up. Both the body and the spirit are refreshed by a temperate climate; the Sarmatian shores are frozen with everlasting cold. In pure water there is a comfort that is begrudged to none; *here*, the water of the marsh is drunk, mixed with the brine of the sea.

I am deficient in all *comforts; and* yet my spirit subdues everything; for 'tis that which makes even my body to exert its strength. To sustain one's burden, you must strive with the head fully erect; but, should you suffer the muscles to bend, it will fall. Hope too, that the wrath of the Prince may be moderated in length of time, prevents me from desiring not to live, and from utterly perishing. And no little consolation do you afford me, ye few *friends*, whose attachment has been proved throughout my misfortunes. Persist in thy resolves, I pray, and abandon not my bark on the ocean; and preserve both thy regard for me, and for the opinion that thou hast formed.

EPISTLE VIII.—TO MAXIMUS COTTA.

He thanks Cotta for having sent him the likenesses of Augustus, Cæsar, Livia, and Tiberius; and says, that as he is forbidden to behold the originals, he will pay his adoration to their resemblances. He then expresses his hope that they will grant him a more endurable place for his banishment; and that they will not suffer their likenesses to remain in a place which must be displeasing to them.

The one Cæsar with the other, Gods whose likenesses thou didst lately send me, have arrived safe, Maximus Cotta; and, that thy present may embrace the number that it ought, Livia is there, added to her Cæsars. Happy is the silver, and more blest than any gold, which, when in its rough state it had its value, will now be as a Divinity *to me*. By presenting me with riches, thou couldst not have given me greater wealth, than *these* three Divinities, that have been set before my face. 'Tis something to behold the Gods, and to think that they are present, and to be able to converse as though with the real Divinity. How great a gift, ye Gods! The remotest region does not confine me *now;* and *once again*, as formerly, I live in safety in the midst of the City. I see the features of Cæsar, as I formerly used to see them; scarcely did I hope for the fulfilment of that prayer; and, as once I did, *so now* I salute the heavenly Divinity. Thou hast nothing preferable, I think, that thou couldst offer me on my return. What is wanting to my eyes, but the Palace alone? a place which, if Cæsar is away, becomes worthless. When I look upon him, I seem to be beholding Rome; for *in himself* he bears the *majestic* features of his country.

Am I deceived; or are the features frowning upon me in the likeness, and has the stern figure a certain threatening aspect? Pardon me, thou hero, by thy virtues elevated above the immense world, and draw in the avenging reins of thy retribution. Pardon me, I pray, thou everlasting glory of our age; whom his own watchfulness makes to be the ruler of the world. By the name of thy country, which is dearer to thee than thyself; by the Gods, who are never deaf to thy prayers; by the partner of thy bed, who alone has been found worthy of thee, and to whom thy majesty *of character* has not proved a source of anxiousness;[19] by thy son, like to thee in the resemblance of his virtues, *and* who, by his morals, can be recognized as belonging to thee; and by thy grandsons, worthy both of their grandsire, and of their father, *and* who, by rapid strides, are realizing thy wishes; do, but in a very small degree, alleviate my punishment and moderate it; and grant me a place afar from the Scythian foe. And, (if so it may be), thou, Cæsar, that art next after Cæsar *Augustus!* be thy Divi-

---

[19] *A source of anxiousness.*]—Ver. 30. The meaning of this phrase is somewhat obscure; but he seems to imply that Livia was naturally so graceful, and so well prepared to adapt herself to circumstances, that she did not feel herself overpowered by the elevated position to which she had been raised.

nity not hostile to *these* my entreaties. May, ere long, savage Germany be borne, with timorous features, before thy triumphant horses. May thy father live to the years of the Pylian *Nestor*, thy mother to those of the Cumæan *Sibyl*, and long mayst thou remain a son. And thou, fitting wife for *a husband so* mighty, listen with no obdurate ears to the entreaties of me, a suppliant. Then may thy husband be *ever* prosperous; then, with thy children, may thy grandsons, and together with thy daughters-in-law, the children which those daughters-in-law have borne, be prosperous. Then may Drusus, whom cruel Germany snatched from thee, be the only portion of thy progeny to perish; then, may thy son, clad in purple, press on his snow-white steeds, in his warfare the avenger of his brother's death. Accede, ye most merciful Divinities, to these my timorous prayers; may it be of some advantage *to me*, to have the Gods in my presence. On the approach of Cæsar, the gladiator quits the entire arena, and his countenance affords no slight aid. Let it be of some benefit to me as well, that, so far as I can, I behold your features; since one house has been visited by three Divinities. Blessed are they who behold, not the resemblance, but the originals; and who, face to face, see the real persons of the Gods. And since unkind fate has denied me this, I worship with my prayers what art has granted *me*, the resemblance *of them*. 'Tis thus that men are acquainted with the Gods whom the lofty skies conceal; and in place of Jove, the form of Jove is venerated. Lastly, have ye a care that your likenesses, which are, and which ever shall be, in my possession, be not in a place displeasing to you. For my head shall sooner part from my neck, and sooner will I allow my eyes to leave my gouged cheeks, than I will part with you torn from me, ye Gods of the commonwealth. You shall be my harbour, and the altar of my exile. You will I embrace, if I am surrounded with the Getic arms; you will I follow as my eagles, you as my standards.

Either I deceive myself, and am deluded by my excessive longing, or a hope does suggest itself, of a more desirable place of banishment; for less and less stern are the features in the likeness, and the countenance appears to assent to my requests. May the presages of my anxious mind be truthful, I pray; and, just though it be, may the wrath of the Divinity become moderated.

EPISTLE IX.—TO KING COTYS.

He writes to Cotys, the King of Thrace; and, after extolling the nobility of his descent, he tells him that it is the duty of Gods and of Monarchs to succour the distressed; and that, as Cotys himself is a poet, he has a double claim on him. He entreats him to show him kindness and hospitality in the misery attendant upon his exile.

Cotys, offspring of kings, the origin of whose noble race extends even to the name of Eumolpus;[20] if garrulous report has now reached thy ears, that I am lying prostrate in a part of the earth that is neighbouring to thee; listen, most merciful of youths, to the voice of a suppliant; and give that aid which thou canst to *me*, an exile (for such thou canst *do*). Fortune has delivered me to thee; this is a thing on which I shall make no complaint; in this thing alone, she has proved not hostile to me. Receive my wrecked ship on no inhospitable shore, that the waves may not prove safer *to me* than the land.

'Tis a regal thing (believe me) to assist the distressed; and it befits so great a man as thou thyself art. This becomes thy fortune, which, glorious though it be, can hardly prove itself equal to thy *greatness of* soul. Power is never beheld under circumstances more favourable, than as oft as it does not allow entreaties to be in vain. This the splendour of thy family requires; this is the task of a nobleness derived from the Gods above. This *course*, Eumolpus, the most illustrious founder of thy family, and Ericthonius,[21] who was before Eumolpus, recommend to thee. This thou hast in common with the Deity; that both of you, when entreated, are wont to give aid to those who supplicate you. For what reason would there be for us to worship the Deities with the usual rites, if you deny that the Gods are inclined to assist us? If Jupiter will turn a

---

[20] *Eumolpus.*]—Ver. 2. He was a son of Neptune and Chione, and reigned over the kingdom of Thrace. Aiding the Eleusinians against the Athenians, he was slain by Erectheus, as we learn from Apollodorus. The king Cotys, to whom this epistle is addressed, is, by some, supposed to have been the same person that is mentioned by Suetonius, under the name of Cotiso.

[21] *Ericthonius.*]—Ver. 20. He was one of the early kings of Athens, and succeeded Amphictyon, whom he expelled. He was fabled to have had the tail of a dragon for his lower extremities, and to have enjoyed the favour and patronage of Minerva. He was the ancestor of Chione, the mother of Eumolpus.

deaf ear to him that entreats, why should the stricken victim fall before the temple of Jupiter? If the sea will give me no rest on my voyage, why should I offer the useless frankincense to Neptune? Why should Ceres receive the entrails of a pregnant sow, if she denies the unavailing prayer of the toiling husbandman? No he-goat will, as a victim, present his throat to the long-haired Bacchus, if no new wine flows under the pressure of the foot. I pray that Cæsar will guide the reins of empire, because so well does he consult the advantage of his country. 'Tis interest, then, that renders both men and Gods illustrious; each *of us* esteeming his own *especial* benefactor. And do thou, O Cotys, offspring worthy of thy parent, give some assistance to one who lies prostrate within thy camp. 'Tis a becoming pleasure for one man to save another; and by no act is favour more readily sought. Who does not execrate Antiphates the Læstrygon? Or who disapproves of the manners of the munificent Alcinoüs?[22] He of Cassandria[23] is not thy father, or one of the race of Pheræ;[24] or he who roasted the inventor in his own contrivance; but one, as valiant in battle, and as unused to be subdued in arms, as he is averse to bloodshed, when peace is concluded.

Besides, to have thoroughly studied the liberal arts, softens the manners, and suffers them not to be brutal. And no king has been better prepared by them *than thou*, or has given more time to the pursuits of peace. Thy verses testify *this*; if thou wast to conceal thy name, I should not say that a young man of Thrace had composed them. That Orpheus might not be the only poet of this region, the Bistonian land is rendered proud by thy genius. And, as thou hast the courage, when circumstances demand it, to take up arms, and to stain thy hands with the blood of the enemy; and as thou art skilled at hurling the javelin with thy extended arm, and at guiding

---

[22] *Alcinoüs.*]—Ver. 42. He was a king of the Phœacians, who most hospitably entertained Ulysses when he was shipwrecked on his coasts.

[23] *He of Cassandria.*]—Ver. 43. This is supposed to refer to Apollodorus, a bloodthirsty tyrant of Cassandria, in Macedonia, who, in revenge for his cruelties, was first flayed alive, then thrown into a boiling cauldron, and while still living, entombed. His character, as remarkable for cruelty, is often referred to by the classical writers.

[24] *Race of Pheræ.*]—Ver. 43. Alexander, the tyrant of Pheræ, in Thessaly, was also noted for his cruelties, and was slain by his wife Thebe, with the assistance of her brothers.

the neck of the swift steed; so, when due time has been devoted to the pursuits of thy country, and when the task of valour is at rest from off thy shoulders, *peculiarly* its own; in order that thy hours of retirement may not waste away in sluggish sleep, thou seekest the bright stars by the path of the Piërian maids. This thing, too, creates some tie between thee and me: we are both of us worshippers at the same rites. To a poet, do I, a poet, extend my arms in supplication, that thy land may prove hospitable to my exile. I have not come to the Pontic shores as one guilty of murder, nor have any fell poisons been mixed by my hand; and no seal of mine has been convicted of *impressing* a forged mark on strings within which any documents are enclosed.[25] Nor have I done any thing, which I am forbidden by the laws to do; and yet, a graver fault than *all* these must be confessed by me.

But, lest thou shouldst ask what it is, I have written a silly *work on the* Art *of Love.* 'Tis that, which forbids my hands to be guiltless. *But* ask not on what other subject I have erred; and let my fault be concealed under my Art *of Love* alone. Whatever it is, I have been sensible of the moderation of the anger of the avenger, who has deprived me of nothing but the land of my birth. Since I am deprived of that, let thy vicinity now cause me to be in safety in *this* hated place.

---

[25] *Documents are enclosed.*]—Ver. 69. ' Subjecta tabella;' literally, 'a tablet being placed underneath.' The 'tabulæ,' or 'tabellæ,' were thin pieces of wood, often of an oblong shape, covered over with wax, on which an impression was traced with the iron 'stilus' These tablets were also made of ivory, but more frequently of citron-wood, beech, or fir. The inside only of the tablet was covered with wax, the outer part consisting solely of wood. The leaves were fastened with wires at the back, and opened and shut, like in the books of the present day. There was a raised margin to each leaf of the tablet (similar to our school slates), to prevent the wax of the one from rubbing against the other. From two to five, six, or even more of these leaves, were joined together. Two being so joined, were called 'diptucha,' three, 'triptycha,' and so on. Those tablets which contained legal documents, such as wills, had the outer edges pierced with holes, through which a triple thread, or string, 'linum,' was passed, on which a seal was then placed, to guard against forgery, and, without which, the document was not considered to be legally executed. To this custom the poet here refers, in saying that the crime of forgery cannot be imputed to him, as the cause of his banishment.

EPISTLE X.—TO MACER.

Writing to the poet Macer, he sets forth many reasons why he should remember him and their former terms of intimacy; and he says, that if he recals the many happy hours they once spent together, he will seem to be ever present before his eyes. He concludes by entreating him never to forget him at any future time.

Dost thou know, Macer, from the impression of the seal affixed, that it is Naso who writes to thee these words? And if the *seal* ring is not the discoverer of the writer, are these letters, written with my own hand, recognized by thee? or does length of time deprive thee of the recollection of them, and do thy eyes fail to recall to memory the ancient characters? Although thou mayst have forgotten both my seal and my handwriting, *I* only *hope* that love of me has not forsaken thee. This thou owest both to the intimacy of a length of years, and *to the fact*, that my wife is no stranger to thee, and to thy pursuits which thou hast followed with more prudence than I have, and hast not been guilty of any Art *of Love*, as became thee. Thou singest whatever was left undone by the immortal Homer; that the Trojan wars may not be without a finishing hand.[26]

Naso, a proficient of little prudence, while he is producing the Art of Love, receives a sad reward for his learning. Yet with poets there are common ties among themselves, although we each of us pursue our separate path. Of these, though I am far away, I suspect that thou art not forgetful, and that thou hast a desire to alleviate my calamities. Under thy guidance, I beheld the magnificent cities of Asia; under thy guidance, Trinacria was viewed by my eyes. We beheld the heavens glowing with the flames of Ætna, which the Giant, placed beneath the mountain, belches from his mouth; and the lakes of Henna, and the fetid pools of Palicus,[27] and *the spot* where Anapus joins Cyane with its waters; and, not far thence, the Nymph, who, as she flies from the river of Elis, runs,

---

[26] *A finishing hand.*]—Ver. 14. Homer concludes the Iliad, after the death of Hector. Macer had commenced his poem at that period, bringing it down to the taking of Troy.

[27] *Fetid pools of Palicus.*]—Ver. 25. There were two brothers, named the Palici, said by some writers to have been the sons of Jupiter; but, according to Hesychius, the name of their father was Adranus. From them, two sulphureous lakes of Sicily received the name of Palicus.

under cover, even beneath the waves of the sea. Here, a large portion of the passing year was spent by me. Alas! how unlike is that region to the Getic *land!* And, how small a part is this, of the things which we saw together, as thou didst render the journey delightful to me; whether we were ploughing the azure waves, in the painted ship, or whether the two-wheeled chaise[28] bore us, with its active wheels. Often did our journey appear short, by our interchange of conversation; and, shouldst thou number them, our words were more numerous than our steps. Often was the daytime too short for our discourse; and, while talking, the long hours of the summer day proved too short. 'Tis something, together, to have dreaded the dangers of the sea, and to have offered our united prayers to the Gods of the ocean; to have, at one time, transacted business together, and to be able to recall to memory, at another time, the sallies of wit that followed it, and of which we need not be ashamed. If these things recur to thee, though I am far away, at all hours shall I be before thy eyes, as though that moment seen.

I myself, indeed, though I am under the sky of the extremity of the world, which always stands aloof from the flowing waters, still regard thee with the only feelings that I can, and often do I converse with thee, under *that* freezing firmament. Thou art here, and thou knowest it not; thou art, while absent, repeatedly present: and thou comest, beheld *by me*, from the midst of the City among the Getæ. Make me some return; and since that place is a more happy one, ever retain me there, in thy constant breast.

[28] *The two-wheeled chaise.*]—Ver. 34. 'Esseda.' 'Essedum,' or 'esseda,' was originally the name of the chariots which were used by the natives of Britain and Gaul in warfare. The Romans copied their form for the purposes of luxury and convenience; and the use of them, in the time of Seneca, was very general in Rome. The 'esseda' were always drawn by two horses, and they are supposed to have been kept in readiness for hire, at the post-houses or stations, and to have been similar to the 'covinus,' except that the latter had a cover.

EPISTLE XI.—TO RUFUS.

The Poet is here writing to Rufus Fundanus, the uncle of his wife; he tells him, that, distant as he is, he is fully sensible of his kindness; and he prays the Gods to grant him a commensurate return for his affection.

Naso, the author of the Art *of Love*, an unfortunate work, sends thee this book, hurried off in a short space of time; that, although we are separated by the wide distance of the whole world, thou mightst be enabled to perceive that I keep thee in remembrance.

Sooner shall forgetfulness of my own name come upon me, than thy affection be banished from my breast. And sooner will I give up this breath to the vacant air, than the grateful recollection of thy kindness shall fade. I esteem the tears with which thou didst moisten thy face, when my own was dry in tearless grief, a great mark of kindness. I call *thy* consolation to a distressed mind, a great mark of kindness; when thou didst afford it, both to me and to thyself. Of her own accord, indeed, and of herself, my wife is deserving of all praise; still by thy admonition is she improved. For, what Castor was to Hermione,[29] Hector to Iülus, the same do I congratulate myself that thou art to my wife. Not to be unlike thee in virtue, is her aim; and by her life does she prove that she is of thy family. Therefore, what she would have done without any persuasion, the same does she do more abundantly, having found thee as an encourager. The steed that is thorough-bred, and that of itself would gain the honours of victory in the race, if you encourage it, will run *even* more swiftly. Besides, thou dost perform my requests, *thus* absent, with faithful diligence, and thou deemest it no trouble to bear any burden. Oh! may the Gods give thee a recompense, since I myself cannot: *the Gods*, who will reward, if they witness acts of affection. May thy body, too, last long, for *the practice of* those virtues, Rufus, thou greatest glory of the Fundanian soil.[30]

[29] *To Hermione.*]—Ver. 15. Hermione was the daughter of Helen, consequently Castor and Pollux were her uncles.
[30] *Fundanian soil.*]—Ver. 30. Fundi was a town of Campania, and was the native place of Rufus.

BOOK THE THIRD.

EPISTLE I.—TO HIS WIFE.

He enlarges upon the misery he endures in the region of Pontus; and he tells his wife, that it is not to be wondered at, if he desires a more tranquil place for his banishment; and that, as a good wife, it is her duty to exert all her energies in his behalf. He requests her to make application to Livia, the wife of Augustus, upon whose kindness of disposition he expatiates. He begs his wife to choose a fitting opportunity, and instructs her how she must act, and what request she is to make.

Thou sea, for the first time set in motion by the oars of Jason, and thou land, which art devoid of neither the savage foe, nor of *perpetual* snow, when will the time come, when I, Naso, shall leave you, being commanded to go to a region less exposed to the enemy? Or am I ever to live amid this barbarism? And must I be entombed in the soil of Tomi? With no desire to disturb thy peace[1] (if, land of Pontus, there is any peace for thee, whom the neighbouring foe is for ever trampling under his swift steed), with thy leave, I would say, thou art the most intolerable part of my wretched banishment: thou dost aggravate my woes. Thou dost neither feel the Spring bedecked with the flowery wreaths, neither dost thou behold the naked bodies of the reapers. For thee no Autumn holds forth the clustering grapes; but all seasons retain an intense cold. Thou keepest the sea bound up with ice, and often, in the ocean, does the fish swim inclosed in the covered water. Thou hast no springs, except of running water, almost as salt as the

---

[1] *With no desire to disturb thy peace.*]—Ver. 7. 'Pace tua;' literally, 'with thy peace,' corresponds with our expression, 'by,' or 'with your leave.' It is, however, necessary here to render it as above, to give full effect to the reference which the Poet immediately makes to the mention of 'peace.' His grief did not entirely preclude his indulgence in the pleasures of punning.

sea, and it is a matter of doubt whether that quenches thirst, or increases it. But few trees, and those of no strong growth, appear in the open country, and on the dry land is beheld an *exact* resemblance of the sea. No bird warbles forth its notes, unless, perchance, in the distant forest, a few drink the water of the ocean, with croaking throat. The bitter wormwood grows prickly along the unproductive plains, a harvest, in its bitterness, fitting to the place of its growth. Add, too, *continual* alarms, and the attacks of the fortifications by the enemy, and how the arrow, dipped in the deadly venom, reeks *with it;* that this region is afar, and distant from every route, and is a place where one can travel in safety neither on foot, nor on board ship. 'Tis not, then, to be wondered at, if a different spot is repeatedly requested by me, as I seek *to put* an end to these *evils*. It is still more strange, my wife, that you cannot obtain this favour, and that you can withhold your tears at my woes. Do you enquire what you are to do? You may ask that, forsooth; you will find out, if you really wish to know. To be willing is a slight matter: to obtain a thing, you must set your heart upon it, and this anxiety must curtail your moments of sleep. I believe that many have the will; for who can be so cruel to me, as to desire my exile to be spent without tranquillity? It is your duty to strive with all your heart, and all your strength, and to exert yourself night and day in my behalf. And, that others may render me aid, you ought, my wife, to surpass my friends, and to be the *very* first to fulfil your duties.

A conspicuous name has been conferred on you, in my writings: you are *there* said to be the model of a good wife; take care that you fall not short of it. Be careful that my praises are well-founded; that you may show respect for a work of Fame. Though I myself should make no complaint, yet Fame will complain, in my silence, if you have not that care for me which you ought to have. My destiny has exposed me, in the sight of the public, and has drawn upon me more attention than I formerly received. Capaneus has become better known from being struck by lightning: Amphiaraüs[2]

---

[2] *Amphiaraüs.*]—Ver. 52. He was the son of Oïcles, and was a prophet and soothsayer of Greece. Being forced by Polynices to accompany him to the Theban war, he fled from Periclymenus, who pursued him. Jupiter, on this, hurled a thunderbolt, which opening the ground,

is known, from his horses having been sunk in the earth. Had he wandered less, Ulysses would have been less known; the fame of Philoctetes became great, through his wound. If there is any room for humble names among great ones, my fall makes me too illustrious; and my pages allow not that you should be unknown, in which you have a celebrity not inferior to that of the Coän Battis. Whatever, then, you shall do, you will be beheld on an extensive stage, and you will prove an affectionate wife, with no few *persons for your* witnesses. Believe me, as often as you are praised in my verses, she who reads those praises, enquires whether you are deserving of them. And, as I believe that there will be many to approve of those virtues, so there will be no few ready to criticise your actions. Therefore, do you take care, that Envy may not be able to say, "This woman is slow in helping her afflicted husband." And, since I have lost my strength, and cannot guide my chariot, be it your care alone to keep up the flagging yoke. As my veins become exhausted, in my illness I look to the physician: come to my aid, while the last moments of my life still remain; and, as you are in stronger health, do you give me that assistance, which, if I were better than you, I would *then* give you. Conjugal affection, and the marriage tie, demand this; you yourself, my wife, demand this of your virtues. This you owe to the family in whose number you are reckoned, that you may honour it, not more by your attachment than by your goodness. Though you should do everything *besides*, unless you prove yourself praiseworthy as a wife, it will not be believed that Marcia is esteemed by you. And I am not unworthy *of it;* nor (if you are only willing to speak the truth) are there no thanks due *from you* for my kindnesses: they are repaid me with heavy interest; and Envy has not the power, though she should desire it, to injure you. But still, add this one action to your former ones, and be regardful of your duty in the alleviation of my misfortunes. Exert your energies, that I may be placed in a less hateful spot; and *then*, no part of your duty will be defective. I ask great favours, but nothing to produce dislike, when you entreat *in my behalf;* and though you should not gain your request, your denial will be productive of no danger. And do not blame me, if I request you so often, in my lines,

he and his chariot, with Bato, his charioteer, were swallowed up. After his death, divine honours were paid to him.

to do as you are doing, and to imitate yourself. The trumpeter is wont to be of use to the valiant; and the general, with his voice, cheers on the men that are bravely fighting. Your goodness is well known, and is attested to all futurity: let your courage, too, be no less than your goodness. The battle-axe of the Amazons is not to be assumed in my behalf, nor is the small target to be borne by your active hand. A Deity is to be prayed to, not to become friendly to me, but to be less angered against me, than he was before. If there is no favour *for you*, yet tears will plead in your favour. By this means, or by none at all, can you influence the Gods. It is well provided by my misfortunes, that these shall not be wanting to you; and as I am your husband, you have abundant cause for weeping. And as my fortunes stand *at present*, I think you will have to weep throughout all time. My fate supplies you with such resources *as these*.

If my death could be redeemed at the price of yours (which Heaven forfend), 'tis the wife of Admetus[3] whom you would imitate. You would become the rival of Penelope, if, as a wife, you had occasion to deceive importunate suitors by a virtuous stratagem. If you had to follow, as an attendant, the funeral of a dead husband, Laodamia would be a precedent for your actions. The daughter of Iphis[4] must be placed before your eyes, if you wish to place your body full of life on the lighted pile. There is no necessity for death, none for the web of the daughter of Icarius; but the wife of Cæsar must be implored with your own lips. She, by her own virtues, ensures that hoar antiquity shall not surpass our time in the credit of chastity. While she has *both* the beauty of Venus and the manners of Juno, she alone has been found worthy of the bed of a Divinity. Why are you trembling? Why do you hesitate to approach *her?* Neither unnatural Progne, nor the daughter of Æetes, is to be entreated by your words; no daughter-in-law of Ægyptus, nor the cruel wife of Agamemnon, nor *yet* Scylla, she who, by her lower parts, keeps the Sicilian seas in dread; nor yet the mother of Telegonus,

---

[3] *The wife of Admetus.*]—Ver. 106. Alcestis was the daughter of Pelias, and the wife of Admetus, king of Pheræ, in Thessaly. In her affection for her husband, she consented to die in his stead.

[4] *The daughter of Iphis.*]—Ver. 111. Evadne, the daughter of Iphis, in her grief, threw herself on the funeral pile of Capaneus, her husband.

born for the transformation of shapes; nor Medusa, having her matted hair wreathed with serpents. But 'tis a princely woman; in whose *instance* Fortune proves that she can see, and has removed the false imputation of blindness. This universe contains nothing in the world more illustrious than her, with the exception of Cæsar; *even* from the rising of the sun to its setting. Choose the time for entreating her, which you have often watched for, that your bark may not leave *harbour* with an unfavourable tide. The oracles do not always give out the hallowed responses; and the temples themselves are not thrown open at all times. When the state of the City shall be such, as I now suppose it to be, and when no misfortune shall be contracting the brow of the public; when the home of Augustus, honoured with rites, after the example of the Capitol, shall be joyous (as now it is, and *long* may it be so), and shall be replete with tranquillity; then may the Gods grant you liberty to approach her; then believe that your words will have some effect. If she shall be engaged with something of more importance, postpone your undertaking, and take care, not, by too much precipitation, to ruin my hopes. Again, I do not order you not to seek access to her until she is entirely at liberty; *for* she hardly has leisure to decorate her person. Should the Court be crowded with the venerable Senators, *still* must you go amid the turmoil of business. When it has been thy lot to come into the presence of Juno,[5] take care and remember the character that you are sustaining.

And do not defend my acts; silence must be preserved when a cause is bad: let your words be no other than anxious entreaties. Then there must be no cessation of your tears; and, on the ground, extend your suppliant arms to the heavenly feet. Then ask for nothing else, but that I may depart from amid savage foes; let it be enough for me for Fortune to be my foe. More things, indeed, occur to me; but, struck with awe, you will hardly be able to utter thus much with your trembling lips. I am of opinion that this will not cause you injury; let her understand that you stood in awe of her Majesty. And, if your words are interrupted by your sobs, it will do no harm; tears sometimes have the weight of words. Take

---

[5] *Presence of Juno.*]—Ver. 145. Under this august name, he intends to convey a compliment to Livia.

care, too, that a lucky day[6] is found for your undertaking, and a fitting hour, and a favourable omen. But first, after fire has been placed on the hallowed altars, offer frankincense and unmixed wine to the great Gods; among whom, before all, adore the Divinity of Augustus, and his affectionate offspring, and the partner of his bed. May they, after their usual manner, be kind to you; and may they behold your tears with no severe countenance.

EPISTLE II.—TO COTTA.

He praises the constancy of Cotta; and he says, that, whereas others deserted their friend in his adversity, he always remained firm in his attachment. He tells him that his kindness will always be remembered by him; and that it will not be forgotten after his death, should his writings survive to posterity.

I PRAY, Cotta, that the salutation which thou here readest, sent by me, may come to thee bringing its own fulfilment.[7] For, while prospering, thou greatly diminishest my torments, and thou causest a good part of me to be *still* unscathed. And when others flag, and desert my split sails, thou remainest, as the only anchor of my shattered bark. Thy affection, then, is delightful *to me;* and I pardon those, who, together with Fortune, have turned their backs in flight. Although the thunderbolts strike *but* one, not one *only* do they alarm; the multitude that is near him who is smitten, is wont to tremble. And when a wall has given symptoms of an approaching fall, that spot becomes deserted in anxious apprehension. Who, of the fearful ones, does not avoid intercourse with the sick man, in dread lest he should thereby contract the malady of his neighbour? Me too, in the extreme dread and alarm of my friends, and not through dislike, did some *of my acquaintances* desert—neither attachment, nor affectionate attention was wanting in them; they stood in awe of the hostile Deities. And, although they may appear too cautious

---

[6] *A lucky day.*]—Ver. 159. Not, in fact, one of those days that were called 'atri,' 'black,' as being remarkable for some public calamity.

[7] *Bringing its own fulfilment.*]—Ver. 2. 'Missa vere;' literally, 'sent truly;' alluding to the word 'salus,' 'health,' or, as it is rendered above, 'salutation.'

and timid, yet they do not deserve to be called bad. But my sincerity thus excuses my friends, and is in their favour, that they may have no grounds of reproach on my account. Let them be content with this indulgence; and, *if they like*, they may put it upon record, that, even by my testimony, their conduct was unimpeached. Ye few are the more desirable portion, who, in my adversity, deemed it a disgrace to give me no aid. For that reason, will gratitude for your kindness die at the time, when, my body being consumed, I shall have become ashes. *In that* I shall be deceived, and it shall extend beyond the period of my life, if indeed my works shall be read by attentive posterity. The lifeless body is the due of the sorrowing pile; fame and glory escape the erected pyre. Theseus is dead, and he who was the companion of Orestes; but still each of them lives in his own praises. And you too, shall our remote descendants often praise, and in my writings your fame will be distinguished. Even here, the Sauromatæ and the Getæ have now heard of you; and the barbarian multitude approves of such feelings. And when, lately, I was making mention of your goodness (for, I have learned to speak the Getan and the Sarmatian languages), by chance a certain old man, as he was standing in that company, answered my words to the following effect:—

"We too, stranger, whom the freezing Danube confines, far from you *at Rome*, are well acquainted with the name of friendship. There is a place in Scythia, (the ancients call it Tauri,) which is not so very far distant from the Getic land. Of this land I am a native, and of my country I am not ashamed: this nation worships the Goddess, the sister of Phœbus. Her temple remains to this day, supported on vast columns; and you ascend to it by ten times four steps. The story is, that in this place there was a statue, that had come from heaven; and that you may have the less hesitation *in believing it*, the pedestal still stands there, deprived of the Goddess. The altar, too, which had been white from the nature of the stone, is dyed red, *being* discoloured by the blood which was shed *upon it*. A woman, who is a stranger to the torch of marriage, performs the rites; *one*, who is pre-eminent among the Scythian matrons in noble station. The nature of the sacrifice is, (for thus did our forefathers ordain) that the stranger must die, struck by the sword of the virgin. Thoas ruled the kingdom, *a man* illustrious in the land of Mæotis; and no one was more famed throughout the waters of the Euxine. While he held the Sceptre, they say, that a certain Iphigenia, a stranger, made her way *thither*, through the liquid air. Her, carried under a cloud by the light breezes through the air, Phœbe is supposed to have deposited in these regions. She had *now* presided, in due form, over the temple for many a year, performing the woeful rites with unwilling hand; when two young men came in a sail-bearing ship, and trod our shores with their feet. Their ages were alike, and so *was their* affection; of these, the one was Orestes, the other, Pylades. Fame preserves their names. They are immediately led to the remorseless altar of Trivia, having their two hands bound behind their backs. The Grecian priestess sprinkles the captives with the water of purification, that the long *sacred* band may encircle their yellow hair. And while she is preparing the rites, while she is binding their temples with the fillets, and while she is ever discovering some ground for tardy delay: she says, 'Pardon me, young men, I am not cruel; I perform rites that are more barbarous than their own country. *Yet*, such is the custom of *this* nation. But, from what city do ye come? and whither were ye directing your course, in your unfortunate bark?' She spoke, and the pious virgin, on hearing the name of her country, found out that they were inhabitants of her own city. 'Let one of you,' she says, 'fall as a victim; let the other go, as the messenger of these rites, to your paternal abodes.' Pylades, on the point of death, bids his dear Orestes go: the other refuses; and each, in his turn, strives to die. This is the sole thing, on which they are not agreed: in *all* other respects, the pair are of one mind, and without disagreement. While *these* beauteous youths are waging *this* contest of love; she pens written characters to her brother. She *there* gives a message for her brother, and he to whom it was given (see the accidents of mortals) was her brother. There is no hesitating; from the temple they carry off the image of Diana: and by ship, they are stealthily borne over the boundless waters. *This* wondrous friendship of the youths, although so many years have elapsed, even yet enjoys great celebrity in Scythia."

After this hackneyed story was related by him; all praised their actions and their faithful attachment. In truth, even in this land (than which there is none more uncivilized) the name of friendship moves the hearts of barbarians. What ought ye to do, who are born in the Ausonian City, when such actions affect the ruthless Getæ? Besides, thou hast always a kind disposition, which has thy virtues for a proof of thy high nobility; *virtues*, which Volesus,[8] the founder of thy paternal name, would approve, and which Numa, thy maternal ancestor, would not disavow as his own. The Cottæ too, who are added to thy family name, a house that would have perished,[9] hadst thou not existed, would praise *them*. Oh thou, *thus worthy* of that line, believe that it is befitting such virtues to assist a ruined friend.

EPISTLE III.—TO FABIUS MAXIMUS.

He says, that while reclining on his couch, Cupid presented himself, and that he requested the God, that, inasmuch as through him he had been exiled, he would prevail upon Augustus to grant him a less disagreeable spot for his banishment. He then states the answer that he received from Cupid.

If thou hast leisure to give a little time to thy exiled friend, do thou be present, Maximus, thou star of the Fabian house, while I tell thee what I have seen; whether it was the phantom of a body, or an appearance of reality, or a dream.

'Twas night; and the Moon was entering the windows with their two shutters,[10] as strong as she is generally wont to shine

---

[8] *Volesus.*]—Ver. 105. He was the paternal ancestor of Cotta; being a Sabine, who migrated to Rome with Titus Tatius. Silius Italicus tells us that Volesus was of Spartan origin.

[9] *That would have perished.*]—Ver. 108. From this, it appears that he had been adopted into the Aurelian branch of the house of Cotta, which had, at the time of the Poet's writing this Epistle, become extinct.

[10] *Their two shutters.*]—Ver. 5. This alludes to the fact that many of the windows were openings in the wall, closed by means of shutters, which sometimes had two leaves, or compartments. They were frequently without any other protection or covering than the shutters; but were sometimes covered with lattice or trellis work, and sometimes with net-work. Laminæ of 'lapis specularis,' or 'mica,' were used in later times, to admit the light, while excluding the cold. Glass was also used under the early emperors, as frames of glass windows have been found in some of the houses at Pompeii. It is most probable that the window of the room in which the Poet lay at this period was glazed either with 'mica' or glass; as it is not likely that in a climate, the cold of which, as he often says, he felt so bitterly, he would lie in bed exposed to the chill of the night; as,

in the middle of the month. Sleep, the common respite from care, possessed me, and my languid limbs were stretched over the whole couch; when, suddenly, the air shook tremulously, beaten by wings, and the moved window creaked with a gentle noise. Startled, I supported my body on my left arm; and sleep, dispelled, departed from my trembling breast. Cupid was standing, with a countenance not such as he was formerly wont, in his sadness holding a maple staff in his left hand. On his neck he had no collar,[11] no hair-pin in his hair;[12] nor was he neat, with his locks well arranged, as formerly. His soft hair was hanging over his rough countenance, and his wings appeared all ragged to my eyes: just as it is wont to be on the back of the aërial pigeon, which many fingers of handlers have touched. Soon as I recognized him, (and none was better known to me) my tongue, set at liberty, addressed him in such words *as these:* "Oh boy, the cause of exile to thy beguiled master, whom it had been more to my interest not to have had for my instructor; hast thou come hither, too, where there is peace at no time, and the barbarian Danube freezes with his icy waves? What is the cause of thy journey? unless that thou mightst be the witness of my sorrows, which are, if thou knowest it not, a cause for hatred against thee. Thou wast the first to dictate the poems of my youth; under thy guidance, I have alternated the five feet with the six feet.[13] Thou didst not allow me to soar aloft with the Mæonian verse, nor to celebrate the actions of great generals. Perhaps thy bow and thy flame diminished the powers of my genius, *which, small though perhaps they were, were* still something. For

by his mention of the rays of the moon entering the room, it is clear that the shutters were not closed, as he lay.

[11] *Had no collar.*]—Ver. 15. 'Torquem.' The 'torquis,' or 'torques,' was an ornament of gold, twisted spirally and bent into a circular form, which was worn round the neck by the men of the upper classes among the Persians, Gauls, Britons, and other northern and eastern nations. Cupid is here represented as wearing no 'torques,' as a sign of grief.

[12] *No hair-pin in his hair.*]—Ver. 15. 'Crinale.' This alludes to the custom of the women, and probably the children among the ancients, of platting the hair, and then fastening it behind with a hair pin. This was called either 'acus crinalis,' or 'crinale,' absolutely, as in this instance. They were made of metal, wood, bone, or ivory, and resembled a needle or bodkin with a sharp point. This fashion still prevails in Italy and Germany, and has been adopted in some degree in England.

[13] *With the six feet.*]—Ver. 30. 'That is, when he composed his 'Amores,' in the Elegiac measure, in his younger days.

while I was singing of thy sway, and that of thy mother, my mind never had leisure for any work of magnitude. And that was not enough; in my folly, too, I wrote verses, that thou mightst, through my books on the Art *of Love*, become not inexperienced. In return for these, exile was given as a recompense to wretched me; that, too, in regions the most distant, and without *the enjoyment of any* peace. But Eumolpus, the son of Chione, *did* not *prove* such towards Orpheus, nor was Olympus such towards *Marsyas*, the Phrygian Satyr. Chiron received no such reward from Achilles, and they do not say that Numa did any injury to Pythagoras. And, not to repeat names collected over a long space of time, I am the only one who have been ruined by my own scholar. While I am providing thee with weapons, while, wanton one, I am instructing thee; the master receives such a gift as this from his scholar. *And* yet thou knowest, and thou mightst say it, sworn to the truth, that I plotted not against lawful wedlock. These things did I write for those whose chaste hair the fillet does not touch, nor the long gown their feet. Tell me, I pray, when didst thou learn to beguile the matrons, and, through my precepts, to cast a doubt on *the legitimacy of* their offspring? Is not every woman strictly repulsed from these books, whom the law forbids to entertain men by stealth? But of what avail is that, if I am considered to have composed precepts for adultery, forbidden by severe laws? But thou, mayst thou have arrows that strike all things, and may thy torches never be without the burning flame; may Cæsar, who is the descendant of thy brother Æneas, rule the empire, and hold sway over the whole earth; *but* do thou cause that his wrath against me be not implacable, and that he allow me to be punished in a place more agreeable."

These things did I seem to say to the winged boy; these words did he seem to utter to me. "By the torches, *that are* my weapons, and by the arrows *that are* my weapons, and by my mother, and by the head of Cæsar, do I swear, that, under thy instruction, I learned nothing but what was lawful, and that there is no ground for accusation in thy books on the Art *of Love*. And would that, like this, I could defend thee in other respects! Thou knowest that it is rather another thing that caused thy ruin. Whatever it is (and that grief ought not to be disclosed) thou canst not say that it was unattended with fault on thy part. Although thou mayst screen the change under the appearance of error, still the anger of the Avenger was not greater than was deserved. But yet, that I might behold thee, and that I might console thee thus prostrate, my wings have glided through immeasurable tracts. These regions did I first behold, at the time when, at the request of my mother, the Phasian damsel *Medea* was pierced by my weapons. Thou, soldier that art a friend to my camp, art the cause of my revisiting this land, after a length of ages. Lay aside, then, thy fears; the wrath of Cæsar will be assuaged, and a more joyous time will come, at thy entreaties. And fear not delay; the time that we look for, is at hand; and triumph makes every *place* to be filled with joy. While thy house, and thy sons, and their mother Livia are happy; while thou art happy, great Father of thy country, and of the *triumphant* General; while the people is feeling an inward joy, and, throughout the City, every altar is glowing with the perfumed flames; while the venerable temple is affording an easy access; 'tis to be hoped that our prayers may *at length* be enabled to prevail."

He spoke; and either he disappeared in thin air, or my senses began to awake. If I doubted, O Maximus, of thy approval of these words, I could believe that there are swans of the colour of Memnon.[14] But neither is the milky stream changed into black pitch; nor does the ivory, which was white, become the turpentine tree. Thy birth is befitting thy spirit; for thou hast a heart that is noble and endowed with the honesty of Hercules. Envy, that spiritless vice, attacks not *such* high feelings; like a viper, it crawls lurking on the ground beneath. Thy lofty spirit rises superior to thy very descent; and thou hast not a name that is more illustrious than thy character. Let others, then, injure the distressed, and desire to be dreaded; and let them wield their arrows, tipped with the corrosive venom; thy house has *ever* been accustomed to aid the prostrate: in the number of these, I pray thee to allow me to be.

[14] *Colour of Memnon.*]—Ver. 96. That is, black. The ancients considered that a black swan was the very ideal of an impossibility: modern enterprise has corrected this mistake, and has shown us, by ocular demonstration, that such a bird exists in the Australasian continent.

EPISTLE IV.—TO RUFINUS.

Ovid, having sent to Rome his Poem on the Triumph of Tiberius, after the conquest of Illyria, requests his friend, Rufinus, to take it under his protection. He excuses himself on many grounds, because he feels that he has not done justice to his subject. He then addresses Livia, the mother of Tiberius, and foretells that he will shortly have another triumph, and that over Germany.

Thy friend Naso sends thee, from the city of Tomi, these words that bear no insincere salutation; and he bids thee, Rufinus, to show favour to his Triumph; if indeed, it comes into thy hands. 'Tis *but* a little work, and unequal to its vast subject; but, such as it is, I entreat thee, take it under thy protection. *Bodies* that are healthy are strong of themselves, and seek *the aid of* no Machaon: the sick man, in his uncertainty, has recourse to medical aid. Great poets have no need of an indulgent reader, they captivate one, however unwilling and difficult *to please*. I, whose talents protracted toils have impaired, (or may be, I had none even before), infirm in strength, recover health by thy kindness; shouldst thou withhold that, I should think myself deprived of every thing. And, whereas *all* my productions rely upon partial support, this book has an especial claim to indulgence.

Other poets have written of a temple which they beheld; 'tis something to set down what we have seen with a recording hand. I write of these things, with difficulty caught by me in public with greedy ear; and rumour has been *in place of* eyes for me. Does, forsooth, the like enthusiasm, or the same inspiration arise from things when *only* heard of, as from them when seen? I complain not that the splendour of the silver and of the gold, and the purple which ye beheld, was wanting to me; but still the *various* places, the nations modelled in a thousand forms, and the battles themselves, would have invigorated my lines. The countenances, too, of the kings, the surest indexes of their feelings, would perhaps, in some measure, have aided that work. Every genius is able to grow warm at the applause of the public, and at its transports of joy. As much vigour should I have acquired, amid such acclamations, as the raw soldier does, when he hears the trumpet sound to arms. Although my heart were made of snow and ice, and were colder than this region that I am *now* enduring; yet the features of that Chief, as he stands in his ivory chariot, would dispel every chill from my senses. Defective in these respects, and furnished with uncertain authorities, with good reason I have recourse to the aid of thy favour. Neither the names of the leaders nor those of the places are known to me; my hands with difficulty met with subject matter. Of events so great, how large a part was there that Fame could repeat, or that any one could write to me? With greater reason, then, O reader, thou oughtst to pardon me, if there is anything there omitted by me, or in which I am mistaken. Besides, my lyre, that has dwelt upon the everlasting complaints of its master, was with difficulty brought round to a song of joy. Words of gladness hardly recurred to me seeking them after so long a time: to be at all joyful, seemed to me a novelty. And as the eyes dread the sun, to which they are unused, so was my mind averse to joyousness. Novelty is the most endearing of all things, and thanks for a kindness, which delay retards, are lost. I suppose that other works, written in a spirit of emulation about the great triumph, have already been read by the lips of the public. The reader drinks of those cups when thirsty, when *now* satisfied, of mine; that stream is drunk of when fresh, mine becomes nauseous.[15] I have not been idle, nor has slothfulness made me tardy: the remotest shore of the wide ocean confines me. While report is arriving hither, while my hurried verses are being composed, and, when composed, while they are travelling to you *at Rome*, a whole year may have passed away. And it makes no slight difference, whether you first pluck the roses *before* untouched, or whether, with a late hand, when there are scarcely any left. What wonder is there, when the garden is exhausted, the flowers having been picked, if a chaplet has been formed, not worthy of its chief!

I entreat no poet to think that this is said against his verses: in her own behalf has my Muse spoken. I have kindred ties with you, ye poets; if it is allowed to the wretched to be of your number. Ye, my friends, have lived with me, as *being* a large portion of my *very* life; even in this region, I, *still* ever present,[16] hold you in esteem. May my verses then be commended to your

---

[15] *Becomes nauseous.*]—Ver. 56. 'Tepescit;' literally, 'grows warm.' Warm water, when drunk alone, is generally productive of a tendency to nausea.

[16] *I still ever present.*]—Ver. 70. 'Non absens:' literally, 'not absent.'

favour, in behalf of which I cannot address you personally. Writings generally please after death; because envy is wont to attack the living, and to tear them with unfair tooth. If it is a kind of death to live in wretchedness; the earth *only* awaits me, and the sepulchre alone is wanting to my end. Lastly, although this result of my labours should be blamed on every side, there will be no one to blame my zeal. Although strength is wanting, yet the inclination is to be commended; with this, I trust, the Gods are content. This is the reason, why, even the poor approach the altars acceptably; and *why* a lamb pleases not less than a slaughtered ox. The subject, too, was so great, that it would have proved a burden even for the great poet of the Æneid to support it. The weak Elegiac measure, too, was not able to bear on its unequal wheels the excessive weight of a triumph.

I am doubtful in opinion, what kind of measure I shall now use; for another triumph is approaching; one over thee, O Rhine. The presages of the truth-telling poets are not deceptive. A laurel must be offered to Jove, while the former one is still green. Thou art not *now* reading my words, who am far removed to the Danube, to streams that are drunk of by the unsubdued Getæ. 'Tis the voice of a Divinity; a Divinity resides within my breast: I foretell and I prophecy this under the influence of a God. Why, Livia, art thou delaying to prepare the chariot and the procession for the triumph? Wars do not now cause thee any delay. Germany throws aside her spear, which she curses; now wilt thou say that my prophecy has its weight. Have faith, and soon will thy confidence be realized; thy son will reiterate his honours, and will, as before, go in procession with the yoked steeds. Prepare the purple, which thou mayst place on the victorious shoulders: the very laurel is able to recognize the head to which it is accustomed. Let the shields and the helmets sparkle with gems and with gold; let the trophies on the lopped trunks stand above the men in fetters. Let the towns in ivory be surrounded with the turreted fortifications; and let an imitation of a thing be supposed to be performed after the manner of the original. Let the squalid Rhine have his hair gathered under his broken reeds, and his waters tinged with blood. Now, captive kings are demanding the ornaments of barbarism, and woven vestments of more worth than their own lot. *Prepare*, too, the things which the invincible valour of thy family, both has caused, and will cause, to be prepared by thee.

Ye Gods, by whose command I have given utterance to the future, verify my words, I pray, by a speedy fulfilment.

EPISTLE V.—TO MAXIMUS COTTA.

He launches forth in praise of the speech of Maximus Cotta, which he had delivered before the judicial court at Rome, a copy of which he had sent the Poet to read; and he begs him often to send him his productions. He says that, in his absence, he ever seems present to him; and that he fancies himself at Rome, in his company, as though in the enjoyment of heaven. When he remembers that he is in Scythia, he says that he seems to return to the infernal regions.

Dost thou inquire, whence the letter was sent to thee, that thou art *now* reading? *'Tis* from here, where the Danube joins the azure waves. When the place has been mentioned, the author, too, ought to recur to thee, Naso the poet, who was ruined by his own talents. *'Tis he* who sends thee, Maximus Cotta, from among the shaggy Getæ, the salutation which he would rather give thee in person.

I read, O youth that hast not degenerated from the eloquence of thy father, the fluent language that has been spoken by thee in the crowded court. Although this has been read by me with a hastening tongue, throughout several hours, my complaint is, that there was too little. But this I have made more by often reading it again; and never was it less pleasing to me, than it was at first. And since, when so often read, it loses nothing of its interest, it pleases by its own merit, and not by its novelty. Happy were they, whose lot it was to hear it in reality, and to enjoy *the pleasure of* language so eloquent! For although there is a pleasant taste in water that is fetched, water is drunk with greater pleasure at the spring itself. It is more gratifying, too, to pluck the apple from the bough pulled downward, than to take one from a sculptured dish. And, unless I am mistaken, had not my Muse caused my exile, thy voice should have given utterance *in my presence* to the work which I have read. As was my wont, perhaps as one of the hundred men, I should have been sitting as a judge over thy words; and a greater pleasure would have filled my heart, when I was influenced by thy language, and yielded my assent to it.

Since fate, yourselves and my country being left behind, has preferred that I should be among the barbarian Getæ, often send me, I beg, as it is permitted thee to do, the pledges of thy pursuits, to be read *by me*, that I may seem still more to be with thee: follow, too, my example, unless thou despisest it—*a thing* which, more properly, thou thyself shouldst show me. For I, Maximus, who for some time have been dead to you, *my friends*, endeavour, through the medium of my genius, not to perish *utterly*. Give a commensurate return; and let my hands receive no few memorials of thy labours, that will be *so* pleasing *to me*. But tell me, O youth, so devoted to my pursuits, art thou not, by those very *pursuits*, reminded of me? When either thou art reciting the poem which thou hast just composed, to thy friends, or when, as thou art often wont, thou art requesting them to recite, does not thy heart grieve, forgetting what it is that is absent? Assuredly it does feel that an indefinite portion of itself is wanting. And as thou wast wont to speak much of me when among you, is now too the name of Naso *often* on thy lips? May I, indeed, perish, wounded by the Getic bow (and may that be the punishment of my perjury which thou seeest thus near me), if I do not in thy absence behold thee almost every moment.

Thanks to the Gods, the spirit may range wherever it pleases. *In my imagination*, when, beheld by none, I have arrived in the City, I often hold discourse with thee; I often enjoy thy conversation. At that moment, it is hard to say, how delightful it is to me; and how happy is that hour, in my thinking. At that moment (if I may be at all trusted), I believe myself received into the abodes of heaven, along with the blessed Gods. Again, when I have returned hither, I leave the heavens and the Gods above; and the Pontic soil is not far removed from the Styx. If, against resisting fate, I am struggling to return thence, do thou, Maximus, divest me of an unavailing hope.

EPISTLE VI.—TO A FRIEND.

He writes to one of his friends, who, through fear of Augustus, did not wish his name to be mentioned in his writings; he bids him consider the merciful disposition of the Emperor, and tells him that he has no just grounds for apprehension; but he promises that, without his leave, he will not insert his name in his letters. He asks him, if he cannot venture to do so openly, at least to maintain his former affection towards him in secret.

Naso sends these few lines, from the Euxine waves, to his *old* companion, to which he was nearly adding the name. And why, when others deem it safe, art thou the only one to request that my lines should not name thee? By me, if thou knowest it not, thou mayst be informed, how great is the mercy of Cæsar, in the midst of his wrath. Were I compelled to be the judge of my own deserts, I should be able to subtract nothing from this punishment which I am suffering. He does not forbid any one to remember his companion; he does not prevent me from writing to thee, nor thee to me. Thou canst commit no crime, if thou consolest thy friend, and dost alleviate his cruel fate by soothing words. Why, while thou art fearing in safety, dost thou cause such dread to become a ground of hatred against the august Deities? We have sometimes seen those that have been blasted by the bolts of the lightning, live and recover, Jove not forbidding it. Because Neptune had shattered the ship of Ulysses, Leucothöe did not refuse to aid him as he swam. Believe me, the Deities of Heaven spare the wretched, and they do not for ever and unceasingly persecute the afflicted. And no God is more lenient than our Prince; he moderates his might by justice. Cæsar has lately placed her in a temple built of marble;[17] he did so, long since, in the temple of his mind. Jupiter hurls his lightnings at random against many, who have not deserved punishment for a commensurate fault. When the God of the ocean has overwhelmed so many in his relentless waves, how large a number of them was deserving to be drowned? Were all the

---

[17] *Temple built of marble.*]—Ver. 25. This temple is not anywhere mentioned by the classical authors. Some commentators think that reference is made to the temple which was dedicated to Mars Ultor, or the Avenger, after the defeat and death of Brutus and Cassius. They justify this supposition, on the ground that vengeance, or rather retribution, is a part of justice.

bravest to perish in battle, the choice of Mars, even in his own judgment, would be unjust. But if, perchance, thou shouldst desire to inquire of us *Romans*, there is no one who would deny that he is deserving of what he endures. Besides, no day can again bring to life those that have perished either by the sea, or by warfare, or by fire. Cæsar has pardoned many, or has modified a part of their punishment: and I pray that he may will me to be *one* of that multitude. And dost thou, when we are a people under such a Prince, believe that there is ground for apprehension in the correspondence of an exile? Perhaps, with Busiris for thy master, thou mightst with reason have dreaded this, or with him, who was wont to roast men shut up in the brass. Cease to asperse a merciful spirit with thy vain fears. Why, in the tranquil waves, art thou in dread of the rocks? I seem hardly able to find an excuse for myself, because I first wrote to thee without a name. But fear had taken away the use of reason from me, *thus* stupified, and all judgment had forsaken me in my misfortunes. Dreading my destiny, not the wrath of the Avenger, I myself was alarmed by the superscription of my own name.

Thus far exhorted, indulge the grateful Poet, that he may insert thy dear name in his sheets. It will be a disgrace to *us* both, if thy name, connected with me by long acquaintanceship, is to be read in no part of my book. But, that this apprehension may not disturb thy slumbers, I will not be affectionate beyond thy wishes; and I will conceal who thou art, unless thou thyself shalt have *first* given me permission. No man shall be compelled to receive my gifts. Only do thou, if it is a cause of anxious fear *to thee*, love him in secret, whom thou couldst even love openly without danger.

EPISTLE VII.—TO HIS FRIENDS.

THE Poet writes to his friends, and complains that his letters are eternally on the same subject, and that after he has so often entreated them to obtain of Augustus either liberty for him to return, or to go to a more tranquil place of exile, he knows not what language to use. He says that in future he must change his subject, lest he should appear burdensome to them and to his wife, who, through fear, does not dare to second his wishes. He also says that he will bear his evils with equanimity, as he has endured sorrows even greater; and expresses himself ready to die an exile.

WORDS fail me, asking the same thing so often, and I am at

last ashamed that my useless entreaties have no end. I suppose that weariness is the result of lines all of the same tenor, and that you have all learned by heart what I desire. Already do ye know what my letter brings, although the paper is not *yet* loosened from its strings; therefore, let the purport of my writings be changed, that I may not so often go against the stream that carries me away. Pardon me, my friends, if I have confidently reckoned upon you; henceforth there shall be an end of such mistakes. I will not be called a burden to my wife, who, forsooth, is as timid and as inexperienced in my case, as she is virtuous. This too, Naso, shalt thou endure; for worse hast thou already suffered. By this time *the weight of* no burden can be felt by thee. The bull that is taken from the herd refuses the plough, and withdraws his youthful neck from the galling yoke. I, whom Destiny has been wont to treat with cruelty, have long ceased to be unprepared for any evils. I have come to the Getic land; in it let me die, and let my destiny go on to the end, by the path on which it has begun. Let it delight to adhere to a hope, which does not ever delight *to elude us* by its frustration; and if you desire anything to happen, think it will come to pass. The next step after this, is, entirely to despair of safety; and to feel convinced, once for all, with a certain assurance that we are ruined. In the healing, we see certain wounds become larger, which it had been better not to have touched. He dies a more easy death, who is overwhelmed by a sudden torrent, than he who wearies his arms in the swelling waves.

Why have I imagined that I could depart from the Scythian regions, and be blessed with a happier land? Why did I ever hope for any more leniency in my behalf? Was my fortune thus experienced by me? Behold! I am tormented still more bitterly, and the beauty of places, called to my memory, renews the sadness of exile, and begins it afresh. Still, it is better for the zeal of my friends to have slumbered, than for the entreaties which they have used, to have been of no avail. Great, indeed, is the thing, my friends, which ye dare not do; but, had any one asked it, there was one who would have granted it. If only the wrath of Cæsar has not denied you that, I will die courageously amid the Euxine waves.

EPISTLE VIII.—TO MAXIMUS.

He sends a quiver and arrows to Maximus, from Tomi, and says that, as he has not the means of sending him any better present, he hopes that he will take in good part a gift of such a trifling nature.

I was considering what presents the country of Tomi is able to send thee, testifying my attentive affection. Thou art worthy of silver, more worthy still of yellow gold: but they are wont to delight thee *only* when thou *thyself* givest them. Besides, this soil is not enriched by any metals: the foe scarcely permits it to be turned up by the husbandman. Often has the glistening purple covered thy *under* garments; but that is not dyed by the Sarmatian hand. The sheep bear coarse fleeces, and the matrons of Tomi have not learned to employ the arts of Pallas. The woman bruises the gifts of Ceres, instead of *spinning* wool, and she carries the heavy weight of water, her head placed beneath. The elm here is not clothed with the clustering vines; no apples bend the branches with their weight. The unsightly plains produce the bitter wormwood, and the soil shows, by its productions, how bitter it is.

There was nothing, then, in all the region of Pontus, that lies on the left hand, which my attention could send thee. Still I have sent thee some arrows, enclosed in a Scythian quiver; may they be stained, I pray, with the blood of thy foe. Such pens as these, such books as these, does this land possess: this is the Muse that flourishes, Maximus, in the place of my abode. Although I am ashamed of sending them, because they seem *so* trifling; still I beg thee to take it in good part, that I have sent them.

EPISTLE IX.—TO BRUTUS.

Brutus had written to tell Ovid that a person had blamed his writings for containing nothing but complaints about the place of his exile, and entreaties to be removed to another country; on which the Poet, in answer, admits that there are many faults in his verses, and that it would have been well had there been that one only. He then states the reasons why he has not corrected them, and tells Brutus why he has so frequently repeated the same thing, as his letters were written to different persons, and were not originally intended to be collected in one work.

Thou tellest, me, Brutus, that some one, who, I know not, finds fault with my poems, because in these books the subject is *always* the same; that I pray for nothing but to enjoy *the favour* of a spot not so remote, and that I complain that I am surrounded by a numerous foe. Oh! how is it, that out of so many faults, but one alone is censured? 'Tis well, if my Muse is wrong in this only. I myself am sensible of the faults of my works; whereas, *usually*, every one approves of his own verse more than it deserves. The author *naturally* praises *his own* works. Thus, perhaps, in days of yore, Agrius[18] said that Thersites had good features. But that error does not lead my judgment astray; nor do I forthwith fall in love with anything to which I have given birth. Dost thou ask then, why, if I see my error, I *continue to* commit faults, and suffer grounds for censure to exist in my writings? The art of perceiving and removing diseases, is not the same. The sense of feeling exists in all; by skill *alone*, disease is removed. Often, when I wish to change a word, I leave it; and my ability falls short of my judgment. I often (for why should I hesitate to confess the truth to thee?) feel it a trouble to make a correction, and to endure the tedium of protracted exertion. Enthusiasm itself aids the writer, and diminishes his toil; and, as the work grows, it waxes warm along with his feelings. But, to correct, is a thing as much more difficult, as the illustrious Homer was greater than Aristarchus.[19] It galls the mind, by the languid chill of anxiety, just as the charioteer pulls in the reins of the anxious steed. And so may the benignant Deities mitigate the wrath of Cæsar against me, and may my bones be covered by a soil that enjoys tranquillity; as sometimes, when I endeavour to exert pains, the cruel form of my destiny presents an obstacle. And I hardly appear to myself of sound mind, for writing verses, and for taking care to correct them, amid the savage Getæ.

But there is nothing more pardonable in my writings,

---

[18] *Agrius.*]—Ver. 9. He was the father of Thersites, who, as well as being deformed, was the most cowardly and contemptible character in the Grecian army before Troy.

[19] *Aristarchus.*]—Ver. 24. He was a grammarian of Alexandria, and a commentator upon the writings of Homer. Ælian tells us that he was considered to be a person of such refined and exquisite taste, that those lines were rejected by universal assent, which he had pronounced not to have been written by Homer. His name was applied proverbially, perhaps with some degree of injustice, to those who were inclined to be hypercritical or censorious in their judgments.

than that but one idea almost pervades them all. When joyous, I have usually sung joyous songs; when sad, I compose what is sad. Either season is suitable to its own productions. On what should I write, but on the miseries of this dreadful spot, and entreat that I may die on a more agreeable soil? Oft as I say the same things, I am heard by hardly any one; and my words, unnoticed, fail of effect. And yet, although they are the same things, I do not write them to the same persons; and my single voice seeks aid through many *intercessors*. Ought one only of my friends to have been intreated, Brutus, lest the reader might twice meet with the same subject? It was not of so much consequence *to me*: pardon the confession, ye learned: the reputation of my works is of less value than my own safety.

Lastly, whatever subject-matter any poet has planned out for himself, he varies many things, according to his own judgment. My Muse, also, is a too faithful indicator of my misfortunes; and she carries the weight of an uncorrupted testimony. And it was not either my purpose or my intention that a book should be composed, but that to each person should be delivered his own letter. Afterwards, I united them when collected, without any order, however; that thou mayst not suppose by chance that it was a work of selections by me. Pardon my writings, of which fame was not the cause with me, but self-interest and affection *united*.

BOOK THE FOURTH.

EPISTLE I.—TO SEXTUS POMPEIUS.

He tells Pompeius that it shows a want of affection, not to have mentioned him in his lines; as he has received services at his hands which deserve never to be forgotten. He confesses that through his assistance he was saved, and that by his kindness he still exists.

RECEIVE, Sextus Pompeius, a poem composed by him, who is indebted to thee for his life. If thou dost not forbid thy name to be placed *there* by me, that will be added as the crowning point to thy deserts. But if thou contractest thy brow, in truth, I shall confess that I have done wrong. Still the cause of my fault is a praiseworthy *one;* my feelings could not be withheld from being grateful. Let not thy anger, I pray, be heavy against this affectionate mark of attachment. Oh! how often did I appear to myself ungrateful in these *my* books, because thou wast to be read of in no part *of them!* O! how often, when I was intending to write another *name*, has my right hand unconsciously traced thy name on the wax! My very mistake pleased me, in a slip like this; and with difficulty was the blotting out *of thy name* made with unwilling hand. He must see it at last, said I; though he should complain, I am ashamed that I have not deserved this censure sooner.[1] Give me *the stream of* Lethe, that takes away the memory, *and* yet I cannot be forgetful of thee. I entreat thee to permit it to be so, and not to repel my words, *as though* disdained *by thee;* and do not consider there to be any ground for censure in my attachment. Let this slight mark of affection repay thy

---

[1] *Deserved this censure sooner.*]—Ver. 16. His meaning seems to be, that he felt convinced, that whenever he should write, his friend would certainly answer him, upbraiding him with his neglect; and that he is ashamed that he has so long deferred writing, and thereby bringing upon himself the censure that he merits.

great deserts; but if not, I will be grateful, even against thy will. Thy kindness was never idle about my welfare; thy chest never denied me its bounteous riches. Now too, thy benevolence, not at all alarmed by the suddenness of my downfall, gives aid to my existence, and will do so.

For what reason, perhaps thou mayst enquire, have I so great confidence in the future? Every one has regard for the work which he has completed. As the Venus, who is wringing her hair dripping with the ocean wave, is the production and the glory of the artist of Cos;[2] as the warlike Goddess stands, formed by the hand of Phidias,[3] the guardian, either in ivory or in bronze, of the Athenian citadel; as Calamis[4] asserts the glory of the horses which he has made; as the heifer of Myron[5] resembles life; so I, Sextus, not the slightest portion of thy works, am esteemed to be the gift and the produce of thy protection.

EPISTLE II.—TO SEVERUS.

He writes to the Poet Severus, and excuses himself, on several grounds, for not having yet mentioned his name in his Pontic writings; although he has not omitted repeatedly to send him letters, written in prose.

What thou art reading, O Severus, most illustrious poet of the great kings,[6] comes even from amid the unshorn Getæ. I am ashamed (if only thou wilt allow me to speak the truth), that

---

[2] *The artist of Cos.*]—Ver. 29. This was Apelles, the painter, who was a native of Cos, an island of the Ægean sea. His most famous painting was the one here mentioned, of Venus Anadyomene, or Venus rising from the sea.

[3] *The hand of Phidias.*]—Ver. 32. He was an Athenian, and the most celebrated of the Grecian sculptors. He made a statue of Minerva, twenty cubits in height, and formed of ivory and gold. It was in a standing position, and was erected in the citadel of Athens. He also made a statue in bronze, of the same Goddess, which was remarkable for its extreme beauty.

[4] *Calamis.*]—Ver. 33. Calamis was an artist of great celebrity. His statues of horses were considered to be unrivalled.

[5] *Myron.*]—Ver. 34. He was a famous sculptor, whose most celebrated work was the figure of a heifer. Pliny the Elder makes mention of it.

[6] *Poet of the great kings.*]—Ver. 1. He means, by this expression, to address him as a tragic poet; as kings, and persons of exalted station, were generally the subjects of tragedy, while persons of the humbler classes usually figured in comedy.

as yet my books have not mentioned thy name. Yet the affectionate letter, devoid of *poetic* numbers, has never ceased to be exchanged between us. 'Tis verses alone, signifying my grateful attachment, that have not been sent thee. For why should I send that which thou makest thyself? Who would give honey to Aristæus? wine to Falernian Bacchus? corn to Triptolemus? apples to Alcinoüs? Thou hast a prolific fancy, and for no one among the cultivators of Helicon does that crop spring up more abundantly. To send verses to such a one as this, would be to heap leaves in the woods. This, Severus, was the cause of my delay. Nor yet does my genius favour me, as formerly; but I plough a dry sea-shore with a barren plough-share. As, forsooth, the slime chokes up the springs in the waters, and the stream, obstructed, is kept back in the fountain stopped up, so have my abilities been destroyed by the slime of my misfortunes; and my verses flow from a less prolific source. Had any one placed Homer himself in this country, even he, believe me, would have become a Getan.

Pardon the confession: I have given a loose rein to my pursuits, and few are the letters that are traced by my fingers. That holy inspiration, which fosters the genius of poets, which was once wont to exist in me, is gone. The Muse scarcely attends to her duty; scarcely, when compelled, does she give her tardy hands to the writing tablets when taken up. I have little pleasure in writing, not to say none; and I take no delight in connecting words in *poetic* numbers. Either *it is*, because I have derived no advantage thence, inasmuch as 'twas that thing that was the beginning of my woes; or, *it is* because it is the same thing to dance to time in the dark, as to write verses which you can read to no one. A listener sharpens one's energy; and excellence, when approved of, *still* increases. Applause, too, gives an immense stimulus. Here, to whom can I recite my writings, except to the yellow-haired Coralli, and the other tribes which *the country of* the barbarian Danube contains? But what can I do alone? and on what subject can I wear away my wretched hours of idleness, and beguile the day? For, since neither wine, nor deceiving games of chance, have any charms for me, by means of which time is wont stealthily to pass away in silence; nor, as I could wish, if savage warfare would allow it, does the earth, renewed in its cultivation, amuse me; what remains *for me* but a cold solace, the Piërian maids, Goddesses who have not deserved well of me. But do thou, by whom the Aonian fountain is drunk of with more success, cherish a pursuit which turns out to thy advantage; and deservedly venerate the rites of the Muses, and send hither some production of thy recent labours, for me to read.

EPISTLE III.—TO A FAITHLESS FRIEND.

He rebukes the perfidious and fickle conduct of a former friend, whose name he conceals; since, although he had been on the strictest intimacy with him from his earliest childhood, he has not only deserted him in his adversity, but has even pretended that he knew him not. He concludes, by recommending him to keep in mind the vicissitudes of Fortune, and her inconstancy.

Shall I complain, or shall I hold my peace? Shall I write the charge without the name, or shall I will it to be known to all who thou art? I will not use thy name, lest thou shouldst be graced by my censure; and, lest fame should be obtained by thee, through my verse. So long as my bark was in good condition, with strong keel, thou wast the first to be willing to take a passage by me. Now, because Fortune has contracted her brow, thou withdrawest; at a time when thou knowest that I stand in need of thy aid. Thou feignest ignorance, too, and thou wishest not to seem to have known me; *and*, when thou hearest my name, thou enquirest, "Who is *this* Naso?"

I am he; although thou dost not wish to hear it, who, when almost a boy, was united with thee, *then* a boy, in early friendship. I am he, who was first accustomed to know thy serious *thoughts*, and the first to be present at thy joyous sports. I was thy comrade, and thy friend in the most intimate acquaintanceship; I was the only poet, in thy judgment; I am the same one, perfidious man, of whom thou now knowest not whether I am living, *or not;* about whom 'twas no care of thine to make enquiry. If I have never been dear to thee, *then* thou confessest to have acted the hypocrite; if thou didst not pretend it, thou wilt be proved *to be* inconsistent. Tell me now, come, tell me, what offence it is that has *thus* changed thee; for, unless thy complaint is a just one, mine is just. What thing is it that now forbids thee to be like what thou wast formerly? Dost thou call it a crime, because I began to be unfortunate? If thou didst give me no assistance in reality, and by deeds, *yet* there might have come *from thee* a paper inscribed with *two or* three words. For my part, I hardly believe it; but report says, that thou dost insult me *thus* prostrate, and art not sparing of thy words.

What art thou doing, madman? Why art thou withdrawing tears from thy own wreck, supposing that Fortune should abandon thee? That Goddess confesses how changeable she is on her unsteady wheel, which she ever keeps on its edge, under her wavering foot; she is more fleeting than a leaf or than any breeze. Thy fickleness, thou faithless one, is alone equal to her. All that belongs to man is pendent from a slender thread, and that which was firm falls headlong with a sudden descent. By whom has not the wealth of the rich Crœsus been heard of? and yet, as a captive, he received his life from an enemy.[7] He who was but just now dreaded in the city of Syracuse, with difficulty repelled cruel hunger by a lowly employment.[8] Who was greater than he styled "the Great?"[9] *and* yet, in his flight, with imploring voice, he entreated aid of his dependant; and the very man whom the whole world obeyed, was rendered more needy than all *besides*. Marius, the man who was made illustrious by the triumphs over Jugurtha and the Cimbri, under whom, oft as he was Consul, Rome was triumphant, lay concealed in the mud[10] amid the reeds of the marsh, and endured many things disgraceful to so great a man. The Divine power finds sport in

---

[7] *From an enemy*.]—Ver. 38. Crœsus, the rich and powerful king of Lydia, being conquered by Cyrus the Great, was condemned to be burnt, and being placed on the pile, recalled to mind the remarks of Solon, on the instability of human affairs. Cyrus, being struck with the circumstance, and the wondrous mutation of his enemy's fortunes, pardoned him.

[8] *By a lowly employment*.]—Ver. 40. Dionysius the tyrant of Sicily, being expelled from Syracuse, fled to Corinth, where he earned a livelihood by pursuing the calling of a schoolmaster.

[9] *He styled 'the Great.'*]—Ver. 41. He here alludes to the miserable end of Pompey the Great.

[10] *Concealed in the mud*.]—Ver. 57. Marius, flying from the faction of Sylla, was obliged to seek safety by hiding among the reeds in the marshes of Minturnæ. Being discovered, he was thrown into prison, and a Cimbrian slave being sent there to put him to death, he was so struck by the majestic dignity of his countenance, that he was unable to perform his cruel mission. Marius defeated Jugurtha, the king of Numidia, in Africa, and defeated the Cimbri, a powerful people of Germany, who had invaded Italy.

the affairs of men, and the present moment hardly carries certainty. Had any one said to me, "Thou wilt go to the shores of the Euxine, and wilt be in dread, lest thou be wounded by the bow of the Getan;" I would have said, "Go and drink those potions that cure the mind; and whatever beside is produced in the whole of Anticyra."[11] Yet, this I have endured; and even if I could *have defended myself* against mortal weapons, I could not, as well, have provided against those of the Gods. Do thou then feel apprehensive, and believe, that that can turn out sad, which, while thou art speaking, seems joyful.

EPISTLE IV.—TO SEXTUS POMPEIUS.

He says that no state is so utterly wretched as not to have some intermixture of joy; and he shows how that has been his lot. He says that, as he walked along the sea shore, Fame told him that Pompeius would be Consul for the ensuing year, and that this has afforded him extreme pleasure. He then laments that he cannot be present to see his friend assume the Consulate; but entreats him sometimes to bestow a thought on him in his exile.

No day is so far surcharged with clouds, borne by the South winds, that the showers flow in torrents without intermission. No spot is so barren, that there is not generally in it some useful plant, mingled with the rough brambles. Misfortune has made nothing so wretched, that pleasure does not diminish the evil by some cessation. Lo! I, deprived of my home, my country, and the sight of my family, am driven in my shipwreck, to the waters of the Getic shores; and yet I have found a cause for relaxing my brow and not remembering my lot.

For while, in my sadness, I was pacing the yellow sands, a wing behind me seemed to make a *faint* noise. I looked back: there was no person that I could see; yet, these words were caught by my ear—"Behold, I, Fame, am come to thee, the messenger of joyful things, having glided along immense tracts through the air. The next year will be auspicious and happy, when Pompeius shall be Consul, than whom no one is dearer to thee." She spoke; and soon as she filled Pontus with the

---

[11] *Anticyra.*]—Ver. 54. This was an island near the coast of Phocis. It was remarkable for the quantity of hellebore which grew there, the juice of which plant was supposed by the ancients to be curative of madness.

joyous news, the Goddess hurried her steps thence to other nations. But, my cares dispersed amid my recent joy, the intolerable ruggedness of this place was forgotten by me. Therefore, when, Janus with the two heads! thou shalt have unlocked the long year, and December shall have been expelled by the month sacred *to thee*, the purple of the supreme dignity shall array Pompeius, that he may be deficient in no one of his honours.

I seem already to behold the inmost parts of the house bursting with the multitude, and the people crushed for want of space: and the temple of the Tarpeian abode, for the first time entered by thee, and the Gods readily acceding to thy prayers; the snow-white bulls, too, which the Faliscan grass has fed on its plains, yielding their necks to the unerring axe. And when thou hast begged all the Gods to be propitious to thee, and some most especially; *there* will be Cæsar along with Jove. The Senate-house will receive thee, and the Senators, convoked according to custom, will give ear to thy words. When, with its eloquent utterance, thy voice shall have gladdened these; and, as it is wont, the day shall have produced its words of congratulation; and thou shalt have given the merited thanks to the Gods above, together with Cæsar, who will afford reason for thee often to do so: then thou shalt return home, the whole Senate accompanying thee; thy house being hardly able to hold the respectful multitude. Ah! wretched am I! that I am not to be seen in that crowd; and that my eyes will not be able to enjoy these things! Although far away, I shall behold thee, so far as I can, in my mind: it will look upon the features of its own Consul. May the Gods cause my name, at some time, to recur to thee, and thee to say—"Alas! what is that unfortunate man doing?" Should any one bear to me these words of thine, I will confess that my exile will at once become more endurable.

EPISTLE V.—TO SEXTUS POMPEIUS, WHEN CONSUL.

The Poet is supposed to be addressing his own lines, before sending them to Pompeius, to whom he wrote the last Epistle; he states his message, and the extreme obligations he is under to Pompeius, declaring, that through his kindness he has become his property. He then prays him to continue to preserve that life which he has already saved.

Go, humble Elegiacs, to the learned ear of the Consul, and

bear words to be read by a man, honoured *by his office*. Long is the road, and ye speed onward, with uneven feet; and the earth lies hid, concealed under the wintry snow. After you shall have passed over cold Thrace, and Hæmon capt with clouds, and the waters of the Ionian Sea: in less than ten days you will arrive at the City, the mistress *of the world*, although you should not make a hurried progress. Then, straightway, let the house of Pompeius be sought by you; none is nearer to the Forum of Augustus. If any one of the multitude should inquire who ye are, and whence: let him, with deceived ear, hear any names you please. For, although it may be safe to confess, as *indeed* I think it is, undoubtedly a false account causes less fear. You will have no opportunity, too, of seeing the Consul, some one preventing you when you have arrived at the threshold. Either he will be ruling his own Quirites, by pronouncing judgment, when, on high, he shall be seated on the ivory *chair*, conspicuous with its carvings; or he will be adjusting the revenues of the people by the erected spear,[12] and he will not allow the resources of the great City to be diminished. Or, when the Senators shall have been summoned to the temple built by Julius *Cæsar*, he will be transacting business worthy of so great a Consul. Or, he will be giving the wonted salutation to Augustus and his son, and will be asking advice on the duties not *yet* well-known *to him*. After these, Cæsar Germanicus will occupy all his spare time; to him he pays respect, next after the great Gods.

But, when he shall have rested, after the anxieties of these matters, to you will he extend his beneficent hands: and, perhaps, he will enquire what I, your parent, am doing. I wish you to answer him in words like these: "He is still living, and to thee, he confesses that he owes the life, which, in the first place, he holds as a gift from the benignant Cæsar. With grateful lips, he is wont to repeat, that thou, when he went into exile, didst point out a safe road through the lands of barbarism; that through the anxiety of thy mind it was ef-

---

[12] *By the erected spear.*]—Ver. 19. The public revenues were farmed out, or sold, under the superintendence of the Consul, to the highest bidder. In auctions, a spear was usually erected, which was said to have been a symbol, derived from the old and summary practice of selling under a spear the booty acquired in war. Hence, the phrase 'Sub hasta vendere,' means, 'to sell by auction.'

fected, that he did not make the Bistonian snow warm with his blood. That there were many presents besides added to the preservation of his life, that he might not exhaust his own resources. That *due* thanks may be returned for these kindnesses, he swears that he will be thy property for all *future* time; for that, first shall the mountains be destitute of the shady tree, and the seas shall have no sailing ships, *and* the rivers shall again return to their springs, by streams flowing upward; before gratitude for thy kindness can pass away." When you have said these things, entreat him to preserve what is his gift: and so, the purpose of your journey will have been fulfilled.

EPISTLE VI.—TO BRUTUS.

He says that he has now passed five years in Pontus; and that Fabius Maximus is dead, in whose intercession in his behalf he had centered his hopes. He admits, however, that Brutus has shown equal affection towards him. He enlarges upon the virtues and abilities of Brutus, and declares that he never will be ungrateful for the kindnesses of those friends, who have been faithful in their attachment during his adversity.

The Epistle, which thou art reading, Brutus, comes to thee from those regions in which it would not be thy wish for Naso to be. But that which thou wouldst not wish, my wretched destiny has willed. Ah me! it is more powerful than are thy desires! An Olympiad of five years[13] has been spent by me in Scythia; time is now passing into *the period of* a second lustrum. For stubborn Fortune *still* persists, and insidiously opposes her spiteful foot to my wishes. Thou hadst resolved, Maximus, the light of the Fabian house, to speak to the Divinity of Augustus, with suppliant voice, in my behalf. Thou didst die, before *thou hadst preferred* thy entreaties, and I believe, Maximus, that I was the cause of thy death; not such was my value. I now dread to entrust my safety to any one. Aid itself perished with thy death. Augustus had begun to

---

[13] *An Olympiad of five years.*]—Ver. 5. The Olympiad was a period of four years, which intervened between each celebration of the Olympic games, which were held at Olympia, in Elis. The Olympiads began to be reckoned from the year 776 B.C. Ovid calls an Olympiad 'quinquennis,' as consisting of four complete years, and terminating just at the commencement of a fifth.

pardon my fault, committed through deception: he has abandoned my hopes, and the earth at the same moment. *And yet*, Brutus, I, placed here far away, have placed before thee, a poem, such as I could, on the newly-made inhabitant of the heavens. May that act of piety, be favourable to me; and may there be a limit now to my woes, and may the anger of that holy family be moderated. I could swear for certain, that thou too, Brutus, known *to me* by no uncertain signs, prayest the same thing. For, whereas thou hast ever shown me sincere affection, still did that affection wax stronger in the hour of adversity. Whoever had beheld thy tears and mine together, would have supposed that both of us were about to undergo punishment. Nature produced thee kind to the wretched, and gave not a more benignant heart to any one, Brutus, than to thee. So that, if any one were ignorant what is thy power in the warfare of the courts, he could hardly suppose that the accused are pursued to conviction by thy lips. In truth, it belongs to the same person, although there appears to be a discrepancy, to be gentle to the suppliant, to be terrible to the guilty. When the vindication of the rigid law has been undertaken by thee, each of thy words has, as it were, venom infused. May it be the lot of thy enemies to find how impetuous thou art in warfare, and to feel the weapons of thy tongue. These are sharpened by thee with a care so imperceptible, that all deny that thy genius belongs to that body *of thine*. But if thou seeest any one crushed by cruel Fortune, no woman is more pitying than are thy feelings. This I especially was sensible of; when a great part of my acquaintances denied *all* knowledge of me. I shall be forgetful of them, *but* never forgetful of you, *my friends*, who have anxiously alleviated my misfortunes. And first shall the Danube (too close to me, alas!) turn its course from the Euxine sea to its source; and, as though the days of the feast of Thyestes[14] had returned, the chariot of the sun be driven towards the Eastern waves; before any one of you, who have mourned me *thus* torn away, can prove that I, in my ingratitude, have not remembered him.

[14] *Feast of Thyestes.*]—Ver. 47. When Atreus served up the children of Thyestes, to be eaten by their father, according to the fable, the sun ran back in his course, being struck with horror at the atrocity of the deed. The story has been more fully referred to in a previous Note.

EPISTLE VII.—TO VESTALIS.

Vestalis having been sent to assume the command in the regions of Pontus, Ovid calls upon him to witness the truth of his assertions, as to the wretched nature of that country; he then enlarges upon the valour of Vestalis, and promises that his exploits shall be commemorated by his verse to all futurity.

Since, Vestalis, thou hast been sent to the waves of the Euxine, that thou mayst dispense justice in regions situate under the Pole, thou beholdest, thyself being present, in what kind of a land I am placed; and thou wilt be a witness that I am not accustomed to make idle complaints. Young man, sprung from the Alpine kings, by thy aid undoubted confidence will be given to my words. Thou thyself seeest, no doubt, that Pontus is hardened with frosts; thou thyself beholdest the wine frozen with hard ice; thou thyself beholdest how the Iazygian herdsman leads his laden waggons over the midst of the waters. Thou seeest, too, the poison hurled beneath the barbed steel, and the arrow bearing a double cause of death. And would that this portion had been only beheld by thee, and that it had not, too, been known by thee in personal combat! Thou didst aspire to the office of a Chief Centurion, through many a danger; an honour which of late deservedly fell to thy lot. Although this dignity be abounding for thee in plenteous advantages,[15] yet valour itself will be the first in rank. This the Danube cannot deny, whose waters thy right hand once made red with Getic blood. This Ægypsus[16] cannot deny, which, retaken, when thou didst enter it, was sensible that there was no advantage in the natural resources of the place; for that city was even with the clouds, on the top of a mountain ridge, *and it is* doubtful whether *it was* better defended by position or art. The savage enemy had taken it from the Sithonian king, and, victorious, possessed the intercepted wealth; until Vitellius[17] bore his standards, car-

---

[15] *In plenteous advantages.*]—Ver. 17. The office of Chief Centurion, or 'Primipilus,' was extremely lucrative, in the advantages and emoluments that accompanied it.

[16] *Ægypsus.*]—Ver. 21. This was a well fortified town, situate in the Scythian territory, on an eminence near the banks of the Danube.

[17] *Vitellius.*]—Ver. 27. History is silent as to any further particulars relative to this officer.

ried along the waves of the stream, among the Getæ, his soldiers having landed. But, most valiant descendant of the ancient Daunus,[18] an impulse came on thee to go against the opposing enemy. There was no delay. Conspicuous afar, in glittering arms, thou takest care that deeds of bravery shall not be concealed; and, with rapid strides, thou advancest against both steel and the *fortified* place and the stones, more numerous than the hail of midwinter. Neither the multitude of javelins, hurled upon thee, nor yet the darts which are reeking with the blood of the viper, stop thee; the arrows with their coloured feathers bristle on thy helmet, and hardly is any part of thy shield without a wound; nor does thy body fortunately escape all blows, but pain is inferior to the love of glory. In such manner, at Troy, Ajax is said in defence of the Grecian ships to have warded off the torches *hurled* by Hector. When thou hadst now approached nearer, and the combat was hand to hand, and the fight could be waged with the fierce sword at close quarters; 'tis difficult to say what thy courage there performed, and how many thou didst put to death, and whom, and in what manner. Thou, victorious, didst tread upon heaps made by thy sword; and many a Getan was under thy foot placed upon him. The next in rank fights after the example of the Chief Centurion;[19] and the soldiers both give and receive many a wound; but thy valour as much outshines the others, as Pegasus did in speed the swift horses. Ægypsus is taken, and, Vestalis, thy exploits have been attested in my verse to all *future* time.

EPISTLE VIII.—TO SUILLIUS.

AFTER the death of Augustus, Ovid writes to Suillius, the son-in-law of his wife, and thanks him for his letter, late as it is, which he has just received. He asks him to entreat Germanicus in his behalf, and he promises, not to erect in his honour marble temples, but to sing his praises in his poems. He then shows that it is most becoming to express gratitude to princes in poetical effusions. He extols the merits of poesy, and prays that his verses may conduce to his own advantage; and concludes by saying, that if he is denied permission to return to his country, still, a place of exile, nearer to Rome, will give him a better opportunity of celebrating the exploits of Cæsar.

SUILLIUS, graced by studious pursuits, thy letter arrived here

[18] *Daunus.*]—Ver. 29. He was king of the Rutulians, who settled in Apulia, and was the father of Turnus and Juturna.

[19] *The Chief Centurion.*]—Ver. 49. 'Primi pili.' This was the First,

safe, late, but still pleasing to me. In it, thou sayest that if affectionate esteem can soften the Gods above by entreaties, thou wilt give me assistance. Though hitherto thou hast availed nothing, I am indebted for thy friendly disposition; and I call it a kindness to have the wish to aid. May only this anxiety of thine last to a late period; and may thy affection be not worn out by my misfortunes. The links of connexion make a certain tie between us; and that they may ever remain unbroken, is my prayer. For she who is thy wife, the same is almost my daughter: and she who calls thee son-in-law, calls me husband. Wretched am I, if thou contractest thy brow when thou readest these lines, and art ashamed to be my connexion! But thou wilt be able to find here nothing deserving of shame, except Fortune, who proved blind for me. Shouldst thou trace my pedigree; we shall be found to be Knights, from the earliest stock, even through unnumbered ancestors. Shouldst thou wish to enquire what is my character; take away my *mistake* from wretched me, and it is free from blemish. Only do thou, if thou shalt have a hope that anything can be done by entreaty, implore the Deities, with suppliant voice, whom thou dost venerate. Thy Gods are the youthful Cæsar; appease thy own Divinities; assuredly no altar is better known to thee than this. It never suffers the entreaties of its worshippers to be in vain; hence seek relief for my fortunes. Should it aid me with a breeze ever so small, my sunk bark will rise again from the midst of the waves. Then will I offer the solemn frankincense in the burning flames, and I will testify how great is the power of the Gods. But I will not erect to thee, Germanicus, a temple of Parian marble. This downfall has diminished my property; let thy own family and rich cities erect temples to thee; Naso will show his gratitude with his verses, *which are* his wealth. I confess, indeed, that but small gifts are returned for large ones, when I give *but* words in return for my deliverance granted to me. But he is abundantly grateful, who gives the most he can; affection *thereby* reaches its limits. The frankin-

---

or Chief Centurion, of the first maniple of the Triarii. He was originally called 'Centurio Primus,' and afterwards 'Centurio Primipili,' or, as in the present instance, 'Primipilus.' He was next in rank to the military Tribunes, and sat on the military council. In his charge, too, was the eagle of the legion, whence he obtained the title of 'Aquilifer.'

cense which the poor man offers to the Gods out of the little censer, is not less availing than that which is offered out of a broad charger. The sucking lamb, too, just as much as the victim fed on the Faliscan pasturage, when slain, stains *with its blood* the Tarpeian altars. And indeed, nothing is more pleasing to men of regal dignity than gratitude expressed through the verse of poets. Verses perform the heralding of your praises, and they provide that the fame of your actions be not fleeting. By verse is valour made immortal; and, free from death, it obtains the notice of late posterity.

Decaying age consumes both iron and stone; and no one thing has greater power than time. Writings survive the length of years; through writings hast thou known of Agamemnon, and who bore arms against him, or who, with him. Who, without verse, could have known of Thebes and the seven chiefs, and of what took place after these things, and what before? The Gods, too, (if I may be allowed to say so,) exist through poetry; and majesty so great has need of the voice of one to celebrate it.

'Tis thus we know that Chaos, when divided, derived its parts from that *original* mass of early nature; thus, that the Giants aspiring to the realms of heaven were hurled to Styx by the storm-bearing fires of the Avenger. 'Twas thus that the victorious Bacchus received glory from the conquest of the Indians; Alcides, from the taking of Œchalia;[20] and lately, in some degree, verse hallowed thy grandsire, whom his virtues added to the number of the stars. If then, there is any life *at all* still remaining in my genius, it shall all be at thy service. Thyself a poet, thou canst not despise the homage of a poet; according to thy own judgment, that pursuit has its worth; and had not so great an influence invited thee to loftier *objects*, thou wouldst have been the especial glory of the Piërian maids. But it was more glorious to afford us a subject-matter, than verses; and yet thou canst not entirely abandon them. For at one time thou art waging war; at another, thou art fitting thy words into measure, and what is a business to others, the same is a sport to thee.

[20] *Œchalia.*]—Ver. 62. Hercules made war on Eurytus, the king of Œchalia, whom he killed, together with his sons. He took and plundered the town, and led Iole away captive, to gain whom he had undertaken the expedition.

And as Apollo is slow at neither the lyre, nor the bow, but either string comes in contact with his sacred hands; so art thou defective in neither the arts of the scholar nor those of the Prince; but the Muse is united with Jove in thy intellect. And inasmuch as she has not removed me from that stream, which the hollowed hoof of the Gorgon steed has formed, may she aid me, and may she give me assistance in performing the rites that are common *to us*, and in applying my hand to the same pursuits; in order that I may, at length, escape from the shores too much exposed to the Coralli clad in hides, and from the cruel Getæ; and, if my country is shut against wretched me, that I may be located in any place, that is less distant from the Ausonian City; from which I may be able to sing thy new-born praises, and to relate thy great exploits, with the least possible delay.

Implore for one who is almost thy step-father, dear Suillius, that this prayer may influence the Divinities of the heavens.

EPISTLE IX.—TO GRÆCINUS.

THE Poet, having been informed that Græcinus is Consul elect, laments that he is away from Rome, and cannot share in the general joy, or take part in the ceremonial; and such being the case, he bids his letter perform his part. He requests Græcinus to entreat in his behalf that he may return; and he says that his joy is increased by the fact that Flaccus, the brother of Græcinus, will succeed him in the Consulship, whose good offices he also entreats. He concludes by enlarging upon the miseries of his exile.

NASO sends thee this salutation, Græcinus, from the Euxine waves, from a spot whence it is permitted him, not whence he delights, *to do so*. And may the Gods grant that, *thus* sent, it may arrive on that morn, which shall be the first to present thee with the twice six fasces.[21] And since without me, thou, as Consul, wilt approach the Capitol, and I shall not be a portion of thy retinue; let my letter act the part of its master, and perform the duty of thy friend on the day appointed. Had I

[21] *Twice six fasces.*]—Ver. 4. The Consuls were attended by twelve Lictors, without whom they never appeared in public. These preceded the Consul in a line, one behind another. The one that went last, or nearest to the magistrate, was he to whom the requisite commands were given, and he was called 'Proximus Lictor.'

been born under better destinies, and had my chariot sped onward with unbroken wheel, my tongue would have performed the duty of saluting thee, which now my hand discharges, by means of my writing. Congratulating thee, I would have given thee kisses with complimentary words; and that honour would not have less been mine than thy own. On that day (I confess it) I should have been so proud, that hardly any house could have contained my pride. And while the body of the venerable Senate attended at thy side, I, of Equestrian rank, should have been seen going before[22] the feet of the Consul. And although I could wish ever to be close to thee, I should have rejoiced not to have had my place at thy side. And I should not have been complaining, even if I had been squeezed by the crowd; but it would then have been a pleasure to me to be pressed by the populace. I should have beheld, in my joy, how lengthened was the train of the procession, *and* how dense a crowd occupied the long road. And that thou mayst the better know how trifling matters influence me, I should have looked to see what kind of purple clothed thee. I should also have observed the wrought statues on the curule chair, and all the sculptured work of the Numidian tusk.[23] And when thou shouldst have been escorted to the Tarpeian heights, until the devoted victim should fall by thy order, the great God, who dwells in the midst of the temple, should have heard me in secret giving him thanks. I would also have offered frankincense, with a mind three or four times more bounteous than the charger *containing it*, overjoyed by the honours of thy dignity. Here should I have been numbered among thy friends *then* present: if only my destinies had auspiciously given me permission to be in the City: and that pleasure which now is conceived by my mind, could then have been enjoyed by my eyes. It seemed not thus to the inhabitants of heaven, and perhaps, with justice; for what can it

[22] *Seen going before.*]—Ver. 18. In the Consular procession, it was customary for the Equestrian order to precede the Senators. It appears that it is from the enjoyment of this right of precedence, that the Poet says that he should be required, during the time of the procession, to leave his place by the side of the Consul.

[23] *Of the Numidian tusk.*]—Ver. 28. It has before been observed, that the curule chair was made of, or decorated with, ivory. The greater part of the ivory used by the Romans, was most likely to be the produce of Numidia, and other provinces of the north of Africa.

avail me to deny the cause of my punishment? And yet I will use my mental powers, which alone are not banished from the spot, and so will I behold thy Consular robe [24] and thy Fasces. They only shall behold thee, dispensing justice to the people, and shall feign to be present in thy places of privacy. At one moment, they shall behold thee setting up to auction, under the spear, the revenues of a long lustrum, and letting out each thing with a scrupulous fidelity; at another time, eloquently speaking in the midst of the Senate, discussing what the public welfare requires; at another time, decreeing thanks to the Gods above, on account of the Cæsars, and striking the white necks of the choice bulls.

And would that, when thou shalt have already prayed for things of more consequence, thou wouldst entreat that the wrath of the Deity against me be appeased! May, at these words, the sacred fire shoot upwards from the laden altar, and may the pointed flame, in its brilliancy, give a good omen to thy prayers. Meanwhile, in so far as I may, that I may not ever be in querulous mood, I will celebrate here, too, the festive day on thy Consulship. Another cause of joy, and one that yields not to the first—thy brother shall be thy successor in an honour so great. For, as thy rule, Græcinus, is finished on the last day of December, he commences it on the day of Janus; and, such is the affection between you, you will share your joys alternately, thou in the Consular dignity of thy brother, he in thine. Thus thou wilt have become twice Consul, and twice Consul, he: and in thy family will be beheld a twofold honour: which, great though it is, and *though* Rome sprung from Mars, beholds no sway more lofty than *that of* the supreme Consul; yet the dignity of the giver amplifies this honour, and a thing that is given partakes of the majesty of him who confers it. May it, then, be granted *thy brother* Flaccus, and thyself, to enjoy such *marks of the* good opinion of Augustus at all times. But when you shall have leisure, from the care of affairs more connected with yourselves, I entreat you, add your prayers to mine. And if the

---

[24] *Thy Consular robe.*]—Ver. 42. Literally, 'prætexta.' The 'toga prætexta' had a broad purple border. It was worn by the children of both sexes, and by the magistrates of Rome, the Municipia, and the colonies, and by the priests, and those engaged in the sacred rites. It is said to have been first derived from the Etrurians.

breeze shall at all swell the sail, loosen the ropes,[25] that my bark may take its departure from the Stygian waters. Flaccus was lately the governor of these regions, Græcinus; and, under his rule, the savage banks of the Danube were in safety. He kept the Mysian nations in constant peace; he, by his sword, alarmed the Getæ that trust in the bow. By prompt valour he recovered Trosmis,[26] that had been taken, and tinted the Danube with barbarian blood. Inquire *of him*, what is the aspect of this spot? and *what are* the miseries of a Scythian climate? and by how near an enemy I am kept in alarm? whether or not the slender arrows are dipt in the venom of the serpent? or whether human lives are not the sad victims? whether I tell an untruth, or the hardened ocean freezes with the cold, and the ice extends many hundred yards[27] out to sea? When he has told thee these things, inquire of him what is said of me, and ask in what manner I spend my tedious time. I am not hated here, nor, in truth, do I deserve to be; and my disposition has not changed together with my fortune. That peace of mind remains, which thou wast wont to praise, that former modest demeanour, as usual, on my countenance. Thus am I far away, thus *am I* here, where a barbarian enemy causes cruel arms to have more power than laws; whereas no woman, man or boy, Græcinus, for now so many years, can have any ground of complaint against me. This is the cause, why the people of Tomi wish me well, and assist me, since this land can testify in my favour. They prefer that I should depart, because they see that I wish it; yet, in regard to themselves, they wish me to be here. And shouldst thou not believe me; there are decrees in existence in which the public records praise me, and make me exempt from impost. Although this boasting is not befitting the un-

[25] *Loosen the ropes.*]—Ver. 73. The 'rudentes' were the ropes used to move or fix the masts, sails, or yards of a vessel.

[26] *Trosmis.*]—Ver. 79. This was a city of Mysia, which the Scythians had taken from the Romans.

[27] *Many hundred yards.*]—Ver. 86. 'Jugera multa;' literally, 'many jugera.' The 'jugerum' of the Romans was, as a measure of superficies, 240 feet in length, and 120 in breadth. It was the common measure of road among the Romans. Pliny renders the Greek word πλεθεον, by 'jugerum,' in which case it would be a measure of length of 100 Grecian, or 104 Roman, feet. In the present instance, the word seems to imply a measure of length.

fortunate, the neighbouring towns grant me the same privileges.

My piety, too, is not unknown; this stranger land sees a shrine of Cæsar existing in my house. Together with him, stand his affectionate son, and his wife *as* his priestess;[28] Deities not less than him who has *lately* been consecrated a God. And that no part of the family may be wanting, each of his grandsons stands *there*, the one, next to the side of his grandmother, the other, to that of his father. As oft as the day arises from the Eastern quarter, so often do I offer suppliant words to these, together with frankincense. The whole of the Pontic land, attesting my dutifulness, shouldst thou enquire, will say that I do not invent this. The Pontic land knows that I celebrate the birth-day of the Divinity with sports as worthy as I can, in this country. And not less is my duty, in this respect, known to strangers, if *at any time* the extensive Propontis has sent any persons to these seas. Thy brother also, under whose government were the districts of Pontus on the left, may, perhaps, have heard of these things. My fortune is not equal to my heart, and in such duties, *though* poor, I willingly expend my little property. Nor do I, far removed from the City, present these things to your eyes; but I am content with silent acts of piety. And yet these things will some day reach the ears of Cæsar; there is nothing which passes throughout the whole world concealed from him. Doubtless thou knowest of this, and beholdest it, Cæsar, summoned to the Gods above! since *now* the earth is exposed to thy eyes. Placed among the stars fixed in the arch of the sky, thou hearest my prayers, which I utter with anxious lips. Perhaps, too, those verses may arrive thither, which I have sent, about thee, newly-made an inhabitant of heaven. I divine that, by means of these, thy Divinity will be appeased; and, not undeservedly, dost thou bear the benign name of Father.

---

[28] *His wife as his priestess.*]—Ver. 107. His meaning is, that Livia venerates the memory of her husband Augustus in no less degree than the priest venerates the Deity of whom he is the minister.

ELEGY X.—TO PEDO ALBINOVANUS.[29]

He writes to his friend Pedo Albinovanus, the poet, and refers to the length of time he has lived among the savage Getæ; comparing his troubles with those of Ulysses, he says that his own are the greater. He entreats him to preserve his attachment to him in his adversity; and to imitate the example of Theseus, whose exploits he had made the theme of his verse.

The sixth summer is being passed by me, here, on the Cimmerian shore, to be spent among the Getæ, wrapped in skins. And dost thou, my dearest Albinovanus, compare flint stones, or iron, to my hardships? The drop hollows out the stone; the ring is worn by use, and the curving ploughshare is rubbed away by the pressure of the earth. Will, then, devouring Time consume everything except me? Even death, overcome by my hardships, is tardy *in its approach*. Ulysses is an instance of a mind extremely patient; he who was tost on the fitful ocean during ten years; but yet he did not endure the whole of that term, *full* of the anxieties of his destiny; there were frequently pauses of quietude. Was it a hard thing for him, during six years, to embrace the beauteous Calypso, and to share the bed of a Goddess of the Sea? The son of Hippotas[30] entertained him; *he* who gave *him* the winds as his gift, that a serviceable breeze might bend his impelled sails. It was no hardship to listen to the *Sirens*, damsels that sang so well, and the lotus was not bitter to him that tasted it. I would buy the potions that cause forgetfulness of one's country, at the price of half my life, were they but saleable; nor couldst thou ever compare the city of the Læstrygon, to the nations which the Danube passes with its winding stream. The Cyclop, too, will not surpass Phyaces[31] in cruelty; how large a part of my dread is he wont to form! Although Scylla is lurking, with fierce monsters, downward from her amputated groin; the ships of

---

[29] *Pedo Albinovanus.*]—He was an heroic poet of Rome, and is now generally supposed to have been the author of the Consolation to Livia Augusta, on the death of her son Drusus; a poem which was long attributed to Ovid.

[30] *The son of Hippotas.*]—Ver. 15. Æolus was the son of Hippotas. He hospitably entertained Ulysses, and gave him favourable winds for his return to his own country.

[31] *Phyaces.*]—Ver. 23. This person appears to have been a savage chief of some of the neighbouring Scythian tribes.

the Heniochi[32] do more injury to mariners; and thou canst not compare Charybdis with the hostile Achæi, although she thrice vomits forth the brine that she has thrice sucked up. Although these roam more at large, on the coasts on the right-hand side *of the Euxine Sea*, still they do not allow this side to be free from anxiety. Here are fields without trees, here are arrows dipped in venom, here the winter makes the sea passable even on foot; so that the traveller, despising the ship, may go *with* dry *feet*, where the oar had lately made a path by impelling the waves. Those who come from your parts, say that you hardly believe these things. How wretched is he, who endures things more dreadful than can be believed! Yet, do believe me, and I will not allow thee to remain ignorant of the reasons why the cold winter hardens the Sarmatian Sea. The Constellation that bears the form of a wain, and that brings extreme cold, is near to us. In these parts Boreas arises; he is familiar with these coasts, and he derives his strength from a neighbouring region; but the South Wind, which breathes warmly from the opposite pole, is far away, and comes but seldom and faint. Besides, here mingle the rivers with the inclosed Euxine Sea, and the ocean loses its power, from the multitude of streams. Hither do the Lycus,[33] the Sagaris, the Penius, the Hypanis, and the Crates flow onwards to the sea, and the Halys, whirling with many a pool; and the rapid Parthenius, and the Cynapes, carrying along rocks, rolls on, and the Tyras, that is more sluggish than no *other* river. And thou, Thermodon, well known to the female squadrons,[34] and thou too, Phasis, once sought by the men of Greece. The most pellucid Dryaspes, too, with the stream of the Borysthenes, and the Melanthus silently pacing on his quiet way; *the river*, too, which separates the two lands, Asia

[32] *The Heniochi.*]—Ver. 26. These were a race of pirates, who lived in the neighbourhood of Colchis, and caused great terror by their devastations. The Achæans were a people of Scythia, of a similar rapacious and lawless character.

[33] *The Lycus.*]—Ver. 47. This, and the other rivers here mentioned, are streams which, situate in the north of Turkey, the south of Russia, or in Asia Minor, flow into the sea of Marmora, or the Black Sea.

[34] *The female squadrons.*]—Ver. 51. The Amazons are here alluded to. They were a warlike race of females, who first dwelt in Sarmatia, near the river Tanais, but afterwards in Cappadocia, near the river Thermodon.

and the sister of Cadmus,[35] and makes his path between them both; and innumerable others, the greatest among all which, the Danube, denies that he yields *the palm* to thee, O Nilus. Such an abundance of streams, taints the waters which they increase; and permit not the sea to retain its strength *of current*. Moreover, just like a standing pool, and a sluggish swamp, it is of colour hardly azure, and its *native* hue is modified. Fresh water swims on the surface of the deep, and is lighter than the sea water; which derives its peculiar weight from the admixture of salt.

Should any one inquire why these things are told to Pedo, and what is the use of mentioning them in measured numbers; I will tell them, I have worn away the time and I have beguiled my cares; this advantage has the present hour brought to me. While I have been writing these things, I was far removed from my usual sorrows; and I was not sensible that I was in the midst of the Getæ. But thou, I doubt not, when in thy verse thou art praising Theseus,[36] dost defend the reputation of thy subject, and thou dost imitate the hero of whom thou art singing. He certainly forbids friendship to be the waiter upon times of prosperity. Although he is an hero, mighty in his exploits, and is celebrated by thee, in language in which he ought to be sung, yet in him there is something worthy to be imitated by us, and any one can be a Theseus in attachment. Foes have not to be subdued by thee, with the sword and with the club, by reason of whom the Isthmus *of Corinth*[37] was hardly passable by any one; but affection must be shewn, not a difficult matter to him who is willing. What labour is it not to have violated sincere attachment. Thou must not suppose that these things have been said with complaining tongue to thee, who remainest throughout constant to thy friend.

[35] *The sister of Cadmus.*]—Ver. 55. Europa, who gave name to Europe, which is here signified.

[36] *Art praising Theseus.*]—Ver. 71. Pedo Albinovanus wrote a poem, of which Theseus was the hero.

[37] *The Isthmus of Corinth.*]—Ver. 80. This spot was rendered almost impassable by the atrocities perpetrated by Sinnis, or Scyron, a robber of that vicinity. Theseus slew him, and hung him on a pine tree.

EPISTLE XI.—TO GALLIO.

Having been informed by Gallio of the death of his wife, he apologizes for not having before named her in his writings, in return for the grief which he manifested on his banishment from Rome. He states his own sorrow on hearing of the death of the wife of Gallio, but he says that he will not presume to offer him consolation, as he is already acquainted with all the precepts of the learned on the subject of resignation, and he trusts, that by this time, his grief has subsided. He also thinks it possible that, by the time his letter arrives, Gallio may have married again.

Gallio! the fault will be hardly excusable by me, that thou hast not received praise in my verse; for thou, too, (as I remember), with thy tears didst foment my wounds, that were made by the celestial spear; and, would that, afflicted by the loss of thy friend *thus* snatched away, thou hadst felt no reason besides, why thou shouldst grieve! It pleased not thus the Gods, who, in their cruelty did not think it wrong to deprive thee of thy chaste wife. For a letter lately came to me, the messenger of woe, and thy loss was read of by me with tears. But I would not dare, in my folly, to console so wise a man, and repeat to thee the well-known sayings of the learned; I suppose, too, that thy grief has terminated by this, through the very length of time, if not on principle. While thy letter was arriving, while mine, returning, is passing over so many seas and lands, a *whole* year passes away. To offer consolation, is the duty of a certain space of time; so long as grief is in full career, and while the afflicted seeks relief; but, when length of time has lulled the wounds of the mind, he who unseasonably foments them, renews them.

Besides, (and may this omen be a true one for thee!) thou mayst by this time be happy in a new marriage.

EPISTLE XII.—TO TUTICANUS.

He first tells Tuticanus the reason why he has not hitherto mentioned his name in his writings. He then refers to the intimate friendship that has existed between them from their childhood: and he concludes, by entreating him to use his influence with Tiberius Cæsar in his favour.

It is caused by the nature of thy name,[38] that thou art not

---

[38] *The nature of thy name.*]—Ver. 2. He says that the quantities of the feet in the name of Tŭtĭcānŭs had rendered it impossible for him, with due regard to poetical rules, to name him either in Hexameter or Pentameter lines.

named, my friend, in my books. But I would deem no one worthy of honour sooner than that; if only my verses are any honour. The law of *poetical* measure, and the nature of the name, impede this act of duty; and there is no way for thee to take a place in my numbers. For I am ashamed so to distribute thy name into two lines,[39] that the first one may end, and the second, begin with it. I should be ashamed, too, if, in the part *of the word*, where a stress is laid on the syllable, I should pronounce *thy name* short, and call thee Tŭtĭcănus? and thou canst not be introduced in a line under the form of Tūtīcānus; so that the first syllable be made short out of a long one. Or, *suppose the syllable* is made long, which is now pronounced short; and the second *syllable* is long with an extended pause. If, by these blemishes I should dare to spoil thy name, I should be laughed at, and I should deservedly be denied to be the possessor of judgment. This was the cause of my deferring this tribute, which my resources shall *now* pay with the addition of interest. And under an indication of some sort, I will celebrate thee; I will send thee *my* verses, oh thou that wast known when almost a boy to me when almost a boy *as well;* and that hast been beloved by me not less than as a brother by a brother through a series of years, as long as we both of us have lived. Thou wast my kind adviser, thou wast my guardian and my companion, while I guided the reins but newly assumed with inexperienced hand. Often, under thy criticism, have I corrected my works; often, by my recommendation, was an alteration made by thee; when the Piërian maid instructed thee to write the Phæacian poem,[40] worthy of *even* Mæonian paper. This even course, this unison, commenced in early youth, continued

---

[39] *To distribute thy name into two lines.*]—Ver. 7. He means to say that the only way in which his name can possibly be introduced is by using the first two syllables for the final spondee of the Hexameter, and commencing the Pentameter with the two remaining syllables; but that he would be ashamed to adopt that expedient; thereby implying the limping and mutilated nature of the lines, which would infallibly result from such a step.

[40] *Phæacian poem.*]—Ver. 27. This appears to have been a poem which Tuticanus had composed either in praise of Alcinoüs, the king of the Phæacians, or descriptive of the wanderings of Ulysses, as recounted by him to Alcinoüs, by whom he was hospitably entertained. He compliments Tuticanus on his work, in saying that it was worthy of the paper of Homer.

unimpaired until our hair was grey. And if these things move thee not, I could believe that thy breast is of hard iron, or enclosed in infrangible adamant.

But, first, may war and frosts, which two *evils* Pontus so hateful to me possesses, cease from off this land, and may Boreas become warm, and the South wind intensely cold, and may my lot become more endurable; before thy feelings are hardened against thy ruined companion. May this burden not be added to my woes; and it is not added. Only do thou, by the Gods of heaven, of whom he is the most unwavering, under whose rule thy honours have continually increased, effect by defending me, an exile, with constant attachment, that the desired breeze desert not my bark. Dost thou ask, what I would recommend? May I die, if I am not almost unable to say; if only, the person who is dead can die *again*. I neither know what to do, nor what to wish, or not to wish; and my own interests are not well ascertained by me. Believe me, prudence is the first thing to forsake the distressed, and common sense and judgment take flight together with prosperity. Do thou thyself, I pray, consider in what respect I can be assisted, and through what channel thou canst make a passage to *the attainment of* my desires.

EPISTLE XIII.—TO CARUS.

He tells Carus, the Præceptor of the Cæsars, that he will at once perceive, from the colour of the paper and the structure of the verse, from whom this letter comes. He informs him that he has composed, in the Getic tongue, a letter in praise of Augustus, Livia, and her children. He entreats him, by their ancient friendship, as he is now in the sixth year of his exile, to procure his removal to some other place.

O thou, not to be numbered among my wavering acquaintances, hail thou who art called Carus, a thing which thou really art.[41] The colour *which this letter bears*,[42] and the composition of my verse, can be at once a sign to thee from what quarter thou receivest this salutation; not that *my composition*

---

[41] *A thing which thou really art.*]—Ver. 2. 'Carus' signifies 'dear.' It being the name of his correspondent, he tells him that he is not only Carus in name, but in reality.

[42] *The colour which this letter bears.*]—Ver. 3. The fact of it being worn and thumbed, showing that it has come from a distance.

is wonderful, but neither is it, assuredly, common-place; but, of whatever nature it is, it is evident that it is mine. Thou, too, thyself, though thou shouldst tear off the superscription from the top of the paper,[43] I *still* seem able to pronounce what is thy composition. Placed among ever so many works, thou art recognized, and thou wilt be found, through indications which have been remarked.

The strength which we know to be worthy of Hercules, and equal to *the might of* him of whom[44] thou art singing, betrays its author; my Muse, too, betrayed by her peculiar qualities, may perhaps be remarkable through her own blemishes. As much did his ugly shape hinder Thersites from lying concealed, as Nireus[45] was conspicuous for his beauteous one; and it will not be right for thee to be surprised, if the verses are faulty, which I, now become almost a Getic poet, compose.

Ah! I am ashamed *to own it;* I have composed a work in the Getic language, and barbarian words have been arranged into my measures. I have given satisfaction, too; congratulate me! I have begun to have the reputation of a poet among the savage Getæ. Dost thou enquire what was my subject? I have sung the praises of Cæsar. My new attempt was aided by the inspiration of the Divinity; for I have shewn that the body of our father Augustus was mortal; that his spirit has departed to the æthereal abodes; that he who, by compulsion,[46] has assumed the reins of empire, often refused *by him,* is equal to his father; that thou, Livia, art the Vesta of chaste matrons; and that it is a matter of doubt whether thou art more worthy of thy son, or of thy husband; that there are two youths, the firm supports of their father, who have given sure indications of their

---

[43] *The top of the paper.*]—Ver. 7. 'Frons chartæ' will, perhaps, either mean the top of the paper in a book composed of a scroll, or the first page in one composed of different leaves, like our books; the 'titulus' would be the superscription and address, stating by whom written, and to whom sent.

[44] *Him of whom.*]—Ver. 12. Hercules, who was the hero of his poem.

[45] *Nireus.*]—Ver. 16. He was the son of Charops and Aglaia, and a native of the island of Syme. Homer says that he was the most beauteous of men.

[46] *By compulsion.*]—Ver. 27. This refers to the pretended difficulty which Tiberius made, on being requested by the Senate to assume the reins of government; an offer which, for some time, to suit his purposes, he pretended to refuse to accept.

disposition. When I read through these verses, written not in the song of my country, and the last page came to my hands, all moved both their heads and their full quivers, and there was a prolonged applause in the mouths of the Getæ; and one said, "Since thou writest these things about Cæsar, thou oughtst to be restored by the command of Cæsar."

He, indeed, said so; but now, Carus, the sixth winter beholds me removed under the snowy pole.

My verses avail me not; once did my verses injure me, and they were the first cause of so wretched a banishment; but do thou, by the common ties of our sacred pursuits, by the name of friendship not despised by thee, *aid me;* then may Germanicus afford a subject-matter for the scope of thy genius, the foe being captive in Latian chains. May the youths prosper, the common anxiety of the Gods, whom, it is thy great honour to have had entrusted to thee to educate; do thou give all the influence that thou canst to my preservation, which will not be achieved, except by a change of *my* place *of exile.*

EPISTLE XIV.—TO TUTICANUS.

He writes to Tuticanus, whom he had before addressed, and says that he would prefer any place of exile to Tomi. He says, that the people of that place ought not to be angry at his censures, as they are not directed against them, but the place only. On the contrary, he admits that he has invariably received the greatest kindness from them.

These *lines* are sent to thee, whom I lately complained of as not having a name suited to my measure.

In them, thou wilt find nothing to give thee pleasure, except that I am still pretty well; even health is hateful to me, and my most earnest wish is, forsooth, to depart some way or other from these regions. I have no anxiety but to leave this land; for any one will be more pleasing than this which I behold. Send my sails into the midst of the Syrtes, into the midst of Charybdis, so that I may depart from my present locality. Styx, even, if there is such a thing, will be a good exchange for the Danube; and if there is anything *besides* that the world contains lower than Styx.

The tilled field less dreads weeds, the swallow less dreads the winter, than Naso does the places adjacent to the Getæ, the worshippers of Mars. The people of Tomi are angry with me, on account of such expressions, and the public displeasure has been excited by my lines. Shall I, then, never cease to receive injury through my verses, and shall I be everlastingly punished by an imprudent disposition? Why do I delay cutting off my fingers, that I may not write? and why, in my madness, do I still adhere to the weapons which have been my ruin? Again I turn to the wonted rocks, *and* to those waves, in which my shipwrecked bark was dashed. But, I have done nothing; it is no fault of mine, ye people of Tomi, whom I esteem, although I utterly hate your place.

Let any one examine the records of my labours; my letters have made no complaints about you. I complain of the cold, and of incursions to be dreaded on every side, and that the fortifications are shaken by the enemy. I have uttered charges, most truthful, against the locality, not against the people: even you yourselves often condemn your own soil.

The Muse of *Hesiod*, the old man that was devoted to agriculture, dared to show us why his own Ascra should always be shunned. But he who wrote was born in that land; and yet Ascra was not exasperated against her own poet. Who loved his country better than the sagacious Ulysses? And yet, by his showing, the ruggedness of the place has become known. Scepsius [47] did not attack places, but manners, in his bitter remarks, and Rome *herself* was accused. And yet she bore these false charges with equanimity, and an abusive tongue was no injury to its owner. But an unskilful interpreter excites the wrath of the people against me, and calls on my lines to *answer* a fresh charge. Would that I were as fortunate, as I am pure in my heart. No man is yet in existence that has been wounded by my tongue. Besides, had I been blacker even than Illyrian pitch, the friendly multitude should not have been slandered by me. My exile, kindly entertained by you, people of Tomi, shows that men of such gentle manners are Greeks. The Peligni, my people, and Sulmo, my native place, could not have been more affectionate *to me*, in my misfortune. That honour was lately conferred by you on me, which you would scarcely grant to any one flourishing and prosperous. As yet,

[47] *Scepsius.*]—Ver. 38. It is not known whether this person was a poet or a philosopher, who was thus allowed with impunity to attack the manners of the Roman people.

I am the only one that is exempt from impost in your country; except those who have these privileges by law. My temples have been wreathed with a sacred garland, which the public favour bestowed on me, reluctant *to accept* it. As pleasing, therefore, as the land of Delos was to Latona, which alone afforded her a place of safety, in her wanderings; so dear to me is Tomi; which, in its hospitability, remains faithful up to the present moment to me banished from my country. Oh! that the Gods would only grant, that it might *but* afford a hope of tranquil peace, and that it could be further off from the freezing pole.

EPISTLE XV.—TO SEXTUS POMPEIUS.

He tells him that he is indebted to him for every thing but his life, which he owes to Cæsar. He begs him to ask of the Emperor, whom he so much respects, another place of exile exposed to fewer hardships. He excuses himself for so often making the same request; but he says, that his longing knows no bounds.

If there is still any one in existence not unforgetful of me, or who enquires what I, Naso, sent afar, am doing; let him know that I owe my life to the Cæsars, my safety to Sextus *Pompeius*. After the Gods above, he shall be the first in my esteem. For, though I should embrace all the season of my wretched life, no one part of it is without his kindnesses. These are as many in number as the crimson grains under the thin rind *of the pomegranate*, that blush in the beds of a fertile garden; as the ears of standing corn that Africa, the grapes that the land of Tmolus,[48] the olives that Sicyon, the honeycomb that Hybla produces. I confess it; you may attest it; sign it, ye Quirites. There is no need for the authority of the laws; I myself say *so*. Put me too, but a trifling matter, among thy patrimonial possessions; let me be a part, however small, of thy property. As much as Trinacria is thine,[49]

---

[48] *Tmolus.*]—Ver. 9. This was a mountain of Lydia, famed among the ancients for the excellence of its wine and saffron.

[49] *Trinacria is thine.*]—Ver. 15. It is supposed that Sicily was under the especial protection and guardianship of Sextus, and that he was entrusted by Augustus or Tiberius with the command in Macedonia, or in one of its principal towns.

and *Macedonia*, the land that was ruled over by Philip; as much as thy house, that adjoins the Forum of Augustus; as much as thy Campania, thy country domain, is pleasing to the eyes of its owner, and the rest which thou possessest, Sextus, either as left to thee or bought; so much am I thy *property;* by reason of which melancholy gift thou canst not say that thou possessest nothing in Pontus. And, oh! that thou didst not, and that a more genial soil were granted me; and, that thou wouldst hold thy property on a preferable spot! And since it rests with the Gods, attempt to soothe the Divinities, whom thou worshippest with unceasing veneration: for, it is hard to discover, whether thou art more a proof of my mistake, or its consolation. And I do not entreat thee in uncertainty: but often, the speed of the flowing water, as we go along with the stream, is increased by rowing. I am ashamed, and I dread to be always making the same entreaties, lest a justified tedium should take possession of thy feelings. But what shall I do? Desire is a thing that knows no bounds. Pardon, kind friend, my failing. Often, when I wish to write something else, I glide into that subject: my very letters of themselves ask for *another* place *of exile*.

But whether thy favour is to have effect, or whether cruel Destiny bids me die under the freezing pole; I shall ever recall to mind thy unforgotten services; and my country shall hear that I am thine. Each other country besides, that is situate under this sky, shall hear of it, if only my song travels beyond the savage Getæ; *and shall know* that thou wast the cause and the guardian of my safety, and that I am thine, less only the coin and the balance.[49*]

EPISTLE XVI.—TO HIS ENENY.

He tells his calumniator, that he ought not to revile him, as he ought now to be looked upon as dead; and that envy attacks only the living, but does not molest the dead: he then enumerates a multitude of poets, whom he may assail with as much justice as himself.

Thou envious man, why dost thou pull to pieces the verses of Naso, who is no more? Death is not wont to injure genius. Greater fame, too, arises when we are no more; and I had reputation even when I was numbered with the living. When

[49*] *And the balance.*]—Ver. 42. These were formally used on the sale of slaves.

Marsus[50] was existing, and Rabirius,[51] with his nervous language, and Macer, the bard of Ilium, and Pedo the poet of the stars, and Carus, who, by his Hercules, would have offended Juno, had he not now been the son-in-law of Juno; and Severus,[52] who gave a regal poem to Latium, and either Priscus,[53] with their elegant *poems on* Numa. And thou, Montanus,[54] who excellest either in unequal or equal measures, and who hast a celebrity in two kinds of verse. Sabinus, too, who bade[55] Ulysses, the wanderer for ten years over the raging seas, write an answer to Penelope; and who left his Træzene and his work upon the Days unfinished, by reason of his premature death. Largus,[56] too, who is called by the epithet belonging to his genius, he who brought the Phrygian sage to the Gallic plains. Camberinus as well, who sings of Troy subdued by Hercules; the Etrurian[57] also, who derives his reputa-

[50] *Marsus.*]—Ver. 5. Domitius Marsus was a Roman poet, the contemporary of Ovid and Horace. Only five lines of his works are extant; four of these form part of an elegy on the death of Tibullus.

[51] *Rabirius.*]—Ver. 5. Caius Rabirius was a Roman Epic poet, whose writings were full of spirit and energy, on which account Ovid calls him 'magni oris.' His works have perished.

[52] *Severus.*]—Ver. 9. Cassius Severus was a Roman poet of considerable merit, who wrote several tragedies, to which reference is here made. He also wrote some epigrams and elegies. His works have not come down to our time.

[53] *Either Priscus.*]—Ver. 10. These were two Roman poets of the name of Priscus; each of whom wrote a poem, of which Numa Pompilius was the hero.

[54] *Montanus.*]—Ver. 11. Julius Montanus was a Roman poet, who was patronized by the Emperor Tiberius. He composed both in Heroic and in Elegiac measure, to which Ovid here refers, as the unequal and equal measures.

[55] *Who bade.*]—Ver. 13. Aulus Sabinus, the Roman poet, composed an Epistle, supposed to be written by Ulysses, in answer to that of Penelope, which is the first Epistle in Ovid's Heroides; to this fact reference is here made. It is not known whether the work mentioned here, under the name of Træzene, refers to a poem composed by him in praise of some female of that name, or to some tragedy or didactic work relative to Træzene, in Argolis, of which place Pittheus, the grandfather of Theseus, was king.

[56] *Largus.*]—Ver. 17. This poet, who is here said to have been so called from his fruitful genius, composed a poem descriptive of the settlement of Antenor the Trojan at Patavium, now Padua, in the north of Italy; which was formerly Cisalpine Gaul.

[57] *The Etrurian.*]—Ver. 20. It is not known to whom reference is here made; or whether the poet gained his fame by singing the praises of his mistress Phillis, or those of Phillis the daughter of Lycurgus, king of

tion from his Phyllis. The poet, too,[58] of the sail-covered sea, for whom you might suppose that the azure Deities had composed his verses. He, too, who sang the Libyan armies and the Roman battles; and Marcus, skilled in every kind of composition; and the Trinacrian, author of his song on Perseus, and Lupus,[59] the author of the return home of the descendant of Tantalus, and of the daughter of Tyndarus. *Tuticanus,* too, who translated the Mæonian *song of Alcinoüs the* Phœnician, and together with him, thou too, Rufus, the performer on the Pindaric lyre. The Muse, too, that is supported on the tragic buskins of Turranius; and thy Muse, Melissus,[60] sportive with the sock of comedy. While Varus[61] and Gracchus[62] were describing the fierce boastings of their Tyrants, Proculus was following the wanton path of Callimachus. There was Tityrus,[63] too, who was feeding *his sheep* on his paternal pastures, and Gratius[64] was giving proper weapons to the hunter. Fontanus sang of the Naiads, beloved by the Satyrs, *and* Capella included his words in unequal measures. And though there were others, the names of all of whom 'twould take a long time to

Thrace, who succeeded her father in that kingdom. Some would read 'Fuscus,' instead of 'Tuscus.' Of Camerinus, nothing whatever is known.

[58] *The poet, too.*]—Ver. 21. He alludes to Publius Terentius Varro Attacinus, a Roman satirical poet. He translated the Argonautics of Apollonius Rhodius into Latin verse, to which reference is here made.

[59] *Lupus.*]—Ver. 26. Nothing is known of this poet, or of either of the three that are referred to immediately before him.

[60] *Melissus.*]—Ver. 30. Caius Cilnius Melissus was the freedman of Mæcenas, and was the author of several comedies and mimes, and of a book of jests. Of Rufus and Turranius, no particulars are known.

[61] *Varus.*]—Ver. 31. Quintilius Varius, or Varus, was a native of Cremona, and was of Equestrian rank. He is mentioned by Horace and Virgil, and was one of the persons to whom the Emperor Augustus entrusted the revisal of the Æneid, prior to its publication.

[62] *Gracchus.*]—Ver. 31. He was a Roman poet, who wrote a tragedy on the subject of Thyestes, the same which Varus had chosen. Ovid alludes to the taunts which the poets put into the mouth of Thyestes against Atreus.

[63] *Tityrus.*]—Ver. 33. Under this name he alludes to Virgil; who introduces Tityrus as one of the characters in his first Eclogue. It is generally supposed that the poet intended, under that character, to depict his own fortunes, and the favour he had experienced at the hands of Augustus. Of Proculus, nothing is known.

[64] *Gratius.*]—Ver. 34. Gratius was a Roman poet, whose poem on hunting, called 'Cynægeticon,' has come down to our time.

recount, whose verses the public possesses; and there were *other* young men, whom I have no right to mention by name, as their labours are as yet unpublished; still I could not venture, Cotta,[65] to pass thee in silence in the throng.

Thou light of the Piërian maids, thou guardian of the bar; to whom the highest nobility of the blood on both sides has given the Cottæ as the maternal, the Messalæ as the paternal ancestors. If I may be allowed to say so, my Muse was one of illustrious name, and was one that was read *even* amid *authors* so great. Therefore, Envy, cease to defame one removed from his country, and do not, inhuman man, scatter my ashes. I have lost every thing. Life alone is left, that it may afford matter for my woes and the power of feeling them. Of what use is it to plunge the sword into the lifeless limbs? By this time, a fresh wound can find no place *unhurt* in me *for its infliction*.

[65] *Cotta.*]—Ver. 41. To this poet, the second Epistle in the third Book of the Pontic Epistles is addressed. Of Fontanus, and Capella here referred to, no further information has come down to us.

END OF THE PONTIC EPISTLES.

THE
INVECTIVE AGAINST THE IBIS.

It is not known against whom this shocking poem, which combines a chapter of horrors with a vocabulary of abuse, was written. It is, however, generally supposed that Caius Julius Hyginus, a grammarian of Alexandria, and the freedman of Augustus, an author who has left a work on the ancient Mythology, is the person alluded to. Whoever it may have been, it appears that he had been a friend of Ovid, and that, in his banishment, he had calumniated both the Poet and his wife, and had tried to enrich himself by the confiscation of the property of the exile. The Poet makes allusion to these several facts; and says, that he will follow the example of Callimachus, the Greek poet, who attacked Apollonius Rhodius, another poet, under the fictitious title of Ibis: which was the name of a bird of Egypt, of filthy habits, supposed to live upon scorpions and venomous serpents. The country of the person attacked, or, at least, its vicinity, seems to be denoted by his allusion to Lybia, as being the country of his enemy, and the adaptation of the Ibis, as the object of censure; although Suetonius says, that Hyginus was really a Spaniard, though thought by some to have been a native of Alexandria. Some say, that Corvinus, others that Cornificius, was the name of the unfortunate object of Ovid's vituperation. The former, however, is the more general belief among the learned.*

Up to this time, twice five lustra having now been passed by me, every verse of my Muse has been inoffensive, and not a single letter of Naso's exists, out of so many thousands that have been written, that can be read as injurious. My books, too, have hurt no one but myself; when the life of the author was lost through his Art *of Love*. One man (and that very circumstance is a great reproach) does not permit my credit for inoffensiveness to be lasting. Whoever he is (for I will still, in some measure, be silent on his name) he forces my

* As a full reference to each of the allusions to be found in this poem would suffice to fill a small volume, and as a considerable proportion of them have been already explained in the Notes to the former part of this work, some of the more obscure passages only will be selected for elucidation in the notes.

unused hands to take up weapons. He does not allow me, removed afar to the cold rising of the North wind, to lie concealed in my place of exile. In his cruelty, he torments the wounds that seek for rest, and he bandies my name about the whole of the Forum. Nor does he allow her, who is bound to me by the lasting tie of marriage, to lament the death of her wretched husband. While I am clinging to the shattered remains of my vessel, he strives to seize the planks of my shipwreck. He, too, who ought to extinguish the sudden conflagration, like a plunderer, snatches his booty from the midst of the fire. He strives that subsistence may be wanting to my exiled old age; alas! how much more worthy was he himself of my misfortunes! The Gods deemed otherwise; of whom he is by far the greatest to me, who willed not my wanderings to be destitute. To him, then, whenever I shall be allowed, I shall always return deserved thanks for a disposition so merciful. Pontus shall hear of these things; perhaps the same *Divinity* may cause a nearer country to testify them for me. But I will be deservedly an enemy to thee, however wretched, who hast, cruel man, trod upon me when lying prostrate. Water shall sooner cease to be the antagonist of fire, and the light of the Sun shall be joined with the Moon; the same portion of the heavens shall send forth the West winds and those of the East; and the warm South wind shall blow from the cold *North* pole; a fresh-born concord, too, shall arise between the smoke *of the ashes* of *Eteocles and Polynices,* the brothers, which the old enmity separated *even* on the lighted funeral pile; Spring, too, shall mingle with Autumn, and Summer with Midwinter; and the West and the East shall be the same spot, before, having laid aside the arms which I have assumed, there shall be the friendship, thou wretch, between me and thee which thou hast broken by thy crimes: *before* this resentment can ever cease in length of time, or time and season can moderate my hatred. There will be that peace between us, so long as my life shall last, which there is wont to be between the wolves and the weak sheep. I, indeed, will commence the first warfare in the verse with which I have begun, although wars are not wont to be waged in this measure. And, as the lance of the light-armed soldier, not yet heated *for the combat,* is first aimed at the ground strewed with the yellow sand; so will I not at first aim at thee with the sharp steel; nor shall my spear at once strike at thy hated head, neither will I mention thy name, or thy actions in this book; and I will suffer thee, for a little time, to conceal who thou art. Afterwards, shouldst thou persist, the bold Iambic measure shall provide me with weapons against thee, steeped in the blood of Lycambes.[1]

At present, I curse thee and thine, in the same manner in which *Callimachus*, the son of Battus, curses his enemy, the Ibis. And as he *does*, I will involve my lines in dark fables, although I am not accustomed to practise this kind *of composition*. Emulating his obscurities in his Ibis, I shall be pronounced forgetful of my taste and of my skill. And as I do not disclose to inquirers, for the present who thou art, do thou as well, in the meantime take the name of Ibis. As my lines will contain some obscurity, so be the whole tenor of thy life overcast. I will cause some one to read these lines to thee on thy birth-day, and on the Calends of Janus, with no deceiving lips.

Ye Gods of the sea and of the land, and ye who, together with Jove, possess realms *still* better than these between the opposite poles, I pray all of you to turn hither your attention, and to allow *due* weight to attend my wishes. And do thou, Earth, and thou Ocean with thy waves, and thou Æther on high, receive my prayers; ye stars too, and thou form of the Sun, surrounded with rays; thou Moon too, who never shinest with the same aspect with which thou didst *the day* before; thou Night too, awful in the appearance of thy shades: and ye *Destinies as well*, who spin your appointed task with three-fold fingers; and thou, *Lethe*, river of the water that sanctions no false oath, that rollest through the vallies of hell with terrific roar; and you *Furies*, who they say, are seated before the dark doors of the dungeon, with your locks wreathed with twisted vipers; and you, too, the commonalty of the Divinities, ye Fauns, and Satyrs, and Lares, and Streams, and Nymphs, and thou race of Demigods. And lastly, all ye Gods both old and young, from ancient Chaos down to our time, assist, while imprecatory verses are being repeated against this per-

---

[1] *The blood of Lycambes.*]—Ver. 54. Lycambes having promised his daughter, Neobule, to the poet Archilochus, broke his word; on which the poet inveighed so bitterly in his verse against the father and the daughter that they both hanged themselves.

fidious head, and anger and resentment are performing their part; favour my desires all of you, each in his order, and let no fraction of my wishes be unrealized. Let the things that I pray for come to pass, that he may suppose that they were not my sayings, but the words of the son-in-law of Pasiphaë.[2] May he suffer, too, those punishments, which I shall omit; may he be wretched to an extent beyond my imagination. And let not my prayers that execrate a fictitious name, prevail the less *for that reason*, or influence in a less degree the great Gods.

I accurse him, whom my mind understands *as* the Ibis; who knows that by his crimes he has deserved this execration. I am guilty of no delay; *as* the priest, I will go through the prayers resolved on by me. Whoever ye be, that are present at my rites, aid me, *all of you*, with your words. Whoever ye be, that are present at my rites, utter words of sadness; and approach the Ibis with tearful cheeks; meet him with inauspicious words, and with the left foot *advanced;* and let black vestments clothe your bodies. And thou too, *Ibis*, why dost thou hesitate to assume the mournful fillets? the altar, as thou seeest, is now standing *ready* for thy doom. The procession is prepared for thee; be there no delay in the fulfilment of my vows of ill omen *for thee*. Victim accursed, extend thy throat for my knives. May the earth deny thee its produce, the stream its waters; may the wind, and may the air deny thee their breezes. May the sun be no *longer* bright for thee, nor the moon shining: may all the stars fade from before thy eyes. Let neither Vulcan, *God of fire*, nor air afford thee *their use:* let neither the land nor the sea afford thee a passage. An exile and in need, mayst thou wander; mayst thou visit the thresholds of others; and mayst thou beg a little morsel with tremulous lips. Let neither thy body nor thy weakened mind be free from complaining pain; and may the night prove more tormenting to thee than the day, the day than the night. Mayst thou ever be wretched; and mayst thou be pitied by none. Let both man and woman

---

[2] *Son-in-law of Pasiphaë.*]—Ver. 90. Theseus married Ariadne, the daughter of Pasiphaë; and afterwards, crediting the false accusation of Hippolytus, by his mother-in-law, Phædra, he cursed him, and prayed Neptune to destroy him; on which Hippolytus was dragged by his horses and killed.

rejoice in thy misfortunes. Let hatred be added to thy tears, and when thou art enduring a multitude of woes, mayst thou be deemed worthy of still more. May too, which seldom happens, the hateful appearance of thy sorrow be deprived of the usual interest. May the occasion of death not be wanting to thee, *but* may its opportunity be denied thee: may life, forced *upon thee*, never meet with the death that is longed for. May thy breath, *only* after a prolonged struggle, forsake thy agonized limbs: and may it torment thee first by a lengthened procrastination.

These things will come to pass. Phœbus himself, this moment, gave me signs of the future, and a bird of bad omen flew on my left hand. Assuredly, I will always believe that what I wish will influence the Gods above; and, perfidious *wretch!* I shall ever be nourished by the hope of thy destruction. That day will *come to* pass, which will hereafter take thee away from me; that day will *come to* pass, which comes *but* slowly for me. And may that day, which approaches but tardily for me, first take away this life, often the object of thy attacks, before this resentment ever fade in length of years, or time or season modify my hatred. So long as the Thracian shall fight with the javelins, the Iazyges with the bow, so long as the Ganges shall be warm, the Danube be cold; so long as the mountains shall have their oaks, the plains their soft pasturage, so long as the Etrurian Tiber shall have yellow waters, *so long* with thee will I wage war; *even* death shall not put an end to my wrath, but to one ghost shall it give ruthless arms against *another* spirit. Then, too, when I shall have flitted into vacant air, my lifeless phantom shall *still* hate thy shade; even then, as a ghost, I will approach, not unforgetful of thy crimes, and, a skeleton form, I will attack thy face. Whether I shall be worn out by length of years, a thing I would not desire, or whether I shall depart by a death caused by my own hand; whether I shall be tost in shipwreck along the boundless waves, and the fish from afar shall prey on my entrails; whether foreign birds shall tear my limbs, or whether wolves shall stain their jaws with my blood; or whether any one shall deign to deposit me in the earth, or to give my lifeless body to an humble pile; whatever I shall be, I shall struggle to escape from the Stygian regions, and, *as my own* avenger, I will extend my cold hands to thy features. In thy watchings thou shalt behold me; seeming to be present in the silent darkness of night, I will disturb thy sleep. In fine, whatever thou shalt be doing, I will hover before thy face and thy eyes, and I will wail; in no spot shalt thou be at rest. The twisted thongs shall send forth their sounds, and the torches, wreathed with snakes, shall ever be smoking before thy conscience-stricken face; by these Furies, while *yet* living, thou shalt be tormented, and by the same when dead. Thy life will prove shorter than thy punishment. Obsequies and the tears of thy friends, shall not be thy lot; undeplored shalt thou be thrown out. Thou shalt be dragged by the hand of the executioner, amid the shouts of the people, and the hook shall be fixed amid thy bones. The very flames, which devour everything, shall fly from thee; the retributive earth shall reject thy hated carcase with disgust. With talons and bill shall the sluggish vulture drag thy entrails, and the greedy dogs shall tear asunder thy perfidious heart. Over thy body, too, (although thou mayst be elated at such a compliment), there shall be strife among the insatiate wolves. Thou wilt be banished to a spot far away from the Elysian Plains, and thou wilt inhabit the abodes which the guilty crowd occupies. *Sisyphus* is there, both rolling his stone and catching it *as it falls*; and *Ixion*, who is whirled, fastened to the circumference of the revolving wheel; the *Danaides*, too, grand-daughters of Belus, who bear on their shoulders the water that *ever* flows away, the daughters-in-law of Ægyptus, a blood-stained crowd; *Tantalus*, the father of Pelops, catches at the apples, *ever* at hand, and the same person is ever thirsting for, *yet* ever abounding with the flowing water; *Tityus*, too, who at his crown many hundred yards[3] distant from his feet, there affords his entrails, as the due of the ever-present bird. There one of the Furies will lacerate thy sides with a whip, that thou mayst confess the number of thy crimes; another one will give thy torn limbs to the dragons of Tartarus; the third will roast thy smoking cheeks with fire. Thy guilty shade shall be tormented in a thousand ways, and Æacus shall be *quite* refined in thy tortures. To thee shall he transfer the torments of those men of olden time; thou shalt be a cause of rest to the shades of the ancients. Sisyphus, thou shalt have one, to whom thou mayst

---

[3] *Many hundred yards.*]—Ver. 183. 'Jugeribus novem,' 'nine jugera.' See Note to Pontic Epistles, Book iv., Epistle ix., line 26.

hand over thy burden that ever rolls back again; the rapid wheels shall now whirl the limbs of a new victim. He it shall be, who shall in vain catch at the boughs and the water; he shall feed the bird with his undiminished entrails.

No other end shall terminate the punishment of this death, and no hour shall be the last for miseries so great. I will mention a few of the number; just as though any one were to pick leaves from Ida, or *skim* water from the surface of the Libyan sea. For, I can neither recount how many flowers spring up in the Sicilian Hybla, nor how many ears of saffron the Sicilian land produces; nor yet with how many hailstones Athos is made white, when the ruthless storm rages on the wings of the North wind. Nor yet could all thy woes be enumerated by my voice, even though thou shouldst give me multiplied mouths. Sorrows will come upon thee, O wretched man, so many and so great, that I could fancy that even I could be forced to weep. Those tears will make me happy unceasingly; then will those tears be *far* sweeter to me than laughter. Of ill omen wast thou born; thus did the Gods will; and there was no star favouring or propitious at thy birth. No Venus shone, no Jupiter, at that hour; neither Sun nor Moon was in a favourable position. *Mercury*, whom the beauteous Maia bore to the great Jove, did not afford thee his light situate with any kind influence for thee. The stars of Mars, and of the old man with the scythe, ruthless and foreboding no tranquillity, overwhelmed thee. The day, too, of thy birth, that thou mightst see nothing but what was sinister, was foul and lowering with clouds o'ercast. This was the day to which Calamitous Allia[4] gives a name in the Calendar; a day which produced the Ibis as well, a public disgrace. Soon as he, falling from the womb of his impure mother, came in contact with the Cinyphian ground with his filthy body, the owl of the night sat on an opposite house-top, and uttered his ill-boding notes with funereal voice. Forthwith the Furies washed him in the sedge of the swamp, where the deep waters had overflowed from the Stygian pools. They besmeared his breast with the venom of the serpent of Erebus,

---

[4] *Calamitous Allia.*]—Ver. 221. Allia was a river about fifteen miles distant from Rome, near which the Roman army was cut to pieces by the Gauls under Brennus. The 16th day of July, on which it happened, was ever after considered as 'ater,' or 'unlucky.'

and thrice did they clap their blood-stained hands; they filled, too, his infant throat with the milk of a bitch; this was the first nourishment that entered the mouth of the child. Thence does the fosterling imbibe the savage nature of his nurse; and, throughout all the Forum, does he bark out his canine words. They swathed his limbs, too, with clouts dipped in rust, which they snatched from a funereal pile that had been shamelessly deserted. And, that it might not lie down, supported by the bare earth, they placed his youthful head upon the flint stones. And, when now they were about to depart, they waved near his eyes, and before his face, torches made of green branches. The infant cried, soon as he came in contact with the pungent smoke; when thus spoke one Sister of the three: "Those tears have we destined for thee to endless time, which shall ever flow with a cause to excite them." She spoke. Clotho ordered her promises to take effect, and, with envenomed hand, she spun the black warp. And that she might not have to pronounce the lengthened foreboding of his days, she said, "There will be a Poet who shall foretell thy destiny." I am that Poet; from me shalt thou learn thy sorrows; if only the Gods give their own energy to my words; and if the confirmation of events, which thou shalt find to be true throughout thy griefs, is consequent upon my lines. And that thou mayst not be tortured without the precedents of former ages, may thy woes be no lighter than those of the Trojans. Mayst thou, too, on thy gangrened foot bear wounds as numerous as Philoctetes, the Pæantian hero, the heir of the club-bearing Hercules. Mayst thou feel no less pain than Telephus, he who sucked the udder of the hind, and who received the wound of *Achilles* in arms, his cure as a friend; *or than Bellerophon*, who fell headlong from his horse upon the Aleïan plains, whose beauty was nearly his own destruction. Mayst thou see that which *Phœnix*, the son of Amyntor did; and, deprived of thy eyes, mayst thou tremblingly grope thy way with the assisting stick. And mayst thou see no better, than *Œdipus*, whom *Antigone*, his own daughter guided; whose criminality either parent experienced. *Mayst thou be* just as *Tiresias*, the old man celebrated in the *prophetic* art of Apollo, after he was chosen umpire in the sportive dispute: just, too, as *Phineus* was, by whose directions the dove was given as the forerunner and guide of the bark, the work of Pallas; *and like Polym-*

nestor, who lost his eyes, by which, to his sorrow, he had beheld the gold; *eyes* which the bereft mother⁵ offered as an atoning sacrifice to the shades of her son. Like the shepherd of Ætna, whose future calamities Telemus, the son of Eurymus, had previously prophecied. Like the two sons of Phineus, whom the same person deprived of sight that gave it to them; like Thamyras and the person of Demodocus. May one mutilate thy members, just as Saturn cut off those parts, whence he had derived his origin. And may Neptune be no more favourable to thee on the boisterous waves, than *he was* to *Ceyx*, whose brother and wife suddenly became birds; and to *Ulysses*, the sagacious man, upon whom *Ino*, the sister of Semele, took compassion, as he clung to the shattered remnants of his ship. Or, that one *only*⁶ may not have been acquainted with that kind of punishment, let thy divided entrails be torn asunder by horses going different ways. Or, mayst thou endure thyself what *Regulus*, who thought it shameful to be redeemed, bore from the Punic general. And may no Divinity be present to aid thee; as it was with *Priam*, to whom the altar of Hercean Jove, *as a place of refuge*, was of no avail. And just as Thessalus was precipitated from the heights of Ossa, mayst thou be hurled as well from the rocky steep; or may thy limbs be a prey to greedy snakes, just like those of Euryalus, who received the sceptre after him. Or may the boiling stream of water poured over *thee* hasten thy death, like that of Minos;⁷ and just as Prometheus, mayst thou feed the fowls of the air with thy blood far from guiltless, but not so with impunity. Or, like the son of Etracus, the fifth from the thrice great Hercules, mayst thou be hurled, when slain, into the boundless ocean. Or may some boy, loved with a disgraceful affection, hate thee

---

⁵ *The bereft mother.*]—Ver. 270. Polymnestor, king of Thrace, received under his protection Polydorus, the son of Priam, together with a large sum of money which was entrusted to his care. To gain the money, he murdered the child, on which Hecuba, the mother of Polydorus, tore out his eyes.

⁶ *That one only.*]—Ver. 281. Metius Fuffetius, the king of Alba, having engaged to aid the Romans against the Fidenates, behaved with treachery; on which Tullus Hostilius took a most cruel revenge, by causing him to be dragged to pieces between horses.

⁷ *That of Minos.*]—Ver. 291. Minos was stifled in the vapours of a hot bath by Cocalus, the king of Sicily, to whose court Dædalus had fled, and whither Minos had ursued him.

and wound thee with the ruthless sword, like *Philip*, the son of Amyntas.

May, too, no draughts be mingled for thee, less treacherous, than *were for him*, who was born of Jove wearing the horns.[8] Or mayst thou perish, suspended in the manner of the captive Achæus,[9] who was miserably hanged, the gold-bearing stream attesting it. Or may a tile, hurled by the hand of the foe, crush thee, as it did him, who was famous with the kindred surname [10] of the son of Achilles. And may thy bones repose no more quietly than those of Pyrrhus, which, scattered about, were strewed in the roads of Ambracia.[11] And mayst thou die, just like the daughter of the descendant [12] of Æacus, by the impelled darts; from Ceres it is not possible to conceal this wickedness. And, like the grandson of the King,[13] just now mentioned in my verse, mayst thou drink extract of cantharides, a parent administering it. Or may some adulterous woman be called virtuous for thy murder; just as she was called virtuous, by whose avenging hand Leucon [14] fell. And,

[8] *Jove wearing the horns.*]—Ver. 300. This was the form under which Jupiter Ammon was represented. Alexander the Great asserted that he was the son of Jupiter Ammon, and not of Philip. By some writers he was supposed to have been poisoned by the agency of Antipater.

[9] *The captive Achæus.*]—Ver. 301. Achæus, king of Lydia, for his oppressions and exactions, was hanged by his subjects, with his head downwards in the river Pactolus, whose sands were said to be golden. Another account is, that he was delivered over to king Antiochus by Bolus and Cambylus, and then treated in the manner before mentioned, near the river Pactolus.

[10] *The kindred surname.*]—Ver. 303. Pyrrhus, the king of Epirus, who had the same name as the son of Achilles, was killed by a tile thrown by a woman from the wall, as he was besieging the city of Argos.

[11] *The roads of Ambracia.*]—Ver. 306. Pyrrhus, the son of Achilles, was slain by Orestes; and, as we are told by Hyginus, his bones were scattered throughout Ambracia, on the coast of Epirus.

[12] *Daughter of the descendant.*]—Ver. 307. Laodamia, the youngest daughter of Pyrrhus, son of Achilles, fled in a popular tumult, to the altar of Ceres, where she was slain by a man named Milo; on which the Goddess sent plagues against the country, and the murderer becoming mad, mutilated himself and died.

[13] *Grandson of the King.*]—Ver. 309. This passage is supposed to refer to Pyrrhus, the grandson of Pyrrhus the Great, the antagonist of Rome. Olympius, who was either his mother or grandmother, destroyed his mistress, Tigris, with poison, and is supposed to have despatched him in a similar manner.

[14] *Leucon.*]—Ver. 312. Leucon is supposed to have been guilty of

mayst thou, together with thyself, throw on the pile the dearest pledges *of affection;* an end which Sardanapalus experienced for his life. And may the sands, driven by the South wind, cover thy face, as they did that of *Cambyses,* who attempted to profane the temple of Libyan Jove. May the crumbling ashes consume thy bones, as *they* did of those who were slain by the treachery of the second Darius.[15] Or, may cold and hunger be the cause of thy death, as with Neocles, that once was banished from olive-bearing Sicyon. Or, as he, of Atarna,[16] mayst thou be disgracefully carried to thy superior, sewed up in the hide of a bull. Mayst thou also be stabbed in thy chamber, after the manner *of Alexander* of Pheræ, who was put to death by the sword of his wife. And, mayst thou, like Aleuas[17] of Larissa, find, by thy wounds, those to be unfaithful, whom thou deemest trustworthy. And, just like Milo,[18] under whose tyranny Pisa was tormented, mayst thou be precipitated alive in the subterranean waters. May those bolts, too, strike thee, which were sent by Jupiter against Adimantus, who ruled the realms of Phlius. Or, like, in days of old, Lenæus,[19] from the regions of Amastris, mayst thou be deserted, naked on the ground, that is called by the name

adultery with the wife of Oxilochus, the king of Pontus, who was his own brother, and then, in hopes of gaining the kingdom, to have slain the king, on which his paramour, the wife, in revenge slew him.

[15] *The second Darius.*]—Ver. 317. Darius Ochus, having taken an oath never to slay his confederates by poison, famine, the sword, or violence, invited those of his faction to a feast. In the room was a trap-door, under which hot ashes were placed; when he had made his guests intoxicated, the trap was opened, and they fell into the ashes and were smothered.

[16] *He of Atarna.*]—Ver. 321. Hermias, the king of Atarna, a city of Mysia, having revolted from the king of the Persians, was conquered by Hector, the king's general; and, from what is here stated, he is supposed to have been brought before his master sowed up in the hide of an ox.

[17] *Aleuas.*]—Ver. 325. Aleuas, king of Larissa, the son of Thiodamas, was slain by his guards, whom he had appointed with the view of protecting him against the vengeance of his own subjects.

[18] *Milo.*]—Ver. 327. Milo was king of Pisa, in Elis; who, in return for his cruelty, was drowned by his subjects, in the river Alpheus, a stone being first tied round his neck.

[19] *Lenæus.*]—Ver. 331. Lenæus, or Dionysius, king of Heraclia, being expelled by Mithridates, from Amastris, in Paphlagonia, fled to a place called the course of Achilles; and, being abandoned by his friends, he was there slain. Achilles had formerly pursued Iphigenia to the same spot.

of Achilles. And just as either Eurydamas was thrice dragged around the pile of Thrasyllus, by Larissæan wheels, or, as *Hector*, who, with his body, made the circuit of the walls not destined to last, which he had frequently defended; and as, when the daughter of Hippomenes suffered a new kind of punishment, her adulterer is said to have been dragged on the Actæan soil: so, when thy odious life shall have left thy limbs, may avenging horses drag thy filthy carcase. May some *projecting* rock transfix thy entrails; as were once those of the Greeks, *returning from Troy*, transfixed in the Eubæan strait. And as the bold ravisher, *Ajax, the son of Oïleus*, perished by lightning and the waves; so may fire aid the waves that are to overwhelm thee. May thy infatuated mind, too, be frenzied by the Furies, as with *Marsyas*, who, *when flayed*, had but one wound in the whole of his body. And, as with *Lycurgus*, the son of Dryas, who held the realms of Rhodope, who had not the same regard for both his feet. As it happened, too, in former times, to *Hercules*, at Œta, and to the son-in-law of the Dragons,[20] and to *Orestes*, the father of Tisamenus, and to *Alcmæon*, the husband of Callirhoë. And may thy wife be no more chaste than *Ægile*, that matron, at whom Tydeus might blush for a daughter-in-law; and, *than Hypermnestra*, the Locrian, who had intercourse with the brother of her husband, concealing it by the death of her handmaid. May the Gods also make thee able to rejoice in a wife, as faithful as *Amphiaraüs*, the son-in-law of Talaus, and *Agamemnon*, the son-in-law of Tyndarus, did; and, *as true as the Danaïdes*, the grand-daughters of Belus, who, daring to contrive the death of their cousins, are overwhelmed everlastingly with water up to their necks. May she burn, too, with the flame of Byblis, and of Canace, as though with that of a torch; and be not thy sister known to thee, but in a criminal manner. Shouldst thou have a daughter; may she be as Pelopea was to Thyestes, Myrrha to her own father, and Nyctimene to hers; and may she be no more affectionate, or attached to the person of her father, than thy daughter was to thee, Pterelas,[21] or thine to

---

[20] *Son-in-law of the Dragons.*]—Ver. 349. This was Athamas, who married Ino, the daughter of Cadmus and Hermione, who were fabled to have been transformed into dragons.

[21] *Pterelas.*]—Ver. 364. He was a king of Thebes, who was betrayed by his daughter, Cymetho, or Comætho, in her extreme admiration of Amphitryon, his enemy.

thee, Nisus; and, *than Tullia,* who made the place accursed by the fame of her wickedness, and crushed the limbs of her father with the wheels driven over them. Mayst thou die as the youths did, whose heads the summits of the gates of Pisa[22] once supported; *and,* as *Œnomaüs,* who stained the ground that had been often bathed in that of the wretched Suitors, more deservedly with his own blood. *And,* as *Myrtilus,* the charioteer, did, the betrayer of the remorseless tyrant, who gave its new name to the Myrtoan sea. *And,* as those who, in vain, sought *Atalanta,* the damsel swift of foot; until she was caught, overtaken through the three apples. And as those who entered the irremeable retreats of the darkened habitation, that concealed the form of the wondrous monster, *the Minotaur.* Like those *Trojans,* whose six bodies, along with other six, *Achilles,* the son of Æacus, in his rage, placed upon the lofty pile. Like those, whom we read that the Sphynx devoted to a horrid death, when deceived by the obscurities of her ambiguous language. Like those who were slain in the temple of the Bistonian Minerva; on which account even now the face of the Goddess is covered. Like those, who once, as food, made the mangers of the Thracian king red with blood. Like those who were exposed to the lions of Therodamas, and like those who were sacrificed at the Tauric rites of the Goddess worshipped by Thoas. Like those whom voracious Scylla, and Charybdis, opposite to Scylla, snatched trembling from the Dulichian ship: like those whom Polyphemus despatched into his vast paunch: like those who entered into the houses of the Læstrygons. Like those whom the Punic general[23] drowned in the waters of the well, and made the

[22] *Gates of Pisa.*]—Ver. 368. Œnomaüs, king of Pisa, in Elis, proclaimed that any one who should conquer him in a chariot-race should marry his daughter, Hippodamia; but that the person who was conquered should die. Thirteen were overcome and put to death, and their heads were fixed to the gates of Pisa. Pelops won the race by the help of Myrtilus, the charioteer of Œnomaüs, who, for a bribe, withdrew the lynchpin from the axletree, so that the king fell to the ground; whereon Pelops gaining the race, won Hippodamia. and, for his treachery, threw Myrtilus in the sea that lay between the Ionian and Ægean seas, which thence was called the Myrtoän Sea.

[23] *The Punic general.*]—Ver. 391. This is supposed to have been Hamilcar, who having deceitfully allured the Senate of the town of Acerra into his power, drowned them in wells and ditches, and covered their bodies with stones.

stream white with the dust thrown in. Just as the twice six maid servants of *Penelope*, the daughter of Icarus, and her suitors perished, and like *Melanthius*, too, who furnished those suitors with arms against the life of his master. Just as *Antæus*, the wrestler, who lies prostrate, thrown by the Aonian stranger, one who (wondrous to relate) was conqueror after he had fallen. Like those whom the strong arms of Antæus crushed; and those whom the Lemnian multitude[24] put to a cruel death: like him, who, the discoverer of cruel rites,[25] slain as a victim, brought down the showers of rain after a length of time. As *Busiris*, the brother of Antæus, strewed the altars with that blood which, *in justice*, he ought, and was slain himself, after the example he had set: *and as Diomedes*, who, in his impiety, fed his terrible steeds with human entrails, in place of the blade containing the grain: like the two that were slain, on different occasions, by the same avenger, Nessus, and *Eurytion*, the son-in-law of Dexamenus. Like thy great grandson, Saturn, *Periphetas*, whom *Æsculapius*, the son of Coronis, from his own City saw yield up his life. Like Sinnis and Scyron, *the robbers, and Procrustes*, the son of Polypemon, and the *Minotaur*, who was a man in one part, a bull in another. *Like him, too*,[26] who, surveying the waters of this sea and of that, used to let the pine trees pressed down spring up from the ground into the air; *and like* the body of Cercyon, which Ceres beheld, with joyful countenance, dying by the hand of Theseus. May these curses, which my anger calls down with merited prayers, be thy lot, or *others* not more tolerable than these woes. Just as Achæmenides, deserted on Sicilian Ætna, was, when he beheld the Trojan sails approach.

---

[24] *The Lemnian multitude.*]—Ver. 398. The women of Lemnos, despising the sacrifice of Venus, were made by her so loathsome to their husbands, that they left them, and sought new wives from other regions. On their return home, the former wives slew their husbands, together with their new-found spouses.

[25] *The discoverer of cruel rites.*]—Ver. 399. Thrasius, or Thrasyllus, a soothsayer, when a drought prevailed, told Busiris, the tyrant of Egypt, that if he sacrificed strangers to Jupiter, rain would fall. Busiris, finding him to be a foreigner, ordered him to be sacrificed first.

[26] *Like him too.*]—Ver. 411. This alludes to Pityocamptes, a notorious robber, who infested the isthmus of Corinth, and is generally considered the same as Sinnis, the robber that was slain by Theseus; though Ovid here makes them to be distinct individuals.

Such, too, as was the fortune of the two-named Irus,[27] and *of those* who post themselves *as beggars* on the bridge, *a fortune* which shall be more intolerable to thee. In vain may *Plutus*, the son of Ceres, ever be loved by thee; and may he, ever sought, desert thy fortunes. And as the soft sand gives way under the pressure of the foot, as the water ebbs and flows, so may thy possessions always melt in some indescribable manner; and, slipping through the midst of thy hands, may they ever flow away. Mayst thou, when filled, be wasted by insatiate hunger, like the father of the damsel[28] who was wont to assume various forms. And may no loathing of human flesh come on thee; and in the *only* respect that thou canst, thou shalt be the Tydeus of the present day. And mayst thou perpetrate some *crime*, by reason of which the steeds of the horror-stricken Sun may again be turned from the West towards the East. Thou shalt repeat the foul banquet of the table of Lycaon, and thou shalt attempt to deceive Jupiter by the false appearance of thy viands. I wish, too, that some one would try the power of the Divinity, by serving thee up; that thou mayst be the son of Tantalus, and the boy of Tereus. And may thy limbs be scattered over the wide fields, as those *were* which arrested the progress of the father *of Medea*. Mayst thou imitate the real bulls in the brass of Perillus, with a voice adapted to the figure of the bull. And, like the cruel Phalaris, thy tongue first cut out with the sword, mayst thou lament in imitation of the bull, enclosed in Paphian brass. And whilst thou shalt desire to return to the years of a more youthful age, mayst thou be outwitted like *Pelias*, the aged father-in-law of Admetus. On horseback mayst thou be swallowed, *like Curtius*, in the gulf of the pervading swamp, only so that there be no glory in thy deed. And mayst thou perish, like those sprung from the teeth sown in the Grecian fields by the Sidonian hand *of Cadmus*. May the direful impreca-

[27] *The two-named Irus.*]—Ver. 419. He was a notorious beggar of Ithaca, who is mentioned in the Odyssey. His original name was Arnæus, which was afterwards changed to Irus. He was slain by Ulysses with a blow of his fist, for aiding the suitors of Penelope.

[28] *Father of the damsel.*]—Ver. 427. Erisicthon, a Thessalian, having cut down a grove of Ceres, was punished with insatiable hunger. His daughter Mestra, or Dryops, having the power of transforming herself, consented to be sold in various forms to procure the means of satisfying her father's hunger, which often compelled him to devour his own flesh.

tions fall upon thy head which the grandson of Pentheus uttered, and the brother of Medusa; and those with which, in the little book, the bird was accursed, which purges its own body with water injected.[29] And mayst thou endure as many wounds as *Osiris* is said to have borne, from whose rites the knife is said to be absent. And mayst thou insanely hack thy worthless members to the Phrygian tune, like those whom Mother Cybele influences.

From a man mayst thou be made neither man nor woman, like Atys; and mayst thou shake the jarring tambourine with effeminate hand. Mayst thou, too, suddenly be changed into a *lion*, the beast of the great Mother *Cybele*, just as the conqueror, and she that was conquered[30] in the foot-race, were transformed. And, that Limone alone may not have experienced that punishment, may the horse tear thy entrails, too, with savage tooth. Or, as he of Cassandria,[31] not less cruel than that tyrant, mayst thou, wounded, be entombed in the earth heaped on thee. Or, as *Perseus*, the descendant of Abas, or the Cycneian hero, mayst thou, shut up, be precipitated into the waves of the deep; or mayst thou be slain, a victim at the sacred altars of Phœbus; a death which Theudotus[32] received at the hands of a cruel enemy. Or may Abdera devote thee on the appointed days,[33] and may multitudes of stones, in a shower, be hurled upon thee *so* devoted.

Or mayst thou be struck by the three-forked bolt of Jove, like *Capaneus*, the son of Hipponoüs, and like *Atrax*, the father of Dosithoë; like *Semele*, the sister of Autonoë; like Jasius, whose aunt was Maia; like him, who badly guided the horses that in his rashness he had desired. Like *Salmoneus*, the

---

[29] *With water injected.*]—Ver. 452. The Ibis was said by the ancients to purge its own body with injections of sea-water, by the aid of its bill; and thereby, to have first led to the use of the clyster pipe.

[30] *She that was conquered.*]—Ver. 460. Hippomanes and Atalanta were changed into lions by Cybele, whose temple they had defiled.

[31] *He of Cassandria.*]—Ver. 463. See the note to Pontic Epistles, Book ii. Epistle 9, l. 43.

[32] *Theudotus.*]—Ver. 468. Asserting himself to be king of Bactria, he was conquered by Arsaces, the king of Persia, and was sacrificed by him to Apollo.

[33] *On the appointed days.*]—Ver. 469. The people of Abdera, in Thrace, were accustomed, at the beginning of each year, to vote the death of one individual in behalf of the state; on which, the person so named, was stoned to death.

cruel son of Æolus; like him born of the same parent as she was sprung from, who, as the Bear, *ever* avoids the flowing waters. As Macedo, with her husband, was struck by the swift lightnings, so, I pray, mayst thou fall by the fires of the heavenly avenger. Mayst thou also be a prey to the *dogs*, by which Latonian Delos may not be approached, Thasus, *the priest of Apollo*, having been torn *by them* before his time; and who pulled in pieces him who beheld the bath of the modest Diana, and Linus, the grandson of Crotopus. And mayst thou not be more lightly stung by the venomous serpents than *Eurydice*, the daughter-in-law of the old man Œagrus, and of Calliope; than *Opheltes*, the son of Hypsipyle; than *Laocoon*, who was the first to pierce with his sharp spear the wood of the suspected horse. And mayst thou not approach the lofty stairs more cautiously than Elpenor, and mayst thou feel the effects of wine in the same manner as he did. And mayst thou fall, as much vanquished as each Dryopian[34] that aided the inhuman Thiodamas, who called them to arms; as much as Cacus, who fell slaughtered in his own cave, betrayed by the voice of the heifer shut up *there;* as much as Lichas, who bore the gifts dipped in the Lernæan venom, and who dyed the Eubœan waves with his own blood. Or mayst thou come to Tartarus from the steep rock, like him who read the Socratic book[35] upon death; like him who beheld the deceiving sails[36] of the ship of Theseus; like the boy *Astyanax*, who was hurled from the towers of Troy; like *Ino*, the nurse of the infant Bacchus, who was his aunt; like him, the cause of whose death was

[34] *Each Dryopian.*]—Ver. 490. Thiodamas, having refused food to Hylas, the son of Hercules, Hercules slew some of his oxen. Thiodamas thereupon raised an army against him; on which he was defeated, together with the Dryopians, his allies.

[35] *The Socratic book.*]—Ver. 496. Cleombrotus, an academic philosopher, having read 'Phædo,' the book written by Plato, the scholar of Socrates, on the Immortality of the Soul, in his extreme desire to enjoy the happy state there described, threw himself off a rock into the sea, where he was drowned.

[36] *The deceiving sails.*]—Ver. 497. Ægeus, seeing black sails on the ship of his son Theseus, on his return from the conquest of the Minotaur, supposing that it was a token of his son's death, threw himself into the sea, which thence assumed the epithet of 'Ægean.'

the invention of the saw.[37] Like the Lydian virgin,[38] who threw herself from the lofty rocks, *and* who had uttered opprobrious expressions to the reluctant Deity. May a pregnant lioness, a native of thy country, meet thee on thy paternal soil, and may she be the cause of thy death, resembling that of Phayllus, *king of Ambracia*. May, too, the boar which slew the son of Lycurgus, and *Adonis*, who was born of a tree, and the bold Idmon, tear thee as well; and may he, even when dead, give thee a wound, as with him, upon whose face the head of the transfixed boar fell.[39] Or mayst thou be *like* him whom a pine-nut slew with a similar fate, and mayst thou be as the Phrygian, and the hunter of Berecynthus.[40] Should thy ship touch upon the Minoïan sands, may the Cretan multitude take thee to be a Corcyræan.[41] Mayst thou enter a house about to fall, like the offspring of Aleuas,[42] when the Constellation was propitious to the man who was the son of Leoprepis. And, like either Evenus or Tiberinus, drowned in the rapid stream, mayst thou give a name to the flowing river. And may thy head, a fit prey for wild beasts, be a prey for man, cut off like that of the son of Astacus,[43] from thy muti-

[37] *Invention of the saw.*]—Ver. 500. Perdix, the nephew of Dædalus, invented the saw. His uncle, stung with jealousy at his skill, threw him headlong from the tower of the temple of Minerva, at Athens. The Goddess, however, supported him, and he was changed into a partridge, which was called by his name.

[38] *The Lydian virgin.*]—Ver. 501. Ilex, the daughter of Ibycus, a Lydian, being loved by Mars, was protected by Diana against him. Reviling the God, Mars became incensed, and killed her father, on which Ilex became mad with grief, and threw herself from a rock into the sea.

[39] *The transfixed boar.*]—Ver. 508. Thoas, a hunter of Andragathia, having captured a boar, instead of sacrificing both the head and feet to Diana, kept the feet, and hung up the head only by a string tied to a tree. Falling asleep beneath it, it fell upon him, and smothered him.

[40] *Hunter of Berecynthus.*]—Ver. 510. Atys and Nauclus, two hunters, sleeping under pine-trees, were killed by the pine-nuts falling upon them.

[41] *A Corcyræan*]—Ver. 512. The people of the isle of Corcyra had been guilty of an insult to the bones of Minos, king of Crete. The inhabitants of the latter island were consequently in the habit of sacrificing any native, of Corcyra who might fall into their hands, to the shades of Minos.

[42] *Offspring of Aleuas.*]—Ver. 513. Scopas, the Thessalian, the son of Aleuas, was slain for his impiety, by the fall of his house, from which calamity Simonides, the poet, who was his guest, was saved by the intervention of Castor and Pollux.

[43] *The son of Astacus.*]—Ver. 517. Menalippus, the youngest son of

lated carcase. And, as they say that Broteas did, in his desire for death, mayst thou place thy limbs to be burnt on the lighted pile. Shut up in a cage, mayst thou suffer death, like the compiler of the history,[44] that availed him nothing. May, too, thy insolent tongue prove thy destruction, as it was the ruin of the inventor of the abusive Iambics.[45] Like him, too, who slandered Athens in his limping verse,[46] mayst thou perish, despised, for want of food. And, as the poet of the satirical lyre[47] is said to have perished, may thy breach of faith be the cause of thy ruin. And, as the serpent gave the wound to Orestes, the son of Agamemnon, mayst thou, too, perish from a sting containing venom. May the first night of thy marriage be the last of thy life: Eupolis and his new-made bride died in this manner. As they say that Lycophron[48] the Tragedian perished, so may an arrow stand fixed in thy vitals. Or, torn in pieces, mayst thou be scattered in the woods, by the hands of thy relations; just as *Pentheus* was scattered about, at Thebes, who was descended from *Cadmus changed into* a dragon for his grandsire. And mayst thou be drawn over the wild mountains, a bull dragging thee; just as *Dirce*, the tyrannical wife of Lycus, was dragged. And, that which *Philomela* the unwilling supplanter of her sister suffered, may thy tongue, cut out, fall before thy feet. Like him that was named

Astacus, having been slain in the Theban war, his head, when cut off, was mangled and gnawed by Tydeus, to the great disgust of Minerva.

[44] *Compiler of the history.*]—Ver. 522. Callisthenes, of Olynthus, wrote a history of the exploits of Alexander the Great, in which he launched out into extreme praise of that monarch. Being accused of conspiring against his master, his nose, ears, and lips, were cut off, and his limbs were mutilated, and, after being carried about in a cage, he was put to death.

[45] *Inventor of the abusive Iambics.*]—Ver. 523. This was Archilochus, the poet, who employed the Iambics against Lycambes, as before mentioned. He was afterwards banished, by reason of the numerous enemies that his satirical turn had created against him.

[46] *Limping verse.*]—Ver. 525. This is generally supposed to refer to Hipponax, who, in verses called Scazons, a limping measure, inveighed against Bupalus and Athenis, inhabitants of Athens.

[47] *The satirical lyre.*]—Ver. 527. This is supposed to refer to Alcæus, the Lyric poet, who broke his promised allegiance to Pittacus, by whom he was put to death. By some, Stesichorus is supposed to be here referred to.

[48] *Lycophron.*]—Ver. 533. Contending with an antagonist as to the relative merits of their poetry, he was slain by him with an arrow.

Blæsus, the founder of Cyrrha, late in its erection, mayst thou be found in innumerable parts of the world. And may the industrious bee, as it did to the poet Achæus,[49] fix its hurtful sting in thy eyes. Bound, too, on the hard rocks, mayst thou have thy entrails torn, like *Prometheus*, whose brother's daughter was Pyrrha. Like the son of Harpagus,[50] mayst thou recall the example of Thyestes, and, slaughtered, mayst thou enter the bowels of thy parent. Mayst thou have thy members mutilated, thy parts being lopped off by the cruel sword, just as they say that the limbs of Mimnermus were. And as it was with the Syracusan poet,[51] may the passage of thy breath be closed, thy throat being stopped up. May thy entrails, too, lie exposed, the skin being stripped off; like him whose name the Phrygian river bears. Mayst thou, to thy misery, look upon the face of Medusa, that changes into stone, she who, *though* but one, put to death many of the subjects of Cepheus. Mayst thou feel the bite of the mares of Potniæ like Glaucus, and mayst thou leap into the water of the sea, like another Glaucus.[52] And as, with him who had the same names as the two just now mentioned, may Gnossian honey[53] stop up the passage of thy breath. Mayst thou too drink, with trembling lips, the same which *Socrates*, the most learned of men, accused by Anytus, once drank with serene countenance. May nothing, shouldst thou love anything, happen to thee more fortunately than it did to Hæmon; and mayst thou enjoy thy own sister, as Macareus did his. Or mayst thou behold what the son of Hector saw from his native towers, when now the flames prevailed on every side. Mayst thou expiate

[49] *Achæus.*]—Ver. 543. When composing a poem in his garden, a swarm of bees settled on his head. Trying to drive them away, they fixed their stings in his eyes, and blinded him.

[50] *The son of Harpagus.*]—Ver. 547. Harpagus, not having killed Cyrus, as his grandfather, Astyages, had ordered him, was invited by the king to a feast, when his own son was served up to him as the chief dish.

[51] *The Syracusan poet.*]—Ver. 551. Theocritus is supposed to be here alluded to, who, by some writers, is said to have been hanged for railing against Hiero, king of Sicily.

[52] *Another Glaucus.*]—Ver. 558. Glaucus, a fisherman, seeing the fish when caught, revive on eating a certain herb, ventured to taste of it, on which he leaped into the sea, and became a God of the ocean.

[53] *Gnossian honey.*]—Ver. 561. Glaucus, a Cretan, playing at tennis, or, as some say, following a mouse which he was trying to catch, fell into a vessel filled with honey, and was smothered.

thy crimes with thy blood, like *Adonis*, who was begotten by his father, who was his grandfather, *and* whose own sister, by criminality, became his mother. May such a kind of weapon stick in thy bones as that with which *Ulysses*, the son-in-law of Icarius, is said to have been slain. And as the loquacious throat[54] was stopped up in the horse that was made of maple wood, so may the passage of thy voice be closed by the thumb. Or, like Anaxarchus, mayst thou be brayed in a deep mortar,[55] and may thy bones, when struck, rattle instead of the real corn. And may Phœbus enclose thee in the lowest depths of Tartarus, as he did *Crotopus*, the father of Psamathe; the same as he had done to his own daughter. May that plague, too, attack thy family which the right hand of Chorœbus conquered, and *so* aided the wretched Argives. Like *Hippolytus*, the grandson of Æthra, doomed to perish through the wrath of Venus, mayst thou, in exile, be dragged by thy frightened horses. As the host, *Polymnestor*, slew his foster-child, on account of his great riches, may thy host slay thee, on account of thy want of riches. As they say, too, that his six brothers were slain, together with Damasicthon, *son of Niobe*, so may all thy race perish, together with thee. As the harper, *Amphion*, added his own death to that of his wretched children, so mayst thou have a deserved loathing of thy own life. Or, like *Niobe*, the sister of Pelops, mayst thou become hard with rock growing over thee, and, *like* Battus, who was ruined by his own tongue. If thou shalt cleave the vacant air with the hurled quoit, mayst thou fall, struck by the same circle as the boy, *Hyacinthus*, the son of Œbalus. If any water shall be cleaved by thy alternating arms, may every stream prove more injurious to thee than that of Abydos, *over which Leander swam.* As the Comedian perished in the midst of the waves, while he was swimming, so may the Stygian

---

[54] *The loquacious throat.*]—Ver. 571. This is supposed to refer to a man named Anticlus, who, when shut up in the wooden horse which was carried within the walls of Troy, was seized with a desire to answer Helen, who, standing outside, imitated the voice of his wife. Ulysses stopped his throat, by the pressure of his thumb, and so effectually precluded his utterance that he never spoke again, being suffocated.

[55] *In a deep mortar.*]—Ver. 573. Anaxarchus, a philosopher of Abdera, was condemned by Nicocreon, the tyrant of Cyprus, to be pounded with iron pestles in a mortar, which torment he suffered with the greatest fortitude, and biting off his own tongue, he spat it in the face of the tyrant.

water suffocate thee. Or else, when, shipwrecked, thou shalt have escaped the boisterous sea, mayst thou perish on touching the shore, as Palinurus *did*. And may the pack of watchful hounds, the care of Diana, tear thee too in pieces, like the Poet of Tragedy.[56] Or like *Empedocles*, of Trinacria, mayst thou leap upon the face of the giant *Enceladus*, where the Sicilian Ætna vomits forth flames in abundance. May the Strymonian matrons tear asunder thy limbs with insane nails, thinking they are those of *Orpheus*. As *Meleager*, the son of Althæa, burned with distant flames, so may thy funereal pile be consumed by the flame of a branch. As the new-made bride, *Creusa*, was deceived by the Phasian chaplet, and as the father of the bride, and, with the father, the household. As the venom, diffused, pervaded the limbs of Hercules, so may the pestilential poison consume thy body. May those wounds, from a new-fashioned weapon, await thee too, by means of which his offspring avenged Lycurgus, the son of Pentheus. And, like Milo,[57] mayst thou endeavour to cleave the fissile oak; and mayst thou be unable to remove thence thy hands caught *there*. Mayst thou perish, too, through thy own gifts, like Icarus; against whom the drunken crowd raised their hands in arms. And as Erigone, his affectionate daughter, did, through grief for her father's death, do thou cause the noose of the rope to go round thy throat. Mayst thou too endure famine, the threshold of the house being blocked up, like him to whom his own mother[58] herself gave sentence of punishment. Mayst thou outrage the statues of Diana, after the example *of Agamemnon*, who sped on his rapid path from the port of Aulis. After the example of *Palamedes*, the son

---

[56] *The poet of tragedy.*]—Ver. 597. Euripides, the Greek Tragic poet, having supped with king Archelaus, on returning home, was attacked by the dogs that kept the temple of Diana, and was torn to pieces by them, his enemy Lysimachus having set them on him for that purpose.

[57] *Milo.*]—Ver. 612. Milo of Crotona, a man of enormous strength, endeavouring to withdraw the wedges that had been inserted in a cleft oak, the wood suddenly closed and caught his hands, which were held so fast that he could not withdraw them, and he became a prey to wild beasts.

[58] *His own mother.*]—Ver. 618. Pausanias, a general of the Lacedæmonians, being condemned for treason, was shut up by the Ephori in the temple of Minerva, and the door was blocked up with stones, his mother throwing the first stone against it.

of Nauplius, mayst thou be punished with death on a false accusation: and may it be of no advantage to thee that thou didst not deserve it. As the host, *the priest* of Isis, deprived Æthalius of his life, whom, Io remembering it even to this day, drives afar from her rites. And as the bereft mother, by the aid of her lamp, betrayed Melantheus as he lurked in darkness after the murder; so may thy breast be pierced with the hurled darts; so, I pray, mayst thou be injured by thy own allies. May such a night be passed by thee, as was by *Dolon*, the Phrygian coward, who bargained for the horses which the brave Achilles used to drive. Mayst thou, too, enjoy no better sleep than Rhesus did, and those who were the companions of Rhesus, both in his death and before, in his journey; *and*, than *they did*, whom the active son of Hyrtacus, and his companion, put to death, together with the Rutulian Rhamnes. Surrounded, too, like the son of Clinias,[59] with smoky flames, mayst thou carry thy half-burnt limbs to Stygian doom. May rustic arms also prove the destruction of thy life, as they were for Remus, who dared to pass over the new-built walls. Lastly, I pray, that amid Sarmatian and Getic arrows, thou mayst live and die in these regions. These things have been only sent thee in a hurried work, that thou mayst not complain that I am forgetful of thee. *They are few indeed*, I confess, but may the Gods grant more than is asked for, and, in their kindness, may they multiply my wishes.

Hereafter, thou shalt read still more, and that which shall contain thy true name, *written* in *Iambics*, the measure in which ruthless warfare ought to be waged.

[59] *The son of Clinias*.]—Ver. 635. Alcibiades, the son of Clinias, being, through the agency of Lysander, banished from Athens, fled into Phrygia. Pharnabazus, sending persons to slay him, they set the house on fire, on which he made his way through the flames, but at length fell dead, pierced with darts.

END OF THE INVECTIVE AGAINST THE IBIS.

THE HALIEUTICON;

OR,

TREATISE ON FISHES.

A FRAGMENT.

This fragment is full of lacunæ and corrupt readings. Ovid seems to have intended to depict in this poem the points of resemblance in terrestrial and aquatic animals. From its treating on the nature of fishes, he calls the work Halieuticon, from the Greek word ἁλιεύς, 'a fisherman.' Some writers have attributed this fragment to Gratius Faliscus, a Roman poet, the author of the Cynægeticon, a treatise, in verse, on hunting; but Pliny the Elder (Book xxxii. c. 2) distinctly says, that Ovid is the author; his words are—'The disposition of fishes, which Ovid has mentioned in his work called Halieuticon, appears to me really wonderful.' Commentators generally believe this poem to have been written by him during his exile at Tomi.*

* * * * The world received the law; and he gave arms to all beings, and reminded them of their *self-preservation*; for thus it is that the calf threatens, which, not yet bears horns on its tender forehead; for this reason the hinds flee, the lions fight valorously, the dog *defends himself* by his bite, the scorpion by the sting of its tail, and the light bird flies away with agitated wings.

All have a *vague* fear of a death that is unknown *to* them; to all *it has been granted* to be sensible of the enemy, and the means of defence that have been given them, and to know the power and the manner of using their weapons: and thus

---

* The different versions of this Fragment vary so much, that it has been thought proper to adopt those readings, which seem most likely to imply the writer's meaning, without reference to the text of any individual commentator. A few passages are of very obscure signification, and are open to considerable doubt.

too, the scarus[1] is caught by stratagem, beneath the waves, and at length dreads the bait fraught with treacherousness. It dares not strike the sticks[2] with an effort of its head; but, turning away, as it loosens the twigs with frequent blows of its tail, it makes its passage, and escapes safely into the deep. Moreover, if perchance any kind scarus, swimming behind, sees it struggling within the osiers, he takes hold of its tail in his mouth, as it is *thus* turned away, and so [it escapes.]

* * * * * * *

The cuttle-fish, slow in flight, when perchance, it has been caught under the buoyant wave, and every moment is in dread of the hands of the spoiler, vomits from its mouth a black blood, that tints the sea and hides its path, deceiving the eyes of those that follow.

The pike, taken in the net, though huge and bold, sinks down, crouching in the sand which it has stirred up with its tail. * * * *[3] It leaps into the air, and uninjured, with a bound it escapes the stratagem. The fierce lamprey, too, conscious of the smoothness of its round back, turning *its head*, in preference,[4] towards the loosened meshes of the net, with its slippery body at last escapes clear through the multiplied windings, and, injurious in the example *it has set*, it alone slips through them all. But, on the other hand, the sluggish polypus sticks to the rocks with its body provided with feelers, and by this stratagem it escapes the nets, and, according to the nature of the spot, it assumes and changes

---

[1] *The scarus.*]—Ver. 9. This fish is, by some, supposed to mean the 'parrot-fish;' by others, 'the char.' The scarus was esteemed a great delicacy at the Roman tables. It is not now known to naturalists what were the various fishes to which, in the translation, the Latin name only is given; this circumstance, of course, renders it impossible to give their present names in English.

[2] *The sticks.*]—Ver. 11. Radiis. This alludes to the sticks, or twigs, which formed the sides of the 'nassa,' which was a contrivance for catching fish by the junction of willow rods. This, being somewhat in the shape of a large bottle with a narrow mouth, was placed with the mouth facing the current.

[3] * * * *.]—Ver. 17. The words here are, 'Uber Servato, quem texit, in - - - resulset.' They are not capable of any translation.

[4] *Turning its head in preference.*]—Ver. 27. 'Magis conversa.' These words seem to be used in contradistinction to the word 'aversus,' as applied before to the 'scarus,' when endeavouring to make its escape.

its colour, always resembling that *place* which it has lighted upon; and when it has greedily seized the prey hanging from the fishing-line, it likewise deceives *the angler*, on his raising the rod, when, now emerging into the air, it loosens its feelers, and spits forth the hook that it has despoiled *of the bait*.

But the mullet, with its tail, beats off the pendant bait, and snatches it up when *thus* struck off. The pike, lashed into furious rage, is carried along with its flounderings on every side, and follows the current that carries it on, and wriggles about its head, until the cruel hook falls from the loosened wound, and leaves its opened mouth. The lamprey, too, is not ignorant of its own powers of attack, and is not without its sharp bite on the instant as its means of defence; nor, when caught, does it lay aside its fierce spirit. The anthias uses those arms, which, being behind it, it does not behold; it knows, too, the power of its back-bone, and turning its body with its back downwards, it cuts the line and intercepts the hook fixed *in the bait*.

As to the rest of the animals which inhabit the dense woods, either vain fears are ever alarming them, maddened with terror, or the blind ferocity of their nature is ever throwing them headlong *into dangers*. 'Tis nature itself that prompts them either to take to flight, or to rush into close conflict. See how the intrepid lion rushes on, to scatter the ranks of the hunters, and *how* he presents his breast to the hostile darts. Wherever he approaches, he burns with rage, more and more confident, and more spirited; he shakes his mane, and he adds anger to his *native* strength. He rushes on, and, by his own courage, he hastens his death.

The hideous bear, as it rolls along from its Lucanian[5] dens, what is it but a sluggish mass, ferocious, and of a stolid disposition? The wild boar, hard pressed, signifies his anger by his erected bristles, and, with a bound, rushes amid the wounds of the opposing steel, and, followed up, dies with the weapon transfixing his vitals.

Another portion *of the animals*, trusting in their fleetness, turn their backs on the pursuer; *such* as the timid hares, and the deer with tawny hide, and the stag, flying with unlimited

---

[5] *Lucanian.*]—Ver. 57. Lucania was a district situate in the south of Italy.

terror. 'Tis nature itself that prompts them, either to take to flight, or to rush into close conflict.

The honour of high spirit and the greatest glory belong to the horse; for, in his instinct, he covets the victory, and exults in his conquest. Whether it is that he has gained the wreath, in the seven courses[6] round the Circus; do you not see, how much more erect the victor raises aloft his head, and displays himself to the applause of the crowd? or, whether it is when his lofty back is adorned with the slaughtered lion; how proudly, how remarkable for his stately air, does he walk, and how his hoof, as he returns heavily laden with the spoils of victory,[7] actuated by the generous impulse, strikes the ground?

Which is the especial point of merit in the dog? What intrepid boldness there is in them! What sagacious aptness for the chase: what powers of endurance in following. Now they are snuffing the air with elevated nostrils; now they are examining the track with nose close *to the ground*; and *now*, with their cry, they proclaim that they have found, and urge on their master with their voice. Should *the prey* escape his attack, then, over hills and over plains does the dog pursue. All our toils are centered in their skill; on that do all our hopes rely.

But I would not recommend you to go out into the midst of the ocean, nor to try the depths of the open sea. You will do better to regulate your cable[8] according to each kind of locality. At one time, the spot may be rugged with rocks; such demands the pliant fishing-rod; whereas the smooth shore requires the net. Does some lofty mountain send its deepening shadows over the sea; according to their different natures, some *fish* avoid, and some seek *such a spot*. If the sea is green from the weeds that grow at the bottom   *   *   *
      *   *   *   *

let him apply patience, and let him watch by the soft seaweed.

Nature has designed, in a varied manner, the bottom of the

---

[6] *Seven courses.*]—Ver. 68. The extent of the race in the Circus Maximus, was always seven times round the ' meta,' or goal.

[7] *Spoils of victory.*]—Ver. 74. ' Spoliis opimis.' This literally means the spoil taken from a prince or general of the enemy. It is here applied to the lion, as being the king of the wild beasts.

[8] *Your cable.*]—Ver. 87. 'Funem.' This seems to apply to the rope, by which the boat or punt of the fisherman is moored.

ocean, and she has not willed that all fish should frequent the same haunts; for there are some that love the open sea, such as the mackarel,[9] and the sea ox, and the darting hippurus, and the gurnet with its swarthy back, and the valuable helops, unknown in our waters, and the hardy sword-fish, not less dangerous than a sword with its blow, and the timid tunnies, that fly in large shoals; there is, too, the little sucking-fish, wondrous to tell! a vast obstruction[10] to ships; you, too, the pilot-fish, the companion of the vessels, who always follow the white foam of the track that they make along the ocean, and the fierce cercyros, that haunts the bases of the rocks; the cantharus, too, unpleasant in its flavour, the orphas, like it in colour, and the erythinus, reddening in the azure waves; the sargus, remarkable with its spots and distinguished by its fins, the sparulus, refulgent with its gilded neck, the glittering pagur, the tawny shark, and the ruff that re-produces itself, deprived of two-fold parents; besides; the rock-fish,[11] with its green scales and its little mouth, the scarce dory, the tinted mormyr, and the gilt-head, rivalling the brilliancy of gold; the grayling, too, with its livid body, the darting pike, the perch, and the tragus. Besides; the melanurus, remarkable for the beauty of its tail, the lamprey burning with its spots of gold, the green merling, the conger-eel, cruel with the wounds *which it inflicts* on those of its own kind, the sea-scorpion, injurious from the sharp sting in its head, and the glaucus that is never beheld under the Constellation of summer. But on the other hand, some fishes extend themselves on the sands covered with weeds, as the scarus, which fish alone ruminates the food it has eaten, and the prolific species of the pilchard, the lamyros, the smaris, the filthy chromis, and the salpa,[12] deservedly in little esteem; the fish, too, that imitates,

[9] *The mackarel.*]—Ver. 94. 'Scombri.' This name is supposed by naturalists to have belonged to the mackarel; but it is by no means certain to what fish it was given.

[10] *A vast obstruction.*]—Ver. 99. The 'Echeneis remora,' or sucking fish, was supposed, by sticking to the rudder or keel of a vessel, to be able to stop its sailing.

[11] *The rock-fish.*]—Ver. 110. 'Saxatilis.' This probably is not the name of any fish; but, as the poet had forgotten the name, he uses it as denoting its habits.

[12] *The salpa.*]—Ver. 122. Pliny the Elder tells us that this was a sea

beneath the waves, the pretty nests of the birds; and the squalus, and the red mullet, tinted with a faint blood colour; the sole, too, shining in its whiteness; the turbot, like it in colour; the pearl-fish,[13] admired on the coasts of the Adriatic; the broad epodis, and the frog-fish, with its soft back.

The last appear *   *   *   *
    *   *   *   *   *

The slippery gudgeon, too, that hurts with none of its prickles; the ink-fish, that carries a black liquid in its snow-white body; the tough sea-pigs, and the twisting caris; the cod-fish too,[14] little deserving of a name so ugly; and you, too, the acipenser, famed in distant waters *   *   *

---

fish, which, like a stock fish, required to be beaten with rods in order to make it tender.

[13] *The pearl fish.*]—Ver. 126. 'Rhombus.' This fish is generally supposed to have been the turbot, or pearl;' though 'passer,' which has been just mentioned, is supposed also to have been one of the names of the turbot.

[14] *The cod-fish.*]—Ver. 131. 'Asellus.' This fish was highly esteemed by the Romans, and is generally thought to have been the cod-fish. Its name 'asellus' is, literally, 'little ass,' for which reason, with his usual punning propensity, Ovid says that it does not deserve a name so ugly.

THE END.

J. BILLING, PRINTER, WOKING, SURREY.

CPSIA information can be obtained
at www.ICGtesting.com
Printed in the USA
LVOW04s0719060218
565476LV00009B/109/P